If you are writing a report, would deductive structure (conclusions and recommendations followed by the evidence) be more effective than inductive structure (evidence first, conclusions and recommendations last)?

If chronological order or problem-to-solution order is appropriate, have you been consistent in arranging materials?

STYLE

Is your message clear, using primarily short, familiar words and short sentences in active voice?

Have you been courteous, using the you-attitude throughout? (Compare the number of *you*s and *your*s with the number of *I*s, *we*s, *my*s, and *our*s.)

Have you used positive tone, eliminating as many negative words as possible?

Is the message concise? Have you eliminated common redundancies and wordy expressions?

Have you used a variety of sentence types and lengths?

FORMAT AND MECHANICS

Have you used correct spelling, grammar, and punctuation?

Letters Have you used letterhead stationery or your return address appropriately?
Are your margins set appropriately?
Have you included a date?
Is your inside address complete? Have you used the two-letter state abbreviation?
Does your salutation correspond with the first line of your inside address?
Have you paragraphed for readability?
Is your signature block complete?
Have you included appropriate closing notations?

Memos Have you dated the memo?
Are your heading entries (*To, From, Subject*) entered correctly?
If your memo is long, have you used appropriate topic headings?
Have you paragraphed for readability?
Have you checked to ensure that you have *not* used a signature block?

Reports Have you used the appropriate preliminary parts?
Have you checked your headings to ensure that they correctly indicate major divisions and subdivisions?
Have you included appropriate graphic aids?
Have you provided complete and appropriate documentation?
Have you included the appropriate supplemental parts?
If the report will be bound, have you left additional space on the margin?

BUSINESS COMMUNICATION

From Process to Product

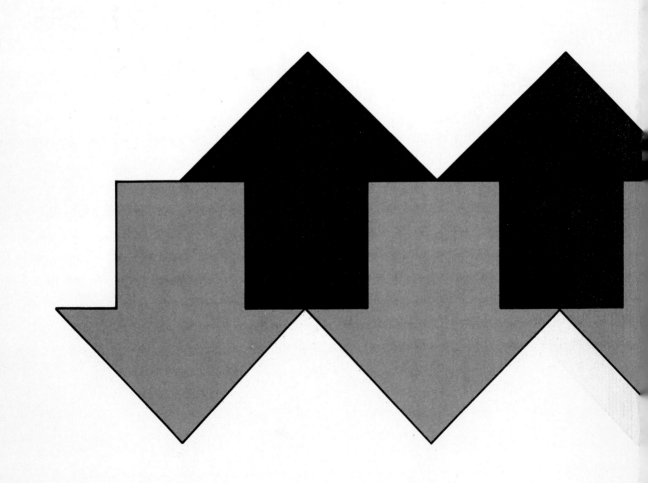

BUSINESS COMMUNICATION

From Process to Product

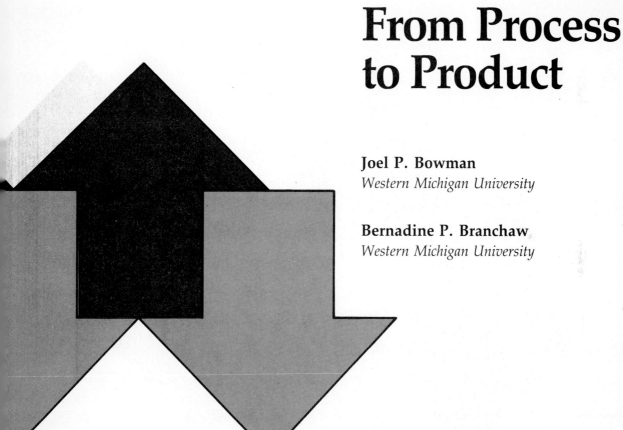

Joel P. Bowman
Western Michigan University

Bernadine P. Branchaw
Western Michigan University

THE DRYDEN PRESS
Chicago   New York   Philadelphia
San Francisco   Montreal   Toronto
London   Sydney   Tokyo   Mexico City
Rio de Janeiro   Madrid

Acquisitions Editor: Joan Resler
Developmental Editor: Rebecca Ryan
Project Editor: Nancy Shanahan
Design Director: Alan Wendt
Production Manager: Mary Jarvis
Permissions Editor: Doris Milligan
Director of Editing, Design, and Production: Jane Perkins

Text and Cover Designer: Quarasan
Copy Editor: Maggie Jarpey
Compositor: Waldman Graphics
Text Type: 10/12 Palatino

Library of Congress Cataloging-in-Publication Data

Bowman, Joel P.
  Business communication.

  Includes index.
  1. Communication in management.   I. Branchaw,
Bernadine P.   II. Title.
HF5718.B668 1987   658.4'5   86-11685
ISBN 0-03-001898-6

Printed in the United States of America
789-016-98765432

Address orders:
111 Fifth Avenue
New York, N.Y. 10003

Address editorial correspondence:
One Salt Creek Lane
Hinsdale, IL 60521

The Dryden Press
Holt, Rinehart and Winston
Saunders College Publishing

The Dryden Press Series in Business Communication

Preface

Users of *Successful Communication in Business* will recognize that this book, *Business Communication: From Process to Product*, has its foundations in our earlier book. Our orientation and philosophy of communication remain the same, and much of our advice about how to write and about what the final product should be remains the same. Nevertheless, although we have retained the features of the earlier text that students and instructors found helpful, this book is more than a revision. Our change in title reflects an increased emphasis on the process involved in producing the final product, in contrast to the first edition's primary emphasis on the final product. In addition, *Business Communication: From Process to Product* contains many new features that both students and instructors will appreciate.

Objectives

The ability to communicate effectively is a skill every person needs. Clear, effective communication makes for successful relationships—both in personal and business life. *Business Communication: From Process to Product* will show students—whether in college or already at work in business—how to increase the effectiveness of their written and oral communication skills.

For this reason, our approach is more humanistic than is often the case with business communication textbooks. Throughout the book we stress the commonalities of communication situations: the context, the ethics underlying communication decisions and relationships, empathy between the sender and receiver of a message, the use of language, and the nonverbal message that accompanies and modifies the meaning of the written or spoken message.

Also throughout, we stress a problem-solving approach rather than the overly prescriptive "recipe" approach common to many business communication textbooks. We provide complete coverage of the important topics and sufficient direction and examples for students to understand both *how* a communication problem should be solved and *why* it should be solved in a particular way.

Special Features

Business Communication: From Process to Product offers the following features to increase its readability and usefulness:

- *Marginal questions.*   In place of typical marginal comments about the text, we have used thought-provoking questions to help focus the reader's attention on key elements in the text. These questions not only help students think about and understand the material but also may be used as quiz or discussion questions.

- *Communication Today vignettes.*   Quotations, stories, and examples are included to help readers understand the relationship between the theory and practice of business communication.

- *Chapter Overviews.*   Each chapter begins with an overview of the contents to help orient readers to the material in the chapter. This method is designed to be both more thorough and more effective than the typical chapter objectives provided by most textbooks.

- *Communication Challenges.*   Each chapter opening includes a challenge for students to think about and solve as they read the chapter. Students may compare their solutions with the one that appears after the chapter summary to see how well they have understood the material.

- *Real-world examples, problems, and cases.*   Both students and instructors can profit from the numerous examples, problems, and cases we provide for each type of message. All examples, problems, and cases have been adapted from actual communication situations in business or industry.

- *Current material on the new trends in communication technology.*   Reviewers have called our chapter on communication technology the most thorough and timely in any business communication text. Most organizations are expanding their use of computers and computer-related equipment for communication purposes. Familiarity with the communication uses of technology is critical for success in modern organizations. *Business Communication: From Process to Product* introduces students to the *what* and the *how* of communication technology.

- *Coverage of international communication.*   In this age of cross-cultural business ventures, businesses come increasingly into contact with people from other countries—as suppliers, as consumers, as employees, and as representatives of regulatory agencies. Today it is not enough for business people to be able to communicate with members of their own culture only; they must be able to communicate effectively with people from virtually every corner of the world.

- *Material on legal considerations of business communication.*   Because much business communication implies a legal contract, this text helps attune students to the implications of the messages they send. In an increasingly litigious society, students and business people must be able to protect themselves and their organizations from the possibility of legal action.

- *Ancillary package.*   In addition to the basic text, *Business Communication: From Process to Product* offers a full range of support materials. This includes an *Instructor's Manual/Test Bank, Computerized Test Bank* (for Apple II® and IBM PC®), and student *Study Guide.* Instructors are sure to find this extensive package helpful in class preparation, student review, and testing. Finally, a *Computerized Assisted Instruction* writing and grammar tutorial is also available.

Overview

Because routine communication situations in business have established methods and procedures, people in business generally spend most of their time communicating nonroutine messages. To help readers prepare for those nonroutine situations, we begin *Part One* with an overview of how communication works, the role it plays in business, and what makes a message—especially a written message—effective. This section contains two new and important chapters on writing skills and the process of writing to help students develop their critical compositions skills early.

Part Two focuses on business letters and memos—the kind of short messages that constitute the bulk of written communication in business. Because effective short messages require an understanding of the communication context, the business and human objectives of the message, and the psychology of the receiver, we have concentrated on showing readers how to analyze communication situations and apply general principles rather than emphasizing specific rules for common letter types. A liberal use of examples helps students understand how the general principles apply to specific message types.

Part Three covers business reports. Reports are such an important job function that most business people write reports from virtually their first week on the job. Every aspect of report writing—from the initial assignment, to research, to writing—is presented in step-by-step detail. We provide examples of all the common short report forms as well as information on the less common but extremely important long, formal report so that students will have a thorough understanding of the report-writing process regardless of their choice of careers.

Part Four discusses what for many students is the most important communication situation they will ever face: the job application process. We have designed the materials to be equally useful to both seniors who already know their career goals and lower division students who are just beginning to think about jobs. That is, it covers the information necessary for the job application process and that is useful in long-term educational career preparation.

Part Five, "Communication Strategies at Work," covers a wide range of managerial communication concerns, including interpersonal communication, conflict resolution and negotiation strategies, international communication, group communication dynamics and techniques for running meetings, and communication technology—all concepts that every manager needs to understand.

Acknowledgments

Whether you are currently a student or working in business or industry, we think that you will find this book thorough, readable, and helpful. Many people have contributed to make *Business Communication: From Process to Product* the high quality textbook that it is.

Some of our intellectual debts are long-standing: We owe special thanks to Francis W. Weeks, Professor Emeritus from the University of Illinois, and to C.W. Wilkinson, Professor Emeritus from the University of Alabama. Membership in the Association for Business Communication has afforded us the advice of colleagues too numerous to name. Our reviewers, however, deserve special mention for their valuable comments and suggestions, which helped us produce a better book. We are indebted to the following colleagues for careful reading and thoughtful commentary:

Arthur H. Bell; University of Southern California

Jo-Carol Fabianke; San Antonio College, Texas

Robert D. Gieselman; University of Illinois at Champaign-Urbana

Retha H. Kilpatrick, Western Carolina University

Shelby J. Kipplen; Owens Technical College, Ohio

Frank O'Brien; Hollins College, Virginia

Scott S. Schroeder, DeVry Institute of Technology

Linda Sharp, Texas Tech University

Craig Snow; Purdue University, Indiana

William N. Shannon III, Saint Mary's College

Annette N. Shelby, Georgetown University

Dickie Spurgeon; Southern Illinois University

Gloria N. Wilson; Arizona State University

Daniel R. Wunsch; Northern Illinois University

We are also indebted to our students, who have helped us improve the text in both major and minor ways. To the best of our abilities we have implemented the many suggestions students have offered for improving examples and explanations. We think that the result would please them. We think that it will please you, too. Good reading.

Joel P. Bowman

Bernadine P. Branchaw

Contents

BUSINESS COMMUNICATION

From Process to Product

PART ONE

Communication in Business

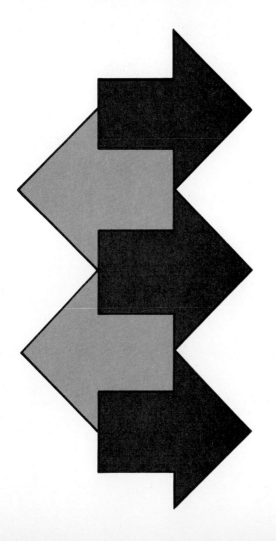

Communication is a complex process in which many possibilities for error exist. Over the past 50 years the centrality of communication to every aspect of human affairs has been increasingly recognized. In Part One we will examine some of the factors that make communication a vitally important area of study in today's world.

Business is now realizing that, to a large extent, success depends on how well certain messages are communicated. Employees need to know what their job duties and benefits are; the public needs to know the advantages of the company's products and services; the government needs to know that the company is complying with regulations and tax laws.

All human interaction—including the work of business—depends on the flow of information that we call communication. Whether the expression of that flow is nonverbal, oral, written, or electronic, each message contains at least two elements: the surface element and the psychological element. In the chapters that follow, we will show you how to control both elements.

CHAPTER ONE
Understanding the Communication Process

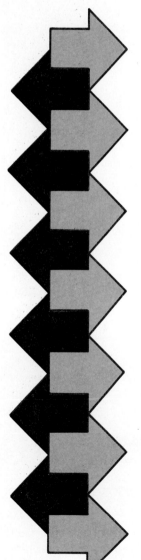

"Submit a memo outlining your ideas."
"Answer this letter for me."
"You're responsible for the sale presentation on Tuesday."
"I'll need an analytical report covering your findings."

Every business transaction requires communication: a phone call, meeting, letter, memo, oral presentation, or formal report. The effectiveness of the transaction depends on the effectiveness of the communication involved. This chapter introduces the basic concepts necessary to understand communication and the role it plays in business.

Topics

Overview: Communication Is
 Central
Communication and
 Relationships
  Harmonious Relationships
  Cooperative Relationships
  Adversarial Relationships
  Hostile Relationships
The Organizational
 Environment
Communication and Human
 Behavior

Communication Variables
 Perception
 Sender
 Message
 Channel
 Receiver
 Feedback
 Noise
 Transfer of Meaning
Communication Objectives
Successful Messages
Summary
Exercises

COMMUNICATION CHALLENGE

Milwaukee Heights Public Schools
Milwaukee, WI 53205

July 28, 19xx

To Our Vendors:

Last year we sent you a letter for the purpose of eliminating unauthorized purchases and to inform you that we were going to pay invoices twice a month.

As a result the incidence of unauthorized purchases improved appreciably, but it did not eliminate the problem. So this is a reminder that any sales made to the District without a purchase order will not be honored for payment.

In regards to our paying invoices twice a month we did accomplish it but not without some problems. We had trouble getting receiving copies into the Business Office and we had to change our payment days to the second and fourth Wednesdays.

We have and will appreciate your cooperation.

Sincerely,

Keith Bartleson

Keith Bartleson
Business Manager

▷ OVERVIEW: COMMUNICATION IS CENTRAL

Communication establishes relationships and makes human organization and cooperation possible. Business organizations differ from social and other non-profit organizations in that earning a profit is their principal objective. Hence, effective business communication not only establishes and maintains relationships but also does so in a cost-effective way.

Communication is the completed transmittal of a message from a sender to a receiver. The act of sending in itself is not communication; the message must be received for communication to occur. Because communication is a complex process involving seven variables, opportunities for errors abound.

Individuals in organizations communicate almost continually — to ask questions, to provide information, to persuade, even to entertain. Because business communication, like nonbusiness communication, maintains relationships, each message should attempt to accomplish two objectives: a *business* objective and a relationship or *human* objective. The business objective determines *what* is said, and the human objective determines *how* it is said.

Take a look at the letter presented in the following Communication Challenge. What are the objectives of this letter? How well does the letter achieve those objectives? In particular, what aspects of the letter interfere with its ability to achieve its objectives? Finally, what is your general impression of the letter as an example of business communication?

As you read the material in this chapter, you may wish to return to this Communication Challenge periodically to see whether you can add to or correct your original observations. Our analysis of the letter follows the chapter summary.

▷ COMMUNICATION AND RELATIONSHIPS

How does communication establish and maintain relationships?

Can you imagine a relationship without communication? Relationships are, in fact, established, maintained, and even defined by the communication that takes place within them. In general, relationships can be harmonious, cooperative, adversarial, or hostile.

Harmonious Relationships

In a **harmonious** relationship the parties involved desire the same goals and agree on the methods to achieve them. They have no serious differences that require resolving. In some ways this is an ideal relationship. Because the parties never have serious disagreements, however, they have little opportunity to learn from each other.

Cooperative Relationships

In a **cooperative** relationship the parties involved have differences about goals or about methods to achieve them, or about both goals and methods, but they are able to discuss their differences and reach an amicable agreement on how to compromise. In a cooperative relationship each party sees the other's opinion as legitimate, and differences of opinion are resolved by rational discussion.

Adversarial Relationships

How can communication improve adversarial and hostile relationships?

An **adversarial** relationship is marked by strong differences of opinion about goals or the methods that should be used to achieve them, or about both goals and methods. Neither party in an adversarial relationship recognizes the legitimacy of the other's opinion. Adversarial relationships often require mediation by a third party and often reach agreement only following legal action. Sometimes the relationship between labor and management in an organization is adversarial, with each side believing that the other is being unreasonable.

Hostile Relationships

A **hostile** relationship is one in which the parties involved deliberately try to injure each other. In this type of relationship all attempts to reach agreement have failed, and the parties try to achieve their objectives by force. Strikes, lockouts, and war are examples of hostile relationships on the organizational and national level. In a hostile relationship, communication has broken down because neither side trusts the other to be truthful.

Communication in harmonious and cooperative relationships is supportive and designed to solve problems and resolve differences. In adversarial and hostile relationships, the communication is accusatory and self-centered, focusing on the sender's point of view only. These differences are important to keep in mind as we look at the organizational environment, the role communication plays in human behavior, the variables that influence the communication process, and specific communication objectives.

◇ THE ORGANIZATIONAL ENVIRONMENT

What is an organization?

An organization is a group of people working together to achieve a common goal. Communication helps structure human relationships so that people can work together in this manner and thus makes organizational life possible. In working together to achieve common goals, people establish the common values, activities, and expectations that make up the organizational life, or environment.

Social fraternities and sororities exist to help college students develop social skills; professional associations exist to help people develop their professional skills; and a business organization exists to help people meet their economic needs. Each of these organizations is characterized by the activities it uses to meet its objectives, and it is successful to the extent that

What common pur-
pose do business
organizations share?

it helps its members satisfy their needs. Any organization must return more to its members than membership costs them—in other words, the benefits of membership must outweigh the costs. This is especially true of business organizations, which exist to exchange products or services for other products, services, rewards, or other items of value.

This common goal of all businesses—to produce benefits outweighing costs—is the basis for understanding the practical culture that governs business activity. To remain in business, an organization must do well in the exchange process: profits must exceed the costs of operation. Consequently, business organizations strive to keep the costs of operation as low as possible.

For many nonbusiness or nonprofit organizations, success is primarily a matter of achieving a particular objective regardless of the time and expense involved. Business organizations, however, need to be concerned with time and expense because their main reason for existence is economic.

Communication is one of the factors that govern the time, expense, and procedures used to achieve business objectives. Organizations measure the effectiveness of communication by whether the communication achieves its particular objective in an economical way. Correctness, technique, and form contribute to communication effectiveness, but the important tests are these two:

How does a busi-
ness measure the
effectiveness of
communication?

1. Whether the audience provides the information, understands an important issue, or adopts the suggested behavior.

2. Whether the result is worth the cost of the communication.

Until recently, business organizations had to be content with controlling the mechanical aspects of communication. The cost of writing and mailing a letter, for example, can be measured in terms of time, equipment, and materials. The cost of telephone calls can be checked on a regular basis.

Why is business
concerned about
communication ef-
fectiveness?

In the past few years, however, businesses have begun to view communication as an operating cost that can be reduced in other ways as well. Most businesses now recognize that communication efficiency can have a tremendous impact on their overall effectiveness. The cost of a letter should not be measured in terms of production only. In fact, the "cost" of a letter has no meaning unless the return is also known. A $2 letter that returns nothing is more expensive than a $25 letter that secures a $1,000 order.

Much of what increases communication efficiently is psychological. The following factors are critical:

1. Who communicates with whom and why.

2. The needs of the organization.

3. The needs and roles of its members.

4. External factors that influence the organization (consumers, competitors, suppliers, governmental agencies, and the like).

COMMUNICATION TODAY. . .

The overwhelming majority of service workers are actually engaged in the creation, processing, and distribution of information. The so-called service sector minus the information or knowledge workers has remained a fairly steady 11 or 12 percent since 1950. . . .

The real increase has been in information occupations. In 1950 only about 17 percent of us worked in information jobs. Now more than 65 percent of us work with information as programmers, teachers, clerks, secretaries, accountants, stock brokers, managers, insurance people, bureaucrats, lawyers, bankers, and technicians. And many more workers hold information jobs within manufacturing companies. Most Americans spend their time creating, processing, or distributing information.

Source: John Naisbitt, *Megatrends* (New York: Warner Books, 1984), pp. 4–5.

Major Conclusions of Research on 1,158 Newly Promoted U.S. Executives, 1980 to 1981:

Oral and written business communication was the course selected as "very important" more often than any of 13 courses as preparation for a career in general management.

Executives in all companies, as based on gross operating revenues, chose business communication as the course best preparing one for a career in general management.

Executives in the following functional areas selected business communication as the course best preparing one for a career in general management: production/operations; marketing/sales; finance/accounting/taxes; personnel/industrial relations; research and development.

Executives in the following major industry groups chose business communication as their first choice in preparing one for a career in general management: durable goods, manufacturing; nondurable goods, manufacturing; retail/wholesale trade; business services; regulated industries; and other groups.

Source: H. W. Hildebrandt et al, "An Executive Appraisal of Courses Which Best Prepare One for General Management," *The Journal of Business Communication*, 19, No. 1 (Winter 1982), p. 5.

In the past 20 years or so the business community has become increasingly aware that many of its problems are directly related to communication. As a result, the demand for professional seminars on communication has increased, as has the number of communication-related jobs in business and industry. Also, the increasing number of required communication courses at colleges and the increasing number of specialized communication courses emphasizing organizational and business needs demonstrate that communication will continue to be an important area of study for a long time to come. Can you imagine a life without communication?

▷ COMMUNICATION AND HUMAN BEHAVIOR

Why does "communication" cause so many problems?

In spite of the recent attention communication has been receiving, it is such a standard, common occurrence in our lives that we tend to take it for granted: We talk to people and they answer. We write letters; we receive replies. We read books, take tests, and write papers. Almost everything we do requires some kind of communication activity. We are talking or listening to someone (if only ourselves) from the time we get up in the morning until we go to bed at night. When we are not talking or listening, we are probably reading or writing.

As is the case with other routine activities, the fact that we communicate so often makes us think that we are experts. When we do not understand or cannot make ourselves understood, we usually blame the other person. Most of the time, however, we use communication fairly well. We are polite and friendly. We get along well with most of the people we know. We are understood (or at least we think we are), and usually we are able to understand the other person (or at least we think we do). So it is only natural for us to consider ourselves experts.

But communication is more complex than it appears. On the surface it seems easy to achieve good communication by using common sense. And much of our current knowledge about communication is based on a common-sense approach. Often, however, common sense is not enough to explain and solve communication problems. Skilled communicators draw on an extensive body of knowledge, including not only semantics—the study of the meaning of language—but also aspects of psychology, sociology, and the graphic arts.

Because communication seems so simple, we tend to forget that it is a process involving a number of variables, each subject to a number of possible problems. Regardless of the number of people involved, the communication process is always more complicated than it seems on the surface because of these variables.

▷ COMMUNICATION VARIABLES

What is communication?

What is communication? We can begin answering that question with a simple definition: communication is the successful transmission of a message to a receiver. Although, obviously, other living species besides human beings are

FIGURE 1.1 Model of the Communication Process

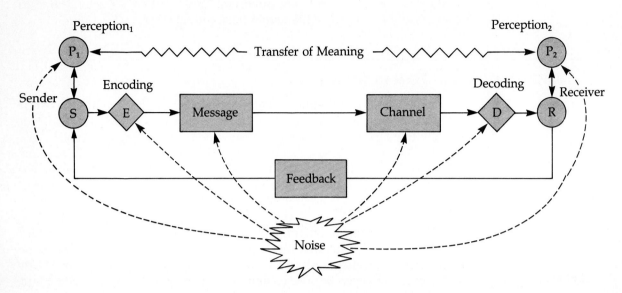

capable of certain kinds of communication, this book will discuss only the human kind. Also, although communication can be "internal" or "intrapersonal" (a mental talking to yourself), it is generally more useful to limit the term to mean the transfer of meaning between and among people.

Communication begins with a *perception* in the mind of a *sender*. This perception is the impetus for a *message*. The sender selects a *channel* that will convey the message to a *receiver*. *Feedback* indicates to the sender how well the meaning has been transferred. *Noise*, anything that interferes with the transfer of meaning, can occur at any point in the communication process. The goal of this process is the *transfer of meaning*. Each of these variables influences the communication process, as Figure 1.1 illustrates.

Although the figure suggests that each factor operates separately from the others, in actuality the factors are interdependent and essentially take place simultaneously. The sender, for example, may be watching the receiver for signs of feedback while she or he is in the process of sending a message. Thus, the sender may be in effect sending and receiving messages simultaneously.

Perception

What factors influence perception?

The first factor in the communication process, perception (P_1), is responsible for all the others. To paraphrase the seventeenth-century philosopher René Descartes, we know we exist because we perceive. Perception is the act of using the senses to become aware of the environment. Although we all live in the same *objective* world, each of us has a different *subjective* view of the world. We see the world with different eyes. No matter how similar two people may be, no two of us are exactly alike, and so each of us perceives the world and events differently.

Human perception is a complicated subject, and we have space to deal with only a small part of it. To be successful as a business communicator, you need to know that perceptions vary according to a wide variety of factors, including age, sex, height, weight, group and cultural identifications, and individual life experiences. Older people and young people, men and women, whites and blacks, will tend to have different perceptions of many events. People tend to perceive what they have been taught to perceive and what they expect to perceive. No one's perception is fully accurate, and everyone's perception is at least partly true.

Effective business communication depends on our ability to recognize that perceptions — both our own and those of others — may be inaccurate and on our willingness to continue the communication process until important differences are understood and problems are resolved.

Sender

How does the sender influence the communication process?

The sender is responsible for *encoding,* or formulating a message that will convey the meaning of the original perception. Encoding is the process of converting the perception—whether it is of an event occurring in the outside world or a new idea — into the gestures or words that will have meaning to another person. One of the main objectives of this book is to help you improve your communication skills by improving the way you, as a sender of messages, encode your perceptions for other people.

In addition to your concern for the accuracy of the message itself, as a sender you must also be concerned with your credibility — the degree to which your reader can believe you. Your credibility greatly influences the kind of reception your messages will receive. Because credibility depends on how well you convey trustworthiness and professional competence, it can be aided by skilled communication, but, of course, it must also be earned by your past performance.

The surface message contained in your communication will always be secondary to the psychological message. The psychological message will be determined by whether you believe what you are saying, and whether you care what your audience will think and feel. A history of speaking the truth and of caring about others virtually guarantees credibility.

Message

What is a message?

The third major factor in the communication process, the message, is what we communicate. Messages consist of verbal or nonverbal symbols containing information, meaning, or intelligence. Each message is an attempt to define and share with our intended receiver some aspect of our perception of the world—what we see, hear, feel, taste, smell, or think—and what that perception means to us.

Of course, messages can vary greatly in complexity, from the infant's cry announcing discomfort to the complicated language of détente. When people's perceptions are similar, simple messages serve; as perceptions become increasingly dissimilar, the complexity of messages must also increase. You know from experience how much easier it is to communicate with your friends than with strangers whose age, occupation, or nationality differs markedly from your own. Messages, then, may be placed on a continuum according to their complexity, with simple messages on one end and complex messages on the other.

Simple Messages.   Simple messages contain few components requiring interpretation. In American culture a sign stating "No Smoking" is an example of a simple message. Our shared perceptions—including the common language, the widespread acceptance of definitions for "no" and "smoking," the brevity of the message, and our previous experience with this and similar messages—contribute to our ability to understand the message without having to struggle with interpretations. Traffic signs, simple directions, and many of our daily conversations with our friends are other examples of fairly simple messages.

Complex Messages.   Complex messages contain many components that must be interpreted before the message can be understood. If we say, for example, "Broad diversification rules out extraordinary losses relative to the whole market; it also, by definition, rules out extraordinary gains," we have three principal terms (*diversification, extraordinary*, and *market*) for which a wide range of interpretations is possible. If we choose to send that message to someone, we are probably safe in assuming on the basis of shared culture that the other words in the message would be relatively clear; but we would need to make sure that our receiver knew exactly what we meant by the three noted terms, or miscommunication would result. Even this message is simple, however, compared to the messages required for building a bridge, selecting a site for a new motel, or programming a new insurance rate schedule on a computer.

Channel

Why does the channel influence the communication process?

Communication channels include nonverbal, oral, written, and electronic methods. Each of these channels has certain characteristics which can either help or hinder the transfer of meaning, depending on the circumstances, the message, and the audience involved.

Nonverbal.   The most important nonverbal components in organizational communication are

1. Space
    a. Between people (*proxemics*)
    b. Allocated to people (*territory*)

2. Time
    a. Amount
    b. Kind (exclusive or shared)
    c. Who waits for whom

3. Kinesics
    a. *Open* postures and signals, inviting communication
    b. *Closed* postures and signals, discouraging communication

4. Appearance
    a. Conforming
    b. Nonconforming

Nonverbal communication serves primarily to communicate attitudes, feelings, status, and other affective (emotional) messages. In business, nonverbal messages help regulate activities, including verbal (both oral and written) communication flow. The "territory" allocated to executives, for example, serves at least two purposes: (1) it protects them from intrusions that would interfere with accomplishing important tasks, and (2) it indicates their status to others. It is much more difficult to see a corporation's chief executive officer than it is to see the director of personnel. And it is harder to see the director of personnel than it is to see a member of his or her staff.

Communicators should be aware of the effects of nonverbal indicators. Space, time, kinesics, and appearance either increase or decrease the distance (physical and emotional) between people; and every increase in distance brings a corresponding decrease in affective communication.

Think about your own communication preferences. Are you most comfortable communicating with people who

1. Come from your part of the country or from some other area? From the United States, Canada, Mexico, Northern Europe, Southern Europe, Asia?

2. Are over 40 or under 40?

3. Are white, black, brown, or red?

4. Wear three-piece suits or blue jeans and tee-shirts?

5. Prefer reading philosophy to watching sports on television, or vice versa?

Differences of the kind in the preceding list often create psychological barriers in the communication process.

Decreases in affective (emotional) communication sometimes result in reduced or inaccurate feedback about matters of organizational importance. Good use of time and kinesics, however, is usually sufficient to maintain high quality communication. It is important to keep, and be on time for, appointments. Body movements and eye contact should indicate openness, inclusion, and willingness to communicate.

Oral.   Even if we exclude extraorganizational oral communication ("Did you see the ball game last night?"), the bulk of communication activity in organizations is still oral and takes place between two people or in small groups. People at work in business spend approximately 75 percent of their time speaking and listening. Much of this oral communication is "preliminary" and concerns decision making. The results of this sort of oral communication usually end up in writing. Other oral communication helps build organizational morale. The work-related conversations people have with each other on the job satisfy social needs. Talking with others about solving common problems is important to most people.

Open and *closed* communication stances affect oral communication just as they affect nonverbal communication. The degree to which communication stances are open or closed is usually referred to as the *communication climate*. Being open orally means being willing to listen as well as to talk, attempting to see the other person's point of view as well as conveying your own. Being closed orally means the opposite and usually represents an attempt to use power to control the relationship.

Students and teachers, for example, may have difficulty communicating with each other because they are "closed" to the other's point of view. Instead of working together to solve their common problems, they too often judge and manipulate each other in ways that hinder reaching common goals.

The characteristics of open and closed communication climates are as follows:

Open	Closed
observational	judgmental
problem solving	manipulative
you-oriented	we-oriented
equal	condescending
flexible	dogmatic
supportive	defensive

Harmonious and cooperative relationships are marked by open communication, whereas much of the communication in adversarial and hostile relationships is closed. Because an organization requires the cooperation of its members for long-term survival, it is management's responsibility to en-

Why is oral communication important to an organization?

Why does an open communication climate result in a more cooperative relationship?

courage open communication. Long-term organizational success requires that all employees in the organization feel that they can express their observations and criticisms to others in the organization, regardless of rank.

What would happen if you went in to see your instructor to convey a criticism? Would it influence your grade? Do you share your criticisms with your classmates? Can you share *positive* observations with your instructor and classmates? Your answers to these questions will tell you what kind of communication climate governs your class. The same characteristics apply in business.

In an open communication climate, employees believe that

1. They will receive credit for their ideas and contributions.

2. Their complaints will be taken seriously, investigated, and either resolved or explained in a satisfactory manner.

3. Those higher in the organizational hierarchy are not manipulating communication flow to control them.

4. Those higher in the organizational hierarchy value them as human beings whose needs and aspirations go beyond their organizational functions.

Written.   Nearly all important business communication is eventually put into writing. The main advantage of written communication is that it provides a fairly permanent record; the main disadvantage of writing is that it does not permit rapid feedback. Writing is a much slower channel of communication than the nonverbal and oral channels. For this reason, clarity is much more important with a written communication than with an oral message. Also, because the absence of prompt feedback deprives the sender of the opportunity to modify the message according to the response observed in the audience, the psychological impact of a written message requires especially close attention.

The psychological climate of a written communication may suggest a helpful, problem-solving attitude on the part of the sender or a defensive, judgmental attitude. Compare the following sentences responding to a request for an extension on a loan repayment because of an emergency operation.

Closed: Because you have been a good customer of ours, we are willing to grant an exception to our policy in this case. (Note that the writer is saying that the reader does not *deserve* special treatment but that the writer will *grant* it grudgingly to avoid losing the reader's business.)

Open: Certainly you may have the extra 30 days. We wish you a speedy recovery. (Note the gracious way the reader's request is approved.)

How will increased use of electronic communication channels influence the communication process?

Electronic.   Electronic channels range from teletype to television, from electronic mail to computer meetings. Some electronic channels serve primarily as transducers, converting one form of energy to another and back again, for written and oral communication. Teletype, for example, converts a written message into electronic impulses and back into a written message, speeding the process of sending a written message. Likewise, television converts an oral message into an electronic message and back again, allowing oral communication to overcome the barrier of distance.

Electronic channels usually have the same basic characteristics as other channels. In some cases, however, the electronic media exert an extra influence on the message. Electronic mail, for example, is frequently more concise and less formal than its written equivalent. Whether this tendency will change as more people use electronic mail on a regular basis remains to be seen. Perceptions of what is courteous, concise, and effective change over time, and new uses of electronic media will undoubtedly alter some of the currently accepted communication practices.

Receiver

How does the receiver influence the communication process?

The receiver is responsible for *decoding* the message transmitted by the sender. In addition to converting the sender's words and sentences into meaningful ideas, the receiver observes nonverbal components of the communication to see whether they confirm or contradict the verbal message. The receiver also measures the current message against his or her previous experience to help determine the meaning of the message.

Like other factors in the communication process, the receiver, or audience, can vary in several ways. The size of an audience, its familiarity with the content of the message, its attitude toward the subject, and its previous relationship with and attitude toward the sender of the message are all important. The audience's distance—both physical and emotional—from the sender also has an important influence on the transfer of meaning. The greater the distance, the more difficult it is to communicate. Communicating with friends is easier than communicating with strangers or enemies. Friends try to keep the communication channels open even when they disagree. Strangers and enemies are more likely to give up when communication becomes difficult.

Feedback

What is feedback?

Feedback is not technically a part of the original process of communication. Rather, it constitutes an entirely new message from a new sender, prompted by a new perception. Feedback is, however, related to the original message in that it indicates how effective the transfer of meaning was. It lets the sender know that *some* transfer has taken place, that a message — if not an accurate conception of the original perception — has been received. Feedback can be as simple as a nod of the head, a brief "yes" or "no," or a quick question; or it can be as complex as a lengthy written response. Feedback is important because we use it to evaluate the effectiveness of the messages we send. Companies judge the effectiveness of their advertising, for example, by measuring the increase in name recognition and sales.

Noise

How does noise influence the communication process?

Noise, a term popularized since the advent of electronic communication, is a factor in the communication process because the process is imperfect. Noise refers to any interference with the transfer of meaning. If you are delivering a speech while a band practices in the next room, you have a noise problem. If you put greasy fingerprints all over a letter, you have created a noise problem. If you are trying to communicate with people from another culture, you may have a noise problem. Anything that hinders the accurate transfer of meaning is noise. Some types of noise cannot be prevented. Those that often can be prevented include

In oral communication
bad acoustics
bad attitude toward speaker or audience
poor sound system
poor appearance of speaker or audience
outside disturbances
    cars
    sirens
    people
    doors
    telephones

In written communication
poor quality paper
greasy thumbprints or fingerprints
smudges
faded ribbon
dirty typewriter keys or print elements
color of paper
water or coffee spots

poor typing corrections

bad grammar

poor punctuation or spelling

long blocks of single-spaced typing

Transfer of Meaning

How can two peo-
ple be sure that
they understand
each other?

The transfer of meaning is the goal of all communication. This goal is not necessarily achieved just because some kind of information is transferred from the sender to the receiver. Because the message selected by the sender may not adequately express his or her perception, and because the message represents a new perception for the receiver, the meaning transferred to the receiver may be quite different from the sender's original perception. A comical statement illustrating the problem is

> I know that you believe you understood what you think I said, but I am not sure that you realize that what you heard is not what I meant.

Although much can go wrong in the communication process, problems can usually be solved by persevering. We need to discover the meanings our messages have for others so that we can alter our messages when necessary to achieve a more accurate transfer of meaning. Because no two people ever share exactly the same experiences or view of the world, communication is *always* imperfect. The receiver's perception (P_2 in Figure 1.1) will *never* be identical with the sender's perception (P_1). The two perceptions can, however, be close enough to make cooperation possible and relationships enjoyable. Good communication, in which all parties have a fairly accurate understanding of what the others think, requires effort and commitment on the part of both senders and receivers.

▷ COMMUNICATION OBJECTIVES

Most models, including the one in Figure 1.1, are useless without a specific application. As an example of a specific application for the communication model, assume that you wish to reduce the degree of conflict you experience with a certain person. By remembering that individual perceptions vary and that language is symbolic, you may be able to listen for what that person *means* rather than to what the person *says* the next time conflict arises.

How does business
communication dif-
fer from personal
communication?

On a personal level our general objectives are to understand and to be understood—and liked—by other people. Successful business messages also focus on a business objective. Broadly speaking, these business objectives fall into three general categories: to inquire, to inform, and to persuade. A fourth communication objective, to entertain, has business applications though it is not purely a business objective. (Obviously, these objectives are often a part of nonbusiness communication as well.)

1. **To Inquire.**   Inquiring messages are designed to obtain information, goods, or services: asking questions, placing orders, and making simple (as opposed to persuasive) requests.

2. **To Inform.**   Informative messages are designed to convey positive, neutral, or negative information to an audience. Information is positive if the receiver will welcome it. It is neutral when the receiver has no special interest in it. It is negative when it will hurt the receiver's feelings or cause the receiver to be angry, resentful, or disappointed.

3. **To Persuade.**   Persuasive messages are designed to alter an audience's behavior. Typical sales messages, of course, are persuasive. In addition, any message that would be resisted by the receiver for any reason needs to be persuasive. If, for example, you are inviting someone to speak at an event but you cannot meet that person's expected compensation, you will need to send a persuasive request rather than a simple request.

4. **To Entertain.**   Entertaining messages are designed to help hold the audience's attention while some other purpose is being achieved. Business messages designed only to entertain are rare.

Business relationships include an aspect that corresponds to the desire to be liked in a personal relationship. Businesses need to convince employees, suppliers, clients or customers, and a variety of external agencies to "care" about them and to desire to establish or maintain a continuing relationship. For this reason, in addition to having a specific business objective, even the most business-like messages also have a human objective: to create or maintain as much trust and goodwill as circumstances allow.

◇ SUCCESSFUL MESSAGES

What is a successful message?

Successful messages achieve both business and human objectives. Achieving both in most business situations requires training and planning. As tempting as it may be sometimes to argue with your audience, you should remember that successful business messages do not accuse people of shortcomings or express personal frustration or anger. Business messages should be communicated to improve business—to help sell products and services—and to build goodwill between sender and receiver.

COMMUNICATION SOLUTION

Although the letter in this chapter's Communication Challenge (See the chapter overview.) does succeed in communicating the informative part of its message (the school system will not pay bills that do not have a corresponding purchase order), and thus achieves its business objective, it neglects the receiver's point of view, and thus fails to achieve the human objective of maintaining a good relationship. Count the number of "we"s in the letter. Notice that the letter focuses on the writer's problems (see the paragraph beginning "In regards to . . .") and conveys the attitude that the relationship between writer and reader is essentially a one-way proposition. Because it focuses so entirely on the writer's problems, the letter suggests that the writer feels that he is more important than his readers. A good relationship is not communicated, regardless of the expressed appreciation of cooperation, and the reader is left with a "so what" feeling.

Note also the way the use of language influences the message. What does the writer mean, for example, when he says that "the incidence

of unauthorized purchases improved appreciably"? Did the incidence get bigger and better? What is wrong with saying "We have and will appreciate your cooperation"? Does the writer mean, "We *now* have your cooperation and *in the future* will appreciate it," or does he mean, "We have *appreciated* your cooperation in the past and will appreciate it in the future too"?

The writer of this letter was no doubt busy and was understandably concerned about his own problems at the time he wrote this letter. He forgot, however, that one of the main functions of communication is to establish or maintain relationships. Any act of communication conveys more than the specific message—it conveys an attitude. The writer of the letter in the Communication Challenge conveys an attitude of being self-centered and uncaring about his readers' needs and problems. Similarly, all acts of communication—whether nonverbal, oral, written, or electronic—reveal something of the sender's attitude about the receiver.

At its best, communication can convert an adversarial or hostile relationship into one of harmony or cooperation. At its worst, it can create hostility where none existed previously. Your business communication will be more successful when you strive to develop cooperative relationships by remembering the dual purpose (business and human) of every message. In the chapters that follow, we will show you how you can accomplish these objectives in a wide variety of business communication situations.

▷ SUMMARY

Communication establishes or maintains relationships and makes human organization and cooperation possible. Communication is the transmission of a message from a sender to a receiver. Relationships may be classed as harmonious, cooperative, adversarial, or hostile.

An organization is a group of people working together to achieve a common goal. Business organizations have some kind of product as a result of exchanging products or services as their objective. For this reason, businesses need to be concerned with the cost-effectiveness of their communications.

Communication may seem easy to understand and achieve, but it is actually a complex process involving a number of variables. A perception in the mind of a sender is encoded into a message that is transmitted by a channel to a receiver who decodes the message to create his or her own perception. Feedback, a new message from the original receiver to the original sender, confirms the accuracy of the transfer of meaning. Noise or distortion may enter this process at any step.

Business communication always has two objectives—a business or practical objective and a human objective. Business objectives are to inquire, to inform, to persuade, and to entertain. The human objective is to maintain or improve the relationship between sender and receiver. Successful messages achieve both the business and human objectives, perhaps even converting an adversarial or hostile relationship into one of harmony or cooperation.

▷ EXERCISES

Review and Discussion Questions

1. Describe the four basic types of relationships.

2. What is an organization?

3. What is the common objective of business organizations?

4. What must be known before the cost of a letter can be measured?

5. What are the seven variables in the communication process? How does each variable influence the process as a whole?

6. What are the differences between open and closed communication climates?

7. Name and explain business and human communication objectives.

8. What makes a message successful?

Problems

Analyze the reader's probable reaction to the business objective and the human objective in the following messages:

a. We have received your letter in which you claim that 5 of the 14 Model 12 portable color televisions arrived in a nonfunctional condition.

We are at a loss to explain how this unlikely event could have occurred because each television is tested thoroughly before it is crated in a specially designed, damage-proof carton. We suspect that faulty handling in your store is responsible for the trouble.

Since you have been a good customer of ours, however, we are willing to send you five more Model 12 televisions, and we will do so as soon as you return the televisions which you claim are defective.

b.   Your letter has been forwarded to this office for reply. I'm very sorry that 5 of the 14 Model 12 portable color televisions arrived in unsatisfactory condition, and I apologize for the inconvenience this has caused you.

Since you have been a good customer of ours, we are sending you five additional Model 12 televisions, assuming, of course, that you will return the five which were probably damaged in shipment.

Again, I apologize for all the trouble this has caused you, and I assure you that in the future, all television sets will be examined thoroughly so an event of this magnitude will never occur again.

c.   You will receive replacements for the five Model 12 portable color televisions by Tuesday, 15 December.

When the carriers arrive, simply give them the original color televisions. We will examine the sets thoroughly to see what caused the trouble, and as soon as we know the cause, we'll let you know. Thank you for bringing the matter to our attention so quickly. Your promptness will help us give you better service.

The enclosed brochure on the Model 12 television is new. I'm sending you 100 brochures along with the new Model 12 televisions for free distribution to your customers. Should you need more before your next order, call me collect at (415) 555-4419.

CASE

The model of the communication process presented in Figure 1.1 has frequently been called the *transmission* model. Where did this model originate? What are its advantages and disadvantages as an explanation of what happens when people communicate? Find at least three articles in professional journals (see *The Journal of Business Communication*, for example) that discuss communication models, and present your findings and conclusions in a paper of two to three typewritten pages.

CHAPTER TWO

Developing Business Writing Skills

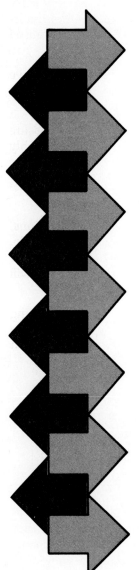

Regardless of the changes in communication brought about by technology, written communication will continue to play a central role in business and in society as a whole. No other form of communication can present complex ideas as clearly and logically as a written message. This chapter reviews the fundamentals of writing and English usage.

Topics

COMMUNICATION CHALLENGE

MOUSER, MOWATT AND MUELLER, INC.
15206 GREENLEAF STREET   SHERMAN OAKS, CA 91403

June 16, 19xx

TO: Alice Carroll, VP Operations

FROM: Roger Jacksa *rj*

ADDING EXERCISE FACILITIES FOR EMPLOYEES

Requesting to do a study to examine the costs associated with installing
exercise facilities for employee use.

Other companies have indicated that a higher morale and employee
satisfaction rate will emerge, the initial amount of facilities would be
small.

By exercising on a continuous basis, employee productivity has been
proven to increase. People that exercise being healthier and more
energetic than those who don't. The attached chart determines the
level of interest our employees have in this facility.

The study would take about one weeks time.

▷ OVERVIEW: FOLLOW THE CONVENTIONS

Language changes over time. Words take on new meanings, expressions
come into and drop out of favor, and even the spelling of a word may change.
The rules for English usage may seem arbitrary, especially in view of the

dynamic nature of language. These rules, however, are necessary if language is to communicate effectively and efficiently. You have doubtless had the experience of communicating with someone who used words with which you were unfamiliar or used words you knew but in an unexpected way. You can imagine how difficult communication would be if everyone had Humpty Dumpty's philosophy of having words mean just what he chooses them to mean.

It is important to know and follow the conventions of English usage for the same reason it is important to know and follow other cultural conventions: it will help keep you out of trouble. Your use of language, like your dress and appearance, is one thing you can't hide. People will judge you by the way you speak and the way you write. Based on your use of language, they will make assumptions about your intelligence and competence to do a job.

The memo in this chapter's Communication Challenge, for example, violates several communication conventions. Can you identify them? After you've read the chapter, compare your observations with those we present in the Communication Solution following the summary.

◁ THE NATURE OF LANGUAGE

What causes language to change? Would we be better off if language never changed? Why or why not?

Anyone who has ever looked at one of Chaucer's poems is aware that language has changed greatly since the fourteenth century.

> Whan that Aprill with its shoures soote
> The droghte of March hath perced to the roote. . . .

Language is dynamic. It changes to meet the changing needs of the people who use it. In general, oral forms of the language change more quickly than written forms, and one function of written language is to provide a fairly stable standard against which change can be measured. Of course, the main function of a written standard of language usage is to facilitate communication by helping to ensure the accurate transfer of meaning from sender to receiver.

The rules governing the way language should be used may sometimes seem arbitrary and unnecessary. For example, in the ungrammatical sentence, "He ain't got no bread," the use of the double negative does not interfere with our ability to understand that the person doesn't have any bread. We are more likely to have trouble understanding how the sender is using the word "bread." Does it mean food or money? Now look at the message, "Smelling like rotten eggs, I gasped as I drove past the factory." Miscommunication here is possible as a result of the message sender's failure to follow a grammatical rule governing the placement of modifiers.

COMMUNICATION TODAY. . .

"Although levels of usage have always been recognized, what is new in the contemporary world is the equal blessing bestowed on all of them. And implicit in that blind blessing is a reluctance to hurt anyone's feelings or to make him feel inferior. This attitude is puzzling. There are more poor fiddlers than good ones, but no one hesitates to say that there is such a thing as good violin playing. . . .

"The change in the twentieth century has been quite noticeable but not revolutionary. Visualize the language as three overlapping glass doors. At the right is a narrow one labeled "formal." In the center is a wide one labeled "reputable." And at the left, broadest of all, is one labeled "casual." What has happened is a gradual shift of two of these to the left.

"There is no need, then, for argument about the existence, the inevitability, and the desirability of change. There is need, however, for argument about the existence of such a thing as good English and correct English. Let us not hesitate to assert that "The pencil was laying on the table" and "He don't know nothing" are at present incorrect, no matter how many know-nothings say them.

"Let us do these things not to satisfy "rules" or to gratify the whims of a pedagogue, but rather to express ourselves clearly, precisely, logically, and directly — and to cultivate the habits of mind that produce that kind of expression. Let us, in short, write carefully and correctly.

Source: Theodore M. Bernstein, excerpted from *The Careful Writer*, pp. xiii–xv. Copyright © 1965 Theodore M. Bernstein. Reprinted with the permission of Atheneum Publishers, Inc.

What is the function of grammar?

The rules of grammar have been established for the same reasons that rules for other human activities have been established. When we all follow the same rules, we can better understand and cooperate with each other. It is also helpful if the rules don't change too quickly. Linguists (language experts) disagree about what constitutes "too quickly." As is the case with any cultural standards, some experts are too eager to change, and some refuse to change at all. When language changes too quickly, its abilities to transcend both time and distance are diminished. The balance between the change necessary to keep language alive and interesting and the stability required for maximum usefulness is built into culture. If you are either too far ahead or too far behind what most people accept as "correct," your speech and writing will attract the kind of attention you would probably rather avoid.

▷ GRAMMAR

Why is it important to know the parts of speech?

Grammar is important—but rather than consider grammatical principles absolute indicators of right and wrong, you should consider them guides to effective communication. We think you will find that grammar is really quite simple when you concentrate on the few absolute essentials you will need to communicate effectively. Any objections you may have to grammar are probably a result of its sometimes arbitrary nature. Certain grammatical rules cannot be logically explained but must simply be accepted. Without them, however, we would not have agreement on how language should be used, and the lack of agreement would hinder communication. Keep in mind, also, that the words we use to express grammatical principles are merely symbols for concepts we have about the ways language functions. To be able to discuss the concepts, we need a common terminology. One important part of this terminology concerns the components of language—the parts of speech—and how they function in sentences.

Part of Speech	Function
Noun	Names something
Pronoun	Takes the place of a noun
Verb	Expresses action
Adjective	Modifies a noun or pronoun
Adverb	Modifies a verb, adjective, or another adverb
Conjunction	Joins one element to another
Preposition	Shows relationship
Interjection	Expresses strong feeling

Nouns

A noun names a person, place, thing, or idea. In sentences, nouns can function as subjects, direct objects, indirect objects, objects of prepositions, subject complements, and appositives. **Proper nouns** name particular persons, places, or things; they are usually capitalized. Examples of proper nouns include *Abraham Lincoln; Washington, D.C.;* and *Blue Ridge Mountains.* **Common nouns** name persons, places or things that are not specific, such as *man, woman, city, state, chair, desk, profits,* and *losses.*

Common nouns may be classified as **abstract** or **concrete.** Abstract nouns refer to intangible things—things that cannot be seen, heard, touched, tasted, or smelled. Abstract nouns refer to qualities or ideas, such as *goodness, freedom, democracy,* and *capitalism.* Concrete nouns refer to tangible things—things that can be seen, heard, touched, tasted, or smelled—such as *chair, noise, skin, fur, apple, smoke,* and *fumes.*

Abstract and concrete are, of course, matters of degree rather than absolutes. Most nouns are only abstract or concrete in relation to other nouns. The word *dog,* for example, is less concrete than a specific breed, *English setter,* and less abstract than the word *mammal.* This concept is often referred to as **the ladder of abstraction.**

Pronouns

A pronoun is a word that takes the place of a noun. The noun for which a pronoun stands is its *antecedent*. Pronouns can be personal, relative, interrogative, demonstrative, or indefinite.

Personal pronouns refer to the person speaking, the person spoken to, or the person spoken about.

When should you use the relative pronouns "who" and "that"?

	Singular	**Plural**
Person speaking:	I went.	We went.
Person spoken to:	You went.	You (all) went.
Person spoken about:	He went.	They went.

Relative pronouns introduce subordinate clauses by referring to antecedents in the main clause. *Who, whom, which,* and *that* are relative pronouns.

Dolores Powers is an executive who works hard.

In this example *who* is a relative pronoun that introduces the subordinate clause; it refers to the antecedent, *executive,* in the main clause.

Interrogative pronouns start direct or indirect questions. *Who, whom, what, which,* and *whose* are interrogative pronouns. (Do not confuse *whose* with the contraction, *who's,* which stands for *who is.*)

Direct question:	Whose account is this?
Indirect question:	I wonder what stock we should purchase.

When do you use the pronoun "that" to refer to a person?

Demonstrative pronouns point out particular persons or things. *This, these, that,* and *those* are demonstrative pronouns. *This* (singular) and *these* (plural) refer to objects that are near. *That* (singular) and *those* (plural) refer to objects that are distant.

Singular:	This is mine.	That is hers.
Plural:	These are mine.	Those are hers.

Indefinite pronouns refer to groups of persons or to things in general. Some indefinite pronouns are

all	every
any	everybody
anybody	everyone
anyone	everything
anything	neither
each	most
either	much

none	somebody
several	someone
some	something

Case.   Pronouns have different cases depending on the role they play in a clause. When the pronoun is acting as the subject of a verb, it is the *nominative* case (because it *names* the subject of a verb). When the pronoun receives the action of a verb or is the object of a preposition, it is in the *objective* case. And when a pronoun refers to a noun or pronoun earlier in the sentence, it is in the *reflexive* case. When it expresses ownership, the pronoun is in the *possessive* case.

Nominative Case	Objective Case	Reflexive Case	Possessive Case
I	me	myself	my/mine
you	you	yourself	your/yours
he/she	him/her	himself/herself	his/her
it	it	itself	its
we	us	ourselves	our/ours
you	you	yourselves	your/yours
they	them	themselves	their/theirs

Incorrect:	*Me* and Carl prepared the work schedules.
Correct:	Carl and *I* prepared the work schedules.
Incorrect:	Just between you and *I*, Susan Crowfoot will be our new president.
Correct:	Just between you and *me*, Susan Crowfoot will be our new president.
Incorrect:	Give a copy of the report to her and *myself.*
Correct:	Give a copy of the report to her and *me.*
Incorrect:	*Them* and *us* designed the brochure for the seminar.
Correct:	*They* and *we* designed the brochure for the seminar.
Incorrect:	It was *me* who called yesterday.
Correct:	It was *I* who called yesterday.
Incorrect:	She believes that Darrell or *him* submitted the plan.
Correct:	She believes that Darrell or *he* submitted the plan.

Incorrect:	Is this book *her*'s?
Correct:	Is this book *hers*?

Incorrect:	Everyone liked *them* acting.
Correct:	Everyone liked *their* acting.

Incorrect:	For *me*, I prefer the longer weekend.
Correct:	For *myself*, I prefer the longer weekend.

Incorrect:	A man like *yourself* should know better.
Correct:	A man like *you* should know better.

Compound personal pronouns are those in the reflexive case, the "self" pronouns (myself, yourself, himself, herself, itself, ourselves, yourselves, themselves). They are used to direct the action of the verb back to the subject.

Sherry bought *herself* a new desk.
They satisfied *themselves* by buying 100 shares of IBM stock.

They are also used when you want to emphasize a noun or pronoun already expressed.

I *myself* shall do the job.
The manager *herself* conducted the workshop.
Mr. Rousch *himself* told us the news.

What is wrong with saying, "Please join Tyrone and myself"?

Do not use a compound personal pronoun unless the noun or pronoun to which it refers is stated in the sentence.

Incorrect:	Give the papers to Joan and *myself*.
Correct:	Give the papers to Joan and *me*.

Incorrect:	A person (any person) such as *yourself* should recognize the importance of deadlines.
Correct:	A person like *you* should recognize the importance of deadlines.

Verbs

Why are verbs so important for effective writing?

A verb is a word that expresses action or being. A verb is essential to complete the meaning of any sentence. A **transitive** verb needs an object to complete its meaning; an **intransitive** verb does not need an object to complete its meaning.

Transitive:	David completed the project.
Intransitive:	Mary Ann sat.

Some verbs are both transitive and intransitive.

Transitive: Fred sells stocks.

Intransitive: Fred sells frequently.

An intransitive verb has no object, but it may have a **complement** (discussed later in this chapter under "Sentences"). An intransitive verb that joins a subject to its complement is called a **linking** verb. Common linking verbs are *be, seem, appear,* and verbs describing the senses, such as *feel, taste,* and *look.*

Profits seemed high.
Profits are good.
The pie tastes wonderful.

Voice.   If the subject of the sentence does the action that the verb describes, the verb is in the **active voice.** If the subject of the sentence receives the action, the verb is in the **passive voice.**

Active voice: Edward prepared the sales report.

Passive voice: The sales report was prepared by Edward.

In active voice sentences the subject of the sentence always performs the action. Passive voice sentences use the verb "to be" and the past participle of an action verb so that the subject receives the action.

Active voice: The *manager decided* to buy a new desk.

Passive voice: It *was decided by* the manager to buy a new desk.

Passive voice: It *was decided* to buy a new desk.

Tense.   The simple tenses (past, present, and future) are easier to understand than the compound tenses. Use them when possible, but make sure that the verbs used for each event accurately depict the time appropriate for the event. See "Progression of Verb Tenses" later in this chapter.

Adjectives

Adjectives are words that modify nouns or pronouns. In the following sentence *short-term* modifies *profits.*

Short-term profits increased.

Adjectives have three degrees of comparison — *positive, comparative,* and *superlative.* Use the positive degree when the word modified is not being compared with anything else. Use the comparative degree when comparing two things; use the superlative degree when comparing more than two things.

Generally, add the suffix -er to form the comparative degree, and add -est to one-syllable adjectives to form the superlative degree. For adjectives of more than two syllables, add the words *more* (for comparative) or *most* (for superlative). For negatives, add *less* (for comparative) or *least* (for superlative). Two-syllable adjectives may take either form to show the comparative or superlative degree.

Positive	Comparative	Superlative
bright	brighter	brightest
angry	angrier	angriest
	more angry	most angry
appreciative	more appreciative	most appreciative

Some adjectives have irregular forms of comparison.

Positive	Comparative	Superlative
bad	worse	worst
good	better	best

What's wrong with saying "most unique"?

Other adjectives cannot be compared; they are absolutes. *Round, square, perfect,* and *unique* are absolute adjectives.

Incorrect: It was the *most unique* party I had ever attended.

Correct: The party was *unique*! (Unique means one of a kind)

Negative comparisons of absolutes are always correct:

Correct: The party was *almost* unique.

Correct: The report was *nearly* perfect.

Adverbs

Adverbs are words that modify verbs, adjectives, or other adverbs. They give information about *when, where, how,* or *how much.* Most adverbs end in *-ly.*

Profits increased rapidly.

Often adverbs can be moved from place to place in a sentence without changing the meaning of the sentence. When the sentence contains more than one word that could be modified by the adverb, however, confusion may result.

The profits that had declined sharply rose the next day.

In this example we cannot tell whether the profits "declined sharply" or "sharply rose." **Limiting adverbs** (*only, nearly, almost, just,* and *hardly*) must immediately precede the word they modify.

Only profits declined 18 percent. (Nothing else declined.)
Profits *only* declined 18 percent. (Profits did not plummet.)
Profits declined *only* 18 percent. (Profits did not decline 20 percent.)

Conjunctions

A conjunction is a word that connects words, phrases, or clauses. Conjunctions are classified as **coordinate, correlative,** and **subordinate.** Coordinate conjunctions — *and, but, or, for, nor* — join elements of equal rank.

Both the executives and their secretaries planned the program.

Correlative conjunctions connect matched pairs. Some correlative conjunctions are *either . . . or; neither . . . nor; both . . . and; not only . . . but also.*

The bank will have its grand opening on either Monday or Wednesday.

Subordinate conjunctions connect elements that are not of equal rank. Some subordinate conjunctions are

after	since
although	so
as	unless
because	when
if	while

After we save enough money, we will buy a new car.

Prepositions

A preposition is a word that shows a relationship of one word in the sentence — its object — to some other word in the sentence. Common prepositions are the following:

about	for
between	into
by	over
down	to
during	toward

This book is about communication.
Evelena is the president of Permanent Press Inc.

Interjections

An interjection is a word that expresses strong emotion and is generally isolated from the rest of the sentence.

> Wow, did you see that?
> Ouch! You hurt me.

▷ SENTENCES

What is a sentence?

The parts of speech just discussed are used to build sentences, the basic units of communication. A sentence is a group of words that expresses a complete thought and contains a *subject* and a *predicate* (verb).

> Profits (subject) increased (predicate).

In addition to the two essential parts—the subject and the predicate—sentences contain other elements that modify or complete those parts. These elements are *complements*, *phrases*, and *clauses*.

Subject and Predicate

The subject of a sentence is that part about which something is being said. Subjects can be simple or compound.

> **Simple:**   *Jessica* works in marketing.
>
> **Compound:**   *Jessica* and *Jerome* work in marketing.

The predicate of a sentence is that part that says something about the subject. Predicates can be simple or compound.

> **Simple:**   Norman *reads*.
>
> **Compound:**   Norman *reads* and *writes*.

Complements

What is the difference between a direct object and an indirect object?

A complement is a word that completes the meaning of the subject and the verb. Complements are of three kinds: direct objects, indirect objects, and subject complements. A **direct object** is a word that receives the action of a transitive verb. Direct objects answer the question *what* or *whom*.

> Patricia sold *trucks*. (what?)
> Alfonso loved *Olga*. (whom?)

An **indirect object** always precedes the direct object; it answers the question *to whom, for whom, to what,* or *for what.*

> Patricia sold *Joshua* a truck. (to whom?)
> Patricia bought *Joshua* a truck. (for whom?)
> I gave the *tire* a kick. (to what?)
> Reggie bought the *company* a plane. (for what?)

A **subject complement** is a noun, pronoun, or adjective that renames or describes the subject. Two kinds of subject complements are the predicate nominative (a noun or pronoun) and the predicate adjective. A **predicate nominative** is a noun or pronoun that follows a linking verb and renames the subject.

> Joshua is the *buyer.* (noun)
> It is *he.* (pronoun)

A **predicate adjective** is an adjective that follows a linking verb and describes the subject.

> Margarite is *intelligent.*

Phrases

What is the difference between a phrase and a clause?

A phrase is a group of related words that do not express a complete thought. A phrase may contain a subject or a predicate but not both. Phrases may be either prepositional or verbal; both modify other parts of the sentence.

A **prepositional phrase** is a phrase beginning with a preposition and modifying other words in the sentence.

> The cover *of the book* is red.
> The book sold *for $5.*

A **verbal phrase** begins with a *verbal*—a verb used as a noun, adjective, or adverb. Three kinds of verbal phrases are gerund phrases, infinitive phrases, and participial phrases.

Gerund phrase:	*Dictating letters* is not an easy task.
Infinitive phrase:	*To become president* was her ambition.
Participial phrase:	*Having dictated letters all morning,* the executive was tired.

Do not confuse gerund phrases with participial phrases. Gerund phrases act as nouns; participial phrases act as adjectives.

Gerund phrase:	*Making a profit* is necessary to stay in business.
Participial phrase:	*Making a profit,* I stayed in business.

Clauses

A clause is a group of words that contains a subject and a verb. Clauses are either main or subordinate. A **main clause** contains a subject and a verb and expresses a complete thought; it is a *simple sentence* (discussed later under "Kinds of Sentences"). A **subordinate clause** contains a subject and a verb but does not express a complete thought; it needs the main clause to make its meaning complete.

> **Main clause:** *Profits increased rapidly* before the Christmas holidays.
>
> **Subordinate clause:** *After our profits increased,* we bought additional property.

Uses of Phrases and Clauses

Phrases and clauses are used in sentences as nouns, adjectives, and adverbs. When a phrase or clause modifies a verb, adverb, or adjective, it is an adverb phrase or clause.

> Profits increased *in the afternoon.* (adverb phrase)
> *Because sales increased,* profits rose. (adverb clause)

When a phrase or clause modifies a noun or pronoun, it is an adjective phrase or clause.

> Profits *on the sales of cars* increased. (adjective phrase)
> Profits, *which had been low,* increased. (adjective clause)

When a phrase or clause is used as a noun, it is a noun phrase or clause.

> Our company makes *cars.* (noun)
> Our company makes *whatever you want.* (noun clause)
> *After the meeting* would be the best time. (noun phrase)
> *Making profits on cars* is easy. (gerund phrase)
> *To make a profit on a car* is easy. (infinitive phrase)

Phrases and clauses may be restrictive or nonrestrictive. A **restrictive** phrase or clause is one that is essential to the meaning of the sentence. A **nonrestrictive** phrase or clause is not essential to the meaning of the sentence.

> **Restrictive:** The man *who is director of research* conducted the seminar.
>
> **Nonrestrictive:** A. W. Wells, *who is director of research,* conducted the seminar.

Kinds of Sentences

Sentences made from the foregoing components may be simple, complex, compound, or compound-complex, depending on what components are

How can a complex sentence be used to subordinate one idea to another?

present. A **simple sentence** contains one subject and one verb.

> Profits (subject) increased (verb).

A **complex sentence** contains a main clause and one or more subordinate clauses.

> Because profits increased (subordinate clause), morale improved (main clause).

A **compound sentence** is two simple sentences joined by a coordinating conjunction.

> Profits increased (simple sentence), and (conjunction) morale improved (simple sentence).

A **compound-complex sentence** contains two simple sentences and one or more subordinate clauses.

> Because we raised dividends (subordinate clause), profits increased (simple sentence), and (conjunction) morale improved (simple sentence).

In constructing sentences, we must consider what kind of influence each component has on the message contained in the sentence. For example, a subordinate clause is "subordinate" because it makes the idea contained in it depend on the idea contained in the main clause.

> Because profits increased, morale improved. (emphasis on morale)
> When morale improves, profits increase. (emphasis on profits)

▷ PROBLEMS OF USAGE

Why would business people and other professionals be concerned about spelling?

More important than terminology is knowing how the components of language should be used. Experts do not agree about all aspects of language usage, but certain rules are so widely accepted that you should consider them absolutes.

Spelling

Misspelled words are the single most common error in business letters. We have found that students frequently misspell the following words:

accommodate	mileage
business	fulfill
convenience	intercede
embarrass	customer
its (it's)	accept (except)
opportunity	loose (lose)

develop	proceed
questionnaire	until
receive	familiar
separate	occurrence
sophomore	maintenance
writing	choose (chose)
benefit	envelope
congratulate	truly
definite	recommend
February	sincerely
morale	to (too, two)
personnel (personal)	written

Subject and Verb Agreement

A verb must agree with its subject in person and number. There is usually no difficulty with making the verb agree with the subject in person. It is the number—singular or plural—that can cause difficulty, especially when words, phrases, or clauses separate the subject from the verb.

Singular subjects require singular verbs.

> The *company was* established in 1902.
> *Each* company *has* its own charter.

Plural subjects require plural verbs.

> The *companies were* established in 1902.
> *Most* companies *have* a charter.

Do not be misled by plural nouns that intervene between the verb and subject.

> The *merchandise* for all the stores *was* delivered on Thursday.

Pronoun and Antecedent Agreement

A pronoun must agree with its antecedent (the word it stands for) in number (singular or plural) and gender (feminine, masculine, common, or neuter).

Singular, feminine:	*Mary* worked on *her* project.
Singular, masculine:	*Bruce* worked on *his* project.
Plural, common:	*They* worked on *their* projects.
Singular, neuter:	The *project* gave satisfaction to *its* author.

Sentence Fragment

What is wrong with using incomplete or run-on sentences? Won't everyone know what you mean anyway?

Every sentence must contain a subject and a verb and must express a complete thought. If a group of words does not express a complete thought, even though it contains both a subject and verb, it is a sentence fragment, which is not acceptable in most business letters or other formal writing.

Fragment:	When we arrived.
Sentence:	When we arrived, they started the session.

Run-On Sentence

Two sentences must be separated by a period, a semicolon, or a comma and a conjunction. If they are not, the result is a run-on sentence, meaning that the two sentences run into each other.

Run-on sentence:	We arrived they started the session.
Correct:	We arrived. They started the session.
Correct:	We arrived; they started the session.
Correct:	We arrived, and they started the session.

Comma Splice

If two sentences are joined by a comma alone, the result is a comma splice. The comma "splices" or joins two sentences that should be separate.

Comma splice:	We arrived, they started the session.
Correct:	We arrived. They started the session.

Mismodification

When used properly, modifiers make the meaning of sentences clearer. But nothing can cause more confusion than misplaced or dangling modifiers. A recent ad for a headache medicine said that the medicine "should not be taken if you've ever had a severe allergic reaction to aspirin or any other pain reliever without consulting your doctor first." The ad writer didn't mean it, but she or he is saying that you can take the medication if you consult with your doctor before having severe allergic reactions to other pain relievers.

Misplaced or dangling modifiers modify the wrong word, phrase, or clause. Avoid mismodification by placing the modifier as close as possible to the word, phrase, or clause that it modifies.

Misplaced modifier:	The client had a large envelope talking to Mr. Polski.
Correct:	The client talking to Mr. Polski had a large envelope.

Dangling modifier:	While trying to repair the typewriter, the telephone rang.
Correct:	While trying to repair the typewriter, he heard the telephone ring.
Dangling modifier:	Entering the store, her eye spotted the sale sign.
Correct:	Entering the store, she spotted the sale sign.
Dangling modifier:	Confirming our phone conversation, our policy and procedures are explained in this letter.
Correct:	This letter confirms our phone conversation about our policy and procedures.
Dangling modifier:	Rolling smoothly along at 55 miles an hour, Detroit arrived sooner than expected.
Correct:	Rolling smoothly along at 55 miles an hour, I arrived in Detroit sooner than I expected.
Dangling modifier:	As a person who is concerned with progress, I hope that I can count on you.
Correct:	Because I am concerned with progress, I'll be counting on you.
Correct:	Because you are concerned with progress, I'll be counting on you.

Progression of Verb Tenses

When you write, be consistent in your use of verb tenses. Avoid shifting from one tense to another unless your meaning requires it. Changing tenses can cause confusion. The verb of the main clause should agree in tense with the tense of the subordinate clause in that the time sequence must be logical.

Incorrect:	After Angela *leaves* the room, Arnold *told* his story.
Correct:	After Angela *left* the room, Arnold *told* his story.
Correct:	After Angela *had left* the room, Arnold *told* his story.

Make sure that your verb tense accurately expresses when the action takes place.

Tense	Use	Example
Present	Action occurring now	I go.
Present progressive	Action ongoing at the present	I am going.
Past	Action completed in the past	I went.
Past progressive	Action ongoing in the past	I was going.
Future	Action that will take place in the future	I will go.
Future progressive	Action ongoing in the future	I will be going.
Present perfect	Action completed at the present	I have gone.
Present perfect progressive	Action continuing from the past into the present and the likelihood of its continuing into the future	I have been going.
Past perfect	Action completed before another past time	I had gone.
Past perfect progressive	Continuing action completed before a second past action	I had been going.
Future perfect	Action that will be completed before a certain time in the future	I will have gone.
Future perfect progressive	Action continuing until a specified time in the future	I will have been going.

Parallelism

Parallelism is the use of the same grammatical construction for two or more parts of a sentence that have the same function—comparing ideas, contrast-

How do correlative conjunctions influence the construction of a sentence?

ing ideas, or coordinating ideas. Match nouns with nouns, verbs with verbs, phrases with phrases, clauses with clauses, and sentences with sentences.

Her duties included *composing, editing, typing,* and *proofreading.*

Faulty parallelism occurs when sentence elements that are alike in function are expressed in different grammatical forms.

Her duties included *composing, editor, typing,* and *to watch for errors.*

▷ PUNCTUATION

What is the function of punctuation?

Words are not the only symbols we use to express ourselves in writing; punctuation helps indicate our meaning by showing how the words, phrases, and clauses we write should relate to each other. Figuratively speaking, punctuation marks are the nuts and bolts that hold a written communication together. We will now examine the most common uses of punctuation marks.

Period

Use the period

1. To end a declarative sentence.

    A distinction exists between brevity and conciseness.

2. To end an imperative sentence (a sentence that gives a command).

    Make your sentences concise.

3. To end an indirect question.

    Sue asked if she could write a report on conciseness.

4. To end a polite request.

    Will you please send me a copy of your bulletin.

5. After abbreviations and initials.

    Mr. J. W. Moltzan   Ph.D.   Mon.   A.M.

Comma

Use the comma

1. To separate items in a series.

    They purchased new furniture, appliances, and accessories.

2. To enclose unessential expressions.

Of course, the company will be closed on July 4.
We will, however, be open on Monday, July 5.

3. To set off appositives (words placed side by side so the second describes the first).

Mr. Leo Attaway, our purchasing agent, secured the raw materials.

One-word appositives or those forming parts of proper names do not require commas. (Some experts, however, recommend commas for one-word appositives.)

My sister Betty bought 40 shares of blue-chip stock.
The manager reminded me of Attila the Hun.

4. To separate two or more adjectives.

She enclosed a stamped, addressed envelope.

5. To separate the parts of dates and addresses.

On July 4, 1976, the United States celebrated its bicentennial.
Dimitri lives at 408 Banburdy Street, Canton, Ohio.

6. To set off nouns of direct address.

Please, Mr. Holtzen, send us your check for $100.

7. To set off introductory phrases.

Wondering about the sudden increase in profits, the manager flew to Texas.

If the introductory phrase is short (no verb and fewer than five words), omit the comma (unless the sentence would be confusing without it).

In the report several management techniques were discussed.

8. To separate two main clauses joined by a conjunction.

The accident occurred in the afternoon, and there were no witnesses.

If the clauses are short, omit the comma.

She asked and he answered.

9. To set off introductory subordinate clauses.

If Jean should call while I'm gone, tell her I'll be back in 20 minutes.

10. To set off nonrestrictive clauses and phrases.

My mother, needing more information, wrote to the director.

11. To separate two unrelated numbers.

On June 1, 400 students enrolled.

12. Between contiguous verbs.

Those who call, call for a reason.

13. To indicate the omission of words.

Last month Allen called two meetings; this month, two.

Question Mark

Use the question mark after direct questions.

Who has the dictionary?

Exclamation Point

Use the exclamation point after exclamatory words, phrases, clauses, or sentences.

Really!   How wonderful!   You're kidding!

Semicolon

Use the semicolon

1. To join two main clauses that are not joined by a conjunction.

Darlene is interested in music; Dennis is interested in drama.

2. After each item in a series with an item or items containing commas.

Agnes visited Ann Arbor, Michigan; Chicago, Illinois; and Gary, Indiana.

3. To separate main clauses joined by a conjunction when both clauses contain a comma or when either clause contains two or more commas.

Our company president, who winters in Florida, arrived this morning; and as soon as she arrived, she called a meeting of the board of directors.

Colon

Use the colon before a list of items.

The purchasing agent ordered several kinds of typewriter ribbons: silk, nylon, cotton, and carbon.

Do not use a colon when the list follows a preposition or a verb.

The report was prepared to (1) identify problem areas, (2) propose solutions, (3) draw conclusions, and (4) make recommendations.

Do not end an introductory sentence with a colon when the sentence is lengthy or when another sentence separates it from the list.

> Hannah Associates submitted the following recommendations. Please note that several of the recommendations are based on the Allison report.
>
> **1.**   Purchase the Ribicon property.
>
> **2.**   Sell the 20 acres adjoining the Hackett property.
>
> **3.**   Construct two plants on the Holsted property.

Dash

Use the dash for greater emphasis or for abrupt interruptions.

> Four of the players — Val VanDyke, Jess Jakowski, Abe Solomon, and Bodo Buelow — were chosen for the national team.
>
> The mistake — if that's what it was — caused a great deal of confusion.

Parentheses

Use parentheses

1.   To separate expressions providing qualifying information not important to the meaning of the sentence.

> Dr. R. Furjanic (Business Education) received his doctorate from Northern Illinois University.

2.   To enclose figures or letters preceding enumerated items.

> The following projects are included: (1) Tax Analysis, (2) Time Management, and (3) Human Relations.

Underscore

Use the underscore

1.   For titles of books, periodicals, plays, and newspapers.

> Business Reports (book)
> Journal of Business Communication (periodical)
> Jacques saw Hamlet three years ago. (play)
> Lillian bought today's issue of the Times Gazette. (newspaper)

2.   For words that would be italicized in print.

> "Not only what you say but also how you say it, is important."

3.   To indicate italics in a manuscript to be printed.

Quotation Marks

Use quotation marks

1.   For direct quotations.

  Vern said, "I'll install your carpeting."

2.   For slang expressions.

  "ain't"   "goofed"

3.   For titles of articles, short poems, songs, subdivisions of books, and unpublished works.

  "Mastery of Typewriting" (article)
  "Ode on a Grecian Urn" (poem)
  "Mack the Knife" (song)
  "Writing Skills" (chapter)
  "A Study to Determine the Significance of Ten-Minute Timed Writings" (dissertation)

4.   Periods and commas are placed *inside* quotation marks. Other punctuation marks are placed outside, unless they are part of the original quotation.

  Mary Ellen has read "Ode on a Grecian Urn."
  Has Mary Ellen read "Ode on a Grecian Urn"?
  Robert asked, "When will I see you again?"

◊ CAPITALIZATION

The most common rules governing capitalization are the following:

1.   Capitalize the first word of
  a.   A sentence.

    Management is an important executive function.

  b.   An elliptical (condensed) expression.

    Congratulations!   Really?   No.   Yes.

  c.   A direct quotation.

    Mary Lou said, "The subsidiary should have an independent budget."

  d.   A salutation.

    Dear Mr. Bussard

e. A complimentary close.

Sincerely yours

f. A list or an outline.
1. Period
2. Comma
3. Semicolon

2. Capitalize proper nouns and adjectives.

Berard Building　　　Baltic　　　Colorado River　　　French

3. Capitalize all titles when they precede the name.

Dr. Reiter　　　Sheriff Saulson　　　Captain Dolez

4. Generally, do not capitalize titles when they follow a name or are used in place of a person's name. Retain the capitalization for a high-ranking official, however.

Lester Salisbury, production manager
Our production manager
Myles Murphy, Senator
Thomas Goodwin, professor
His professor
Charles Powers, Chief Justice

5. Capitalize all titles in addresses and in closing lines of a letter.

Mrs. Patricia Kennard, Principal

Jack Blaha
Director of Research

6. Do not capitalize a title when it is followed by an appositive.

Our supervisor, Mr. Joseph Anropolis, submitted a report.

7. Capitalize names showing family relationship, but not when preceded by a possessive.

Uncle Steve and Aunt Louise　　　my mother　　　Dad

8. Capitalize the main words in titles of publications and literary or artistic works. Do not capitalize an article, conjunction, or short preposition unless it is the first word.

The Silent Majority Speaks up About It. (book)

9. Capitalize the names of specific courses and subjects. Do not capitalize general areas of study unless the word is a proper noun or adjective.

COMMUNICATION SOLUTION

The memo in this chapter's Communication Challenge presents a composite of errors found in actual business letters and memos. It contains the following errors:

> *Requesting to do a study to examine the costs associated with installing exercise facilities for employee use.*

The opening paragraph is not a complete sentence. Who is doing the requesting? A sentence must have both a subject and a verb and express a complete thought. Note also that the words *to do a study to examine* are repetitive. *Requesting to study* or *requesting to examine* would be sufficient.

> *Other companies have indicated that a higher morale and employee satisfaction rate will emerge, the initial amount of facilities would be small.*

This section contains a comma splice. Also, what is a higher morale *rate* or an employee satisfaction *rate*? The word *rate* implies a basis for calculation: The interest *rate* is higher now than it was last year (interest rates are calculated as percentages). Morale and satisfaction can be measured, but they cannot be calculated.

> *By exercising on a continuous basis, employee productivity has been proven to increase. People that exercise being healthier and more energetic than those that don't. The attached chart determines the level of interest our employees have in this facility.*

Continuous means without ceasing, constantly. No one exercises continuously. *Continually* means almost constantly, but with short time-outs, and hardly anyone exercises even that much. *Regularly* would be a better word. Also, the chart cannot *determine* (cause) the level of employee interest but can merely *show* it. The paragraph also uses the relative pronoun *that* incorrectly. The relative pronoun *who* should be used for people. (The demonstrative pronoun *that,* however, may refer to people.) *One weeks time* needs an apostrophe to indicate possession (the time of one week): one *week's* time.

Business Communication 242   Typewriting II
American History 101   English writing
accounting   chemistry
German   Russian history
Marketing 303   management

10. Capitalize a degree after a name or in abbreviations.
Do not capitalize the name of a degree when used as a general term.

John Arnold, Doctor of Medicine
B.A.   M.A.   Ed.D.   D.D.S.   Ph.D.
A bachelor of science degree

11. Capitalize the principal words in the names of associations, business firms, clubs, fraternities, governmental groups, religious bodies, and schools.

The Association for Business Communication
Business Club
Federal Party
Alexander High School
XYZ Corporation
Delta Pi Epsilon
First Christian Reformed Church
Alpha Beta Chi

12. Capitalize days of the week, months of the year, holidays, historical events, and periods of time.

Monday, January 23	Memorial Day
World War II	Middle Ages

13. Do not capitalize the seasons of the year, decades, or centuries.

spring	summer	fall	winter
early thirties	twentieth century		

14. Capitalize points of the compass when they designate definite regions. Do not capitalize points of the compass when they are used for direction.

Midwest	South America	Middle East
Far East	south side of town	east of Detroit

15. Capitalize nouns followed by a number or a letter. Some nouns, however, such as page, paragraph, line, or verse, are not capitalized.

Building 83	page 23
Lot A	paragraph 3
Chapter X	line 8
Flight 807	verse 46

▷ SUMMARY

Language is dynamic, changing to meet the needs of the people who use it. The written language does not change as rapidly as the spoken and provides a fairly stable standard of usage. The rules of grammar help ensure the accurate transfer of meaning from sender to receiver. A knowledge of grammar, including the functions of the various parts of speech and sentence construction, is an aid to clear communication.

Writers should be especially careful to avoid errors of usage—such as lack of agreement between subject and verb, mismodification, and faulty parallel construction — that may result in miscommunication. Punctuation also plays an important role in written communication, and writers should be familiar with the different uses of the various marks of punctuation.

▷ EXERCISES

Review and Discussion Questions

1. Name and define the eight parts of speech.

2. What is the difference between transitive and intransitive verbs?

3. What is the difference between a phrase and a clause?

4. Name the four kinds of sentences, and give an example of each.

5. What is parallelism?

6. How can punctuation influence the meaning of a sentence? Give an example.

Problems

1. Identify the misplaced or dangling modifiers that make the following sentences unclear and unsatisfactory, and rewrite the sentences to improve the modification.
    a. After working for 35 years, retirement was welcome.
    b. To type the resume, the typewriter keys must be cleaned.
    c. When a little boy, my father took me to the office.

2. Rewrite the following sentences to eliminate faulty parallelism.
    a. They were not only happy about the date but the accommodations as well.
    b. Steve's hobbies are sailing, swimming, and tennis.
    c. Either we will rent the bikes or take our own.

3. In the following sentences, correct any pronouns that do not agree with their antecedents.
    a. When anyone has questions, they should see me in the office.
    b. The Stryker Corporation lost their lease.
    c. The committee agreed to file their report by January 1.

4. Punctuate the following sentences correctly.
    a. Seminars will be held in Chicago Illinois Detroit Michigan and Columbus Ohio
    b. Johns supervisor recommended him for a promotion

c. The research committee completed its report therefore you should have it by the end of the month

5. Indicate whether the verb is active or passive. If the verb is passive, rewrite the sentence so that the verb is in the active voice.
   a. Several important decisions were made by Mr. Harmon.
   b. The material was shipped on Tuesday by the company.
   c. Mary was given several choices by her supervisor.

CASE

Books on rhetoric, including English handbooks, manuals of style, and other guides to correctness and usage, abound. Using at least three of these books as sources, define and explain the concept of levels of language usage. Be sure to cover substandard, colloquial, informal, and formal levels of usage and give examples of each. Present your findings in a paper of two or three typewritten pages.

CHAPTER THREE

Developing an Effective Business Writing Strategy

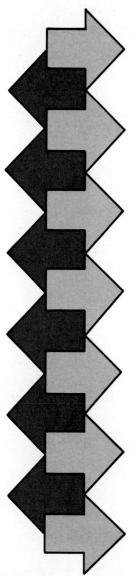

Unlike interpersonal communication, in which the sender and the receiver can use means other than language to communicate both the subject content and the feeling content of a particular message, written communication must communicate these through the use of language alone. This chapter discusses the language and writing style that make effective business messages.

COMMUNICATION CHALLENGE

What is wrong with the following letter, and how would you revise it to make it better?

As you read this chapter, think in terms of an *ideal* reply to an application for employment rather than the typical form letter often necessitated by the volume of applications companies receive. What changes would be necessary for the letter to retain the reader's goodwill?

Gryde Industries • 14 Pace Plaza, 3-B • New York, NY   10038 • 212/555-5552

April 20, 19xx

Mr. Richard Blackstone
480 Jackson Street
Champaign, IL 61820

Dear Richard:

It has been brought to my attention that you did not receive my letter that was sent to the University Placement Office. Please excuse us for we were unaware that the University of Illinois has several placement offices. Therefore, I will review the contents of my original letter.

I had the opportunity to carefully review your qualifications and interest with our Personnel people. Unfortunately, Robert, it appears that they have decided on some other applicants for possible employment.

Although I cannot be very encouraging at this time, I will keep your resume on file for possible future openings. Also, I would like to thank you very much for your interest in Gryde.

Sincerely,

Marvin E. Olag

Marvin E. Olag,
Administrator
Salaried Personnel

MEO:rs

▷ OVERVIEW: THE HUMAN RELATIONS OF BUSINESS WRITING

A knowledge of grammar and punctuation is not enough to ensure an effective written message. A message may be free of error and still fail to communicate in the desired way. In addition, written communications in business, being central to all aspects of modern operations, must be cost effective, paying for themselves directly (by increasing sales, for example) or indirectly (by creating goodwill).

To communicate effectively, a written message needs to be placed in an appropriate communication context so that the reader will quickly recognize the subject of the message. The writing style or use of language also will influence the reader's perception of a message and help determine whether he or she responds to it in a favorable way. For this reason, a business message should be clear, courteous, concise, and positive. Its sentences should be written with variety of structure, emphasizing the most important points and subordinating the less important.

In addition to communicating an idea, each message also communicates the attitude of the writer toward the reader. Each message, then, performs an essential human relations function. An effective business writing strategy includes both a business objective and a human objective (the human relations function). This chapter shows you how to achieve both the business and the human objective through your selection and arrangement of words, sentences, and paragraphs.

▷ WRITTEN COMMUNICATION

Why is writing difficult for many people?

The ability to write effective messages is a skill that everyone needs, and our chief concern is to help you develop that skill. But in addition to presenting the mechanics and principles that will make your messages effective, we also want to show you that writing can be a much easier and more pleasurable means of communicating than it is usually thought to be.

Most people struggle with writing because they know that their mistakes will be more obvious in written communication than they would be in an oral situation. Putting a message in writing tends to amplify its importance so that it receives closer attention. Nonverbal and oral communication are usually considered easier and more natural than written communication. And to a certain extent, this is true. It is not accidental that children learn to talk before they learn to write.

Writing Is Work

The ability to communicate in writing requires more—and better-developed —communication skills than oral communication usually requires. Being aware of this, many people are reluctant to attempt written communication. Also,

COMMUNICATION TODAY...

Better Writing Will Pay Off

Unfortunately, much of the business writing we come across is murky, pompous, windy and unreadable. And the prognosis is anything but optimistic.

What we're fighting is failure to recognize good writing—made worse by the belief that big words and long sentences make one appear more professional. . . .

Fortunately, there's a body of research that shows that simple words and short sentences attract more readers. Consider these findings from various studies:

Best selling books have generally proved to be more readable than those not on the best selling lists.

The most readable stories in newspapers attracted 43 percent more readers.

Articles rewritten to make them more read-able resulted in a 49 percent increase in readership in one instance and in a 66 percent increase in another.

College students read up to 90 percent further into an article when it was made more readable.

Simply put, all of this means that more people will read something that's easy to understand. Conversely, writing that's hard to read cuts down on readership because it's too taxing. . . .

Now some executives might argue that most of their readers are college graduates who are able to handle heavy stuff. Granted, but why take the chance of turning them off because they have to strain to get the meaning? As Mueller noted, "People prefer to get information written at a level below their capacity."

Otherwise why would *The Wall Street Journal* average a Fog Index of 11—just one grade level above *Reader's Digest?*

Source: Frank Grazian, "Better Writing Will Pay Off," *Communication Briefings,* March, 1984, 3:5, p. 3. (Encoders, Inc., 806 Westminster Blvd., Blackwood, NJ 08012.) Reprinted with permission.

most of the writing we do while growing up is for school work. Thus we tend to associate the act of writing with our teachers' criticisms. It is no wonder that by the time we are ready to enter the world of business, many of us are hesitant about writing.

As adults we spend nearly all of our waking lives sending nonverbal and oral messages but comparatively little time writing. Frequently our lack of practice makes writing seem a more difficult means of communicating than it actually is. Many adults, even well-educated adults, would rather make a phone call than write a letter, even when a letter would be the most cost-effective form of communicating. Correctly approached, however, writing is one of the easiest, most efficient means of communicating.

Business messages are often considered a bore to read and write. And sometimes the reason is obvious:

Dear Sir:

Is it obvious that the letter was received?

Your letter of the 20th has been received and forwarded to this office for reply. We have carefully read your letter and beg to advise you that in accordance with our policy we are unable to grant your request.

Why tell the reader no twice?

Pursuant to your request, we examined the document which you find herewith enclosed. Unfortunately, our policy will not allow us to act on this matter.

Have they been of service? What further questions might the reader have?

We hope that we have been of service in this regard, and if you have further questions, please do not hesitate to contact us. We remain,

Yours most sincerely,

Most business letters and memos, fortunately, are not as bad as the foregoing. Letter writers usually manage to say something of interest and say it in a warm, natural way. Even so, much writing in business is based on old formulas and contains too many outdated expressions to make interesting reading.

The Evolution of Business Writing

How did the invention of the typewriter influence business correspondence?

The modern business letter has been shaped by the business use of the typewriter during the last quarter of the nineteenth century. Early typewritten letters followed the older forms of handwritten models—hanging paragraphs (in which the first line begins at the left margin and the other lines are indented beneath it; such paragraphs are occasionally still used when a special effect is called for), flowery expressions (especially in the opening and closing), and language that in no uncertain terms indicated the class distinctions between reader and writer. Around the turn of the century, letters were written in the following style:

My Dear Sir:

Enclosed herewith you will find our copy of the Brillo report that you requested in your letter of recent date.

Regarding the matter of imports, we beg to advise that all our exports are taxed. If you have any further questions, feel free to contact us at your earliest convenience.

I beg to remain your most humble and obedient servant,

As the modern business letter evolved, the language became less formal and the appearance became more streamlined and efficient. Astute business persons kept track of which letters had the best results. They also took note of what psychologists and linguists were discovering about the effects that language had on people. By the mid-1930s the fundamental principles of modern business writing were set.

Untrained writers have frequently used a "model" approach to solve their writing problems — they go to the files to see what was written before. This technique has been used for years. As a result, many letters and reports being written today would sound far more natural to our great grandparents than they do to us.

Even trained writers, however, are not always able to do their best. Time limitations, interruptions, and other work pressures will not permit the attention to detail that writing the best letter requires. When rushed, all of us tend to fall back on what we — or someone else — said before. But we want you to learn how to write without using models. Our goal is to teach you to write the *best* business letters and reports when the circumstances require it and to write acceptable messages always — even when your time is limited.

Writing Is Important

Why is a written message often considered more important than a spoken one?

In spite of the problems many have with writing, written messages are one of the most important means of communicating in business. Of course, some business communication is nonverbal, and a great deal of it is oral: many words are spoken for each one that is written. But the words that are written are usually the most important ones, and no modern business could exist for long without letters and other forms of written communication. If two managers reach an agreement on the telephone, they will write follow-up letters to make sure that there will be no misunderstandings. If an important meeting is held, someone will take notes and write the minutes.

Written communication is important to business — and to civilization in general — because it provides a fairly permanent record. Writing lets people overcome the barriers of time and distance, and it also permits writer and reader to consider carefully the meaning of complex messages. No other means of communication offers this combination of advantages. A telephone call may be much faster than an exchange of letters, but even if the conversation is tape-recorded, the telephone does not leave a readily accessible record.

With oral messages, it is easy to hear what you want to hear in spite of what is actually said. While a written message may be subject to different interpretations, the message will not change over time, so those concerned can refer to it when necessary.

The Advantages and Disadvantages of Writing

What are the advantages and disadvantages of written communication?

The development of writing permitted primitive people to communicate from generation to generation with an accuracy not possible with oral techniques. Because of writing, legend gave way to history. Writing also enabled people to communicate more accurately over longer distances than had previously been possible. Because of writing, isolated villages gave way to city-states and eventually to empires. And it was only through writing that the complex philosophical, legal, and political concepts important in modern life were developed.

Written communication is not important to business by accident or default. The need for efficiency in modern business requires the selection of the best means of communicating in most circumstances. Because the advantages far outweigh the disadvantages, business correspondence remains a principal means of both routine and nonroutine communication in business.

The advantages of communicating in writing are

1.   Writing provides a permanent record. Written messages may be filed for future reference. With a letter or report on file, there can be no question about what was said.

2.   Writing provides proof of agreement. An exchange of letters can constitute a contract. If you write to us ordering merchandise at a certain price and we write back agreeing to send it, we have established a contract.

3.   Writing puts emphasis on logic. Written communication facilitates the controlled use of language to present complex ideas. The writer may revise the message as often as necessary until it says exactly what is intended. The reader may study the message as long as necessary to understand it. For this reason, writing does a better job of conveying complex information than phone calls or other oral channels of communication.

4.   Written messages may be more convenient. Letters and reports can usually be written and read at the times most convenient for the writer and reader, whereas phone calls may be inconvenient for one party.

Written communication has only two disadvantages:

1.   Because writing is a more formal means of communicating than speaking, and because we tend to be more formal when we write than when we speak, a written message may lack warmth and clarity.

2.   We cannot receive the immediate feedback necessary to alter our message if our receiver does not understand our original message.

The Costs of Communication

What does it cost an organization to send a letter?

Written communication is an expensive necessity for business. While the estimates for the cost of an individual letter may vary greatly, letter writing is obviously expensive enough to deserve every business person's attention. In addition to the relatively fixed costs of paper, envelopes, postage, and typewriters (or word processing equipment), it takes time to write and prepare a letter for mailing.

SIDEBAR

The Changing Costs of Business Letters

According to The Dartnell Institute of Business Research, the cost of an average business letter in 1985 increased 5 percent over the $8.10 recorded for 1984.

In 1985 secretaries indicated that they needed 18.5 minutes to prepare a single letter. This is the first drop in a six-year average of 19 minutes, which reflects the increased productivity brought about through the use of electronic typewriters and word processing equipment. Undoubtedly as management and secretaries become more familiar with the new technologies, production will increase even more.

The following table shows the rise in cost of the average business letter from 1930 when Dartnell first conducted such a survey.

1930	$ .30	1975	$3.79
1935	$ .52	1976	$4.17
1940	$ .72	1977	$4.47
1953	$1.17	1978	$4.77
1960	$1.83	1979	$5.59
1964	$2.32	1980	$6.07
1968	$2.54	1981	$6.63
1970	$3.05	1982	$7.11
1973	$3.31	1983	$7.60
1974	$3.41	1984	$8.10

Source: "Dartnell Target Survey," The Dartnell Institute of Business Research, Chicago, 1985.

A midlevel manager earning $45,000 a year makes approximately $23 an hour. A secretary earning $18,000 a year makes approximately $9 an hour. The costs of a letter produced by this particular executive and secretary might add up something like this (not including overhead, fringe benefits, and other fixed charges):

Machine dictation time:	15 minutes	$5.75
Transcription time:	20 minutes	3.00
Revising draft:	10 minutes	3.83
Typing final copy:	10 minutes	1.50
Materials, postage; mailing costs (gathering, sealing, stamping, etc.):		.75
		$14.83

How does modern word processing equipment influence the costs of letter production?

Some letters, of course, take more time and are more expensive to write than others. Routine, recurring business transactions can usually be written for far less than the hypothetical $14.83. With modern dictation and word processing equipment and the increased use of standardized paragraphs and form letters, many business writing problems can be solved quickly and easily —over and over again.

The Dartnell Institute of Business Research estimates that the average cost of a business letter in 1985 was $8.52.[1] Other estimates are higher. In comparing the costs of writing and mailing a letter to those of using an electronic mail system, a special education supervisor said that the total cost in personnel time, materials, and postage was about $24 for a letter that was dictated and typed. The cost for the same letter prepared and sent by computer, however, was about 50 cents.[2]

Reports are even more expensive to write than letters. In addition to the expense of researching a problem and deciding on a solution, reports frequently go through several drafts before being prepared in final form.

Even when you take full advantage of modern word processing equipment and other innovations, your writing skills will remain an extremely important factor in the cost-effectiveness of your written communication. Many business situations still call for individualized letters and reports, and not every company has the latest in time-saving equipment. Also, you may be the person in your company selected to write standardized paragraphs for others to use; and you may be assigned the job of ensuring that the paragraphs are current, coherent, correct, and considerate.

Why is oral communication not a complete solution to the high cost of written communication?

Oral communication, including telephone calls, may seem like a way to avoid some of the high costs of written communication. In some cases this may be true. Two parties may reach an agreement for a $5 phone call, when that same agreement might have required a $50 exchange of letters. Oral communication, however, has its own costs. Because it is easier to misunderstand an oral message, expensive mistakes more often result from oral communication. Also, oral communication may lead to wasting time through missed phone calls, interrupted meetings, and personal conversations on business time. Finally, if the agreement resulting from the $5 phone call mentioned previously is important, a $50 exchange of letters may still be required to confirm the arrangements.

The Profit Potential

How can you measure the cost-effectiveness of a letter?

Every message has a *profit potential* — that is, it represents an investment that you make in anticipation of gaining something or of preventing some loss. Many messages can return a profit when handled in a simple, routine way. Other messages require more care.

Suppose, for example, you must refuse a request made by your company's best customer. If you are careless with your letter, you might offend

---

[1] "Dartnell Target Survey," The Dartnell Institute of Business Research, Chicago, 1985.

[2] Kathy Jessup, "Electronic Mail System: A Boon for Intermediate Schools," *The Kalamazoo Gazette*, April 29, 1984, p. D11.

the customer and lose her or his business. Because the profit potential is high, such a letter requires extra care—a larger investment to prevent an even larger loss. Or suppose you have to write a negative job evaluation on a member of your staff. How can you tell the person exactly what he or she is doing wrong without discouraging him or her and thus ruining the chances of helping the person become a more effective worker?

Although the profits of communication cannot always be measured in dollars, every business message will have an impact on the company's profits, and every message should provide a return for its investment.

Letters and reports represent both the writer and the writer's company. Customers, clients, and associates frequently form their entire impression of you and your company from your written communication. A successful message communicates not only the information but also the image you wish conveyed. A written message should make its purpose clear and at the same time establish empathy between the reader and writer, making the reader feel that the writer is an enjoyable person with whom to do business.

▷ ELEMENTS IN SUCCESSFUL WRITTEN COMMUNICATION

It sounds simple enough. To be successful, a message must make its purpose clear and establish empathy between the reader and writer. But to accomplish these goals, you will need to consider the following four variables that will influence the success of a message:

1.   The communication context.

2.   The writing style or language usage.

3.   The purpose of the message.

4.   The appearance of your message.

The Communication Context

Why is it important for the reader to understand the subject of the letter after reading the first sentence?

All communication occurs in a context that includes a sender and a receiver, including the history of their previous experiences and expectations, and a reason for communicating.

The Reader.   The person or persons to whom you are writing should be a major influence on what you say and how you say it. Whether your reader will understand your message and cooperate with you will depend on how well you are able to anticipate his or her expectations, attitudes, and needs. Obviously, if you know someone well, you will have a much better idea of what he or she will expect, want, and need in any given situation than if you don't know the person well.

Adaptation for the Reader.   Whenever you write, you need to *adapt* your message and writing style to communicate successfully with your particular audience. When you are writing to friends and business acquaintances of long standing, you can — and should — be less formal than when you are writing to someone you do not know.

Your friends may forgive you if your message is not as considerate as it might be, but they will certainly enjoy your message more if you anticipate correctly how it will affect them. When writing to your friends, you can visualize them and imagine yourself delivering the same message in person.

What would your greeting be?

Would you put business first and pleasure second?

Would you socialize a bit first and save business until later?

Would you use formal or informal language?

How would you convey good news? Bad news?

How would you ask for your friend's help?

Knowing what to say in a message is much easier when you can visualize your reader and imagine her or his response to what you want to say. The more we know about a person, the easier it is to make accurate assumptions about that person's behavior. What does your reader want? What are her or his interests? You can at least partially answer these questions by knowing whether your reader is

A customer (the end user of a product or service).

A dealer.

A friend.

A representative of a particular group or organization.

Dependent on you.

Independent of you and your organization.

Well educated.

Financially secure.

How can you deter-mine what your reader wants to know?

Each of these factors will influence the reader's interests and needs. A customer or user of a product, for example, would be interested in the utility and value of the product. A dealer would be interested in utility and value primarily as they pertain to how quickly the product would sell, how satisfied the customers would be, and how much profit could be made.

While no prediction that we may make about behavior — either our own or someone else's — can be absolutely certain, the more facts we have about our reader, the more likely our assumptions will prove correct. Even when we do not know our readers personally, we can usually make fairly accurate predictions about how they will react to our messages if we consider everything we do know before we write. Certain needs and expectations are universal:

1.   We are all cheered by good news.

2.   We are all disappointed by bad news.

3.   We all tend to resist performing actions that will cost us either time or money.

The degree to which a person would be cheered, would be disappointed, or would resist acting may vary. But all of us want things to go well for us and expect the benefits (however measured) of our actions to exceed their costs.

Our intuition and previous experience with people help us predict how readers may react to a message even if we are unacquainted with those readers. To increase the accuracy of our prediction, however, we should give careful consideration to the rather wide variety of expectations readers may have.

What happens when you violate someone's expectations?

The Reader's Expectations.   Certain expectations common to most readers are not always recognized by the writer, although they may have great impact on how a message is received. For example, most readers expect to see a standard format in a business letter. When you violate that expectation, you attract the reader's attention to the appearance of your message, which may cause the reader to pay less attention to your content. On the other hand, such a violation of expectation may cause the reader to notice a message that would otherwise be ignored. To help determine some of your readers' expectations, ask yourself the following questions:

1.   What are my readers' previous relationships with me?
    a.   Do they know who I am?
    b.   How well do they know me?
    c.   How well do they like me?
    d.   Do they trust me?

2.   Is my relationship with them primarily personal?
    a.   Do I view them as friends?
    b.   Which is more important to me—our mutual business or our friendship?
    c.   Do we meet socially? Would I like to?
    d.   Do I know anything about their lives away from the job?

3.   Is my relationship with them primarily a business relationship?
    a.   Have I ever communicated face to face with them?
    b.   Do I ever correspond with them just for the fun of it?
    c.   Do I ever exchange personal information with them?
    d.   For what reasons do I correspond with them?

4. What kind of business relationship do I have with them?
   a. Are they business persons who understand business terminology and practices?
   b. Are they customers who work in nonbusiness jobs?
   c. Is our business relationship new or well-established?
   d. Have I always been honest and fair with them?
   e. Have they always been honest and fair with me?

5. How important is the future of the relationship?
   a. Do I wish the relationship to continue?
   b. Do my readers wish the relationship to continue?
   c. Has the relationship been profitable?
   d. Has the relationship been enjoyable?

As you ask yourself the preceding questions in relation to a particular reader, you can determine whether that reader will welcome your letter and how she or he is likely to react to your message. When you are writing to someone for the first time, for example, you should be especially careful with your explanation of why you are writing — your purpose must be stated clearly and explicitly. When you have a well-established relationship with a reader, the history of your communication with that reader will help place each new message in a meaningful context.

How do people's emotions influence their communications with each other?

In addition to having certain expectations based on their previous experiences with you, whether face to face or through written messages, your readers will also have certain emotional needs that will influence the way they respond to your message. The most important of these are

1. **People are self-centered.**   Your readers will always want to know what the message will do for them. They will expect your letter, memo, or report to have a specific point or purpose. Your reader's first question will usually be, "How will this message benefit me?" Successful letter writers answer that question by specifying the kind of satisfaction — material, emotional, psychological, or intellectual — the message offers the reader.

2. **People are defensive.**   Readers are frequently suspicious of promises made in messages. Readers also tend to perceive some kinds of messages as threatening. They may, for example, perceive constructive criticism as a personal attack, and a careless choice of words in important correspondence may cause serious problems.

3. **People are not perfect.**   Human error is a part of life, but no one — neither you nor your readers — enjoys having mistakes pointed out and criticized. We all like to consider ourselves a bit "more perfect" than the next person, and we all find it easier to discover and correct the

errors of others. Your readers will respond more favorably to your messages if you concentrate on the positive aspects of a situation, deemphasize mistakes, and focus on doing better in the future. Be especially careful to avoid directly accusing your readers of shortcomings. Accusations will cause them to become defensive and to resist your message.

4. **People need specific information.**   Most people do not feel comfortable with generalities, abstractions, and vague statements. Your messages will be more successful if you explicitly identify your own goals and help your readers establish clear, definite, and positive goals for themselves. Let your readers know what is going to happen next, who should take what action next, and by what date.

5. **People do the best they can.**   Even though your readers may have disappointed you and you may suspect that they are being less honest or less intelligent than they should be, grant them the benefit of the doubt as long as you possibly can. Assume that your readers are acting honestly and intelligently in relation to *their* perception of the situation, even if *your* perception is different. If you can learn to see the situation from your reader's point of view, you will be in a better position to explain your own point of view to them.

Does every message contain an emotional component? Why or why not?

The Reader's Attitude and Knowledge.   Individual readers' expectations are determined to a great extent by their individual attitudes and knowledge. As explained earlier, each message you write will have both a *subject content* (business objective) and a *feeling content* (human objective). Successful communicators do their best to match the subject content of the messages with their readers' knowledge and the feeling content with their readers' attitudes. The feeling content, or *human objective,* of any business message should be to make the reader feel as good as possible about the message expressed in the business objective.

You can better achieve both your business objective and your human objective in any message by asking yourself the following questions about your reader before you write.

1. What does my reader already know about the subject?
   a. Have we communicated about this subject before?
   b. Is my reader familiar with the specialized language of the subject?
   c. Is my reader familiar with basic business terminology?
   d. Will my reader require a full explanation of the subject, a simplified explanation, or no explanation at all?

2. What does my reader want to know about the subject?
   a. Is the subject already important to my reader?
   b. Can knowing about the subject benefit my reader?
   c. Does my subject have built-in reader interest, or must I create interest in some way?

3.   How does my reader feel about the subject?
   a.   Does my reader have a positive, negative, or neutral view of the subject?
   b.   What previous experience has my reader had with the subject that would influence his or her feelings about it?
   c.   Are my feelings about the subject the same as my reader's?

4.   How does my reader feel about me and my company (or my department)?
   a.   Does my reader have a positive, negative, or neutral view of me and my company?
   b.   What previous experience has my reader had with me or my company that would influence his or her feelings?
   c.   Are my feelings about my reader the same as his or her feelings about me and my company?

5.   How does my reader feel about other people, business, and life in general?
   a.   Is my reader optimistic or pessimistic?
   b.   Does my reader tend to be accurate and precise in business dealings?
   c.   Is my reader generally willing to grant the benefit of the doubt?

Why should you analyze the purpose of a message and its intended audience at the same time?

Message Purpose.   The audience to whom you will be writing is one of the fixed aspects of your communication situation. The other aspect, the one you will usually begin with, is the purpose of your message—the reason you are writing. These two elements are usually interdependent: you are writing to a particular reader or group of readers for a particular reason, and to alter either the audience or the purpose would be to change the entire communication context. The audience and the purpose of the message should be analyzed simultaneously.

To attain both its business objective and its human objective, the message must not only make its purpose and any required action clear, but also make the purpose and action seem desirable. Before you write, you should clarify your purpose by asking yourself the following questions:

1.   Why am I writing the message?

2.   Who will receive the message?

3.   Where and when (in what context) will the reader receive the message?

4.   What do I want the reader to know?

5.   What do I want the reader to do?

6.   When do I want the reader to do it?

7.   How should the reader do it?

8. Why should the reader do it (what benefits can I offer)?

9. How can I make it easier for the reader to do it?

10. How can I help the reader achieve his or her goals?

To accomplish your business objective, whether it is to inquire, to inform, or to persuade, you will need to consider your reader's probable emotional reaction. Some messages may have more than one business objective. When you need to write such a message, you should consider your reader's probable response to each objective separately.

After you have established your business objective, ask yourself the following questions:

1. Will the message disappoint the reader or hurt his or her feelings?

2. Is the reader likely to ignore or resist the message?

How can you determine whether to emphasize the business objective or the human objective in a message?

The answers to these final two questions determine how much attention you should pay to achieving the human objective of establishing or retaining the reader's goodwill and cooperation. Your analysis of the audience and the communication context will also determine the appropriate structure for the message. Message structures are discussed in Chapter 4.

Writing Style

In written communication, *how* something is said (the writing style) is frequently as important as *what* is said. The *how* controls the feeling content of the message, while the *what* controls the subject content. Regardless of the purpose of the message, effective business writing is always clear, courteous, concise, natural, and positive.

What is a writer's first obligation to the reader?

Clarity.   The writer's first obligation to the reader is to be clear. An unclear message causes even the most tolerant reader to feel irritated. Even when the news is bad, a reader will appreciate being able to understand the message and thus make an informed decision based on it. In fact, in recent years attempts have been made to legislate the use of plain language in government and business documents. The legal profession in particular has been attacked for using obscure language that often confuses readers. The "plain language movement" is likely to continue, because all people want to be able to understand what they are reading. Clarity in writing is achieved by using an appropriate vocabulary, keeping sentences and paragraphs short and readable, and using a logical structure.

Vocabulary.   Which of these two statements is more easily and quickly understood?

1. Refrain from implementing aggressive behavior until the opponents' sclera has been observed and duly noted.

2. Don't fire until you see the whites of their eyes.

How does vocabulary influence clarity?

Vocabulary — the words you choose to use — has an important impact on clarity. Certain words will be unfamiliar to some people. In general, short, familiar, everyday words communicate more effectively than longer, less well-known words. Of course, a well-educated audience will have a better-developed vocabulary than a poorly educated audience, but even the best-educated audience will not appreciate having to struggle with your vocabulary. Choose the short, simple word rather than the long, complicated word.

Complicated word	Simple word
ameliorate	improve
interrogate	ask
cognizant	aware
consummate	complete
subsequent to	after
institute	start
with regard to	about
be kind enough	please
give consideration to	consider
under date of	on
as of this writing	now

Experts in a given area often forget that the audience for a message may not be equally expert. This is especially true for people working in technical areas who must write to higher-level managers, who tend to be generalists rather than specialists, and to those outside the organization.

What is the difference between denotations and connotations?

In addition to examining your writing to eliminate words that may be unfamiliar to your audience, you should check to make sure that the words you have selected will mean the same thing to your audience as they do to you. Words have both *denotations* (dictionary meanings) and *connotations* (associated, personal meanings). The words *inexpensive* and *cheap* can both denote the same thing, but their connotations are decidedly different. For most people, *inexpensive* simply means low in cost while *cheap* means poorly made or a poor value.

Many words have connotations that are fairly well agreed upon. The neutral word *smell*, for example, has synonyms with both positive and negative connotations. Compare *odor, stink,* and *stench* with *aroma, fragrance,* and *bouquet.* Many words, however, have associated meanings that vary greatly from person to person. For example, depending on family background and income, *inexpensive* could mean anything from $1 to well over $1,000.

The word *friend* may mean an intimate companion to one reader, a casual acquaintance to another, and a Quaker to yet a third. In fact, it may have all three meanings for the same reader depending on the context in

SIDEBAR

Keep It Simple

One classic and often quoted illustration of miscommunication because of lack of clarity involves a plumber and the National Bureau of Standards. The plumber had written to the Bureau to say that hydrochloric acid was effective for cleaning out clogged drains. Someone at the Bureau replied in typical bureaucratic language.

> The efficacy of hydrochloric acid is indisputable, but the corrosive residue is incompatible with metallic permanence.

The plumber wrote back, thanking the Bureau for *agreeing* with him. Another member of the Bureau tried to straighten out the plumber with the following message:

> We cannot assume responsibility for the production of toxic and noxious residue with hydrochloric acid and suggest you use an alternative procedure.

The plumber thanked the Bureau a second time, saying that he was getting fine results and that the Bureau should suggest the use of hydrochloric acid to other people. Finally, the problem got passed to the department head, who wrote:

> Don't use hydrochloric acid. It eats the hell out of the pipes.

The first two bureaucrats did not analyze their reader well enough to communicate a clear message. They selected words that were clear enough to them without thinking about whether the plumber would also know the words. The department head saw the communication problem from the plumber's point of view and selected words that would be effective in that particular context.

which the word is used. That the writer means a particular thing by a particular word is not a guarantee that the reader will also attach the same meaning to that word.

While it is impossible to preclude a reader's private interpretations and associated meanings for words, a writer should attempt to select words that will result in a correct interpretation of the message as a whole when they are considered together in a particular context. By selecting the right word, the writer reduces the number of possible interpretations; and by placing that word in the right context, the writer further reduces the possibility of miscommunication.

Another possible cause of miscommunication is misuse of words by the writer because of faulty understanding. Before you use a word, make sure that you know what it means. Some words are widely misused because the writers do not check a dictionary before using them. What, for example, is the difference between *disinterested* and *uninterested?* Many people do not know that *disinterested* means *impartial* and is not a synonym for *uninterested,* which means *without interest.*

Why should writers pay particular attention to nouns and verbs?

Because nouns and verbs carry the essential information in your sentences, pay particular attention to the words you select for them. These words should be *specific* rather than *general* because specific language enables the reader to visualize the action of your letter, and it also helps create believability.

General:	This television set is high quality.
Specific:	All components in this television meet or exceed government specifications for use in manned satellites.
General:	I completed a long report for one of my management classes.
Specific:	In Managing Human Resources, I completed a 50-page study of the impact of quality circles on productivity in the automotive industry.

As a rule, exact facts, figures, details, and examples communicate more clearly than vague generalities. Be especially careful to avoid general words that may have different meanings (connotations) for different people: *large, small, good, bad, a few, many,* and so forth. How large, for example, is a *large profit?* Further examples of general versus specific words and phrases follow.

General	**Specific**
soon	March 15, tomorrow
number	nine
city	Atlanta
contact (as a verb)	call, write, visit
somebody	Dr. Kitty Locker
dog	Fido
high profits	a 42 percent markup
our product	The Norton Blender
a magazine	*Woman's Day*

Abstract language also detracts from clarity because it omits specific details that may be required for the reader to understand a message. In most cases *concrete* language, which refers to specific facts or events, communicates more clearly.

Abstract:	It has been brought to my attention that you did not receive your check. (*How* was it brought to the writer's attention?)

Concrete:	Thank you for calling to let me know that you had not received your check.

Many abstract expressions are simply wordy versions of their more concise equivalents. See the following list and also "Wordy Expressions" later in this chapter.

Abstract	**Concrete**
Consideration was given	I considered
Prior to the termination of your policy	Before your policy ends
My analysis of your situation	I think that
The electrical potential may be injurious	Danger. High voltage.

Try to avoid words that have become essentially meaningless (or annoying) through overuse or imprecise use. Among the worst offenders in this category are *very, done, get, deals with,* and *involves.*

Not this:	Our chances of succeeding are *very good.*
But this:	Our chances of succeeding are *excellent* (or simply *good*).
Not this:	The report is *done.*
But this:	The report is *finished* (or *complete*).
Not this:	Did you *get* the materials yet?
But this:	Did you *obtain* (or *receive*) the materials yet?.
Not this:	This memo *deals with* the problem of employee turnover.
But this:	This memo *discusses* (or *analyzes* or *presents*) the problem of employee turnover.
Not this:	The high rate of employee turnover *involves* both poor morale within the company and better opportunities elsewhere.
But this:	The high rate of employee turnover *is caused by* both poor morale within the company and better opportunities elsewhere.

Your message will also be clearer if you state it explicitly rather than implicitly. That is, your message should be definite and straightforward, leaving nothing to be inferred or assumed by the reader, stating rather than implying information. Using specific and concrete words will help you make explicit statements.

Implicit: The items you ordered will be arriving soon.

Explicit: You will receive the Minolta SRT-202 and POW-27 electronic flash attachment in about 10 days. I shipped them by United Parcel Service this morning.

When is it better to imply your point rather than state it explicitly?

An explicit message, however, not only answers *who, what, when,* and *where,* but also answers the important question *why.*

Implicit: It will be to your advantage to order now.

Explicit: By ordering now, you will receive two issues absolutely free.

A message should be implicit rather than explicit only when the explicit statement would be unnecessarily negative or offensive.

Explicit: You forgot to specify the color and size of the shirt you ordered.

Implicit: The shirt you ordered is available in several colors and sizes. Please use the enclosed card to indicate your choice of color and size.

In the foregoing example, the explicit statement is unnecessarily negative because it accuses the reader of being forgetful. The implicit statement is clear because it asks for a specific action, yet it avoids a direct accusation.

Explicit: Spring is coming. You'll need to replenish your stock of Lawnamatic Power Mowers now.

Implicit: Because spring is coming, the demand for Lawnamatic Power Mowers will soon be increasing. To ensure beating the spring rush, use the enclosed order blank to replenish your stock.

In this example, the explicit statement offends the reader by emphasizing something that is obvious to the reader (spring is coming) and by giving the reader instructions for managing his or her business. The implicit statement subordinates the obvious (*because* spring is coming) and emphasizes *why* rather than *how* the reader should act.

How does sentence length influence clarity?

Sentence Structure.   Sentence structure is also an important consideration in achieving clarity. The easiest sentences to read and to understand are short, simple sentences that use the active voice and the past, present, or future tense, and that make an explicit statement. To avoid monotony, sentence length should be varied, but short sentences are easier to read and are therefore usually clearer than long sentences. Use short sentences for your main ideas, and place supporting information in the longer sentences.

The simple tenses (past, present, and future) are clearer than the compound tenses (present progressive, past progressive, future progressive, present perfect, past perfect, and future perfect). Naturally, some ideas require the compound tenses, and you will need to use them to express your idea accurately. But when possible, use the simple tenses. And when you are using a compound tense, make sure that your tense progression is logical and clear so that your reader will know when each event takes place. See Chapter 2 for an illustration of verb tenses.

Active voice also aids clarity by simplifying the description of the events taking place. It is easier to read and to understand than passive voice because it is more direct and focuses on people in action.

How does the voice of a sentence influence its clarity?

Active: You will receive the items listed on the enclosed invoice by April 7.

Passive: The items listed on the enclosed invoice will be shipped by April 3.

Passive voice results from using a form of the verb *to be* in combination with the past participle of an action verb (usually ending in *ed*). The subject of a passive sentence receives, rather than does, the action. Often the doer of the action is indicated by the preposition *by*.

Passive: The accounts were examined by the auditor.

Active: The auditor examined the accounts.

Passive: The folders were sorted by Susan.

Active: Susan sorted the folders.

Active voice is clearer than passive voice because it places an explicit subject early in the sentence so that the reader knows exactly who is responsible for the action. Compare the following sentences:

Passive: It was concluded that new word processing equipment should be purchased.

Active: I concluded that B & B Enterprises should purchase new word processing equipment.

Note that in the passive sentence the *doer of the action*, the person responsible for concluding, is not clear. Note, too, that a reader cannot tell who should purchase the new word processing equipment. In the active sentence, however, both these factors are explicit and clear.

Writers are sometimes tempted to use passive voice to avoid responsibility for their decisions or to disguise their own mistakes:

Passive: It was felt that you should seek employment elsewhere.

Active: You're fired.

Passive: It was discovered that the check had not been sent.

Active: I discovered that I forgot to include your check.

As a rule, this technique does not work because readers (and audiences for oral messages, too) can determine who is doing the concluding, feeling, or deciding. The writer has not disguised her or his responsibility but has simply written an unclear, weak sentence.

When should pas-
sive voice be used?

Although passive voice should not be used to avoid responsibility for a decision or to disguise one's own mistakes, it can be used effectively to subordinate a reader's mistake.

Active: You failed to complete both sides of the form.

Passive: Both sides of the form should be completed.

Active: You did not send your check along with your application form.

Passive: A check was not included with your application form.

Passive voice is also useful when the doer of the action is unknown or unimportant. When neither the writer nor the reader know or need to know who is doing the acting, a passive voice sentence can be clearer and more logical than an active voice sentence. In the following sentences, note the way the passive sentences emphasize the subject of greatest importance, whereas the active sentences emphasize unknown or unimportant subjects.

Passive: The concrete was poured today. (Emphasizes what happened.)

Active: Some people poured the concrete today. (Emphasizes *some people*.)

Passive: The office was burglarized during the night. (Emphasizes what happened.)

Active: Someone burglarized the office during the night. (Emphasizes *someone*.)

How does sentence
type influence clar-
ity?

Your sentences should also accurately reflect the relationship between the ideas expressed in them. This is achieved by proper choice of simple, compound, complex, or compound-complex structure for each sentence. **Simple sentences** contain separate, independent thoughts.

> I will meet you at the airport. We can go directly to dinner.

Compound sentences contain related and equal ideas, either similar or contrasting.

> I will meet you at the airport, *and* we can go directly to dinner.
> I will meet you at the airport, *but* I will not be able to join you for dinner.

Complex sentences contain unequal thoughts, with one subordinated to (dependent on) the other.

> Although I can't meet you at the airport (dependent clause), I will join you for dinner at the hotel (independent clause).

Compound-complex sentences contain equal and unequal thoughts.

> Although I can't meet you at the airport, I will join you for dinner at the hotel, and we can discuss the contracts at that time.

How does para-
graphing influence
the clarity of a mes-
sage?

Paragraphing.   Paragraphing also greatly influences clarity and readability. Simply defined, a *paragraph* is a series of related sentences about a particular topic. Because short paragraphs are easier to read than long paragraphs, most paragraphs in business messages should be short. In single-spaced material (letters, memos, and most short reports), the first and last paragraphs should be no longer than about four lines (not four sentences but four lines) long. Middle paragraphs should be not much longer than eight lines. The length of the paragraphs, however, should be varied to avoid a choppy appearance.

Paragraphs are also more readable when the first sentence is the *topic sentence* and announces the main idea presented in the paragraph. The rest of the sentences in the paragraph should relate to, support, and explain the idea presented in the topic sentence.

What is wrong with
beginning a letter
by saying, "I have
received your let-
ter"?

Logical Structure.   Clear writing depends on logical structure (which is closely related to paragraphing). A message should have a definite beginning, middle, and end. To provide this kind of structure, begin by placing the message in a particular *communication context.* In old-fashioned business letters, writers would say, "I have received your letter of the 12th," or "In reference to your letter of the 5th instant," (this month), to place the communication in context. Modern business communicators try to place their messages in context without being so stilted or obvious.

> Here, Clyde, is the information you requested. Model Y, which you asked about, offers many advantages.

> You're right to expect many years of trouble-free service from Guardsman surveillance equipment.

Once the message as a whole is placed in a specific context, each of the elements within the message should also be placed in its own specific context so that the reader receives a unified message that moves clearly from point to point.

A unified message has continuity of thought and singleness of purpose. Unity, like structure, requires planning. You should group related ideas together and then arrange the groups into a logical sequence. Eliminate ideas that do not pertain to either your subject content (business objective) or your feeling content (human objective). So that your reader will always know where your message has been and where it is going as you move from idea to idea, provide your reader with a clear, specific reference to the preceding idea or anticipate your next idea with an explicit statement of direction. The four principal ways of establishing the *unity, coherence,* and *transition* required for clarity are

Why is it important for each idea in a written message to be logically connected with the preceding idea?

1.   **Repetition.**   As you move from sentence to sentence, repeat key words or ideas or use pronouns to stand for key words and concepts.

     You're right to expect many years of trouble-free service from *Guardsman surveillance equipment.* Our *equipment* provides. . . .

     Congratulations on your upcoming *graduation.* To celebrate this *joyous occasion.* . . .

     Repetition of sentence structure can also be used to give added emphasis to the ideas put into parallel structure.

     First, examine everything you've written for clarity. Second, examine everything you've written for proper tone. Third, examine everything you've written for proper emphasis. Finally, examine everything you've written for completeness.

     Although repetition of words and ideas is an effective means of showing transition, unnecessary repetition makes for dull reading. Avoid using two words that say the same thing (close proximity), and avoid communicating the same idea twice (*thank you again.* . .).

2.   **Cause and effect.**   A second way of establishing unity, coherence, and transition is by showing a cause-and-effect relationship between two or more events. Words such as *thus, therefore, due to,* and *because* indicate that one event is the cause of another. (Although some writers use the word *since* to indicate cause and effect, it is best used to indicate the passage of time.)

     Because Fran bought 42 shares of American Business stock, Arno purchased 45.

     Because you said that I should take whatever steps were necessary to save the money, I assumed that I had the authority to close the plant in Pontiac.

Writers need to take special care with cause-and-effect statements. Whenever you use this method to establish transition, make sure that the one event is the cause of the other. The following statement may or may not be true:

The low morale on the assembly line is due to the antiquated equipment.

Until the writer knows for certain that the antiquated equipment is the direct and only cause of the low morale, the sentence should be less absolute.

The low morale on the assembly line is at least partly due to the antiquated equipment.

The low morale on the assembly line may be due to the antiquated equipment.

3.   **Comparison/contrast.**   You can also establish unity, coherence, and transition by pointing out the similarities and differences between two concepts or events.

Douglas McGregor and Rensis Likert have both developed methods of analyzing managerial characteristics. McGregor calls the basic styles of management Theory X and Theory Y, and Likert calls them Job-centered and Employee-centered.

The difference between a university and a trade school is that the university is more concerned with the *why* than the *how*, while the trade school is concerned more with the *how* than with the *why*.

Business communication is more complicated than other kinds of communication because the communicators must not only worry about communicating, but also worry about the cost.

Foreign cars offer better gas mileage than American cars, but American cars offer more options.

4.   **Time and place.**   Because our thinking ability depends so heavily on chronological order, it is important for a reader to know when and where the events you refer to in your message are taking place.

You should receive the marble faun Tuesday, 17 November. I shipped it by United Parcel Service this morning.

By making your references to time and place as specific as you can, you are establishing a logical order for events that will be clear to your reader.

Before deciding which car to purchase, I looked at Mazdas, Fieros, Toyotas, and Hondas. *After* driving the cars, I narrowed the possibilities to either the Fiero or the Toyota, and I made my *final* decision on the basis of the Toyota's better gas mileage.

Time and place transitions are best indicated by referring to *steps 1, 2, 3,* or *points 1, 2, 3.* Frequently you can use a *numbered list* to show that the steps or points are related parts of a larger whole.

In addition to ensuring that each message begins at a logical place and proceeds logically from point to point, you should structure the message to increase its overall effectiveness. Business messages, as has been true of effective communication since Aristotle, are arranged either *deductively* or *inductively.*

What is the difference between inductive and deductive messages?

Deductive order begins with the main point (or points), which is followed by supporting details. Inductive order begins with the details and concludes with the main point (or points). Business communicators have adapted these basic structural patterns for use in specific circumstances, which we will discuss in Chapter 4.

Timing.   As is true for all communication situations, the timing of messages is important. It is timing that places a message in a particular communication context. Depending on the situation, a direct or an indirect presentation might be more effective. When your message is important, it should be timed for greatest success.

Why is it important to answer business correspondence quickly?

Because business letters and memos are written for a specific purpose, it is important that they be written in time for the reader to take whatever action is necessary. To make it easy for your reader to reply, consider dividing complex tasks into a series of simpler items so that the reader can reply to each item separately.

As a general rule, **you should answer any letter you receive within 48 hours** even if you cannot provide a complete answer and will need to write again later. This rule does not apply to memos as much as it does to letters.

Why should you be concerned with the readability of your messages?

Readability.   To be clear, a message must be readable — easy to read. Readability is a broad term that covers most of the suggestions we have offered thus far for clarity, such as short paragraphs and sentences, specific language, and simple vocabulary.

To increase the readability of your messages, remember that no one likes to work at understanding a message. Readers appreciate messages that they can read quickly, easily, and without misunderstanding. Keep your messages as simple, straightforward, and uncluttered as you can without talking down to your reader. If you cannot read your own message quickly and easily, your reader probably won't be able to do so either. Obviously, you will have to spend a little extra time and put forth an extra effort to ensure a readable message. But the time you invest will provide a better return than the time you might otherwise spend writing a second message to clarify the first.

Two writing authorities, Robert Gunning and Rudolf Flesch, have established formulas for determining the readability of a piece of writing based on the number of words in each sentence and the number of syllables in the words. Because the resulting figure roughly corresponds with the educational level required to read a given piece of writing, the Gunning Fog Index has become one of the most widely used formulas. Figure 3.1 describes the procedure for using the Fog Index.

Such objective measurements of readability have their applications. You may use the Gunning Fog Index as a quick and convenient measure of the readability of your writing, but you should be aware that such formulas are not consistently accurate as predictors of readability. As Jack Selzer and other researchers have pointed out, the formulas are based only on factors that are

---

**FIGURE 3.1
Application of the
Gunning Fog Index**

1. Using a sample of at least 100 words, determine the average number of words in a sentence by dividing the total number of words by the total number of sentences. Count each independent clause as a separate sentence. For example, "Personal computers offer greater flexibility than stand-alone word processors, and they can perform all but the most sophisticated word process operations just as well as the much more expensive WP equipment" would be counted as two sentences.

2. Count the number of polysyllabic words (three or more syllables). Omit from this count proper nouns (primarily names of people and places), verbs containing three syllables as a result of the addition of *-es* or *-ed*, and combinations of short, easy words (*insofar, however, undertake,* and so forth).

3. Determine the percentage of so-called difficult words by dividing the number of polysyllabic words by the total number of words in the passage.

4. Add the average number of words in a sentence to the percentage of polysyllabic words. Multiply the total by 0.4.

5. The resulting figure shows the readability of the passage in terms of the level of education (grade) required to read the passage.

    EXAMPLE: A passage contains
       152 words
        11 sentences
        21 polysyllabic words
    Average sentence length = (152/11) = 13.8
    Percentage of difficult words = (21/152) = 14%
    Average length + percentage × 0.4 (13.8 + 14 × 0.4) = 11.12
    Reading level = 11.1 (about 11th grade)

---

easy to count and do not include enough variables for an accurate estimate of readability.[3]

Usually your best guide to readable writing is your own common sense: Are your paragraphs short and inviting? Are your topic sentences specific and in the active voice? Is your vocabulary appropriate for your audience? Do your sentences average about 17 words? A "yes" answer to these questions practically guarantees readable writing.

What can writers do to include courtesy in their messages?

Courtesy.   A courteous message takes its reader's feelings and point of view into consideration. A courteous message, like a courteous person, is polite, considerate, and empathic. Courtesy is extended primarily through the feeling content (human objective) of your message, though the subject content (business objective) may also be influenced by your consideration for your reader. The basic assumption of a courteous message is that writer and reader are both reasonable people with good intentions who can solve problems, make decisions, and understand each other without resorting to any form of psychological or physical force. Courtesy depends on the writer not only understanding the reader's viewpoint, but also assuming that the writer and reader will be able to cooperate as equals.

What is empathy?

The You-Attitude.   The questions listed earlier in this chapter are designed to help you see a business communication situation from your reader's point of view. Empathy is only possible when you can see a situation from the other person's perspective. A courteous message has empathy; it takes the reader's thoughts, feelings, and point of view into account. It anticipates the emotional response a reader might have to a message and takes the steps necessary to help the reader feel good about the message. It anticipates the reader's needs and questions and offers explanations and answers accordingly.

You can establish empathy with your reader even when your message will be unpleasant. Remember that your messages will be more successful if you **put your readers and their problems first.** Your readers will expect you to have legitimate interests and concerns, and it is courteous for you to specify where your own interests lie. Your readers, however, will appreciate your showing them, by emphasizing the ways in which they will benefit, that you also understand their needs.

One measure of the you-attitude in your message is to count and compare the number of "*you's*" with the number of "*I's*" and "*we's*." When you can, make the reader or the reader's company or product the subject or object of your sentences. The you-attitude is impossible to achieve without using

---

[3]Jack Selzer, "Readability Is a Four-Letter Word," *The Journal of Business Communication* (Fall 1981), 18:4, pp. 23–34, esp. p. 25.

second-person pronouns, although, of course, their use will not automatically
guarantee it.

Writer viewpoint:	We are happy to have your order. We shipped it this morning.
Reader viewpoint:	You will receive your solid walnut desk by Tuesday, October 23.
Writer viewpoint:	We have been making Model 12 radios for over ten years.
Reader viewpoint:	Your new Model 12 radio is backed by ten years of testing and improvements.
Writer viewpoint:	I have ten years' experience in management.
Reader viewpoint:	My ten years' experience in management would enable me to make an effective contribution to your planning board.
Writer viewpoint:	We regret that you've had so much trouble with your Soob automobile, and we apologize for not solving your problem sooner.
Reader viewpoint:	You were right to ask me about the troubles you've been having with your new Soob. Thank you for giving me this opportunity to answer your questions.
Writer viewpoint:	I am enclosing a brochure describing our new software.
Reader viewpoint:	The enclosed brochure shows you new software that can save you countless hours at home and on the job.

When your statement is accusatory, the you-attitude is better served by
omitting the *"you."* In such cases passive voice and implied statements show
more empathy.

Writer viewpoint:	You neglected to take care of the requirements of Form 123.
Reader viewpoint:	To enjoy the full benefits of your new ABC, follow the procedures on Form 123.
Writer viewpoint:	You failed to tell us the color of the dress you ordered.

Reader viewpoint:	The dress you ordered comes in seven brilliant colors. Please indicate your choice on the enclosed card.
Writer viewpoint:	Your conclusion is incorrect because our contract clearly states that. . . .
Reader viewpoint:	Paragraph 7 of our contract seems to state that. . . . Do you agree?
Writer viewpoint:	You forgot to check the color coordinator adjustment on the 24″ television sets.
Reader viewpoint:	The color coordinator adjustment on the 24″ television sets should be checked before final assembly.

Each part of a message presents certain hazards in conveying the you-attitude. In the opening of the letter, writers are frequently tempted to begin with a statement of what they have done or why they have done it. Always attempt to use the word *"you"* early in your first sentence. When possible, avoid *"I"* and *"we"* beginnings.

Writer viewpoint:	I have approved your request to substitute Coorson fire extinguishers for the Lablatts extinguishers.
Reader viewpoint:	Yes, you may substitute Coorson for the Lablatts extinguishers.

Because the middle of a message usually contains some kind of explanation, the writer may be tempted to focus on the explanation and neglect the way the reader is affected—although the effect on the reader is naturally what interests the reader. Remember to keep your reader in the picture by making him or her the subject or the object of the sentence when possible.

Writer viewpoint:	Lewis and Clark has been in the expedition business for more than 100 years. We've guided successful tours of Asia, Africa, Europe, and the Louisiana Territory. We make every effort to cover all the points of interest, and we always offer first-class accommodations.
Reader viewpoint:	With Lewis and Clark, you will receive a guarantee backed by more than 100 years of successful expeditions. Whether you wish to see Asia, Africa, Europe, or the Louisiana Territory, Lewis and Clark is able

to provide first-class accommodations close to all the points of interest.

The ending of a message presents problems because the writer is tempted to focus on his or her own needs rather than focusing on how the action, information, or decision will influence the reader.

Writer viewpoint: I need this information by March 12 to make a decision about where we should have our convention.

Reader viewpoint: Your answer by March 12 will enable me to consider your hotel as a possible convention site.

Writer viewpoint: I will be glad to receive your future orders and look forward to doing more business with you.

Reader viewpoint: Thank you for your order. When we can serve you again, call our toll-free number (800) 555-3295.

How is "showing" different from "telling"?

Throughout the message, you will serve the readers' needs better by *showing* the readers how they will benefit rather than simply *telling* them that they will benefit.

Writer viewpoint: You will benefit by owning a Big Byte Personal Computer.

Reader viewpoint: A Big Byte Personal Computer will keep your financial records, manage your stock portfolio, write your reports, and even start your coffeepot in the morning.

Writer viewpoint: You will save time by ordering a Kitchen Magic Food Processor.

Reader viewpoint: A Kitchen Magic Food Processor will reduce the time you spend dicing vegetables by 80 percent.

Why should you treat your reader as an equal?

Cooperation of Equals.   Correspondents should usually consider each other — and treat each other — as equals. Business relationships are interdependent: sellers cannot exist without buyers; buyers cannot exist without sellers; manufacturers cannot exist without distributors; distributors cannot exist without manufacturers. And regardless of the goods or services being offered, one of the parties in any business transaction can always do without these goods or services or can go elsewhere. Any letter you write should demonstrate your knowledge that the reader is doing business with you because he or she has *chosen* to do business with you at that particular time.

Anything that interferes with the one-to-one relationship of equals is usually detrimental to the success of a message. Even when you are writing the same message to many people—as with direct mail advertising and some types of insurance correspondence—you can still write to one person at a time. Use a form message to reduce the expense of writing, printing, and mailing the messages, but use *you* singular rather than *you* plural. Avoid generic terms that lump individual readers into a common pile.

Poor:	Dear Stockholder:
	This letter is to inform all stockholders of an important change in our policy concerning dividends.
Better:	Because you own stock. . .
	in Gibson Guitars, we're writing to let you know about an important policy change.

The reader will still recognize your letter as a form and will understand that it is going to a number of other people, but your message will be more effective because each of your readers will feel that you are considering him or her as an individual rather than as a member of a particular group.

It is important that your language demonstrate not only your respect for your readers as individuals, but also your expectation of mutual respect. A careless choice of words and phrasing could convey an attitude of either superiority or inferiority toward your reader, either of which will interfere with the success of your message. The following negative attitudes are the principal offenders:

What would be wrong with telling a reader, "We are pleased to grant you credit at Trudy's Department Store"?

1. **Indignation.**   Do not let your emotions interfere with your ability to achieve a particular objective. Do not accuse the reader of a deliberate offense or show resentment at having to write or to explain a situation. The seemingly harmless statement, "Your letter has been referred to this office for a reply," may imply that you resent having to answer the letter.

2. **Mistrust.**   When you have a reason to doubt your reader, give your reason explicitly. When you are unsure of something, ask a question. Never use language that implies mistrust. The statement, "You claim that five ceramic figurines were damaged in shipment," implies that the reader was lying about how the figurines were damaged.

3. **Paternalism.**   Do not grant favors, give orders, or lecture your reader. The statement, "We are pleased to grant you permission," places the

writer in a superior position. The statement, "You must complete the enclosed application and return it by Wednesday," implies that the reader is not free to choose an alternate course of action. The statement, "You will need to stock more than one dozen Kingly Electric Blankets because they sell so quickly," implies that you know more about the reader's business than he or she does.

Instead of simply telling the reader to do something, emphasize the benefit associated with the desired action. Instead of simply announcing that something is so, provide the reader with an explanation. The most offensive words are *must, should, ought,* and *need to.*

Not this:	You must complete the enclosed form to initiate your insurance coverage.
But this:	To initiate coverage, simply complete and return the enclosed form.
Not this:	Company policy prohibits our granting requests like yours.
But this:	Because our insurance policy provides coverage for employees only, we are unable to extend use of the company picnic area to outside organizations.
Not this:	You should stock Genius diskettes.
But this:	The combination of low cost and high quality would make Genius diskettes a profitable item for the Software House.
Not this:	When you carefully consider all investment options, you'll decide to entrust your money to Williamsburg Brokerage.
But this:	We invite you to compare Williamsburg Brokerage with your other investment options — and let us know what you discover.

4. **Undue Humility.**   Do not place yourself in a position inferior to that of the reader. Remember that business relationships are interdependent, and your reader usually needs you just as much as you need your reader. The statement, "I hate to bother somebody as important as you are with this little problem of mine," implies that the problem — and the writer — are not worth the reader's attention.

5. **Flattery.**   No one likes a sycophant. Legitimate praise for a job well done is one thing, but do not try to win your reader with flattery. Give

your reader credit for knowing how much praise is appropriate for a particular accomplishment, and give your reader credit for being able to recognize self-seeking motivation hiding behind unearned praise. The statement, ''You are *the only person* in the United States who knows enough about television to . . .,'' attributes a uniqueness to the reader that a reader with intelligence (and knowledge of other experts in television) would recognize as false.

What is the difference between "brief" and "concise"?

Conciseness.   In many ways, conciseness is an extension of the first two elements of clarity and courtesy. You should be concise primarily to help make your message clear and to show consideration for your reader's time. A concise message, however, is not necessarily short. It is one that does not waste words. It is a message in which each word and each sentence accomplish something for you. But in your effort to trim the fat from the meat of your message, do not forget that each message has two objectives: a business objective and a human objective. A message cannot successfully accomplish its business objective without meeting the reader's human needs. Your readers do not want to wade through three or four pages when one will do, but neither do they want to feel as though you could hardly wait to get their letters, memos, or reports out of the way. Compare the following messages:

Wordy: We're so glad that you've written your letter of the 12th to ask about our Jetliner service to Japan. I have your letter before me in which you ask whether we offer such a service and how much the cost would be for a party of two adults and three children for the Jetliner service to Japan.

Our Jetliner flights leave from San Francisco International airport at 12:00 noon every day, seven days a week. The flight time is about 16 hours, and the flight is nonstop from San Francisco to Japan. The airplane will land in Tokyo, and the cost for two adults and three children is only $8,700 for ten days.

You may reserve a reservation on our Jetliner service to Japan by completing the enclosed reservation card. We'll be glad to process your application when we receive a 10 percent deposit of $870.

Too Brief: The Jetliner service you asked about leaves San Francisco International airport every day at noon. The cost for two adults and three children is $8,700 for ten days. The flight to Tokyo takes 16 hours. Please complete the enclosed application and return it with your 10 percent deposit.

Concise: The Jetliner service you asked about leaves San Francisco International airport every day at noon. The 16-hour flight is nonstop, and the airfare includes two dinners, a breakfast, and a lunch.

The cost of round-trip airfare, seven days in Tokyo, and the extended tour of Honshu, including overnight stays in Yokohama, Osaka, and Sakai, is $8,700 for two adults and three children.

Complete the enclosed application and return it with your deposit of $870 to ensure reservations for the tour in June. Should you have questions about the Jetliner service, about Japan, or about your passport, just write. I'll be glad to help.

What is redundancy?

As you can see from the foregoing examples, the wordy letter uses more words than necessary. It contains many redundancies — that is, the letter says the same thing two or three times. In the case of "reserving a reservation," the repetition is obvious. The second letter, on the other hand, is too brief; it does not provide complete information, nor does it accomplish the human objective of an effective message.

Avoiding Wordy Expressions.   Many of the redundancies that make messages wordy have become so common that people use them unconsciously. Some examples are

Wordy	Concise
arrive at a decision	decide
the month of April	April
at the present writing	now
in the amount of	for
effect an improvement	improve
in the neighborhood of	about
new innovation	innovation
assembled together	assembled

exact replica	replica
true facts	facts
widow of the late	widow of
postponed until later	postponed
qualified expert	expert
entirely complete	complete
square in shape	square
basic fundamentals	fundamentals
the color red	red
a bad disaster	a disaster
the most unique	unique
first of all	first
in order to purchase	to purchase
due to the fact that	because
because of the fact that	because
the reason why is	the reason is
the reason is because	the reason is
needless to say	(omit—and consider omitting the rest of the sentence as well)
it goes without saying	(omit—and consider omitting the rest of the sentence as well)
as you know	(omit—and consider omitting the rest of the sentence as well)

Completeness. In your effort to be concise, do not leave your message incomplete. Examine it to make sure that you have covered everything you intended to cover and that you have provided sufficient detail for your reader to know what you expect of him or her. **Make sure the reader knows who is to do what next.** Ask yourself the following questions:

1. Have I answered all my reader's questions?

2. Have I anticipated additional questions my reader may have?

3. Have I provided all the information necessary for my reader to make a logical decision?

4. Have I explicitly asked the reader to perform the action that I want him or her to perform?

5.   Is the subject content sufficiently clear to accomplish my business objective?

6.   Is the feeling content suitable to accomplish my human objective?

Naturalness.   The most effective writing sounds natural to the ear. An effective style is inconspicuous — it does not attract attention to itself. Also, an effective style emphasizes the most important points and subordinates items of less importance.

Inconspicuous Style.   A clear, concise writing style is natural, conversational, unpretentious, and inconspicuous. Although your purpose for writing is to achieve specific goals, your writing style can be lively and interesting without detracting from the content of your message. Business letters and reports are not scholarly dissertations, and your readers will be more impressed with your abilities as a communicator if they understand what you are saying than if you attempt to impress them with your vocabulary or to sway them with rhetoric. Be especially careful to avoid legalese and business jargon.

What is wrong with using a "fancy" writing style (big words, long sentences, and unusual constructions) to entertain, impress, or catch the attention of your reader?

Rather than this	Say this
beg to advise	tell
prior to, subsequent to	before, after
cognizant of	know
please find enclosed	the enclosed booklet
in order to utilize	to use
peruse	read
remunerate	pay
thanking you in advance	I would appreciate
endeavor	try
interrogate	ask
educational resource center	library
in that time frame	then
a viable alternative	a possibility
the subject company	we, the company
as to	of, about
in regard to	about
under separate cover	by parcel post
return same to this office	send it back
this will acknowledge receipt	(omit)
please be advised that	(omit)
in the final analysis	finally

What is jargon?

In addition to the common phrases of legal and business language that too frequently are passed from generation to generaton of business writers, jargon includes "in" words that can be just as offensive to some readers as teenage slang is to those over 30. Such word usage is popular because it lets people sound knowledgeable without requiring them to be specific. Many words that fit into this category are perfectly good technical words that have been ill-adapted to nontechnical situations. Others have been created by writers to suit their own needs. The following are examples:

paramaters	formalize
conceptualize	prioritize
systematized	contact (in place of write or call)
logistical	
consequate	profitwise
finalize	employee-type
interface (as a verb)	time-oriented
	impact (as a verb)

Words of this variety go in and out of fashion so rapidly that a current, definitive (authoritative and complete) list would be impossible. If you are tempted to use a word that you cannot define quickly and easily, you should suspect that the word may not mean to your readers what it seems to mean to you. Check the words in the foregoing list in the dictionary. How many can you find? How many mean what you thought they did?

Your writing will be both less conspicuous and more interesting if you find new expressions to replace clichés. The following are only a few of the trite phrasings you should avoid.

bolt out of the blue	lock, stock, and barrel
hook, line, and sinker	fast as lightning
clear as crystal	hard as nails
pretty as a picture	good as gold
last but not least	sly as a fox
nose to the grindstone	shoulder to the wheel
green with envy	burn the midnight oil
first and foremost	father time
crack of dawn	sober as a judge
home sweet home	man about town
his true colors	generous to a fault

The trouble with such expressions is that they have been worn out with overuse, and now they have no real meaning. As is the case with legalese and business jargon, readers skip over trite figures of speech without paying attention to what you are trying to say. To prevent your style from creating a barrier to communication, say what you have to say simply, using fresh terminology.

Emphasis and Subordination.   Natural writing requires more than the elimination of jargon and pompous language. It also requires the same kind of variation and emphasis you provide naturally in oral communication. As you write, vary your words, sentence structure, and paragraph length to keep your message from becoming monotonous.

Why is variety important in business writing?

1.   Rather than repeating the same words, find acceptable synonyms, use pronouns, or restructure the sentence to avoid unnecessary repetition.

2.   Most of your sentences should be short and direct, but if all your sentences are short, your writing will be choppy and your readers will think either that you are a simpleton or that you are talking down to them. Your sentences should average about 17 words.

3.   The standard order for sentences in English is subject-verb-object. Use modifiers, subordinate clauses, and a mixture of sentence types to achieve variation.

4.   Your first and last paragraphs should be about four lines long. Your middle paragraphs should be about eight lines. Keeping the opening and closing paragraphs short helps ensure that they will be read. A four-line paragraph *looks* easy to read. Eight-line paragraphs are not so easy to read, but most readers will attempt them when they have reason to believe that the material is important to them. Paragraph length, however, should be varied—messages written entirely in four-line paragraphs would have a choppy appearance, and messages written entirely in eight-line paragraphs would appear heavy and uninviting.

How can you control emphasis and subordination of ideas in your written messages?

Oral communication allows you to emphasize the ideas you wish to stress by raising your voice, gesturing, and soliciting feedback from your audience to confirm the importance of a point. The means of controlling emphasis in written communication are as follows:

1.   **Placement.**   Where you place an idea in a message influences the amount of attention a reader will pay to it. The opening and closing paragraphs usually receive the most attention.

2.   **Proportion.**   How much space you give an idea indicates your degree of concern. Take extra time—and space—to explain the ideas that are most important to you and to your reader.

3.   **Language.**   Sentences are most emphatic when they are about people doing things. They are less emphatic when they have ideas as subjects. Nouns should be concrete and specific, and verbs should be in the active voice for greater emphasis. Remember that some ideas should be sub-

ordinated rather than emphasized. If the reader will find part of your message accusatory or negative, subordinate that part by using abstract, general words and passive voice.

4. **Mechanics.** You can also emphasize important ideas by underscoring, using capital letters, using color, putting key ideas in a numbered list, and surrounding main points with extra white space.

In general, emphasize ideas or actions that the reader will find positive or beneficial and those things that you or your reader *can* do. Subordinate ideas or actions that the reader will find negative or unpleasant and those things that cannot be done.

Not this:	We do not permit plant tours on Mondays. (Emphasizes the negative response.)
But this:	Although plant tours are not available on Mondays, you may tour our facilities any Tuesday, Wednesday, Thursday, or Friday. (Emphasizes what the reader can do.)
Not this:	I have enclosed your refund check. (Emphasizes what the writer has done.)
Not this:	Please find enclosed your refund check. (Emphasizes the act of finding.)
But this:	The enclosed check is your refund for overpayment on your recent order. (Emphasizes the reader benefit.)

What is wrong with using the phrase, "As you know"?

Also, avoid subordinating parts of your message the reader should know by adding unnecessary phrases like *as you'll recall, as you know,* and *let me remind you.*

Not this:	As you'll recall, last year you ordered two dozen cartons of the 20# cockleshell finish.
But this:	Did you wish to increase your last year's order of two dozen cartons of the 20# cockleshell finish?
Not this:	As you know, we discussed this on the phone last week.
But this:	After we discussed this on the phone last week . . .
Not this:	Let me remind you that we are scheduled

to discuss this at our sales meeting next week.

But this: When we discuss this at our sales meeting next week . . .

What is positive tone?

Positiveness.   The most effective messages are positive rather than negative. Your messages will be more successful when you show confidence in yourself, confidence in your reader, and confidence in your message. Optimistic messages do not neglect problems or negative factors; rather, they approach problems as solvable when reader and writer work together. Confidence is frequently called *positive tone.*

Confidence in Yourself.   To have confidence in yourself, you must feel that you have made the best business decision possible. Such confidence is necessary to create a positive tone to your letter. When you have faith in the fairness of your decisions and actions, it is easier to explain them without becoming defensive or apologetic. A self-confident attitude will help you present to your reader a decisive, positive straightforward image. Structure your message and select your words and phrases to emphasize its positive aspects. Subordinate negative ideas as much as you can without sacrificing clarity.

Negative: We cannot comply with Part II of your request.

Positive: We agree completely with Parts I, III, and IV of your request. Because our delivery schedule is already established for the next fiscal year, implementation of Part II will begin next January.

Negative: I regret that you were caused such a terrible inconvenience and hope that the enclosed refund will restore your faith in Goldsmith products.

Positive: You're right, Mr. Schneider. We inadvertently overcharged you. The enclosed check doesn't show it, but our face is red.

Your choice of words indicates to your reader how you feel about yourself and your ability to get a job done. People with a negative outlook on life frequently use negative words, such as the following:

apologize	difficult
bad	don't
can't	impossible
damaged	inferior

misfortune	regret
mistake	trouble
misunderstand	unable
never	unfortunately
no	unwilling
problem	won't

People with confidence in their abilities to do a job and do it correctly focus on *what* they can do and *when* they can do it. Realism dictates that problems and limitations receive the attention they deserve, but confidence in yourself dictates that you go beyond the problems and limitations to provide your reader with solutions and alternatives.

Confidence in Your Reader.   An attitude of confidence in your reader is as important as confidence in yourself. Assume that your reader will do what is right unless and until you have absolute proof that he or she will not, and assume that your reader is capable of overcoming obstacles. Naturally, confidence in your reader does not include an automatic granting, without question or clarification, of every request a reader might make. You should, however, always give the reader the benefit of the doubt.

What is the relationship between positive tone and the you-attitude?

Do not say "no" when you can legitimately say "maybe." Remember that your reader's perception of your situation and of the communication context will not be the same as yours. Before you make a decision that will affect your relationship with the reader, you should **try to see the situation from the reader's point of view.** Be especially careful to avoid words and phrases that imply that you doubt your reader's truthfulness or ability to get the job done correctly.

You claim (state, imply, suggest) that
If what you say is true
We are at a loss to understand
It's unlikely that your explanation is
You forgot (failed, neglected) to
You must (should, ought, need) to

Threats and bribes will also be offensive to your reader. Expressions that attempt to exert psychological force, grant undeserved favors in return for something, or appeal to the reader's worst motives will usually backfire.

This is done with the understanding that you will
What would your neighbors think if you
You will certainly regret
Because you have been a good customer of ours, we are willing
Even though you don't meet all of our requirements, we will
How much would it be worth to you
Great wealth can be yours
Imagine everyone falling at your feet, willing to do whatever you ask

What is wrong with
concluding a letter
with the expression,
"I hope that I have
answered all your
questions"?

Confidence in Your Message.   You should also show confidence in your
message. To have such confidence, of course, you must spend the time necessary to ensure that your message accomplishes both its business objectives
and its human objectives. Avoid expressions that suggest uncertainty about
the clarity of your message or about how your reader will accept it. *I hope, I
trust, if,* and *why not* imply that you do not think your message has done
everything it should.

> *I hope* that this letter answers all your questions.
> *Why not* send in your order today?
> *I trust* that this will prove satisfactory.
> *If* you want to order, complete the order blank at the back of the brochure.
> *If* you have further questions, do not hesitate to contact me.

Confident messages eliminate the implication of doubt.

> I'm glad to have been of help.
> To order, simply mark your choice and drop the enclosed card in the mail.
> Call me again when I can help.

Under what circum-
stances is it possible
to be too positive?

Overconfidence.   When aiming for confidence, however, remember that
overconfidence leads to presumptuousness, which is a violation of courtesy.
Do not *presume* that your readers will act or think in a particular way just
because you want them to. When your readers have a choice, make sure that
you do not take that choice away from them. Acknowledge the choice, and
make it sufficiently clear that the reader *can* choose.

Presumptuous:	You must complete your application to-day.
Positive and courteous:	By completing your application today, you will be assured a reservation for June 20.
Presumptuous:	Your inventory is not complete without one dozen bottles of Flash perfume, so order some now.
Positive and courteous:	The combination of 42 percent markup and a fast turnover would make Flash perfume a profitable addition to your stock.

▷ YOU ARE WHAT YOU WRITE

Even though the content of your messages may be more important to your
readers than your manner of expression, all readers appreciate an attitude of
warmth. Your letters, memos, and reports should sound as if they were

written by a caring human being. In today's synthetic, mechanized, computerized society, it is especially important that writing be human rather than technological communication.

What does your writing style say about you as a person?

Use written messages as a means of establishing human relationships. See your readers first as people and second as customers, dealers, or manufacturers. We are all people first, and our roles in society are merely superimposed on our basic, common humanity. Help when you can, and when you cannot, be nice about it. We are not suggesting that you should let the feeling content of the message detract from the subject content, but we guarantee that your messages will be more successful if they are obviously written from one human being to another rather than from one machine to another.

Do not let our suggestions — or those of anyone else — for effective letters, memos, and reports become formulas or law. Do not let your old writing — or anyone else's — become models for all future correspondence. Learn the basic principles well enough to apply them automatically in your own business communication, but retain enough flexibility and independent thinking to be able to adapt to situations that may require a unique approach.

Your writing style should be an extension of your personality, and your messages should read much the same way you would talk to your reader were you communicating face to face rather than in writing. Even though one of the main advantages of written communication is its ability to convey complex information better than oral communication, the best writing sounds natural to the ear.

▷ SUMMARY

Everyone needs to know how to write effective messages, but written communication may seem more difficult than it actually is because we spend relatively less time practicing it. Untrained writers often copy the style of messages written previously, which may result in boring letters and memos.

Writing plays an important role in business because it provides a permanent record, provides proof of agreement, puts the emphasis on logic, and may be more convenient than a phone call or personal visit. The costs of written communication are difficult to determine as they include not only postage and the various materials involved but also the time spent writing, rewriting, and typing. The possible return of profit on the message is another important factor in determining its cost.

The most effective messages are those placed in a specific communication context for a specific writer and reader. Consumers and dealers, for example, would have different concerns about a product or service, and the writer should show that he or she understands their different needs and expectations. If the message will disappoint or hurt the feelings of the reader, or if it is one that the reader might ignore, the writer will need to pay close attention to achieving the human objective.

In written communication, how something is said is frequently as important as what is said. The *how* controls the feeling content (human objective) of the message, while the *what* controls the subject content (business objective). The elements of written communication that help us achieve both objectives are clarity, courtesy, conciseness, naturalness, and positiveness.

Clarity, the transfer of a writer's thoughts to a reader without misunderstanding, is the single most important factor in written communication. Because a misunderstood message is worse than no message at all, use the short, simple word rather than the long, complicated word. Ask yourself whether the words you have selected will mean the same thing to your reader as they do to you. Choose concrete and specific words rather than abstract and general words. The easiest sentences to read and to understand are short, simple sentences using active voice in the past, present, or future tense. Clear messages require a logical structure, including a definite beginning, middle, and end. Four principal ways of establishing the unity, coherence, and transition required for clarity are repetition, cause and effect, comparison/contrast, and time and place.

A courteous message takes its reader's feelings and point of view into consideration. A courteous message, like a courteous person, is polite, considerate, and empathic. Empathy is possible only when you can see a situation from the other person's perspective. Courtesy also requires that you put your readers and their problems first. In addition, your language should demonstrate respect for your readers and your expectation of mutual respect. The wrong choice of words and phrasing may convey an attitude of either superiority or inferiority toward your reader that will interfere with the success of your message. The following negative attitudes are the principal offenders: indignation, mistrust, paternalism, humility, and flattery.

Conciseness is an extension of the first two elements, clarity and courtesy. A concise message is one that does not waste words. It is one in which each word and each sentence accomplish something for you. In striving for conciseness, however, beware of incompleteness.

Your letters, memos, and reports will be more successful if you use a positive tone and show confidence in yourself, your reader, and your message. A self-confident message is more likely to be accepted. Structure your message and select your words and phrases to emphasize its positive aspects. Subordinate negative ideas as much as you can without sacrificing clarity. Assume the best of your reader. Assume that your reader will do what is right until you have absolute proof that she or he will not, and assume that your reader is capable of overcoming obstacles. Also show confidence in your message. Spend the time necessary in composing your message to accomplish its business objectives and its human objectives. Remember, however, that overconfidence leads to presumptuousness, which is a violation of courtesy.

COMMUNICATION SOLUTION

The letter presented in this chapter's Communication Challenge has several problems. First, the writer probably does not know the reader well enough to call him by his first name, so the salutation is condescending. Second, although the first sentence places the message in its appropriate communication context, it does so in an illogical way. *How* was it brought to the writer's attention that Richard did not receive the original letter? The most logical way would be for Richard to have called or written to ask why he had not received a response.

Third, note the way the writer shifts responsibility for the negative decision away from himself and places the blame on the *Personnel people.* Note, too, the unnecessarily negative word *unfortunately* and the use of the incorrect name.

Finally, if you were Richard, how much faith would you have in the writer's statement that he will keep the resume on file? What would be necessary for you to believe that the writer actually would review the resume? Compare your solution with the following letter.

Be specific about how you know that he did not receive your previous letter.

Do not "pass the buck." Avoid blaming others for the negative decision. If you do not have too many letters to write, be specific about each applicant's area of interest: "As you are primarily interested in a management trainee position, and our openings are in sales, we have decided on other applicants for further consideration."

Gryde Industries • 14 Pace Plaza, 3-B • New York, NY   10038 • 212/555-5552

April 20, 19xx

Mr. Richard Blackstone
480 Jackson Street
Champaign, IL 61820

Dear Mr. Blackstone:

Thank you for calling to let me know that you had not received my letter in response to your application for employment with Gryde. I inadvertently sent your letter to the incorrect placement office.

I carefully reviewed your application and qualifications with members of our Personnel Department. At this time, Richard, your qualifications and interests do not match the requirements of our available jobs.

I will keep your application on file for six months and automatically review it should new openings occur.

If you are still interested after that time, please let me know.

Sincerely,

Marvin E. Olag

Marvin E. Olag
Administrator
Salaried Personnel

MEO:rs

The reader knows that you will not keep his application on file forever, so be specific about how long you will keep it. That way, the reader will believe you. If you have absolutely no interest in the reader, do not promise future consideration. Simply wish the applicant luck in finding suitable employment.

Your writing should be an extension of your personality, and your letters, memos, and reports should read much the same way you would talk to your reader were you communicating face to face rather than in writing. Your writing style should be natural, conversational, unpretentious, and inconspicuous. Your style can be lively and interesting without detracting from the content of your message. Be especially careful to avoid legalese, business jargon, and clichés. Your messages should sound as if they were written by a warm, caring human being. Use written communication as a means of establishing a human relationship. See your readers first as people and second as customers, supervisors, or subordinates.

▷ EXERCISES

Review and Discussion Questions

1.   What are four advantages of written communication?

2.   What are two disadvantages of written communication?

3.   What is the human objective of any business message?

4.   What are four principal ways of establishing unity, coherence, and transition?

5.   What should be the average length of a sentence?

6.   How do you control emphasis in written communication?

7.   What are four variables that influence the success of a message?

8.   What is a writer's primary obligation to a reader?

9.   What are denotations? Connotations?

10.   When can passive voice be used effectively?

Problems

1.   Revise the following sentences to make them clear.
   a.   We would like to order some desks.
   b.   Terminate the illumination.
   c.   Before his incarceration, the criminal was interrogated by the officers.
   d.   In reply to your recent missive, we wish to state that included herewith are the reports you requested.

2.   Rewrite the following sentences to make them more courteous.
   a.   I must have your response no later than February 1.
   b.   You forgot to specify the sizes of the hinges you ordered.
   c.   You claim that you never received the desks.
   d.   I'll be glad to ship your order when I receive it.

3.   Rewrite the following negative sentences to make them positive.
   a.   We cannot ship your order until Monday.
   b.   Our store will be closed Saturday.
   c.   Our products are not defective.
   d.   Our products do not contain any preservatives.

4.   Find modern, conversational substitutes for the following words and expressions.
   a.   Prior to
   b.   Under separate cover
   c.   Beg to advise
   d.   Please find enclosed

5.   Find modern, conversational substitutes for the following clichés.
   a.   Last but not least
   b.   Crack of dawn
   c.   First and foremost
   d.   Burn the midnight oil

6.   Rewrite the following sentences so that they emphasize the you-attitude.
   a.   To help us fill your order, please send us the size for the sweaters you ordered.
   b.   We shall ship your order as soon as we hear from you.
   c.   We are glad to have your order for six desks.
   d.   We are happy to announce our grand opening, and we would like you to come and register for door prizes.

7.   Rewrite the following sentences in the active voice.
   a.   Your resignation should be made in writing.
   b.   The package is being returned on Wednesday.
   c.   High prices were charged by that company.
   d.   The papers should have been filed by now.
   e.   Banks were closed because of the legal holiday.
   f.   The merchandise should be delivered by Acme Trucking.
   g.   Martha is being awarded a medal for her achievements.
   h.   The contract should have been signed before this.
   i.   The new items will be displayed in the conference room.

CASES

1. Rewrite the following message to make it more concise.

I have your letter of May 27, 19xx, in which you did register your complaint concerning the length of time which you associated with driving to and from your residence. The reason why the delay in answering your correspondence is that one of the gentlemen involved in your move, Mr. Rudolphski, has been on the road driving for us and we had to wait for him to return to query him concerning the conditions relative to your move.

After discussing with Mr. Rudolphski the circumstances, we find that he did leave the warehouse at 7:30 and, in proceeding to your residence on Royal Road apparently encountered some difficulty in locating the correct number as there is a jump in numbers as Royal Road apparently crosses Route #47. This caused him to not be able to locate the residence, and therefore, have to call you for instructions. Mr. Rudolphski indicates that subsequent to the call he did arrive at the house a little before 8:15 and this was the reason for the length of time involved in arriving at the house. In consideration of the fact that you have every reason to believe that we should be able to locate the residence expeditiously, we will credit your account in the amount of one half hours time since Mr. Rudolphski indicates that he lost approximately twenty to twenty-five minutes in locating the residence and further, since it is our policy to charge to the nearest quarter of an hour. As pertains to the return trip from your residence, Mr. Rudolphski indicates that the time is extremely close to being accurate, once again since we charge to the nearest quarter of an hour, we do feel that the time consumed is correct.

Further checking with Mr. Rudolphski, it is my understanding that you were very pleased with the time that it took to perform the actual loading and unloading and, in consideration of the discrepancy above acknowledge, we are enclosing our check to you in the amount of $16.50 representing one half hour's refund resulting from the questionable time in locating the residence.

We regret that you were caused to have to express your complaint but we do appreciate your registering it and we hope that we have answered your question satisfactorily.

2. Rewrite the following message to make it more confident.

Although you are not presently in the very first priority group of persons whom we hope to invite to our campus for further consideration, we are still interested in you. Our position is an Assistant Professorship with a starting salary of $18,500. We are interested particularly in your abilities as a technical writer, at least initially, although we do give some thought to working people in their other areas of interest as soon as possible.

Should we later invite you to the campus, we would want you to make a presentation—perhaps a paper (which would not need to be so formal as one given at a professional meeting) or perhaps to discuss some aspect or aspects of your dissertation. The audience would be faculty and graduate students. About 30 or 40 minutes would be a proper length. Some questions and discussion would follow. Otherwise we would expect only that you not be committed elsewhere and that you retain genuine interest in us.

I would appreciate learning whether or not you have accepted an appointment and the status of your interest in us, if any.

3. Rewrite the following messages so that they contain all the elements of effective communication.
   a. The items which were ordered by you are going to be shipped sometime soon. They all have many fine features which you are sure to enjoy, and their efficacy is indisputable. If you have any questions about their

use, do not hesitate to contact me at your earliest convenience.

b. We have received your letter in which you claim that the crystal wine glasses you ordered from the House of Glass arrived broken.

We are at a loss to understand how this unlikely event could have happened. The House of Glass has over 100 years of packing and shipping experience, and we have never had a complaint. We always use great care in packing and shipping.

You also state that the glasses had been packed without adequate packing material, which we find hard to believe because all our packing material — we now use a special polystyrene plastic of our own manufacture — is added by hand.

Since you have been a good customer of ours, however, we are willing to take back the wine glasses which you claim are damaged and replace them.

c. I know it's a terrible imposition of me to ask a person as important as you to do this, and I apologize for bothering you.

Again, I regret very much having to ask, but if you could please do us the inestim-

able honor of speaking at our annual conference, we would be forever in your debt.

Won't you, therefore, write me and say yes? I apologize again for any inconvenience this may have caused you, and I hope you'll forgive me for it. If you have any questions, do not hesitate to contact me.

d. I have your letter before me and I'm happy to answer it for you. You asked me about our company policy on preparing checks written by our company.

Effective July 1st and thereafter, because of the request by our company president and the company's Board of Directors, checks written in the amount of over one thousand dollars must be co-signed by the controller of our company in addition to the signature of the head of the accounts payable department.

We take this necessary precaution so that in order to prevent misuse of our company checks and funds we have two signatures which would help to alleviate this misuse of company funds and checks.

If you have any further questions you would like to ask us, do not hesitate to contact us.

CHAPTER FOUR
Understanding the Process of Writing

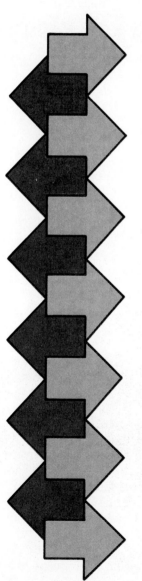

Business writing involves both a *process*—analyzing the situation, developing ideas, writing, revising, and evaluating the results—and a *product*—a letter, memo, or report. In addition to the specific skills presented in the previous chapter, you need an overall strategy for writing an effective business letter—what to say first, what to say second, and how to conclude. This chapter will help you formulate that strategy. Chapter 5, which follows, illustrates appropriate letter and memo formats, and Chapters 6 through 11 will show you how to apply the general techniques to common business letters and memos.

Topics

Overview: Facing the Blank
  Page
Writing: A Four-Step Process
  Planning
  Arranging
  Composing
  Rewriting
Potential Legal Problems
  Defamation

Fraud
Discrimination
Coercion
Unmailable and Unordered
  Items
Use of Copyrighted
  Materials
Summary
Exercises

COMMUNICATION CHALLENGE

Imagine that you are Gregory Landrum, Vice President of Planning and Budgeting for Wang and Wang Architects and Engineers. You have been directed by Charlie Wang, President of the firm, to recall all company-issued credit cards and institute a system of expense vouchers.

Currently, department heads, assistant department heads, project consultants, and project managers all have company credit cards, which they use when traveling and entertaining. Almost from the day they were issued, the credit cards have been a problem. In spite of the company's efforts to hold travel and entertainment costs down, cost-overruns have been excessive. It seems as though the company credit cards encourage employees to spend more than they normally would. Two employees in particular have been guilty of spending more than they should. Jean Bellarmann, Assistant Head of the Engineering Department, and Mario Granada, a project service manager, always seem to order expensive dinners and have room service more often than necessary.

Although the expenses of these two stand out as excessive, you and Wang believe that everyone is guilty of overspending to some extent. The new expense report forms will help remind employees of how much they are actually spending by requiring them to submit forms for specific amounts which will be charged against specific projects. Employees may receive cash advances for travel, accommodations, and entertainment. If they prefer, they may use their own credit cards and use the form to request reimbursement. The new forms will be available March 15, so they should return the company credit cards by that date.

See if you can solve this problem before reading this chapter. Do the best you can, and then make changes in your solution as you read through the chapter. Compare your final version with the one that follows the chapter summary.

▷ OVERVIEW: FACING THE BLANK PAGE

In many ways writing business letters and memos is like any other writing task—whether a high school or college term paper, a short story, or even a poem. For example, whatever the project, a person who writes must begin with a piece of blank paper (or its electronic equivalent). Often the most difficult part of a writing task is knowing how to begin. Each individual needs to develop her or his own techniques for dealing with the blank page.

Because it is an easy way to begin, business writers in particular are tempted to copy something that they—or someone else—have written earlier. In some cases this is an acceptable and economical solution: form and guide letters have a definite purpose in business. As mentioned previously, however, business writers need to be able to make informed decisions about when to use form letters and what kind to use.

The writing process, for any type of writing, begins with planning. In business writing the final product—whether letter, memo, or report—is a solution to a communication problem. This solution can be divided into three general parts: (1) the purpose of the message, (2) the reader's point of view in the situation, and (3) specific techniques that apply to the situation.

This chapter shows you how to plan a letter or memo by analyzing typical communication situations and how to begin the writing process by developing a specific message structure and outline. It also provides some specific advice for turning your outline into a final product and describes specific techniques for writing the first draft, revising to achieve excellence, and overcoming writer's block. Additionally, this chapter covers an aspect of writing unique to business communication: legal problems that may result from careless writing.

▷ WRITING: A FOUR-STEP PROCESS

What four steps does a writer go through in the process of writing?

Many kinds of writing, from high school and college themes to newspaper and magazine articles, use a four-step process of inventing, arranging, composing, and rewriting to solve a problem. The first step, inventing, is a part of planning. The writer decides on a thesis or purpose and selects appropriate support. In the arrangement stage, materials are placed in the order that the writer believes will prove most effective. The writer then composes (writes), and finally, she or he rewrites to improve the theme or article.

In many ways, business writing employs the same process. The writer must determine the purpose of the message, *invent* a thesis statement to communicate it, and then select appropriate support material and arrange it in the most effective order. The writer then composes the letter, memo, or report and completes the process by rewriting to improve the document before preparing the final copy.

Planning

What are the two phases of planning?

Planning is a two-phase process. The first phase is, of course, the kind of general preparation discussed thus far in Part One: it requires that you understand the communication process, know the audience, and understand (and be able to apply) the techniques of effective communication. The second phase of planning is problem-specific—it requires working through the details of solving a particular problem.

Problem Solving.   Because a business communication problem is not solved unless the communicator achieves both the business objective and the human objective of the situation, both objectives require specific attention. And frequently the situation is more complex—and requires more atten-

COMMUNICATION TODAY...

The final version of a letter, memo, or report represents the results of diverse intellectual activities:

gathering information

selecting relevant information

generating ideas

discovering relationships

recording ideas, relationships, and information

organizing material

communicating ideas, relationships, and information clearly, economically, and persuasively

examining ideas and their expression critically

What's more, these activities are "messy." Although we must go through all of these steps each time we write, we usually jump back and forth from one step to another and rarely complete a step before going on to the next. For example, gathering information stimulates thought and generates ideas; the ideas we formulate direct us toward additional information and help us decide which information is relevant. Getting new information, however, may stimulate our thinking and result in new ideas. Then, as we organize material, we may discover gaps in our thinking that send us back to brainstorming in search of new relationships. Even as we compose a draft, we may think of new ideas or better patterns of organization than those we had charted for ourselves prior to writing.

Source: Geraldine Henze, *From Murk to Masterpiece: Style for Business Writing* (Homewood, IL: Richard D. Irwin, 1984), p. 10.

tion—than it appears at first. For example, place yourself in the following situation:

> You have been having trouble starting your new, imported car in cold weather. The dealer has been very helpful in trying to solve this problem but hasn't been successful. The dealer has written and telephoned the U.S. distributor to find out what the factory recommends but so far has not been able to get anything specific. The dealer thinks that a letter from you would help get a faster response from the distributor. Because you are eager to have the problem corrected, you write to the distributor and send a copy of the letter to the dealer.

How do you determine what points to include in your letter, and how do you determine the most effective arrangement of those points? First, you analyze the communication context by asking yourself the following questions:

1.   What is the letter's purpose?

2.   What is my reader's point of view?

3.   How do the techniques of effective business communication apply in this case?

The Letter's Purpose (First Example).   As explained in Chapter 2, each letter has two categories of purpose: business objectives and human objectives. You need to consider both.

1.   Your business objective is to obtain the information that will help your dealer help you.

2.   Your human objective is to establish empathy with the distributor so that the spirit of cooperation will prevail.

Your Reader's Point of View (First Example).   To your reader, your problem is just one among many. It is probably being considered by someone, but it may not be a high-priority problem. Your dealer has already written and telephoned about it, so the distributor may feel a little resentful that you are writing. But it is in the distributor's interest to help solve your problem, and you can probably help speed up the process by reminding the distributor that the problem is sufficiently important to receive immediate attention.

The Techniques of Effective Communication (First Example).   After you have determined the purpose of the letter and the reader's point of view, you can prepare to apply the techniques of effective communication.

1.   **Clarity.**   What information do you need to include to be clear? Exactly what do you expect your reader to do? What is the specific problem (is it *your* problem or *your reader's*)? What language and vocabulary should you use to be best understood? About which matters should you be explicit and which matters implicit? What should be emphasized, and what should be subordinated?

2.   **Courtesy.**   What is your reader's point of view? In this hypothetical case, you would need to obtain the distributor's name from the dealer so that you can write to a specific reader. Remember that the reader is not responsible for your problems. It is, however, in your reader's best interest to help you. Express yourself using "reader viewpoint" language. You should also give the dealer proper credit so that the distributor knows that your dealer has been trying to help. Courtesy requires that you provide the dealer with a copy of the letter as well.

3.   **Conciseness.**   Your reader will not have time to read a long letter. Do not include extraneous material. Focus on the problem and on what should be done about it rather than on how frustrated or angry you are. In your desire to be brief, however, do not overlook the need for achieving the human objective. Because the situation is potentially negative from the reader's perspective, you should focus on the objective details so that the reader can see that you are being fair. Be complete: make sure you have provided all the information your reader will need to help find a solution to your problem.

4.   **Naturalness.**   Begin at a point that will make sense to your reader and then arrange all the details in logical order, providing good transition from point to point. Use conversational language.

5.   **Positive Tone.**   Avoid accusing the reader of not responding quickly enough and expressing other negative attitudes. Assume that your reader is willing to do whatever is necessary to solve your problem. Use positive language throughout, and avoid lecturing or giving orders.

After you have considered each of the foregoing steps (and after you have practiced a little), you will end up with a letter something like the one illustrated in Figure 4.1.

Complex Problem Solving (Second Example).   The letter in Figure 4.1 is simple, straightforward, courteous, and concise. It should result in an answer that will either help or promise to help. Many problems, however, are more complex than the one in our first example. They may require both a more complex analysis and a more complex solution. Or your first letter might not get results, so your second letter might have to be more complex. Place yourself in the following communication situation.

What do you do if your first letter is unsuccessful?

> You own a small ceramics business specializing in high quality dinnerware. Some of your dinnerware is sold by a few high quality stores across the country, but most of your products are made to order and sold directly to customers who appreciate fine craftsmanship. You have received a letter from a new, wealthy, and influential customer stating that her shipment—a $3,500 order for a handmade 5-piece place setting for 12—was completely ruined in transit. She has requested replacement in six weeks so that she can use the dinnerware for an important party where the guests would all be potential customers for your quality ceramics.
>
> The shipment was insured for $500, and because of the care you take with packing, you question whether the entire shipment could possibly have been damaged. Until now, you have never lost more than a few pieces of any one shipment in your 15 years of doing business. Your carrier, however, inspected the damage and reported that the packing crates were "in bad shape" and has agreed to pay you the $500.
>
> You cannot possibly duplicate the entire shipment in six weeks because each piece must be hand-turned on a wheel (and you must produce at least 25 to end up with 12 that are close matches), given time to dry, individually glazed, and kiln-fired twice before you can crate and ship them.

Obviously, this is a rather nasty problem; fortunately, most letter-writing problems are not this complex. But all problems in business correspondence, whether simple or complex, are solvable with the same kind of analysis.

What is a mixed message?

The Letter's Purpose (Second Example).   This letter actually has several purposes. It is a *mixed message*. (Mixed messages are discussed in Chapter 11.)

1.   You must inform the reader that you will replace the entire shipment. The carrier said the shipment was a total loss, so you have no choice.

**FIGURE 4.1
Sample Letter**

The subject line
identifies the
problem.

The "name" open-
ing places the letter
in a specific context
and shows that you
and the dealer are
cooperating rather
than arguing.

Provide the neces-
sary explanation in
the secondary posi-
tion. The distributor
may know most of
this already.

Provide the specific
details so that the
reader knows what
has already been
done.

Close by letting the
reader know who is
to do what next.

6824-G Hyde Park Drive
Joplin, MO 63700

February 14, 19xx

Mr. Clinton McCarty
Vice President--Customer Service
Renabbit, USA
3961 Loganberry Drive
Massapequa, NY 11758

Dear Mr. McCarty:

SUBJECT: Starting a 19xx Renabbitt in Cold Weather

My Renabbitt dealer, Hermann Bussmann of Bussmann's Renabbitt in
Joplin, Missouri, suggested that I write to you about the problem
I've been having starting my 19xx Renabbitt in cold weather.

When I first purchased the Renabbitt in October, the car started
quickly and easily every time. When the weather turned colder in
late November, however, starting the car in the mornings has
become nearly impossible. The critical temperature seems to be
about 20 degrees. Once the car has been started and has warmed
up, restarting is no problem.

Since the starting problem developed, Bussmann's has replaced
the battery, tuned the car twice, and replaced the fuel pump.
Nothing has helped. Mr. Bussmann thought that you might be
able to provide some pertinent information.

I would certainly appreciate it if you would investigate the
starting problem and suggest possible causes and cures.

Sincerely,

Marie E. Rankin

Marie E. Rankin

2.   You must inform the reader that you are unable to replace the entire shipment in six weeks.

3.   You must inform the reader how much of the shipment you can replace in six weeks and when you can replace the remainder.

4.   You must retain the reader's goodwill even though you suspect that she is being less than fully honest with you.

5.   You need to find out whether she has sufficient good pieces from the first shipment for you to provide enough replacements for use at the dinner party without implying that she lied.

Some of these purposes are strictly business objectives. Some require that special attention be placed on the human objective in that they are likely to evoke an emotional response in the reader. The reader, for example, will be disappointed that you cannot replace the entire shipment in six weeks, and she would be angry if you accused her of having some good pieces left. You need to consider which objectives are strictly business and which have sufficient feeling content to deserve special treatment.

Your Reader's Point of View (Second Example).   Your reader probably does not realize how time consuming it is to produce ceramic dinnerware. She undoubtedly thinks that six weeks is ample time for you to complete the order. If the reader does possess some good pieces from the first shipment, she probably feels entitled to keep them without paying for them because of the irritation she has been caused. Your reader would undoubtedly like to have the special dinnerware for use at the party and might be willing to cooperate by telling you which pieces are absolutely essential and which can wait — if you can ask her without implying that she has good pieces from the first shipment and is trying to cheat you.

The Techniques of Effective Communication (Second Example).   Because of the complexity of this problem, it is going to be more difficult for you to achieve clarity, courtesy, conciseness, naturalness, and positiveness. Your reader will need to know something about how ceramic dinnerware is made if she is to understand why you cannot replace the entire shipment in six weeks. But she is more interested in her problem than in yours and will not want to hear too much about turning, glazing, and double-firing. Figure 4.2 illustrates one possible solution to this problem.

Other Examples of Problem Solving.   The same kind of analysis is appropriate for all business writing situations, even when you are writing routine intracompany correspondence. Suppose, for example, you are writing a memo to your district manager reporting on the results of your winter sales trip.

Your memo's purpose would be to convey the important information.

Your reader would undoubtedly already have a good understanding of the nature of sales trips and would appreciate a concise message focusing on results, problems, and possibilities for improving sales.

**FIGURE 4.2
Sample Letter**

Twice Turned Ceramics
3242 Brookview Avenue
Waco, TX 76710

1 November 19xx

Senator Bobbie Jones
8011 Colesville Road
Silver Springs, MD 20910

Dear Senator Jones:

The beginning concentrates on feeling content rather than on subject content.

Thank you for writing so promptly about your dinnerware. We have already begun duplicating your order and will work as quickly as we can without sacrificing quality.

The explanation is given before the subject content and is connected to a reader benefit.

As you may know, our handcrafted dinnerware and other specialty ceramic products must receive careful, individual attention at each stage of their production from artisans who care about quality workmanship. The kind of quality you expect requires us to produce more than twice the pieces actually purchased so that we may sell you only those pieces that are truly perfect.

Clarify what you can do. Stress the reader benefit associated with the delay.

In the next six weeks we will be able to manufacture and ship duplicates of about half the pieces in your original order without sacrificing quality. It will take us another six weeks to produce the remainder. Because you would like to use the dinnerware for the party you are having, we will concentrate on producing those pieces that will enable you to set your table with elegance.

Clarify what you are doing. Try to talk the reader into cooperating.

We have begun work with the dinner plates and will have all 12 finished in plenty of time. Please use the enclosed card to indicate your priority for completion. Because each piece is individually produced, we do not have to work in lots of 12. Should 6 or 8 of one item be enough for the purposes of your party, we could produce 6 or 8 now and the remainder later.

Assure the reader that she will receive a complete duplicate set. Remind her to complete and return the card.

We will, Senator Jones, work as quickly as fine craftsmanship permits, and you'll receive a complete set of the dinnerware you ordered. When we receive your instructions, we'll do everything possible to finish the essential items in time for your party.

Sincerely,

Leeander Schewe

Leeander Schewe

enc

Clarity and conciseness would be the most important elements of effective communication.

Figure 4.3 focuses on important statistics:

**FIGURE 4.3
Sample Memo**

Copeland Restaurant Supplies
Internal Use Only

Memorandum   Interoffice Use

Date: 4 January 19xx

To: Susan Goodwin

From: Denise Caplane

Subject: FEBRUARY SALES, AREA 14

In February I called on 237 restaurants and obtained contracts with 32. In January, 9 restaurants that had been with us picked up contracts with other suppliers.

Area 14's annual business for 19xx will amount to approximately $1,041,000 volume with 143 restaurants. See the attached table for details.

att

Direct message. Begins with the main details.

Secondary information follows. Details are put in a table for easy reference.

Under what circumstances should you write a memo simply to protect yourself?

As another example, place yourself in the position of a new automobile insurance underwriter who has been ordered to renew a policy for a driver who has a history of minor accidents and two arrests for driving while intoxicated. Your department manager agrees with you that the policy should be canceled, but because the driver has policies with the company worth more than $200,000 a year to the company, your manager's superior told her to make sure that the policy is renewed on schedule.

You believe that the company is taking too great a risk. The chances are that the driver will have another accident and that the next one will not be minor. It is possible that the company could be involved in a long and expensive lawsuit. Were that to happen, you know who would be blamed. What kind of message should you write?

What is your purpose? While you believe that you should try to persuade the company to allow the policy to expire, your main purpose in writing a message at all is to protect yourself.

Who is your reader? Should you write a memo to your department manager or to her superior?

What is your reader's point of view? Your department manager agrees with you. Her supervisor, as far as you know, believes that the renewal is a good idea.

How do you incorporate the techniques of effective communication? Each element provides hazards. You are facing an issue difficult to deal with directly. It will be difficult to establish a clear purpose and to write about it with confidence.

We cannot claim that the example in Figure 4.4 represents the best possible solution to this problem. The best solution would depend on the specific people involved, and in this case no message, however good, would guarantee success.

Most business communication situations are unique. The people and the circumstances are sufficiently different that each message requires separate analysis. What works in one situation with one reader, may not work the next time with the same reader or in a similar situation with another reader.

Combining Purpose, Plan, and Content.   All business writing situations can be analyzed according to the foregoing method. And as infinitely varied as the possibilities are, all business messages should answer the same general questions and contain the same basic elements. Check every message you write for answers to the following questions:

1. Is the message structured to emphasize its main purpose?
   a. What is its business purpose?
   b. What is its human purpose?

2. Does the message have secondary purposes?

3. Does the message take the reader's point of view into account?
   a. What does the reader already know?
   b. What does the reader want to know?
   c. What is the reader hoping to hear?

4. Does the message contain enough information to be clear?

FIGURE 4.4
Sample Memo

AMERICA FIRST INSURANCE
945 CLOVERDALE NORMAL, IL 61761-7443

Date: February 21, 19xx

To: Loraine Petroski, Department Manager LP

From: Craig Oosterhouse

Subject: Michael Thorsberg   Policy #: 12-1908-3318

Message:

Your department deserves to be included in the information loop. Write to the supervisor only if your manager tells you to.

Since our conversation on Tuesday, I've reviewed the insured's character references, driving record, and claims history.

Indirect opening. Try to enlist reader's sympathy by referring to information the reader is familiar with.

I believe that the record shows that Thorsberg is likely to have more accidents and that the next one may be serious. Because of the potential for a lengthy, expensive lawsuit, we should make an effort to avoid renewing Thorsberg's auto insurance.

Suggest an acceptable alternative.

Perhaps Jim Spring (Petroski's supervisor) could arrange a package deal with Thorsberg that would retain his nonauto insurance policies.

Ask for the action you expect.

Will you discuss the matter with Jim once more before we issue the renewed policy? I would appreciate it.

5. Does the message maintain a courteous tone throughout?

6. Is it concise?

7. Is it grammatically, mechanically, and factually correct?

8. Does it express confidence in the reader and the message without being overconfident?

9. Does it have a pleasant, conversational tone?

10. Have you specified how your reader will benefit from your message?

How can answering a number of specific questions about a message actually reduce the time required to write it?

It may seem as though checking each message you write against these objectives would be a terribly time-consuming process — one that will rob your writing of creativity and naturalness. Actually, the reverse is true. Having specific questions to answer will greatly reduce the time it will take you to write effective messages. And by making sure that you have answered each of the questions in a message, you will frequently avoid having to write a second message to clarify points you may have neglected in your first message.

What aspect of a message should the reader find of greatest interest?

As a business writer, you owe it to your reader to write interesting, conversational messages. Most business messages, however, do not require creativity to be interesting. The content and purpose of your message should receive the reader's attention. You do not write business messages to entertain. You write them to convey information to your reader quickly, clearly, and pleasantly. Your messages will be successful and interesting when you concentrate on achieving the business and human objectives inherent in the communication context.

Arranging

Once you know what you wish to say, arranging material for best effect in most business situations follows a few well-known and well-accepted principles. Note that the structure of the sample solutions in Figures 4.1, 4.2, 4.3, and 4.4 is either *deductive* (most important point first) or *inductive* (most important point presented *after* the supporting evidence), depending on the nature of the business objectives in each problem.

Why should a negative message be presented only after the supporting evidence?

When the business objective is positive (something the reader will welcome), the message begins with it. When the business objective is unpleasant, or something that will require persuasion of the reader to act, the message begins with something your reader will respond to more favorably, and the business objective is presented after the supporting evidence is clear. This principle is the foundation for the message structures used in business correspondence.

Message Structures.   When the business objective of your message will neither hurt your reader's feelings nor be resisted, you should emphasize it by placing it at the beginning. Messages that emphasize the business objective (subject content) are called *direct messages*. The main point — the purpose — of the message is stated immediately.

When the business objective of your message will either hurt your reader's feelings or be resisted, you should emphasize the human objective (feeling content) of the message. Messages that emphasize the human objective are called *indirect messages* because they delay presentation of the business objective until the reader has been prepared emotionally and the human objective accomplished.

How do message structures take advantage of the principles of emphasis and subordination?

Both the direct and indirect structures take advantage of the fact that readers pay closest attention to the beginning and the ending of a message and tend to pay the least attention to the middle. Consequently, the beginning and ending are emphasized, while the middle is subordinated. All messages, whether they are direct or indirect, follow the same general structural principles.

The *primary element* presents information that the reader will consider positive or important. In letters and memos this element is usually one or two paragraphs long. In longer reports it may be a few pages long. It may contain

1.   An important question.

2.   Good news.

3.   Important information.

4.   A statement of agreement.

5.   A statement complimenting the reader.

6.   Information that will benefit the reader.

Secondary elements present information that the reader will consider negative or less important. In short messages this section may be several paragraphs long. Because it supports or explains, it may constitute the bulk of the material in longer messages. It may contain

1.   Explanations.

2.   Supporting, secondary details.

3.   Additional questions.

4.   Negative information.

5.   Reasons the reader should act.

The *closing element* presents information that the reader will consider positive or important. In short messages this element is usually one or two paragraphs long. In longer messages it may be a few pages. It may contain

1.   A clarification of who does what next.

2.   Information that will benefit the reader.

3.   Suggestions for specific, positive courses of future action.

4.   Summaries, conclusions, and recommendations.

Formal outlining procedures are discussed in Chapter 12, but most letters and memos do not require formal outlines. It is enough simply to organize information around the concepts of a beginning, a middle, and an end (an informal outline).

Direct Messages.   Several types of common business letters and reports usually call for a direct presentation because the business objective is more important than the human objective.

Letters.   Letters of inquiry and letters that convey positive and neutral information, for example, are almost always direct messages because the content of the message has built-in reader interest. These messages almost always begin with an explicit statement of — or question about — the letter's business objective.

Please send me one dozen copies of Understanding and Using Communication in Business by Bowman and Branchaw.

Would the Grand Hotel be able to accommodate the 300 persons attending The Association for Business Communication annual convention from 29 to 31 December?

Yes, Mr. Bach, Motown Records would be glad to consider your concertos for publication.

Beginning February 15, George, order all replacement parts by part number and factory number.

The human objectives are secondary in these messages, not because they are unimportant, but because the positive nature of the business objectives helps the reader and writer establish the empathy required for good communication.

Memos and Business Reports.   Most memos and reports are direct messages. The subject line or title tells the reader what the message is about, and the first sentence or paragraph conveys the information most important to the reader.

Because of their special achievement, the following personnel will receive merit salary increases this year.

Cathy Carlson

Wade Carlson

Linda Lambert

Paul Madelinsky

Debra Page

Dan Sculthorpe

Longer reports usually begin with conclusions and recommendations or a summarizing overview including the conclusions and recommendations. Because they follow different rules than those for letters and memos, we will discuss longer reports separately, beginning in Chapter 12.

How can psychological preparation help a reader accept bad news?

Indirect Messages.   When the reader is likely to find the subject content of a message unpleasant, either because it will hurt his or her feelings or because it requires the reader to expend time or money, the situation calls for an indirect message. The subject content is delayed until the writer has prepared the reader for it psychologically. Messages that convey negative information and messages that persuade a reader to act require the writer to pay special attention to the feeling content of the letter or memo. The human objective is still to establish empathy between the reader and writer—to convince the reader to agree with the writer. The subject content of such letters, however, is likely to anger, offend, disappoint, or bore the reader.

When the subject of a letter is a point of disagreement, delay the disagreement by finding something you *can* agree with.

> You're certainly right about the kind of management problems facing people in business today.

When the subject of a letter is that you cannot—or will not—participate in something, delay the negative aspect by finding a compliment you can pay the reader.

> Your idea for a fund-raising pancake breakfast is a good one.

> Your clients would undoubtedly benefit from the communication seminar you are planning, Ms. Schumacker.

How can psychological preparation make a persuasive message more successful?

When you are asking the reader to spend either time or money on something that will benefit you, give the reader a reason to act. Begin the letter by promising something that will benefit the reader more than the time or money you are going to ask for.

> Are you tired of the same old daily grind?

> Why throw money down the drain?

> Could you use an extra four hours a day?

Indirect messages should begin with something to create empathy between reader and writer. The how, why, and what of the message are presented after the reader feels that the message contains something of value. Memos and short reports follow the same basic principles as letters. Longer reports use an indirect structure when the reader will resent or resist the subject content, but their reason for doing so is to help ensure an objective evaluation of the information. Reports are discussed further in Part Three.

Messages with More Than One Purpose.

Many business messages have just one clear-cut objective, but many others do not. When your objectives are completely unrelated, you are usually better off writing two messages, each with its own specific goal. When your objectives are related, however, you should combine them into a *mixed message*—a single letter, memo, or report containing two or more objectives.

In some cases the writer must select from two or more possible objectives the one that seems most important for emphasis in a mixed message. For example, you may need to decide whether you should *inform* your readers that you are offering a new product or service, or whether you should *persuade* them to purchase the product or service. You may need to decide whether you should *inform* your readers of a delay in shipment, or whether you should *persuade* them to wait to purchase until you can fill the order.

In such cases honesty usually dictates that you clarify the situation well enough to enable the reader to make a good decision. When your reader has a choice, be sure to indicate what that choice is. Honesty, however, does not preclude your constructing your letter, memo, or report to emphasize the objectives that will be best for you. Take advantage of the extra attention your reader will pay to the beginning and ending of your message to stress positive human elements and the business objectives you would like to achieve. Place negative information and the alternatives you wish to discourage in the middle.

In some mixed messages both of your business objectives may be equally important but may require different treatment because of the way your readers would react to the associated feeling content. Your subject content may, for example, contain both positive and negative information. You may need to tell a reader both that you are sending part of his or her order and also that the reader failed to provide sufficient information for you to complete the order. Or your subject content may contain both negative and persuasive information. For example, you may need to inform your employees of a new method of submitting reports that will require more work of them and also persuade them to accept the new method because it will ultimately save the company a great deal of money.

What should you emphasize when you have two or more important and related objectives?

Whenever you must combine objectives into a single message, put the emphasis on the aspects of the message that the reader will consider positive by placing them in the beginning and closing positions in the message. Use the positive or persuasive aspects of the subject content to help you establish and maintain empathy with the reader in spite of the negative information that will be included.

Composing

Composing—the actual writing of a letter, memo, or report—is easier when you have followed all the preliminary steps of planning and arranging. Your *general preparation* for writing (composing) should include a knowledge of (1) basic writing skills, (2) the communication process, and (3) techniques of effective business communication. Such knowledge prepares you not only to write well, but also to write more easily and quickly because it provides confidence. When you know that your grammar, punctuation, and word usage are correct, you do not have to spend time worrying about whether all your modifiers are in the right place or whether you have sufficient and logical transition between paragraphs.

Your *specific preparation* should include an analysis of the communication problem your letter, memo, or report will address and its context; a determination of the purpose of your message; and an analysis of the best application of the techniques of effective communication to the specific problem, purpose, and reader.

Even with equal preparation, no two people are likely to approach the task of writing in exactly the same way. Some people prefer to begin by jotting down ideas as they occur during the preparation phase of solving the problem; some prefer to write a complete draft, which they intend to restructure and revise later; and some prefer to attempt a final version the first time, taking time to select each word and structure each sentence to accomplish a specific purpose in the best way possible.

Usually working from an outline and a series of notes or producing a rough draft with the idea of revising makes the writing process easier. Knowing that you will change what you produce enables you to work at formulating your message without simultaneously having to evaluate each word, sentence, and paragraph to see if it is the best for your purpose. Selection of better words, sentences, and paragraphs can be your next step. Experienced writers can often perform several operations—analyzing, outlining, and writing—at once, especially when writing short messages. Inexperienced writers, however, should perform each step separately until the procedures are thoroughly familiar.

What problems might result from attempting to prepare a perfect first draft?

The main hazard in attempting to produce a perfect first draft is that the effort may result in *writer's block.* Even though one must analyze the communication problem and context and write a logical outline, the act of writing is essentially a creative process. You must *create* the sentences necessary to express your specific ideas. Attempting to write a perfect first draft may inhibit the creative process by continually interrupting it to evaluate each idea produced. If enough ideas are rejected, the creative part of the brain may stop producing ideas for a while.

Usually the best procedure is to attempt to produce a draft of the entire document (or a complete section of a long document) in one sitting. Try to avoid evaluating during this process, even if something does not "sound right." Get your ideas down on paper (or entered in a word processor). If two ways of saying something occur to you, record them both. Remember that just because you have written it does not mean that you cannot change it or even eliminate it.

Rewriting

After you have finished composing, it is best to let the document sit for a while before you attempt to revise it. A delay in rereading it will help you approach it with a fresh mind and see it more objectively. In general, the less writing experience you have, the longer you should let it sit.

How many times should you revise a business letter?

Many business situations require promptness, so you may not always have as much time to rewrite as you would like. But even when time is short, take a second look at anything you write. Most writers need to revise their first drafts. Even careful, experienced writers make mistakes. Obviously, the longer the document you are writing, the greater the chance that you will need to revise. Even the shortest message, however, may be improved by revision. In revising a business message, keep the relationship between cost and effectiveness in mind. No message is ever perfect, and if you continue to revise with the idea of achieving perfection, the cost of the message will quickly exceed its value to you or the organization.

The only rewriting necessary may be to correct obvious errors in grammar, punctuation, and spelling, especially if you are preparing a relatively unimportant internal document for a sympathetic reader. If you are preparing an important letter or report, however, you may need to spend a great deal of time revising to ensure that the message is not only mechanically correct but also psychologically correct.

When revising, you may improve a document by adding, deleting, changing, or rearranging materials.

Adding.   The process of revision allows you to insert material that you may have inadvertently omitted. Have you included all the information required for your reader to understand your business purpose? Have you included appropriate psychological preparation for a negative or persuasive message? After reading your message, will your reader know who is responsible for future actions, and will she or he know when those actions should take place?

Deleting.   The final version of a business message should be as concise as possible while retaining clarity and while achieving both the business objective and the human objective. Eliminate extraneous ideas, redundancies, and wordy expressions. Until you are thoroughly familiar with what constitutes redundancy and wordiness, you may wish to refer to the section on conciseness presented in the previous chapter when you revise.

Changing.   In addition to adding and deleting material, you may need to change some material when you revise. Have you used the right word to express your ideas — did you say *soon* when you really meant *by noon tomorrow?* Have you emphasized positive, important points and subordinated elements your reader will find negative or obvious? Have you used too many simple sentences — or too many compound sentences? Does each of your paragraphs have a clear and forceful topic sentence? Have you avoided giving orders or lecturing your reader? Have you used correct grammar and punctuation throughout?

Rearranging.   You may find that you need to restructure your message for greater effectiveness. Is the general subject (though not necessarily the specific purpose) of your message clear from the first sentence? Do the beginning, middle, and end of your message include appropriate materials?

▷ POTENTIAL LEGAL PROBLEMS

What is a contract?

Business communicators also need to be aware that a variety of laws cover many aspects of communication. An exchange of letters, for example, may establish a legally binding contract. In some cases letters, memos, personnel documents, and other written communications may constitute an *implied contract.* In our increasing litigious society, in which people often take their differences to court, writers need to ensure that the words they choose do not suggest more (or less) than is intended. If a personnel manual, for example, says that a person may be fired only "for cause," that may constitute a contract that takes precedence over other employment documents. If a brochure says that a special clutch makes your company's chain saw "completely safe to use," your company may be liable for *any* accident that occurs with the saw.

When should you solicit the advice of an attorney before mailing a letter?

Honesty is usually sufficient protection from prosecution under the law or civil action, and an overview of some of the legalities of business communication will alert you to some of the more common legal considerations. For some of the situations you encounter in business, however, you may need the advice of an attorney because the legal system is so complex. Laws may have their source in a state or federal constitution, a statute (local, state, or federal), a regulation (based on a governmental agency's interpretation of a law), or a court decision. What seems logical to a lay person may not be what a court would decide. For example, although the law allows a person to keep unordered merchandise, it is not clear whether the law applies to truly accidental mailings or only to deliberate mismailings that attempt to force recipients to pay for merchandise they do not want. Cases must be examined and decided on individually.

Some guidelines are available to help keep business writers out of trouble. Laws concerning the following areas are of greatest concern to business communicators:

Defamation.

Fraud.

Discrimination.

Coercion.

Unmailable and unordered items.

Use of copyrighted materials.

Defamation

Defamation is the false or unjustified injury to the reputation or character of another by *slander* (oral defamation) or *libel* (written defamation). If a statement can be proven true, it is usually not considered grounds for legal action. Even if it is true, however, you may be sued if you made your statements with malicious intent. Also, remember that what you know to be true and what can be proven true in court may not be the same.

What is *malicious intent,* and why should business writers avoid it?

Be especially careful to ensure that you avoid making potentially damaging statements (either orally or in writing) about someone to a third party. You can tell a person that she or he is incompetent or dishonest to her or his face, but if you *publish* that statement by making it known to a third party (whether by a written or an oral statement), you may be sued.

Credit and employment references pose the greatest damage for most business writers. When you answer inquiries about people, make sure that the information you supply is as accurate as possible. For more information about answering inquiries about people, see Chapter 7.

Fraud

The term *fraud* covers a broad range of situations in which deceit is used to gain an unfair advantage over others. If you were to misrepresent your product or service to a customer, and the customer were damaged (physically, emotionally, or financially) as a result, you would be guilty of fraud. The so-called truth-in-advertising and truth-in-lending laws cover specific kinds of fraud that pertain to business communication. Special laws also cover the fraudulent use of the U.S. postal system.

Under what circumstances might a failure to reveal a defect constitute fraud?

Because business communication, especially persuasive communication (advertising) relies so heavily on emphasizing the positive (see "Positiveness" in Chapter 3), you should remember that the failure to reveal a defect may constitute fraud even in the absence of a deliberate misstatement. The critical tests from a legal point are whether injury may result from the deception and whether the other party would have agreed to your terms if he or she had known the truth. In the example of the "absolutely safe" chain saw mentioned previously, almost any accident would indicate fraud.

Discrimination

Discrimination on the basis of race, color, religion, sex, national origin, and—in many cases—age is illegal. Title VII of the Civil Rights Act of 1964, as amended in 1972 and 1978, prohibits discrimination in a wide variety of employment matters. To avoid the possibility of legal action and the virtual certainty of poor public relations, most organizations have established specific guidelines to help employees avoid even the appearance of discrimination. Chapter 17 lists preemployment questions that should be avoided because they might be discriminatory.

Coercion

It is illegal to unreasonably oppress, harass, abuse, or intentionally cause mental distress to anyone. As a business communicator, you may attempt to persuade someone to act in a particular way. If the person does not respond to reasonable persuasion, however, the only *force* you may take is legal action through the courts. In attempting to collect on an overdue bill, for example, you can use persuasion (appeal to the reader's sense of fair play), but you cannot threaten (tell the reader that people who do not pay get their legs broken). For more information about collection procedures, see Chapter 10.

Unmailable and Unordered Items

Would you have the right to keep an expensive and unordered fur coat sent to you through the mail? Why or why not?

Certain items (firearms, alcoholic beverages, and a variety of printed matter) cannot be mailed. A complete list of unmailable items is available from your local postmaster. Sending unordered merchandise through the mail is not illegal, but it may be unwise, because the recipient of unordered merchandise may consider it a gift and simply keep it. In that event, you will probably have no legal recourse to recover the cost of the merchandise.

Use of Copyrighted Materials

The U.S. Copyright Law (effective January 1, 1978) protects copyrighted materials (including books, articles, poems, essays, cartoons, photographs, graphic aids, and computer software) from being copied without the prior permission of the copyright owner. Single copies made for personal (noncommercial) use and brief quotations (primarily for educational purposes) are exempt.

What is plagiarism?

Business persons are likely to have trouble in this area by using previously published materials in reports or other documents that are eventually published. When such materials are used without providing adequate documentation, such borrowing is called *plagiarism.* Even with documentation, however, using copyrighted material without permission may be illegal.

◁ SUMMARY

Writing is a four-step process of planning, arranging, composing, and rewriting. The first step, planning, has two phases: general preparation and problem-specific preparation. Writers need to understand the communication process, know the audience, and be able to apply the techniques of effective communication. In addition, they need to be able to achieve the business and human objectives of a specific situation. You can determine what points to include in a message by asking yourself (1) What is the purpose of the message? (2) What is the reader's point of view? and (3) How do the techniques of effective communication apply in this case?

Business objectives can be divided into three general categories: to inquire, to inform, and to persuade. To accomplish any of these objectives, you need to consider your reader's probable reaction to them and adapt the arrangement of your message accordingly. When your business objective will neither hurt your reader's feelings nor cause your reader to resist your message, you should emphasize it.

Messages that emphasize the business objective (subject content) are called *direct messages.* When your business objective will either hurt your reader's feelings or be resisted, you should emphasize the human objective (feeling content) of the message. Messages emphasizing the human objective are called *indirect messages.*

Many business messages have just one business objective, but many have more. When your business objectives are unrelated, write two messages. When they are related, however, you should combine them into a *mixed message.* Once the specific objectives, both business and human, are set, the message should be planned to maximize the chances of the writer's achieving them.

Each person approaches the writing task differently. Some prefer to prepare a draft, while others attempt to produce a perfect copy the first time. Writer's block may result from attempting to write a perfect first copy. It is easier for most people to produce a first draft with the intention of improving it later by adding, deleting, changing, and rearranging materials as necessary.

Business writers also need to be aware of a variety of legal considerations. Usually honesty is sufficient protection from prosecution under the law or civil action. Some language, however, may imply a contract where none was intended. Business writers should be aware of laws concerning defamation, fraud, discrimination, coercion, unmailable and unordered items, and the use of copyrighted materials. Because laws governing these areas can be complex, writers should consult a lawyer when in doubt.

Compare the following solution with your own.

The situation in the Communication Challenge at the beginning of the chapter requires an indirect message, because the message will contain information that will disappoint the reader and cause resistance to the requested action. For this reason, you should prepare the reader psychologically before presenting the unwel- come information. Also, you should make the requested action (filling out expense forms) seem as attractive as possible. Be especially careful to avoid implying that only a few (or — worse — only two) people are responsible for the cost overruns. Were you to imply that, people would want you to "punish" only the offenders and to allow the others to keep their credit cards.

Timkin Steel Company

1900 Banning Road
Bethlehem, PA 18015
215/555-6164

26 February 19xx

Interoffice Memorandum

TO: Department Heads, Assistant Department Heads, and
      Travelers

FROM: Gregory Landrum, V-P Planning and Budgeting **G.L.**

COST-OVERRUNS ON EXPENSE ACCOUNTS

State the problem in general terms.

Company credit cards for expense accounts always present problems. No matter how well a company tries to anticipate expenditures, cost-overruns always occur. Because credit cards encourage spending, those with them are prone to assume expenses in the company's name even when the expense may not directly benefit the Company.

Review the facts before your purpose is clear. Mention a reader benefit when possible.

Each year for the past five years, expense account overruns have increased. This past year expenditures exceeded the budgeted amount by 37 percent. To bring expense account expenditures under control, we've decided to institute a new procedure for handling these expenditures. The new method will help you improve your departmental budget and help ensure that expense accounts are used to benefit the Company and your department.

Emphasize the positive aspects of the new system.

As part of the new system, the Company is recalling all Company-issued credit cards. In place of the credit card, you will receive a supply of new Expense Report Forms. With the forms you will be able to receive cash advances for travel, accommodations, and entertainment expenses should an advance be necessary. If you prefer, you may use your own credit card and use the Expense Report Form to request reimbursement.

Stress a reader benefit.

The information provided by the new forms will be entered in the computer so that each department will be able to review how much money has been spent for what purpose. The computer will also show you how much money is left in your expense account budget, thus preventing cost-overruns.

Set and justify an end date for the required action.

As the new Expense Report Forms will be available 15 March, please return your Company credit card by that date. With the new system, we can all look forward to a more productive year.

d

▷ EXERCISES

Review and Discussion Questions

1. In what way is planning a two-phase process?

2. How do you determine what points should be included in your message?

3. How do you determine the best structure to achieve the objectives of your message?

4. What elements or techniques must you consider to be able to coordinate the purpose, plan, and content when writing business messages?

5. How do individual approaches to the writing process differ, and what are the advantages and disadvantages of the common approaches?

6. What is the purpose of rewriting, and what techniques are employed to achieve that purpose?

7. Under what circumstances is revising not cost-effective?

8. Define the following legal concerns and discuss their importance to business communicators.
    a. Defamation
    b. Fraud
    c. Discrimination
    d. Coercion
    e. Unmailable and unordered items
    f. Use of copyrighted materials

Problems

1. Write outlines for messages informing someone of a promotion, denying someone a promotion, and persuading someone to make a donation to a political campaign. Use complete sentences to indicate what you would say first, what second, and what third. Rather than use a formal outline, merely indicate the number and contents of each paragraph that would go into each of the messages.

2. Analyze the following messages and rewrite them so that they will have a better chance of achieving their business and human objectives.
    a. I am president of the Bond Club in Goshen, IN. This is a professional women's service club. We do many good things for the city of Goshen in the state of Indiana. We meet the first Monday of every month. Sometimes we meet twice a month. Sometimes we meet at noon. Most of the time we meet at six o'clock for dinner at some restaurant in Goshen. We usually have a social hour before

the dinner hour if we meet for dinner. After the dinner, we have a speaker. We get our speakers from all over—anyone who will give us a talk. Could you give us a talk? You can talk on any subject you like. Since we don't have any funds to pay you, would you mind if we just served you the dinner free? Can you give us a talk the first Monday in June? If you come before 6 p.m., we'll buy you a drink before dinner. You can talk for about 45 minutes. We might have some questions after the talk. If you have any questions, feel free to contact us. We sure would like for you to be our speaker. Thanks a whole bunch.

b. I would like to take this opportunity to introduce myself. I am a 1975 graduate of Western University. I am currently enrolled in the department of Counseling and Personnel here at Knoxville University. It gives me great pleasure to assume the responsibilities of Coordinator of Campus Visits in the Undergraduate Admissions Office.

I am a native of Dearborn, Michigan, and a graduate of Central High School. After graduating from Western, I was an elementary school teacher before beginning graduate school in January, 1977.

I would like to take this opportunity to reacquaint you with our campus visits program. The Undergraduate Admissions Office will again be providing regularly scheduled campus tours originating from the office reception area on Monday, Wednesday, and Friday at 10:00 a.m. and 2:00 p.m. for prospective students and/or visiting dignitaries. If this time is inconvenient, a special tour may be arranged upon seven days' prior notice. We hope that you will utilize our campus tour program, whenever you have occasion to entertain campus visitors. If I can be of further assistance, please do not hesitate to call me at the office.

c. We are in receipt of your letter of the 25th of last month in which you claim that the one dozen crystal wine glasses you ordered from us arrived in unsatisfactory condition.

You stated that all of the glasses were either broken or cracked. We are at a loss to understand how this unlikely event could have happened, as we carefully inspect and pack each shipment before shipping it. You may have noticed that our packing materials are specially designed to prevent damage, and we always include a surfeit of styrofoam popcorn as extra insurance.

Understanding that you have been a good customer, you'll be glad to know that we are willing to make an exchange in your case. This is done with the understanding that you will return the broken glasses in their original packing so that we can determine who is responsible for the damage.

d. As a student, you simply have to buy a Crypto mechanical pencil.

You do homework, don't you? Well, the Crypto is ideal for homework because it is the only fully erasable pencil guaranteed never to run out of lead. A special liquid lead makes using the Crypto as convenient as using a ballpoint pen — except you can erase. And everyone needs to erase from time to time.

For a mere $9.95 — less than the cost of many of your useless textbooks — you can have the Crypto, which will ensure high grades for you, as your instructors will be impressed with the neatness of your homework.

Imagine how neat your math homework will be. Imagine having a handy pencil for all your writing needs. The Crypto is also beautifully styled, in gold, silver, or flat black — be sure to indicate your preference.

We use Crypto's here all the time, and we've never had a problem. Refills are available for $1.50 plus a small fee for mailing.

If you want to order, complete the order blank at the back of the brochure which I am enclosing for your reading pleasure. Also, send your check. We're sorry, but to make this special pencil available at this special price, we can't take COD or charge card orders.

CASES

1. What evidence confirms the effectiveness of indirect structure for negative and persuasive studies? Find at least two articles in professional journals (you might begin with *The Journal of Business Communication*) that discuss message structures, and summarize their findings in a typewritten (or word processed) paper one or two pages long.

2. Collect several (five or six) brochures or other business documents (direct-mail ads would be ideal) and examine them for language that either presents a potential problem or is designed to prevent a problem. Analyze the ways in which the writers have left themselves open to legal action or protected themselves. Present your findings in a typewritten paper one or two pages long.

PART TWO

Common Business Writing Situations: Letters and Memos

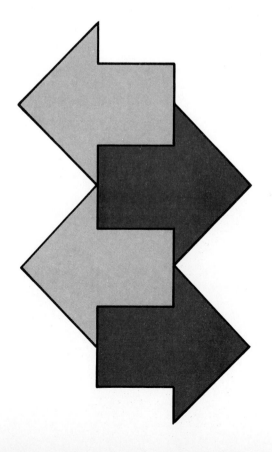

Most written communication in business falls into two general categories: letters and reports. Letters usually transmit information between separate business entities, that is, from an individual to a company, from one company to another, or from a company to one or more individuals. While letters are also used to transmit information within an organization, reports are the usual means of conveying information from one part of a company to another part. Memos are the most common kind of report.

In Part Two we will discuss the kinds of letters and memos you will encounter most frequently on the job, and their appropriate format and appearance. Business reports are discussed in Part Three.

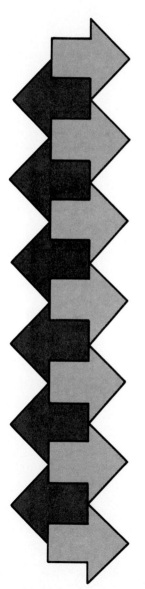

CHAPTER FIVE

Letters and Memos: Format and Appearance

In general, the appearance of a business document should be inconspicuous. If the appearance attracts attention to itself, it may do so at the expense of the message—the reader focuses on how the message *looks* rather than on what it *says*. This chapter shows you the standard formats for letters and memos, all of which are unobtrusive because they are used so often.

As mentioned in Chapter 2, letter format changed with the business use of the typewriter. Since then, it has changed still further as new formats have been introduced to make letter production more economical. Suppose you had the job of making your company's standard letter format more economical . . . what would you do? The example below is presented in the format that was most widely used in the early 1950s. What changes would you make to reduce the cost of such a letter? Compare your ideas with those presented in the chapter.

Timkin Steel Company

1900 Banning Road
Bethlehem, PA 18015
215/555-6164

March 15, 1950

The Roan Corporation
6666 Lindero Canyon Road
Westlake Village, California

Attention: Mr. Richard Daly

Gentlemen:

    Subject: Modified Block Style With Indented Paragraphs

    Here is the information you requested on the modified block letter style with indented paragraphs that is commonly used in business today. The enclosed sample letters illustrate the modified block letter style with blocked indented paragraphs.

    Notice that the date line is typed beginning at the centering point. The attention line is typed a double space below the inside address and the subject line is typed a double space below the salutation. The attention line begins at the left margin, whereas the subject line is indented five spaces. Each paragraph in the body of the letter is indented five spaces.

    The complimentary close is typed beginning at the centering point. The company name in the closing lines is typed in all capital letters a double space below the complimentary close. The dictator's name and title are blocked four spaces below the company name.

    The initials of the dictator followed by a colon and the initials of the typist are typed at the left margin. When additional materials are enclosed with the letter, an enclosure notation is typed two spaces below the reference notations.

    Very truly yours,

    TIMKIN STEEL COMPANY

    Susan B. Brenner

    Susan B. Brenner
    Office Manager

SBB:tm

Enclosures

▷ OVERVIEW: WHAT THE READER EXPECTS

First impressions do count. By the time a reader is actually reading one of your letters, for example, he or she will have already made some preliminary decisions about you and your company. The kind of envelope, the way in which the letter has been addressed, the quality of the stationery and the print, the presence or absence of obvious corrections (strikeovers, whiteouts, or erasures), and the placement of the letter on the page all say something about you and your company.

1. An inappropriate type of envelope and stationery may say you or your company are ostentatious or cheap.

2. Obvious typing corrections may say you are sloppy.

3. An irregular letter format may say you are inexperienced or incompetent.

Readers expect certain things when they open an envelope, and you always risk offending readers when their expectations are violated. For this reason formats — especially for letters (which are by nature more formal than memos) — change slowly. The appearance of memos is usually less critical than that of letters, and on occasion, short memos may even be handwritten without offending the reader.

Because readers inevitably make judgments about you based on the appearance of your documents, it is important for you to know the conventions — the standard formats — and to follow them unless you *choose* to do something unusual to achieve a specific effect.

▷ LETTERS

What is a letter?

By definition a letter is a written message in a particular format — that is, the message is presented using one of several standardized physical arrangements that we generally take for granted. The appearance of a letter is determined primarily by convention — we use a particular form for a letter because over the years a particular form has become accepted as "a letter." As arbitrary as a letter's format is, however, it plays a vital role in how your reader will react to your message.

The first impression your reader will form of you, your company, and your message will be the result of your letter's appearance. Readers simply do not give the same respect and attention to a sloppy letter as they do to a neat one. Even if you have done everything else correctly, a messy, unattractive appearance may indicate to your reader that you are a careless, unconcerned person. The opposite is also true: a neat, carefully prepared letter suggests that you are well-organized and that you have concern for your reader.

In addition to the neatness of the message—freedom from typographical errors, strikeovers, smudges, and other disorders—you need to consider the impact of the following other factors:

1.   Stationery.

2.   Letter layout.

3.   Parts of the letter.

4.   Punctuation styles.

5.   Letter formats.

▷ STATIONERY

How could the stationery used for a letter influence the reader's response to the message?

If it is your job to select stationery for your company, do it with care. Choose a paper that will best represent you and your company. You should consider these features:

1.   **Quality.**   Although paper can be purchased with a rag content of 100 percent, the most widely used paper for letterhead stationery in offices today has 25 percent rag content. Rag-content paper is more durable than wood-pulp paper and makes a better impression. Good quality stationery is worth the investment because it helps create a favorable image for your company.

2.   **Size.**   The standard size for office stationery is 8½″ × 11″. Some businesses and executives may choose the Monarch-size sheets that measure 7¼″ × 10½″. Half-sheets, 5½″ × 8½″, are used by some companies for short notes and intracompany messages.

3.   **Watermark.**   For added prestige, many companies have a translucent design impressed on the paper during manufacture. This design is called a watermark. Watermarks may be the logo or official emblem of the company.

4.   **Weight.**   Although paper for office stationery can be purchased in weights from 7 to 32 pounds, the generally accepted weight is from 16 to 20 pounds.

5.   **Color.**   White is the most acceptable color for business letters; however, pastels are gaining increased acceptance.

▷ LETTER LAYOUT

Your letter should be balanced. "Picture-frame" your message by surrounding it with ample white space. The margins "frame" the message. Although the length of the message generally determines the width of the margins, it's usually best to maintain margins of 1½ inches, compensating for the loss or gain of space by adjusting the spacing within the parts of the letter. The top margin of a letter is usually 2 inches; the bottom margin should be about 2 inches or more, depending again on the length of the message. If the letter is two pages, the bottom margin on the first sheet should be about 1½ inches.

▷ PARTS OF THE LETTER

Why should you use a standard format for correspondence?

The names and positions of the parts of the letter are conventions, made customary by common usage. Readers expect letters to contain certain elements and to look a certain way. Because an unusual appearance detracts from the content of the letter, your letters should be fairly conventional in appearance. Figure 5.1 illustrates all the parts of a standard business letter. The parts as shown are correct, but some aspects are changing (especially the salutation and company signature) to meet the needs of a changing society.

Letterhead

Almost every business firm uses letterhead stationery for the first page of every letter. The letterhead occupies the top 2 inches of the paper. In addition to the company's name and address, it may include the telephone number and official emblem of the company. Some firms also include the names of their officers or top executives. Because a company wants to create a favorable impression, it will generally hire a professional designer to create its letterhead.

If you use plain paper for your message, include your return address. Because your name appears at the end of the letter, it should not be included in the return address.

The succeeding pages of the letter and the envelope should have the same quality, color, and weight as the letterhead page.

Date

Every piece of correspondence requires a date line. The date consists of the day, the month, and the year. Two widely used styles are acceptable:

July 15, 19xx   or   15 July 19xx

FIGURE 5.1
The Parts of a Letter

Letterhead

Date

(4 Line Spaces)

Inside Address

Attention Line

(Double-space)

Salutation

(Double-space)

Subject Line

(Double-space)

Body (Single-space
lines in paragraphs.
Double-space be-
tweeen paragraphs)

(Double-space)

Complimentary
Close

(Double-space)

Company Name for
Legal Signature

3 Line Spaces

Signature

Typed Name

Title

(Double-space)

Reference Initial

(Double-space)

Enclosure Notation

(Double-space)

Copy Notation

(Double-space)

Postscript

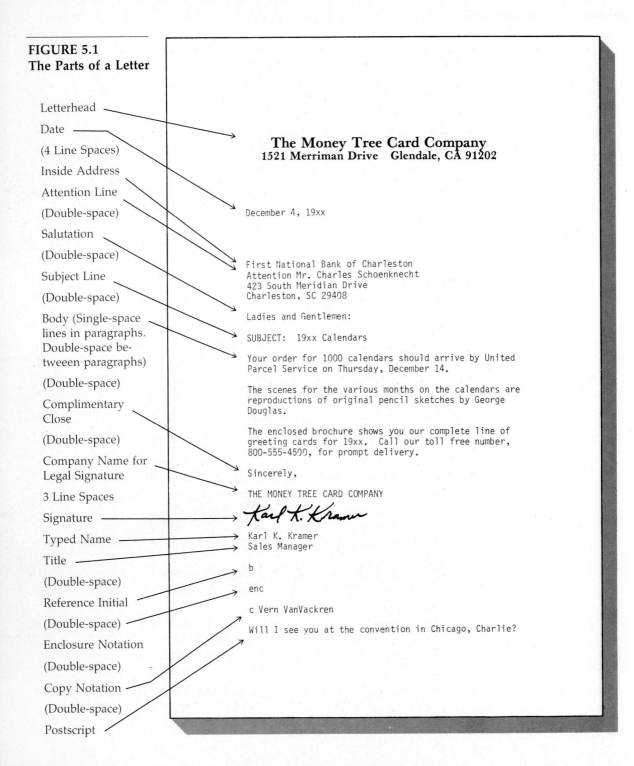

The Money Tree Card Company
1521 Merriman Drive   Glendale, CA 91202

December 4, 19xx

First National Bank of Charleston
Attention Mr. Charles Schoenknecht
423 South Meridian Drive
Charleston, SC 29408

Ladies and Gentlemen:

SUBJECT: 19xx Calendars

Your order for 1000 calendars should arrive by United
Parcel Service on Thursday, December 14.

The scenes for the various months on the calendars are
reproductions of original pencil sketches by George
Douglas.

The enclosed brochure shows you our complete line of
greeting cards for 19xx. Call our toll free number,
800-555-4500, for prompt delivery.

Sincerely,

THE MONEY TREE CARD COMPANY

Karl K. Kramer
Sales Manager

b

enc

c Vern VanVackren

Will I see you at the convention in Chicago, Charlie?

Do not use all figures in the date (as in 6/7/79), because not all English-speaking people agree about whether the month or the day appears first. Do not abbreviate the month in the date line, though you may abbreviate other dates later in the letter. Depending on the length of the message, type the date line two or more line spaces below the letterhead or the typewritten return address.

Some formats for electronic mail require a third form of the date which places the year first, the month second, and the day last:

    1986 October 15   or   1986 10 15   or   1986 Oct 15

In general, do not use this date form for printed correspondence.

Inside Address

The inside address directs your letter to the recipient. Because envelopes are seldom retained, the inside address is essential to every letter. The inside address includes the following:

1. **The courtesy title of the addressee.**   For example: Mr., Mrs., Miss, Ms., Dr., Rev., Captain.

2. **The addressee's full name.**

3. **The professional title of the addressee.**   For example: Dean, Chairperson, Director, President, Consultant.

4. **The name of the organization.**

5. **The street address or mailing address.**

6. **The city, state, and zip code.**   The state may be spelled in full or abbreviated using the standard abbreviation or the two-letter zip code abbreviation. See Figure 5.2 for a complete list of two-letter abbreviations for state, district, and territory names recommended by the U.S. Postal Service. Postal officials recommend only one letter space between the two-letter state abbreviation and the zip code.

If you are not sure how the lines in the inside address should appear, remember that the most specific item — the name of the person or company — always appears first. The most general items — the state and zip code — appear last.

The inside address is typed below the date line. The number of lines between the date and the inside address is determined by the length of the letter. Four to six line spaces are typical.

Whenever possible, direct your letter to an individual rather than to a company. If you do not know the individual's name, then direct the letter to the person's professional title such as Office Manager, Personnel Director, or Purchasing Agent. Personalizing your letters by addressing them to an

Why is it usually better to write to a specific person at a company?

FIGURE 5.2
Two-letter State
Abbreviations

Alabama	AL	Kansas	KS	Ohio	OH
Alaska	AK	Kentucky	KY	Oklahoma	OK
Arizona	AZ	Louisiana	LA	Oregon	OR
Arkansas	AR	Maine	ME	Pennsylvania	PA
California	CA	Maryland	MD	Puerto Rico	PR
Canal Zone	CZ	Massachusetts	MA	Rhode Island	RI
Colorado	CO	Michigan	MI	South Carolina	SC
Connecticut	CT	Minnesota	MN	South Dakota	SD
Delaware	DE	Mississippi	MS	Tennessee	TN
District		Missouri	MO	Texas	TX
of Columbia	DC	Montana	MT	Utah	UT
Florida	FL	Nebraska	NE	Vermont	VT
Georgia	GA	Nevada	NV	Virgin Islands	VI
Guam	GU	New Hampshire	NH	Virginia	VA
Hawaii	HI	New Jersey	NJ	Washington	WA
Idaho	ID	New Mexico	NM	West Virginia	WV
Illinois	IL	New York	NY	Wisconsin	WI
Indiana	IN	North Carolina	NC	Wyoming	WY
Iowa	IA	North Dakota	ND		

individual speeds the mail-routing process within the company and will help your letter receive a careful reading.

When you do not know whether a woman prefers Mrs. or Miss for her courtesy title, use Ms. When you do not know whether the name is masculine or feminine, for example Kyle, Kim, Jackie, Pat, or Erin, use M. When you address your letter to two or more men, use, for example, Mr. Smith and Mr. Adams; to two or more married women, use Mrs. Smith and Mrs. Adams; and to two or more unmarried women, use Misses. You may choose to use the courtesy title of Mses. (plural of Ms.) when you are not sure which title the women prefer or when you know that some are married and others are not.

The following are examples of inside address.

Mr. Gordon Godder
Director of Sales
Godder Guitars Inc.
3802 Karl Avenue
Paw Paw, MI 49079

Wagner Plumbing and Heating Supply Company
Attention Mr. Cris Carpenter
569 Antiago Road
Albuquerque, NM 87105

Mrs. Mary Ann Wells
3021 Winchell Avenue
Crawfordsville, IN 47933

Dr. James Petkin, Dean
College of Business
Texas A & M University
College Station, TX 77843

What is a simulated inside address?

Simulated inside addresses are often used instead of specific inside addresses in large-scale mailing campaigns. If you are sending the same letter to many people, the cost of addressing each letter individually would probably exceed the profit that such personalization would achieve. Inserting a name and address on a printed form letter is also expensive and usually does not improve the results of a letter.

A simulated inside address retains the traditional appearance of the letter and avoids the use of a salutation based on an obvious mailing list category or the extremely artificial *Dear Friend.*

In place of an expensive to produce personal address, such as

Mr. John A. Woods
1700 Montgomery Street
San Francisco, CA 94111

Dear Mr. Woods:

or in place of an inexpensive but dull salutation, such as

Dear Homeowner:

begin the letter with three or four lines personalized for *one* reader and in the usual position of the inside address. For example,

You can sleep soundly
When you know your home is
Protected by Sound Alarm . . .

Because you are
One of Portland's
Busiest Executives . . .

Attention Line

Traditionally, the attention line directs a letter to a person; to a professional title, such as Sales Director, Production Manager, or Service Manager; or to a department when the letter is addressed to a company. Modern usage is moving away from the attention line. When you can, address your letter to a particular person, department, or job title.

Traditional: The Williamsburg Hat Company
Attention: Director of Personnel
1492 Columbus Avenue
Ft. Myers, FL 33900

Modern: Director of Personnel
                 The Williamsburg Hat Company
                 1492 Columbus Avenue
                 Ft. Myers, FL 33900

Should you need to use an attention line, type it on the line *after* the name of the company. (Formerly the attention line appeared two line spaces below the inside address, but new postal regulations require that the city, state, and zip code appear last.) Several styles for typing the attention line are still acceptable:

Attention Mr. Joseph Lancaster

ATTENTION: Personnel Department

Attention of the Sales Director

ATTENTION — MS. SARAH SANDSKILL

Salutation

The salutation is the conventional greeting that begins the message. Some letter formats, however, omit the salutation. The type of salutation used depends on the inside address and the relationship between the sender and the receiver. Type the salutation two line spaces below the inside address. Salutations in business letters are usually followed by a colon. Examples of typical salutations are

Dear Mrs. Omli:

Dear Mr. Jones:

Dear Miss Jaskovak:

Dear Ms. Powers:

Dear Mr. Todd and Mr. Koestner:

Dear Messrs. Meehan, Rudman, and Jenco:

Dear Mmes. Schroeder, Moreman, Knudtson, and Chang:

Dear Mses. Karpel and Murphy:

Dear Misses Grinton and McGrath:

Gentlemen: (*never* Dear Gentlemen)

Ladies: (*never* Dear Ladies)

Ladies and Gentlemen: (*or* Ladies or Gentlemen)

Dear Mrs. Spaulding and Mrs. Folz:

Mesdames: (*never* Dear Mesdames)

Dear Personnel Director:

Dear Sir: (When name and title are unknown. *Never* use Dear Sirs.)

Dear LeRoy:

Dear Kathleen:

Dear Doctor Arnold: (Dear *Dr.* Arnold is gaining in popularity.)

Dear Professor:

Dear R. D. Dimitri: (*or* Dear M. Dimitri when sex of addressee is unknown)

How can simplified letter form help avoid sexist salutations?

As a result of the increasing number of women in business, modern usage is moving away from the use of the salutation *Gentlemen* as the proper form of address for corporations. No acceptable substitute, however, has been found. Some writers have been using the term, *Gentlepersons,* but it has not gained wide acceptance — probably because it seems to neuterize both men and women. *Ladies and Gentlemen* is meeting with somewhat better success, but many resist it as a salutation because it is cumbersome and suggests that the letter will be read by many people instead of just a few.

To avoid addressing businesswomen as *Gentlemen,* and to avoid the awkwardness of *Ladies and Gentlemen,* address your letter to either a specific person or a specific title (Personnel Director, Manager, Vice President of Marketing). When you do not know to whom or to what office your letter should be addressed, you can avoid the salutation by using simplified letter form.

Subject Line

A subject line tells your reader what your message is about and serves as a guide for filing. Keep subject lines short, never longer than one line. Regardless of the content of the letter, the subject line should be positive. The subject line is placed two line spaces *after* the salutation. Many styles are acceptable.

Subject: Expense Vouchers

SUBJECT: Vacation Schedule

Subject: Pay Increments

SUBJECT — POLICY 4503-2317

LETTER STYLES (The word "subject" is really unnecessary.)

Promotion Procedures

Expressions such as *re, in re, in regard to, about, reference,* and *regarding* are becoming increasingly outdated.

COMMUNICATION TODAY...

TO WHOM IT MAY CONCERN

Whatever else women's rights groups have done, they most certainly have complicated letter salutation choices.

Women have been moving into the business world since the invention and introduction of the typewriter in the 1870s, but it wasn't until well into this century that women's demands for job equality started getting some attention — when businesses, whether by legislation or by public pressure, began to share some of the traditionally all-male jobs.

It was inevitable that at this time language would be looked at with a critical eye — the stereotypes of the male boss and the female secretary, the job titles and names containing *-man,* and, of course, the letter salutations: *Gentlemen* to a firm employing both men and women and *Dear Sir* to a title when both the name and sex were unknown. Even the masculine pronouns *he, him* or *his* were objectionable when they were used to refer to an indefinite pronoun or an ambiguous antecedent such as *somebody* or *anyone,* teacher, or student, employer or employee. Unfortunately, a lot of these problems still haven't been sensibly solved. We did away with *-man* — laws were passed that desexed job titles — and a *janitorial foreman* became a *janitorial supervisor;* a *nurseryman,* a *horticulturist; chairmen, chairpersons;* even the schools found themselves with *freshpersons* (in more than one sense of the word).

But no one seems to have a good substitute for *Gentlemen. Gentlepersons? Gentlepeople? Dear People? Ladies and Gentlemen? To Whom It May Concern?* . . .

The American [sic] Management Society has long promoted its Simplified letter style, eliminating both salutations and complimentary closes. And although this may be a cowardly solution — if in doubt, leave it out — it is one way of sidestepping the problem. Besides, many have long agreed that AMS has a point: *Dear Mr. Black* is not so dear when he doesn't pay his bills, and the writer of a letter making extravagant claims for a product might not seem so *Sincerely yours.* Too, someone usually brings up the point that, if *Dear Mr. Anderson* and *Very truly yours* are not the way we talk, why are we using such old-fashioned expressions? . . .

My own personal opinion — for what it is worth — is that some will switch to the AMS Simplified style but that a lot of firms will go right on doing what they've been doing for the past thirty years. Once people assume letter writing habits, it's hard for them to change. It's going to be up to women to promote changes, particularly when they have some authority to do so.

Use what most secretries have been using for a long, long time and that is common sense and courtesy. Empathy, too, should be a factor. How would you like your mail addressed?

Source: Doris H. Whalen, "Dear To Whom It May Concern," *News,* Vol. 1, No. 3, (Orlando: Harcourt Brace Jovanovich, Inc.) Reprinted with permission.

Body

Why should first and last paragraphs in a letter be kept short?

The body contains the essential information of the message. Single-space the body of the letter and double-space between paragraphs. Your letter will look better if you keep your paragraphs short. First and last paragraphs should be no longer than four lines. Middle paragraphs should be about eight lines.

Be sure, however, to vary the paragraph length to keep your letter from having a choppy appearance.

Complimentary Close

The complimentary close is the conventional closing of the letter. It should agree with the degree of formality of the salutation. (When the salutation is *Gentlemen,* for example, *cordially* is inappropriate as a complimentary close.) When you omit the salutation in your letter, you should also omit the complimentary close. Type the complimentary close two line spaces below the last line of the body of the message. The most frequently used complimentary closes are the following:

Sincerely,	Sincerely yours,
Cordially,	Cordially yours,
Best regards,	

The following complimentary closes are used less frequently:

Yours truly,	Yours very truly,
Very truly yours,	

Company Signature

For legal reasons, some companies prefer to include the typewritten name of the company in the signature block. The signer is then assumed merely to be acting as an agent for the company, and the first name appearing after the body of the letter assumes the legal responsibility for the contents. Because the company's name appears in the letterhead, most companies prefer to avoid the redundancy and to assume responsibility for letters in other ways.

When you include your company's name in the closing lines of the letter, type it in all capital letters two spaces below the complimentary close.

Cordially yours,	Sincerely,
ZAPPO PRODUCTS INC.	B & B ENTERPRISES

Writer's Signature

Every letter must be signed. The writer of the letter signs her or his name in the space between the complimentary close (or company signature if one is used) and the typewritten signature.

Typewritten Signature and Title of the Writer

In informal situations the writer may choose to omit the typewritten signature. Most business letters, however, contain the typewritten signature and the title of the writer. This helps the reader decipher illegible signatures. The

SIDEBAR

The "Legal" Signature Block

A "legal" signature block may not always be sufficient to protect a writer in all cases. If a writer ordered products using the company letterhead and the company signature, and the company refused to pay, the writer could be held liable for payment if it were determined that she or he intended the items for personal use.

typewritten signature appears on the fourth line below the complimentary close (or company signature if one is used). The writer's title or department is typed on the line below the typewritten signature. If the writer's title is short, it may be typed on the same line as the typewritten signature with a comma separating the two.

Carmos Alveraz, Auditor	William Kennard
Accounting Department	Service Manager
Benedict Beno, Dean	A. S. Zola, Bursar

Typewritten signatures lines never include the courtesy title *Mr.* Typewritten signature lines of women may include the courtesy title to indicate how the women would prefer to be addressed, but it is not required. The title may be enclosed in parentheses.

Miss Karen Prynn	Mrs. Cecilia Branch
(Ms.) Janet Kwarta	Nancy Molzan

Reference Initials

What are the functions of closing notations on a letter?

Usually, if the closing lines include the typewritten signature of the writer, his or her initials may be omitted in the reference initials. If the closing lines do not include the typewritten signature of the writer, his or her first and/or middle initials and last name precede the initials of the typist. The typist's initials, or the initial of the typist's last name only, are typed at the left margin one or two spaces below the last line of the closing. If the initials of the writer are given, then a diagonal or a colon separates the typist's initials from the writer's initials. The following examples are acceptable:

CJJEFFERSON:tjk	ABK/mfd
sr	k
ckd	JPB:b

Enclosure Notation

If enclosures accompany the letter, a notation is typed one or two spaces below the reference initials. The following examples are all acceptable, but the lowercase *enc* without punctuation is the most economical.

Enclosure	Enc.
Check enclosed	Enclosures (2)
2 Enclosures	Enclosures: 1. Check
enc	2. Contract
	3. Invoice

Copy Notations

To show that a copy of the letter is being sent to one or more persons, type a copy notation one or two spaces below the reference initials (or enclosure notation if one is used). Because carbon paper is no longer the primary means of making copies of letters, the single letter *c* is now preferred to the older form *cc*. It is more economical and refers to a copy made by any means. Any of the following forms are acceptable:

> C Miss Susan Zimmerman
> CC: Accounting Department
> Copies to J. Kovacik
>   A. Shutty
>   L. Zajac
> C Jack Myrberg
> C: Personnel Department
> c Donna Jacquies
> cc Cheryl VanDam

Blind Copy Notations

When should you send a blind copy to a third party? Under what circumstances could a blind copy cause problems?

Some companies still send copies of letters to an individual other than the addressee without wanting the addressee to know that this is being done. Such copies are called *blind* copies because the addressee does not know that someone will receive a copy of the letter. The blind copy notation is typed on the copies of the letter *but not on the original*. It appears one or two spaces below the copy notation.

> bc Alex Sowa
> BC: A. Zouganellis
> bcc G. Peterson

Mailing or Addressee Notations

To indicate special mailing or addressee notations on the letter, type these notations in all capital letters or in initial capitals with the rest lowercase and place them either two line spaces above the inside address or two spaces below the copy notation or whatever line was typed last.

CONFIDENTIAL	Special Delivery
Personal	Please Forward
REGISTERED MAIL	CERTIFIED MAIL

Postscript

Why is a postscript often a sign of poor planning?

A postscript is an afterthought, and in formal letters it is usually a sign of poor planning. The postscript, however, has two legitimate functions:

1. To add a personal comment to a business letter.

2. To reemphasize a reader benefit in sales letters.

The abbreviation *P.S.* is not necessary to indicate a postscript. The position of the postscript tells the reader that it is one. The postscript is the last item in a letter, and it may be handwritten.

The Second Page

With the exception of sales letters, business letters are usually one page long, but sometimes a message is sufficiently complex to warrant two or more pages. When you have a second page, use one of the following second-page headings:

Horizontal Headings:

Mr. Gerald Vanderkoff	15 July 19___	2
The ABC Company	2	July 15, 19___

Vertical Headings:

Mrs. Mildred Goodwin
Page 2
August 15, 19___

Cacaterra Company
January 16, 19___
Page 2

The second and succeeding pages of a letter are usually typed on plain stationery of the same quality, size, and color as the letterhead. Rather than use plain paper, however, some companies prefer to have an identifying mark, such as the company name, in small print across the bottom of the page, or a company slogan across the top of the sheet of the second page.

The date appearing on the second page is always the same date as is on the first, even though the second page of the letter may be typed on a different day. The heading for the second page begins 1 inch from the top of the page. The second-page side margins are the same as the first-page side margins. Begin the message of the second page three line spaces after the heading. A signature block cannot appear on a page by itself. **At least two lines of the body of the message must be carried over to the second page.** The bottom margin is determined by the length of the letter.

▷ PUNCTUATION STYLES

The two most common styles of punctuating the salutation and the complimentary close of a letter are

1. **Open punctuation.** No punctuation appears after the salutation or the complimentary close.

Gentlemen	Sincerely yours
Dear Mr. Byers	Sincerely

2. **Mixed punctuation.** A colon follows the salutation, and a comma follows the complimentary close.

Gentlemen:	Sincerely yours,
Dear Mrs. Beveridge:	Cordially,

▷ LETTER FORMATS

Why have business organizations been slow to adopt the simplified letter form in spite of its greater economy?

The usual formats for business letters include block, modified block, AMS Simplified, personalized, and specialty, which are listed in order of their current popularity. Block format is the most widely used because it is relatively economical and has a traditional appearance. Many conservative companies still choose to use modified block, although it is gradually becoming outdated. The simplified letter form is the most economical of the formats, but many companies resist adopting it because it does not contain all the traditional letter parts. The personalized and specialty formats are used for special effect.

Block

In the full block letter format, all parts of the letter and all lines begin at the left margin. See Figure 5.3 for an illustration of the block format.

FIGURE 5.3
Block Format,
Mixed Punctuation

Vermont Manpower Center
202 West Maple Street
Whitney, VT 02135

January 30, 19xx

Dr. Patricia Marcum
Department of Business Education
  and Administrative Services
Illinois State University
Normal, IL 61761

Dear Dr. Marcum:

This letter is an example of a letter typed in block
format with mixed punctuation. The block format is a
more economical format than modified block.

Notice that all lines begin at the left margin--the
date, inside address, salutation, body, and closing lines.
Observe, too, that the spacing between letter parts is
standard.

The block style is popular because it retains the
traditional appearance established by the modified block
format while providing a definite economic advantage.

Cordially,

W. I. Grogg

W. I. Grogg
Manager, Education and Training

b

(This is the most common format and punctuation style.)

Modified Block

The modified block format has two versions. Modified block with blocked paragraphs has all lines beginning at the left margin except the date and the closing lines, which begin at the center of the page, as Figure 5.4 illustrates.

Modified block with indented paragraphs is the same as the first version except that the paragraphs are indented. See Figure 5.5 for an example of this format.

Simplified

In the Administrative Management Society's simplified letter format, all lines begin at the left margin. This format omits the salutation and the complimentary close. See Figure 5.6 for an illustration of the AMS simplified format. NOTE: The simplified format is frequently used for electronic mail.

Personalized

The personalized format is a combination of the block and the AMS simplified formats. Like the simplified, it omits the salutation and complimentary close, but it retains the traditional block appearance by providing personalized facsimiles of those two standard letter parts. See Figure 5.7 for an illustration of the personalized format.

Specialty

In some situations special forms may help attract reader attention. The most common of these formats uses hanging paragraphs, color, italic print, or other mechanical means of catching a reader's attention. Direct-mail advertising makes the most extensive use of specialty formats. Other possible uses might be for company invitations, special announcements, or seasonal greetings. See Figure 5.8 for an illustration of a specialty format.

▷ ENVELOPES

Return Address

The return address is generally printed in the upper-left corner of the envelope and matches the letterhead printing. If the envelope does not have a printed return address, type your return address in the upper-left corner, not on the back, of the envelope. Single-space the return address and use the block style. Addressee notations—*confidential*, *personal*, or *attention*—are typed three line spaces after the return address in all capital letters, initial capital letters with the rest lowercase, or underscored.

**FIGURE 5.4
Modified Block
Format, Blocked
Paragraphs, Open
Punctuation**

*Susan Rice
14 Fulton Street
Ross, CA 94011*

                                       November 16, 19xx

Ms. Louise Steele
Administrative Assistant
100 English Building
608 South Wright Street
University of Illinois
Urbana, IL 61801

Dear Ms. Steele

This letter is an example of a letter typed in
modified block format with blocked paragraphs
and open punctuation.

Notice that all lines begin at the left margin
except the date and the closing lines, which
begin at the center of the page. The spacing
between letter parts is standard.

Even though it is more expensive to use than
the block format, modified block is still used
by many conservative American businesses. It is
the only letter format that gives the writer the
choice of indented paragraphs.

                         Sincerely yours

                         Susan Rice

                         Susan Rice

FIGURE 5.5
Modified Block
Format, Indented
Paragraphs, Mixed
Punctuation

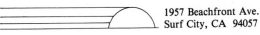

1957 Beachfront Ave.
Surf City, CA 94057

December 23, 19xx

Mr. Roger Downs
1400 Ocean Blvd.
Halfmoon Bay, CA 94019

Dear Roger:

    This letter is an example of modified block with indented
paragraphs and mixed punctuation.

    Though it was once a common form, it is becoming in-
creasingly outdated because it is an expensive form to use.
Every indentation takes the typist additional time, and
that extra time can add up over the year.

    A few companies still prefer this format because some
people feel that it gives a warmer appearance than block
format.

                 Cordially,

                 Woody Petroski

                 Woody Petroski

FIGURE 5.6
AMS Simplified
Format

ADMINISTRATIVE MANAGEMENT SOCIETY
5211 Chagrin Blvd.   Cleveland, OH 44114

April 14, 19xx

Mr. Lester P. Salisbury, Manager
Perry Manufacturing Company
3802 Karl Avenue
Nashville, TN 37203

AMS SIMPLIFIED FORM

This letter form, Mr. Salisbury, is typed in the simplified format recommended
by the Administrative Management Society. To use this modern, time-saving
format, follow these suggestions:

1. Use block format.

2. Omit salutation and complimentary close but try to use the reader's name
    in the first sentence.

3. Use a subject line. Type it in ALL CAPS two line spaces below the
    inside address; triple-space from the subject line to the first line
    of the body.

4. Type enumerated items at the left margin; indent unnumbered listed
    items five spaces.

5. Type the writer's name and title in ALL CAPS at least four line
    spaces below the body of the letter.

6. Double-space closing notations--reference initial and enclosure and
    copy notations--after the writer's name.

AMS simplified letter format, Mr. Salisbury, is not only very efficient but
also quite attractive.

Charles Powers

CHARLES POWERS, PERSONNEL DIRECTOR

m

c Thomas Goodwin
  Myles Murphy

Mailing Address

Why should the mailing address on the envelope be the same as the inside address in the letter?

The mailing address is the same as the inside address. Type the mailing address about five spaces to the left of the center of the envelope and about halfway down from the top. Single-space the lines of the mailing address and use the block style.

Mailing Notations

Mailing notations—*certified mail, registered mail,* or *special delivery*—are typed three line spaces after the stamp position in all capital letters, initial capital letters with the rest lowercase, or underscored. See Figure 5.9 for an illustration of the large (No. 10) envelope and the small (No. 6¾) envelope. Figure 5.10 illustrates the folding and inserting process.

▷ MEMOS

Although memorandums, commonly known as memos, are technically a short report form, they are worth considering here for two reasons: (1) they use the same basic organizational patterns to achieve the same kinds of objectives as letters; and (2) like letters, they are usually brief, rarely being longer than a page. The memo format, however, is less formal than letter format because memos are used to exchange information within an organization, whereas letters are sent to persons outside the organization. If, for example, you work for the Los Angeles branch of a New York company, you will probably use memos instead of letters to correspond with the home office in New York. Figure 5.11 illustrates the memo format.

Appearance

Why are memos usually less formal than letters?

Because memos do not leave the organization, you need not be very concerned about public relations—you can use stationery that differs from letterhead stationery in color, printing, quality, and size. Use inexpensive wood-pulp paper rather than expensive rag-content paper. Sizes of memo stationery range from full sheets, 8½" × 11", to half-sheets, 5½" × 8½". Some businesses prefer half-sheets for economy; other companies choose full sheets for ease in filing.

Although most companies prefer white paper for their letters, they may prefer using colored paper for memos to distinguish them from other business papers. Colors may designate particular departments.

FIGURE 5.7
Personalized Format

CONNECTICUT COLLEGE OF BUSINESS
10002 Post Road • Fairfield, CT 06694

September 8, 19xx

Dr. Henry McKeown
3150 Reynolds Road
Jackson, MI 49201

Yes, Henry,

standard letter formats are still correct, but many letter
writers are choosing to personalize messages with breezy,
"open" beginnings and closings in place of stilted, formal
salutations and complimentary closings.

These personal openings and closings have the advantage of
retaining the appearance of traditional formats while
substituting something useful for the dull salutation and
complimentary close.

Why say	Dear Mr. Dorsaneo:
	Here's a copy of the material you requested.
When you can say	Here, Mr. Dorsaneo,
	is a copy of the material you requested.
Why say	Dear Dr. Mascolini:
	The crushed velvet pantsuit you ordered is available in red, blue, black, and magenta.
When you can say	The crushed velvet pantsuit, Dr. Mascolini,
	is available in red, blue, black, and magenta.

```
        Dr. Henry McKeown     September 8, 19xx

        Why say               Dear Bob:

                              We enjoyed your visit and the lovely
                              dinner at the Black Swan.

        When you can say      Thanks, Bob,

                              for the lovely dinner at the Black
                              Swan.  We thoroughly enjoyed your
                              visit.

        Why say               Sincerely yours,
                              Sincerely,
                              Cordially yours,

        When you can say      When you're in town again. . .

                              Please call,

                              I'm so glad you got the job. . .

                              Congratulations,

                              Call me at (415) 555-9608. . .

                              When I can help again,


        When you use the personal style, you show your reader that
        you are a thoughtful letter writer and a person who can
        think for himself.

        Naturally, if you are writing to a very conservative
        company, you would want to use a more traditional format
        to make sure that you don't offend your reader.  Your
        format, as well as your language, should indicate your
        empathy for your reader.

        We'll be glad to help again when you have questions. . .

        Anytime,

        Joel P. Bowman        Bernadine P. Branchaw
```

FIGURE 5.8
Specialty Format

American Heritage Company
12 Avenue of the Americas
New York, NY 10020

July 4, 19xx

SPECIALTY FORMATS

When you need to make a special effort to attract your reader's
    attention, consider devising your own format. Hanging
    paragraphs are one way of attracting attention.

Other mechanical means would include the use of color, or

> you might box the important
>
> information to show the
>
> reader what to look at first.

The main rules to follow in devising a specialty format are the
    following:

1. Keep it simple.

2. Include all the appropriate letter parts.

3. Be consistent--use the same techniques throughout.

4. The arrangement of the material on the page should
    usually correspond with the shape of the paper.

Specialty formats are most often used in sales letters and
    invitations.

Cordially,

Walter J. Thompson
Director

FIGURE 5.9
Large and Small
Envelopes

```
F. Robert Walczak
Scientific Research, Inc.                                        STAMP
1540 Page Mill Road
Palo Alto, CA 94304

CONFIDENTIAL

                                                        SPECIAL DELIVERY

              Mr. Lynn H. Molzan
              Woollen Associates
              604 Ft. Wayne Avenue
              Indianapolis, IN 46204
```

```
Sheila Furjanic
8 Oak Place                                     STAMP
Croton-on-Hudson
New York, NY 10520

PERSONAL                                REGISTERED MAIL

          Mr. James E. Bennett
          4514 Ellenita Avenue
          Northridge, CA 91324
```

NOTE: The area below the address must be free of notations so that the Optical Character Reader in use at major post offices can "read" the address automatically, starting with the zip code.

FIGURE 5.10
Folding and
Inserting Process

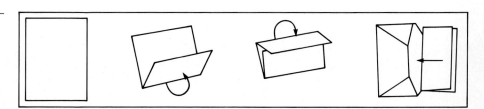

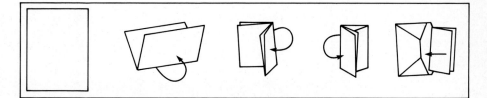

FIGURE 5.11
Memo Format

Timkin Steel Company

1900 Banning Road
Bethlehem, PA 18015
215/555-6164

Interoffice Memorandum

15 August 19xx

TO: Gertrude Sonnevil, Office Manager

FROM: Jean Mutchall, Personnel Director *jm*

SUBJECT: Annual Review of Hazel Kramer

Please tell Hazel Kramer that her appointment for
annual review is Monday, 1 September, at 9 a.m.

Please complete the attached form and return it
to me by Thursday, 30 August.

att

Headings

Unlike letters, which use the formal inside address, salutation, complimentary close, and typed signature, memos require only informal headings. Normally, four informal printed headings appear on memo stationery: *To, From, Date,* and *Subject.* Although the arrangement and design may vary among companies, these four headings appear on most forms. Printing of the heading lines may be either vertical or horizontal.

Horizontal Heading:	TO:		DATE:	
	FROM:		SUBJECT:	
Vertical Headings:	DATE:	TO:	TO:	DATE:
	TO:	FROM:	FROM:	
	FROM:	DATE:	SUBJECT:	
	SUBJECT:	SUBJECT:		

If your organization does not provide printed forms, you may omit the word *date* and simply type the date. The word *subject* may also be omitted, as Figure 5.12 illustrates.

◇ SUMMARY

A letter is a written message in a particular format — that is, the message is written in one of several standardized physical presentations that we generally take for granted. The first impression your reader will form of you, your company, and your message will be the result of your letter's appearance.

The appearance of your letter depends on five elements: (1) stationery, (2) letter layout, (3) parts of the letter, (4) punctuation style, and (5) the letter format itself.

When selecting letterhead paper, you should consider the quality, size, watermark, weight, and color. The parts of the letter are letterhead, date, inside address, attention line, salutation, subject line, body, complimentary close, company signature, writer's signature, typewritten signature and the title of the writer, reference initials, enclosure notations, copy notations, and postscript. The two most common styles of punctuating the salutation and the complimentary close are open punctuation and mixed punctuation.

The usual formats for business letters include the block, modified block, AMS simplified, and personalized. Each of these has certain advantages. Modified block is the most conservative. Block and personalized are more efficient than modified block and are usually considered more personal than the AMS simplified, which is the most efficient.

FIGURE 5.12
Memo Format
without the
Heading *Subject*

Timkin Steel Company

1900 Banning Road
Bethlehem, PA 18015
215/555-6164

Interoffice Memorandum

16 November 19xx

TO: All Employees

FROM: Don DeLong, Personnel Department *D.D.*

GROUP HEALTH INSURANCE

Mrs. Alice Flint, our representative from the
Green Shield Insurance Company, will be here on
Monday, 28 November, to answer any questions you
may have on our new medical coverage insurance
plan.

Mrs. Flint will meet with all interested employees
at 9 a.m. in Room 405. Should you wish an
individual appointment to discuss your personal
needs, call me at Extension 22.

The memo is a short, informal message that provides a rapid, convenient means of communication between employees within the same organization. It is a company's principal written medium for internal communication.

◇ EXERCISES

Review and Discussion Questions

1. On what factors does the appearance of a letter depend?
2. What features should you consider when selecting stationery?
3. What are the parts of a letter?
4. What does the letterhead contain?
5. What is included in the inside address?
6. What is the purpose of the subject line?
7. What is a blind copy notation?
8. What is the purpose of a postscript?
9. What are the two most common styles of punctuation for the salutation and complimentary close of the letter?
10. What are the five usual formats for business letters?

Problems

1. Using separate sheets of paper, type the following letter in
   a. Block format and address it to Ms. Sandra Palumbo, 228 Glen Road, Lafayette, CA 94549.
   b. Modified block format with blocked paragraphs and open punctuation and address it to Mr. Charles Quible, 208 Cypress Street, Lakewood, OH 44107.
   c. Administrative Management Society Simplified format and address it to Mrs. Judith Pauly, 143 Summit Avenue, Fargo, ND 58102.
   d. Personalized format and address it to Dr. Wanda Aus, Dawson Community College, Box 421, Glendive, MT 59330.

   Here is a slightly more positive solution to the negative letter you gave us. The situation is really negative, but for legal reasons you must be explicit. The reader knows (or should know) that the check is outstanding and either does intend to defraud or expects to hear something. Can you say what the reader might do to pay—$5 a week or some other step-at-a-time plan? If so, you should do that—to give the reader hope.

COMMUNICATION SOLUTION

If you had the job of making your company's standard letter format more economical, you might consider using the block style, which is more efficient than the modified block. You might also consider using the AMS simplified style, which is the most efficient.

To make letters less expensive to use, you would type the date at the left margin, and the attention line below the name of the company in the inside address. You would use the two-letter state abbreviation rather than spelling out the name of the state. The word *subject* could be omitted in the subject line. Paragraphs would not be indented; they would begin at the left margin. The complimentary close would begin at the left margin, and the company name would be omitted. The reference notation would include only the initial or initials of the typists. The word *enclosure* would be abbreviated and typed with lowercase letters.

Following are the two most economical solutions: block and simplified letter forms.

Block

LETTERHEAD

March 15, 1985

Mr. Richard Daly
The Roan Corporation
666 Lindero Canyon Road
Westlake Village, CA 96100

Dear Mr. Daly:

BLOCK LETTER STYLE

All paragraphs would be blocked.

* * * * * * * * * * * * *

* * * * * * * * * * * * * *

Sincerely,

Susan B. Brenner
Office Manager

m

enc

AMS Simplified

LETTERHEAD

March 15, 1985

Mr. Richard Daly
The Roan Corporation
666 Lindero Canyon Road
Westlake Village, CA 96100

AMS SIMPLIFIED LETTER STYLE

In AMS letter form, Mr. Daly, all paragraphs are blocked.

* * * * * * * * * * * * *

* * * * * * * * * * * * *

The typed name appears four line spaces following the last line of the letter.

SUSAN B. BRENNER, OFFICE MANAGER

m

enc

2. Using separate sheets of paper, type the following message in
   a. Memo format with vertical headings. Send the memo to Kathryn Oates and select an appropriate subject line.
   b. Memo format with horizontal headings. Send the memo to Duane Bennett and select an appropriate subject line.

   The attached materials represent my effort to restructure the company manual. The new structure represents a radical departure from the former manual, but it has proven effective in our branch office. The critical aspect of the restructuring for your purposes is detailed on the reverse of the opening statement. Please let me know if I can provide other materials you would find useful.

CASE

What kinds of formats are being used for electronic mail? Using at least three sources (either electronic or hard copy), evaluate formats being used for electronic mail. Are any of them adaptable to paper mail? What advantages would the electronic formats offer over traditional formats? What disadvantages would they present? Submit your analysis and conclusions in a three- to five-page paper.

CHAPTER SIX

Placing Orders and Asking Questions

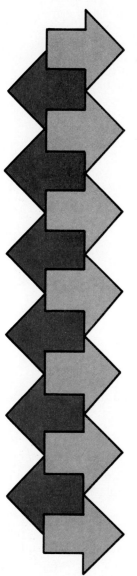

Letters or memos requesting goods, services, or information are known as *direct requests.* Your readers will welcome most messages of this type because your order or inquiry will give them the opportunity to sell goods or services, build goodwill, or share information about something of common concern. This chapter shows you how to write effective orders and inquiries (direct requests).

Topics

COMMUNICATION CHALLENGE

Suppose that you are the Vice President of Operations for the Second National Bank, 14 East River Drive, Seattle, WA 98104. You need to request an adjustment on three new modular office systems you recently purchased from Coppercase Products, 111 Telegraph Avenue, Oakland, CA 94603.

While the modular offices were being installed, the company representative, Roger Horrein, was called back to Oakland for a family emergency. Before leaving, Roger explained the installation process to the crew chief, who was hired locally. After Roger departed, the modular panels were evidently installed incorrectly, because instead of reducing the noise between offices, the panels seem to amplify it. You would like to have Roger or another Coppercase representative return to the bank and correct the problem at Coppercase's expense. Also, because the level of noise is annoying (conversa-

tions carry easily from one of the modular offices to the next), you would appreciate having the problem corrected immediately.

Ellen Kuiper, sales manager for Coppercase, is the person who made all the arrangements previously. You and she have been playing "telephone tag" for three days now, so you have decided to send a letter. Write a letter that will result in the corrective action you desire.

As you plan your letter, ask yourself exactly what you would like Coppercase to do. You will have a better chance of obtaining the action you desire if you clearly specify it to Coppercase. Also, ask yourself what kind of attitude you should convey in your letter toward Coppercase to increase your chances of receiving immediate assistance. Read through this chapter, solve the problem, and compare your solution with the one that follows the chapter summary.

▷ OVERVIEW: HELPING THE READER HELP YOU

When you place an order by mail or write a letter or memo requesting information, your principal concern should be to provide any information your reader will need to help you. Such information may include

1.   Description of the product: size, model number, color, function, design, date of manufacture, and quantity.

2.   Description of service: who, what, when, where, how, and perhaps why.

3.   Explanation of information use: *what* information is required, *why* is it required, *how* will it be used, *when* is it required, and *why* is it required by that date.

When writing letters or memos of this variety remember that your explanation of who you are and why you want something will be less interesting to your reader than what you want. Begin with a clear statement of what you want, either placing an order or asking your most important question. Then provide any necessary explanation.

Another type of direct request is the letter you write when you are dissatisfied with a product or service and want a correction or a refund from the company responsible. Most organizations want their customers or clients to be satisfied, and if something is not right, they want to know about it so that they can correct it. For this reason, you can usually use a direct structure for this type of letter (called a *direct claim*). If possible, you should specify exactly what action you want the company to take.

Regardless of the kind of business or occupation you are in, you will need to write direct requests. Some will be fairly easy to write. For example, you may need to order a dozen ribbons for your printer. As long as you specify the type of ribbon you want (probably by product number) and the quantity and enclose satisfactory billing information (check, money order, or credit card or account number), your letter will accomplish its goal, and you will receive the product you want. Some direct requests, however, are more complex. You may need to order a product but not know its correct name or model number, or you may need to complain about a problem but not know exactly what action the company should take to correct it.

What letter would you write, for example, to solve the problem presented in this chapter's Communication Challenge?

▷ GENERAL STRUCTURE AND CHECKLIST FOR DIRECT REQUESTS

Which structure (direct or indirect) is more suitable for placing orders and making routine inquiries? Why?

Because orders and inquiries are almost always well received, you should use a direct structure for such messages, stressing an important business objective in the opening sentence. The most common mistake writers make in orders and inquiries is failing to provide sufficient information — the specific details — for the reader to perform the requested action.

The human objective in this type of message does not require special attention because the reader will be glad to receive the order or inquiry. Nevertheless, keep your reader's point of view in mind; that is, ask yourself what the reader needs to know to answer your questions or fill your order.

To summarize, when you write direct requests (orders and inquiries), make the opening question or statement absolutely clear; include all the information your reader will need to help you; and clarify who is to do what next and by when.

The general structure for all direct requests is as follows:

1. **Direct opening.**　　Begin with a specific request for what you want or with your most important question. Your request places your message in a specific communication context.

COMMUNICATION TODAY...

The sample order blank presented here shows you the kind of information catalog sales companies require. When you order by mail, you should provide as much information as necessary to ensure receiving exactly what you want.

CONVENIENT PHONE ORDERING:
Credit card holders, call (800) 555-1212 Monday through Friday, from 8:00 A.M. to Midnight, EST.

Please provide the following information

To send this order to a different address
NAME _____
ADDRESS _____ APT. _____
CITY _____ STATE _____ ZIP _____

NAME _____
ADDRESS _____ APT. _____
CITY _____
STATE _____ 57577
ZIP _____

We offer five convenient methods of payment:
☐ CHECK OR MONEY ORDER ENCLOSED PAYABLE TO GARDEN OF EDEN

☐ **VISA** (3)   ☐ **MasterCard** (4)   ☐ **AMERICAN EXPRESS** (5)   ☐ **DINERS CLUB INTERNATIONAL CITICORP** (6)

_____ GOOD THRU _____
CARD NUMBER
SIGNATURE _____ DATE _____

For your own protection, please do not send cash or stamps.
Sorry, we can accept no COD's.
For orders shipped outside the continental United States, please add a surcharge of 10% of the total.

Just in case we need to call ...
DAYTIME PHONE:
AREA CODE (   ) _____

PAGE	ITEM	QTY.	CATALOG NUMBER	COLOR	SIZE	PRICE EACH	TOTAL PRICE

TOTAL ITEMS

Merchandise Total		
Handling Charge	1	95
Subtotal		
N.Y. and VA Residents ONLY Sales Tax on Subtotal		
Shipping charge 75¢ per item		
ORDER TOTAL		

Thank you for your order

GUARANTEE OF SATISFACTION
You must be completely satisfied with every item purchased from Garden of Eden. If for any reason an item does not live up to your expectations, return it to us for an immediate no-questions-asked refund or exchange, whichever you prefer.

Why should any ex-
planations be in the
secondary position?

2. **Explanation.**   Explanations *always* belong in the secondary position. Your reader needs to know the purpose of the letter before reading about who you are and why you want something. As you explain, be sure to keep your reader in the picture by referring to the reader and the reader's company, product, or service.

3. **Secondary matters.**   Other questions or specifications should follow the explanation. Using a numbered list for secondary matters will help focus the reader's attention on each item separately. When each question requires its own explanation, however, do not use a numbered list. Instead, put each question and its explanation in a separate paragraph.

4. **Who does what next.**   Many orders and inquiries should conclude with an *end date* or deadline that lets the reader know when you need the information or goods. Be polite and give a reason to justify the deadline. When end dating is inappropriate, be sure to let your reader know who is responsible for what happens next.

▷ ORDERS

How specific should
you be when order-
ing a product or
service?

Buying and selling by mail is big business. Sears, JC Penney, Marshall Field, and many other retailers use catalogs and the mail to sell their goods and services to those customers who do not have direct access to stores. Also, publications ranging from the *International Yellow Pages* to *The Whole Earth Catalog* to the classified sections in popular magazines encourage ordering by mail. Most of the companies that sell by mail provide customers with well-designed catalogs, order blanks, and reply envelopes.

Why is "Please
send me" the best
beginning for an or-
der?

When an order blank is not available, make sure that you include all the specific information your reader will need to fill the order quickly and easily. Remember that your offer to buy will constitute a contractual agreement, so it is important that it be accurate and complete. Check for the following:

1. Have you specified that your letter is an order and not a request for information? The best beginning for an order is *Please send me.*

2. Have you specified the goods completely? In addition to the quantity, catalog number or issue, name of the product, and price, you need to specify all the details appropriate for each particular item, including color, size, grade, machine or part number, pattern, finish, style, or weight. Omission of these details will delay your order.

3. Have you specified how you intend to pay? When you enclose a check or money order, be sure to say that the enclosed check is in payment

for the goods. When you request credit, make sure that you provide the appropriate credit information with the order.

4.   Have you specified where, when, and how you want the goods shipped? Each year retailers receive hundreds of orders complete with money orders (and sometimes even cash) which do not provide either a shipping destination or a return address.

Note the way Figure 6.1 illustrates the foregoing points:

FIGURE 6.1
Sample Order Letter

```
            5409 Summer Circle
            Boston, MA 02106

            May 15, 19xx



            Garden of Eden
            Mail Order Department
            47 Linwood Avenue
            Newton, NJ 07860

            Ladies and Gentlemen:

            Please send me the following items listed in your spring/
            summer 19xx catalog:

            1 National Semiconductor 8-Digit "Data-
              checker" Calculator Model NS103              $ 24.95

            1 Sharp 10-Digit LCD Pocket Scientific
              Calculator Model EL 5806                       29.95

            1 Panasonic Electric Pencil Sharpener            29.95

            1 "Governor" Desk Set                            35.00

                    Subtotal                               $119.85

                    Tax                                       4.79
                                                           $124.64

                    Parcel Post Charges                       3.56

                    Total                                  $128.20

            The enclosed check for $128.20 covers the cost of my order.  I
            would appreciate receiving the merchandise by June 27 because
            I will be leaving on vacation that day.

            Sincerely,

            Shunitsu Okuda

            Shunitsu Okuda
```

When no catalog or parts list is available, take special care to supply the reader with the information necessary to determine your particular needs. In some cases you may have to order a catalog or parts list before you can order the item you need. You cannot expect your reader to know what you want unless you specify it exactly. Even in the most complicated case, however, you can expect your reader to be helpful; if you cannot specify exactly what you want, at least provide sufficient information for the reader to help you find more specific ordering information.

▷ INQUIRIES

Why should most inquiries be structured as direct messages? Under what circumstances would you need to write a persuasive request?

Companies welcome letters asking about their goods, services, operations, and (usually) personnel. Such letters offer businesses an opportunity to make a sale or to build goodwill. Individuals welcome letters asking about matters of common concern, especially when they have particular expertise in the area asked about. Most such requests should be structured as direct messages because the reader is already motivated to reply. Because the human objective is not a problem, the business objective receives the main emphasis.

Asking about Goods and Services

The business objective in inquiries as with orders, is letting the reader know what you want in a way that will permit a quick and easy reply. You should almost always begin with your most important question.

> What are the differences between the 16-foot Hydrofoil and the 16-foot Hydroplane sailboats? I saw your ad in the December *Sail*.

> How much experience does a hobbyist need to assemble a Heathkit GR-101 color television set?

Why is the best opening for a direct request a specific question?

Your opening question should *always* be specific. Whenever possible, let the reader know what information you already have by mentioning where you saw the ad or heard about the product, service, or subject. Remember, too, that vague questions and requests result in vague answers. For example, if you write *Please send me any information you have about the GR-101 television set*, your reader is not likely to tell you how much experience is required for assembly. So if that is the question you want answered, be sure to ask it specifically. General requests for additional information should *follow* all your specific questions and necessary explanations:

> In addition to answering the foregoing questions, please send me any other information you think I would find helpful.

The information you want most should be requested in your opening sentence — the sentence that will receive your reader's closest attention. When you don't know exactly what information you want, guess. Ask the question you think will *most likely* give you the information you want. Keep in mind that the most important question is almost never cost. When you are tempted to use cost as your first question, ask a question related to *value* instead. Ask about cost later in the letter.

> What is the guarantee covering the Autoelectric Zig-Zag sewing machine you advertised in the July issue of <u>Family Circle</u>?

After you have asked your most important question, provide the reader with the explanation required for a complete answer. Your opening question will place your letter in a specific communication context, and your explanation, in the secondary position, will not only clarify your opening question, but will also serve as a transition to your other questions. When possible, arrange your letter so that you can use a numbered list, which will increase the clarity of your letter.

When should you use a numbered list for your secondary questions?

A numbered list is good for questions that require only a short explanation or that can be made specific and clear by a single, inclusive explanation following your opening question. But if each question requires a separate explanation, a numbered list will lose its impact. In that case separate paragraphs are a better arrangement than a numbered list.

By asking specific questions and emphasizing each one separately, you greatly increase your chances of receiving specific answers to each question. You also increase your chances of receiving the information when you want it by setting and justifying an end date — or deadline — for your reader's response.

When should you set and justify an end date (deadline)?

Of course, if you have no need for the information by a specific date, you should not manufacture an end date and justifying reason. Show confidence in your reader's willingness to respond promptly.

What is wrong with thanking the reader "in advance" for her or his compliance with your request?

You should also assume that the reader is well acquainted with the benefits of a cordial response, so you do not need to draw special attention to those benefits. Also, do not use the phrase *thanking you in advance*. If the reader's reply warrants a word of thanks, send it *after* you have received the reply. Thanking in advance is discourteous because it shows that the writer assumes that the reader will respond in a particular way. Such an assumption is presumptuous.

Compare the examples in Figures 6.2 and 6.3.

Asking about Operations

Whether you are writing to someone in another department or branch of your company or to someone in another company, a message asking about operations usually calls for a direct structure. While some operations, such as government contracts, marketing strategy, and product development are confidential, most are not. Companies will usually share information about routine operations in the interest of promoting business harmony. Figure 6.4 illustrates a request for information about operations.

Asking about People

Why do letters requesting information about people present special hazards for writers?

Requests for information about people present special hazards for letter writers because of the so-called sunshine laws, which permit access to many kinds of personal information. Information that formerly could be kept confidential is now available to the person asked about and, in some cases, to other interested parties as well. The most common requests for information about people are concerned with employment, school applications, and credit. In each case the person asking for the information should be asking because he or she has a legitimate interest to protect, and the person asking should also be prepared to keep the information received as confidential as the law will permit. Whenever you inquire about somebody, you should protect yourself and your reader as much as possible by observing the following precautions:

1. State whether the person being inquired about authorized your request for information.

2. State whether the person being inquired about has waived right of access to the reply.

3. State whether you will keep the information confidential.

4. Show your reader that you are asking for the information because you have a legitimate interest to protect.

5. If your inquiry concerns employment, ask questions only about the person's ability to handle the job being applied for.

Figure 6.5 illustrates these points.

▷ INVITATIONS

What kinds of invitations are direct requests? What kinds are persuasive requests?

Most invitations are a special category of direct requests because it will be primarily to the reader's advantage to attend or participate in the event you are planning. When it is primarily to your advantage—as when you invite a "name" speaker to appear before your group—you will need to write a *persuasive request* according to the principles presented in Chapter 10. When invitations are special goodwill messages involving no persuasion, they should use a direct structure. State the main idea, the invitation, first. Explanations and a request for confirmation (when necessary) follow. Be sure to cover the five W's—*who, what, when, where,* and *why.* When the *how* is important, be sure to describe it fully as well. Most invitations are fairly short because the advantages for the reader are obvious, as Figure 6.6 illustrates.

**FIGURE 6.2
Sample Letter
of Inquiry**

Vista *Advertising Concepts*
1602-21 Macdonald Drive, ACC 215
Corvallis, OR 97331
503/555-5880

28 May 19xx

Republic Business Machines
3370 Colonial Avenue
Los Angeles, CA 90066

Subject: L-100 AND M-101 WORD PROCESSORS

Ask the main question. Tell your reader how you learned about the product, service, or idea.

What are the differences between your Model L-100 and Model M-101 word processing centers? One of these models, advertised in the July issue of Business Education Forum, may be the answer to my problem.

I own a small direct-mail advertising company, employing five copywriters, a business manager, and three secretaries. Because all of our work must be carefully done, one of your word processing centers may provide the solution to our extensive editing problems.

Explain your situation fully, but keep the reader in the picture.

Currently all the written work produced by the copywriters and the business manager is dictated to one of the secretaries. The material is transcribed in draft form and may undergo more than ten revisions before it receives approval. We have reached the point where we may need to hire an additional secretary to keep up. Would either the Model L-100 or M-101 help us reduce the time we spend revising?

Put the secondary questions in a numbered list.

Answers to the following questions would help me decide about purchasing one of your machines:

1. How much of an increase in efficiency can we expect with a word processing center?

2. What is the total cost--including tax, shipping, and service contract-- for each model?

3. How much training is required for dictating and transcribing with the machines?

Ask for other information after you've asked specific questions. Set and justify an end date. DO NOT THANK THE READER IN ADVANCE.

Republic Business Machines   28 May 19xx   2

4. Are both models compatible with IBM Personal Computers?

5. Which machine would you recommend for my office?

In addition to answering these questions, please send me any other information you think might help me. As our busiest season begins in August and I will need to decide whether to hire additional help by 1 July, I would appreciate receiving your reply by 15 June.

LEROY HAGGE--PRESIDENT

FIGURE 6.3
Sample Letter
of Inquiry

Ask a main ques-
tion first. Tell the
reader how you
know about the
product.

Explain the situa-
tion, subordinating
elements the reader
already knows.

Explain each ques-
tion separately.

Encourage a prompt
response even
when you do not
need the informa-
tion by a specific
date.

```
                    11014 Whitehorn
                    Cincinnati, OH 45221

                    May 25, 19xx


                    Lake Michigan Electronics
                    50 North Pascack Road
                    Spring Valley, MI 49087

                    Gentlemen:

                    How much experience does a hobbyist need to assemble an
                    LM-101 color television set?  A friend of mine owns an
                    LM-101, and I'm very impressed by its performance.

                    Although your catalog states that only experienced kit
                    builders should attempt to build color televisions, my
                    friend thought that I would be able to do a satisfactory
                    job by taking my time and paying close attention to
                    your directions.

                    Admittedly, my kit building experience is limited.
                    Nearly 20 years ago I built an LM hi-fi, and almost
                    as long ago I built an LM portable radio.  I can still
                    make a decent solder joint.  Do you think I should
                    attempt an LM-101?

                    If you think that I should practice kit building first,
                    will you recommend projects that will prepare me for
                    building one of your color televisions?

                    Would reading a book on electronics help?  Can you
                    recommend a book that would be useful?

                    May I have your answers to these questions soon?  I'm
                    eager to begin.

                    Sincerely,

                    Carol Watson Pomerenke

                    Carol Watson Pomerenke
```

**FIGURE 6.4
Sample Inquiry
about Operations**

Timkin Steel Company

1900 Banning Road
Bethlehem, PA 18015
215/555-6164

Interoffice Memorandum

1 June 19xx

TO: Marvin Vandencamp

FROM: Connie S. Johnson *csj*

CHANGES IN AFFIRMATIVE ACTION POLICY

What are the new guidelines governing interviewing and
hiring women and minorities?

Because many of the applicants for Director of Communication
are women, I am especially concerned that our screening
practices be objective. Would a complete copy of our
Company policy on Affirmative Action help? If so, please
send me one.

As we will begin screening candidates on 20 June, I would
appreciate your sending appropriate materials by the 10th.

Direct Request. Ask
most important
question first.

Provide any infor-
mation necessary
for the reader to
help you solve your
problem.

Set an end date
when appropriate.

FIGURE 6.5
Sample Inquiry about a Person

North Central University
Pemberton Hall, Mills Road   Ames, Iowa 50012

Graduate Admissions   *515/555-1908*

March 15, 19xx

Dr. Margaret Porter
Management Information Systems
College of Business
California State University
Long Beach, CA 90840

Dear Dr. Porter:

Please use the space below to give us your opinion of Linda M. Mishall's chances of succeeding in graduate school. She listed you as a reference on her application for admission and has waived right of access to your reply.

  --When Linda was your student, did she demonstrate superior academic skills?

  --Did she do her work promptly?

  --How would you rate her in comparison with the other students you have taught: upper 5 percent, upper 10 percent, upper 25 percent, upper 50 percent?

  --What would you predict are her chances for success in graduate school?

Please use the reverse of this form to give us any other information you think will help us decide about Linda's admission to our graduate program. We will keep your reply strictly confidential.

Sincerely,

Calvin Luther III
Director of Admissions

Direct opening followed by the explanation.

Secondary questions in an unnumbered list.

Request for additional information and offer to keep reply confidential.

**FIGURE 6.6
Sample Invitation**

The invitation, in-
cluding purpose,
place, and time.

Explanation and
details.

Request for confir-
mation is last.

═══════ **HOUSTON RENAISSANCE CENTER** ═══════

1 November 19xx

Dear Friend:

Please be our special guests at the grand opening of the
Houston Renaissance Center on Saturday, 14 November, from
10:00 a.m. until 2:00 p.m.

Celebrate our opening with us by enjoying a champagne
brunch and tours of the 67 stores and specialty shops in
the Center. The enclosed SPECIAL GUEST identification
tags will admit you and your family to the Houston
Renaissance Center and the champagne brunch free of
charge.

Come celebrate with us. To help us prepare for you,
please call 555-6000 and let us know whether you plan
to attend.

Cordially,

Larry M. Pettit

Larry M. Pettit, Public Services

enc

FIGURE 6.7
Invitation to Renew
Membership

Greater Rawlins Chapter
ASHD   American Society for Human Development

15 December 19xx

TO: Jack Toole

FROM: Dean Malos, Treasurer *dm*

MEMBERSHIP

You're cordially invited to renew your membership in
the Greater Rawlins Chapter of ASHD. Our yearly dues
are still $10, payable 1 January each year.

Our Chapter has enjoyed a good year, with many fine
programs and a continued exchange of ideas and
suggestions. Our new officers are now making plans
for the coming year. Next year's meetings promise
to be better than ever.

Plan now to attend each meeting, held on the third
Wednesday of the month, September through May.

Please use the enclosed reply envelope to mail
your check.

enc

▷ Direct Claims

Why do most companies welcome complaints?

Requests for refunds, replacements, and adjustments on goods or services can usually be structured as direct messages, because companies know that the only way they can stay in business is by satisfying their customers. Reasonable requests are granted automatically, as long as the letter writer is careful to communicate the reasonableness of the request. Only when your reader has demonstrated an unwillingness to respond to reason or when your request is based on your emotions rather than logic, should you write a persuasive request. Persuasive requests are discussed in Chapter 10.

Show Confidence in the Reader

When you make a claim, your basic assumption should be one of confidence in your reader. You should assume that your reader will do the right thing if you explain the situation accurately. Remember that your reader is not personally responsible for the trouble you have had with the company's product or service, and remember that your reader—and the reader's company—will most likely be pleased to receive information that will permit an improvement in goods and services.

Be Specific

Why should most direct claims include a request for a specific action?

Always make your claim as specific and as definite as you can. When you know what the problem is and what is required to correct it, state the problem explicitly—giving all the details—and ask for the specific correction. When you do not know exactly what is wrong, explain the situation as best you can. Figures 6.8 and 6.9 show the basic technique for writing a direct claim letter when you know exactly what you want. The sample letter shown in Figure 4.1 is an example of a direct claim when the writer does not know what specific action will solve the problem.

▷ Summary

Letters or memos that request goods, services, or information (orders and inquiries) are well received by the reader because they give the reader an opportunity to sell goods or services, build goodwill, or share information about something of common concern. Consequently, this type of message should have a direct structure and is referred to in this text as a *direct request*. The writer's main task with all orders and inquiries is to provide the specific details necessary for the reader to perform the requested action.

**FIGURE 6.8
Sample Direct
Claim**

Begin with a
straightforward,
positive, description
of the problem. As-
sume that your
reader wants to
help.

Give as complete an
explanation of the
problem as possi-
ble.

Close by asking for
what you want. If
you need it by a
certain date, say so.

1400 Barrydowne Road
San Diego, CA 92110

October 4, 19xx

C-Tronics
324 North Woodland Drive
Marietta, GA 30064

Ladies and Gentlemen:

The Ranger pocket calculator in the attached package does
not correctly compute problems containing the number 8.

I purchased the calculator at Dyers two weeks ago, and
the store manager thought that I would receive faster
service by sending the calculator to you.

While it always solves other problems correctly, even
simple problems containing 8 result in a wrong answer.
A simple problem like 2 x 8, for example, can result
in an answer as low as 9 or as high as 108.

As I am an engineer and need a reliable calculator
every day on my job, I would appreciate a prompt
replacement.

Sincerely,

Barbara Pedersen

Barbara Pedersen

**FIGURE 6.9
Sample Direct
Claim**

Timkin Steel Company

1900 Banning Road
Bethlehem, PA 18015
215/555-6164

Interoffice Memorandum

15 August 19xx

TO: Darlene Eerdmans, Purchasing

FROM: Joe Gorzalski, R&D *jg*

SUBJECT: Company Car 114, Voucher 2740

State the problem → Company Car 114 doesn't meet the needs of the R&D department,
first.   Darlene.

Provide a complete → We really need a full-size station wagon with heavy-duty
explanation.   suspension because nearly all our travel includes
                    transporting bulky equipment. The compact sedan
                    described in Voucher 2740 does not have enough cargo
                    space to meet our needs.

Close by asking for → Please assign the sedan to another department and check
what you want.   on the station wagon R&D special ordered on 12 May. Will
                     you give me a call between 9 and noon next Monday to let
                     me know your progress? I'd appreciate it.

att: Voucher 2740

COMMUNICATION SOLUTION

Compare your solution to the Communication Challenge with the one presented here. Be prepared to discuss the differences between your solution and this one. Are parts of your solution better? What makes them better? If parts of your solution are not as good, what could you do to improve them?

Second National Bank
4 East River Drive
Seattle, WA 98104

May 20, 19xx

Ms. Ellen Kuiper
Sales Manager
Coppercase Products
111 Telegraph Avenue
Oakland, CA 94603

Dear Ms. Kuiper:

Begin by introducing the problem. → The three Coppercase modular office systems recently installed in the Second National Bank require an adjustment. They are not reducing noise the way they should. In fact, the panels actually seem to amplify sound, as conversations in one office are easily overheard in the next.

Provide a full explanation. → When the Coppercase representative, Roger Horrein, was called back to Oakland because of a family emergency, he entrusted final assembly to the local crew chief, who then supervised the completion of the office systems. The panels look nice and add a great deal to the appearance of the Bank, and if it weren't for the noise problem, we'd be fully satisfied.

Clarify what you want. → Please have Roger or one of your other field representatives return to the Bank to check the installation and correct the problem. Because the noise is annoying and because so much bank business is confidential, I would appreciate having the problem corrected by the end of the month.

Ask for a specific action. → Please call to let me know when the field representative will be here. If I am not available, leave the message with my secretary.

Sincerely,

Henry Goldbloom

Henry Goldbloom

The general structure for all direct requests is (1) direct beginning, (2) explanation, (3) secondary matters, and (4) who does what next.

When ordering by mail, be sure to (1) specify that your letter is an order, (2) describe the goods completely, (3) state how you intend to pay, and (4) specify where, when, and how you want the goods shipped.

Begin direct requests with your most important question. After you have asked your most important question, provide the reader with the explanation required for a complete answer. Use a numbered list for your questions when they require no explanation or when your questions can be made specific and clear by a single, inclusive explanation following your opening question. To increase your chance of receiving a response when you want it, give an end date and justify it.

Most invitations are a special category of direct requests. When, however, an invitation is to the writer's advantage, it becomes a *persuasive* request and should be written according to the principles in Chapter 10. For invitations that are special goodwill messages involving no persuasion, state the main idea — the invitation — first, and follow it with the explanation and a request for confirmation.

Requests for refunds, replacements, and adjustments on goods and services should usually be handled as direct messages, because companies know that the only way they can stay in business is by satisfying their customers. When you make a claim, explain the situation accurately. Make your claim as specific and as definite as you can. State the problem explicitly — giving all the details — and ask for the specific correction or an investigation.

▷ **EXERCISES**

Review and Discussion Questions

1. What is a direct request? Give four examples.

2. What type of structure does an order or inquiry have? Why?

3. State the general structure for all orders and inquiries.

4. When ordering by mail, you should check your letter for four specific points. What are they?

5. Why do requests for information about people present special hazards? What precautions should you observe?

Problems

1. You and your family are planning a one-week vacation and would like a two-bedroom cabin with kitchen, living room, and bath facilities. Be-

cause the prices listed in the brochure you received are reasonable, write to Scott's Ranch, 1457 Trail Lane, Estes Park, CO 80517, and make reservations. Ask for a confirmation.

2.   Order for your firm, Flair Electric Company, 1204 Milham Road, Hayden, AZ 85235, three Model 239 executive desks, three Model 485 swivel chairs, and one Model 7896 conference table from Bon Office Furniture, 126 Peekstok Road, Phoenix, AZ 85000. The desks are walnut and sell for $675 each. The chairs sell for $110 each. The 12-foot conference table sells for $789. Have the items shipped COD by Ready Truck Lines.

3.   Look over the advertisements in a trade publication or a discount catalog, and write a letter ordering four or five items. Be sure to supply all the necessary information. Enclose a check (simulated enclosure only) for the items, and specify how you want the items shipped. Submit a photocopy of the advertisement for the items along with your letter.

4.   As purchasing agent for Arco Chemical Company, 324 Second Avenue, Midland, MI 48640, order 5 tons of used paper from Ferlinsky Paper Company, 2450 Hillcrest Street, Midland, MI 48640. You want a ton delivered each Monday for five consecutive weeks. Ask for the 5 percent discount for ordering 5 tons or more.

5.   Write to the personal shopper at Marshall Field, One State Street, Chicago, IL 60610, and order three pairs of white Isotone (one size fits all) gloves for Christmas gifts for your friends. Items are to be sent three weeks before Christmas, gift-wrapped, and accompanied with a greeting card. Your charge plate number is 460-14-649. Names and addresses of your friends are

Mrs. Agnes Daly, 4514 Ellenita Avenue, Tarzana, CA 91356
Mrs. Lorraine Blaha, 1521 Merriman Drive, Glendale, CA 91202
Mrs. Joann Reiter, 815 Valley Lane, Lockport, IL 60441

6.   Sandra Kasan, 1409 Morrow Lane, Jud, ND 58454, ordered three $6.50 red cotton T-shirts for her nieces as follows: one size small with the printed name Judi; one size medium with the printed name Becki; and one size large with the printed name Kathy. When Sandra opened the package from the Teen Tee-Shirt Shop, Box 12144, Atlanta, GA 30319, she found one size small with the printed name Becky, one size medium with the printed name Kathi, and one size large with the printed name Judy. Write the shop and ask for replacement of the shirts with the correct sizes to correspond with the correct spelling of the names. Also ask the shop what you are to do with the three shirts that are unacceptable because of improper sizes and incorrect spelling of names.

7.   As president of the Alpha Kappa Psi Fraternity, 735 Fraternity Village Row, Bloomington, IN 47401, write an inquiry to Nicholas Brothers,

1012 Avondale Drive, Louisville, KY 66450, asking about trophies. Ask for descriptions, sizes, and prices. You need to have all the trophies in time for your awards banquet. Is there an additional charge for engraving?

8. You are the office manager of Kiep Associates. You've been looking over your various office forms and realize that they are inefficient. You decide to write a letter to Tripleday Brothers, 222 Douglas Avenue, Marietta, OH 45740, asking for prices and possible delivery dates for the following forms: petty cash disbursements, expense report sheets, requisition slips, interoffice memorandums, and telephone message pads. Do the forms come in various colors? Sizes?

9. You are interested in certificates of deposit. You have heard that the First National Bank in Los Angeles, CA 90242, offers them at interest rates from 9 percent to 13 percent. Write the bank and ask what the minimum deposit is and the number of years the certificates must be held. Is there a penalty for early withdrawal of the money?

10. As Ms. Quinta Mandez, real estate agent, write a letter inviting a prospective home owner to an open house on Sunday, May 5, at 2:00 P.M. The house is at 2317 Outlook Street, Pittsburgh, PA 15202. Write your letter to Marilyn J. Janis, 427 Statler Street, Forest Hills, NY 11375.

CASES

1. Assume that you are the program chairperson for the annual convention of The Association for Business Communication, which will be held two years from this October 20–24. Write the Hilton Inn, 301 Park Avenue, New York, NY 10011, and request information about convention facilities. Because you expect about 500 conventioneers, ask if the inn would be able to accommodate a group this size. How many conference rooms would be available, and what is the seating capacity of each? Does the inn have facilities for serving a banquet? What recreational facilities are available? Is there a charge for meeting rooms? What is the cost for a single room? Double? Suite? Are complimentary suites available for convention officials? What special convention arrangements are available?

2. Paul Apson purchased an 8-ounce package of dried apricots for $2.59 from a local supermarket. When he arrived home and opened the package, he found black "specks" that resembled dead insects. Rather than return the package to the local supermarket, Paul asked you to help him write to the distributor, Foodco Products, 1494 Riverview Drive, Cincinnati, OH 45200, and ask for an explanation and a refund. Write the letter for Paul and return the empty cellophane package with the price marked on it.

3. Sheila Rae Thompson, 411 Whitney Avenue, Louisville, KY 40200, received her monthly statement along with duplicate copies of gasoline and oil purchases from Stancrest Oil Company, 9034 Broadway, Centerville, NE 68724. After checking her copies with the

duplicates, Sheila found a copy dated March 19 for $15.58 that she could not match with her receipts. On the copy she noticed the name Sheila Mae Thompson, 902 Roseland Street, Louisville, OH 44641. Write a letter for Sheila, returning a copy of the duplicate to Stancrest and asking for an adjustment on her next statement.

4. Perhaps you (or someone you know or heard about) have been dissatisfied with a recent purchase. Write a claim letter to the company explaining the situation and requesting action.

5. Write the Foline Linen Company, 200 Spring Street, Dayton, OH 45401. You recently purchased a 52″ × 70″ red-and-white checkered polyester kitchen tablecloth. After the first washing (you followed the washing instructions explicitly), the colors ran together. You want a replacement. Return the original tablecloth to them.

6. Using the information in Problem 5, write to Foline Linen Company and request a refund.

7. Write a letter to a college, university, or graduate school of your choice and ask for information about a specific course of study. Ask about the cost of a school catalog and about the procedure for ordering one.

8. As personnel director of Rimco Manufacturing Company, 3311 Douglas Avenue, Memphis, TN 38118, write to Professor Jamie Summers, Department of Business and Technical Writing, Rensselaer Polytechnic Institute, Troy, NY 12181, and ask about Mark Goodwin, a graduate of Rensselaer, who listed Dr. Summers as a reference. You not only want to know what kind of student Mark was, but you would also like to know how well Dr. Summers knows Mark, how well Mark gets along with others, and something about Mark's attitude toward school and work.

9. As Director of Marketing for Marvelous Plastics Company, 1412 Pico Blvd., Riverside, CA 92521, write to David Wells, Director of Product Development for Marvelous, and ask about the new line of model rocket ships being developed. You will need to know when the new line will go into production, when prototypes will be available, and when the models will be ready for distribution. You should also ask about the features that will help you market the models and about packaging requirements. Use your imagination to come up with appropriate questions about the features model rockets might have.

10. As Director of Personnel for Marvelous Plastics Company (see previous problem), write to the directors of all departments and ask for their employment statistics. You are in the process of compiling your quarterly report on Affirmative Action, and you need to confirm ages and ethnic backgrounds of all Marvelous employees.

11. Answer an inquiry from Mr. Art Capriotti, Western Tape, P.O. Box 69, Mountain View, CA 94042. Mr. Capriotti is inquiring about Ms. Sally VanHoven, who is seeking employment as an administrative assistant. As Sally's former employer, you write and say that for the two years that Sally worked for you, she was dependable, trustworthy, and accurate. She seemed to get along well with her supervisors, her peers, and her subordinates. Sally was an energetic person who was always eager to learn.

12. As a professor of business communication, write a letter to the president of the Kiwanis Club, Mr. Herbert Keenan, 3098 Kingsgate Street, Memphis, TN 38118, telling him that you accept his invitation to speak on "Writing Winning Letters" at the September 12 club luncheon meeting. You will need an overhead projector and screen for your presentation. You plan to speak for 45 minutes and

to allow 15 minutes for questions and answers. The Kiwanis Club should donate your $100 honorarium to its scholarship fund.

13. As a faculty member of the physical education department, you have been asked by the sponsors of the cheerleaders to judge the tryouts. Twelve men and women are trying out, and you and two other judges need to select four persons for next year's squad. Write a letter to the sponsors, Dr. and Mrs. Bruce Kemel, Foothill College, 12345 El Monte Road, Los Altos Hills, CA 94022, saying that you will be happy to be a judge.

14. A friend just wrote to you asking how he or she should go about writing a letter requesting a replacement for a defective cassette tape recorder just purchased through the mail. Using your own words, describe the general procedure your friend should use to obtain a replacement. Put your description into proper format.

15. On your last two visits to Nichols' Department Store, you have been treated rudely by the sales clerks. On Monday, 27 October, you went in the store to buy a pair of shoes. You tried on several pairs but found none that you liked. As you were leaving, the clerk said, "Thanks for wasting my time." On Thursday of that same week, you went in to return a set of towels because the towels had been packed in such a way that you were unable to see that one of the towels was defective, having an orange stain on it. When you requested an exchange or refund, the clerk said, "Don't you think that you're being awfully picky?" Only after several minutes of arguing were you able to obtain a refund. Write a letter of complaint to Mr. Roger Nichols, owner of the department store.

16. Write to a company of your choice and request information about a service or particular line of products. Along with your letter, submit to your instructor the company's reply and your analysis of its effectiveness.

17. As Director of Personnel for the Second National Bank, 14 East River Drive, Seattle, WA 98104, send a memo (on a separate sheet of paper) to Charles T. Alred, Head of the Bank's Legal Department, asking for hiring guidelines in view of recent Affirmative Action legislation and court rulings involving quotas and reverse discrimination. How many people will you need to interview for each opening? How specific must job descriptions and personnel qualifications be?

18. As Director of Personnel for the Second National Bank (see previous problem), write a letter (on a separate sheet of paper) to Gerald J. Oliu requesting information about Veronica Jackson. Ms. Jackson has applied for a job as a teller at Second National and listed Mr. Oliu as her supervisor at the Bank of California, 1492 Columbus Avenue, San Francisco, CA 94110. You should let Mr. Oliu know that Ms. Jackson has applied for a job and that she has waived her right of access to his reply. Offer to keep the information he sends confidential.

19. Find a magazine advertisement for a product or service in which you are interested. Write a letter to the manufacturer requesting additional information. Price, name and address of the local dealer(s), guarantee, service, and specific applications or details of the product or service are some of the items you might ask about. Ask at least five questions and provide any required information. Submit the ad (or a photocopy) with your letter.

20. As the public relations director for the First National Bank, 120 North Cedar Road, New Lenox, IL 60451, write a letter inviting the community—especially people in their fifties and sixties—to attend a free pre-retirement

planning seminar. The letter will be an advertisement in the Sunday edition of the local newspaper. The seminar will be on Monday, September 9, from 7 P.M. to 9 P.M. at the bank. People interested in the seminar may call 555-7879 for more information or to make reservations. The program includes the following topics: reasons planning for retirement is necessary, investments, financial planning (including wills, trusts, and estate taxes), housing, medicare and health insurance, and leisure time and lifestyle. The program will feature discussion groups with an emphasis on an informal, personally meaningful approach to the topics covered.

CHAPTER SEVEN
Conveying Positive Information

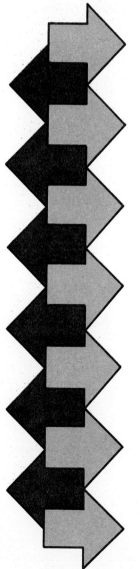

Messages conveying routine or positive information are both the most common messages in business and the easiest to write. Whether you are answering a reader's request or supplying unrequested but positive information, the reader will welcome your message. This chapter presents the techniques for writing typical positive messages.

Topics

Overview: Good News Needs
   No Introduction
General Structure and
   Checklist for Conveying
   Positive Information
Acknowledgments
   Acknowledging Orders

Acknowledging Requests
Announcements
Special Goodwill Messages
Apologies
Transmittals
Summary
Exercises

COMMUNICATION CHALLENGE

How would you respond to the following request for information? Note that the request contains all the information you need to answer, but it is wordy and poorly organized. You will need to locate the writer's critical questions and answer them.

You will be glad to send your report, "The Psychology of Assertiveness," which has been published by your college as a monograph. It sells for $3.50, and your department will be glad to pay the postage.

The report is a one-year study of 142 subjects who underwent assertiveness training during the period of 1984 to 1985. The study begins with their self-analysis at the time of entry in the training program and concludes with their self-analysis one year later.

In addition to sending the brochure, you wish to emphasize your most important conclusions:

1. All applicants increased in positive self-esteem.

2. Those who increased most in self-esteem took part in the eight-week training program requiring out-of-class exercises.

3. Even the participants in the four-hour training programs underwent measurable, positive changes in self-esteem.

4. The cost of the training program did not influence the effect it had on its participants.

Compare your solution with the one that follows the chapter summary.

---

315 Henry Street
Scotch Plains, NY 07076

June 15, 19xx

Dr. Fred L. Kreitner
Department of Psychology
North Central University
Worley Hall, Brighton Road
Ames, Iowa 50012

Dear Dr. Kreitner:

I am a psychology student (graduate) doing research on self-esteem, which, as you know, is a main topic of interest in many schools of psychology these days.

I read (in a current issue of Psychology Today) that you have published a report of a study on assertiveness. As I am now taking a course on the psychology of passivity and aggression, I would like to have a copy of your report, and I'm enclosing $5 to cover the cost of the report and postage.

I am especially interested in whether you learned anything about the relationship between self-esteem and assertiveness and whether self-esteem can be changed (improved) by training.

Thank you in advance for your cooperation.

Sincerely,

Scott W. Kleppner
Graduate Student

◇ OVERVIEW: GOOD NEWS NEEDS NO INTRODUCTION

Whether expected or not, good news is always welcome. Because the good news itself — the subject of the message — creates goodwill, you do not need to focus special attention on the human objective when writing a positive message. In general, your main concern when conveying good news is clarity, so that the reader can immediately tell that the news is good, and so that she or he will know how to take any necessary follow-up action.

Remember to present the information from your reader's point of view, focusing on information that *your reader will consider positive* rather than on information *you consider positive*.

◇ GENERAL STRUCTURE AND CHECKLIST FOR CONVEYING POSITIVE INFORMATION

Why is the human objective less critical in positive messages than it is in negative ones?

Letters and memos conveying positive information may be either reader-initiated (your reader wrote to you first and asked for something) or writer-initiated (you are writing first, and your reader does not expect your message). In either case, when your message contains information to which the reader will respond in a positive way, you should use a direct structure and present the business objective first. The human objective is not critical in positive messages because the reader will welcome the information. Indeed, in a positive message the business objective helps the writer achieve the human objective.

As is true for orders and inquiries (direct requests), the writer's main task in writing messages containing positive information is to convey the information clearly, concisely, and completely. The opening should be positive and direct, placing the message in a specific communication context. The message needs to answer all the questions the reader may have asked and should anticipate questions that may occur to the reader after the message is received. The closing of the letter or memo should either make clear who should do what next and/or help establish a better business relationship.

The general structure for all positive messages is as follows:

1. **Direct opening.** Begin either with a positive answer to one of the reader's questions or with your most important item of information, which may be a summarizing introduction to the rest of the message. The *first* sentence should place the message in a specific communication context by clarifying the purpose of the message.

2. **Explanation.** When an explanation is necessary, it should be in the secondary position, following the important opening statement.

COMMUNICATION TODAY...

Here is one of the best bits of advice ever given about the fine art of human relationships. "If there is any one secret of success," said Henry Ford, "it lies in the ability to get the other person's point of view and see things from that person's angle as well as from your own."

That is so good, I want to repeat it: *"If there is any one secret of success, it lies in the ability to get the other person's point of view and see things from that person's angle as well as from your own."*

That is so simple, so obvious, that anyone ought to see the truth of it at a glance; yet 90 percent of the people on this earth ignore it 90 percent of the time.

An example? Look at the letters that come across your desk tomorrow morning, and you will find that most of them violate this high canon of common sense. Take this one, written by the head of the radio department of an advertising agency . . . (I have set down, in parentheses, my reactions to each paragraph.) . . .

> *"Dear Mr. Blank:*
> *The _____ company desires to retain its position in advertising agency leadership in the radio field."*
>
> (Who cares what your company desires? I am worried about my own problems. . . .)
>
> *"This agency's national advertising accounts were the bulwark of the first network. Our subsequent clearances of station time have kept us at the top of agencies year after year."*
>
> (You are big and rich and right at the top, are you? So what? . . .)
>
> *"We desire to service our accounts with the last word on radio station information."*
>
> (*You* desire! *You* desire. You unmitigated ass. I'm not interested in what *you* desire . . . Let me tell you once and for all that I am interested in what *I* desire. . . .)

Source: Dale Carnegie. *How to Win Friends and Influence People* (New York: Pocket Books, 1962), pp. 37–38.

3.   **Secondary matters.**   Answer any questions your reader may have. In addition to providing specific answers for those questions your reader has asked, you should anticipate and provide answers for questions your readers should have asked but did not. Complete, thoughtful answers show your courtesy and willingness to cooperate. Your explanation and secondary matters should be in a logical sequence, with explicit transitions from point to point. Enumerated (numbered) lists help in the same way they do in orders and inquiries (see Chapter 6).

4.   **Positive close.**   After reading your message, the reader should know who is going to do what next. When no further action is required, you may either stop or use the closing element of the letter to improve the future of the business relationship. When appropriate, resell the product or service the reader has already purchased (*resale*) or sell the reader a new product or service (*new sales*).

◇ ACKNOWLEDGMENTS

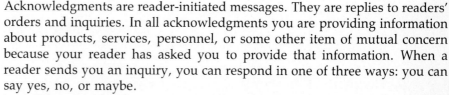

What is a reader-in-
itiated message?

Acknowledgments are reader-initiated messages. They are replies to readers'
orders and inquiries. In all acknowledgments you are providing information
about products, services, personnel, or some other item of mutual concern
because your reader has asked you to provide that information. When a
reader sends you an inquiry, you can respond in one of three ways: you can
say yes, no, or maybe.

When you decide to say yes, use a direct structure to convey the positive
answer. Even when you are not fully satisfied with your positive decision,
take advantage of the situation—and your decision—to build a better business relationship. When you cannot give an immediate positive answer, your
acknowledgment is a negative message, which we will discuss in Chapter 8.

Acknowledging Orders

Readers expect prompt, courteous replies to their requests for goods and
services, and by fulfiling that expectation you can increase the positive feelings your readers have for you and your company. Acknowledgments of
orders are directed toward either dealers or consumers, and—as is true for
all business messages—the writer needs to adapt the message to the particular needs of the audience. The writer also needs to consider the cost of the
acknowledgments relative to the goods or services ordered. It makes no sense,
for example, to send a $9 personalized acknowledgment for a $2 order. On
the other hand, a customer who places a $2,000 order deserves a well-written,
personal reply. Most orders should be acknowledged with a carefully prepared form message that

1. Lets the reader know that the correct merchandise is on its way by
    specifying the items shipped and the method of shipment.

2. Expresses appreciation for the reader's business.

3. Suggests possibilities for future business transactions.

When should you
reply with a printed
form? When should
you use a comput-
erized form letter?
When is an individ-
ually prepared reply
worth the expense?

While printed forms, along with a specific invoice, are effective in many
cases, computerized letters and letters composed from standard paragraphs
stored magnetically (as with modern word processing equipment) are generally more useful because they reduce costs and convey more personal concern for the reader.

Whether you use one of the form replies or a personal letter, be sure
to include as much you-attitude as possible. Resale material, which stresses
the benefits of goods or services already purchased, will help convince the
reader that she or he has made the correct decision. Sales material, which
suggests that the reader would do well to purchase something else from you,
helps reinforce the idea that the business relationship will continue.

Note the way Figures 7.1 and 7.2 adapt the general structure to meet
the needs of different readers with orders of different sizes.

FIGURE 7.1
Printed Form

Specify the merchandise and method of shipment.

Express appreciation for the order. Stress reader benefits.

Resell the product, service, or your business in general.

Suggest possible future business. Sell a new product or service.

Suggest a specific and positive course of action.

Garden of Eden
Mail Order Specialists Since 1974
47 Linwood Avenue, Newton, NJ 07860
1-800-555-1212

May 18, 19xx

Ms. Shirley B. Nord
1400 North Cooper Drive
Arlington, TX 76011

Dear Ms. Nord:

You should receive the merchandise listed on the enclosed invoice in about ten days. We are sending your order by parcel post.

Thank you for your order. We're glad to provide the Mail Shopper service for you.

In addition to the convenience of home deliveries, Mail Shopper gives you an absolute ten-day guarantee on all merchandise ordered through us. We want you to be fully satisfied.

Next month, Mail Shopper's summer white sale will offer you the opportunity to stock up on sheets, pillow cases, and towels. All linens and towels listed in our winter catalog will be reduced 50 percent beginning June 1.

Use the enclosed special "red flag" order blank to order the sale merchandise.

Sincerely,

Gloria Paxon

Gloria Paxon--Catalog Sales

**FIGURE 7.2
Individual Reply**

Royal Papers   *Specialty Papers for Every Use*
852 Rim Crest Drive
La Crosse, WI   54601

May 11, 19xx

Ms. Tarina Wan Salleh
Good Deal Business Center
120 East Prairie Drive
Morehead, KY 40351

Dear Ms. Wan Salleh:

Specify the merchandise and method of shipment. →

You should receive four dozen reams of the Royal Papers specified on the enclosed invoice early next week. As you requested, we sent them by United Parcel Service.

Explain any necessary financial details. →

Your total bill was $288, and the enclosed check for $22 is your refund. Because you paid in advance, you received our 3 percent cash discount, and we paid for shipping and handling.

Express appreciation for the order. Adapt the letter to the interests of your specific reader — dealer or consumer. Resell the product. →

Thank you for your order. Royal Papers is glad to add you to its list of dealers. You'll find that the combination of a quality product and national advertising will make Royal Papers a profitable line for you.

Along with your shipment of Royal Papers, you'll receive 500 copies of a colorful brochure announcing Royal products for distribution to your business friends. The brochure cover carries the embossed name, address, and phone number of your store.

Sell a new product. →

Should you wish to take advantage of our regular terms of 3/10, n/60, complete and return the enclosed credit application. Mr. William McPherson, our sales representative in your area, will be in to see you in about two weeks. He will be glad to help you with store displays and will explain our volume discount to you.

Stress reader benefits. →

Suggest possible future business. →

Another product that would do well in your store is Royal's new line of color-coded memo forms. To receive your samples, complete the enclosed reply card and drop it in the mail.

Sincerely,

Denvern Perotti

Denvern Perotti
Customer Service

enc

Acknowledging Requests

When should a reply to a reader's request attempt to sell a product or service?

Positive acknowledgments of requests fall into three general categories: those that give you the opportunity to sell your goods or services to your reader, those that emphasize positive information but may include some sales material, and those that should contain no sales material. Obviously, if you are in a business that exists by selling products or services, you will want to use every opportunity to increase your chances of making a sale. Before you answer any request for information about your products or services, ask yourself whether you should concentrate on the objective of supplying the information or the objective of selling a product or service.

The two objectives call for different treatment. A message concentrating on supplying the information, even though further sales opportunities may also be mentioned, is a direct message because its true business objective can be stated in the opening sentence. A message concentrating on selling a product or service is an indirect message because its business objective is delayed until the reader is prepared psychologically for your request for action. These replies with sales opportunities that concentrate on the selling objective rather than on the objective of supplying information are *persuasive messages* and are discussed in Chapter 10.

What is the best beginning for a positive reply to a request?

General Procedures.

When you have determined that the communication context does not offer you the opportunity to include sales material, you should still use your acknowledgment of your reader's request to build goodwill. When you can provide what the reader has requested, you should say so in the opening sentence. A positive answer to a reader's question will place the message in a specific communication context and will be of more interest to the reader than statements of receipt or appreciation.

Poor:	We have received your request for a copy of our manual, "How to Assert Yourself on the Job Without Being Fired."
Improved:	Here is your copy of "How to Assert Yourself on the Job Without Being Fired."
Poor:	Thank you for asking me to speak at the monthly meeting of the Marshall Hospitality Chapter of the Professional Secretaries International.
Improved:	I'll be glad to speak at the monthly meeting of the Marshall Hospitality Chapter of the Professional Secretaries International next April.

Be sure to answer all of your reader's questions, including those questions asked explicitly, those implied, and those that should have been asked but were not. Be specific in supplying information, and interpret any facts and figures that may not be absolutely clear to your reader. Should some of your information be negative, deemphasize it by placing it in the middle of the letter. Your closing should be forward-looking and positive. Avoid clichés and statements that show a lack of confidence.

Poor:	If I can be of further service, do not hesitate to contact me.
Poor:	Feel free to call on me again.
Improved:	Call me again when I can help.
Improved:	Let me know when I can help again.
Poor:	I hope that this letter answers your questions.
Improved:	I'm glad to have been of help.

Because the closing lines of the message receive so much reader attention, it is especially important for you to make those lines work for you. Readers tend to ignore clichés, and statements lacking confidence tend to undermine the objectives you are trying to achieve.

Avoid these	**Use these**
I hope	We're glad
We trust	I'll be glad to
Do not hesitate	Write me
If you have any questions	When you're in town
Why not call	Visit our showrooms
Thank you again	You've been a big help

Simple Replies.　　Most acknowledgments without sales opportunities are fairly straightforward — you simply agree to do or provide what your reader has requested, as Figure 7.3 illustrates.

Replies to Claims.　　Positive replies to requests for adjustments and replies to requests for credit require more thoughtful treatment because the reader's ego is more involved in the situation. When the reader has requested an adjustment or credit, she or he has a strong interest in the action you take on the request. Even though your positive reply to the reader's request makes it a direct message, such messages present important human objectives to consider.

FIGURE 7.3
Simple Reply

Timkin Steel Company

1900 Banning Road
Bethlehem, PA 18015
215/555-6164

Interoffice Memorandum

June 10, 19xx

TO: Sally Kurtz

FROM: Pat McNally *pm*

SUBJECT: Affirmative Action Guidelines

When the enclosure or attachment is the reason for writing, mention it first.

The attached summary of Company policy on Affirmative Action will answer your questions about interview procedures.

Answer the reader's specifc questions.

You'll find a list of illegal questions on page 14. Other illegal screening procedures are outlined on pages 5-7.

Avoid cliché endings. The reader may have legitimate questions, but do not suggest that your message is inadequate.

Call me if you have questions about any of the guidelines.

ah

What is the difference between resale and new sales material?

The business objective of a positive reply to a claim is to grant the requested adjustment, but the human objective of restoring the reader's confidence in your company, product, and service is equally important. Positive replies to claims should contain resale (emphasizing the product or service already sold) and some new sales material (emphasizing a new product or service) to demonstrate your confidence in your products and the future of the business relationship. Because the reader is more concerned with the fair and complete resolution of the complaint, too much sales material would be offensive. Figure 7.4 illustrates the basic pattern for a positive acknowledgment of a request.

Replies about People.

Acknowledgments of requests for information about people and credit are usually a matter of completing the forms supplied by the company making the request. Occasionally, however, you will need to write a letter — either because the requester did not supply a form or because the circumstances are sufficiently unusual to make a standard form inadequate.

Why is the term "letter of recommendation" not always appropriate?

Replies to requests for information about people are frequently called *letters of recommendation* because the writer is asked whether he or she would *recommend* that a certain person should be admitted to college, be offered a scholarship or job, be granted credit, and so on. The reader intends to take into account the writer's opinion when making the decision about the person. (The term *letter of recommendation* is not always appropriate, because the writer may choose *not* to recommend the subject of the inquiry. *Letter of reference* is a more accurate term.)

When you can recommend the person in question, your recommendation should be stated immediately. When you cannot, the negative material preventing your recommendation, like all negative material, should be placed in the middle of the letter and in as positive a way as possible. Honesty, however, dictates that negative information that would influence the reader's decision be presented clearly. Letters of reference reflect on the writer and his or her judgments as much as they do on the person recommended or not recommended. Replies to requests about people should state whether the information is confidential and whether it was requested (see Figure 7.5).

What is wrong with saying you are *granting* credit?

Replies about Credit.

Another kind of acknowledgment is a reply to a request for credit. When you have determined that your reader deserves an extension of credit, it is because your reader's character, ability to pay, and business conditions all indicate his or her willingness and ability to handle credit transactions honestly.

Your reply approving the request for credit should acknowledge the reader's having earned the privilege of doing business by credit. Telling the reader that you have *granted* or *approved* credit is condescending. Tell the reader rather that he or she has *earned* credit or that you are *extending* credit based on the reader's reputation. When the credit approval is accompanied by the shipment of goods, you should begin the letter by saying that you

FIGURE 7.4
Positive Reply to a Claim

Direct opening—make the adjustment.

Some resale here, but avoid the specific topic of the complaint. A word of thanks helps build goodwill.

Get the problem out of the way early in the letter. Make any required action easy. Avoid the word "defective" when writing to consumers.

When possible, give a full, honest explanation for the problem.

Resell the product by stressing its features and the benefits the reader will receive.

Your closing should look forward rather than backward. New sales material shows confidence in the future of the business relationship.

Moonbeam Products
P.O. Box 4530, Lagina Hills, CA 92653

Consumer Services
Frank T. Olsen, Director

Mr. Whitney E. Morrison
59 West 12th Street
Liberty, MO 64068

Dear Mr. Morrison:

You will receive a replacement for your Moonbeam Blender 23 in two or three days. It will arrive by United Parcel Service.

Each Moonbeam product is fully guaranteed, and we're glad to make this adjustment for you. Thank you for writing so promptly.

When your new Blender 23 arrives, please send us the original blender so that we can determine the exact cause of the difficulty. Your description leads me to believe that there is a break in one of the motor windings.

One of the ways Moonbeam is able to achieve 23-speed flexibility in the blender you purchased is by using a special motor-winding technique. While our technique is more complex and delicate than that usually found in blenders, it results in superior performance.

The Blender 23 is the best that Moonbeam makes, and its versatility is unmatched. It is the only blender on the market that can whip cream without turning it to butter and fluff egg whites. It is also the only blender that can make peanut butter without requiring additional oil. Your new Blender 23 will make cooking a pleasure for you for many years to come.

Along with your new Blender 23, we're sending a brochure of other Moonbeam products. Each Moonbeam product carries an absolute five-year warranty. The Deluxe Food Chopper shown on p. 23 of the brochure would be a perfect kitchen companion for your blender.

Sincerely,

Frank T. Olsen

December 30, 19xx

**FIGURE 7.5
Sample Reply
About a Person**

North Central University
Axley Hall, Harvey Road   Ames, Iowa 50012

College of Business   *515/555-1685*
Business Education and
Administrative Services

April 1, 19xx

Begin with the rec-
ommendation or
other positive state-
ment.

Mr. Lionel D. Wunsch
Director of Personnel
Sprinkle Equipment Company
333 North Glassell
Olathe, KS 66062

Use first or last
name depending on
how well you know
the person and
NOT on the basis of
age or sex. Tell the
reader how you
know what you
know about the
person.

Dear Mr. Wunsch:

I'm glad to recommend Ms. Carmen Montagano for the job of
secretary to the President of Sprinkle Equipment Company.

When Carmen was my student in a one-semester business communication
course, she consistently demonstrated superior ability, willingness
to work, and a positive attitude. She always did her work on time
and was willing and eager to learn. Her happy, energetic nature
made her a joy to have in class. Carmen demonstrated her ability
to write a variety of business letters in a clear, concise manner
and earned an A for the semester.

Subordinate nega-
tive elements.

Because of her eagerness to complete tasks, Carmen occasionally
did less than accurate work, and she had not yet fully developed
her proofreading skills. She did want to do a job right,
however, and was fully capable of absolute accuracy if its
importance was stressed.

Provide additional
information that
your reader will
find useful.

Since the completion of the course, I have had the opportunity
to know Carmen on a more personal basis. She continues to be
the same cheerful person who brightened my class.

Your closing should
be positive.

I'm certain that Carmen would make an excellent addition to
the offices of Sprinkle Equipment Company, too, and I'm glad to
supply this confidential information at your request.

Sincerely,

Margaret Heckler

Margaret Heckler, Ph.d.

SIDEBAR

Avoid Being Sued

Writers of reference letters and personal evaluations need to remember that the information they provide is not completely privileged (exempt from being sued for libel or slander). If information has been solicited, writers may state what they believe to be true in good faith without worrying about being sued even if something later proves untrue. With unsolicited information, however, writers must be more careful to ensure that the information is true and pertinent.

Suppose, for example, you were asked to provide an employment reference for a sales representative who used to call on your firm. You know that the sales representative had just spent six months in prison, and you had heard that the crime was fraud. If you were to mention fraud in your letter, you would be giving unsolicited information (the inquiry was about employment; you were not asked whether the sales representative had been imprisoned). And if your information proved false, and the sales representative had actually been in jail for drunken driving on a suspended license, you might be held liable for damages. The test would be whether you were careless or malicious in reporting the unsolicited information or whether you were reporting what you believed to be true in good faith.

have sent the merchandise. Sending the merchandise implies the extension of credit, and except for the credit information, a credit approval letter is similar to an order acknowledgment.

When writing to consumers, you should always clarify your credit terms and the procedure for paying. When you are writing to dealers, adapt your language to avoid an explicit explanation of terms the dealer probably already knows.

Figure 7.6 illustrates these points. As shown in the figure, after the explanation of credit terms, you can provide resale and new sales material as for an order acknowledgment.

Messages to individual consumers are essentially the same as those to dealers except that the credit terminology will be different. An individual consumer usually receives a charge card and a "revolving" account that extends limited credit ($500, $1,000, $2,500 and $5,000 limits are typical) based on the person's character, ability to pay, needs, and previous credit experience. Messages approving personal credit accounts need to explain the use of the charge card, the method of billing (usually once a month with an end date and minimum amount due), and the finance charges. Because these messages are often form letters, resale and new sales material are limited to service, the advantages of credit purchasing, and seasonal sales information.

**FIGURE 7.6
Sample Reply to a
Request for Credit**

Send the merchan-
dise.

Welcome the reader
and make clear that
credit is earned, not
granted.

Explain the terms,
but subordinate all
details the reader
should know. Be
explicit about dis-
count savings.

Marian Wood Cosmetics
11 Frontage Road • Milledgeville • Georgia • 31061

January 16, 19xx

Mr. Stanford P. Leland, Manager
Crossoak Center
5545 Morro Blvd.
Lafayette, LA 70504

Dear Mr. Leland:

You should receive the items listed on the enclosed
invoice in time for your Saturday morning sale. We
shipped them by Air Express this morning.

The charges for the cosmetics and air freight total
$460, which we've billed to your new account. Be-
cause of your excellent record of prompt payment,
we're glad to have you as a credit customer.

With our usual credit terms of 3/10, n/60, you
can save $13.80 by paying the discount price by
the date specified on the invoice. The full
amount is due 60 days after the invoice date.

▷ ANNOUNCEMENTS

In what way are announcements similar to invitations?

Messages that announce sales, special events (such as conferences, meetings, formal parties, or other celebrations), and special awards are direct messages because readers will welcome receiving them. When the reader will respond favorably to them, messages that announce changes in policy, procedure, or responsibilities are also direct messages and are usually written in memo form. (Some announced changes in policy, procedures, or responsibility are *mixed* messsages. See Chapter 11).

Because many announcements imply an invitation, they are written in much the same way as invitations. The difference between them is that an invitation always contains an explicit *please attend,* whereas an announcement merely announces the event and suggests that the reader should attend because of the benefits she or he will receive.

Most business announcements are printed or photocopied and are sent to regular customers (frequently charge customers) with the objective of building goodwill. Because they are usually sent to many people at once, business announcements are often prepared as a form and may use a *simulated inside address.* Note the way the first three lines in Figure 7.7 have the appearance of a traditional inside address and use *you* in singular case to refer to the reader.

Announcements sent within the company to co-workers follow the same basic pattern. Common uses for these messages are to announce retirements, parties, staff meetings, promotions, special achievements (board appointments, publications, sales awards, and project completions), policy statements, procedures, new products and services, and changes in benefits. The announcement may go to the entire company or to a specific department. Some of these situations call for personal letters as well.

What is message overload?

Unfortunately, many business people receive so many announcements that they do not read them all. The problem of too many messages is known as *message overload.* To help ensure that your announcements are read (1) announce only truly important events, (2) color-code your announcements for instant recognition, and (3) do not send too many.

While the communication context will, of course, govern the tone and formality of these announcements, they are all direct messages in which the positive, important information is stated first. Explanations and secondary details belong in the middle of the message, and the closing should specify who is to do what next, making the suggested action as easy as possible. These messages frequently use the memo format. See Figure 7.8 for an example.

Because announcements go to groups of people, they are prepared as forms. Very formal announcements (some wedding invitations and new business partnerships) are engraved. Other announcements, depending on formality, are printed or photocopied. Very formal announcements are more a

**FIGURE 7.7
Sample
Announcement**

Gilmore's
515 Suburban Way   DeKalb, IL 60115

April 21, 19xx

Use a simulated in-
side address to
avoid a mailing list
salutation.

> Because you are
> One of Gilmore's
> Special customers...

Specify the who,
what, when, where,
and how. Write to
one reader at a
time.

> We're glad to give you a head start on our annual Spring Sale.
> Tuesday, February 25, from 6:00 p.m. until midnight, you and a
> few other select customers may take advantage of our "by
> invitation only" evening at our downtown store. Simply present
> this letter at the door when you arrive.

Provide necessary
explanation, details,
and sales material.

> As a regular credit customer at Gilmore's, you're entitled to
> something special. This invitation gives you the opportunity
> to shop at leisure, have first pick of the sale items, and
> receive discounts up to 75 percent on nearly everything in
> stock.

Make the action as
easy and as attrac-
tive as possible.

> To make your shopping even easier, we'll provide a free-parking
> pass for you, free babysitting service while you shop, and free
> coffee and cookies. Because you're special...

This sale is for you.

Cordially,

Jeanette Gilmore

Jeanette Gilmore

FIGURE 7.8
Announcement in
Memo Format

Timkin Steel Company

1900 Banning Road
Bethlehem, PA 18015
215/555-6164

Interoffice Memorandum

March 12, 19xx

To: Production Department

From: R. Dan Sallee *R.S.*

Subject: Vacation Schedule

Here is the summer vacation schedule. This year (for a
change) everyone received his or her first choice.

NAME	DATES	SIGNATURE
L. Burry	Jun 19-23	_____
A. Calhoun	Jul 11-15	_____
D. Dowling	Aug 8-12	_____
S. Mazade	Jul 5-9	_____
C. Welborn	Aug 22-26	_____
M. Wheeler	Jul 18-22	_____

Please confirm your schedule by signing your name next to
your dates, and return this sheet to my office by March 26.

matter of etiquette than of business communication and usually use old-fashioned, stylized English. For more information about these announcements, consult a printer or books on etiquette.

▷ Special Goodwill Messages

What kind of message has no specific business objective?

Messages that do not have a particular business objective are known as special goodwill messages because their only purpose is to improve the relationship between writer and reader. These messages can be especially meaningful to a reader precisely because they do not have any other purpose. To include sales material of any sort in these messages would defeat their special goodwill. Typical categories of special goodwill messages are

1. **Messages of congratulation.**   Significant accomplishments, such as promotion, retirement, election to an office, winning a competition, or marriage, deserve special messages of recognition and praise.

2. **Messages of appreciation.**   Whenever someone does you a favor, you owe that person a word of thanks. When the favor is large enough, the person deserves a letter. Many businesses send routine thank-you messages to customers for prompt payment, patronage, or recommendations to others. These messages are most effective when they conduct no business.

3. **Messages conveying season's greetings.**   Special business relationships merit an exchange of greetings at appropriate times of the year. Most businesses limit season's greetings to specially prepared cards.

4. **Messages of welcome.**   Businesses use messages of welcome to make new customers, prospective customers, and new employees feel at home. Messages of welcome should emphasize useful information and a willingness to help the newcomer.

5. **Messages of sympathy.**   Messages extending condolences are difficult to write, but your business friends will appreciate your having cared enough to express your sympathetic feelings. Even though the subject is melancholy and seems negative, messages of sympathy are direct messages. Your reader will already know of the misfortune, so your opening should acknowledge the unhappy event and place your message in the proper communication context. When writing a message of sympathy, take special care to match your vocabulary to the situation. *Greatly distressed*, for example, is more appropriate for a death than a broken toe.

Except for season's greetings, each of these messages requires specific, personal details to be convincing. Messages of congratulation and appreciation should focus on the reader's accomplishment or efforts. Messages of welcome should provide helpful information, and messages of sympathy should mention the deceased person's fine qualities, or, in case of illness or accident, express wishes for a speedy recovery from the specific illness or injury. Your readers will appreciate your awareness that relationships are human as well as business in nature.

▷ APOLOGIES

Under what circumstances is an apology required?

When apologies are called for, they are often positive, direct messages. In many cases, however, apologies are unnecessary because the reader will be more concerned with whether you have corrected the error than with how sorry you are that it happened in the first place. When you can correct the difficulty, you should begin the message with your statement correcting the problem.

Poor: I'm sorry that you were inconvenienced by having to return your Astrosonic clock radio for repairs.

Improved: You'll receive your fully repaired Astrosonic clock radio in just a few days. I've sent it by United Parcel Service. When our technicians examined the radio, they discovered. . . .
[Give a full explanation and provide resale and new sales material.]

Apologies are required when you, your company, or a company representative has made a mistake that cannot be corrected. Having caused a minor inconvenience is not in itself a reason to apologize. People in business and the general public expect things to go wrong once in a while. Nothing—and nobody—is perfect. Faulty products and mistakes are bound to occur. Apologies for solvable problems usually serve no purpose and may be perceived as insincere. When you can solve the problem, solve it. When you cannot solve the problem, apologize.

Apologies are required in the following circumstances:

1.   You have taken too long to answer a letter.

2.   You tried to solve the reader's problem once and failed; the reader had to ask a second time.

3. A defect in your product injured a customer. (For legal reasons you should avoid admitting guilt. Let your lawyer see your message before you mail it.)

4. A representative of your company was rude to someone.

5. A defect in your product was of such a nature that the consumer will not be interested in a correction. (A cockroach in a jar of peanut butter; a dead mouse in a bottle of beer.)

6. A problem in your business operations has cost someone else time, money, and exasperation.

What would be wrong with subordinating an apology by placing it in the middle of a letter and using passive voice?

Why is "I" an appropriate way to begin a letter of apology?

When your reader deserves an apology, put it first in the message. Never try to subordinate an apology by placing it in the middle of a message, and—even more important—*never* apologize at the end of a message. The secondary elements in a message of apology should include a full, positive explanation of the problem, and the closing element should look forward to a positive, continuing business relationship, as Figure 7.9 illustrates. (When an apology is a *negative announcement* and comes as a surprise to a reader, treat it as a negative message as discussed in Chapter 8).

▷ TRANSMITTALS

What is a transmittal?

Letters and memos of transmittal are used to transmit (send) something else—a report, a resume, or some other enclosure—to a reader. A message is a letter of transmittal when the item transmitted provides the principal reason for the letter. In most cases the transmittal begins with a reference to the item transmitted, which places the communication in the proper context.

Here is the report you requested.

Here are the brochures you asked for.

The enclosed schedule, Mr. Swados, shows you what I propose for the summer scouting program.

Be sure to emphasize the importance of the enclosure to the reader rather than the mere fact that something is enclosed (which would be obvious in most circumstances).

Not this: Please find enclosed the descriptive brochure

Not this: I am enclosing a brochure

But this: The enclosed brochure describes

FIGURE 7.9
Sample Apology

Standard Brush Inc.
One Ridgely Place, N.W.
Harverhille, MA 01830
617/555-1210

20 May 19xx

Mrs. Victoria O'Brien
1606 Park Street
Newport, RI 02841

Dear Mrs. O'Brien:

I was sorry to hear that Mr. Myles Malanchuk, a
Standard Brush salesperson, was rude to you.
Thank you for bringing this matter to my attention.
Your letter will help us improve our service.

I will have the field manager talk to the salesperson about his behavior. While I can't explain
his rudeness, I can assure you that Standard
Brush sets high standards for courtesy and expects
every salesperson to meet those standards.

Because you were nice enough to take the time to
write, I'm sending you a complimentary set of
Standard brushes. You'll receive them in about
two weeks.

Cordially,

Stanley Waller

Stanley Waller
Customer Service

Apologize first. Let the reader know that you care. Note *I* and *we* beginnings are appropriate in only a few in-stances. *I'm sorry* is an effective way to begin an apology.

Do what you can to make things better.

When appropriate, do something nice to make the reader feel better.

Why should the reference to an enclosed brochure appear late in a sales letter?

Sales letters transmitting enclosures and letters transmitting resumes are the exceptions. They are indirect rather than direct messages and do not refer to the enclosure until late in the letter (see Chapter 10).

The secondary elements of a typical transmittal letter explain or summarize the contents of the item transmitted, and the closing element specifies who is to do what next, as Figure 7.10 illustrates.

◊ SUMMARY

Letters or memos conveying information are either reader-initiated or writer-initiated. When your message contains information to which the reader will respond in a positive way, you should use a direct structure and present the business objective first. Human objectives are not critical in positive messages because the reader will welcome the information. The general structure for all positive messages is (1) direct beginning, (2) explanation, (3) secondary matters, and (4) positive close.

Acknowledgments are responses to specific requests. In all acknowledgments, you are providing information about products, services, personnel, or some other item of mutual concern because your reader has asked you to provide the information. When a reader sends you an inquiry, you can say yes, no, or maybe. When you decide to say yes, use a direct structure to convey the positive answer. When you cannot give a direct positive answer, your acknowledgment is a negative message.

Readers expect prompt, courteous replies to their responses for goods and services, and by fulfilling that expectation, you can increase the positive feelings your readers have for you and your company. Most orders should be acknowledged with a carefully prepared form letter that (1) lets the reader know that the merchandise is on its way, specifying the items shipped and the method of shipment, (2) expresses appreciation for the reader's business, and (3) suggests possibilities for future business transactions.

Positive acknowledgments of requests fall into three general categories: those that give you the opportunity to sell your goods or services, those that emphasize positive information but may include sales material, and those that should contain no sales material. A message concentrating on supplying the information is a direct message because its true business objective can be stated in the opening sentence. A message concentrating on selling the product or service is an indirect message because its business objective is delayed until the reader is prepared psychologically for the request for action.

Acknowledgments of requests for information about people and credit are usually a matter of completing forms supplied by the company making the request. When you write a positive letter of reference, your recommen-

**FIGURE 7.10
Sample Letter of
Transmittal**

America First Insurance
945 Cloverdale • Normal, IL • 61761-7443

15 March 19xx

Mr. Darrin Swados
620 West Ringold Street
Freeport, IL 61032

Dear Mr. Swados:

Direct opening.

The enclosed schedule, Mr. Swados, shows you what
I propose for the summer scouting program.

Explanation and
summary of high-
lights.

The three weekend outings--11-12 June, 9-10 July,
and 30-31 July--will prepare the boys and girls for
the week-long Jamboree scheduled for 13 to 20
August.

As the schedule shows, on each of the weekends
and during the Jamboree, nearly all of the scouts'
time will be structured and supervised.

Specify who should
do what next.

When I receive your approval and suggested changes,
I will have the schedule printed and distributed
to area leaders.

Let me know what else I can do to help.

Cordially,

Craig Oosterhouse

enc

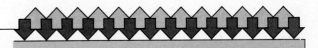

COMMUNICATION SOLUTION

This chapter's Communication Challenge is best solved with a letter of transmittal. The reader wants your report, and you are sending it to him. That is the best place to begin. Compare your solution to the one presented here.

North Central University
Worley Hall, Brighton Road   Ames, Iowa 50012

Department of Psychology   *515/555-0095*

6 July 19xx

Mr. Scott W. Kleppner
315 Henry Street
Scotch Plains, NY 07076

Dear Mr. Kleppner:

Transmit the report. Refund the extra.

Here is the report you requested on the "Psychology of Assertiveness." The cost of the report is $3.50. The enclosed check for $1.50 is your refund.

Provide the necessary explanation.

The enclosed report contains a one-year study of 142 subjects who underwent assertiveness training in 1984-85, beginning with their self-analysis at the time of their entry in the training program and concluding with their self-analysis one year later.

List the secondary information.

For the purposes of your study, Mr. Kleppner, the most interesting aspects of the study are the following:

1. All applicants increased in positive self-esteem.

2. Those who increased most in self-esteem took part in the eight-week training program requiring out-of-class exercises.

3. Even the participants in the four-hour training programs underwent measurable, positive changes in self-esteem.

4. The cost of the training program did not influence the effect it had on its participants.

Keep the ending positive and forward-looking.

Let me know when I can help again.

Cordially,

Fred L. Kreitner

w

enc

dation should be stated immediately. When you must respond negatively, place the negative material in the middle of the message and state it in as positive a way as possible.

A message approving a request for credit should acknowledge the reader's having earned the privilege of doing business by credit. When the credit approval is accompanied by the shipment of goods, you should begin the message by saying that you have sent the merchandise. Sending the merchandise implies an extension of credit.

Messages announcing sales, special events, and special awards are direct messages because readers will enjoy receiving them. Messages that do not have a particular business objective are known as special goodwill messages because their only purpose is to improve the relationship between writer and reader. No sales material should be included with them.

When apologies are called for, they are positive, direct messages. When you can correct the difficulty, you should begin the message with your statement correcting the problem. When you cannot correct the difficulty, apologize first and then make a positive, forward-looking statement.

Letters and memos of transmittal are used to transmit something—a report, a resume, or some other enclosure—to a reader. A message is a letter of transmittal when the item transmitted provides the principal reason for the letter.

▷ EXERCISES

Review and Discussion Questions

1.   What is the general structure for all positive messages?

2.   What information should be included in letters acknowledging orders?

3.   In acknowledging requests, when do you use a direct structure? An indirect structure?

4.   Name the various categories of special goodwill messages. What is the purpose of these messages?

5.   When are apologies required?

6.   When do you use a transmittal? Are letters and memos of transmittal direct or indirect messages? Why?

7.   What is wrong with the following letter?

LAMDA
Lamda Music Division

February 1, 19xx

Roger P. Wilcox
1108 Briarcliff Drive
Urbana, IL 61801

Dear Mr. David Perry

Thank you for your letter informing us of the defective
product which you have returned to us for replacement.

Enclosed, please find your replacement at no charge.

We trust this arrangement will meet with your approval
and maintain your faith in LAMDA products.

Very truly yours,

LAMDA MUSIC DIVISION

Leonard J. W. Tait
Supervisor
LMD Quality Assurance

LJWT:rsd

Problems

1. Because of your expertise in business communication, you have been asked to speak to the English classes at your local high school. Although accepting the invitation means that you will be responsible for speaking for about 40 minutes (and a 10-minute question-and-answer period) to five English classes beginning at 9:00 A.M. and ending at 3:00 P.M., you are willing to take the time because of the importance of the topic. The dates you have been offered, however, are not convenient. You were given a choice of November 14, 15, or 16, and you have important appointments on these days. You would be glad to visit the classes on November 17 or 18. Write your letter of acceptance to Mr. William Atkins, English Coordinator, Houston High School, 7722 Braesview, Houston, TX 77071.

2. Mr. Atkins (see preceding problem) has again asked a favor. This time he would like to borrow several issues of *The Journal of Business Communication* to show his students. You agree to lend him five issues. You want them back in about three weeks so your own students can use them to research their team projects. Write the letter and send the journals separately by parcel post.

3. As owner of the Wilkins Real Estate Agency, 498 Kilbourn Avenue, Provo, UT 84602, you decide to write a letter of welcome to all newcomers to your home town. For a fee, the Chamber of Commerce furnishes you with a list of newcomers. Because you receive a limited number of names, you will compose a form letter but will write as if you were addressing each person individually. So that your readers will remember you and your firm when they decide to look for a home, you want your letters to be of real service. Provide the most useful information about your community. You will also enclose a map of your home town provided by the Chamber of Commerce. Write a letter of welcome to Mr. and Mrs. Charles Cowman, 451 Grandview Drive, Kirkland, WA 98033.

4. It is your job as sales manager for Tot Toy Shop, 6437 Pierce Street, Albia, IA 52531, to acknowledge the order received from Mrs. Dolores Dahl, 2311 Curtis Court, Benton, KY 42025, for the following items: two model FX 1186 Fox Super Sport Trainers, one Tonka Mighty Grader, and three 12″ Musical Lullabye Baby Dolls. Tell Mrs. Dahl that she'll have the items in time for Christmas.

5. Assume that you are an assistant to the sales manager of the Oaks Pharmaceutical Company, 150 Spring Street, Euclid, OH 44717. You just received a request from Wyer's Pharmacy, 9714 Washington Avenue, Providence, RI 02911, for a gross of 2-ounce bottles of desiccated liver pills, 12 tubes of O-P medicated shaving cream, and 24 8-ounce bottles

of O-P cough syrup. Acknowledge the order. Tell how and when ship-ment will be made.

6. Write a letter to Mrs. Irene Tarkinson, Tarkinson Clothiers, 408 Hen-derson Avenue, Boston, MA 02109, telling her that you'll be shipping her order for the following:

1 doz Style 33 K391 100% Quiana nylon, panel pattern tie, blue and rose.
1 doz Style 33 K392 100% Quiana nylon, panel pattern tie, green and rust.
1 doz Style 33 K393 100% Quiana nylon, panel pattern tie, silver and brown.

Tell how and when you plan to ship the items.

7. After 26 years with National Incorporated, Allyn Bacon, Senior Auditor, is retiring. Announce his retirement to the staff of the home office. Be sure to include a brief history of his major accomplishments at National and his plans for retirement. Use a separate sheet of paper for your message.

8. As the manufacturer of glass and aluminum containers, your company, Spartan Bottle and Can Company, 83 Lincoln Avenue, Hammond, LA 70401, receives a great many letters from ecology-minded people who complain about the harmful effects of your throw-away bottles and alu-minum cans. They complain about the waste of glass and metal re-sources and the waste of energy caused by continual production of new containers that will be used only once and thrown out. Until recycling technology improves, however, manufacturing new containers is less expensive than recycling, and most consumers prefer the convenience of no-deposit, no-return containers. Your company does not condone littering or other misuse of your products. Write a form letter to send to people who write letters of complaint about your lack of concern for the environment.

9. As the director of public relations for Majestic and Taylor, write a form thank-you letter to be sent to your regular charge customers around the country. Because you have stores in 15 major cities, you will need to avoid regionalisms—references to particular cities, climates, or styles appropriate for one region only. Majestic and Taylor specializes in fine fashions for men and women.

10. As personnel director of Midwest Insurance Company, 5167 South Main Street, Charleston, IL 61920, write a form letter to send to the benefi-ciaries of life insurance policies held by your company. The beneficiaries may collect the money from the policy in either one lump sum or monthly installments. Or if the beneficiary prefers, you will hold the money—invested at 9 percent a year—until he or she wishes to collect. Such an arrangement can help with children's college expenses or the benefici-ary's own retirement.

CASES

1. Mr. Patrick Busey, owner of Central Hardware, 980 Landau Avenue, Hattiesburg, MS 39401, has ordered $800 worth of 10-gauge electrical wire from you (Williams Die Casting and Wire Company, Bainbridge, GA 31717) and has requested rush shipment. You called Busey's credit references, who confirm that he always pays his bills on time. Busey needs the rush shipment because a new Crunchy Cereal factory is being constructed in Hattiesburg, and the construction will require a great deal of electrical wiring. Send the wire by United Parcel Service, and extend Busey a $1,500 line of credit with terms of 2/10, n/30. Tell Busey that you also make high quality 12- and 14-gauge electrical wire, and encourage his future business.

2. Mrs. Adrienne Balboa, 1927 Highland Avenue, Durango, CO 81301, applied for a revolving charge account with a $5,000 line of credit with your store, Crepe's of Chicago, 7500 S. Pulaski Road, Chicago, IL 60652. Your credit check reveals that Mrs. Balboa is sometimes a little slow to pay, but she always pays eventually. You decide to grant her credit, but limit her to $1,500. You also want to remind her that the finance charge on revolving accounts is high (1½ percent on the unpaid balance every month or 18 percent a year). Encourage prompt payment. You will also include some standard paragraphs describing your personal service, exclusive merchandise (everything a woman could want), and your custom-made jewelry. Tell her, too, that your new mail order catalog is now being printed and that you'll send it in about ten days.

3. Your company, J & J Ballbearings, 410 East River Drive, Ames, IA 50011, has grown large enough that you have purchased group health insurance for your 35 employees. The new policy provides coverage for all hospitalization and doctor's office calls up to $100,000 for each off-the-job accident or illness. (On-the-job accidents are covered by your Worker's Compensation policy.) In addition, the policy pays for 80 percent of all prescribed medication costs. To qualify for the benefits, your employees will need to complete a medical expense form (a sample of which you will enclose with your letter) for each accident or illness. Your employees will also need to send the *original* bill for medical treatment or the *original* copy of their receipts for prescription drugs. Marcia Miller in personnel will help with claims. You should remind them to keep a copy of any bills and receipts for their own records. Write a form letter to be mailed to each employee at home.

4. As Luella Fritzler, manager of customer relations for World Insurance Inc., you receive several inquiries a day for information about your various insurance packages for health, auto, life, and home. Even though your national advertising instructs people to call or visit their local World agent, they write to you because they are afraid that your agents will pressure them into buying insurance that they do not really want. Prepare a letter that will explain that:
   a. You have forwarded their inquiries to a local agent (give a specific name and address).
   b. The agent is in a better position to help them because he or she can better determine their individual needs.
   c. World agents do not use high-pressure techniques but are genuinely concerned with providing the kind of coverage that will ensure lasting satisfaction.
   While the letter will be prepared as a form letter, each person will receive a personal copy. Send a sample letter to Becky Giffin, 369 Indian Mound, Cincinnati, OH 45212. Enclose a brochure describing World Insurance package coverage.

5. As Gerald J. Oliu (See Problem 18 in Chapter 6), answer the letter asking about Veronica Jackson, who worked as a teller for you

for five years while her husband completed graduate school. Ms. Jackson was an excellent teller. In the five years she worked for you, she never missed a day because of illness, she was never late, and she rarely took personal time. She was friendly, helpful, and accurate in her transactions. You would have liked to have kept her, and she would undoubtedly have been promoted to branch manager had she decided to stay in San Francisco. Use a separate sheet of paper for your answer.

6. Your boss, Susan Silverman, is the new head of the Public Relations Department in your company, InfoShare, an electronic information service (One By Land Avenue, Boston, MA 02116). Her first assignment to you was for you to prepare a scrapbook containing copies or photocopies of all the news stories about InfoShare you could find.

   The previous head of the department did not believe in systematic record keeping, so you have had to go back through five years worth of newspapers (especially *The Wall Street Journal, New York Times,* and *Boston Globe*), trade publications, computer magazines, newsweeklies (*Time, Newsweek, U.S. News and World Report*) and business magazines (*Business Week, Forbes, Barons,* and *Fortune*). But your five weeks of work have paid off, and you have a collection of more than 600 articles that mention InfoShare, beginning with its inception five years ago up through last week's feature article in *Business Week.*

   You have placed either the original (when the original copy was yours) or a photocopy (when you had to borrow from the library) in a scrapbook, arranged in chronological order. Each entry includes the bibliographic data so that the document could be relocated if necessary.

   Send a memo to Susan along with the scrapbook, letting her know what you have accomplished.

7. Susan Silverman, your boss at InfoShare (see previous problem) has asked you to answer a letter of complaint from one of InfoShare's customers. It seems as though something went wrong with your billing procedure, and for the first week in March, many customers were charged a higher rate than they should have been. For one reason or another, your billing computer automatically charged everyone at the 1200 baud rate of $10 an hour instead of the 300 baud rate of $5 an hour, regardless of which speed they had used.

   Conchita Marano (Member ID Number: 4001-72212) caught the mistake in her billing and complained using your "Electronic Feedback" service. For that week in March, she has 12 hours of connect time billed at the incorrect rate. Prepare a message for Conchita telling her that you will credit her account for the amount of the overcharge. Also, thank her for bringing the problem to your attention. More than 500 of your customers were affected, and her complaint has allowed you to correct their charges as well. To show your appreciation, you will provide her with 10 hours of free connect time. Send your message electronically using memo format. (Remember to prepare hard copy for your instructor.)

8. As Ms. Betty Levy, Manager, Consumer Relations, Kool Kola Company, 286 Greencrest Drive, Wilmington, NC 28401, you have just received a letter of complaint. You have been making Kool Kola for more than 20 years, and while you have received a few letters of complaint, the one you received today is the nastiest you have ever read. Using unrepeatable language, your customer informed you that he discovered a partially smoked cigar in a bottle of Kool Kola. Chemical analysis of the cigar (which the customer enclosed, telling you what you could do with it) revealed that the cigar indeed had been extinguished in the bottle of Kool Kola before

the bottle was capped. You suspect that one of the workers you had to lay off because of a business downturn about three months ago was responsible. Write a letter to Mr. John Pauley, 307 W. Brooks, Norman, OK 73069, and explain the situation in a way that will help reestablish his good feelings about Kool Kola.

9. You are Edward LaMere, Personnel Manager of Micro-Electronics, 6321 Natural Bridge Road, St. Louis, MO 63121. You and the other managers decide that you could improve company morale and reduce personnel turnover by writing letters commending employees on their noteworthy community accomplishments. The company has two employees who deserve special recognition. Write letters to them.

   a. Ms. Judy Williams, 1107 Darton Avenue, St. Louis, MO 63121, who works in your word processing center, just completed her college degree by taking courses at night. She has demonstrated a lot of initiative and perseverance and is now eligible for a promotion. She should come see you and fill out the proper forms so she can be considered for a job as administrative assistant or secretarial supervisor.

   b. Mr. Thomas Ryan, 601 South Union Street, St. Louis, MO 63121, who supervises circuit board assembly, was recently credited with saving the lives of a St. Louis family. He was on his way home from the company bowling tournament when he spotted smoke coming out of a house. He immediately stopped, turned in the fire alarm, and with disregard for his own safety, broke the bedroom windows and helped rescue the residents who were overcome by the smoke.

10. When you applied for a part-time writing and editing job to help pay for your college expenses, you listed one of your professors, Dr. Francis W. Weeks, Chairman, Division of Business and Technical Writing, University of Illinois, Urbana, IL 61801, as a reference. Upon being hired for the job, you learned that Dr. Weeks had written an excellent letter of recommendation for you, which was the main reason you were hired. Write a thank-you letter to Dr. Weeks.

11. In your job as dean of the College of Business, Western Kentucky University, Bowling Green, KY 42101, you are frequently asked to write letters recommending students for employment. Each letter must be individually written to be effective. For each of the students, you need to discuss academic achievement, participation in Alpha Kappa Psi (a well-known business fraternity), participation in other paraprofessional activities (Marketing Club, Administrative Management Society, Finance Fraternity, Women in Business, and Pi Omega Pi), and personal qualities. Write a letter recommending Ms. Susan Tice for a job as administrative assistant at Gibson Guitar Company, 225 Parson Street, Kalamazoo, MI 49001. Her qualifications are a straight-A average in her major, administrative services, and an A− average in her minor, general business. Her all-university average is B+. She has an admirable list of extracurricular activities, including membership in Alpha Kappa Psi. She has also served as president, vice-president, and treasurer of Pi Omega Pi. In addition, during the four years she was in college she worked part-time as a secretary in your office to finance her education. She is personable and well-qualified for the administrative assistant's job. As the letter will be placed in Susan's placement file, address it *To Whom It May Concern.*

12. As P. K. Dresser, owner of Johnson Moving and Storage Company, 442 Broadway Street, Lincoln, NE 68516, you receive the following letter:

   I believe that I'm entitled to a partial refund on the moving job Johnson Moving and Storage did for me Friday, 23 August 19____.

As you can see from the enclosed copy of the bill, I was charged for 5 hours, and I should have been charged for 3 hours and 45 minutes. The bill shows that the driver left your warehouse at 7:00 a.m., but he didn't arrive at my house until 8:15, even though my house is less than one mile from your warehouse. I don't mind paying for the driver, his assistant, and the truck while they were working to move me, but I strongly object to paying for the time the driver and his assistant took to have a leisurely breakfast before they began work.

Please send my refund of $85 to my new address: 1127 Rambling Road, Lincoln, NE 68516.

You agree that the customer, Mr. Johnny Rankin, deserves a refund. The refund, however, will be $50 for the unnecessary hour. You are going to charge him at your usual rate ($50 an hour) and include a reasonable amount of transportation time. You investigate and discover that the reason for the delay in your driver's reaching Mr. Rankin's home was that the moving van broke down, and it took the company mechanics nearly an hour to fix it. Mr. Rankin should not have been charged for that time, and you are glad that he has given you the opportunity to correct the error.

13. Mr. Rodney Stipes, 1441 Banbury Lane, Austin, TX 78700, wrote to you because the fine bone-china imported tea set he purchased thorugh your store (Pier 4 Imports, 1700 Aberdeen Street, San Francisco, CA 94133) was broken in shipment. The tea set (valued at $400) was insured, and you are immediately sending a new set. Because of your experience with Mr. Stipe's set, you will use an improved carton and additional packing for all future shipments.

14. As Henry Bixby, owner of Bixby Imports, 703 Linck Street, Cazenovia, NY 13035, you've just received a call from Mr. James Richards, P.O. Box 691, Indiana Hills, CO 80454, who told you that two months ago he ordered a Spanish silver serving tray for the twenty-fifth anniversary of his sister and her husband, Mr. and Mrs. William Grady, 422 Summit East,

Seattle, WA 98102. Mr. Richards did not receive a bill for the purchase and became curious. Mr. Richards called his sister to see whether the gift had arrived. It had — gift-wrapped, accompanied by an anniversary card and a bill for $497 plus $18 COD charges. Mr. Richards has sent the Gradys a check to cover the cost, and he wants you to send them a letter of apology and full explanation. You investigate and discover that the tray was sent COD because Mr. Richard's name did not appear on the order slip and the Gradys did not have a charge account with the store. You will redesign your order forms to show both the person to be billed and the person who is to receive the merchandise. Write letters to the Gradys and to Mr. Richards. Send Mr. Richards a copy of your letter to the Gradys and refund the COD charge. Send an appropriate memo to your purchasing department so that new forms can be ordered.

15. As personnel director of Indiana State Bank, Bloomington, IN 47401, write to Ms. Mary Lou Berard, 469A Nobles Hall, Bloomington, IN 47401. Ms. Berard is an honors graduate in finance and banking from Indiana University in Bloomington, and you want to invite her to an interview. You wish to see her at 10 A.M. on June 2. You will interview her and then introduce her to the officers of the bank. At noon, you and the bank president will take her to lunch. Write the appropriate messages.

16. As Ms. Alice Harris, manager of consumer relations at Natural Foods Inc., 1906 Cheshire Lane, Greeley, CO 80631, write a letter of apology to Mr. Herman Grotzinger, who found a (dead) cockroach packed in a box of your 100-percent whole-grain cereal. Use information about your favorite cereal to provide appropriate resale material.

17. Your secretary has just brought you a letter more than six months old. How the letter got lost and where it has been are a mystery. It

is from a new and important customer, Mr. Curtis Matthews, General Manager, Rollin Manufacturing Incorporated, 4242 Western Avenue, Superior, WI 54880. In the letter Matthews says that if he can have immediate written confirmation that your company, Williams Tool and Die, Main and Race Streets, Emporia, KS 66801, can supply the required machine parts, Rollin Manufacturing will be eligible for a large government contract. Matthews clearly states that he wants your letter — and not a phone call — in seven days. If he does not have your letter by then, he will have to take the business to another firm. Write a letter to Mr. Matthews, apologizing for your late response, and try to win his future business.

18. As sales manager for Toastie Cereals Inc., 8450 Ravine Road, Battle Creek, MI 49000, you receive a letter from Mrs. Agnes Richards, 1133 Benjamin Road, St. Louis, MO 63122, who enjoys your natural cereals but says she does not understand why the boxes of this cereal are only three-fourths full when she opens them. Write Mrs. Richards and explain to her that each box of cereal you produce does contain the weight specified on the box and is full when it leaves the plant, but because of the settling of the cereal flakes during shipment and handling, some of the boxes may appear to be not quite full.

19. As head of payroll, you have the task of computing sick leave and vacation days accrued by each person in your firm. Because you have recently switched computer systems, you want to double-check the figures entered for all employees. Prepare a memo to send to department heads, which they should then route to each employee in their departments so that each person can check his or her own record. If both sick leave and vacation time are correct, the employee should sign in the space provided. If either sick leave or vacation time is incorrect, the employee should make an appointment with Lester Salisbury, your assistant.

20. As the head of the marketing at Olsen Graphics Company, 711 Suffolk Place, Streamwood, IL 60103, you conduct year-end performance appraisal interviews with each of your 12 staff members. The past year you have had a high turnover in staff, and your 7 new staff members might feel threatened by the upcoming interviews. Write a memo to your staff that, in addition to setting up specific times for the interviews, will convince the new staff members that the interviews are designed to help them by answering questions, establishing goals, and identifying problems.

CHAPTER EIGHT
Conveying Negative Information

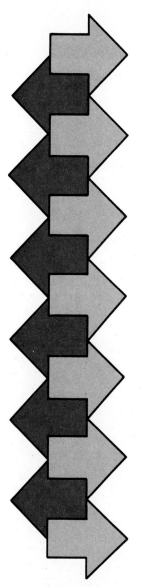

Any message that will hurt the reader's feelings or cause her or him to lose face is a negative message. To keep hurt feelings to a minimum, the writer should provide enough psychological preparation for the reader to understand the reason for the negative aspect of the message. This chapter discusses the strategies for writing typical negative messages.

COMMUNICATION CHALLENGE

As the director of financial aid for Major University, you are responsible for administering several hundred graduate teaching and research assistantships and fellowships each year. So that all awards can be made and accepted by the start of the school year (which will be September 10 this year), you must receive the applications by May 1. You automatically inform those whose applications are late that they have missed the deadline and encourage them to reapply next year. Send such a letter to Ms. Susan Sanheim, 3110 Bobolink Lane, Woodland Hills, CA 91371, whose application you received on May 8.

▷ OVERVIEW: PREPARE THE READER FOR BAD NEWS

In old movies bad news is often preceded by the advice to "have a seat" — perhaps so that the person would not have far to fall when the bad news was delivered. While most people do not faint when they receive a negative message, the proper psychological preparation can reduce the negative impact of bad news.

Untrained business writers are tempted to forget that psychological preparation is as important in a letter as it is when the bad news is delivered in person. For this reason, messages conveying negative information are usually longer and require more careful preparation than positive messages. They are *indirect* rather than direct messages. Two main concerns of such messages are to deliver the right kind of psychological preparation and the right amount.

In general, the amount of psychological preparation needed depends on how deeply the reader's feelings will be hurt. How personal is the negative information? The more the negative information concerns the reader as a person, the greater the need for psychological preparation. Your refusing an order because you are out of stock will not hurt a reader's feelings as much as your refusing to extend credit, for example.

What do you say to someone before you deliver bad news? The best preparation you can provide is a logical and believable reason for the negative message, clearly indicating that it is in the reader's best interest. If the situation does not allow that approach, at least show that your reason is legitimate.

Help your reader save face when the reason for the negative message involves his or her shortcoming. If possible, show the reader how to compensate for the shortcoming, or suggest a positive alternative to the negative situation. The fact that a positive alternative exists, however, cannot be offered as a reason for a refusal. The advantages of buying with cash (discounts), for example, are *not* a reason to refuse credit.

How would you solve this chapter's Communication Challenge? Try writing a draft of a solution now and then revise it as you read this chapter. Compare your final solution to the one that follows the chapter summary.

▷ GENERAL STRUCTURE AND CHECKLIST FOR CONVEYING NEGATIVE INFORMATION

What makes a message negative?

The reader's response determines whether a message is negative. Even though a message may contain negative information, it is not a negative message unless its business objective will anger, upset, or hurt the feelings of the reader. Use an *indirect* structure for this type of message. Because the human objective is critical here, you need to emphasize it.

The writer's main task in conveying negative information is to present it in a way that will help the reader preserve a positive self-image and maintain the reader's positive attitude toward the writer and the writer's company.

Why is an indirect structure used for a negative message?

An indirect structure helps prepare the reader for the negative aspect of the message by placing the emphasis on the reasons for the negative decision and, where possible, on the positive alternatives to the original course of action. It places greater emphasis on the feeling content (human objective) of the message than on the subject content (business objective).

It is very important to present negative messages with confidence. Because you should send a negative message only when you are fully convinced that you have made the correct decision, explain the decision with confidence. Assume that your reader will understand and accept your point of view if you explain it adequately. Never apologize for a negative decision,

Why should you avoid apologizing for a negative decision?

and do not imply that you wish you could have done otherwise (*I really wish I could, but*). Focus instead on the rightness of your decision and on the other courses of action available to the reader. Remember, you are saying no because it is a good business decision. You and your reader should both benefit from what may seem negative. A loan denial, for example, usually means that the reader would risk loss of his or her credit rating if extended credit.

The general structure for all negative messages is as follows:

1. **Indirect opening.** Deal first with the human objective — retaining the reader's goodwill. Delay your presentation of the business objective — the negative message. Begin with something the reader will respond to positively, but be sure to place the message in its specific communication context. Find something to agree with, pay the reader an honest compliment, give a positive answer to one of the reader's questions, or — as a last resort — thank the reader for having written to you. Do not mislead the reader into thinking that the letter will contain

COMMUNICATION TODAY...

A Few Ways to Say 'No'

How you say "no" plays a vital part in whether or not the outcome will be successful. Here are a few ways that work. Pick the ones that best suit you and the situation.

Follow the "no" with a straightforward explanation of what you are feeling or willing to do. *Examples:* "I'm uncomfortable doing that." "I'm not willing to do that."

Offer an alternative after saying "no." *Example:* "I don't have time today, but I could help you out first thing in the morning."

Clarify your reasons after saying "no."

But avoid giving long-winded excuses or rationalizations. Just provide the other person with more information to better understand your position.

Say "yes," then give your alternative solution. *Example:* "Yes, I'd be willing to go along with your second idea but not with the first one you suggested."

Make an empathetic listening statement, *then* say "no." *Example:* "I can see that it's important to you that one of my secretaries get your report done. I'd like to have someone do it, but my staff is already overburdened with . . ."

Source: Madelyn Burley-Allen, *Managing Assertively: How to Improve Your People Skills*, (New York: John Wiley & Sons, Inc., 1985). Reprinted with permission.

positive information, but also avoid giving the negative aspect away too soon. The words *however, but, although,* and *even though* indicate a turn for the worse. An indirect opening is frequently called a *buffer beginning* because it "buffers" the negative business objective that follows.

2. **Explanation.**   Give good, logical reasons in a positive way. Whenever possible, connect the reasons to a long-term reader benefit (for example, keeping prices low, providing better service to all customers, receiving the exact item of choice, or avoiding credit difficulties). Be sure to give *real* reasons rather than hiding behind company policy or the small print in your warranty. When giving more than one reason for the negative message, provide some rational transition from reason to reason. But avoid overkill: If one of your reasons is an absolute, you do not need to list all the other reasons you have for your decision. When you do not have all the facts, delay the decision—avoid saying no until you can provide a good reason.

What is wrong with attributing a negative decision to company policy?

3. **Subordinated refusal.**   Subordinate the refusal as much as possible without sacrificing clarity. Make sure that at least one good reason precedes the refusal, and use positive language in making the refusal. To avoid accusing the reader, you may need to use passive voice (see Chap-

ter 3). When you can do so, make the refusal by implication—give your reasons for a refusal, and suggest alternatives, but omit an explicit statement of refusal.

4. **Positive close.**   Whenever you can, suggest ways in which your reader can achieve the objective that you are at present refusing. When there is no way for the reader to achieve that objective, offer positive alternatives, resale or new sales material, or goodwill. Always show your intention to maintain a positive business relationship. Frequently new sales material will demonstrate your confidence in the future of the relationship. When further action is required, specify who should do what next.

▷ NEGATIVE ACKNOWLEDGMENTS

What circumstances would justify declining a request for goods or services?

A negative reply to a request for goods, service, an adjustment, or credit is bound to upset the reader. Because your reader will expect to have the request approved, your negative reply will come as a disappointing surprise. When you decide that the negative reply is the only one possible under the circumstances, you need to make the best of the situation by

1. Working to maintain a positive human and business relationship.

2. Making certain that the reader understands the reasons for your decision and knows what other courses of action are possible.

Delayed or Declined Orders

How and why should a writer subordinate a reader's mistake?

One type of negative acknowledgment is a letter stating that an order cannot be filled or that there will be a delay in filling it. The fault may be either the reader's or the writer's (or the fault of the writer's company). When the reader has been at fault by not supplying complete order information, the writer's principal task is to obtain the information required to complete the order without accusing the reader of having written an inadequate order.

Poor:	You forgot to specify which brand of diskette you desired.
Improved:	So that you can receive the diskettes of your choice, please use the enclosed card to let us know which brand you prefer.

When the writer or writer's company is responsible for the delay or refusal, the writer's principal task is to persuade the reader to wait until the order can be filled or to retain faith in the writer's company or its products in spite of having to order elsewhere.

Poor: Due to manufacturing difficulties we will be unable to send the two dozen 5-inch attaché cases for about three weeks.

Improved: We will be able to send the 5-inch attaché cases in about three weeks, as soon as the new alarm system is perfected.

Letters regarding delays in shipment for which the reader is at fault (by omitting necessary information) require (1) careful, positive wording of a request for the missing information, (2) inclusion of resale material, and (3) a request for specific, prompt action on the part of the reader. Figure 8.1 illustrates these principles. While the message is a long one in view of the small profit on one blender, modern word processing equipment makes it possible to use the same basic message for a wide variety of products over an extended time. The cost of individual letters would be low compared to the goodwill and increased sales that would result.

Letters announcing a delay caused by problems at the writer's company should have the objective of keeping the order in spite of the negative content of the message (announcing a delay). The writer needs to explain the reason for the delay, let the reader know how long the delay will be, and persuade the reader to wait. When the delay is going to be a long one (and what constitutes "long" will vary depending on the nature of the product or service involved), the writer should acknowledge the reader's right to make the decision about whether to wait, as Figure 8.2 illustrates. When the delay will not be long, you may assume — with confidence — that your decision to complete the order later will meet with the reader's approval.

Under what circumstances should you be explicit about the reader's right to choose whether she or he will wait for your product or service?

When you must decline an order because business conditions make it impossible for you to supply the goods or service (or a reasonable alternative), you need to explain the situation in a straightforward way. Your reader will appreciate it if you supply information about where and how the requested goods or services can be obtained. You should offer resale or new sales material when such material would be appropriate for your reader.

It is more usual, however, that you will need to decline customer orders because you market your products through a system of established dealers. In this case, your business objective is to persuade the reader to visit a local dealer. Your human objective is to retain the reader's goodwill in spite of the disappointment that your negative reply will create. Both objectives call for an indirect structure. Follow these general principles when writing a letter to refuse a customer who has ordered directly through the mail.

1. **Indirect opening.**   Find a positive opening that will place the message in its correct communication context before delivering the negative subject content (your business objective).

2. **Explanation.**   Explain clearly the reader benefits associated with your

**FIGURE 8.1
Sample Delayed
Order**

Use an indirect opening, but place the message in a specific communication context. When possible, send part of the order. Do not thank the reader for the order or say that you are glad to have it. Thanking for an incomplete or declined order is insulting.

Keep the reader's interest in your product by using resale material and focusing on the reader's choice rather than the mistake.

Not "You neglected to tell us which model" and not "We need to know which model."

The amount of resale (and the length of the letter) should be appropriate for the product or service involved. Word processing equipment can make fuller treatment economical.

Close by telling the reader exactly what to do and by encouraging prompt action.

Moonbeam Products
P.O. Box 4530, Lagina Hills, CA 92653

Consumer Services
Frank T. Olsen, Director

Ms. Jane Salmon
492 Oceanside Drive
Santa Monica, CA 90402

Dear Ms. Salmon:

You will receive the Moonbeam Model 14 electric can opener you ordered in just a few days. We shipped it by United Parcel Service on July 16.

The Model 14 is the best can opener Moonbeam makes, and it is well known for its rugged dependability. All of Moonbeam's blenders have the same kind of rugged construction, and one of them is sure to be right for your needs.

To meet the variety of kitchen demands, Moonbeam makes six different models of blender, each of which comes in four vibrant colors.

The enclosed brochure fully describes the models, their uses, and some of their unique features. So you may receive the blender that best meets your needs, please review the brochure and complete the order card on the last page.

The Model 14 and all of Moonbeam's blenders come with an absolute five-year warranty for your added assurance of quality.

We designed Moonbeam electric kitchen aids to make all your kitchen duties a pleasure. The Model 14 electric can opener will handle any size can regardless of shape. It's also completely submersible for easy cleaning. Whichever Moonbeam blender you select, you will receive a highly versatile product which will cut in half the time required to scramble eggs, make pancakes or waffles, and crush ice.

As soon as we receive the card indicating your choice of blender, we'll send it to you by UPS. By returning the card now, you can be enjoying the speed and convenience of automatically mixed, chopped, and pureed foods in about ten days.

Sincerely,

Frank T. Olsen

July 17, 19xx

enc

FIGURE 8.2
Delayed Order with
a Long Delay

Guardsman

1900 East Lake Avenue
New York, NY 14604
718/555-3003

February 21, 19xx

Mr. Thomas L. Wendell
553 Aberdeen Road
Chattanooga, TN 37402

Dear Mr. Wendell:

When you cannot
send part of the or-
der, find a positive
opening with which
the reader will
agree.

Your order for a Guardsman 10-horsepower, 40-inch, electric-start Lawn
Tractor shows your concern with quality. The Guardsman exceeds the
American National Safety Institute's standards and offers the ruggedness
and durability of solid steel construction.

Begin your explana-
tion fairly soon.
Your reader will
want to know why
you have not said,
"Your order is on
its way."

We usually try to fill orders for Guardsman Lawn Tractors in about two
weeks, and we can understand your desire to have your Guardsman when
the grass begins its spring spurt in April. Because of the steel
workers' strike and an unprecedented demand for Lawn Tractors this
season, it will take us six to eight weeks to fill your order.

You'll find the Guardsman 10 worth the wait. The electric-start,
35-cubic-inch, 10-horsepower engine has plenty of reserve power for
tackling the toughest of home-mowing needs. The engine governor
automatically increases gas feed to maintain blade speed in tall
grass and weeds--even on steep hills.

Use resale material
to discourage the
reader from buying
elsewhere.

In addition to the many features designed to make the Guardsman 10 the
most versatile home lawn tractor on the market, any family member old
enough to drive it can use it with complete confidence. The Guardsman
10 comes with a safety interlock which permits the engine to start
only with the mower in neutral and the blades disengaged. Another
safety feature you'll appreciate is the automatic cutoff that dis-
engages the blades and kills the engine should the driver leave the
tractor seat while the tractor is in gear. Guardsman is the only
lawn tractor available with this important feature.

Because the delay is
a long one, you
should make clear
that you know the
reader has a choice.
You should also en-
courage the deci-
sion you want the
reader to make.

Please use the enclosed card to let us know your decision. We will
continue with our evaluation of your application for credit but will
hold your deposit until we hear from you.

Mr. Thomas L. Wendell   February 21, 19xx   2

Now that the steel workers' strike is over, we're building Guardsman 10
Lawn Tractors as fast as possible without sacrificing the famous
Guardsman quality. Because we want you to be fully satisfied with your
Guardsman, we assemble each one carefully so the Guardsman you receive
will work flawlessly--and looks good, too.

Specify who is to ——————→ By returning your card today, you can receive your Guardsman 10 before
do what next. The   15 June--in plenty of time to help you with those midsummer and early
last sentence should   fall chores.
mention a reader
benefit.   Sincerely,

                           Kimberly Yeager

                           Kimberly Yeager
                           Marketing Manager

                           enc

system of dealers (such as direct, personal service; free installation; or the need to examine products before purchase).

3.   **Resale.**   Include the same kind of resale material as you would in delaying an order. Resale material will help retain your reader's interest in your product.

4.   **Positive close.**   Conclude by telling the reader exactly what to do and where to go to complete the purchase.

Figure 8.3 illustrates these points.

Should you need to decline an order from a dealer, it will be for one of the following reasons:

1.   The dealer has not established sufficient credit. Because in this case your business objective is to retain the order on a cash basis, this type of letter is a credit refusal and not an order refusal. We discuss credit refusals later in this chapter.

2.   You already have an exclusive dealer in the area. In this case your explanation of the arrangement you have with the existing dealer will justify your declining the order. Your positive close should be limited to simple goodwill and should avoid resale, new sales, and positive alternatives. (Do not send your readers to the competition — they will get there on their own.)

3.   The dealer does not meet your requirements. This is a broad category, covering financial matters (the dealer insists on a larger markup than you offer) and character (the dealer has a reputation for not providing the high quality of customer service you expect from your dealers). You must base your letter of refusal on the particular circumstances and on your analysis of the communication context.

Negative Replies to Requests

Under what circumstances should you say "maybe" rather than "no"? Under what circumstances would a "maybe" be misleading?

Most people make requests and claims only when they feel that they truly deserve a positive reply. Any time you must refuse a request or claim, the human objective — retaining your reader's goodwill — should receive the emphasis. You should delay the presentation of the business objective — that is, the refusal — until you have prepared the reader by stating your reasons. In a negative reply, the refusal itself should always be subordinated as much as possible without sacrificing clarity. In Figure 8.4 note the way the writer says *maybe* rather than *no* even though the refusal is clear.

The example in Figure 8.4 contains one business objective (refusing the request for the present) and one human objective (retaining the reader's goodwill). Frequently, negative replies to requests will contain more than one business objective. For example, in addition to denying the request, you

**FIGURE 8.3
Sample Letter
Declining an Order**

SINDELAR CORPORATION
16767 Bumble Bee Avenue
Logan, UT 84322
801/555-5552

6 January 19xx

Dr. Georgia Lynch
800 Magnolia Street
New Orleans, LA 70114

Dear Dr. Lynch:

You may thank the reader for "interest," but not for the order.
→ Thank you for your interest in Sindelar Computer Products. The equipment you saw advertised is the best Sindelar makes, and it is capable of performing all the tasks you listed in your letter.

State the refusal in terms of a reader benefit.
→ Because Sindelar equipment and software are available in a wide variety of configurations, we have established a nationwide chain of dealers who are in a better position to determine individual needs. So that you can be sure of receiving the best combination of equipment and software to meet your needs, visit the Hard & Software Store at 1121 Goodwin Street in Erie, where a complete line of Sindelar equipment is on display.

Include resale to retain the reader's interest.
→ The enclosed brochure will provide more information about Sindelar products. The new integrated business package described on page 32 should prove ideal for a small business like yours.

Sincerely,

Dale Lukon

Dale Lukon
Assistant to the President

enc

Note: Be sure to notify retailers of interested customers in their areas. They should perform their own follow-through as well.

**FIGURE 8.4
Sample Claim
Refusal**

The opening must place the message in its context without suggesting approval or refusal of the request. Provide a clear transition to the reasons that follow.

Keep expressions of appreciation short and simple. To avoid misleading the reader or sounding vain, and to help establish empathy instead, focus on the reader rather than on yourself.

Make sure the refusal is clear. Note the use of specific dates in this example.

Show the reader that you understand his or her problem and do what you can to help with a solution.

The close must be positive. Do not return to the negative aspect. In view of the refusal, an offer of "further" help would sound sarcastic.

Woodhaven
6133 King Highway   Aptos, CA 95003   408/555-4200

Commercial   Residential   State-wide Relocation Service

September 3, 19xx

Mr. Jon Doyle
Diller Realty
10105 Trinidad
Bloomsburg, PA 17815

Dear Jon:

Every professional realtor should benefit from the session titled "The After Market Created by the Selling of Land Contracts in the Second Mortgage Money Exchange" at the coming convention of the National Association of Realtors.

Your idea for the session is a good one. Through continued association with the major banks and lending institutions, Woodhaven has confirmed that the "after market" is ignored by a great number of realtors. Most members of our association would be honored to head a session of such importance. I am no exception.

Woodhaven usually supports attendance at professional conventions, and I have already submitted my request for travel funds. My employer will determine the amount of my support as soon as all requests are submitted.

Because Woodhaven has not yet assigned me funds for attending the convention and because of schedule conflicts arising from the convention's falling so close to Christmas, I won't be able to give you a definite answer until December 1, well past your November 10 deadline.

I still hope to attend the convention and would be pleased to head the session, but because you need a firm commitment soon, I suggest that you ask Anthony Bishop of our St. Louis branch to head the session. As you already know, Tony is an excellent public speaker and would make a fine addition to the program.

The convention promises to be first rate. The ideas you have outlined for the program look very good. The results of your planning and hard work are already obvious--keep up the good work.

Cordially,

Michele Conley

Michele Conley

may wish the reader's business in a way other than the one the reader has suggested. Whether you can accomplish the second business objective — obtaining the reader's business — depends on how well you accomplish your human objective in the letter. Note the positive approach and the full explanation in Figure 8.5, which was written to an 18-year-old student who had requested that his insurance premium be reduced because his father's premium was lower.

Negative Replies to Claims

How can you avoid calling the reader a liar in a negative reply to a claim?

When a customer has written to you claiming that your product or service was deficient in some way, you obviously need to consider the situation carefully. Some companies have decided that it is in their best interests to act on the assumption that the customer is always right and approve every adjustment requested. Other companies feel that unwarranted claims should be refused because it is unfair to make all customers pay for the unreasonable requests of a few.

If you decide that a reader's request is unwarranted and should be refused, you need to be careful to avoid accusing the reader of carelessness, misrepresentation, or fraud. Rather than assume that the reader is trying to cheat you deliberately, assume that your reader truly does not understand your service or the operation of your product. Your principal objective is to resell the product or service in question and, to show confidence, sell a new product or service at the same time. Your human objective is to retain the reader's goodwill. Figure 8.6, a letter refusing a refund for a tour, illustrates these points.

Credit Refusals

Why is a letter refusing credit more of a persuasive message than a negative message?

A letter refusing credit is more of a persuasive message than a negative message because its objective is not so much to refuse credit as it is to obtain the customer's business on a cash basis. The human objective in a credit refusal is to show the reader that while a credit purchase might look attractive at the moment, it is in the reader's long-term interest to avoid risky credit obligations.

When refusing credit, make your reasons clear and suggest ways the reader can go about improving credit eligibility. Tell the reader what your requirements for credit are, and invite the reader to apply for credit again later. Do not, however, suggest that you will automatically extend credit the next time the applicant writes.

Because you still want the customer's business, but on a cash basis, much of your letter will consist of resale. Emphasize the advantages of doing business on a cash basis, but remember that these advantages are *not* reasons for refusing credit; they are an alternative, so they should follow the refusal. The following structure applies whether you are writing an individual reply

FIGURE 8.5
Sample Claim
Refusal

Use an indirect opening that agrees with something the reader has said.

Provide a full explanation for your decision.

When possible, show that the refusal is based on impersonal evidence.

Avoid accusing the reader, and use positive language to subordinate the negative aspect.

Offer positive alternatives.

Your close should be positive and forward-looking.

Carlson Insurance
An Independent Insurance Agency

3317 Greenleaf Blvd.   Personal, Commercial
Palo Alto, CA 94301   Auto, Home, Life and
415/555-4200   Business Packages

June 11, 19xx

Mr. Charles X. Shull
1501 Newell Road
Palo Alto, CA 94303

INSURANCE RATES

Yes, Mr. Shull, we do make money on policies carried by good drivers like your father, and your father should be proud of the fact that he has not had an accident in ten years.

Insurance companies keep careful statistics on different kinds of cars and drivers. These statistics are the basis for determining insurance rates. Drivers with very few or no accidents, like your father, receive the lowest rates.

Because unmarried drivers under 25 account for the highest frequency of accidents of any age group, they are charged higher rates than any other age group. Also, the Cobra-Jet which you drive has had one of the highest frequency of accidents and is charged a higher rate than a car like your father's.

The driving record of the individual driver is also one of the most important factors in computing the premium charged. The premium you received is correct for your age, car, and driving record.

One way to lower your premium would be to drop the collision coverage on your car. But, should you have an accident that was your fault, you would have to pay for the damage to your car. Or you might trade your Cobra-Jet in on a compact car.

I am happy to have your father as a policyholder, and I'm sure that you will be just as good a driver as your father. As you grow older and accumulate a few years of accident-free driving, your insurance premiums will drop accordingly. Give me a call or stop by to discuss some of the ways you might reduce your insurance premiums now.

Cal Davis

Cal Davis

FIGURE 8.6
Letter Refusing a Refund

Use an indirect opening that agrees with something the reader said. As a last resort, thank the reader for having written.

Explain the reasons for the refusal carefully.

Subordinate the negative aspect by emphasizing the positive elements of the situation.

When possible, avoid saying no directly. Stress reader benefits.

Your close should be positive. Focus on future business.

Parkview Travel and Tours
A Full Service Agency

5600 Portage Road, Charleston, NC 29424

August 5, 19xx

Mrs. Frances Crenshaw
114 Quarter Horse Drive
Charleston, NC 29420

Dear Mrs. Crenshaw:

You're right to expect superior accommodations when you arrange tours through Parkview Travel and Tours. We do stake our reputation on providing the best accommodations available.

Because you are a seasoned traveler, you know that different countries have different customs. Not all countries have the same concepts of courteous service as we have in this country. Do you remember how upset you were on your tour of Japan last year when you returned to your hotel only to discover that the hotel manager had moved you to a different room? When you discovered that being moved in that way is a common occurrence in Japan and shows no disrespect, you accepted your next unscheduled move like a native.

It is the same with Kenya and Tanzania. I'm sure you'll agree that your accommodations in Nairobi were as plush as you would expect to find in any major city anywhere in the world. When you signed up for the "Primitive Safari," we informed you that the journey around Lake Victoria would be under primitive conditions, and the materials we sent you before your trip described the emergency equipment required for the journey.

As difficult as the Primitive Safari was for you, I'm sure you'll agree that to be fully appreciated, the beauty of nature must be observed close at hand. You've had an opportunity, Mrs. Crenshaw, to see a part of Africa that few Americans will ever see, and to see it in a way that will be impossible in just a few years.

Perhaps this next year you should consider a vacation a little less strenuous. We have several European tours scheduled that should appeal to you. The enclosed brochures describe the steamship lines, countries, and accommodations available.

Use the enclosed card to request further information. We'll be glad to complete all the arrangements for you.

Cordially,

Samuel T. Rex

Samuel T. Rex

enc

**FIGURE 8.7
Sample Credit
Refusal**

The indirect open-
ing focuses on
something the
reader will agree
with while men-
tioning the purpose
of the letter.

The explanation
gives the reasons
clearly and logi-
cally, emphasizing
the reader benefit of
not using credit at
this time.

The refusal is clear.
Passive voice helps
avoid accusing the
reader of any short-
coming.

Offer positive alter-
natives when
possible.

Subordinate the
negative aspects of
the alternatives. To
omit them com-
pletely would mis-
lead the reader.

Encourage the ac-
tion you want the
reader to take.

Sun Glow, Inc.
1330 Healy, Macomb, IL 61455
Solar Heating Specialists Since 1950

January 29, 19xx

Mr. Robert Wilson
Best Buy Hardware
2825 Stadium Drive
Boise, ID 83725

Dear Mr. Wilson:

Your order and application for credit indicate your awareness of
the current demand for solar heating equipment. We're glad to
hear that you anticipate increased sales in your area.

In making the routine checks you authorized, we discovered that
your present level of indebtedness exceeds the 2 to 1 ratio
generally considered safe for credit transactions. Until that
ratio is met, cash transactions would help you avoid further
indebtedness while improving your assets-to-liabilities ratio.

We'd like to work along with you as you improve your ratio. By
taking advantage of our express shipping, you could offer Sun
Glow solar heaters to your customers without needing to maintain
a large inventory.

Our store display and catalog should help to sell Sun Glow products
without increasing your indebtedness. Even with the added charge
for express shipping, your profit margin would still be above a
healthy 20 percent.

The two quarter-page ads a year in the newspaper of your choice
which we provide all dealers would increase your customer traffic
and help you sell Sun Glow equipment.

By completing the enclosed request form, you'll receive Sun Glow's
catalog and our 3' x 6' wall display. Let us know your decision.

Sincerely,

Sylvia Everard
Marketing
enc

to a dealer who has ordered a large amount of goods on credit or a form reply to a customer who has requested a credit card.

1. **Indirect opening.** Begin with something the reader can agree on, such as the market conditions, the usefulness of the product(s), or the reader's choice of product(s). Include some resale to maintain reader interest in your product(s). Do *not* thank the reader for the order; to do so would sound selfish in view of the credit refusal.

2. **Explanation.** Explain your requirements for credit explicitly. Without sacrificing clarity, subordinate as much as possible the ways in which the reader does not meet your requirements. When you can offer useful advice (a local bank loan based on collateral, for example) without sounding paternalistic, do so. Your reader will appreciate genuine helpfulness.

3. **Refusal.** Make clear that you will not extend credit at this time, but leave the door open for future consideration. Do *not* promise to extend credit later.

4. **Positive alternatives.** Use resale material to encourage completing the order or otherwise doing business on a cash basis. Inform the reader of cash discounts and other advantages of cash. Smaller orders, layaway, and other helpful suggestions will encourage the reader to continue doing business with your company. Do not suggest that the reader apply for credit elsewhere, which would imply that your decision to deny credit was arbitrary.

5. **Positive close.** Make it easy for the reader to reply. Remember that the reader has the choice of continuing the business relationship, so you cannot take action until your reader decides. Make clear what you would like the reader to do, and end with a reader benefit.

Figure 8.7 illustrates the foregoing principles.

▷ NEGATIVE ANNOUNCEMENTS AND REMINDERS

Why are negative announcements usually more difficult to write than negative acknowledgments?

When your negative message is written in reply to something the reader has requested, you at least have a logical starting point for your letter. Readers who have requested favors, adjustments, or credit expect your reply and know that their request may be denied. Negative announcements and reminders present a more difficult problem. Even when your readers know that they have not fulfilled some obligations, they do not fully expect to receive your announcement. Also, negative announcements and reminders are frequently prepared as form letters to keep their costs low. This makes personalization difficult.

If negative announcements and reminders are to be read at all, they must offer the reader something of value. When you can, offer real and specific benefits. At the least, you should offer to discuss the situation with the reader so that you can reach an agreement about a satisfactory solution for the particular problem.

In writing negative announcements and reminders, you may be tempted to neglect a positive approach to the problem. Compare the following sentences from letters to college students:

Poor:	I regret to inform you that your admission to candidate status has been delayed until you complete the following requirements.
Improved:	Before your admission to candidate status, you will need to complete the following requirements.
Poor:	On March 3, we sent you the accidental injury forms and requested that you return the forms to the Health Center. It's now March 27, and we have not yet received your reply.
Improved:	To receive your check from Student Insurance, you will need to file the accidental injury forms we sent you on March 3.

Note the brevity and the positive approach of Figures 8.8 and 8.9.

What are the legal implications of letters of reprimand?

Letters of reprimand also fall into this category. Even though these messages stay within the company, letter format is appropriate because of the formality of the situation. Such letters are usually preceded by less formal warnings, so the reader should be expecting the negative message. Even so, when circumstances require you to reprimand an employee for her or his behavior, delay the most negative aspects of the message until you have reviewed the facts. To help the person do a better job in the future, be specific about what the person has been doing wrong (too much absenteeism, too many personal phone calls, poor quality control, or other failures to meet job requirements). You should also specify in the letter what the person needs to do to perform satisfactorily. Letters of reprimand are often delivered during a personal interview so that their contents can be discussed. Use the following structure:

1. **Review the facts.**   Use positive language to specify what the reader is doing wrong, and explain the reasons the reader should be aware that the behavior is wrong.

**FIGURE 8.8
Sample Negative
Announcement**

Use an indirect opening when the reader does not really expect bad news.

Explain quickly because the negative message will be obvious. Personal information can be added to a form letter.

Focus on the future when possible.

PERRY'S PACKAGING
110 Factory Avenue
Kent, Ohio 44240

April 12, 19xx

Mr. George Rambo
Cardboard Container Division

Dear George:

As you know from reading the daily newspapers, local business has been hit rather hard by the recession. Perry's Packaging has tried hard to retain all personnel during this difficult period.

Because of another recent downturn in business, we find that some layoffs have become necessary if the company is to remain solvent. The layoffs were determined strictly by seniority. Because you have low seniority, George, your layoff will be for 90 days. Your work has been excellent, and the layoff is not a reflection of your abilities.

Should the market improve soon, you can be sure that we'll notify you. We will be glad to have you back at Perry's as soon as possible.

Sincerely,

Perry Mason

Perry Mason, President

**FIGURE 8.9
Sample Negative
Announcement**

When the fact that
you are writing
makes it obvious
that the news is
bad, omit the indi-
rect beginning.

Be as positive as
possible, and offer
whatever help you
can.

BANK OF THE AMERICAS

5 Timber Lane • Woodridge, CT 06525

December 20, 19xx

Ms. Janice Steiner
1401 Foucher Street
Woodbridge, CT 06525

Dear Ms. Steiner:

Subject: Account # _____   Due Date _____
           Amount Due _____   Late Charges _____

Although your payment is overdue, your previous record
indicates a sincere desire to keep your account up to date.
We assume that something has happened which makes it
difficult for you to pay. We'd like to help.

Solving money problems, whatever they might be, is our
business. If you do have a problem, chances are that it
will be easier than you think to find a solution. We
would like to help you protect your credit standing. So,
please make your payment or let us hear from you soon.

Sincerely,

Adrian Everts

Adrian Everts, Manager

SIDEBAR

Fire Me, and I'll Sue!

Thirty years ago, business managers were relatively free to hire and fire as they pleased. A person who did not perform up to expectations or whose manner or dress was displeasing could be fired quickly and easily. Times have changed. A variety of federal, state, and local laws now protect employees from being unfairly dismissed, and the burden of proof frequently falls on the employer, who must be able to supply documented evidence that the individual was ineffective on the job.

Does your employee manual state that employees will receive fair and impartial hearings before being discharged? If so, you will need to ensure that they receive such hearings before you fire them. Job descriptions, personnel policy statements, and employee evaluation forms and letters are all legal documents that may be used against you in court proceedings.

To reduce the chances of being sued if it be-

comes necessary to dismiss someone, take the following steps:

1. Help the person save face. Follow good communication practices.

2. Provide clear job descriptions, being careful to cover any areas open to interpretation. Describe minimum standards of performance.

3. Establish a regular system of performance reviews, being careful to document areas requiring improvement.

4. Document specific job failures and provide written warnings. Require the employee to respond to any warning in writing. Require professional consultation by an outsider when appropriate (as for drug or alcohol abuse).

5. Do what you can to help the individual find more suitable employment, either in another part of your company or elsewhere.

2.   **State the expected behavior.**   Tell the reader exactly what should be done to correct the problem.

3.   **Offer to help.**   Keep the communication channels open. Offer to discuss the situation with the reader. Ask the reader to come up with his or her own solution to the problem.

Figure 8.10 illustrates the foregoing principles.

▷ APOLOGIES

Under what circumstances is an apology an indirect message?

Sometimes you must apologize for a negative announcement. If you have to postpone or cancel an engagement at the last minute or otherwise renege on a commitment to a reader, an apology may be necessary and appropriate.

Unlike most apologies (see Chapter 7), apologies for negative announcements should be delayed until after the reason has been presented (use an

**FIGURE 8.10
Sample Letter
of Reprimand**

Timkin Steel Company

1900 Banning Road
Bethlehem, PA 18015
215/555-6164

14 October 19xx

Mr. Robert Reitenbach
Production Department

Dear Bob:

As you know from our discussion Friday, many of your staff have expressed
unhappiness with the way you treat them.

Because our many conversations about this subject haven't helped you change
your behavior, I'm writing this letter so that you'll know that this is an
important problem and deserves your immediate attention. A copy of the letter
will be placed in your personnel file.

Your long and excellent record with the Company indicates that you have the
potential to succeed in management. Since you have become Production Manager,
however, the unusual number of complaints from your staff suggests that
something serious is wrong. The complaints that bother me the most are the
name calling and the public ridicule to which you frequently subject your
staff.

For you to be successful as Production Manager, you'll need the cooperation
of each employee in your Department. To those employees, you are the
Company's spokesperson. Their loyalty to you is an important factor in
their motivation to do a good job for the Company.

To earn their loyalty, you'll need to take the time to listen to them and to
take their problems seriously. You'll find that most production problems can
be traced to a simple solution when management and staff work together.

My main concern is to help you solve the problem of your relationship with
your staff. It's important to the company and to your career that we come
up with a workable solution quickly. To help you decide on a course of
action, I've arranged for you to meet with Dr. Leo Buscaglia on Tuesday,
November 11, at 10:00 and for you to take a week of your vacation beginning
today.

Review the facts in an unemotional way.

Let the reader know that the situation is serious. NOTE: The writer should have documented the "many conversations."

State the expected behavior.

Offer to help. Specify possible courses of action.

Mr. Robert Reitenbach   14 October 19xx   2

Your appointment with Dr. Buscaglia will be at company expense, as will any future appointments he feels might be necessary.

Tell the reader exactly what you expect. →

When you report back to work a week from today, see me first. I'd like to hear your plans for improving your working relationship with your staff at that time.

Cordially,

Robert Meyers, VP--Personnel

indirect structure). Beginning such a message with *I'm sorry* would reveal the negative content before the reader was prepared to receive it. In cases like these, use the following structure:

1. **Indirect opening.**   Begin with something the reader can agree on, but keep it brief. The reader is not expecting your message and will wonder why you are writing.

2. **Explanation.**   Why are you breaking your commitment? When possible, stress business reasons (which are impersonal). Personal reasons, unless they are extremely serious (such as illness or death in the family) often sound insincere.

3. **Negative aspect.**   Tell the reader explicitly that you cannot keep your promise. Do not allow any opportunity for the reader to misunderstand.

4. **Apology.**   Apologize either immediately before or immediately after clarifying the negative aspect. Keep the apology brief to avoid encouraging the reader to feel worse than he or she already does.

5. **Positive alternatives.**   Do what you can to help the reader solve the problem caused by your inability to keep your commitment.

6. **Goodwill close.**   Be positive and forward-looking. Be careful about making new promises, which may not be taken seriously at this point. Do *not* restate the apology.

Figure 8.11 illustrates these principles.

▷ SUMMARY

Negative messages contain a business objective to which the reader will respond in a negative way. When your message will hurt, anger, or upset the reader, you should use an indirect structure. An indirect structure helps prepare the reader for the negative information by placing the emphasis on the reasons for the negative decision and on the positive alternatives to the original course of action. The general structure for all negative messages is (1) indirect beginning, (2) explanation, (3) subordinated refusal, and (4) positive close.

A negative acknowledgment of a request for goods, service, adjustment, or credit is bound to upset the reader. You need to make the best of the situation by (1) working to maintain a positive human and business relationship and (2) making certain that the reader understands the reasons for your decisions and knows what other courses of action are possible.

Any time you must refuse a request or claim, the human objective — retaining your reader's goodwill — should receive the emphasis. You should

**FIGURE 8.11
Sample Negative
Announcement
Including an
Apology**

Seattle Construction Supplies
10 Mackenzie Avenue • Seattle, WA 98195

June 6, 19xx

Dr. Lucy Baines
College of Business
Redwood University--Oceanside
Grants Pass, OR 97526

Dear Lucy:

Keep the indirect opening brief. → The Sales/Marketing convention you are planning for July appears to be shaping up nicely, Lucy.

Introduce the reason quickly. → When you first asked me to speak, I was glad to agree because July has always been our slack month here in Seattle. Because July usually is so slow, this year my boss has decided to send me to Anchorage, Alaska, where I will spend the entire month calling on construction companies. For this reason, I will be unable to

Keep the apology brief. → speak at the convention as planned. I'm sorry to be giving you such short notice, but I learned only yesterday that I would be going to Alaska.

Help the reader when possible. → My assistant, Roger Jackson, would be available to speak in my place. He is young (23) and inexperienced, but he is rapidly learning techniques for marketing heavy machinery and would work hard to provide a high-quality presentation. I will be glad to ask him to speak if you wish.

The close should be positive and forward-looking. Do not restate the apology. → Please let me know whether you would like me to speak to Jackson about presenting in my place, and good luck with the convention.

Cordially,

Mary Lou Mealor

Mary Lou Mealor, Director
Sales and Marketing

COMMUNICATION SOLUTION

Compare your solution to this chapter's Communication Challenge with the one that follows.

The foregoing letter is one possible solution to the problem. Another possible solution is to offer some kind of financial assistance—student loan, tuition deferment credit, or part-time employment—for *this* year.

Note that this letter can seem individual, even though it would likely be handled as a form. You would simply place the date, name, address, salutation, and date received into a database, and the mail-merge function on a word processing program would do the rest.

The "Thank you" opening is appropriate here because there is little else to comment on that pertains to the subject. You will not have read her application, so you cannot comment on its contents.

Establish the reason for the deadline, and express it as a long-term reader benefit. She will want her application to receive full and impartial consideration next year.

Be clear about her ineligibility, even at the expense of being a little negative. Subordinate the negative aspect as much as possible, and look forward to a positive future.

Show confidence in the future of the relationship, and provide as much help as possible.

North Central University
Pemberton Hall, Mills Road   Ames, Iowa 50012

Financial Assistance   *515/555-1908*

May 15, 19xx

Ms. Susan Sondheim
3110 Bobolink Lane
Woodland Hills, CA 91371

Dear Ms. Sondheim:

Thank you for your application for financial assistance at North Central University, Ms. Sondheim.

This year we received far more applications than we have financial aid available and making the selections will be difficult. To ensure that each applicant receives full and impartial consideration, we have set May 1 as the deadline for consideration.

As we received your application May 8, you are ineligible for financial assistance this year. You may wish to apply again next year, when the deadline will again be May 1. We will begin accepting applications on January 15.

Should you require assistance completing the form, please stop by the Financial Aid Office in Pemberton Hall.

Sincerely,

Guy Gibson

Guy Gibson

delay the presentation of the business objective—the refusal—until you have prepared the reader by stating your reasons.

When you decide that a reader's claim is unwarranted and should be refused, you need to be careful to avoid accusing the reader of carelessness, misrepresentation, or fraud. Your principal business objective is to refuse the request; your secondary business objective is to resell the product or service in question and—to show confidence—sell a new product or service at the same time. Your human objective is to retain the reader's goodwill.

In most respects a letter refusing credit is more of a persuasive message than a negative message because its objective is not so much to refuse credit as it is to obtain the customer's business on a cash basis. The human objective in a credit refusal is to show the reader that while a credit purchase might look attractive at the moment, it is in the reader's long-term interest to avoid risky credit obligations.

Negative announcements and reminders are frequently prepared as form letters to keep their costs low. If they are to be read at all, they must offer the reader something of value. When you can, offer real and specific benefits. At the very least, offer to discuss the situation with the reader.

When you must apologize for a negative announcement, as with a broken promise, keep the indirect opening brief. Stress business reasons when possible. Subordinate the negative aspect and the apology, and help the reader solve her or his problem when possible. The closing should be positive and forward-looking.

◇ EXERCISES

Review and Discussion Questions

1. What makes a message negative? What general structure should be used for all negative messages?

2. When the reader is at fault for not supplying complete order information, what is the writer's principal task? What is the writer's principal task when the writer (or the writer's company) is at fault?

3. Name three reasons you might need to write a letter to decline an order from a dealer.

4. What do you need to avoid when refusing a reader's request for an unwarranted claim? What are your business objectives in such a letter? Your human objectives?

5. Why is a message refusing credit more of a persuasive message than a negative message? What should you make clear to your readers in such a letter?

Problems

1. Mrs. Sue Dickens, your boss at Dickens and Jackson, 9411 Pico Blvd., Santa Monica, CA 90400, has asked you to prepare for her signature a form letter to be sent to all customers who send incomplete orders for clothing to the department store. Dickens and Jackson is currently using a form postcard that contains neither resale nor new sales material. Mrs. Dickens thinks that a form letter will provide sufficient opportunity to build goodwill and will be worth the added cost.

2. Assume that when Mr. Patrick Busey (see Case 1 in Chapter 7) wrote to you ordering the electrical wire, he failed to specify the gauge of the wire. When you tried to call him, you learned that an electrical storm had disrupted phone service in town. To avoid further delay, acknowledge his order by mail, but suggest that he call you collect with the necessary information.

3. Your company, William Orange Publishing, 901 West Benjamin Street, Richmond, VA 23284, just received an order for 100 copies each of seven books from the Campus Book Store, Tiffin University, Tiffin, OH 44883. You can send five of the books now. The listed prices are retail, and the wholesale discount is 20 percent:

    You Can't Go Home Again, Thomas Wolfe, $4.95 ea., paper
    You Gotta Be Kidding, Henry McKeown, $8.95 ea., cloth
    The Prodigal Son, Richard Milhous, $14.95 ea., paper
    Moses and Monotheism, Sigmund Freud, $2.95 ea., paper
    Ain't No Way, Aretha Franklin, $11.95 ea., cloth

    For two books, however, *Psychology and Phraseology,* by Mary Goldman, and *Fun with the Semantic Differential,* by Vern Marietta, the Campus Book Store failed to specify the cloth or paper editions. The hardbound edition of *Psychology and Phraseology* sells for $10.95 and the paperback for $4.95. The hardbound edition of *Fun with the Semantic Differential* sells for $15.95 and the paperback for $6.75. Write the Campus Book Store.

4. Answer Mr. William Atkins (see Problem 1 in Chapter 7) with a negative reply. You would like to be able to help him, but your schedule is completely full for the next six months. If he would contact you earlier next year, you would be glad to consider speaking about business communication to the English classes next fall.

5. As an assistant professor of marketing at Franklin and Marshall College, Lancaster, PA 17604, you have just published your first book, *The Shrinking World and the International Market.* Already you have received letters from three of your former students requesting autographed copies. The letters do not say so directly, but their implication is that you are to send the books without charge from your limited supply from the pub-

lisher. Write a sample letter to John Keats, 712 Lamia Way, Syracuse, NY 13210, and refuse. John can obtain a copy of the book from Shelly Press, Englewood Cliffs, NJ 07632, for $11.95 (includes postage and handling), and you will be glad to autograph it for him should he visit Lancaster, PA, or send it to you by special fourth-class insured mail.

6. Because of your new book, *The Shrinking World and the International Market* (see preceding problem), you have been invited to interview for an associate professorship at the University of Bridgeport, Bridgeport, CT 06602. The offer is very attractive and includes a substantial raise, but you wish to remain at Franklin and Marshall College until you complete work on your second book, *Principles of International Marketing*, which will take about a year. Decline the interview for the present, but leave the door open for future negotiations. NOTE: Simply wishing to remain at Franklin and Marshall (as opposed to being required to remain there by some special circumstance or for a special reason) is not a reason to decline the interview unless you are sure you will never be interested in the University of Bridgeport. Find — and use — a logical reason for being unable to move until you have finished your book.

7. Rewrite the following letter:

Dear Student

We regret that our records indicate that you have failed to meet the requirements for graduation.

Please notify the graduate office if you plan to graduate in _____. If we do not hear from you IMMEDIATELY, we shall place your original diploma application in your folder with the understanding that you will notify us when you wish to have it reactivated for a future commencement.

The Graduate College

Requirements Not Met:

8. When you accepted an invitation to speak for free to your local chapter of Parents Without Partners (PWP), it was with the understanding that if you later received an invitation to speak for your usual fee of $500, you would be free to cancel your engagement with PWP. Such an opportunity has arisen. Send Mr. Wayne Dwyer, president of PWP, 157 Hillside Drive, Rosell, IL 60172, your notice of cancellation. Include whatever specifics (title of talk, time, place, or names of possible replacements) you think are necessary.

9. Rewrite the following letter:

I regret to inform you that your admission to candidate status has been delayed until you complete the following requirement:

Please let us know when you have completed this requirement so that your application for candidacy can be considered for approval. Let me emphasize that your candidacy will be denied if you fail to complete this requirement.

Sincerely,

Eileen S. Dostal
Associate Dean

P.S. Let me remind you of the regulation that graduate students are required to elect six hours of credit after their application for candidacy has been approved.

10. As Head of Purchasing, tell Elisa Cranford, the Director of Marketing, that her department does not have permission to purchase its own word processing equipment. Instead the marketing department is authorized two self-correcting typewriters. For other work, it will have to use the centralized word processing equipment of the company.

CASES

1. Your company, Wholesale Electronic Supply Company, 4270 Peach Street, Atlanta, GA 30330, has just received a rush order for 15,000 200-ohm precision rheostats built to specifications supplied by Anderson Manufacturing, 47 Bethel Street, North Newton, KS 67117. You would like to retain the order, but because you have just begun a special order for the U.S. Navy that will take 90 days to complete, you must decline the order for the present. However, you do not want to lose Anderson as a customer. While other companies are capable of building the rheostats, your company has been building electronic equipment to individual specifications longer than anyone else in the country. Write the letter.

2. As the manufacturer of Lennox Sewing Machines, you frequently receive letters from customers who would like to purchase the machine directly from you rather than through one of your dealers. Prepare a form letter you can send as a reply that will direct the readers to their local dealers. Rather than specify dealers in the letter itself, you will enclose a brochure listing all your dealers in the 50 states.

3. As the manufacturer of Cowan Color Televisions, 716 Coamo Street, Hato Rey, PR 00917, you have received a letter from Mr. Marty Cox, owner of Cox's Appliances, 3911 Murray Street, Hennessey, OK 73742. Mr. Cox would like to be a dealer for you. While you do not have a dealer in Hennessey (the closest dealer is in Enid), Cox's Appliances does not have the right image for high-quality (and high-priced) Cowan Color Televisions. You only merchandise through high quality department stores, and Cox's Appliances is a rather strange conglomeration of fix-it shop, small town hardware store, and junk shop. Write a letter refusing Mr. Cox without offending him. Your investigation reveals that he is well-known and well-liked in Hennessey, and if he would remodel his store or perhaps purchase a new property, he might qualify for a dealership.

4. As owner of the Fruit Basket, RR4, Orlando, FL 32810, you advertise special gifts of fruit

in several national magazines. Because you have found it much more convenient to do business for cash only, you always include a complete description of the baskets available and their prices in your ads. Nevertheless, today you have received an order for your $200 basket from Mrs. Ronda Young, 986 Gaviotta Drive, Los Angeles, CA 90000, requesting that the basket be sent COD. A quick check of your records indicates that Mrs. Young has purchased a $200 basket each year for the past five years. This is the first time she has requested a COD shipment. You do not want to lose her business, but you must write to her and request payment before you can send the fruit basket to her.

5. As assistant to Mr. Herman I. Brogg, Manager of Education and Training at Walla Walla Insurance Companies, One Walla Walla Plaza, Walla Walla, WA 99362, prepare a letter for Mr. Brogg's signature refusing to sell a copy of Walla Walla's video program, "Effective Sales Techniques," to Dr. Sally J. Larkin, College of Business, North Central Bible College, Minneapolis, MN 55404. All of Walla Walla's training films are for intracompany use only because they are made with Walla Walla employees rather than professional actors and actresses.

6. You are Douglas Downing, Credit Manager of Blair Radio Equipment, 501 Wellington Drive, Denton, TX 76201. You have on your desk a letter and credit application from Mark McMerill, 2678 Crandall Court, Austin, TX 78734. Mark wants to order a $300 Panasonic Tri-Mode Stereo Sound System complete with an 8-track tape player and full-feature record changer with dust cover. Your credit check on Mark tells you that he is slow in paying his debts. In fact, he has an outstanding balance of $500 with another creditor. Write a letter to Mark, denying him credit. Try to sell the stereo to him on a cash basis.

7. You are Sam Harrison, owner of Harrison Department Store, One South Chicago Street,

Searcy, AR 72143. Your store has been in the family for five generations and has a fine reputation in the city. The mayor writes you a letter requesting a contribution of $30,000 for the new civic center that is to be built near your store. You will be glad to contribute $5,000 of corporate funds and to solicit another $5,000 from your employees. Write a letter to the mayor of the city, Ms. Alice Walden, City Hall, 1540 Page Mill Road, Searcy, AR 72143.

8. You are the office manager of Hoffman-LaRoche Inc., 133 Glentree Drive, Madison, WI 53706, and today you receive a letter from a communications student at the University of Wisconsin. The student (Jana Jefferson, 578 Sanford Drive, Madison, WI 53706) said her professor assigned a project of auditing a local firm's correspondence for a three-month period and she would like permission to do so for your firm. Because of the confidentiality of your correspondence, you refuse. However, you will be glad to let Jana tour the company and interview several of your employees who routinely write letters and reports.

9. As the personnel director of E. I. Liddy Pharmaceuticals, 4721 Montgomery Lane, Joliet, IL 60436, prepare a form letter you can use to inform job applicants that they have not been hired. Each letter will be individually typed, which will permit you to personalize the opening paragraph and the reasons for the refusal. Write a sample letter to Ms. Judith Senne, 819 Weber Street, Huron, OH 44839. Although she will receive her degree in marketing (one of job's requirements), other applicants have demonstrated better leadership skills by their participation in campus organizations.

10. Ms. Janice Roberts, 22 Darlington Apts., Ponce, PR 00731, has applied to your bank, the Industrial City Bank, 10 Clinton Square, Ponce, PR 00731, for an auto loan, telling you that she needs the car to look for work.

Ms. Roberts is recently divorced, and when she was married she established credit in her husband's name only. Because she has no marketable skills and no job, you decide to refuse her application for credit. Because recent court decisions have tended to support divorced women in their claim to credit established when they were married, you will need to word your refusal carefully. Be sure to tell her that because of her previous experience with your bank, you will be glad to extend credit as soon as she obtains a job.

11. One of your least pleasant jobs as a department head is reprimanding members of your staff. Naturally you try to reprimand in as nice a way as possible. You begin by referring to the employee's deficiency in casual conversation, focusing on ways of improving job performance. Only when the situation is critical do you put anything in writing. Today you must write and deliver a letter of reprimand to Abraham Fenwick, who works for you in the Advertising Department. Your staff of professionals is composed roughly of half men and half women, who must work together closely. Fenwick, unfortunately, is unable to accept the women's professional competence. While he is not outright insulting, he manages to get in enough digs to ruin the harmony of your office. You have mentioned Fenwick's churlish attitude to him several times now, and each time he has promised to cooperate more fully with everyone in the office. This morning, however, Fenwick disrupted office procedures for what must be the last time. When Ms. Arlene Farrone, your best copywriter, was in the middle of presenting a new campaign to corporate management, Fenwick told her to go get coffee for everyone. Ms. Farrone continued her presentation in a professional manner, but, as she told you later, she found the remark extremely offensive. You have determined that the next time Fenwick fails to acknowledge the professionalism of the women on

your staff, he will be fired. Prepare his letter of reprimand.

12. As the Production Manager for Sun Glow Products, 270 Jay Street, Chillicothe, OH 45601, refuse an employee's request for a vacation during your peak production period. Don Mulder, one of your line supervisors, won $10,000 in the state lottery and has now requested that you permit him to combine his 19xx and 19xx vacations and take all of November off. You need him at work in November because of Christmas sales. If he is willing to wait, you can arrange for him to take the double vacation in February.

13. As Production Manager for Sun Glow Products (see Case 12 in this chapter), you have received a request to double your output of Sundail watches. After studying the situation, you have determined that even by hiring the additional authorized personnel, the two assembly lines now operating are not capable of such an increase in production. At best, you can increase production 25 percent. Your current plant facilities do not have room for an additional line, and even if space were available, a new line would cost approximately $800,000 to install. Write a memo to Paul Dunlap, president of Sun Glow, informing him of the situation.

14. As the owner and president of Wholesale Electronic Supply (see Case 1 in this chapter), you have a sad announcement to make. Your contracts with the U.S. Navy have not been renewed, and you will need to release several employees. You have already made a general announcement, so your memo to those affected will not be a complete surprise. Prepare a memo for William Anderson that can serve as a model for the others you must write.

15. Your company's suggestion box produces far more suggestions calling for refusals than it

does ones that are accepted. As chair of the Suggestion Committee, refuse a suggestion from Albert A. Harper, Foreman of the Loading Dock. Harper suggested that the two Heslop forklift trucks used in Shipping and Receiving be replaced by Altmans. In some ways the Altman is a better forklift. It has greater lifting capacity, has fewer repair problems, gets slightly better gas mileage, and has a longer life expectancy. It is, however, a much more expensive forklift.

This is the third suggestion this year from Harper that you need to refuse. Each of his suggestions has had merit and has given the committee something worth considering. It took the committee several hours to discover that the higher initial investment for the Altman forklifts would never be offset by the day-to-day savings. Harper will have to continue to use the Heslop forklifts, and when they are replaced, it will be with something less expensive than the Altman truck.

16. Because your company, Werner Fashions, needs to protect its designs, you frequently must refuse requests for information about your plans for next year's clothes and for tours of your offices. As you are now in the midst of planning your designs for next fall, you must refuse a request for a tour. On a separate sheet of paper, write to Ms. Marla Hague and tell her that she and her eighth-grade home economics class will not be able to tour your offices at this time. Her address is Room 7, Robert E. Lee Junior High, Centerville, PA 16404.

17. Since the publication of your recent book, *Successful Human Relations,* you have received numerous requests for speeches and public appearances. One of the recent requests, from the Zonta Club of Canton, conflicts with your trip to New York to appear on the "Today Show." On a separate sheet of paper, write to Ms. Carole Collins, the President of Zonta, and refuse her request. Be-

cause your schedule has been so busy lately, you are unable to suggest an alternate time, though she could call you again in about six months. In the meantime, Dr. Dwayne Heires of the Department of Psychology at Malone College does a good job speaking about the psychology of human relations. Ms. Collins might give Dr. Heires a call.

18. As a major manufacturer of sporting goods, your company—Heart Incorporated, Vail, CO 81657—often receives letters from individuals ordering merchandise directly from you. After they see an ad for one of your products, they write to you and ask for the product at your wholesale price. Because you have determined that the most profitable way for you to do business is through established, reputable retailers, you must refuse all such requests. Customers also receive advantages through this system of distribution. They can examine the merchandise before purchasing, determine whether it meets their needs, and have someone at the local level who will guarantee their satisfaction. Of course, for these advantages customers have to pay the full retail price.

On a separate sheet of paper, write to Edward T. Colton, 1917 Clark Avenue, Raleigh, NC 27695, and refuse his order for a pair of your cross-country skis, boots, and bindings. Two of your dealers are in Colton's town: Williams Sporting Goods, 911 Randolph, and The Sport-About, 217 Franklin.

19. As a loan officer for the American National Bank, 201 South Grand Avenue, New Orleans, LA 70122, you process hundreds of applications for car loans every year. Applications are usually approved on the basis of regular employment. Every now and then, however, a person with a regular job will not have sufficient income to meet all her or his financial obligations. Such is the case with Sarah Sontag, who has applied for a loan to purchase a used car. In spite of the fact that

she is a full-time student at the University of New Orleans, she works full time as night manager of a local McDonald's restaurant and earns $180 a week. Her take-home pay is $120, and she pays $375 a month to rent a luxury one-bedroom apartment. That leaves her with only $141 to meet other expenses. She wants to borrow $2750 for 24 months. That would leave her with practically nothing to live on. It would be in her best interest to avoid borrowing money for a car at this time. After she completes her degree, her credit will be much more valuable. She should be careful to protect it now. On a separate sheet of paper, write to Sarah at 418 Royale Avenue, New Orleans, LA 70122, and refuse her application.

20. As a result of increased fuel costs and inflation, your company, Peck Glass Works, finds it necessary to lay off about 20 percent of its hourly employees. The layoff will be indefinite and based strictly on seniority. Rumors have been circulating through the plant, and the employees know that the layoffs are coming, but they do not know how many— or who—will be affected, or when the layoffs will begin. You have already decided to begin laying off next week at the rate of 5 percent a week until the 20 percent have been laid off.

a. On a separate sheet of paper, prepare a memo for distribution to supervisors explaining the reasons for the layoffs, the methods by which you will determine who is laid off, and when the layoffs will begin.

b. On a separate sheet of paper, write a letter to Rodney Tilton, telling him that he will be laid off indefinitely beginning in two weeks. Rodney has a good work record, and you will be glad to have him back when business conditions permit.

CHAPTER NINE
Persuading Your Reader to Act

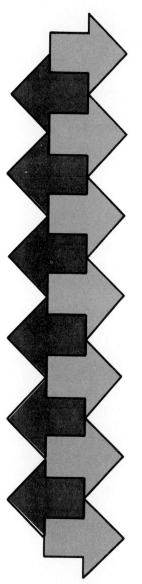

Why do you buy something or change your mind about a subject? What kinds of advertising do you read? What kinds do you ignore? The reasons people are motivated to act are complex and varied. The advertising that appeals to you may not appeal to someone else—and vice versa. This chapter focuses on the psychology of persuasion.

Topics

COMMUNICATION CHALLENGE

Suppose that you are responsible for selling a new, inexpensive ($15.95), solar-powered AM-FM radio to a variety of audiences. The radio runs on solar power during the day and also uses sunlight to charge batteries for use at night. Unlike most radios, it uses a computer chip to ensure the highest quality sound reproduction and best reception. It is even waterproof, and it will have a complete one-year guarantee. Why might each of the following groups be interested in such a radio?

High school students

College students

Homemakers

Businessmen

Businesswomen

Retired persons

Travelers

Also, what interests, needs, or wants might apply to all these categories? How would you go about persuading people to purchase the radio? As you read through this chapter, you may wish to add to or modify your original ideas. Compare your analysis with the one that follows the chapter summary.

▷ OVERVIEW: WHAT IS PERSUASION?

Of all aspects of business communication, persuasion is perhaps the most studied — and the least understood. From Aristotle until today, persuasion has been the focus of tremendous interest and study because it plays such a central role in life. We would all like the power to persuade others — to buy from us rather than from our competitors, to see movie A rather than movie B, to help us fix our car, or even to marry us.

Persuasion is not simple, and we should be grateful that it is not. Can you imagine a world in which someone had so mastered persuasive techniques that he or she could talk anybody into anything? Fortunately, most people resist persuasive messages most of the time. Also fortunately, each persuasive message must vie with a number of competing messages — if I help you fix your car, I will not be able to go to the beach; if I buy product A, I will not be able to buy product B. For this reason, persuasive messages work best — are most persuasive — when they meet the preexisting needs of the audience. In other words, you can talk me into giving up my day at the beach and helping you fix your car only if I have some need that can be satisfied by doing so. Perhaps I

Believe that work is better (healthier, morally superior) than play.

Believe that I owe you a favor.

Am short of cash, and you will pay me $25.

Want you to help fix my roof next week.

Believe that friendship is important.

Am curious about the problem you have been having with the car.

Need to maintain my image as a person who can fix anything.

Whatever my need is, you will not be able to persuade me unless you can make me sufficiently aware of it so that helping you becomes more desirable than going to the beach.

▷ THE NATURE OF PERSUASION

What is persuasion?   All communication is persuasive to the extent that it attempts to influence behavior and thinking. Almost everything we have said about writing thus far pertains as much to your need to "sell" a favorable image of yourself or your company as it does to communicating a particular idea. *Persuasive messages,* as we use the term here, however, differ from the other message types discussed so far in that their purpose is to produce a specific behavior in a reader who may ignore or resist the message or the suggested behavior.

You thus run a greater risk of failing to communicate in persuasive situations than you do in informational situations. In communication situations involving positive information, your business objective and human objective are both served by communicating your message simply and clearly. In communication situations involving negative information, your business objective includes not only communicating your message clearly, but also having your reader accept it. In negative situations you cannot achieve your business objective without taking your reader's feelings into account and thus achieving your human objective; in other words, you must achieve your human objective to achieve your business objective.

In addition to the problems presented by negative messages, communication situations requiring persuasion also present the problem of having the reader simply not care about or actively disagree with your message. Persuasive messages, like negative messages, require indirect structure because you must prepare the reader for the business objective by focusing on the human objective first.

Why are people suspicious of persuasive messages?   Before you can ask your reader to take a particular action, you must convince your reader that your message has something worthwhile to offer and that what you say is true. Furthermore, you must achieve these objectives in spite of the fact that your reader may suspect persuasive messages—yours included—of being untruthful to some degree.

One of the least recognized facts about persuasion is that the most successful persuasive messages are those that can offer the audience real benefits or other positive information. The more the reader has to gain, the easier it is to prepare a persuasive message.

▷ READER RESISTANCE AND APPEALS

When a reader is likely to ignore or resist your message, you need to analyze your reader according to the principles discussed in Chapter 1, paying particular attention to the possible reader benefits. Also, you need to evaluate your reader's perception of you and of the subject of your message and compare these perceptions with your reader's probable self-interests.

What the Reader Perceives

Many factors influence your reader's reception of your persuasive message. Although you do not need to understand all the current theories of how persuasion works to be able to write an effective persuasive message, you do need to consider your credibility, the reader's degree of interest in the subject of your message, and the content of your message.

What is credibility?

Credibility.   Your ability to persuade will depend heavily on whether the reader perceives you as an expert on the topic of the message and on whether the reader believes that you are honest. You can have

> **Long term credibility.**   You are a well-known authority, and you have always been honest before.
>
> **Short-term credibility.**   You offer facts and figures to prove that you are an expert, and your evidence is sound.
>
> **Carry-over credibility.**   You know a lot about one subject and have been honest about it, so you will probably be honest about a new subject, too.
>
> **Official credibility.**   Your particular position or office shows that you should be credible.

It is an unfortunate fact of modern life that people have become accustomed to being lied to. No single group (business leaders, politicians, military leaders, teachers, doctors, the press, or even scientists) has consistently high credibility. The public tends to lack trust because these groups have provided false information in the past, covered up mistakes, and otherwise misled people who relied on them.

How can you improve your credibility?

Because credibility is currently in such short supply, it may well be the single most important factor in persuasion, and the most important factor in credibility is *character.* Fortunately, you have virtually absolute control over your character. If you want to be believed, do not lie or withhold important information, or otherwise mislead those who look to you as an authoritative source of information.

First, be sure that you are authoritative. Your *expertise*, or knowledge of a particular subject, plays an important role in whether you are perceived as credible. Make sure you know your subject thoroughly, but when faced with a question you cannot answer, be honest and admit you do not have an answer. No one expects even an expert to know everything. When you need additional time to answer a question, say so, and then follow through.

Second, you will also be perceived as more credible if you are friendly, warm, and open. Indeed, for the short term, the audience's perception of your credibility may hinge more on your attitude of friendliness and openness than it does on your actual record of expertise and honesty. Remember, however, that the opposite is true for your long-term credibility. That will depend on a consistent record of honesty.

Reader's Interest in the Subject.   You cannot expect someone who has no interest in your subject to be persuaded by even a first-rate letter. To paraphrase Lincoln, you can persuade all of the people some of the time and some of the people all of the time, but you can't persuade all of the people all of the time. Whenever you write a persuasive message, your success rate can be calculated as a percentage. While a typical success rate is impossible to predict, in some instances (direct mail advertising, for example) a *success percentage* of 4 or 5—that is, 4 or 5 out of every 100 readers are persuaded to act—would be an excellent response. In other cases (persuading your boss to add another employee to your department) such a low success percentage would be a disaster.

Why should your reader care about your message?

Content of the Message.   The same arguments and appeals will not work equally well with all people or for all products and services. You should select the content of each message according to your perception of your reader's wants and needs.

Importance of You-Attitude.   To complicate matters further, it is frequently difficult to learn much about your reader's perceptions before you must attempt to persuade her or him. Naturally, before you attempt to persuade, you need to assess your credibility with your intended audience and determine your reader's degree of interest in your topic. But even if your credibility with a reader is low through no fault of your own, and the reader has no particular interest in your message, you may be able to create interest and credibility by paying close attention to what you can do for the reader. By applying the you-attitude to the persuasive situation and focusing on what you can do for the reader—rather than on what she or he should do for you—you can develop the reader's natural interest in personal benefit.

What the Reader Wants

Why are readers likely to resist persuasive messages?

More so than other messages, a persuasive message prompts the reader to ask, "How will this message benefit me?" You will need to provide an answer to that question quickly, interestingly, and believably if you are going to

COMMUNICATION TODAY. . .

People don't buy a newspaper. They buy news.

It isn't spectacles that are bought. It's better vision.

Nobody wants goopy chemicals called cosmetics. But handsome prices are paid for them to bring beauty and good looks.

Millions of drills have been sold. Yet not a single person wanted one. They were buying holes.

People do not buy goods or services. They buy what those things will do for them.

That became dimly apparent as I helped Joe identify the emotions within him, sort them out, and come up with a way to satisfy them. He was motivated to a course of action that I had hoped he would take. I was also taught one of the most valuable lessons of my sales and management career.

Persuasion takes place by helping people meet their emotional needs.

Source: Robert Conklin, *How to Get People to Do Things* (Chicago: Contemporary Books, 1979), p. 100.

---

overcome your reader's natural resistance to being persuaded. Such resistance may be caused by one or more of the following four reasons:

1. **Negative previous experience.**   Your reader may have had a bad experience with you, your idea, your company, a similar product or service, or with other persuasive messages.

2. **Time.**   Your reader may not wish to take the time to read an unexpected message, or your message may require the reader to spend time in a way he or she would not normally choose.

3. **Money.**   Acting on your message may cost the reader (or the reader's company) money that the reader would rather spend in some other way.

4. **Belief systems.**   Your reader may hold beliefs incompatible with the action you desire him or her to perform. People are not easily persuaded to change their religious beliefs, for example.

Unless a reader has had some positive experience with the suggested behavior, he or she will be inclined to focus on the negative aspects of previous experience and on the associated costs. To overcome the reader's tendency to accept the negative in the absence of a strong belief in the positive, you need to appeal to the reader's self-interest. You need to convince your reader that the action you are suggesting will prove desirable and will be more beneficial than the many other ways that the reader's time and money could be spent.

Why are specific
benefits ("a one-
year guarantee")
more persuasive
than general prom-
ises ("you'll be fully
satisfied")?

Appeals to Self-interest.   Because appeals to the reader's self-interest
are more convincing when they are practical and specific, your best approach
is to base your appeals on people's needs for health, wealth, pleasure, and
curiosity. As psychologists have pointed out, human needs are hierarchical;
some are more important to our survival than others. A persuasive message
should base its appeal on the strongest need that can be associated with the
behavior, idea, or product suggested.

One of the best known hierarchies of needs was developed by Abraham
Maslow,[1] who hypothesized that human needs fall into five categories.

Why are appeals to
lower-level needs
more persuasive
than appeals to
higher-level needs?

1.   **Physiological needs**   include food, water, air, sleep, shelter, and other
       requirements for sustaining life.

2.   **Safety and security needs**   include protection from physical and psy-
       chological injury.

3.   **Social needs**   include relationships with others, human affection and
       acceptance, and group membership.

4.   **Ego needs**   include self-esteem and recognition from others.

5.   **Self-actualization needs**   include the desire to become all that one is
       capable of becoming.

Maslow's theory is that after we satisfy the basic (lower-level) needs —
that is, categories 1 and 2 in the foregoing list — we turn our attention to
satisfying the higher-level needs. The theory of a hierarchy of needs helps
explain the reasons people will or will not respond to persuasive messages.

People need to have the basic needs satisfied all the time. If you are
able to satisfy a basic need, your message will appeal to a larger audience
than if you are appealing to a higher-level need. Also, if you can show that
you can satisfy several needs at the same time, your message will have a
greater chance for success.

In general, appeals to *health* — which corresponds with Maslow's first
category and part of the second — are the strongest appeals. Appeals to *wealth*
— which correspond with Maslow's second category — are second in strength.
Appeals to *pleasure* — which corresponds with Maslow's social needs and ego
needs — are third. Appeals to *curiosity* — which corresponds with self-actualization needs — would appeal to the fewest people in most circumstances.

You must, however, begin by selecting your appeals from the standpoint of what the suggested behavior, idea, or product will do for someone
rather than by examining the range of human needs. You cannot arbitrarily

---

[1]Abraham H. Maslow, *Motivation and Personality*, 2d ed (New York: Harper and Row, 1970), pp.
35 – 58.

assign attributes to the behavior, idea, or product simply because those attributes would fill a human need.

How should you begin planning for a persuasive message?

Begin by asking yourself how the behavior, idea, or product will contribute to your reader's health, wealth, pleasure, or curiosity. List as many appeals as you can think of for each category. Your appeals can be either positive or negative. Positive appeals focus on the gain that will result from taking a particular action. Negative appeals stress *avoiding a loss*. Life insurance, for example, can be sold as a means of saving for the future (positive appeal) or as a means of protecting one's family against loss of income in the event of death (negative appeal). Both positive and negative appeals encourage the suggested action. Figure 9.1 illustrates the possibilities.

The four broad and sometimes overlapping categories in Figure 9.1 contain all possible appeals, such as

Making or saving money.

Protecting an investment.

Establishing a reputation.

Saving time or effort.

Playing fair and cooperating.

Achieving a goal.

Wanting to be well thought of.

Wanting to feel good about one's self.

Wanting to be successful.

Being afraid.

Needing to know.

Wanting to be attractive to the opposite sex.

Avoiding unattractive characteristics (such as bad breath).

Fearing illness, old age, and death.

These categories permit an easy frame of reference in deciding what benefits you can offer your reader.

What is the difference between positive and negative appeals?

The general rule is that positive appeals, which focus on what the reader will gain, are more successful than negative appeals, which focus on what the reader might lose. Negative appeals have been effective in selling insurance and some related concepts, and they are currently being used to promote seat-belt use and the 55-mile-an-hour speed limit. Unless the threat of loss is perceived as both real and fairly immediate, however, readers frequently ignore negative appeals. For example, negative appeals have been unsuccessful in persuading people to stop smoking. The threats of disease and an earlier death seem too remote to concern most people.

		Health	Wealth	Pleasure	Curiosity
FIGURE 9.1 Positive and Negative Appeals	*Positive:*	Acting will make your reader feel better or live longer.	Acting will help your reader earn or save money or time.	Acting will make the reader think better of him- or herself, or the reader will enjoy acting.	Acting will answer questions the reader would like answered.
	Negative:	Not acting will make your reader feel worse or die sooner.	Not acting will cost your reader time or money.	Not acting will deprive the reader of enjoyment or make the reader think worse of him- or herself.	Not acting will leave important questions unanswered.

What are the differences between emotional and rational appeals?

Emotional and Rational Appeals.   Appeals are also classed as either emotional or rational, depending on whether they appeal primarily to the reader's emotions or reason. Emotional appeals display the following characteristics:

1.   **They use emotionally laden words.**   Two persuasive messages may contain the same factual elements, but one may use words that appeal to the reader's emotions and the other may use words that appeal to the reader's sense of logic.

> **Emotional:**   You can quit *wasting precious* fuel and *polluting* the air by switching to *modern, pollution-free* electrical heat.

> **Rational:**   An all-electric home gives you clean, efficient heating.

2.   **They use explicit and implied analogies as proof.**   Analogies—that is, comparisons—can be either emotional or rational, depending on how they are used. When analogies are used as proof, they are emotional. When they are used to illustrate and explain, they are logical. The following examples are taken from recent magazine ads:

> **Example:**   The GLC's instrument panel looks like an instrument panel you'd expect to see in a car costing a grand more.

> **Analysis:**   The analogy implies that the instrument panel is high quality.

Example: Like a fine musical instrument, Marantz [stereo equipment] is designed to be at one with the music.

Analysis: The analogy implies that the product is able to reproduce music with the same quality of sound as the original instruments.

Example: The U.S. Environmental Protection Agency reports that charcoal is the best available method for filtering water. It's also used to mellow the taste of the finest bourbons. Plain white filters remove taste. Tareyton's charcoal filter actually improves flavor.

Analysis: The analogy implies that the charcoal filter on the product will filter smoke as well as EPA says it filters water and that the charcoal will mellow the taste of cigarette smoke the same way it mellows the taste of bourbon.

Example: Let Arthur [Ashe], Tom [Watson], and Roger [Staubach] tell you how to improve your grip: "Get Armstrong Tires. They grip the road!" On the court, on the course, and on the field, the right grip gives these winners the control they need. On the road, the Armstrong grip does the same thing.

Analysis: The analogy implies that there is a high degree of similarity between a person holding a tennis racquet, a golf club, or a football and a tire holding the road.

3.   **They appeal to the physical senses.**   Messages that focus on seeing, smelling, tasting, hearing, and touching are emotional. Messages that focus on ideas are rational.

Emotional: Don't tell me taste isn't everything. Taste. And only Winston gives me the taste I like. Winston is all taste all the time. And for me, taste is everything.

Rational: The Trimlite 28 camera has a sharp f/9.5 lens, sliding lens cover, electronic shutter that goes from 1/160 to 1/30 second, CdS

meter for automatic exposure control and
a low-light signal.

4.   **They omit steps required by logic.**   A logical argument proceeds
carefully from point of proof to point of proof. An emotional argument
draws conclusions without providing the complete evidence.

Example: If your schedule [is busy], it's probably hard
                  for people to get hold of you. So you have
                  two choices. You can become a hermit and
                  camp by your telephone. Or you can get
                  yourself a Code-a-phone.

Analysis: The writer of the message has omitted tell-
                  ing the reader why it is necessary for the
                  phone to be answered every time it rings.
                  The reader's third choice is to assume that
                  people will call back if the message is im-
                  portant.

Why should per-
suasive writers con-
cern themselves
with the ethics of
using emotional
appeals?

Emotional appeals, as you can see, tend to manipulate the reader. They
lead the reader to draw conclusions based on insufficient evidence or for the
wrong reasons. Emotional appeals also tend to be more effective for achieving
certain kinds of short-term persuasion. Emotional appeals work best for inexpensive products and intangible services that would be attractive to the
reader primarily because of the momentary pleasure they would provide.

For most situations, however, the best approach is to combine emotional
appeals with more logical arguments. The most persuasive argument you can
provide for an idea, a product, or a service is a true reader benefit. An
emotional appeal may be useful to create reader interest in your message,
but a clear presentation of facts beneficial to the reader is the most persuasive
argument you can use.

In addition to a firm grounding in truth, successful persuasive messages
concentrate on one primary appeal that is based on the writer's analysis of
a strong want or need of the reader. Secondary appeals are used to support
and supplement the primary appeal but are not as fully developed as the
primary appeal.

▷ GENERAL STRUCTURE AND CHECKLIST FOR PERSUASIVE MESSAGES

In what way is the
structure for per-
suasive messages
indirect?

The general structure for all persuasive messages is as follows:

1.   **Attention.**   It is impossible to persuade someone unless that person
will pay attention to you. You can get a reader to focus attention on

SIDEBAR

Show, Don't Tell

Whatever you're selling, find a way to demonstrate it. Whatever you are teaching, look for examples and ways you can present the material by demonstration. Look back on your education.

Which have you remembered the longest, the words you read in the books or the things you learned by involvement and demonstration, mental pictures?

Source: Robert Conklin, *How to Get People to Do Things* (Chicago: Contemporary Books, 1979), p. 108.

We [have] discussed the cardinal rule for securing agreement: Start where THEY are, not where YOU are. The emphasis of this is on the *start,* but it implies movement *toward* something. This "something" can be one of two things: The *actions* you want the audience to take when you are finished; the *attitudes* you want an audience to embrace when you are finished. These are not, of course, mutually exclusive. Actions always signify certain attitudes, and attitudes set up potential action. But from a presentation point of view, it is best to decide on one or the other. Let the momentum built up by such concentration drag along the subtle overtones of the one not selected.

Source: Henry M. Boettinger, *Moving Mountains or the Art and Craft of Letting Others See Things Your Way* (New York: Collier Books, 1979), p. 223.

your message by stating a problem that affects her or him or by promising something of benefit. Emotional appeals frequently catch attention better than rational appeals. The attention element should introduce the primary appeal. Questions that cannot be answered yes or no (that is, questions that begin with *what, how, why, who, where,* and *when*) usually make the best openings for persuasive messages. Because they tend to invite negative responses, *yes* or *no* questions are a second choice for an opening, as are statements of reader benefit.

2.   **Interest.**   You can maintain reader interest by showing your reader that a solution to a problem is possible or by picturing him or her enjoying the benefits promised. Answer the questions asked in the attention element. Use the interest element to provide clear transition from the attention element to the conviction element.

3.   **Conviction.**   The conviction element of your persuasive message consists of the facts, figures, testimonials, tests, samples, guarantees, or other proof your proposal requires. Some of this material may be pro-

vided in a descriptive brochure rather than in the letter to help keep the letter from being too cluttered. (Refer to the brochure late in the message.) The conviction element should fully develop the primary appeal and perhaps contain secondary appeals as well.

4. **Action.**   The close of a persuasive message should tell the reader exactly what action to take, give a reason for acting promptly, and provide a postage-paid reply envelope or other aids to make that action easy. The action element should contain a reference to the primary appeal.

▷ MESSAGE DEVELOPMENT

As you can see from the foregoing discussion, persuasion is a complicated process. Communicating clearly and presenting a definite reader benefit are not in themselves always sufficient to persuade a reader to change his or her behavior. Successful persuasion requires very skillful audience analysis, careful application of the principles of persuasion in an artfully constructed message, and—because human behavior is not wholly predictable—a fair share of luck.

Why is persuasion always a matter of percentages?

As mentioned earlier, persuasion is always a matter of percentages. A letter that is technically perfect (in grammar and style) may fail to persuade, whereas a letter that is poor in many respects may succeed. The differences between successful and unsuccessful persuasive messages are not always obvious. Technical perfection, however, is rarely a principal factor.

What counts the most is the reader's perception of how much he or she will benefit from acting as you suggest. In addition to writing the best letter you are capable of—to avoid losing those readers who expect technical perfection—you need to control your reader's perception by *image building.*

Building the Image

Successful persuasive messages usually have a quality of *life* not found in routine positive or negative letters. This quality of life comes from the mental image the writer has of the objective of the message; the audience; the product, service, or idea; and the possible benefits. The clearer and more positive the writer's mental image is, the more persuasive the message will be. The goal is to create a clear, positive picture in the reader's mind.

What does it mean to "begin where they are"?

The general structure for persuasive messages—attention, interest, conviction, action—and the categories of appeals—health, wealth, pleasure, and curiosity—provide the basis for image building. Your first task as a persuasive writer is to create an image of the benefit that will be clear enough and dramatic enough to catch the reader's attention. To do this successfully, you must begin where the reader is. You cannot build an image for which a foundation does not already exist in the reader's mind. In many ways the persuasive process is a journey from a foundational image the reader already has to the image you wish to create. For your reader to "see" your finished image, you need to begin with the one the reader sees already and alter it in a step-by-step process until the new image is created. Some typical beginning images are

1. **A problem that needs solving.**   Describe a problem that plagues your reader and promise a solution.

    What can you do about the rising costs of office supplies?

    Since January 1, 1980, 10 people have died in 42 accidents at the intersection of Drake Road and Stadium Drive.

    Because American culture is changing from a role-centered to a goal-centered society, Carthage Industries should anticipate changing patterns of organizational communication.

2. **A well-established cultural image.**   When the reader already accepts an image, you can use it as a starting point.

    Because your family is important to you . . .

    Are you working too hard when you should be enjoying yourself more?

    Saving time is just as important as saving money.

    Your family will appreciate cleaner smelling clothes.

    How do *you* measure success?

3. **A specific benefit.**   When the benefit you can offer your reader is definite and obvious, you can use it as an opening image.

    By reorganizing our typing pool and installing modern word processing equipment, TRV can save $26,000 in the first year.

    You can increase your gas mileage by 46 percent regardless of the kind of car you drive.

    Imagine yourself enjoying Cadillac's luxury . . .

    Flying gets you there faster.

    With Sweeto Mouthwash, you'll never have to worry about your breath again.

4. **A desired benefit.**   Benefits less specific and obvious can still make effective opening images.

    What mysteries of life can we solve by exploring Mars?

    When was the last time you took the time to learn something new?

    Would you like your job better if you had the chance to help make some of the decisions?

With today's rate of inflation, your house may be underinsured.

Because comfort is important to you . . .

Moving the Reader

Why is transition especially important in persuasive messages?

In each of the foregoing examples — regardless of whether the appeal is to health, wealth, pleasure, or curiosity — the beginning image is one that an interested reader can readily accept. As we said earlier, not all people will respond to a given persuasive message. People who are afraid to fly, for example, will not only fail to respond to airline ads, but will actively avoid reading them. Persuasion depends on the right opening image for the selected audience.

Once you have selected an attention-getting image appropriate for your audience, your next step is to begin moving the reader from the starting point to your goal — the image that will elicit the desired action. This process requires skill. Introduce changes in your opening image slowly, and keep your reader in the picture as you build on the original image. The following techniques help keep your reader with you as you move from the opening image to the final image.

1.   **Make sure that the opening image is appropriate for your message.** Each sentence should lead naturally to the next.

> **Poor:**   Flying gets you there faster. But why fly when you can enjoy a train ride.

> **Better:**   Flying gets you there faster. But more important than how fast you get there is how ready you are to work once you arrive.

2.   **Subordinate physical description and explanations to the accompanying reader benefits.** (Focus on *value*.)

> **Poor:**   The Moonbeam paint mixer has a ½ horsepower motor. (Physical description only.)

> **Better:**   With its ½ horsepower motor, the Moonbeam paint mixer lets you mix two gallons of paint in only 60 seconds.

> **Poor:**   Currently each office has a secretary who is responsible for all staff support functions, including . . . (Explanation only.)

> **Better:**   Our current office organization is costing us thousands of dollars a year. By having individual secretaries for each separate department . . .

What is a central
selling point?

3.   Focus on one main appeal and develop it fully. The main appeal, often
called the *central selling point*, presents the reader with the final image.
Select your appeal—health, wealth, pleasure, or curiosity—based on
your reader's needs. Introduce other appeals as they relate naturally to
your main appeal, but stress one appeal so that the reader's final image
will be complete. In Figure 9.2, the underlined words and phrases are
the main appeal.

**FIGURE 9.2
Illustration of
Central Selling
Point**

Flying gets you there faster.

But more important than how fast you get there is how <u>ready to work</u> you
are when you arrive. Because flying not only saves you time but also allows
you to arrive <u>fresh and ready to work</u>, you naturally fly whenever you can.
When your business takes you to New York, Chicago, San Francisco, or even
to San Jose or Kalamazoo, you're in good shape.

But what happens when your business takes you to Albion, Michigan, or
to Coyote, Utah? After covering three-quarters of your trip in a couple of hours,
you drive . . .

. . . and you drive

. . . and you drive.

<u>By the time you finally reach your destination, you're tired</u> and more ready
for a shower than a business meeting.

The solution? Your own airplane.

Think of how much <u>time you could save</u> if you could fly directly into all
the cities where you need to do business.

With a Blair Business Jet, you'd not only <u>save the time</u> you currently spend
driving from a metropolitan airport to your point of destination, but also <u>arrive
fresher</u> and ready for work.

And you can own a Blair for less than you might think, especially when
you consider the <u>costs of time lost driving to meetings</u> when calculating your
travel expenses. An executive earning $50,000 a year costs you nearly $30 an
hour—can you really afford to have your key people <u>waste time driving or
waiting for connections in airports?</u> But even more important, <u>can you afford
to have your company represented by tired, grouchy decision-makers? Can you
afford to spend time driving or to arrive tired?</u>

Because <u>time and efficiency</u> are important to you, consider an investment
that will be paying for itself with every trip you or your key people take. A
Blair Business Jet can make a difference.

For more information, call our toll-free number, 1-800-666-9000. You can
begin getting there faster today.

The appeal to wealth—saving time and being more efficient—is stressed
throughout. Secondary appeals—to the pleasure of flying in a private plane
or owning a status symbol—might well be added to a full sales message,

but the focus should remain on the single, primary appeal throughout the message.

Securing Action

What is required for an ending that will secure the desired action from the reader?

As you move your reader from the original image to the final image, you are setting the stage for requesting the action you desire. Your final image should lead naturally to the action you want your reader to take, but unless you provide a gentle push, the image you have so carefully established is likely to fade before the reader acts. The push, however, must be gentle. If your language is too strong, you will increase your reader's natural resistance to acting.

> Don't delay; act today!
>
> You simply must order one now!
>
> You'll have to hurry on this one!
>
> You have no choice but to change the office structure immediately.

If your language is not strong enough, however, your reader will lose confidence in your message.

> If you'd like to try one, . . .
>
> Why not place an order today?
>
> By now you should be able to see the advantages . . .
>
> I hope that this has convinced you . . .

In general, the best request for action tells the reader explicitly what to do and how to do it, makes that action as easy as possible, provides a reason for acting promptly, and gives the reader one last view of the benefit to be gained, as illustrated in Figure 9.3.

**FIGURE 9.3
Sample Action
Endings**

To order, simply complete the enclosed postage-paid reply card and drop it in the nearest mail box. You'll receive your first issue of The Human Psyche in about three weeks.

By signing the enclosed purchase form for the Mentor Information System, you'll enable the market research staff to complete analyses in less than half the time it now takes.

When your audience's belief system differs greatly from yours, you may have to be content with asking for "smaller" actions. Because a small commitment will often lead to a larger one, it's often better to ask for a series of smaller commitments than to ask for the final action you desire, as shown in Figure 9.4.

**FIGURE 9.4
More Action
Endings**

Send no money now. Examine the books for 15 days at no risk. If you're not absolutely convinced that <u>Big Ideas</u> is the best collection of the world's great writing available, simply return the books and pay nothing. To keep the books, send only $19.95 a month for the next 12 months. . . .

The installation of word processing equipment is an important decision which needs careful consideration. If the equipment works as anticipated, we could save thousands of dollars a year. Because of the potential savings, I recommend that we install the equipment in the Personnel Department on a trial basis. . . .

▷ AUDIENCE AND APPEALS

Why is it important to write to one reader at a time?

When you are writing to one specific person, you have a much wider choice of appeals than if you must address a group of people. You can refer to the reader by name and include the kinds of details that will help the reader accept your image of the proper action. When you are sending the same message to many people, you have not only all the problems of persuading one person, but also the task of overcoming the impersonality of form communications.

Because we all consider ourselves unique, we have a natural tendency to be skeptical of messages that do not seem to address needs that are uniquely ours. One of the standard ways persuasive writers attempt to recognize individuality is by identifying the reader by group membership.

Dear Reader:

Dear Homeowner:

Dear Californian:

Dear Voter:

Dear Student:

But the problem with group identifications is that in today's society most of us do not identify strongly with the groups to which we belong. Homeowners, for example, do not all perceive their needs as the same, and the same appeals would not work equally well with all of them. A message to homeowners in general may fail to acknowledge the uniqueness of the individual reader.

When should you use a simulated inside address?

To make sure that each of your readers feels that you understand his or her situation sufficiently well to be able to help, address your readers one at a time. Write your letter for one person, not for a group, using a *simulated inside address*. The simulated inside address looks like a traditional inside address and salutation, making the letter seem less like a form.

Not:	Dear Homeowner:
But:	Because your home is Important to you . . .
Not:	Dear Student:
But:	As a student You know how Frustrating it is . . .

Naturally, your reader will still recognize your message as a form and will suspect that your message may not apply to him or her. To overcome this natural suspicion, design your message for easy readability and mention your main benefit early.

When should you use special mechanical devices to help catch a reader's attention?

When appropriate, mechanical techniques such as color, narrow columns of type, paragraphs of varying widths and lengths, and numbered and unnumbered lists may help increase reader attention to your message.

By now you know that each communication situation calls for an individual approach. This is especially true for persuasive messages. The following chapter presents several common problems calling for persuasive messages. Each of the problems represents a type, but while the principles may be the same for each problem within the type, the application of the principles will vary from problem to problem. No two people perform the same action for the same reason. Your persuasive messages should take this into account.

▷ SUMMARY

To the extent that all messages attempt to influence behavior and thinking, all messages are persuasive. In this text, however, we use the term *persuasive message* to mean one that aims to produce a specific behavior in the reader who may ignore or resist the message.

The following factors will influence your reader's reception of your persuasive message: (1) your credibility as an authoritative and reliable source, (2) the reader's degree of interest in the subject of your message, and (3) the content of your message. Your reader will be likely to resist your message for one of four reasons — negative previous experience, time, money, and belief systems.

You will need to appeal to the reader's self-interest to overcome a negative previous experience or to convince your reader that the action you are

COMMUNICATION SOLUTION

Even though there would be wide variation from individual to individual, members of each of the categories would have several interests in common. You might sell the radio on any of the following bases: low cost, portability, low maintenance (always works, no batteries to replace), technological innovation, high quality sound, durability (waterproof), safety (no shock hazard), reliability (guarantee).

The best sales message would emphasize only one or two of these benefits, briefly mentioning the others. The point that receives the greatest emphasis, the *central selling point,* might be the following:

High school students:	low cost, durability, or portability.
College students:	low cost, portability, or high quality sound.
Homemakers:	low maintenance, portability, safety, reliability.

Businessmen:	low maintenance, technological innovation, high quality sound, reliability.
Businesswomen:	low maintenance, technological innovation, high quality sound, reliability.
Retired persons:	low cost, low maintenance, portability, durability, safety, reliability.
Travelers:	low cost, portability, durability, safety, reliability.

Do any of these appeals surprise you? You might wish to compare your list with that of others in your class and discuss the similarities and differences among the lists.

suggesting will be more beneficial than the many other ways the reader's time and money could be spent. You will also need to analyze the reader's belief systems to determine the degree to which they are compatible with your message.

People's needs fall into four general categories: health, wealth, pleasure, and curiosity. Your appeals to these needs can be either positive or negative.

The general structure for all persuasive messages is attention, interest, conviction, and action.

Successful persuasive messages usually have a quality of *life* not found in routine positive or negative letters. This quality of life comes from the mental image the writer has of the objective of the message; the audience, the product, service, or idea; and the possible benefits. Your first task as a persuasive writer is to create an image of the benefit that will be clear enough and dramatic enough to catch the reader's attention.

Once you have selected an attention-getting image appropriate for your audience, your next step is to begin moving the reader from the starting point to your goal—the image that will elicit the desired action. Use the following techniques to keep your reader with you as you move from the opening image to the final image: (1) make sure that the opening image is appropriate for your message, (2) subordinate physical description and explanations to the accompanying reader benefits, and (3) focus on one main appeal. Your final image should lead naturally to the action you want your reader to take; unless you provide a gentle push, however, the image you have so carefully established is likely to fade before the reader acts.

To make sure that each of your readers feels that you understand her or his situation sufficiently well to be able to help, address your readers one at a time. Write your letter for one person, not for a group.

▷ EXERCISES

Review and Discussion Questions

1. When is a persuasive message necessary?

2. How do persuasive messages differ from other messages?

3. What three factors should you consider in writing a persuasive message?

4. Give four reasons a reader might resist a message.

5. Name the four general categories of self-interest. Explain how they can be either positive or negative.

6. Name and explain Maslow's five categories of human needs.

7. Name the four characteristics of emotional appeals.

8. What is the general structure for an effective persuasive message?

9. Name four typical beginning images.

10. Name three techniques to keep your reader with you as you move from the opening image to the final image.

Problems

1. Write a one-page memo to your instructor explaining the differences between the following letters. Be sure to cover appeals (health, wealth, pleasure, and curiosity) and structural elements (attention, interest, conviction, action).

Dear Teacher:

  We have just the product you'll be interested
in, and it's only $29.95.

  Imagine! Our briefcase is designed to hold a
ton of books, papers, and other work. It's a
simulated leather executive model and measures
24" x 20" x 6". It has a special compartment
for papers, a special compartment for notebooks,
and a special section to hold a cassette tape
recorder or an electronic calculator. It also
has a secret compartment in which a checkbook
or important papers could be hidden.

  Enclosed you will find a brochure. This
brochure describes the briefcase in detail and
has some pictures of it.

  Teachers all over the country are telling one
another about our wonderful, exciting briefcase.
Everyone who has received one has written back
expressing tremendous satisfaction with the
briefcase.

  If you want to receive one, you had better
act today. The supply is going fast, and it
won't last much longer. Order yours now!

      Cordially,

      Everett Kessler

      Everett Kessler

      enc

Every teacher needs
a briefcase that can keep
papers and books nice and neat...

From experience you know how maddening it is to
open your briefcase at the end of a hard day of
teaching, only to discover that your students'
papers are so thoroughly shuffled that you need
an extra 45 minutes just to get each paper back
into its proper place.

With the Executive Teacher briefcase you won't
have that worry. We've taken the special design
features of our Executive briefcase and put them
in a larger model that will hold all the books
and papers you need to carry.

We've made sure that you'll have room for...

         ... your cassette tape recorder
         ... your electronic calculator
         ... your checkbook
         ... important papers you want kept
             separate from your school work

The pictures in the enclosed brochure show you
just how versatile the 24" x 20" x 6" Executive
Teacher briefcase actually is. To order yours,
just complete the order blank and send it with
your check for $29.95 in the postage-free
envelope provided. In ten days you can be
enjoying the...

neatest papers in town.

Cordially,

Everett Kessler

Everett Kessler

As a bonus for ordering in the next seven days,
we'll send you a special edition of the famous
Teacher's Calendar to help you keep your
appointments straight.

enc

2. Using the better letter in Problem 1 as an example, describe the changes you would make if you were attempting to sell the same briefcase to college students. What changes would you make for businessmen? Businesswomen? Write a one-page memo to your instructor explaining your choices.

3. What appeals would you use to sell a trimline pocket calculator to business people? To engineers? To college students? Explain your choices in a one-page memo.

4. What appeals would you use to persuade your boss to let you hire an additional person for your department in spite of a company-wide job freeze? How would the other department heads be likely to respond? Explain your choices and rationale in a one-page memo.

5. What appeals would be appropriate for the following products and services:

Life insurance.

Desk lamp-radio combinations.

A self-help book.

A rock concert.

A Shakespeare festival.

"Bargain" clothes.

Island vacations.

Long-life spark plugs.

Encyclopedias.

A "Giant Screen" color television set.

A fraternity kegger.

Latest fashion designs for men and women.

A new kind of shoe that will not wear out.

A new sports car (choose your own price range, but be specific)

Are the appeals you selected emotional or rational, positive or negative? Why?

6. What evidence would you present in the conviction section of the letter for the products you selected from Problem 5?

7. In a one-page memo, explain the meaning of the sentence, "Sell the sizzle, not the steak."

8. What are the differences between persuasion and manipulation? Explain in a memo of whatever length your instructor requests.

9. George Douglas is manager at The American Heritage National Bank, the only bank left in the country without a computer. The owner of the bank, Mrs. Pat P. Lanthrop, hates computers because a computer once billed her incorrectly for a $2.99 phone call she did not make. The bank is now about to fold because depositors are going to banks with more modern services. How can George go about persuading Mrs. Lanthrop to install a computer in the bank? Should he attempt to persuade her with only one message? If not, what should he try to accomplish in each one? Explain your ideas in a one-page memo.

10. Are there some cases where the facts alone would be more persuasive than any persuasive argument you could make? Give and justify examples.

CASE

How long should a persuasive message be? Collect five or six examples of direct mail advertising (letters you receive selling various products and services). How long are the letters? What sorts of supplemental materials are included? Are the letters longer than you think they should be? What is (are) the function(s) of the supplements?

Do you think that most readers of the direct mail advertising you have selected for study would quit reading before reaching the end of the message? Why might the writers of these letters not care if some people quit reading before reaching the end of the letter?

In a two- to three-page memo, answer as many of these questions as you can. Your instructor may require you to do additional secondary research.

CHAPTER TEN
Writing Persuasive Messages

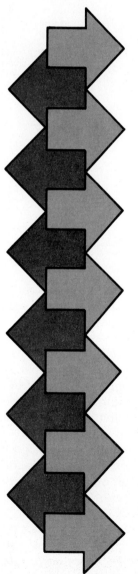

Even though each situation requiring a persuasive message is unique in its particulars, certain general types of situations occur with regularity. This chapter presents the types of persuasive messages required most often.

Topics

COMMUNICATION CHALLENGE

How would you answer a letter from Reginald Jackson (1776 Riverview Drive, East St. Louis, IL 62203) asking about the Recline-O-Matic orthopedic chair you manufacture? His doctor recommended the chair for him.

The chair is designed to reduce strain on the lower back and is especially suitable for those with chronic back pain. Here are some facts about the chair:

Its orthopedic design distributes body weight evenly and fully supports the back.

It has a fully automatic lift-and-recline mechanism that prevents strain on the back.

When a doctor recommends this chair, its purchase price may be covered by insurance. The remainder is tax-deductible.

It blends with any decor, traditional or modern.

It sells for $1,500 and the charge for shipping to East St. Louis will be $158.

It comes in seven colors in four fabrics.

Enclose a brochure that will illustrate colors, fabrics, and the unique steel frame construction. Also, enclose an order form and a physician's form so that Jackson's doctor can specify any special requirements.

Write a draft of your letter now, and then make appropriate changes as you read this chapter. Compare your selection to the one that follows the chapter summary.

▷ OVERVIEW: MOTIVATING THE READER TO ACT

The previous chapter introduced the fundamentals of persuasion. This chapter shows you how to apply those fundamentals to common business situations calling for persuasive messages. Whenever you are writing to someone who has no compelling reason to do (or think) as you ask in your message — and perhaps even no reason to read or reply to your message — you need to write a persuasive message. How persuasive you need to be depends on how obvious it will be to your reader that she or he stands to benefit from acting in the manner you suggest. The three broad categories of persuasive messages are persuasive requests, sales messages (including those that sell ideas), and collection letters.

Just as is true with negative messages, the amount of psychological preparation should be appropriate for the situation. Too much preparation can be as ineffective as too little. A persuasive request, for example, in which you were asking a favor, would require more psychological preparation for the request than would a letter trying to sell an expensive product.

In any persuasive situation, most readers want information about how the product, service, idea, or suggested action will benefit them. Be sure to have a clear conception of those benefits before you begin. Also, make sure

preparation

benefits

action

that you know exactly what you would like your reader to do as a result of your message so that you can ask for that action in the message.

Sales messages, especially letters used in direct mail advertising, tend to be longer than most other business correspondence. It is true that some readers will ignore a longer message, but the most important consideration for a persuasive message is not how many people *read* the message, but how many people *act* as a result of the message. More people may read a short sales letter, but it may be less effective at persuasion than a long one; and in general, it is better to have fewer readers and more "buyers."

Some situations may require more than one persuasive message. When this is true, the entire series of messages follow the basic persuasive structure, with each message containing a more forceful push for action than the preceding one. Messages selling ideas, especially when the audience holds an opposing viewpoint, often use this strategy because it gives the reader time to adjust to a new idea before he or she is asked to act on it.

Sales campaigns and collection letters frequently use this technique as well. In general, the more difficult the persuasive task, the more slowly the writer should proceed. People do not like to be pushed into things. Give them time to decide for themselves that they will benefit from acting on your message.

▷ PERSUASIVE REQUESTS

What is a persuasive request?

Everyone needs to write a persuasive request at one time or another. Are you trying to obtain a "name" speaker for a meeting? Do you need to secure donations for a charity? Have you had a problem convincing a company to replace a defective product? Each of these situations would call for a persuasive request. The four types of persuasive requests are requests for favors, adjustments, credit, and fund-raising letters.

Persuasive Requests for Favors

What are the differences between asking for a favor in person and asking in writing?

Asking a favor by mail is not the same as asking a favor from a friend in person. Friends enjoy helping each other and know that as the relationship continues, the favor will probably be returned. When you write to someone requesting a favor — which will usually cost the reader either time or money — you must offer the reader a benefit that will serve as a substitute for a continuing friendship.

Because your persuasive request should be placed in a specific communication context quickly, you should introduce the reason you are writing early in the message. You should, however, mention the main reader benefit (health, wealth, pleasure, or curiosity) before the specific nature of the re-

COMMUNICATION TODAY...

Giovanni Battista Vico (1668–1744), an Italian philosopher, distills a lifetime of wisdom in a short statement on human temperament: "Men at first feel without observing; then they observe with a troubled and agitated spirit; finally they reflect with a clear mind." Notice the implication of time passing by the use of "at first," "then," and "finally." If Vico is right, as I think him to be, then by linking his insight to the concept of learning by imitation we have a key both to the nature of drama and to methods for the presentation of ideas.

What is the lesson here for us? ...

Simply this. Present your idea in this structure and sequence: statement of the problem, development of its relevant aspects, and resolution of the problem and its development. Use this structure and you send your idea rolling down the well-worn grooves of the human mind. Ignore it and you send it into rocky, unknown canyons from which it may never return.

Source: Henry M. Boettinger, *Moving Mountains or the Art and Craft of Letting Others See Things Your Way* (New York: Collier Books, 1974), pp. 36–37.

There is only one way under high heaven to get anybody to do anything. Did you ever stop to think of that? Yes, just one way. And that is by making the other person want to do it.

Remember, there is no other way.

Of course; you can make someone want to give you his watch by sticking a revolver in his ribs. You can make your employees give you cooperation — until your back is turned — by threatening to fire them. You can make a child do what you want it to do by a whip or a threat. But these crude methods have sharply undesirable repercussions.

The only way I can get you to do anything is by giving you what you want.

Source: Dale Carnegie, *How to Win Friends and Influence People*, rev. ed. (New York: Pocket Books, 1981), p. 18.

quest is clear. Be sure to keep the reader in the picture as you explain why the favor is necessary. Your closing should ask the reader to make a specific commitment by a specific date. It also should reiterate the main reader benefit. Figure 10.1 illustrates these principles of attention, interest, conviction, and action (discussed in Chapter 9).

Be sure to make your message appropriate for the situation and audience. Do not overdo the persuasive content. A message that is more persuasive than it needs to be is often less successful than a message that is less persuasive than it should be. Figure 10.2 illustrates a simple request for a favor when the request is based primarily on friendship.

**FIGURE 10.1
Sample Request for
a Favor**

Open with a question about a common concern or with a statement about a common problem to attract the reader's **attention.** Avoid high-pressure openings and bribes.

Maintain the reader's **interest.** Specify the problem, the benefit (reader's pleasure), and the request in general terms.

For **conviction,** keep the reader in the picture as you provide all the necessary details.

Specify the compensation in positive terms, even when what you can offer is less than the reader expects. Do not apologize for insufficient compensation.

Encourage **action** by setting an end-date and justifying it. Mention the reader benefit once more.

Telephone contact may be required for speed, but written confirmation is usually more dependable.

Associated Chicago Accountants
P.O. Box 4135, Chicago, IL 60646

June 1, 19xx

Dr. Alicia Lauderman
College of Commerce
Department of Accountancy
Illinois Institute of Trade
Ruston, IL 61272

Dear Dr. Lauderman:

How many accountants actually understand the principles of business communication? Your article in THE JOURNAL OF BUSINESS COMMUNICATION pointed out some rather serious shortcomings in letters and reports written by accountants.

The Associated Chicago Accountants agree with you that the typical accountant writes cold, formal letters which can be understood only by other accountants. We'd like to change that, and your expert opinion would be a big help in persuading our members to write better letters.

As the speaker at our annual accountants' banquet, you'd have the pleasure of presenting your ideas to 150 receptive accountants who would be willing to share their letter-writing problems with you.

You'll be our guest at the magnificent banquet, which will be more than just another convention meal, to be held at the Palmer House at 6 p.m., Saturday, September 14. The schedule for the program is

    Cocktails: 6:00 - 6:30
    Dinner: 6:30 - 8:00
    Presentation: 8:00 - 8:45
    Questions and Answers: 8:45 - 9:00
    Entertainment and Dancing: 9:00 - 1:00

Greater than our $100 honorarium is our sincere appreciation for your contribution to the education of our accountants. In addition to the honorarium, we'll reimburse you for air travel and hotel accommodations at the Palmer House. We'll have someone waiting for you at O'Hare if you'll just let us know your arrival time.

Because the program must go to the printer on August 15, we'd appreciate receiving your decision by the 1st. Use the enclosed postage-paid reply card to let us know. The Associated Chicago Accountants look forward to hearing your presentation of the principles of business communication when we meet on September 14.

Sincerely,

Roger Clarke, CPA
enc

FIGURE 10.2
Request for a Favor
Based on Friendship

Timkin Steel Company

1900 Banning Road
Bethlehem, PA 18015
215/555-6164

Interoffice Memorandum

6 Oct 19xx

TO: Jack Fordyce

FROM: Raymond Wright *rw*

SUBJECT: November's Staff Meeting

Rely on the relationship to attract **attention.**

I'd appreciate it, Jack, if you'd present the training
package for me at our November staff meeting.

Maintain **interest** and establish **conviction** by explaining the reason for the request.

My nephew Tim, who you met last Christmas at my house, will
be getting married in November, and I'd like to be there.
The only major item on my calendar that can't be rescheduled
is the training package. Will you take it for me?

Encourage **action** by setting an end-date, but do not push for a definite answer. The small commitment (lunch) may lead to the larger commitment.

I will, of course, have the materials ready and organized
for easy presentation. Shall we discuss it over lunch on
the 10th? Give me a call.

Persuasive Requests for Adjustments

Under what circum-
stances should a re-
quest for an adjust-
ment be a
persuasive mes-
sage?

Most claims and requests for adjustment can be handled as direct-structure informational messages (see Chapter 6). Sometimes, however, you will need to write a persuasive message to achieve the results you desire. You may, for example, have written one request as an informational message and received an unsatisfactory reply. Or you may feel that your reader will be inclined to ignore or resist your message because of the circumstances involved.

In requesting an adjustment, you can appeal to the following qualities in your reader:

1. Sense of fair play (an appeal to psychological pleasure).

2. Desire for customer goodwill (an indirect appeal to wealth).

3. Need for a good reputation (an appeal to continued wealth).

4. Sense of legal or moral responsibility (an appeal to wealth or pleasure).

Why should ap-
peals in persuasive
requests for adjust-
ment be logical
rather than emo-
tional?

When writing a persuasive request for adjustment, you need to remember that your goal—your business objective—is to have the adjustment granted. You may be angry with your reader and tempted to accuse and insult, but your reader will be more inclined to approve your request when you present your case in a calm, logical manner. That does not mean that you cannot let your reader know how you feel. Your disappointment with the products, policies, or services provided by the reader or the reader's company may well be the most important part of your argument.

The main part of your argument, however, must be a clear and logical presentation of the facts. Your reader must know exactly what you expect and why you expect it if you are to receive the adjustment. See Figure 10.3 for an example of an effective persuasive request of this type.

Persuasive Requests for Credit

What is required
for a persuasive
request for credit to
succeed?

Persuasive requests for credit must be based on circumstances that genuinely warrant the extension of credit in spite of the requester's inability to pass certain credit tests. For example, you may be opening a new store and need to purchase inventory on terms longer than your supplier's usual terms. Or you may be refused a credit card at a department store when you believe that your record indicates that you are fully capable of meeting credit card obligations.

Persuasive requests for credit need to demonstrate to the reader that the writer has a good understanding of how credit works, an intention of fulfilling credit obligations, and an ability to pay. Be sure to cover the following points:

1. **Attention.**   Place the message in context by referring to previous correspondence ("Your letter refusing my application for credit came as

FIGURE 10.3
Persuasive Claim

State the problem from the reader's point of view to attract **attention.**

Maintain **interest** by introducing the problem. Remember that your reader is not personally responsible for your trouble.

For **conviction**, give specific dates, figures, and other facts to prove your point.

Encourage **action** by asking for the specific action you desire. Restate the reader benefit.

1501 Hennepin Avenue
Minneapolis, MN 55403

September 23, 19xx

Scandi Motors
20 Exeter Street
Forest Hills, NY 11375

Gentlemen:

What better advertising could Scandi have than satisfied customers? Just as satisfied customers say nice things about Scandi cars, those who aren't satisfied like to talk about their problems.

That's why I'm writing to you. Right now I'm very unhappy with my Scandi because of the unusual difficulties I've been having with it. Since I purchased the car in August 19xx, I've had practically the entire car replaced or rebuilt. In the first 12 months the car has required a new water pump, new fuel pump, two new fuel injectors, new disc brakes, and a new battery. Also, the transmission had to be rebuilt. The warranty covered everything except my cab fare, inconvenience, and loss of time.

But last month the warranty ran out. Just 19 days after the warranty expired, the Scandi dropped a valve and required a complete engine overhaul. The dealer says that he's sorry I've had so much trouble but insists that I pay the $895.49 for repairs.

Under usual circumstances, Scandi's 12 month/24,000-mile warranty would have been sufficient for defective parts to turn up and be replaced. In the case of my dropped valve, however, a part that obviously had been defective for some time didn't reveal itself for 12 months and 19 days. Had my car not been in the shop so often the first year, I would have driven it more than the 12,000 miles it now has, and the defective valve would have been obvious sooner.

Because of the unusual difficulties I've had with my Scandi, I believe that Scandi Motors should extend my warranty to cover the dropped valve. Your check to me for $895.49 will restore my faith in Scandi's reputation for fine cars and fair dealing.

Sincerely,

Ingmar Bergmann

Ingmar Bergmann

enc

a surprise . . .") or by focusing on the way the reader can benefit from extending you credit (primarily, increased sales). Normal interest on the loan is not enough of a benefit to mention, because it is outweighed by the greater than usual risk that you obviously pose to the creditor; otherwise, you would have been extended credit on the basis of your ability to pass normal credit tests.

2.   **Interest.**   Show your reader that you understand that credit is a privilege, not a right. Be positive and confident even though you have been refused credit once already.

3.   **Conviction.**   Explain your financial position and the method by which you expect to pay. Be specific. List credit references, employment and income, any assets and outstanding obligations, and other pertinent facts. Show how the reader will benefit by extending credit.

4.   **Action.**   State your request specifically and confidently.

Figure 10.4 illustrates the principles in the foregoing list.

Persuasive Requests for Funds

What are the differences between asking for donations from major givers (foundations, for example) and from individuals?

Raising funds by mail is increasingly a specialized business. Most political, activist, and public service organizations require donations to stay in business. Many churches, schools, and colleges would operate at a loss without donations. Though you may not choose to work for an organization that makes a regular practice of soliciting funds by mail, during your lifetime you may belong to several nonprofit organizations that could benefit from a few extra dollars. Fraternities, sororities, social clubs wishing to undertake worthy causes, youth clubs, and senior-citizen groups are a few examples.

People who respond to requests for funds fall into two general categories: (1) major givers (wealthy donors, foundations, and corporations), who respond primarily to rational appeals, and (2) donors of small amounts, who respond primarily to emotional appeals. Major givers wish to have a full explanation of how the money will be used, and they will want to see a detailed operating budget. Major givers expect you to demonstrate a real need. Most people, however, give primarily for emotional reasons. They give because they want to help others who are less fortunate than they are; they give because they can see an opportunity to spend a little of their money doing good for others.

Like all persuasive messages, requests for funds must be carefully considered from the standpoint of cost-effectiveness. Each letter costs printing and postage, but not everyone will respond. Your mailing list should be selected carefully on the basis of what audience will have a special interest in your particular project.

**FIGURE 10.4
Persuasive Request
for Credit**

The Rainbow Center

**3483 Creighton Road Southwest
Woodbridge, CT 06525**

March 29, 19xx

Mr. Adrian Everts, Manager
Bank of the Americas
5 Timber Lane
Woodbridge, CT 06525

Dear Mr. Everts:

Your letter refusing my application for credit came as a surprise. Over the past 15 years, my husband and I had four car loans, a home-improvement loan, and a vacation loan with your bank. The mortgage on the house I'm living in is also with your bank.

We repaid each of these loans on time. I suspect that you refused my application because I am now divorced. Even though my husband and I are divorced, my willingness and ability to repay loans have not changed. My income is still more than $20,000 a year. And with the approval of the business loan, I'll be able to add the equipment and hire the help necessary to double my income.

The enclosed financial statements show you my current assets. I have no outstanding obligations. My company's potential for growth is stated clearly in the report by Lambert and Sculthorpe, Management Consultants.

Because recent legislation gives me the right to retain the credit standing my husband and I established over the years, I believe that you should reconsider my recent application for credit.

As my option on the equipment listed in the application expires on November 15, I would appreciate receiving your answer by the 1st.

Sincerely,

Lynn Corrie

Lynn Corrie

After placing the letter in its communication context, review the facts.

Be calm and logical. Demonstrate willingness and ability to repay.

Ask for the action you expect.

End date and justify.

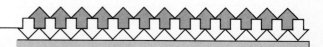

SIDEBAR

The Importance of Mailing Lists

A high quality mailing list is important for all persuasive messages that warrant a *mass mailing.* Direct mail advertising and fund-raising letters should be sent to a selected group of people. An ideal list is *accurate* (correct and current), *pure* (containing all true prospects — those interested in your product, service, or cause), and *homogeneous* (having specific characteristics in common).

Compiling and maintaining a mailing list is usually a job for professionals, and most writers purchase or rent a mailing list. In general, the cost of the list, which is usually measured in terms of the cost for each name, goes up as the selectivity — and purity — of the list increases.

In some cases, a large list of low purity would be the best investment. Low-cost items of wide appeal would do well with such a technique. You might, for example, sell an inexpensive smoke alarm to homeowners in Iowa by purchasing a list of all homeowners in that state. On the other hand, if you wanted to sell expensive burglar alarms, you would use a more selective list, consisting perhaps of names of owners of homes worth more than $100,000 in which the head of the household had an annual income of over $50,000.

Requests for funds follow the same basic organizational pattern as other persuasive messages:

1. **Attention.**   State the problem in such a way that the reader can identify with it. Whether you are writing to a major giver or to the general public, use a people-oriented, personal beginning.

2. **Interest.**   Explain the problem in a way the reader can appreciate. Your main task is to provide enough human interest to keep the reader reading.

3. **Conviction.**   Show what you will do with the money. Major givers are interested in your overall budget. Most people are interested in how you have helped (or will help) individuals. Consider enclosing a separate budget statement.

4. **Action.**   Ask specifically for a donation. If the donation is tax-deductible, say so. Provide a postage-paid reply envelope to make the action easy, and remind the reader of the importance of the contribution. A postscript will frequently improve your return. In the postscript, mention a new reader benefit or a special benefit for acting promptly.

See Figure 10.5 for an illustration of the foregoing principles.

**FIGURE 10.5
Sample Fund-
raising Letter**

Note that mass
mailings may not be
dated.

A simulated inside
address avoids the
tired "Dear Friend"
salutation.

State a problem.

Include the reader.

Promise a solution
to the problem.
Then show how
that promise will be
kept.

**Committee To Elect
Ellen Farrago**
1824 Greenview, Sunshine, CA 94086   (415) 555-4418

Are you concerned
About the high rate
Of crime in Sunshine?

Last year we had more than 9,000 burglaries...

          ...more than 2,000 muggings,
          ...more than 300 rapes,
          ...more than 200 stolen vehicles,
          ...more than 1,000 cases of serious vandalism.

Most of us moved to Sunshine to avoid the problems of big city
living. Unfortunately, over the past several years, big city
problems have also moved to Sunshine.

Our current City administration has been unable to slow the
increase in crime, which is up more than 200 percent over the
last five years. Last year alone, nearly one home in ten--
right here in Sunshine--was touched by crime.

Ellen Farrago wants to make our city safe again, and with your
help, she can do it. Based on her previous experience in the
office of the Mayor of San Francisco, Ellen has a specific plan
for using the same techniques for reducing crime in Sunshine
that have been used effectively in other cities.

If elected Mayor, Ellen will work to

     *   Combine the Police and Fire Departments into a Department
         of Public Safety, which will put more uniformed officers
         on the streets.

     *   Establish a Local Area Network for Law Enforcement with
         neighboring communities, which will make it more difficult
         for criminals to flee the scene of a crime in Sunshine.

     *   Establish Neighborhood Watch, Crime Busters, and Silent
         Observer programs, which have proved successful in other
         communities.

2

    *   Encourage the City Attorney to prosecute to the fullest
        extent of the law rather than engage in plea bargaining,
        which lets too many criminals off the hook.

    *   Obtain federal funds to help finance these important anti-
        crime measures.

Ellen Farrago has the political savvy necessary to make our city
safe again, but she can't begin working to reduce crime in Sunshine
unless she is elected. And she needs your help. Your donation--
for $1,000, $500, $100, or whatever amount you can best afford--
can make a difference in next year's crime rate in Sunshine.

To help reduce crime, please use the enclosed envelope to send
your check to the Committee to Elect Ellen Farrago. You'll
breathe a little easier knowing that you've done what you can.

Cordially,

Walter Taylor

Walter Taylor
Chairman

Margin annotations:

Always put the smallest amount last — most readers try to give more than the minimum.

Be specific about the action. Remind the reader of the benefit.

▷ SALES LETTERS

What are the differences between solicited and unsolicited sales letters? How might those differences influence the structure of the letters?

From one point of view, every letter you write will be selling something. For example, requests sell your responsibility and credibility. Even letters conveying information may be said to "sell" a business relationship based on trust and fair play. When you are deliberately using a letter to sell a product or a service, or when the sole purpose of the letter is to promote future business, your message requires a special strategy. In addition to analyzing your audience, you must know your product or service thoroughly before you can write an effective sales letter. What will your product or service do for your reader? How will it satisfy your reader's need for health, wealth, pleasure, or curiosity?

Sales letters fall into three general, overlapping categories: unsolicited, solicited, and soft-sell. Unsolicited sales letters are also known as direct mail advertising; they are a form of advertising sent by mail directly to the prospective buyer. Solicited sales letters are replies to inquiries about products or services. Soft-sell letters are special goodwill letters designed to maintain cordial relations with important customers.

Unsolicited Sales Letters

How can an envelope teaser overcome the reader's attitude toward "junk mail"?

What is a prospect?

Because many who receive unsolicited sales letters consider them "junk mail," your first objective must be to convince the reader that opening the envelope and reading the letter will be worthwhile. Consider using an *envelope teaser* — a few words on the envelope to suggest a reader benefit — to encourage the reader to continue. Remember that your main concern is with those people in your audience who are true *prospects* — people who want your product or service and can afford to buy it. Write your letter to persuade those with a real interest in your product or service to buy it. Do not make the mistake of writing your letter to entertain everyone who may receive it.

Is it better to emphasize the features of a product or the benefits those features will provide? Why?

Successful sales letters display the following characteristics:

1. **They emphasize the benefits** rather than the features of the product or service.

2. **They use active voice and personalize** the letter to the extent of making the reader the subject or object of many sentences. They picture the reader enjoying the use of the product or service.

3. **They focus on one main appeal.** See the previous discussion of the central selling point.

4. **They subordinate the price,** unless it is an obvious bargain, by mentioning it after most of the benefits have been listed. They state the price in terms of small units ($2 a glass rather than $24 a dozen), compare the price with the cost of something else with which the reader is more familiar, or, when the price is high, suggest extended payments.

5. **They use enclosed brochures** to illustrate the product or service and to supplement the details presented in the letter.

6. **They are specific in their request for action,** specifying exactly what the reader should do (complete the order blank, send a check, or visit a dealer), making that action easy by providing simple order blanks and return envelopes, and encouraging the reader to act promptly.

Figure 10.6, a letter written to homeowners in Ohio, Michigan, and Indiana illustrates these points.

Solicited Sales Letters

What is the best way to begin a solicited sales letter?

In many ways it is easier to write a solicited sales letter than an unsolicited sales letter, because your reader has invited you to send the letter. Consequently, you do not have to worry that your message will be ignored completely.

Whenever someone has written to you asking for information about your products or services, you have a fine opportunity to encourage that person to buy from you. Your message should display all the characteristics of the unsolicited sales letter, but it should be prepared individually rather than as a form. Use the following structure:

1. **Attention.**   Your reader is already interested in your product or service, so begin by answering one of your reader's main questions. Find the most important question in your reader's letter of inquiry that you can answer in a positive way. If you have been asked to make a recommendation, do it first.

2. **Interest.**   Answer all of your reader's questions as clearly and specifically as you can. Subordinate negative answers. Adapt your letter to meet the needs expressed in the reader's inquiry.

3. **Conviction.**   Supply the details and evidence that seem most appropriate for your individual reader. Use an enclosed brochure for additional information to keep the letter from becoming too cluttered.

4. **Action.**   Just as in an unsolicited sales letter, you need to tell the reader exactly what to do, make the required action seem easy ("visit your neighborhood dealer"), and encourage the reader to act quickly. NOTE: Never use a postscript in a solicited sales letter because it would indicate a lack of planning.

The solution to this chapter's communication challenge is an example of a solicited sales letter.

Soft-Sell Letters

Soft-sell letters are special goodwill letters intended to remind the reader that your firm provides a particular product or service. Because of the cost in-

**FIGURE 10.6
Sample Unsolicited
Sales Letter**

Sun Glow, Inc.
1330 Healy, Macomb, IL 61455
Solar Heating Specialists Since 1950

Attention. When
the letter is a form,
use the simulated
inside address to
catch the reader's
attention.

Interest. Keep the
reader in the pic-
ture. Use lists and
vary paragraph size
to make the appear-
ance of the letter in-
teresting.

Conviction. Provide
the facts, figures,
and testimonials.
Focus on one main
appeal—in this
case the appeal is to
wealth.

What can you do
To reduce your rising
Fuel costs?

The cost of heating homes in Ohio, Michigan, and Indiana has, as
you know, increased tremendously in the past few years.

Even with added insulation and a reduced thermostat setting, your
own bills have probably tripled since 19xx. And there's no relief
in sight for the increasing costs of fuel. Gas, oil, electricity,
and even coal are only going to cost more in the future.

But Sun Glow Products has developed an inexpensive and completely
safe solution to home heating problems. Our Energy-Savers can
cut the cost of your winter fuel bill by as much as 31 percent,
and you can install them yourself simply, easily, and without
special tools.

Here's what some satisfied owners have had to say:

"Energy-Savers made a real difference in my bill." Iris
Mannis, Butte, Montana.

"I should have had these years ago." Louis Schumacher,
Yuba, Wisconsin.

"Cut the fuel cost in my store by 32 percent." Elmer Gantry,
Chicago, Illinois.

The Energy-Savers can save you hundreds of dollars in heating
costs next year--and every year thereafter--for only $7.95 each.
All you need to do is place one or two Energy-Savers next to your
heat sources. Energy-Savers should be placed behind radiators,
above forced air outlets, and next to electrical heating elements.
The self-stick backing makes them easy to install.

Made of a special ceramic substance, Energy-Savers are able to
store and reflect heat in a much more efficient way than wall
and ceiling plaster. Studies have shown that rooms with Energy-
Savers stay warmer and require less fuel than rooms of the same
size and shape without Energy-Savers. After you've had the
opportunity to read about the studies in the enclosed brochure,

2

calculate the number of Energy-Savers you'll need for maximum heating efficiency this next winter according to the formula on page 4. You'll be amazed at how inexpensive it will be for you to reduce your fuel costs.

Action. Make it specific, make it easy, and encourage promptness.

To order, simply complete the order blank at the back of the brochure. Should you wish extended payments, complete and return the brief credit application at the same time in the postage-paid envelope provided. Your Energy-Savers will pay for themselves in no time--before next winter is over for typical homes-- and you'll be more comfortable too.

Cordially,

Alice Ajax

Alice Ajax

enc

P.S. A postscript will increase the letter's pull.

Order in the next 10 days, and we'll give you one free Energy-Saver for every 10 you purchase.

What is necessary
for soft-sell letters
to be successful?

volved, soft-sell letters are primarily used at the industrial level to keep a
company's name familiar to important clients and customers. Some organizations use *newsletters* as soft-sell correspondence with a specific audience.

To be successful, soft-sell letters must be welcomed and appreciated by
the reader. The reader must look forward to receiving and reading the message month after month. To create that kind of reader appreciation, you need
to give the reader information of value or provide entertaining material. The
bulk of the letter should consist of information or entertainment, and only
at the end should the writer insert a reminder of the business involved. See
Figure 10.7 for an illustration of this type of letter.

Letters That Sell Ideas

How is selling an
idea different from
selling a product or
service?

Nearly everything we have said so far about selling products and services
applies equally well to selling ideas. When you need to add a new person to
your staff, convince higher management to adopt a new procedure, propose
a feasibility study, or persuade your staff to conserve supplies, you should
follow the same basic procedure you would use to sell a product: analyze
your reader in the same way and select appeals based on the reader's needs.
Also, selling ideas by letter requires the same kind of structural planning as
that used for selling products and services. To sell an idea, however, you
need to take a few additional precautions as follows:

1. **Attention.**   You not only need to begin with a problem of interest to
    your reader, but also must begin with a premise your reader readily
    accepts. If the reader disagrees with your opening, he or she will be all
    the more inclined to resist the rest of your message.

2. **Interest.**   How quickly you can develop your argument depends on
    your reader's degree of resistance. People usually have a vested interest
    in maintaining their current beliefs, and before they will adopt new
    ideas, they must be fully convinced that it is in their self-interest to do
    so. Corporations, for example, are notorious for accepting reports that
    agree with current policy and rejecting reports that disagree with cur-
    rent policy.

3. **Conviction.**   Rely on truth and logic. When there are two sides to an
    issue, present both sides. You can emphasize your own side of the
    argument, but your reader will resent your message if you fail to men-
    tion other obvious possibilities. Always give your reader all the facts
    that might influence his or her decision. Long-range results are usually
    more important than short-range success (concentrate on winning the
    war, even if you must lose the initial battle).

4. **Action.**   Let your reader know exactly what you expect. When your
    reader's resistance is high, it is better to persuade by degrees rather

**FIGURE 10.7
Soft-Sell Letter**

Words of Wisdom . . .
Brought to You by Northern Michigan Paper

Attention. Offer
something of value
or tell an interesting
story.

Interest. Show the
reader how to im-
prove the way he or
she does business,
or provide enter-
tainment.

Conviction. Briefly
remind the reader
of who you are and
what you can do for
him or her. Keep it
simple.

Action. Remind the
reader how to get
in touch with you.

WHY WASTE WORDS?

Ten years ago the average letter was 250 words long. Today the
average is about 125 words. Yet the 125-word letter costs more
to write.

BE CONCISE...

You can generally tell your whole story in a few words and make
the reader feel good about you and your company by concentrating
on the essentials.

KNOW YOUR PURPOSE...

State the purpose of your letter in one clear, simple sentence.
If the reader will welcome that sentence, put it first and explain
later.

If the reader will resent that sentence, explain first to make the
reader feel better, and follow the purpose sentence with some kind
of positive advice.

If the reader will ignore or resist your purpose sentence, save it
until near the end of your letter, after you've explained the
situation thoroughly.

ELIMINATE NONESSENTIALS...

In addition to avoiding wordy expressions (<u>the color</u> red, square
<u>in shape</u>, <u>in the month of</u> August, etc.), eliminate all words and
sentences that do not help make your idea clear or make your
reader feel better about you and your company.

AND ASK THE EXPERTS. . .

When you have real communication problems, remember that
COMMUNICATION CONSULTANTS INC., 2525 Wilshire Blvd., Los Angeles,
CA 90002, is here to help. Whether your problems are letters,
reports, interpersonal, small group, or labor-management, we
can help you solve them. We're as near as your phone. Call us
collect at (213) 389-9000.

than to make your message an all-or-nothing proposition. Remind the reader of the benefits to be gained (or lost) by adopting (or not adopting) your idea.

Figure 10.8 illustrates the principles in the foregoing list, using a format comma in electronic mail systems.

◇ COLLECTION LETTERS

How should a writer incorporate the you-attitude into a series of collection letters?

Because doing business by credit always involves a certain degree of risk, it is sometimes necessary to persuade people who owe money to pay. Collection has become an increasingly specialized business. Everyone in business, however, should have a basic understanding of collection procedures, because collection problems influence the entire operation of the organization. A sale is not complete until the seller is paid.

As you will recall from our discussion of confidence (see Chapter 2), a letter writer should always assume that the reader is going to do the right thing until it has been proven otherwise. When customers are slow to pay, letter writers are sometimes quick to forget this important principle.

The collection procedure is one of gradual escalation in forcefulness. When a bill becomes overdue, the writer should first assume that the reader intends to pay but has forgotten. If the reader does not respond to a reminder (or reminders) to pay, the writer should assume that the reader is not paying because of financial, personal, or medical problems. The writer can help the reader solve his or her problems by making new financial arrangements that will ease the reader's burden. Most people who are slow to pay do so after a reminder or two. Only after these efforts have been made should the writer assume that the reader will have to be persuaded to pay.

Reminders

Reminders of overdue bills usually consist of

1.   Duplicate copies of the original bill.

2.   Duplicate copies of the bill stamped *Reminder* or *Past Due*.

3.   A short note (usually a form) specifying the amount due, the due date, late charges, and the account number.

A company usually sends one or more reminders to a customer because most people who are going to pay will do so when they are reminded gently. Sometimes companies choose to combine a final reminder with an inquiry about the reasons for not paying. Reminders of overdue bills are negative messages. An example of a reminder is shown in Figure 10.9.

**FIGURE 10.8
Sample Letter
Selling an Idea**

Note the electronic
mail format.

```
> Mail
* Send
To:  Michael Bracher
Subj:  Reducing Expenses
Enter message below.  Enter Control-Z to end message.

Hello, Mike.

In the next couple of months, Customer Relations will face a potentially
serious problem, but with the right action now, Lamia could not only avoid
problems, but also save quite a bit of money.

Later this month our senior secretary, Alice Nuttall, will retire.  Under
current company policy, her salary of $24,250 will revert to the general fund.
Her line [job slot] also must remain frozen for at least one year.

To complicate matters further, Sheila Mann has submitted her resignation
effective in March.  Her salary of $16,600 also reverts to the general fund,
and her line will remain frozen for a year, too.

With six highly competent secretaries, we are able to answer every customer's
letter within 72 hours.  We answer 56 percent within 48 hours of receipt.
With both Alice and Sheila gone, however, the department's ability to
maintain its record of prompt, accurate responses will be severely hampered.

With two Memorflex Word Processors, however, the three remaining secretaries
would be able to handle all the correspondence the department now receives.
In addition, the Memorflex typewriters would do perfect work each time so
that the secretaries and I could spend more time deciding what to say in
those cases calling for individual messages.

The two Memorflex Word Processors, including a five-year service contract, will
cost $32,300.  For $1,450 more than the amount the two departing secretaries
take home in pay each year, Lamia Inc. could modernize its Customer Relations
Department.  And by the end of the second year, Lamia would be nearly $20,000
ahead for having made this one investment.

Mike, I would like to meet with you and Vice President Carlson early next xt
week to discuss the purchase of the Memorflex Word Processors. Will you
arrange it for me?

Because our customer relations have been so important to our sales over the
years, Lamia should take positive steps to maintain the prompt, courteous
replies it has always been known for.

Cheers,


Paula Sponseller
```

FIGURE 10.9
A Reminder

BROWNSTONE
PUBLISHING COMPANY, INC
Des Moines, IA 50310

May 31, 19xx

Mr. Ferdinand Payne
1838 North Rowan Avenue
Portland, OR 97230

Invoice No.:   M53083

Amount Due: $15.95

Our Reference No.: 490M01

Have you overlooked the small balance from your recent
purchase? Maybe you've been too busy to notice, but the
balance on your account remains unpaid.

If your payment is already in the mail, please accept
our thanks. Otherwise, please take a moment now to send
us your check in the return evelope.

Sincerely,

Chris Raymond

Chris Raymond
Credit Department

enc

Inquiries

How can a writer help a reader solve his or her financial problems?

Before the writer decides that the customer needs to be persuaded to pay, the writer should try to discover whether special circumstances are preventing payment. Many people are embarrassed when they cannot pay their bills, and instead of taking positive action to solve their financial problems, they hope that if they ignore their problems long enough, they will solve themselves. When the writer demonstrates a genuine willingness to help such readers solve their financial difficulties, most will respond by agreeing to new terms that will allow the company to collect its money and the customers to remain solvent. Inquiries are written with the assumption that it is better to collect your money a little late than not to collect it at all.

Inquiries are divided into two categories. A first inquiry can be simple as the one in Figure 10.10; a second inquiry may contain an appeal for a prompt partial payment and some suggestions for taking care of the obligation in ways other than the original agreement called for. Keep inquiries positive: never suggest that reader satisfaction with your goods or services might be responsible for late payment.

Appeals

When the reader has failed to respond to one or more reminders and to one or more inquiries, the writer must assume that the reader will not pay unless he or she is persuaded — perhaps even forced legally — to do so. Because you would not be writing an appeal unless you had gone through the reminder and inquiry stages, you should assume that the reader is going to be well prepared to resist your message. Should you choose to send more than one appeal, you can begin with at least one positive appeal, such as an appeal to cooperation, fair play, or pride. Because the reader has failed to respond to your earlier messages, however, the chances are that unless you can give the reader a very good reason for paying, he or she will continue to ignore your efforts to collect. We therefore recommend that your letter of appeal be a strong one, appealing directly to the reader's self-interest.

Because the reader has failed to respond several times, negative appeals are usually required at the appeal stage. The reader should be told that by not paying, she or he is likely to lose the following:

1. Credit privileges.

2. The goods or services not paid for.

3. Additional money or property.

4. Good reputation and self-respect.

Figure 10.11 illustrates the foregoing principles.

FIGURE 10.10
First Inquiry

Mielhe's Appliances
413 Ruth • Kent • Ohio • 44240

Everything in Appliances   *Sales & Service*

January 14, 19xx

Mr. Norman B. Bateman
275 Broadview Avenue
Kent, OH 44240

Dear Mr. Bateman:

Attention. Resell the goods or services; remind the reader what he or she is currently enjoying.

Remember how thrilled you were the day we installed your General Appliance color television set? Your wife and children just couldn't wait to see their favorite shows in full color.

Interest. Review the facts for the reader.

When you agreed last August to purchase the $698 General Appliance television set for $42 a month, we were glad to allow you a generous $75 in trade for your used Zephyr to help you qualify for our monthly payment plan.

We were glad to give you the benefit of the doubt because we had faith in you. And we knew that you and your family would enjoy your television viewing more with a new color set.

Conviction. Remind the reader that the consequences for nonpayment are unpleasant.

You are now more than 90 days behind in your payments, and you must think about this each time you sit down to watch television. That can't be very enjoyable. As a favor to yourself and to your family, take care of this credit obligation before the situation becomes more serious.

Action. Tell the reader what you expect and when you expect it.

Right now you can solve your problem by using the enclosed envelope to send us your check for $140 to take care of the amount past due plus the charges for late payment. Send us your check today, and you'll enjoy your television viewing more tonight.

Sincerely,

Paul Mielhe

Paul Mielhe

enc

What is an ultima-
tum?
Should your reader fail to respond to your appeal (some companies send more than one appeal, but we question the cost-effectiveness of doing so), you should give him or her one more opportunity to pay, along with a notification of the action you will take if payment does not arrive. This final letter is known as the *ultimatum.* Your assumption in writing it is that the reader will have to be forced to pay.

In this last effort to collect, you should review the facts, set an end date, and notify the reader that on that date you will turn the debt over to a collection agency or to a lawyer. Do not threaten the reader, and do not accuse the reader of personal shortcomings. Even at this point you may be able to retain your reader's goodwill and cash business, so remain fair, reasonable, and logical throughout.

▷ SUMMARY

Persuasive requests fall into four basic categories: favors, adjustments and claims, credit, and fund-raising letters. When you write to someone requesting a favor, you must offer a benefit. In requesting an adjustment, you can appeal to your reader's sense of fair play, desire for customer goodwill, need for a good reputation, or sense of legal or moral responsibility. Persuasive requests for credit must be based on circumstances that genuinely warrant the extension of credit in spite of the requester's inability to pass certain credit tests.

Requests for funds must demonstrate a real need. Before major givers will make a donation, they need to see a logical explanation of need — including a sample of your budget. Most people, however, give for emotional reasons and prefer to see your need expressed in terms of help for particular individuals.

Sales letters fall into three general categories: unsolicited, solicited, and soft-sell. Unsolicited sales letters are also known as direct mail advertising. Solicited sales letters are replies to inquiries about products or services. Soft-sell letters are special goodwill letters used to maintain cordial relations with important customers.

Collection letters are necessary to persuade people who owe money to pay. The collection procedure is one of gradual escalation in forcefulness. When a bill becomes overdue, the writer should first assume that the reader intends to pay but has forgotten. If the reader does not respond to a reminder to pay, the writer should assume that the reader is not paying because of financial, personal, or medical problems. Only after an inquiry has been ignored should the writer assume that the reader will have to be persuaded to pay.

FIGURE 10.11
Sample Appeal
Letter

Megaphone

6833 Woodcrest Drive   Fort Wayne, IN 46815

16 January 19xx

Ms. Shirley Kropp
1033 S. Fancher Street
Warrensburg, MO 64093

OPEN INVOICE

You must be swamped with paperwork just as we are. So let's put
our heads together and resolve an unpaid balance that is slightly
overdue. The invoice(s) involved is/are as follows:

DATE   1/Nov/xx
INVOICE NO.   M8024778
REASON FOR CHARGE Talk Tank Purchase
AMOUNT $1606.80

Usually overdue invoices result from one of several situations.

1. You've mailed your check in the past 30 days. If so, please
   give us: Check No. _____ Amount _____
   Date _____ Deposit Date from back of canceled
   check (if available) _____.

2. Check issued under different company name than on the
   invoice(s) in question. If so, please explain.

   _____

   _____

3. You don't understand what you've been billed for. If this
   is the case, call me, or jot down a note on the reverse
   side.

4. Once in a while it's something else. Service Problem.
   Maintenance Problem. Waiting for Credit. Other.

   _____

   _____

Ms. Shirley Kropp   16 January 19xx   2

    Jot down what it is, and we'll try to help. Use reverse
    side if necessary.

When your checking is complete and if payment is to be made, please
send your remittance directly to my attention so that I can record
it and then forward it to our Accounting Office with an explanation.
If you should have any questions, please call me directly.

Please list your name, department, and telephone number at work.

_____

_____

_____

Sincerely,

Arvin S. Kopinski

COMMUNICATION SOLUTION

RECLINE-O ORTHOPEDIC FURNITURE
2317 Weaver Avenue
Madison, WI 53702

March 13, 19xx

Mr. Reginald Jackson
1776 Riverview Drive
East St. Louis, IL 62203

Dear Mr. Jackson:

Attention. Answer a question.

The Recline-O-Matic chair you asked about is designed to reduce strain on the lower back and to make sitting more comfortable for those with chronic back pain.

Interest. Keep the reader in the picture as you introduce the features and benefits of the product. Note the references to "your doctor" and "before your injury."

Your doctor may have recommended a Recline-O-Matic chair because it is the only chair designed to permit sitting immediately after most kinds of back surgery. Recline-O-Matic chairs also help prevent the recurrence of back problems because their unique, orthopedic design distributes body weight evenly and fully supports the back. In addition, the automatic lift and recline mechanism allows you to sit and stand without strain to the back. With a Recline-O-Matic, sitting will be as natural and as comfortable for you as it was before your injury.

Conviction. Try to overcome the reader's objections. Be sure to answer all of her or his questions—including those that should have been asked but were not.

You'll be glad to know that because your doctor recommended a Recline-O-Matic, purchase and shipping costs may be fully or partially covered by your insurance program. Also, any portion of the cost of the chair not covered by insurance will be tax-deductible as a medical expense.

But just because the chair is orthopedic, doesn't mean that it's not attractive. The Recline-O-Matic will blend with any decor whether traditional or modern. It comes in seven colors and four fabrics. The enclosed brochure shows you the colors and fabrics available and gives you the details on our unique steel frame construction.

Mr. Reginald Jackson   March 13, 19xx   2

Clarify the price and any special instructions. →

As soon as you complete the enclosed order form, we'll begin constructing a chair to meet your needs. Because the cost of a Recline-O-Matic is $1,500, please complete and return the financial statement and insurance forms provided. Shipping charges to East St. Louis will be $158.

Restate the main reader benefit. →

Just imagine how comfortable you'll feel, Mr. Jackson, when you can sit naturally for watching television, reading, and conversing with friends. Whichever version of the chair you buy, you're sure to enjoy the uncompromising quality and comfort.

Action. Make the action seem as easy as possible. →

Should you have special requirements, have your doctor complete the Physician's Form. You can be enjoying the comfort of a Recline-O-Matic about six weeks after we receive your order.

Sincerely,

James Morrison, President

h

enc

How did you do? Was your version better or worse than the sample presented here? Not all solutions to this problem would need to follow this same form, but you should have included all the details, and you should have followed the same basic structural pattern.

▷ EXERCISES

Review and Discussion Questions

1. What are persuasive requests? Name four types.

2. Explain why asking a favor by mail is not the same as asking a favor from a friend in person.

3. What do persuasive requests for credit need to demonstrate?

4. Explain why the following statement is true: Every letter you write will be selling something.

5. Name the three categories of sales letters.

6. Name the six characteristics of successful sales letters.

7. Why is it easier to write a solicited sales letter than an unsolicited one?

8. Why are collection letters important to business?

9. Explain the following statement: The collection procedure is one of gradual escalation in forcefulness.

10. Why are negative appeals usually required at the "appeal" stage of the collection series?

Problems

1. As a doctoral student in the Department of Business Education and Administrative Services, Kent State University, Kent, OH 44240, Bruce Bailey, 224 Laurel Lane, Kent, OH 44240, needs to send out 600 letters to personnel directors asking them to complete a one-page questionnaire on job requirements for initial office employment. Write the cover letter for Bruce.

2. As Ms. Anita Sullivan, 148 Sixth Street, Knoxville, TN 37916, fundraising committee chairperson for a local charitable organization (name one of your choice), write a letter inviting friends to a $100-a-plate dinner. To persuade friends, tell them what the funds will be used for (use your imagination). To entice them, you might want to mention what the mouth-watering menu will be. You might mention that the Vagabonds

(choral group from a local university) will provide entertainment during the meal.

3. As Chris Wanamaker, president of Pi Omega Theta (a national honorary society), write a letter inviting Dr. Charles Overton, 503 Fifth Avenue, Meriden, CT 06450, to speak for about 30 minutes to the national convention of your group. You will be meeting at the Biltmore Hotel in New York City six months from now. Overton is a well-known expert in advising how to achieve academic success.

4. You are Bill Thompson, 9087 South Gate Street, Orono, ME 04473, and you have just been graduated from the University of Maine. You have decided you no longer will need your IBM electric typewriter, and you wish to sell it. You learn from a friend that Jill St. John, a freshman at the university, needs a typewriter. Because she has not yet moved to campus, write her a letter describing your typewriter and emphasize the benefits of owning an electric typewriter.

5. As the direct mail writer for *Psychology Today*, P.O. Box 2990, Boulder, CO 80323, you (Harold P. Crandall) have been asked to prepare a form letter that will be sent to former subscribers. Your letter is meant to induce them to subscribe to the magazine once again. Be sure to give plenty of reader benefits. (You might want to look at a copy of the magazine in the library to see what the magazine offers.) You can offer four issues free to those who subscribe within ten days.

6. As president of Goldenrod Pharmaceutical, 206 Berwick Road, Columbia, SC 29210, you have been asked to write a letter to your employees on behalf of the United Fund's annual fund-raising drive. All the money collected will be used locally for a variety of good causes—Heart Fund, Cancer Society, The Family Counseling Center, Boy Scouts, Girl Scouts, and the YMCA. The goal for Goldenrod is $18,000. If each person would give just one percent of his or her annual income, Goldenrod would exceed that goal easily.

7. You have been hired by Jake's, a local department store, to write a letter of welcome that will be sent to all newcomers in your community. The letter will be soft-sell, emphasizing useful information and stating that Jake's (118 Cambridge Street, Fairfield, CT 06430) is a friendly, helpful member of the community.

8. As president of the Student Association at Boise State University, 1910 College Blvd., Boise, ID 83725, you are planning a week's sun-sea-sand vacation to Bermuda for all students during the Easter break. The $600 package trip includes the following:

Airfare by United Airlines

Six nights in Bermuda's Surf Hotel

Special area sightseeing tour

All airport transfers

All baggage handling

All tips and taxes

Complimentary meals and beverages enroute

The trip originates from your campus on April 16 and returns on April 22. Reservations are made through the Student Association Tour Committee, Student Services Bldg. Write the creative letter that will be used as an ad in your school's student paper. Interested students may pick up a brochure and more information in the Student Association office.

9. As promotion manager for Sonneville Sisters Department Store, 736 Leland Road, Ellisville, MS 39437, write a form letter to your charge customers encouraging them to do their Christmas shopping at your store. You'll be having daily specials for the week of December 12–17.

Monday	— Gifts for the toddlers to teens
Tuesday	— Gifts for him
Wednesday	— Gifts for her
Thursday	— Gifts for the teens
Friday	— Gifts for those who have everything
Saturday	— Gifts for the home

10. As Mr. Todd Thompson, credit manager of Vos's Department Store, 1092 Main Street, Baltimore, MD 21224, write a letter to your charge customers who have not used their accounts in six months. If they make a $5 charge purchase within the next three weeks, you will give them a free gift—a 14″ × 15½″ × 6″ softly grained vinyl tote bag in a color of their choice (red, orange, gray, green, or gold) with top zipper and tuck lock. You might want to mention your new store hours—daily from 10 a.m. to 10 p.m. and on Saturday from noon until 6 p.m.

CASES

1. You are in charge of sales for the branch office of the Utah Insurance Company, 5089 Warner Road, Akron, OH 44325. The home office just announced a new sales incentive program. If you can sell $500,000 worth of insurance within a six-month period, you'll be eligible for a two-week vacation in Hawaii. You decide to write a letter to the parents of newborn babies (as listed in the birth announcements in the local newspapers) persuading them to buy additional coverage based on their new family responsibilities. Prepare a letter that can be used as a sample, and send it to Mr. and Mrs. Arden Farquhar, 10727 Sprague Avenue, West Haven, CT 06516. Submit the description from the catalog with your letter.

2. As sales director for SweepPower (manufacturers of vacuum cleaners), 498 Stanford Avenue, Newark, NJ 07106, answer Ms. Karen Cayo's (1876 Beverly Drive, Metairie,

LA 70002) inquiry about the SweepPower, an upright vacuum cleaner. SweepPowers move with only the slightest touch of the hand; a motor does the work. SweepPowers sell for $185 each. SP Motor: powerful 2-speed motor delivers 53 air power. Cleaning features: motor-driven vinyl beater brush revolves 4500 rpm. The SP has seven adjustment positions. Construction: hi-impact plastic housing. Push-button suction speed controls. Attachments: rear-mounted attachment port. Electrical information: 20-ft. cord with automatic rewind. UL Listed; 110-120 volts. Order will be processed within ten days of receipt of order. Enclose a brochure for a more detailed description and illustrations.

3. Write a letter to the superintendent of your local school system persuading him or her to add a course in business communication to the high school curriculum.

4. Write a letter persuading the mayor of your city to take action on an important local issue (for example, install a traffic light at a dangerous intersection, repave a particular street, increase pay for fire fighters, and so forth).

5. As Jason Holland, 394 Meadowbrook Lane, Huron, OH 44839, you recently wrote a claim letter to Cold Air Refrigerators, 309 Berwick Road, Columbia, SC 29210, explaining that you wanted reimbursement for the $30 door gasket you had to replace on your one-month-old refrigerator. You were refused your request. You decide to write a persuasive request. This time you mail the original gasket to the company by certified mail. In your letter you explain that obviously the gasket was contaminated by a petroleum product during manufacture.

6. Assume that your friend, Ms. Rose B. Tully, 806 South Highland Avenue, Forest City, IA 50336, has asked you to help her with a claim. Six months ago Rose purchased a 45-piece service-for-eight Royal China "Chantilly" from Pier 4 Imports, 5133 Glentree Drive, San Jose, CA 95129. She received the service for eight, but instead of the Royal China, she received Royal Ironstone. While the Royal Ironstone is very nice, Rose wants the Royal China. She wrote once and was told by Pier 4 that because the Royal China and Royal Ironstone are of equal value, company policy would not permit an exchange. Write a letter for Rose's signature that will secure the exchange.

7. Write a series of soft-sell letters (two, four, or six) appropriate for the kind of company you plan to join when you have finished your education. On a separate sheet explain to your instructor the kind of company involved and the specific audience for your soft-sell campaign. Remember that soft-sell letters are expensive, so you must restrict them to important clients or customers.

8. As Ms. Aretha Flack, write to Wee Ones Inc. and request a donation of Wee One Wetless Disposable Diapers for use at your charity auction. The names of the donors will be listed in the *Yorkshire Record,* your local newspaper, and the money earned at the auction will be used to support the Family Christmas Program, which sees to it that families unable to afford presents for their children receive something good for Christmas.

9. Because your job requires a great deal of travel and entertaining, you have a company expense account. Your company, Orlando Construction and Land Development, 113 Meadowlark Drive, Santa Fe, NM 86501, is very good about paying for travel in advance, but its current method of handling your car rental and entertaining expenses is to reimburse you for money actually spent. You must use your own credit cards and then request reimbursement from the company. The company has resisted providing company credit cards because once one person has one, everyone else will want one to maintain status. You are getting awfully tired, however, by having to delay paying some of your bills

until the company check arrives. Write to Ms. Helen Orlando, the president of your company, and persuade her to issue you a company credit card.

10. Assume that you are Ms. Janice Roberts (see Case 9 in Chapter 8). You believe that as a responsible, adult woman who has done business with the Industrial City Bank for nearly 15 years, you should receive the $2,300 you need to buy a car. While you are willing to concede that you were not gainfully employed during your 15-year marriage, you learned many job-related skills (how to organize, supervise, delegate, and manage) doing volunteer work. You are sure that you can use these skills to find a job, and you already have several interviews lined up. Having the car — which would be yours just as soon as the loan goes through — would make it easier for you to make it to interviews on time.

11. Because of your abilities as a business-letter writer, you have been asked to write a letter for your local animal shelter. Each year people bring you more than 3,000 dogs and cats (and about 200 rabbits, hamsters, turtles, and snakes — and one three-foot alligator) and expect you to find homes for the animals they do not want or cannot care for. You receive some city and county funds, but to meet your operating expenses you must rely on the donations you receive from animal lovers. This year the animal shelter will add a direct mail campaign to its other fund-raising efforts. Prepare letters for (1) major givers — including local businesses and the town's wealthy citizens who have an established reputation for giving, and (2) the general public. Describe the enclosure you would include with each of the letters.

12. Assume that you have been on a particular job for five years. Your company, like many others, is fighting inflation. One of the ways it intends to fight is by not giving salary increases unless the increase can be fully jus-

tified in writing. Support your claim for an increase in a memo to your immediate supervisor.

13. Assume that you are the manager of the Credit Department for Grantos Boutiques, a Wisconsin-based string of stores featuring fashions for women. Design form letters that can be used to collect overdue revolving charge accounts. You will need at least the following:
   a. a 30-day reminder.
   b. a 60-day inquiry.
   c. a 90-day appeal.
   d. a 120-day overdue ultimatum.
   Design your form letters so it will be easy for you to insert the personal information required to make the letters convincing.

14. Invite a "name" speaker to address the annual convention of a professional association or club of which you are a member (or of which you would like to be a member). Because your nonprofit organization has limited resources, you will be unable to pay the speaker his or her usual fee. You will be able to pay the speaker's transportation and lodging expenses and to provide an honorarium of $100, an engraved plaque commemorating the event, and dinner at the evening banquet you have planned. You can also guarantee the speaker an interested audience of about 250 people, many of whom would be interested in purchasing autographed copies of his or her book.

15. As the president of the Professional Women of Oklahoma City, you are planning the annual convention for the Professional Women International. Women from all 50 states and 15 foreign countries will gather in Oklahoma City for the week-long convention. As part of your plan to make the women feel welcome, you are assembling materials for welcome packets for the 1,000 attendees expected. In addition to the convention program, notepaper, and pens, the welcome packets usually contain city maps, key chains, coasters,

and other items of small value. Companies usually donate these items in exchange for the goodwill they create. In the welcome packets you provide, you would like to include small bottles of vitamin pills produced by Vita Corporation, a local pharmaceutical company. You think that the advertising Vita Corporation would receive would more than offset the cost of the donation of 1,000 bottles of Every Day, its new multivitamin pill. Write to Albert J. Lilly, Director of Public Relations, Vita Corporation, 52 The Embarcadero, Norman, OK 73069.

16. Write a solicited sales letter for a product or service with which you are familiar. Address the letter to yourself. You might wish to write a letter asking for information about the product or service first and then respond to the inquiry.

17. Write an unsolicited sales letter for the same product or service selected for Problem 16. Address the letter to yourself.

18. Write an unsolicited sales letter to people in your community who bought new cars three or four years ago. As the sales manager at Gateway Chevrolet, you would like to have their business when they are ready to trade. If they bring your letter with them when they visit, you will take $100 off the sticker price of any new car they decide to purchase.

19. You are the credit manager for Beven's Furniture Store, 4503 W. Main Street, Knoxville, TN 37918. Drs. Raymond and Darlene Farkas, 5404 Malibu Drive, Knoxville, TN 37918, applied for credit when they moved to town a year ago so that they could purchase furniture for their new house. Both are professors at the University of Tennessee and earn good salaries. With their credit, they purchased $3,700 worth of furniture, putting $1,700 down and agreeing to pay $105.26 a month for 24 months. They made 10 monthly payments before missing one. Send a reminder, an inquiry, an appeal, and an ultimatum. Assume no response as you proceed through the collection series.

20. As director of sales for Midwest Insurance Company, 5167 South Main Street, Charleston, IL 61920, you are concerned because the independent insurance agents who sell your policies have let their sales lag over the last three months. Your sales are off by about 15 percent. In investigating the problem, you have discovered that several of your competitors have initiated new sales incentive programs. For the agent with the most sales each month, one company offers a weekend in Las Vegas and another offers a weekend at Disney World. You decide to give a 19-inch color television each month to the agent with the most sales. Persuade the independent agents to sell more of your life, homeowners, fire, auto, accident, and health insurance packages.

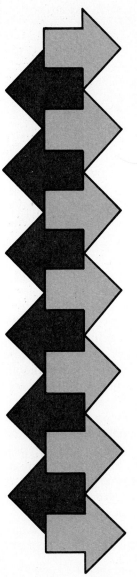

CHAPTER ELEVEN

Writing Messages with More Than One Purpose

Some messages must combine more than one business objective. When these objectives will cause different emotional reactions in a reader, the letter or the memo is a mixed message. This chapter presents the techniques for writing effective mixed messages.

Topics

COMMUNICATION CHALLENGE

A customer has returned a Sav-A-Call cassette phone-answering recorder, Model 6000, and asked for her money back. According to Jean Woods, 699 Water Street, Detroit, MI 48221, the unit has never worked properly. She returned it to the dealer twice for repairs since purchasing it three months ago. Each time the problem has been the same—the Sav-A-Call does not record incoming calls. The examination by your technicians reveals an intermittent short in a diode, something the dealer would not be likely to find because finding it requires either special equipment or many hours of testing the machine in operation. Because the Sav-A-Call has a one-year warranty, Ms. Woods is entitled to free repair or replacement. She is very angry, however, and said in her letter that she wants the refund so that she can purchase one of your competitor's phone-answering recorders. You are willing to give Ms. Woods her refund, but you would like to send her a new Sav-A-Call recorder to replace the defective one. As Director of Company Relations, AC DC Electronics, 3210 North River Street, Watertown, NY 13601, write to Ms. Woods and offer your counterproposal. Make appropriate changes in your first draft as you read through the chapter, and then compare your solution to the one that follows the chapter summary.

▷ Overview: Organize for Proper Emphasis

Not every letter or memo has one clear-cut business purpose. Some business communication situations are complex, and they require carefully planned and organized messages of more than one business objective. Many of these mixed messages attempt to negotiate for a compromise solution to a problem—perhaps a partial refund or an exchange instead of a refund. Success with messages of this type depends on skillful application of the techniques prescribed in the previous chapters to unusual and complex situations.

The basic rules of business communication still apply: subordinate negative information, use the you-attitude, and emphasize the reader benefits for any action you want the reader to take. The organizational pattern for mixed messages, however, is less structured than it is for other message types. Controlling emphasis and subordination is especially important in mixed messages. The trick is in knowing *what* to emphasize, and that decision is not always easy to make. This chapter will help you recognize mixed-message situations and help you select an appropriate strategy for each.

Consider the problem presented in the following Communication Challenge. What are the objectives? Are any of the objectives more important than any others?

▷ GENERAL STRUCTURE AND CHECKLIST FOR MIXED MESSAGES

What is a mixed message?

A mixed message is not the same as a positive message that includes a negative aspect or a negative message that includes some persuasive material. To be considered a mixed message, a message must contain two or more equally important business objectives. Compare the following examples:

> **Positive Message:** Yes, you are covered by insurance, but before we can pay your claim, you'll need to complete the enclosed form.

> **Mixed Message:** Your insurance covers you for *A* but not for *B*.

How does the general structure for a mixed message follow the basic rules for structuring other messages?

While the specific structure for mixed messages will vary depending on the components included, the general pattern is as follows.

1. **Benefit.** The best beginning for a mixed message is a reader benefit. When you do not have a specific benefit to offer, begin with something the reader will respond to favorably that will also place the communication in its proper context. Positive information, a statement of agreement, or an acknowledgment of a common problem will help establish empathy between reader and writer.

2. **Information.** Like all explanations, the informative part of the mixed message belongs in the secondary position because it is less interesting. To help overcome resentment and resistance, provide justifying reasons for the change that is involved. In addition to saying what you want to change or what the reader must do, tell the reader why the action is necessary. When a compromise is involved, explain and justify the reasons for the compromise before stating the compromise itself.

3. **Requested action.** Because mixed messages always require the reader to make a decision or change a behavior, you should make sure that the reader knows exactly what to do and when to do it. Also, make the action seem as easy as possible by providing clear instructions, blank forms, and other appropriate aids. Be sure to connect the action to the reader benefit. When the reader has a choice, however, make sure that you do not ignore that choice.

▷ PRIORITIES IN MIXED MESSAGES

Earlier chapters considered communication situations in which the reader might *welcome, resent, or resist* the message. Not all letter-writing situations fall neatly into one of these categories, however. Some fall into more than

COMMUNICATION TODAY. . .

The case of Israel and Egypt negotiating over who should keep how much of the Sinai Peninsula illustrates both a major problem in negotiation and a key opportunity.

The problem is a common one. There seems to be no way to split the pie that leaves both parties satisfied. Often you are negotiating along a single dimension, such as the amount of territory, the price of a car, the length of a lease on an apartment, or the size of a commission on a sale. At other times you face what appears to be an either/or choice that is either markedly favorable to you or to the other side. In a divorce settlement, who gets the house? Who gets custody of the children? You may see the choice as one between winning and losing — and neither side will agree to lose. Even if you do win and get the car for $5,000, the lease for five years, or the house and kids, you have a sinking feeling that they will not let you forget it. Whatever the situation, your choices seem limited.

The Sinai example also makes clear the op-portunity. A creative option like a demilitarized Sinai can often make the difference between deadlock and agreement. One lawyer we know attributes his success directly to his ability to invent solutions advantageous to both his client and the other side. He expands the pie before dividing it. Skill at inventing options is one of the most useful assets a negotiator can have. . . .

Yet all too often negotiators end up like the proverbial sisters who quarreled over an orange. After they finally agreed to divide the orange in half, the first sister took her half, ate the fruit, and threw away the peel, while the other threw away the fruit and used the peel from her half in baking a cake. All too often negotiators "leave money on the table" — they fail to reach agreement when they might have, or the agreement they do reach could have been better for each side. Too many negotiations end up with half an orange for each side instead of the whole fruit for one and the whole peel for the other. Why?

Source: From *Getting To Yes* by Roger Fisher and William Ury, pp. 58–59. Copyright © 1981 by Roger Fisher and William Ury. Reprinted by permission of Houghton Mifflin Company.

How does the reader's response determine whether the emphasis in a mixed message should be on the business objectives or the human objective?

one category at the same time. Indeed, mixed messages are fairly typical in business situations. While our earlier discussion of the communication context (Chapter 4) and the discussion of the preceding specific message types (Chapters 6 through 10) imply a methodology for handling mixed messages, certain kinds of mixed messages occur often enough to merit specific explanation, as this chapter will provide.

A message to which the reader's response will be mixed presents a special hazard for the business communicator because people have a special propensity for perceiving what they want to perceive. Thus, in a mixed message the reader is likely to ignore the aspect of the message that causes resentment or resistance. As you can tell from the discussion of negative and persuasive messages, when your reader is likely to resent or resist a business objective (subject content) you must emphasize the human objective (feeling content) to retain the reader's goodwill and ensure accurate communication. Until you achieve the human objective of establishing empathy with your reader, you cannot achieve the business objective.

Why are mixed messages more difficult to structure than negative or persuasive messages?

In the case of a mixed message, problems with structuring occur because the writer has more than one business objective. While it is generally true that negative aspects should be subordinated by being placed in the middle of the letter, it is not always possible to arrange the subject content of a mixed message according to the general formula for subordination. The writer of a mixed message must choose between business objectives and human objectives in ways that do not occur in single-purpose messages. For example, when you convey negative information to your reader, you try to simultaneously retain his or her goodwill. Your main objective, however, is to convey the negative information. When the situation forces you to choose between conveying the negative information and retaining the reader's goodwill, you state the business objective clearly, even at the expense of failing to achieve the human objective. Mixed messages pose more of a dilemma as they contain no single main objective. Two or more objectives must be achieved.

Why might the announcement of a change call for a mixed message?

Many mixed messages involve some kind of unexpected change. Even though the change may benefit the reader, he or she is likely to resent or resist the message because this is the way most people react to unexpected change. The general objective of a mixed message is to overcome the resentment or resistance that the unexpected change is likely to create.

When your analysis of the communication situation as outlined in Chapter 3 indicates that you will need to write a mixed message, you must begin with a list of priorities for your message. Essentially you need to know which is more important: the business objectives or the human objective. To help clarify your goals, ask yourself the following questions:

1. How will my reader feel about the change I am suggesting? How will the change affect my reader's business? How will the change affect my reader's self-image?

2. Is it more important to make my reader happy than it is to achieve these particular business objectives?

3. When my reader's happiness is more important than my business objectives, what can I offer to make the business objectives more attractive?

4. When the business objectives are more important than my reader's happiness, what can I say to help my reader save face or accept the business objectives?

Your answers to these questions will help you determine the best structure for communicating your message. While it is impossible to anticipate the wide variety of letter-writing situations that will fall into the mixed-message category, illustrations of three common types will show you how to proceed.

▷ POSITIVE AND NEGATIVE INFORMATION COMBINED

What is a compromise offer?

Communication situations involving compromise require mixed messages. Whenever you suggest a compromise to your reader, you have two business objectives: (1) you want to show the reader that her or his proposal is not fully acceptable, and (2) you want the reader to accept your counterproposal. Your reader will resent and resist these objectives. When you present your counterproposal in a logical, positive way, however, the reader may be willing to overlook the negative aspect and accept the compromise.

What are the advantages and disadvantages of presenting a counterproposal with emphasis on the business objectives? With emphasis on the human objective?

In presenting a compromise offer, you have to decide whether to assign greater importance to the business objectives or to the human objective. The objectives you emphasize are the ones you are more likely to achieve, as the following comparison makes clear. The following structure places the **emphasis on the business objectives:**

1. **Indirect beginning.**   Because the reader will be disappointed that you are refusing the original request, find some aspect of the situation with which you and the reader can agree.

2. **Explanation.**   Give your reasons for not being able to accept the reader's proposal or request. Use your reasons and your counterproposal to imply the refusal. Make your counterproposal sound logical and reasonable. Avoid being paternalistic (*We are willing to grant you* or *We can permit you*) or humble (*We can only offer* or *The best we can do in this case*). Include all the reader benefits associated with your counterproposal.

3. **Action.**   You need to convince the reader to agree to your counterproposal, but you must avoid taking choices away from your reader. When your reader has a choice, take no action without your reader's permission.

The following structure places the **emphasis on the human objective:**

1. **Direct beginning.**   Approve the reader's request or agree to the original proposal. Offer the reader everything he or she has asked for. Avoid apologies, and do not admit to a mistake.

2. **Explanation.**   Even though your opening shows your willingness to let the reader have his or her way, your explanation should make clear your belief that your counterproposal is more reasonable, logical, and equitable than the reader's proposal or request. Include all the reader benefits associated with your counterproposal.

3. **Action.**   While you need to make clear that the choice is the reader's, encourage the reader to reject your original offer and to accept your counterproposal by emphasizing the reader benefits associated with the counterproposal.

The same communication situation can be handled in either way. Figures 11.1 and 11.2 illustrate the different approaches.

**FIGURE 11.1
Compromise with
Emphasis on
Business Objectives**

You're right to expect quality when you buy Moonbeam products. Thank you for returning the toaster for our examination.

For your Moonbeam toaster to work properly, the two thermostats must both be set properly. The one thermostat lets you adjust the toaster to your own taste, from very light to very dark. The other thermostat, located inside the clean-out plate, is the main control. The main control on your toaster, Ms. Muchel, malfunctioned because the toaster had evidently been cleaned with a knife or other sharp instrument, which removed the insulation from some of the wires and caused a short.

We've replaced and adjusted the main thermostat in your toaster, and it now works perfectly. It will continue to provide years of trouble-free service as long as the cleaning and operating instructions provided with each new toaster are followed. Because the cleaning instructions did not specifically prohibit scraping with a knife, we'll let you decide the best course of action.

**FIGURE 11.2
Compromise with
Emphasis on
Human Objective**

The enclosed refund check for $39.95 is our way of saying that we want to treat you right, Ms. Muchel. We want you to know that we stand behind the guarantee that you receive with Moonbeam products.

For your Moonbeam toaster to work properly, the two thermostats must both be set properly. The one thermostat lets you adjust the toaster to your own taste, from very light to very dark. The other thermostat, located inside the clean-out plate, is the main control. The main control on your toaster, Ms. Muchel, malfunctioned because the toaster had evidently been cleaned with a knife or other sharp instrument, which removed the insulation from some of the wires and caused a short.

We've replaced and adjusted the main thermostat in your toaster, and it now works perfectly. It will continue to provide years of trouble-free service as long as the cleaning and operating instructions provided with each new toaster are followed. Because the cleaning instructions did not specifically prohibit scraping with a knife, we'll let you decide the best course of action.

continued

FIGURE 11.1 *continued*

While we would be happy to refund your money as you requested, we believe that you'll want the toaster back now that it is working perfectly. The Moonbeam toaster can provide you with reliable service—and toast the way you like it—for years to come. Should you choose to have the toaster back, we'll pay your shipping charges. Please use the enclosed card to let us know your decision.

FIGURE 11.2 *continued*

The enclosed check shows you that we want you to be entirely satisfied, but now that your toaster is working perfectly, we think that you'll want it back. The Moonbeam toaster can provide you with reliable service—and toast the way you like it—for years to come. Should you choose to have the toaster back, we'll gladly pay all your shipping charges. With your repaired toaster, you'll receive a new, one-year guarantee. To receive your toaster, simply return the check to us in the envelope provided.

Why is fairness so important to the success of compromise offers?

Whether the letter is structured to emphasize the business objectives or the human objective, the basic content of the letter will be essentially the same. In the foregoing examples, however, the letter that encloses the refund check is more likely to make the reader happy. It is also *less* likely to encourage the reader to ask for the toaster back. Once the reader has the refund check, he or she will probably keep it. The letter that emphasizes the business objectives subordinates the possibility of the refund and encourages the reader to request the return of the toaster; but at the same time, it is more likely to make the reader feel that the company is taking advantage of her.

Which is the better letter? That depends on your primary objective. Do you believe that your company will be better off in the long run if you demonstrate conclusively that you stand behind your guarantee, or do you believe that your company will be better off in the long run if you can persuade the reader to give the toaster one more try? As long as the compromise you offer is honest, fair, and reasonable, either approach should prove successful in achieving the human and business objectives.

▷ NEGATIVE AND PERSUASIVE INFORMATION COMBINED

Because people usually resist change even when that change may prove beneficial for them in the long run, messages announcing changes are fre-

Why do people
tend to resist
change even when
the change will
prove beneficial to
them in the long
run?

quently mixed messages. How much persuasive information needs to be included in these messages depends on how resentful the reader will feel about the announced change, how much resistance your message will encounter, and how important your relationship with the reader is to you.

Unlike situations in which you have a compromise to offer, situations that require the combination of negative and persuasive information are those in which no real compromise is possible. The reader may have a legitimate choice, but it usually is an all-or-nothing choice in terms of the relationship between the reader and writer. If the reader does not accept what the writer is offering, the only alternative is to go elsewhere. A company may, for example, decide to install a new computer system. Company employees — and customers — will have to adjust to whatever new procedures that computer requires. Messages written to announce the changes and to explain these procedures would be mixed messages. Changes in billing dates, changes in report procedures, and cancellation of certain courtesy privileges would also require mixed messages that attempt to convince the reader that the change will prove beneficial for both the writer and the reader.

When you have decided that you can neither give the reader what he or she wants nor offer a compromise or choice, your main concern is to present the proposed change in a way that will persuade the reader to accept it. Obviously you would not be proposing the change if it did not offer you and your business advantages, some of which you should be able to pass on to your reader. Whether you are selling a substitute product for the one a reader has ordered or selling an alternate procedure, the basic structure of your message is essentially the same, as follows:

1. **Benefit.**   Because you are going to offer something other than the product or procedure that the reader expects, you need to mention a benefit associated with the change before the reader can guess that you are not doing as expected. Be sure to begin close enough to the subject to place the message in its proper communication context.

2. **Explanation.**   Remember that your reader has a vested interest in the original idea, product, or procedure. To achieve your business objectives, you will need to present your alternative without calling your reader's judgment into question. Avoid the negative words *substitute* and *substitution*. Rather than disparaging the original idea or product, concentrate on the positive aspects of the alternative. Although to be fair, you should state the disadvantages associated with the alternative (they would become clear to the reader later anyway), you should subordinate them as much as possible without sacrificing clarity.

What image is conveyed by the word
substitute?

3. **Action.**   When the reader has a choice, make sure that choice is clear, and do not take unasked-for action (such as sending a substitute product), unless you can do so without placing a burden on your reader.

When the reader has no choice (to continue doing business with you, the reader must follow a new procedure, for example), make the action you expect clear, but subordinate it by reemphasizing the reader benefit in closing.

Why should a letter selling a substitute product use an indirect beginning?

One typical situation that calls for this kind of mixed message is the selling of a substitute product, though the process is the same whether you are dealing with a product, an idea, or a procedure. When you cannot offer the product a customer has ordered (perhaps because you carry a different brand) but you can offer what you feel is a perfectly adequate alternative, your message to your reader has two business objectives: (1) to inform your reader that you cannot sell the product ordered, and (2) to persuade your reader to purchase the alternative.

Your reader may resent your inability to sell the product ordered and may resist your effort to persuade him or her to purchase the alternative, so you will need to emphasize the feeling content of the message and achieve the human objective before you can accomplish your business objectives (an indirect structure), as shown in Figure 11.3.

▷ POSITIVE, NEGATIVE, AND PERSUASIVE INFORMATION COMBINED

What can you do when the communication situation is too complex for standard structural patterns?

When communication situations are complex, writers frequently need to make some difficult decisions about the best organizational patterns for accomplishing a variety of business and human objectives. In general, the basic structural pattern for mixed messages provides a useful guideline. Sometimes, however, the nature of the communication situation requires a chronological arrangement or a problem-solution presentation. In such cases, writers need to remember their obligation to present the information in a manner that is both clear and courteous.

In some situations calling for a mixed message of this kind, the writer can subordinate the negative aspects and arrange the message to meet both the business and human objectives effectively. An example would be an acknowledgment of an order for which the writer can send some items immediately, needs to delay shipment on others, cannot provide some of the items at all, and would like to substitute for yet other items. In acknowledgments of this sort, the organizational pattern is fairly predictable.

1.   Begin by sending those items you can send. Be specific.

2.   Explain the delay.

3.   Give the reasons that you cannot supply certain items, and tell the reader where the items might be available.

4.   Sell the substitute items.

5.   Ask the reader to confirm the required choices, and close by emphasizing the benefits the reader will receive by deciding in your favor.

What is the writer's principal responsibility to the reader?

When the nature of the communication situation requires a chronological arrangement or a problem-solution organizational pattern, you need to remember that your primary responsibility as a writer is to be clear. Your second responsibility is to be courteous. While you should subordinate those aspects of your message that will cause your reader to feel resentment, you should do your best to structure your message to reduce your reader's resistance to announced changes or to your counterproposals. In complex situations of this sort, remember that your message will be most effective when you

1.   Adequately present and discuss all sides of the situation.

2.   Distinguish and clearly label facts, opinions, and value judgments.

3.   Emphasize points of agreement *before* you discuss points of disagreement.

4.   Find and emphasize the benefits the reader will receive by accepting your point of view or course of action.

5.   Acknowledge your reader's right to choose when a legitimate choice is possible.

Why would informing management of a defalcation call for a mixed message?

The example in Figure 11.4 illustrates the presentation of details in a difficult situation. Note that the writer is the assistant manager, who is filling in for the vacationing manager. The assistant has discovered a possible defalcation (misuse of funds) in the department, and the evidence seems to indicate that the Production Department manager is responsible.

Figure 11.5 shows one approach to introducing changes within a department. In this case the memo would have been preceded by discussions, so the contents of the memo would not be a complete surprise to the reader.

▷ SUMMARY

Mixed messages are those that combine more than one business objective when those objectives will cause different reactions in your reader. You need to write a mixed message when your reader will consider part of your message good news and another part of your message bad news. Many mixed messages involve some kind of unexpected change. Even though it may benefit the reader, an unexpected change is generally resented or resisted. The general objective of a mixed message is to overcome the resentment or resistance that the unexpected change (or other negative information) is likely to create.

FIGURE 11.3
Selling a Substitute

Use an indirect beginning that stresses a benefit. Place the message in its specific communication context, but do not mislead the reader into thinking that he or she will receive the product ordered.

Begin your explanation before the reader starts to wonder why you haven't said that the product is on its way. Minimize and subordinate references to the product originally ordered. Give your reader the information required to make a logical decision.

Handle the sales information on the alternative product as you would were you writing an invited sales letter (see Chapter 10).

Use a brochure to keep the letter from becoming too cluttered. When the price is higher or there is some other negative factor, subordinate it as much as possible.

Haas Office Equipment
425 Spring Street
Lexington, MA 02173

3 July 19xx

Ms. Judith C. Sills, Purchasing
International Security
830 Romence
Lexington, MA 02173

Dear Ms. Sills:

Your recent order for one dozen letter-quality printers shows that you've been satisfied with the office equipment we've provided you in the past. High-quality printers will certainly improve the appearance of your business correspondence and reports, and their increased speed and efficiency will make life easier for your secretaries, too.

In our continuous effort to provide only the best equipment at the lowest possible cost, we now carry the MNO Wheelwriters exclusively. Our customers have reported that the MNO printers need fewer repairs and do high-quality work longer without adjustments than the Corone Daisies you ordered. While the Corone Daisies are still available from Hatch Distributors, in Denver, Colorado, we believe you'll find that the MNO Wheelwriters are a better buy.

The solid steel frame and a powerful but quiet heavy-duty motor standard on the MNO Wheelwriters, enable us to offer you an unusual five-year warranty on these high-quality printers.

After you've read the complete description of the Wheelwriters in the enclosed brochure, we think you'll agree that the superior performance and construction of the MNO printers more than justify their slightly higher purchase price. The reliability and longevity of the MNO Wheelwriters make them a sound investment.

Make the reader's choices clear, but emphasize the reader benefits associated with the decision you want your reader to take. Make the action seem easy.

Your closing should be positive. *Do not take unasked for action.* Let the reader decide the best course of action, but show confidence in the future of the business relationship.

Ms. Judith C. Sills, Purchasing   3 July 19xx   2

Because we're so convinced that you'll prefer the MNO printers, we'll be glad to send you one on a trial basis. Our representative in your area could set it up and demonstrate it for you on 15 August. Please use the enclosed card to let us know your decision. We'll hold your check until we hear from you. To complete your order for one dozen MNO Wheelwriters, simply return the card with your check for an additional $14,075 in the reply envelope provided.

Whatever your decision, Haas Office Equipment will always strive to bring you the best products at the lowest possible cost. For your convenience, we're sending a copy of our latest catalog by parcel post.

Sincerely,

Albert Haas

enc

**FIGURE 11.4
Mixed Message
Using Chronological
Arrangement of
Details**

Timkin Steel Company

1900 Banning Road
Bethlehem, PA 18015
215/555-6164

Interoffice Memorandum

22 February 19xx

TO: Nancy Barber, President

FROM   Christopher Reardon, Assistant Manager *CR*
           Production Department

SUBJECT: Inventory Discrepancies

In the past two weeks, I've discovered several discrepancies in
Production's inventory that deserve further investigation.

On 5 February, after a press failure on line 2, I pulled the
requisitions file to order a new press and dies. According to
the records, the press and dies were ordered in December and
replaced in January. The attached copy of the shipping voucher
indicates that the press and dies were signed for on 9 January.
The press and dies cost $27,572.

After this discovery, I decided to compare other vouchers with
current equipment. So far I have found the following additional
discrepancies:

Item	Voucher	Date	Cost
Plates	12-074	16 Oct 19xx	$6,540
Press	12-962	21 Nov 19xx	$16,890
Typewriter	13-003	6 Dec 19xx	$1,247

In all cases, the records show that new equipment has been bought
and paid for. All the heavy equipment was requisitioned through
Houghton Industrial Supplies. The typewriter was purchased
through the local IBM office. None of the listed items seem to
be in the Department, either on the line or in storage.

I believe that this is a serious problem, and I would appreciate
your assistance in investigating it.

I recommend that the Comptroller audit the Production Department
within the next two weeks to determine whether there is a good
explanation for the discrepancies in the inventory.

The subject line and
opening paragraph
should catch the
reader's attention
without offending
him or her. Clarify
the problem that
needs to be solved.

Present the facts
clearly. Present
opinions and con-
clusions after the
details have made
the situation clear.
Passive voice helps
to avoid a direct ac-
cusation.

The opinion is
given as opinion
and not presented
as fact.

Recommended so-
lution and request
for action are last.

FIGURE 11.5
Message Introducing Changes

The subject line and opening paragraph should catch attention in a positive way.

When the reader knows that the change is probable, present it early to avoid building his or her anxiety.

Acknowledge problems honestly. Show how it is to the reader's benefit to help solve problems as they occur.

Stress the benefits associated with the change.

Let the reader know what action is necessary and encourage cooperation. Consider doing something extra to help overcome reader resistance to change.

PARKSIDE

Memorandum   Internal Use Only

July 14, 19xx

TO: Department Heads

FROM: David Berry   *db*

SUBJECT: The Word Processing Center

After our many meetings about installing a centralized word processing center, you should have a good idea of its potential advantages and disadvantages.

Because the potential savings of $67,000 a year are so great, Parkside will begin changing to the Megaphone equipment specified in the systems report of May 15. Installation will begin August 1 and be complete by September 1.

The new system will take some getting used to. As the equipment is installed and departmental secretaries are moved to the word processing center, offices will seem a little empty and less congenial. The increased efficiency should make that a small price to pay.

The new system should make it possible for us to accomplish written work in about two-thirds the time we have been spending. This should reduce evening and weekend work for everyone involved. Also, the substantial savings will mean increased allocations in other areas, which will help us increase efficiency in other ways as well.

The attached schedule shows you the order of installation. When the Megaphone personnel are in your office, they will show you how to use the dictation equipment to best advantage.

As a special inducement to encourage a successful changeover, Parkside is offering a $1,500 bonus to the Department showing the greatest increase in efficiency for the first six months following installation.

The organizational pattern for a mixed message is (1) benefit, (2) information, and (3) requested action. When you do not have a specific benefit to offer, begin with something the reader will respond to favorably that will also place the communication in its proper context. The informative part of the mixed message belongs in the secondary position because it is less interesting or negative. Make sure that the reader knows exactly what to do and when to do it.

When your reader is likely to resent or resist the subject content of your letter, you must emphasize the feeling content to retain the reader's goodwill and ensure accurate communication. Until you meet the human objective of

COMMUNICATION SOLUTION

The situation presented in this chapter's Communication Challenge is, of course, a compromise in which the reader has the right to choose. We place the emphasis on the *business objectives* rather than on the *human objective* because we believe that it is important to persuade her to give our product one more try. If we send the refund check at this point, she is likely to cash it, and we will never hear from her again. If we explain the situation carefully and convince her that our product quality is high, she may decide that it is easier to try the new Sav-A-Call than to make that purchasing decision a second time.

In our solution, note that we have added some specific details in the resale paragraph. Your letter should also contain some specific resale, although you may have selected different features, depending on how familiar you are with phone-answering machines. Note, too, that it would be presumptuous to simply send the new Sav-A-Call at this point. She will be more willing to accept it if you indicate clearly that you recognize her right to choose.

For emphasis on the business objectives, use an indirect opening and establish a cordial relationship. If you place the emphasis on the human objective, your first paragraph would mention an enclosed refund check.

Explain what went wrong and why the dealer could not find the problem. Provide assurance that the problem was unusual.

Acknowledge her feelings, and subordinate the reference to the refund. Introduce your compromise offer.

Resell the Model 6000 by reminding her of its best features. Especially mention features that other phone-answering machines might not have.

Acknowledge her right to choose, and make any required action as easy as possible. End on a positive, forward-looking note.

AC/DC Electronics
3210 River Street
Watertown, NY 13601

Director of Company Relations

November 15, 19xx

Ms. Jean Woods
699 Water Street
Detroit, MI 48221

Dear Ms. Woods:

Thank you for returning your Model 6000 Sav-A-Call. Whenever a customer has a problem with an AC/DC product, we want to know so that we can determine the cause and correct it.

When our technicians examined your Sav-A-Call recorder, they discovered an intermittent short in one of the diodes. As our supplier is very careful to send us only the highest quality components, this sort of problem is extremely rare. Your dealer was unable to locate the faulty diode because special test equipment or many hours of testing the machine in operation would be required.

I know that this has been a frustrating experience for you, and under the circumstances, I would be glad to refund your money. I would also appreciate the chance to show you that a Sav-A-Call can meet your needs. You obviously need and deserve a phone answering machine you can rely on. For this reason I would like to send you a brand new and thoroughly tested Sav-A-Call Model 6000.

The Model 6000 has a larger capacity than any other answering machine on the market and is capable of storing more than 100 30-second messages. It provides for both high-fidelity speaker sound and the privacy of handset listening. It also is fully programmable, recording up to seven different answering messages and using them according to the schedule you select.

Please use the enclosed card to let me know your decision, Ms. Wood. I have a new Sav-A-Call packaged and ready to send--it would be answering your phone for you in just a few days.

Sincerely,

Joseph Lundy

Joseph Lundy

establishing empathy with your reader, you cannot achieve the business objectives.

Communication situations involving compromise require mixed messages. Whenever you suggest a compromise to your reader, you have two business objectives: (1) to show the reader that his or her proposal is not fully acceptable, and (2) to persuade the reader to accept your counterproposal. In presenting a compromise offer, you have to decide whether to assign greater importance to the business objectives or to the human objective. Whether you structure the letter to emphasize the business objectives or the human objective, the basic content of the letter will be essentially the same.

Situations that require the combination of negative and persuasive information are those in which no real compromise is possible. Whether you are selling a substitute product for the one a reader has ordered or selling an alternate procedure, the basic structure of your message is essentially the same: (1) benefit, (2) explanation, and (3) action.

When communication situations are complex, writers frequently need to make some difficult decisions about the best organizational patterns for accomplishing a variety of business and human objectives. In general, the basic structural pattern will provide a useful guideline. Sometimes, however, the nature of the communication situation will require a chronological arrangement or a problem-solution presentation. In such cases writers need to remember their obligation to present the information in a manner that is clear, courteous, concise, confident, correct, and conversational.

▷ EXERCISES

Review and Discussion Questions

1. What is a mixed message?

2. Give the general pattern for all mixed messages.

3. Whenever you suggest a compromise to your reader, you have two business objectives. Name them.

4. In a compromise offer, what structure should you use when you want to emphasize the business objectives? The human objective?

5. When you cannot provide the product a customer has ordered but you can offer an adequate alternative, you have two business objectives. Name them.

6. When a complex communication situation requires you to combine positive, negative, and persuasive information, what factors govern the message's organizational pattern?

Problems

1. As customer relations manager for Edison Electronics, 82 Poe Avenue, Roxie, MS 39661, answer a letter from Roger Dutton, 22 Gaviotta Way, San Francisco, CA 94126. Mr. Dutton complains that the AM-FM portable radio he purchased by mail from your sales catalog has not worked since it arrived, and he demands his $42.75 back. When you examine the radio, you discover that the only thing wrong with it is a dead 9-volt battery. You believe that the radio, which usually sells for $59.95, represents a real bargain and that Mr. Dutton will want it back. Placing the emphasis on the business objectives, offer to return Mr. Dutton's radio.

2. Using the information provided in the preceding problem, write a letter to Mr. Dutton in which you place the emphasis on the human objective.

3. At the Hickory Nut, 4211 Maple Avenue, Albuquerque, NM 87100, you have received the following order from Mr. Hamilton Burr for cheeses, candied fruits, flavored nuts, and specialty jams and jellies.

Five pounds smoked chedder @ 2.79/lb	$13.95
Five pounds Monterey Jack @ 2.49/lb	12.45
Two four-pound packages of assorted candied fruits @ 9.95 ea	19.90
Six four-pound cans of barbecued almonds @ 10.99 a can	65.94
Three $9 packages of specialty jams and jellies @ 9.00/pkg	27.00
Total	$139.24
Tax and Shipping Charges	11.96
Total	$151.20

    Write to Mr. Burr, 748 Arroyo Road, Los Altos, CA 94022, and tell him that you are sending the cheese and the specialty jams and jellies right away by United Parcel Service, that there will be a two-week delay for the candied fruits, and that because of a severe drought, the almonds are not available this year. In place of the almonds, sell Mr. Burr your barbecued walnuts at $6.76 for a 4-pound can.

4. Until recently, your company, Wilcox and Rogers, Investment Counselors, 2954 Helber Street, Flint, MI 48504, sent a monthly newsletter, *Financial Planning for Families,* free to anyone who asked for it. The idea behind the newsletter was to provide useful advice and to establish cordial contact with those who receive it. Because of the increased costs of publishing and mailing the newsletter, you now send one free issue as a sample, but subscribers must pay $6 a year or maintain a $1,000 account with your firm to remain on your mailing list. Answer a letter from Ms. Elizabeth Kranz, 67 Appian Way, Bloomington, IL 61701, requesting you to add her name to your subscription list.

5. As Richard Dallas, Field Supervisor for Southern Construction Company, 1175 Nashville Highway, Murfreesboro, TN 37132, you have en-

countered a problem with one of your clients, The National Bank of Georgia, 197 Lizella Road, Macon, GA 31207. The drawings and the contract specify a 4-foot retaining wall 15 feet behind the building, allowing two access lanes for the bank's two drive-in windows. The bank manager, Carl H. Boyd, now wants 30 feet of access, which will require an 8-foot retaining wall. The additional construction costs amount to $46,000, and you are willing to do as Boyd has requested. The extra lanes and higher costs, however, will be wasted unless the bank adds two drive-in windows ($37,000 each in construction costs) and can build enough business to justify the expense. Write to Boyd recommending that he wait to expand the drive-in access until his volume of business will justify the additional drive-in windows.

6. When Richard Dallas accepted a job as Field Supervisor for your company, Southern Construction Company, 1175 Nashville Highway, Murfreesboro, TN 37132, it was with the understanding that the company would provide him with a new car every two years. Because he must drive 35,000 miles a year from construction site to construction site, you have always provided him with a large, comfortable car. Because of the increase in the price of gasoline, however, you intend to buy a smaller car for his use and are considering a new Oldsmobile Omega. Because the Omega would be more economical than the car he is currently driving, you would be able to increase his expense account by $1,200 a year. The Omega should be comfortable enough, and the extra money in the expense account should allow Dallas to do a better job of entertaining clients when he is on the road. Write a memo to Dallas announcing the changes.

7. As Photon Inc., 105 Grand Street, Burlington, IA 52601, you have developed a unique duplicating machine that can use any paper and requires no chemicals or ink. You have been deluged with orders. The only model you currently have in stock is the PT 109, your tabletop model. You are 90 days behind on deliveries with Model PT 1119, a floor-standing model with double the capacity and speed of the 109, and you are six months behind on deliveries for Model PT 2019, which automatically collates and staples up to 60 pages of material. You no longer manufacture PT 99 because the Model PT 109 produces much superior copies and costs only $55 more. Acknowledge an order from Kermit G. Palmer, Purchasing, Eastern Washington State College, Cheney, WA 99004, for the following duplicators:

8 Model PT 99 at $375 each	$ 3,000
8 Model PT 109 at $430 each	$ 3,440
6 Model PT 1119 at $2600 each	$15,600
2 Model PT 2019 at $6560 each	$13,120
TOTAL	$35,160

Palmer sent the college's check for the full amount, plus $820 for shipping costs, along with the order.

8.   As Doris L. Bruno, Manager of St. Elmo's Medical Center, you have received a list of "nonnegotiable" demands from the hospital nursing staff, including both RNs and LPNs, who feel that they are overworked and underpaid. The nurses especially resent that their schedules do not rotate on a regular basis but are determined by the needs of the hospital. They also want wage increases averaging 14 percent, free use of the clinic, nursing staff increase of 10 percent, and a reduction in their work week from 40 hours to 37½ hours.

   While you can understand the nurses' demands, the clinic budget is already strained to the limits. The amount you charge patients for medical care is already higher than the state average by 17 percent. And because the doctors actually own the clinic, the largest share of the income goes to pay their salaries. For these reasons, you are unable to increase wages or to reduce the work week. You can, however, use the clinic's computer to improve scheduling, and you have the money to hire eight nurses — an increase of 6 percent. The state Nursing Board is currently investigating salaries for nurses and nurses' aides, and perhaps the result of that study will justify higher wages for the clinic's nursing staff at a later date. Write a letter to Pamela Ladendorf, RN, who is acting as spokesperson for the nurses, and present the clinic's position.

9.   As the vice-president of the Midwest Region for Great Lakes Insurance Company, 4589 Lakeview Drive, Marquette, WI 53947, you have received several letters from your agents protesting your new policy of requiring weekly written sales reports. The agents wish to return to the old method of calling in sales figures at the end of each month. The new system, though more economical for the home office, is more time-consuming for the agents. You are willing to go back to the old method, but because the reports must be written eventually, your office will have to prepare the reports if the agents do not. For this reason, you would like to arrange a compromise. Write to your agents and suggest the compromise.

10. Mr. Clayton Hinkel, Hinkel's Hardware, 37 Dart Road, Ithaca, NY 14850, has ordered 12 wood-burning stoves from your company, Energy Systems Inc., 640 Bison Blvd., Butte, MT 59703. The model he ordered, H-107, is no longer in production. You have replaced it with Model I-110, which is 30 percent more efficient. The physical appearance of the stoves is the same, but tighter seals, improved draft, and an improved heat reflector make the new stove worth much more than the additional $75 it costs wholesale. Its higher selling price, $512, as compared to $329, results in an improved profit for dealers. The new model has been selling well in colder climates. Write to Hinkel and sell the newer model.

CASES

1. Ms. Mary Shelley has complained to you, Director of Customer Relations for the Nota Automobile Company, that her new Nota, purchased from Frank's Automotive Center, 42 Northwest 73 Street, Gainesville, FL 32603, is getting only eight miles a gallon. She reports that two different service station mechanics have told her that the carburetor is defective but that mechanics at Frank's have told her that it is not "bad enough" to replace under the warranty. Shelley wants the carburetor replaced.

   You have called Frank Fitzsimmons, owner of Frank's Automotive Center, who told you that he had checked the carburetor himself, and while it was not as good as it should be, it was within specified tolerances. You suspect that poor driving techniques may account for part of Shelley's bad gas mileage. You also suspect that the service station mechanics are not fully reliable and that Shelley may not even know how to calculate gas mileage correctly. In the interest of goodwill, however, you are willing to provide a new carburetor if Shelley will agree to pay for the cost of installation. Convince her to have her car tuned and to improve her driving habits before she invests in the new carburetor. Her address is 2537 Southwest 7 Place, Gainesville, FL 32603.

2. You have just been assigned the job of audit supervisor for Commonwealth Industries. This is your first audit as supervisor. You are particularly eager to succeed. Commonwealth Industries (CI) is one of your office's largest clients. One of your worries is the rumor that CI is going to be party to a large lawsuit.

   You have had one meeting (on September 12, 19xx) with Roger Horinstein, controller of CI. Roger is easygoing, but he is meticulous about details. He shrugs off all questions related to CI's possible legal problems. During the meeting, you concentrated on the requirements for the upcoming audit. You mentioned that you will need a specific time schedule (stipulating when you can expect accounts payable data, long-term debt data, and a copy of the October 30, 19xx accounts receivable master file for confirmations) by September 30, 19xx.

   You also discussed the importance of Carlson and Carlson (your CPA firm) having all records concerning the recent acquisition of Jackson Construction Company. Jackson was the second largest construction company in the state.

   You concluded the meeting with a rundown of the working arrangements and equipment you will need while working at CI. You and your four assistants will need desks, identification cards, and keys to the office spaces. You will bring your own personal computer with you, but you will also need access to Commonwealth's computer the weeks of November 14 and December 10. You asked Roger for about 30 hours of computer time each week.

   You are now confirming the details of your meeting by letter.

3. You are supervisor for the Boston audit of Queen Anne Department Stores, a large retail chain. Your contact is James Secrest at the Queen Anne home office, 1776 Boston Square, Boston, MA 02132. The phone number is (617) 555-6464, extention 242.

   You have just learned that Queen Anne has acquired Surf and Sand (S&S), a small sporting goods store at 45 Sea View Road, Santa Monica, CA 90402. S&S is headed by Skip Johnson. You are somewhat suspicious about S&S. In the back of your mind you seem to remember reading newspaper items about embezzlement problems.

   You are writing to Bennet Erikson, a manager in your firm's Los Angeles office, to ask for information about S&S so you can complete your pre-audit planning of Queen Anne. You would like the Los Angeles office to flowchart S&S's accounting systems and evaluate its internal control.

You need the information immediately. You must have all working papers by March 31, 19xx. Erikson should charge all time, at standard rates, and out-of-pocket expenses to Boston contract 479-38317-03. The rush is because James Secrest at Queen Anne neglected to tell you about the acquisition before he left on a two-month assignment in Paris.

4. Dr. Janice Lester, a professor of international marketing at Indiana University, Bloomington, IN 47401, has written to Ms. Linn Andrews, the president of your company — Andrews Manufacturing Inc., 143 Lakefront Avenue, Holland, MI 49423. Lester proposes that your company finance a field study of the market potential for the new kind of flame-retardant, permanent-press fabrics your company produces. Dr. Lester wants $30,000 to study the market possibilities in England, France, Germany, Italy, and Japan. While you think that the study might well open new and valuable markets for your company, you do not want to finance a luxury vacation for Dr. Lester, either. Based on what you know of Dr. Lester's work, you are willing to make an outright grant of $5,000 and match any funds she is able to obtain elsewhere. You are also willing to pay legitimate expenses associated with the study itself (design and printing of questionnaires, computer analysis time, shipping of sample materials, taxi fares, and the like). Prepare a letter for Ms. Andrews' signature that will make Dr. Lester want to accept your counterproposal.

5. When you installed the Sol-Craft solar heating unit on Mr. L. H. Molzan's swimming pool at 401 W. 46th Street, Indianapolis, IN 46201, you told him that the heating unit would maintain a water temperature of 82° only if an old maple tree, which prevents the afternoon sun from hitting the solar heating unit, were removed. You thought that Mr. Molzan

had agreed to remove the tree, but now you receive a letter saying that the solar heating unit is insufficient. Mr. Molzan wants you to install a propane supplemental heater (which you manufacture). Mr. Molzan agrees to pay for the propane heater, but he wants you to pay for installation because the solar heater is not doing the job. Write Mr. Molzan and explain that the solar heater alone will do the job from early June through the end of September provided the old maple tree — which probably will not live much longer anyway — is removed. Tell him that if he prefers, you will add the propane supplemental heater, but that he will have to pay the full cost for the heater and installation ($854).

6. Mr. Raymond J. Johnson, owner of Johnson Jewelers, 986 Stanford Plaza, Menlo Park, CA 94025, writes to you, Jade & Things, 1492 Columbus Avenue, Tempe, AZ 85281, saying that the large order ($2,500) of silver and turquoise pendants, belt buckles, rings, and earrings arrived too late for Johnson Jewelers to take advantage of the annual Indian fair held in Menlo Park. Johnson requested that the jewelry be sent air express, but because of an oversight in your shipping department, the order was sent by United Parcel Service. As a result, much of the order remains unsold. While the mistake was yours and you are willing to take the order back, you think that it would be better — primarily for you but also for him — if you gave Johnson permission to hold a sale on your merchandise (something you have never done before) and split the advertising costs with him. Johnson would be able to sell most of the jewelry quickly and make necessary room for Christmas specialty items, and you would avoid having to handle the jewelry again. Emphasize the human objective in writing to Johnson.

7. Using the information in the preceding case, write to Johnson and stress your business objectives.

8. As sales manager for Wyland Electronics, 1200 Newkirk Street, Baltimore, MD 21244, acknowledge an order from Ms. Lois Land, 1780 Hudson River Road, Monsey, NY 10952. Ms. Land has ordered your Model QT 12 All-channel CB radio for use in her customized Chevy van. Because of the change from 23 channels to the new 40-channel units, you have discontinued the Model QT 12 and replaced it with the Model QT 14. In addition to its extra communication capabilities, the QT 14 offers several features not available on the QT 12. It has a built-in automatic noise limiter, an illuminated meter to indicate sending and receiving signal strength, and a frequency synthesizer to eliminate crystals. Like the QT 12, it provides 4 watts of power for a strong signal, it has a 100-percent solid-state chassis for long life and reliability, and it has an adjustable squelch control. It includes a bracket for mounting under the dash and a complete instruction manual. The QT 14 does cost more; Ms. Land will have to send another $37.50 for it. Hold her check for $149.50 until she lets you know her decision.

9. Henrietta's Hardware Store, 101 W. Main Street, Duluth, MN 55815, ordered six Waste Queen Garbage Disposals from you, Electrical and Plumbing Supplies, 932 Portage Road, St. Paul, MN 55103. Because you specialize in products for the home handy-person and the Waste Queen requires installation by a professional plumber, you have received several complaints from dealers who purchased the Waste Queen to sell to do-it-yourselfers. You still have plenty of Waste Queen Disposals in stock, but you think that Henrietta's Hardware might prefer the new Grind-All Disposal, which has been especially designed for do-it-yourself installation. The Waste Queen and the Grind-All have many features in common. Both have solid steel construction, a ¾-horsepower motor, a foolproof safety interlock, and an automatic shutoff to prevent silverware and other metallic objects from damaging the disposal. The Grind-All comes with complete installation instructions and a short piece of a new kind of flexible, metal (not plastic) pipe to make installation easier. The Grind-All costs more —$12 more wholesale and $16 more retail. The retail prices are $79.99 for the Grind-All and $63.99 for the Waste Queen. Both the Waste Queen and the Grind-All come with a complete one-year warranty, and you'll be glad to sell Henrietta's Hardware either disposal. You do, however, want to make sure that the differences between the two are clear. Your terms are 2/10, n/30.

10. As manager of the Personnel Department for Doutt Pharmaceuticals, you are required to prepare letters of evaluation on your staff members each year. The person being evaluated receives the letter, a copy is placed in her or his personal file, and a copy goes to the vice-president. Write the letter of evaluation for Mary S. Inacker, who has now been with Doutt for one year.

In her six-month oral review you told her that you admired her energy and the number of screenings she was able to complete in a day, but that she is too brusque with interviewees and does not pay close enough attention to completing interview forms on the job applicants. Inacker agreed to slow her pace a bit and to be more careful with the interview forms, which are essential to your Affirmative Action program. On the basis of her willingness to work on improving, she passed the six-month probationary period.

For a while, the improvement was quite noticeable. Inacker took more time with interviewees, and her reports were complete, accurate, and carefully prepared. In the last six weeks or so, you have noticed a change for the worse. Inacker is now taking too long with each interviewee, and her reports, too, are much longer than necessary. To make matters worse, Inacker is somehow giving each job applicant the idea that she or he will be hired, and you have received several complaints from those you have had to turn down.

Inacker is still an energetic, cheerful person. You think that perhaps she is worried about her upcoming review and is trying to be too careful with clients and reports. You remain convinced that she can make a valuable contribution to the department and to the company.

You will, of course, talk to Inacker when you give her the letter of evaluation, but the letter must contain the bad as well as the good, and you will need to offer Inacker the kind of advice that will help her work for advancement with the company.

11. As the president of General Watch Works, 77 Sheila Street, New York, NY 10001, you have just discovered that several of your dealers have been taking the parts from your less expensive Chronomatic watches and placing them in the more expensive Oldsake watch cases. While the Chronomatic parts are perfectly all right and keep good time, they are not as well made as the Oldsake parts. The Chronomatic parts are noisier and not quite so accurate. Write a letter to all your dealers explaining that the substitution is unethical and, in some states, illegal. Should a dealer continue to substitute parts, you will have to discontinue doing business with him or her.

12. As director of sales for the Midwest Division of the American Cash Register Company, 1920 Clark Avenue, Raleigh, NC 27605, write a letter to your district sales managers informing them of a change in reporting procedures. Currently each district manager assembles the total sales figures each week and telephones them to you before noon each Monday. The telephone reports are followed at the end of the month by a written report specifying the sales by salesperson, district, purchaser, product, and price. The new procedure calls for a written report each week. As director of sales, you believe that because the new procedure will enable you to follow up on each sale more quickly, you will be able to establish a better relationship with your customers, which will lead to increased future sales.

13. Write a letter to your business communication instructor telling him or her
   a. What is wrong with the class.
   b. What you like about the class.
   c. What improvements should be made in the class.

14. As president of the local chapter of Professional Secretaries International, you recently wrote to Professors William Murphy and Nancy Engemann, who work at a nearby university, inviting them to conduct an all-day communication seminar for you. You offered them $500 for the seminar. In their reply, Professors Murphy and Engemann said that they would be glad to conduct the seminar but that their fee would be $800 plus travel, accommodations, and material expenses. Write back to the professors suggesting a compromise: you'll pay the $800 and take care of their lodgings and meals but not their other expenses.

15. You're John Misak, credit manager for Cyclists Inc., 42 East 53 Street, New York, NY 10016. You recently received a letter from Andrea Wilston, 917 Poplar Hill Road, Baltimore, MD 21210. She tells you that two weeks ago she purchased your Women's Model 5M 4829N 26-inch five-speed Midlight Bicycle for $98.99 as advertised in *National Sports*. She expresses much dissatisfaction with the five-speed bike. Because she needs to pedal uphill several times a day, she now prefers a ten-speed bike. She wants you to take the five-speed back at the price she paid for it and to send her a ten-speed bike. She says she only used the bike one week, and it is still as good as new. Because Andrea has used the bike, even though it was only for one week, it is still a used bike. She may trade the bike in for a ten-speed. You will allow 75 percent of the original price of the five-speed bike as credit on the second purchase.

16. Mr. William Morrison, 14 Grand Street, Lynchburg, VA 24502, wrote to you as representative of the Last National Bank of Lynchburg, 458 Scott Street, Lynchburg, VA 24502, and asked whether he could change the date of his mortgage payments from the 1st of the month to the 15th. Because delaying the payment from the 1st to the 15th would change the amount of interest due and alter the amortization schedule, you would have to charge Mr. Morrison $30 for the change. A simpler — and less expensive — solution would be for Mr. Morrison to pay a month early and send his check on the 15th. Write a letter to Mr. Morrison and explain his options to him.

17. As manager of the Western Division of the Continental Oil Company, 111 Plaza Street, New York, NY 10002, you have general responsibilities for all West Coast operations. Recently, however, the main office has been putting a great deal of pressure on you to cut expenses — even though they are also insisting on increased exploratory drilling. Today you have received a letter — signed by Mr. Lawrence Hokezma, the company president — asking you to justify your recent expenditures for drilling equipment. All the equipment is necessary for you to meet company deadlines for your drilling operations on the 16 exploratory wells the company wants sunk in the next 60 days. In your reply, you will, of course, need to justify the expenditures on the basis of need, but you should also persuade the company to set some specific priorities so you can determine the relative importance of cutting back on expenses and maintaining normal drilling operations.

18. As manager of Zoland's Discount Store, write a form letter to all your charge customers announcing the installation of a new computer billing system. Instead of receiving bills on the 1st of the month, customers will now receive their bills based on where their last names fall in the alphabet.

A – F will receive bills on the 1st
G – L will receive bills on the 10th
M – Q will receive bills on the 20th
R – Z will receive bills on the 30th

In addition to announcing the change in billing dates, caution your customers to watch for errors that are bound to happen with such a change in procedures and equipment.

19. For the last ten years, all executives working for American International have been issued American Express credit cards for charging legitimate expense account items. Lately, however, the bills have far exceeded reasonable business expenses, and the board of directors has decided to recall all the credit cards. From now on executives will have to use their own credit cards and submit a form requesting reimbursement. Write a form memo explaining the new policy. Be sure to set an end-date for returning the credit cards.

20. As head of the Advertising Department (see Case 20 in Chapter 8), you must write formal personnel evaluations once every six months until the employee has been with the company two years. It is time for you to rewrite Abraham Fenwick's formal review. In the past six months Fenwick has caused you a lot of trouble because of his sexist remarks and behavior. Fenwick has been improving, however, and he is obviously trying to overcome his rather strong prejudices against women colleagues. Other than the hard feelings Fenwick has caused, his work has been excellent. Your letter of review to Fenwick must mention his sexist behavior and remind him that such behavior will be cause for dismissal, but you should also mention his successes and encourage him to make every effort to acknowledge and accept the professional competence of his women colleagues.

PART THREE

Business Reports

Nearly everyone in business writes reports on a regular basis. An organization communicates with itself through its reports, and its reports serve as a record of its activities so that goals can be set and measured.

Report-writing skill is an important avenue for recognition and promotion. Those in higher management learn about promising employees through their reports. The ability to convey information quickly and clearly often leads to advancement.

The following chapters present the basics of business reports, including classification, appearance, research methodology, writing, and presentation, in both written and oral form.

CHAPTER TWELVE

Business Reports: Form and Function

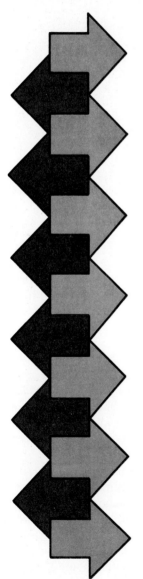

Sooner or later, you will be required to write your first business report. When that day arrives, you may begin by writing short memos or by completing standard entries on routine forms. On the other hand, you may be required to write a formal, analytical report early in your business career. This chapter shows you how businesses and most nonprofit organizations classify and use written reports so that you will be prepared for whatever report writing assignments you receive. Chapters 13 and 14 provide specific information about conducting research for and writing a variety of common business reports.

Topics

Overview: What Do Readers Want?

Advantages of Written Reports

Purposes of Written Reports
Maintenance Reports
Task Reports
Human Reports

Reports and the Decision-making Process

Methods of Classifying Reports
Classification by Function
Classification by Length
Classification by Formality
Classification by Frequency of Issue
Classification by Reader-Writer Relationships

Classification by Type or Form

Requisites of Reports
Proper Organization
Special Techniques
Formal Writing Style
Summarizing Statements

Abstracts and Executive Summaries
Abstracts
Executive Summaries

Life Cycle of Reports

Summary

Exercises

COMMUNICATION CHALLENGE

As a field sales representative for a new manufacturer of industrial cleaning products for walls and floors, you are required to send monthly sales reports to your district manager. During the past month you made 192 calls, which resulted in 44 sales worth $11,000. Your breakdown on sales is as follows:

	Calls	Sales	Amount
Supermarkets	46	14	$3,299
Pharmacies	42	12	3,100
Hardware stores	38	10	2,400
Clothing stores	28	3	763
Real estate offices	22	3	740
Miscellaneous small businesses	16	2	698

How would you present this information if your district manager had requested an informational report? What changes would you need to make if the manager had asked for an interpretive report? An analytical report? Prepare one report of each type.

As you read through the chapter, ask yourself what information might be useful to the district sales manager as he or she plans sales strategy. What might account for the higher sales of industrial cleaning products in supermarkets, pharmacies, and hardware stores? Compare your solutions to the ones that follow the chapter summary.

▷ OVERVIEW: WHAT DO READERS WANT?

Most reports are written because the readers want and expect them. Reports usually go up the chain of command in an organization and are used to help managers make decisions. Managers expect reports to contain helpful, accurate information and to present that information in a suitable—often prescribed—style and format.

Reports may be used to keep track of routine organizational activities, such as sales and personnel matters (promotions, for example), or they may be assigned to solve a specific problem. Routine reports are often called *periodic reports* because they must be submitted periodically. Special reports are usually called *task reports*. Proposals and justification reports may be requested or volunteered and, like task reports, are written to help solve a specific problem.

So that readers can locate the most important information quickly and easily, reports use a variety of special techniques to emphasize that information. First, reports are usually (though not always) structured so that the most important information is presented first. Second, topic headings help readers locate sections of greatest importance. Third, such graphic aids as tables, charts, drawings, and photographs may help clarify and illustrate important facts and figures. And finally, most reports contain some kind of summary (which may be called an *abstract*) for readers who require only a brief overview of the report.

How would you write a report to solve the problem presented in the following Communication Challenge?

▷ ADVANTAGES OF WRITTEN REPORTS

Why are written reports important to modern organizations?

Report writing is probably as old as writing itself; much of what we know about ancient civilizations comes from their business and governmental reports. Certainly no organization of any size can exist for long without some kind of formal report-writing system. And the larger and more complex an organization is, the more it tends to rely on written reports to aid in the decision-making process.

Of course, many reports in all organizations are oral. For example, if your supervisor stops by your office and asks you how you are doing with a certain account, your reply is an oral report. If your supervisor's boss in New York calls your supervisor in San Francisco and asks for last month's total sales figures, your supervisor provides an oral report.

Nearly all important reports, however, are put into writing. This is because (1) written records are fairly permanent; (2) written records help overcome problems caused by time and distance; and (3) written records help managers handle the complex information required to evaluate and make decisions about situations, ideas, and employees.

Why do reports usually go up rather than down the chain of command?

Reports are assigned and written to provide management with the information needed to make decisions. Most managers cannot directly observe the materials, personnel, and other factors involved in running an organization. They must rely on the observations of others to make their decisions when

1. They are too far removed from a particular operation to observe it directly.

2. They do not have time to supervise an operation directly.

3. They do not have the technical expertise to make accurate observations.

Reports go from a person who is in a position to make direct, accurate, reliable, and objective observations to a person or persons who will make decisions about the observations. This means that reports usually go up the chain of command from lower-ranking personnel to those of higher rank. Some reports, however, are exchanged between people of equal rank. As a rule, reports are distributed down the chain of command only as a means of disseminating information.

COMMUNICATION TODAY...

Few tasks arouse more apprehension than writing a report, especially a formal long report. Business people write numerous letters and memos daily and think nothing of it. Report writing, however, seems to fall into a different category, the level of apprehension increasing with the length and formality of the report.

Such a reaction is natural. Here is a piece of your writing that may influence major decisions and will certainly be in the hands of people who determine your future within the organization. Business people, however, should view report writing as an opportunity, not a burden, because a well-written report will leave a lasting impression that will enhance the writer's opportunity for advancement. Likewise, a poorly written report will leave a lasting impression that can change or even forestall the writer's advancement.

Source: Wesley C. King, Jr., J.D., "Approaching and Writing the Business Report," *Readings and Applications in Business Communication,* 2d ed. Richard C. Huseman, *et al.* (Hinsdale, IL: The Dryden Press, 1985), p. 147.

Business report writing skill has been identified as one of the essential areas for leadership success in the business world of the 1980s. Many corporations, in recognition of this need, are requiring their employees, including top executives, to attend report-writing seminars in order to improve their writing skills.

Source: Thomas Inman and Steven Golen, "Business Report Writing Competencies," *Communication Training and Consulting in Business, Industry and Government,* ed. William J. Buchholz, (Urbana, IL: American Business Communication Association, 1983), p. 127.

▷ PURPOSES OF WRITTEN REPORTS

How do reports contribute to achieving basic organizational objectives?

Reports are rarely written without some consideration for how they contribute to the organization's needs to maintain its existence (maintenance reports), to complete certain tasks (task reports), and to satisfy the human needs of the members of the organization (human reports). These basic organizational objectives are more important for reports than they are for letters. Because most business letters are written to solve particular problems as the need arises, their specific purposes are more important than their general objectives.

Routine reports are established because the organization has a continuing maintenance need. Special reports are assigned when a problem or task exists. Many reports written for maintenance and task reasons are assigned jobs—for example, weekly sales reports, periodic audit reports, and personnel evaluations. Reports written to satisfy human needs are usually volunteered by the writer—for example, requests for additional personnel and suggestions on how to revise a current procedure.

Maintenance Reports

Why are maintenance reports frequently called periodic reports?

Maintenance reports are usually a regular part of a job, such as reports submitted by sales representatives on each week's sales. Reports involving such routine information are also known as *periodic reports.* These reports may be written daily, weekly, monthly, quarterly, annually, or at any set interval—even hourly if circumstances require it. The main function of maintenance reports is to monitor and regulate the sustenance of the organization. Most organizations use printed forms and/or specific guidelines to help writers present the required facts quickly and easily in the desired form. Inventory and manufacturing reports are common examples of maintenance reports.

Task Reports

Under what circumstances would a person be required to write a special report?

Task needs usually require special reports, prepared on a one-time basis to deal with a particular problem. The writer must present the information without the aid of a printed form and with only general guidelines. When you are assigned a special report, it will be because you are in a position to make direct observations and to provide management with answers to the following three important questions:

1. **Can we?**   The first logical question about any project is whether it is possible. Can a certain thing be done? Many business projects are obviously possible, but some are not. For example, current technology may not permit the accomplishment of a desired goal. Some projects may be possible for one company but not for another because of the new capital, resources, and technology involved.

2. **Should we?**   If a project is possible for your company, the next question is whether it should be undertaken. Will the expected benefits outweigh the costs? The benefits, of course, may not always be in terms of profits, though profit cannot be ignored. Will the project contribute to the well-being of the company in the long run?

3. **Which way is best?**   Once it has been determined that the project is worthwhile, the means of achieving the goal must be examined to determine the way that will provide the greatest return for the least investment.

Human Reports

Because management is frequently too far removed from certain operations to know everything about them, intelligent managers are open to suggestions. The people dealing with particular situations on a day-to-day basis can

What might moti-
vate a person to
write a report that
higher management
neither required nor
solicited?

frequently foresee problems before they occur and find better solutions than managers, who are not so well acquainted with the project. Reports of this kind are not assigned, but managers may provide incentives (a percentage of the first year's saving, perhaps) to encourage employees to volunteer them when appropriate.

▷ REPORTS AND THE DECISION-MAKING PROCESS

What is the rela-
tionship between
reports and the de-
cision-making
process?

In addition to contributing to the general needs of the organization, reports, like letters, have specific objectives. While we cannot cover all the objectives reports may have, the main function of any report is to provide readers information they need to make a decision. Because management almost always uses the information in reports to allocate funds, personnel, and other resources, that information must be accurate, impartial, and reliable for an organization to operate properly.

Why is it important
for reports to be
accurate, reliable,
and objective?

It is not always easy to write accurate, impartial, and reliable reports. Our own biases may tempt us to alter or omit information that would influence management's decisions. Also, our perceptions are often less than perfect. In preparing even the simplest informational report, you should ask yourself if you have included all pertinent facts, or if you have mentioned only those facts that fit certain preconceptions of yours.

What factors might
interfere with a
writer's ability to be
accurate, reliable,
and objective?

The problem of accuracy and objectivity is compounded in analytical reports, in which the writer must not only present the facts but also interpret them and provide conclusions and recommendations. All of us have certain biases that interfere with our objectivity. For example, when things go wrong, we usually prefer to believe that someone else is responsible. It is easy for us to overlook facts when they go against our prejudices or wishes.

Preconceptions ("Don't confuse me with the facts; my mind is already made up.") can cause a writer not only to ignore some facts but also to overvalue others. And if the writer desires a particular outcome, he or she will be tempted — consciously or unconsciously — to slant the facts so they lead to the conclusion favoring that outcome.

To achieve accuracy and objectivity in your reports, pay particular attention to the following guidelines:

1. Identify — for your reader and for yourself — statements of fact, inferences based on fact, and value judgments. You can use natural, personalized language and still convey objectivity and believability by telling your reader when you are stating a fact, when you are drawing a conclusion, and when you are stating an opinion. Make sure that you have sufficient evidence to warrant your conclusion, and include this documentation in the report. Avoid hasty generalizations and unsupported opinions.

2.   Use accurate, reliable, and objective sources. Books and articles quickly become dated. Also, their authors may not have been as accurate, reliable, or objective as you must be. Use recent sources, and avoid relying on a single source. Compare the information in one source with that found in other sources. People used as sources for questionnaire, survey, or interview data may be uninformed or prejudiced. Check the accuracy of all sources.

Why are analogies sometimes misleading?

3.   Use analogies to explain and illustrate, but not to prove. Because no two things — however similar — are exactly alike, no analogy can be complete enough to constitute proof. False analogies are a form of deception.

4.   Examine all cause-effect statements for completeness and accuracy. Might the effect have more than one cause? Can you identify the specific cause of the effect with certainty? Or might you be dealing with a concurrent effect (one that happens at about the same time and seems related to the main effect) rather than the cause?

5.   Be specific. Avoid unnecessary modifiers and conditional clauses. Too many adjectives and adverbs make your argument seem emotional rather than logical; too many conditional clauses weaken your argument. Use concrete nouns rather than abstract ones. When possible, use people rather than ideas as the subjects of your sentences.

6.   Provide adequate documentation. Cite your sources and clarify your methodology so that your reader will be able to estimate your accuracy and objectivity with some confidence. Be sure to use a method of documentation acceptable to your audience. See Chapter 13 for the common methods of documenting secondary sources.

▷ METHODS OF CLASSIFYING REPORTS

Unlike business letters, which may be classified primarily according to function, business reports may be equally well classified by several other ways in addition to function. Reports, much more than letters, tend to be specialized according to the needs of those who use them. The methods of classification we discuss here are the ones most frequently used, but the names given particular types of reports may vary from company to company.

Classification by Function

Reports may be classified according to the following functions: (1) they may provide information (*informational*); (2) they may provide information and

What are the differences among informational, interpretive, and analytical reports?

interpret it (*interpretive*); or (3) they may provide information, interpret it, and offer conclusions and recommendations based on that information (analytical).

Informational Reports.   Informational reports provide information, often in the form of raw data, without interpretation, analysis, or recommendation. Most maintenance (periodic) reports are purely informational. Some task (special) reports are also purely informational. For example, an oil company might assign a representative the task of discovering and reporting on the feelings of the residents of a particular town about exploratory drilling in the town's only park, without wanting the representative to draw conclusions or make recommendations.

Interpretive Reports.   Interpretive reports provide information and interpret it for the audience. Such reports are primarily useful for helping a general audience cope with technical data. Interpretive reports perform the same basic function in organizations as informational reports. The difference between them is that without the interpretation of the technical details, the audience would probably fail to understand the significance of the information. Interpretive reports explain rather than analyze, and they do not include recommendations.

What would be wrong with offering conclusions and recommendations in every report written?

Analytical Reports.   Analytical reports provide information and also the writer's opinion. It is important to know whether a report should be informational or analytical. Offering conclusions and recommendations when they are not wanted is presumptuous; not offering them when they are expected makes a writer appear careless.

Because most task reports are analytical and because each report must satisfy the needs of a special task, writing task reports is often difficult. Each company specifies certain requirements for reports that address common kinds of problems (for example, an engineering firm would have a particular set of guidelines for analyzing and recommending dam sites), but the guidelines for analytical reports are usually general. They must be sufficiently flexible to deal with many special tasks.

Classification by Length

What are the differences between short and long reports?

Special (task) reports are often classified by length—short or long. Although this method of classification is neither precise nor appropriate for many business report-writing situations, it is fairly common. Its main advantage is that it lets the writer know how much energy management wants invested in a particular report. If your boss asks for a short, analytical report on the fire in the Sunnyvale plant, you know that he or she wants the best information you can provide quickly and wants your conclusions and recommendations based on what you discover, but an exhaustive study is not desired.

The division between short and long is arbitrary. As a rule, short means fewer than ten pages. Also as a rule, short reports are single-spaced and long reports are double-spaced, but there are exceptions, which we will discuss later. Short reports are much more common in business than long reports, but when a long report is necessary, it is usually because the project or problem is critical.

Classification by Formality

What are the differences between informal and formal reports?

As is true with length, formality is a matter of degree. Reports are either informal or formal depending on how the information is expressed and presented. Informal reports are useful to convey routine information to others within the company who will benefit from it. They may be a regular part of the communication process between writer and reader, or they may be sent as *intracompany letters*—sent by the writer to convey a special message to the reader.

Formal reports are advisable when the situation calls for serious treatment, when the relationship between writer and reader is formal, or when the report will be read by a large audience, perhaps over a long time. Informal reports are often discarded after the reader has read them; formal reports are often kept for years.

Classification by Frequency of Issue

Routine (periodic) reports may be prepared hourly, daily, weekly, monthly, bimonthly, or annually. Companies often refer to reports by a combination of frequency of issue and subject matter: for example, *weekly sales report, annual audit report, production report for August*. Nonroutine reports are called *special reports* when this system of classification is used. Special reports are written to help solve nonroutine problems and are special assignments.

Classification by Reader-Writer Relationships

What are the differences between internal and external reports?

Reports may be either internal or external depending on whether the writer and reader both work for the same company. Internal reports, as the name implies, stay within the company. External reports go from a writer in one company to a reader in another company. Internal reports are often less formal than external reports, which must convey an appropriate image of the writer's company to the reader.

Classification by Type or Form

In many companies reports are classified simply according to type or form. The memorandum (memo) is probably the best known of these forms. We discuss the commonly used types and forms in Chapter 14.

▷ REQUISITES OF REPORTS

Good writing style for reports is essentially the same as for other kinds of writing. Reports, however, place demands on writers that are not always present in other communication situations. The information contained in reports is usually much more complex than that in other messages, and that information must be presented both clearly and quickly.

Because reports usually go up the chain of command and because the person receiving the report has requested it for the purpose of making a decision, reports require greater attention to organization and accuracy than most other kinds of writing.

Figure 12.1 illustrates the typical flow of reports in an organization. Note in Figure 12.1 that each level of the hierarchy tends to reduce the number of reports it sends to the next higher level. This means that information is consolidated, and some information may be omitted. A negative situation that figures prominently in a report at the operations level, for example, may be reduced to a sentence or two at the mid-management level, and omitted entirely when the executive sends her or his report to the president. As a result, the president may make a bad decision. For this reason, reports need to follow certain rules to help ensure that important information is not omitted or deemphasized as it moves up the organizational hierarchy.

FIGURE 12.1
Reports and the Organizational Hierarchy

Annual report.

Primarily informational reports — reporting decisions and the results of decisions.

Informational and analytical reports based primarily on information provided by lower-level management.

Informational, interpretive, and analytical reports.

Primarily informational reports, many using printed forms.

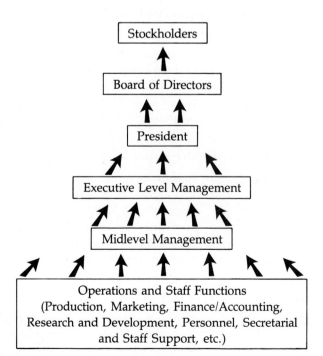

Stockholders

Board of Directors

President

Executive Level Management

Midlevel Management

Operations and Staff Functions
(Production, Marketing, Finance/Accounting,
Research and Development, Personnel, Secretarial
and Staff Support, etc.)

Proper Organization

What are the differences between deductive and inductive order?

Organization is the communicator's primary means of achieving clarity. To achieve proper organization, the writer must anticipate and answer the receiver's questions. Without the aid of immediate feedback, this is sometimes a difficult task.

The purpose of a written message governs its basic structure. Letters, for example, have definite organizational patterns based on the writer's specific objectives. Messages to which the reader will react favorably are presented directly; messages the reader will resist use indirect structure. Similarly, the purpose of a report determines its structure. The basic purpose of all reports is to convey information that may influence decisions; the overall organizational patterns for reports reflect this.

What is the relationship between deductive order for reports and direct order for letters and memos?

Deductive Order.   Reports are arranged to present the most important information either first or last, depending on the reader's expected reaction to it. If the reader will welcome the contents of the report, a deductive order of presentation is better. The writer should put the most important part of the information, including the conclusions and recommendations, first. Deductive order begins with a general principle, offers a specific application, and then provides a conclusion.

The report would *begin* with

General principle:	The company needs to reduce operating expenses by at least $10,000.
Specific application:	The only possible source of this saving is a reduction in personnel.
Conclusion:	Morris L. Burner, the company's least productive employee, should be fired.

The rest of the report would contain the specific facts and other supporting details. You would for example, show why the company needs to reduce operating expenses by $10,000 and that the only source of the saving would be a reduction in personnel. You would also need to supply some evidence that Morris Burner was the least productive employee.

The advantage of this structure is the reader knows exactly what to expect from the report after reading the first few sentences. If the reader has confidence in the writer, he or she may need to read only the first paragraph before making a decision.

What is the relationship between inductive order for reports and indirect order for letters and memos?

Inductive Order.   If the reader is likely to resist the information, the report writer should use an inductive order of presentation, working from specific facts to a general conclusion and saving the recommendation for last. Although the inductive pattern of presentation is similar to the pattern used for persuasive messages, the purpose of the inductive order is not to persuade. The purpose of all reports is to communicate accurate, reliable, and objective information; but sometimes report writers will reach conclusions and make recommendations that management will resist. The inductive pattern of presentation may help to ensure an objective evaluation of the information.

Specific fact:	Last year the company lost $9,500.
Specific fact:	This year the company will lose about $9,750.
Specific fact:	Manufacturing costs have risen; production levels cannot be increased because sales have peaked.
Specific fact:	The plant will need to be retooled before manufacturing costs can be reduced.
Specific fact:	Personnel reduction is the only means of reducing costs until retooling takes place.
General conclusion:	The least productive person should be fired.
Recommendation:	The president's son-in-law, Morris L. Burner, should be fired.

In general, inductive order should be used only when the writer knows that a direct, deductive order will likely result in a poor decision. Many readers resent the slowness of inductive order and read the conclusions and recommendations sections first, regardless of where they appear in the report.

What is an outline, and what are its functions?

Outlining.   After selecting the overall structure for the report, the writer needs to organize the data. Except for the briefest reports, which usually follow the same organizational patterns as letters, making an outline is essential. An outline forces the writer to divide the topic into approximately equal, logical subdivisions emphasizing the most important points. Full-sentence outlines are generally more useful than noun, adjective, or phrase outlines because they force the writer to say something specific about each topic and establish clearly the relationships among topics.

The report writer can usually use some version of the initial statement of the problem for the title of the outline and the finished report. The title should cover the entire subject and should be suitable for the overall pattern of presentation. For example, the report title "New Presses Will Reduce the Accident Rate in the Production Department" might not receive a fair hearing because management resists the expenditure of money. A better title for such a report might be "Reducing the Accident Rate in the Production Department."

Whether the report is deductive or inductive, the title usually implies a certain **basis of classification.** The writer must use that basis of classification for each of the subdivisions, making all subdivisions mutually exclusive. For example, if you are going to report on the ways religious affiliation influences buying habits, it would not be logical to classify your subjects as *Protestants, Catholics, Jews, Atheists, Women,* and *Republicans,* because the categories overlap. A better division would be *Protestants, Catholics, Jews, Muslims, Buddhists, Agnostics,* and *Atheists.*

What kind of expectations could a report title create?

If your title establishes certain expectations in your reader, your subdivisions should satisfy those expectations. If your title begins "Reasons that," your main subdivisions should form a list of reasons. If your title establishes a comparison leading to a choice, your main subdivisions should form a list of the criteria used to evaluate the choices.

Your outline should clearly indicate the relationship among divisions and subdivisions. Either of the following methods of outlining works well:

1.0	Main division	I.	
1.1	Subdivision		A.
1.2	Subdivision		B.
1.3	Subdivision		C.
2.0	Main division	II.	
2.1	Subdivision		A.
2.1.1	Sub-subdivision		1.
2.1.2	Sub-subdivision		2.
2.2	Subdivision		B.
3.0	Main division	III.	

What is the difference between a main division and a subdivision in an outline?

The following conventions used in outlining are designed to help writers avoid problems with the logical presentation of information:

1. Divisions should be organized for relative balance. Because equal divisions indicate equal importance, similar divisions should require about the same amount of space. Each roman numeral or whole number, for example, should be treated equally. This rule is not absolute, but if one of your divisions requires three times as much space as another of supposedly equal rank, your organization may not be well balanced.

2. No single subdivision should occur, since a topic is not divided unless at least two parts result. If you subdivide a part, you must have at least two subdivisions. You cannot have I.A. unless you also have I.B.

3.   Main divisions must be expressed in parallel grammatical form. Sub-
     divisions must be parallel within each division, but they need not be
     parallel with subdivisions of other divisions. Thus A., B., and C. under
     main division I. must be parallel with each other, but they need not be
     parallel with A., B., and C. of main division II.

4.   The total of the subdivisions must equal the main division; the whole
     of each division must be the sum of its parts. For example, the roman
     numerals must cover everything implied by the title.

5.   Divisions and subdivisions should be selected to help the reader grasp
     the information quickly and easily. The ideal number of parts in any
     classification is from three to seven. If you have fewer than three sub-
     divisions, they may be too broad or incomplete; and if you have more
     than seven, your reader will have a hard time remembering important
     points. Use a classification that permits a favorable division of parts.

One common difficulty in outlining is ensuring that all major divisions
are of relatively equal importance and mutually exclusive (that is, they should
not overlap). A second common problem is ensuring that subdivisions are
assigned to the appropriate main division.
     Suppose you are responsible for analyzing the transportation available
at a possible location for a new plant for your company. What should your
major divisions be? You might begin by listing the various forms that occur
to you:

Trucks

Trains

Automobiles

Airplanes

Helicopters

Boats

Or you might think in terms of that which will require transportation: people,
raw materials, and products. Either way, you need to decide what should
constitute your major divisions, and what might constitute subdivisions in
each. Perhaps you would decide on something like the following outline:

I.   Transportation requirements

II. Ground transportation
     A. Truck routes
     B. Automobile routes
     C. Rail spur tracks

  III. Air transportation
    A. Regional airport
    B. Helicopter shuttle service

  IV. Water transportation
    A. Saunders River
    B. Gulf access

Note that each of the major divisions is of roughly equal importance. You should avoid a situation in which you would have something like the following:

What would be wrong with making "Ground transportation" and "Train transportation" equal divisions?

  II. Ground transportation
    A. Trucks
    B. Autos

  III. Train transportation

In this case, train transportation is really a subcategory of ground transportation, and the outline should reflect that.

Special Techniques

The special techniques that make report writing different from other kinds of writing are necessary because reports are almost always longer than letters, and they usually contain more complex information. Help the reader follow your argument, understand your organizational pattern, and keep track of items of special importance by using the following special techniques:

What is a heading? What makes a heading good?

Headings. Headings are a report writer's main aid to easy readability. A heading is a group of words set off from the text that identifies the content following it. Writers are frequently tempted to use a heading as the antecedent of a pronoun, but because headings are not actually a part of the text, the report must make sense even if all headings were removed. Consequently, headings should *never* be used as pronoun antecedents.

   Not this: *Headings.* These are an important technique for all but the shortest reports.

   But this: *Headings.* Headings are an important technique for all but the shortest reports.

  A good heading is both brief and specific, not only stating the topic to be discussed but also giving an important piece of information. "Advantages of Small Cars" makes a better heading than "Small Cars."
  Use headings according to the same basic rules that apply to outlining; make the relative importance of each heading clear by using a uniform system

of form and position. In general, headings entirely in capital letters are superior to headings that include lowercase letters, and centered headings are superior to marginal headings in the same form.

The title of a report should be in a form clearly superior to all other headings in the report. The system illustrated in Figure 12.2 is convenient for use with typewritten material requiring five levels of headings for any one section of the report.

Very few reports require five degrees of headings. Though many acceptable formats exist, when four levels are used, the forms shown for first-, second-, third-, and fourth-degree headings in Figure 12.2 are the most common. When only three degrees are needed, the forms shown for second-, third-, and fourth-degree headings are the most common. When only two degrees are needed, the forms shown for third- and fourth-degree headings are the most common. Most short reports require only two or three levels of headings.

Itemizations.   Lists are another technique report writers use to make their writing clear, precise, and concise. When you put important points in a numbered list, you call attention to each fact in two ways: separately and as part of a whole. The entire list must be separated from the text, and each item in the list should be grammatically parallel with every other item. Capitalize each item displayed in a list.

When are unnumbered lists more appropriate than numbered lists?

Numbering the items in a list usually implies a hierarchy — the first point is considered more important than the second, and so forth. Unnumbered lists are useful when all the items are of equal importance, but they may require some other means of drawing attention to each item, such as underscoring, an asterisk, or a dash.

What are the functions of graphic aids?

Graphic Aids.   Graphs, charts, photographs, tables, drawings, maps, and pictograms are often necessary to illustrate specific points. Such aids can keep the report from becoming cluttered with statistics and lengthy descriptions. So that your reader will understand your graphic aid, remember to do the following:

1.   Introduce the aid *before* your reader encounters it.

2.   Emphasize what the reader should get out of the aid rather than focusing on its existence.

3.   Number and title each graphic aid. Use arabic numbers, and number the aids consecutively.

4.   Ensure that the graphic aids are self-explanatory. Just as the text should be clear and complete without the graphic aids, the aids should be clear and complete without the prose explanation.

FIGURE 12.2
Sample Headings

R E P O R T   T I T L E

For the title of a report, use solid capitals underlined or solid capitals typed with spaced capitals. Type one space between every two letters and three spaces between words. Report titles are centered horizontally and followed by a triple-space.

FIRST-DEGREE HEADING [I. or (1.0)]

Your first-degree headings, which correspond to the roman numerals in your outline, should be in solid capitals and centered. Triple space (two blank lines) before and after a first-degree heading. In single-spaced material, paragraphs are *not* indented but are indicated by a double-space. In double-spaced material, paragraphs are indicated by a five-space indention.

Second-Degree Heading [A. or (1.1)]

Second-degree headings correspond to the major subdivisions of each section in your outline. They should be centered and typed in capital and lowercase letters. Capitalize the first word and all words with four or more letters. Also capitalize words with fewer than four letters except articles (the, a, an), conjunctions (and, but, or, for, nor), and prepositions (to, of, at, in). Capitalize prepositions of more than four letters (above, beyond, etc.). Triple-space before a second-degree heading, and double space after it. When reports require only two or three levels of heading, the second-degree heading may be used for its title and then the third- and fourth-degree headings would be used for the subheadings.

Third-Degree Heading [1. or (1.11)]

Begin a third-degree heading at the left margin. Use capitals and lowercase letters and underscore it. Capitalization is the same as that for the second-degree heading. Triple-space before a third-degree heading, and double space after it.

Fourth-Degree Heading [a. or (1.111)]. The fourth-degree heading begins the paragraph; it is typed on the same line as the paragraph. Capitalization is the same as that for the second-degree heading. Double space before a fourth-degree heading.

The fifth-degree heading [(1) or (1.1111)] is an integral part of the paragraph's first sentence. It consists of the key word or words in that sentence. Capitalize the first word and proper nouns in the heading; underscore the entire heading, but not the entire sentence. Double-space before a fifth-degree heading.

5.   Ensure that the graphic aids are attractive, readable, and clear. Programs are available for most microcomputers to assist in the production of graphic aids. They will automatically convert statistical data into line charts, pie charts, bar graphs, and histograms. If you need to produce a graphic aid by hand, observe the following conventions:

   a.   Allow plenty of room for the aid, and use a generous amount of white space.
   b.   Type all information.
   c.   Use a ruler, compass, and protractor when necessary. Avoid free-hand drawing.

The three most widely used charts are the line chart (Figures 12.3 and 12.4), the pie chart (Figures 12.5 and 12.6), and the bar graph (Figure 12.7). Many other charts and pictograms are variations of these fundamental types (See Figure 12.8).

Line charts are used to show trends or changes over time, such as price changes or relationships between two or more variables. A line chart has two axes—a vertical axis (or Y-axis) and a horizontal axis (or X-axis). To prevent

FIGURE 12.3
A Typical Line
Graph

Figure 1. Net Profits, Cale Inc., 1967–1974

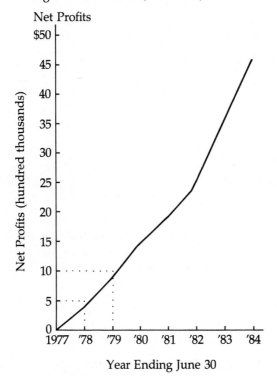

Net Profits

Year Ending June 30

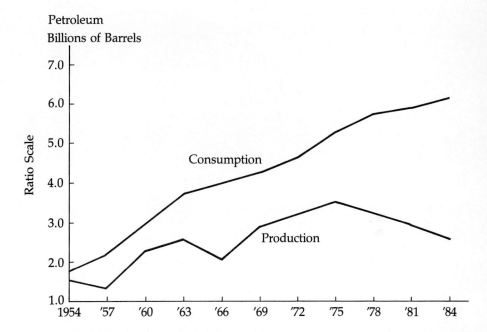

Figure 2.   Oil Production and Consumption Rates

distortion, keep the vertical and horizontal gradations equal. Keep plot lines to a minimum; five plot lines on a single grid should be a maximum.

Pie charts are so called because they divide a whole (100 percent) into segments the same way one cuts a pie. Always begin at the 12 o'clock position and move clockwise, starting with the largest segment and proceeding in descending order. The final section should be either the smallest section or "other," regardless of how large a percentage may be included in the category of "other." Because it is difficult to judge relative sizes, include the value in each "slice." If a section is too small to include its value and label, place the value and label outside the chart and use a line to show the relationship between the value and the appropriate section. Do not use separate pie charts to compare separate wholes. Use a dramatic pie chart to emphasize a particular segment.

Bar graphs are used to illustrate comparisons, especially changes in quantity. The bars can be horizontal or vertical (column). Use horizontal bar graphs to compare data over a single period of time or to represent length or distance. Use vertical bar graphs to compare data over a period of time or to represent height. Bar graphs may be multiple, bilateral, or segmented. Use a multiple-bar graph when you want to compare two or three variables within a single bar graph. A bilateral bar graph shows increases on one side of a

FIGURE 12.5
A Typical Pie Chart

Figure 3.   Ownership of Stock, Dawson Furniture Co.

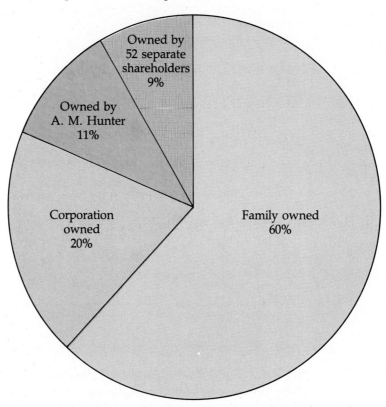

zero line and decreases on the other side of the zero line. Use bilateral charts whenever data to be presented have both positive and negative values. Segmented bar graphs are used to show the composition of the variables being compared.

What are the differences between formal and informal tables?

Tables are useful for presenting a wide variety of statistical and technical information. They are classed as formal or informal. Formal tables are numbered, titled, and have lines surrounding and separating the items (Figure 12.9). Informal tables are not numbered, titled, or ruled (Figure 12.10).

A pictogram, a variation of the bar chart, uses pictures or symbols rather than lines or bars to represent data. To prevent distortion, keep pictures or symbols the same or of equal size. Pictograms may help a reader visualize the importance of the concept being presented.

Formal Writing Style

Because of their importance to an organization, reports may require a more formal style than either letters or memos. Longer analytical reports in particular, which may be read by many people over several years or which may

**FIGURE 12.6
A Dramatic Pie
Chart**

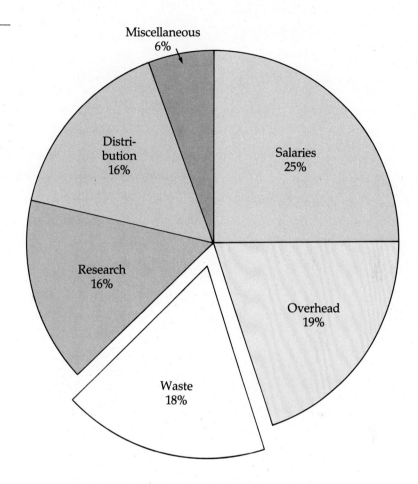

Why do reports often require a more formal writing style than either letters or memos?

be released to the press for general publication, tend to require a formal writing style. In general, formal style is characterized by the absence of first- and second-person pronouns; an increased number of compound, complex, and compound-complex sentences; and an absence of contractions.

Informal:	When I asked Smith how much he wanted for the property, he said that he'd consider selling for $100,000.
Formal:	Smith confirmed that he would consider selling the property for $100,000.
Informal:	I concluded that compound A (which you suggested) worked better than compound B.
Formal:	Compound A proved superior to compound B.

FIGURE 12.7
A Multiple-Bar
Graph

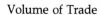

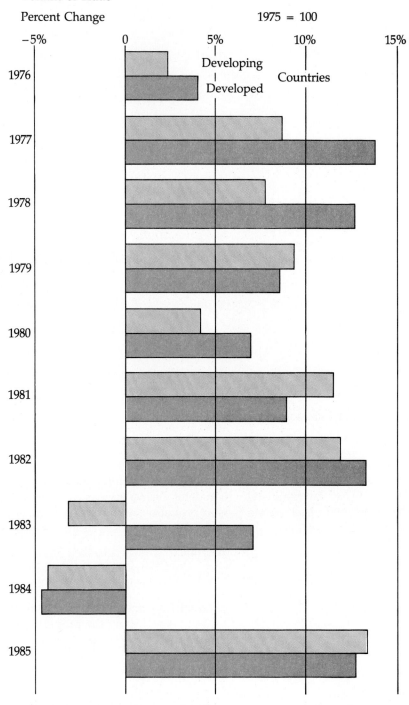

Figure 4. Volume of Trade and Percent of Change
in Developing and Developed Countries

Volume of Trade

Percent Change   1975 = 100

FIGURE 12.8
A Pictogram

Figure 5.   Estimated World Crude
Oil Reserve Percent Distribution 1984

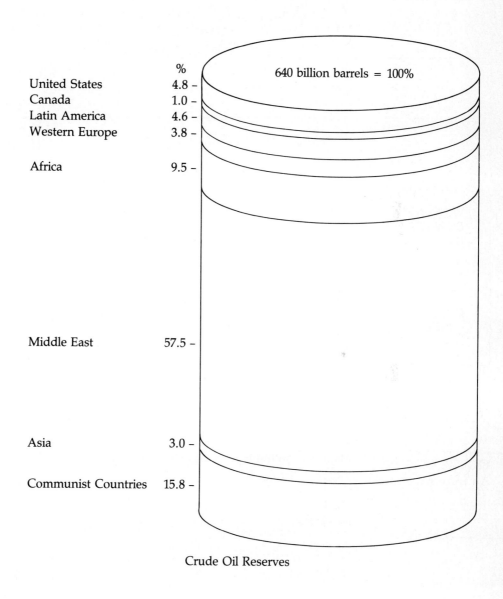

Crude Oil Reserves

FIGURE 12.9
A Formal Table

TABLE 6
Cost-Efficiency Estimate

	GROUP		% DIFFERENCE REM VALUE − NO-REM VALUE / NO-REM VALUE
	REMEDIATION	NO REMEDIATION	REM RELATIVE TO NO REM
1. TOTAL STAFF COST A SEMESTER	$692.80	$504.64	+37%
2. PERCENT CORRECT ON DV	71	33	+115%
3. "UNIT COST" = $ / DV = (1) / (2)	$9.75	$15.29	−36%
4. COST-EFFICIENCY INDEX = DV / $ = (2) / (1)	.1	.07	+43%

DV = Probe Test (mean score)
REM = Remediation
NO REM = No Remediation

FIGURE 12.10
An Informal Table

Make the following changes in your production schedule for April:

Delete

Nomenclature	Product Number	Quantity
Washer, flat, 1/4"	W17425	1,000,000
Washer, flat, 1/2"	W17426	1,000,000
Washer, flat, 3/4"	W17427	1,000,000

Add

Nomenclature	Product Number	Quantity
Washer, lock, 1/4"	W18425	1,000,000
Washer, lock, 1/2"	W18426	1,000,000
Washer, lock, 3/4"	W18427	1,000,000

When you need to be formal, try to do so without resorting to passive voice and awkward circumlocutions to avoid first- and second-person pronouns.

Not this: It was concluded that

But this: I concluded

Not this: The writer is therefore herewith transmitting the attached samples to the reader for his inspection.

But this: For these reasons, I'm sending you the attached samples for your inspection.

Do not sacrifice clear, concise writing to the formality of the situation. A common error in formal writing is to use the passive voice excessively. Check your writing to ensure that your reader will not get lost trying to determine who is going to do (or has done) what to whom when. At the same time, check to ensure that you have not used slang or inappropriate contractions.

Summarizing Statements

How can forecasts and summaries help a reader understand report material?

Brief overviews and recapitulations also help readers grasp important concepts in a report quickly and easily. Because of the length and complexity of most reports, it is difficult for readers to keep the important aspects of your argument clearly in mind as they read from section to section. To help your reader, begin each paragraph with a topic sentence that clearly indicates what you intend to do in that section. For longer sections, provide a concise forecast of what you intend to cover, and show the reader how the new material will contribute to her or his understanding of the topic. Conclude each section with a summarizing statement that shows (1) how the material just presented adds to what was promised and (2) how it relates to the material that will follow.

▷ ABSTRACTS AND EXECUTIVE SUMMARIES

What is an abstract, when is a separate abstract required, and how does an abstract serve the reader?

Just as individual portions of reports require summarizing statements to help the reader keep track of the information in the report, the entire report (especially if it is longer than three pages), also requires a summary. Shorter summaries are often called *abstracts*; longer ones are called *executive summaries*. The abstract (also called a *synopsis, précise,* or *epitome*) may be the first paragraph in a short report, part of the letter or memo of transmittal in a longer report, or a separate page in a still longer report. Executive summaries are usually three to five pages and include more supporting detail than an abstract.

A good abstract or executive summary is a miniature version of the entire report and is prepared *after* the report is completed. It may save the reader the time required to read the entire report; it will certainly make the rest of the report easier to read.

Any kind of summary places special emphasis on conclusions and recommendations, with proportionally less emphasis on the supporting details. After reading a summary, a manager ought to know the following:

1.   The nature of the problem or hypothesis of investigation.

2.   The methodology and results of the investigation.

3.   The advantages and disadvantages of alternative solutions.

4.   The writer's conclusions and recommendations.

Abstracts

What is a summarizing introduction?

Informal reports of five pages or less rarely require more than a summarizing introduction for an abstract, stating the main conclusion and recommendation and providing a brief overview, or forecast, of the rest of the report. The summarizing introduction tells the reader where the report is going (the final destination) and the way in which it will get there (the route). Having the destination and route in mind helps prevent the reader from losing track of the important points in the report.

Reports of between five and about fifteen pages may incorporate an abstract into the letter or memo of transmittal. The first paragraph of the transmittal would transmit the report and clarify the authorization for the report. The middle paragraphs would provide the actual summary, and the final paragraph would conclude the letter. See Figure 12.11 for an example of a memo of transmittal.

What are the differences between descriptive language and summarizing language?

Abstracts are usually more helpful to the reader when they use summarizing language rather than descriptive language. Summarizing language tells the reader what the report says, whereas descriptive (topical) language — as in a table of contents — only tells what the report is about. In general, avoid descriptive language for abstracts.

Descriptive language: This report is about desalinization of ocean water.

Summarizing language: Desalinization of ocean water will become practical within the next decade.

Usually an abstract should be about 10 percent the length of the entire document, but no longer than one page. The abstract, however, may be single-spaced (with double-spacing between paragraphs) even when the report proper is double-spaced. Because the abstract should emphasize the important points, rely primarily on the ideas presented in the topic sentences

**FIGURE 12.11
A Memo of
Transmittal**

The first paragraph
is the *transmittal*, in-
dicating the sending
of the report to the
reader and the au-
thorization for the
report.

The middle para-
graphs provide the
abstract of the re-
port, with emphasis
on conclusions and
recommendations.

Letters and memos
of transmittal tradi-
tionally end on a
positive, forward-
looking note.

MERCY HOSPITAL
ONE SILVER LANE • HOUSTON • TEXAS • 77251

September 9, 19xx

TO: Arron Toplinger

FROM: Mary Leubecker *ml*

REPORT ON GENERAL LEDGER SOFTWARE

Here is the report you authorized on the three software packages
I investigated to replace our current general ledger system.

The software package with the system most capable of meeting
Mercy's needs is the McCormack & Dodge G/L PLUS. Its variety of
applications and the quality of its performance offers a sound
investment at a reasonable price. The G/L PLUS is a completely
advanced computer software system, as you will see in the report.

The other software systems included ADS G/L Software and Wheaton
Systems' Oracle. Both are capable of handling almost any
hospital and its area of need, but the G/L PLUS offers the most
for the money.

You gave me quite an opportunity to see the latest in computer
technology by approving my request to attend the computer conferences. I had the privilege of hearing guest speakers Tom
Peters, author of In Search of Excellence, and Commodore Grace
Hopper, Pioneer of COBOL.

Perhaps we can have lunch together soon to discuss some of the
highlights of the conventions. I thoroughly enjoyed this research
and hope to have a similar opportunity soon.

in the various sections to provide the ideas for the abstract. Remember that the reader needs to know primarily what he or she should *do* as a result of the information presented in the report. You need to provide only enough of the *why* so that the *what* makes sense. If the reader wants more supporting details, he or she will read the entire report.

Executive Summaries

What are the differences between an abstract and an executive summary?

In recent years, the three-to-five page executive summary has become popular, especially for long reports. An executive summary should emphasize important conclusions and recommendations and include the most important supporting evidence. An executive should be able to make an informed decision after reading the executive summary.

Executive summaries are, in fact, short reports, and they employ all the basic report-writing techniques, including headings and graphic aids. The principal difference between an executive summary and the more traditional one-page abstract is in the amount of supporting detail provided. Executive summaries are useful when the conclusions and recommendations are ambiguous and based on complex data or when the reader has a special need to be familiar with the contents of a long report.

▷ LIFE CYCLE OF REPORTS

What is the life cycle of a report?

Reports often outlive their usefulness. It is easy to see how this happens. Reports are usually initiated because someone in management wants to receive particular information. The first stage in the life cycle of a report is *conception*. If the benefits of the report seem to outweigh its probable costs, the report is initiated. This second stage is the report's *inception*. Should the report prove beneficial, it may become a regular part of someone's workload. In its *mature* stage, a report plays a vital role in the decision-making process. Its intended audience reads it and uses the information.

Reports in the *moribund* stage, however, have outlived their usefulness. The information they contain serves no purpose. Such reports are largely unread, yet many such reports are written daily in business. At the 43rd Annual American Business Communication Association Convention, a colleague of ours, Dr. James Lahiff, told an interesting story about a time-use report required of many college professors. These reports required professors to report on how much time they spent on such activities as teaching, advising students, research, and "other."

Tired of spending extra time trying to complete the report accurately, one instructor decided to assign 100 percent of her time to teaching. The report went through without question. The following semester, the instructor indicated that 100 percent of the time had been spent advising students. Management still did not respond. The next two semesters, the report showed 100 percent of the time spent on research and then on "other." The university was not even curious about what the "other" might include. After the 100-percent "other" report, the instructor decided to omit the report entirely. But within a few days after the deadline, she received a call asking for the report. Someone wanted it — even though the information it would contain was useless.

This sort of waste happens in business because routine procedures are part of people's jobs and because of inertia. Once established, reports may prove difficult to eliminate without changing job descriptions or perhaps even without offending certain people on the distribution list.

As a report writer, you should consider the possibility of eliminating reports that seem moribund. You can take action either directly or indirectly. You can tactfully ask your supervisor, the readers of the report, or other appropriate people whether the report still performs a useful function. If the answer is likely to be no, you may wish to request an alternate job responsibility. Should the direct approach be impractical because of your circumstances, try preparing the report but not submitting it. If no one misses the report, omit preparing it the next time and assume new responsibilities.

▷ SUMMARY

Reports are assigned and written to provide management with the information needed to make decisions. Reports go from a person who is in a position to make direct, accurate, reliable, objective observations to a person or persons who will make a decision based on the observations.

Reports are written to satisfy the demands of each of the basic kinds of organizational objectives — maintenance, task, and human. Many reports written for maintenance and task reasons are assigned jobs. Reports written to satisfy human needs are usually proposals on the part of the writer — the kind of report that is frequently dropped into the company suggestion box.

According to function, reports may be classed as informational, interpretive, or analytical. Informational reports provide information only, interpretive reports provide information and interpret it for the audience; analytical reports provide information and the writer's opinion.

Special (task) reports are often classified by length — long or short. The division between short and long is arbitrary; as a rule, "short" means fewer than ten pages.

Reports are either informal or formal depending on how the information is expressed and presented. Informal reports are useful to convey routine information to others within the company who will benefit from it. Formal

COMMUNICATION SOLUTION

Compare your solutions to the sample case presented in the chapter overview with the ones presented here. Be prepared to discuss the differences between your solutions and these. Are parts of your solutions better? What makes them better? If parts of your solutions are not as good, what could you do to improve them?

SHELDON CLEANING SUPPLIES
5240 MT. OLIVET ROAD, SPOKANE, WA 99213

8 September 19xx

To: David Cowan, Sales Manager, District III

From: Gwendolyn Dresselhaus, Sales Representative   *gd*

SALES MONTH: AUGUST 19xx

> Informational reports begin with the most important information.

Here are the figures for last month's sales.

Calls	Sales	Amount
192	44	$11,000

The sales breakdown is as follows:

> Informational reports provide *only* the information.

	Calls	Sales	Amount
Supermarkets	46	14	$3,299
Pharmacies	42	12	3,100
Hardware Stores	38	10	2,400
Clothing Stores	28	3	763
Real Estate Offices	22	3	740
Miscellaneous Small Businesses	16	2	698

SHELDON CLEANING SUPPLIES
5240 MT. OLIVET ROAD, SPOKANE, WA 99203

8 September 19xx

To: David Cowan, Sales Manager, District III

From: Gwendolyn Dresselhaus, Sales Representative *gd*

SALES MONTH: AUGUST 19xx

Here are the figures for last month's sales.

```
Calls      192
Sales       44
Amount   $11,000
```

The sales breakdown is as follows:

	Calls	Sales	Amount
Supermarkets	46	14	$3,299
Pharmacies	42	12	3,100
Hardware Stores	38	10	2,400
Clothing Stores	28	3	763
Real Estate Offices	22	3	740
Miscellaneous Small			
Businesses	16	2	698

As the figures illustrate, supermarkets, pharmacies, and hardware stores account for 80 percent of the sales even though they constitute only 19 percent of the calls.

Interpretive reports begin with the most important information.

Interpretive reports provide some interpretation of important facts.

SHELDON CLEANING SUPPLIES
5240 MT. OLIVET ROAD, SPOKANE, WA 99203

8 September 19xx

To: David Cowan, Sales Manager, District III

From: Gwendolyn Dresselhaus, Sales Representative *gd*

SALES MONTH: August 19xx

Most analytical re-
ports begin with the
most important in-
formation.

Here are the figures for last month's sales.

Calls   192
Sales   44
Amount $11,000

The sales breakdown is as follows:

	Calls	Sales	Amount
Supermarkets	46	14	$3,299
Pharmacies	42	12	3,100
Hardware Stores	38	10	2,400
Clothing Stores	28	3	763
Real Estate Offices	22	3	740
Miscellaneous Small			
Businesses	16	2	698

Analytical reports
include interpreta-
tion and present
conclusions and
recommendations.
Analytical task re-
ports often put rec-
ommendations first.

As the figures illustrate, supermarkets, pharmacies, and
hardware stores account for 80 percent of the sales even
though they constitute only 19 percent of the calls.

I believe that the reason supermarkets, pharmacies, and
hardware stores account for the bulk of the sales is that
they usually have linoleum or asphalt tile floors that
require our industrial cleaning products, whereas the
other businesses usually have carpeted floors.

I recommend that in the future we concentrate sales calls
on supermarkets, pharmacies, and hardware stores. In my
opinion, sales personnel should call on other businesses
only as time permits.

reports are necessary when the situation calls for serious treatment, when the relationship between writer and reader is formal, or when the report will be read by a large audience, perhaps over a long time.

Routine (periodic) reports may be prepared hourly, daily, weekly, monthly, bimonthly, or annually. Companies often refer to reports by a combination of frequency of issue and subject matter: for example, *weekly sales report, annual audit report, production report for August.*

Reports may be either internal or external depending on whether the writer and reader both work for the same company. Internal reports stay within the company; external reports go from a writer in one company to a reader in another.

Reports are arranged to present the most important information either first or last, depending on the reader's expected reaction to it. If the reader will welcome the contents of the report, a deductive order of presentation is better. If the reader is likely to resist the information, the report writer should use an inductive order of presentation.

Abstracts and executive summaries should use summarizing language rather than descriptive language. Abstracts and executive summaries should be faithful to the complete report in content and emphasis, while making sure that the conclusions and recommendations are clear. Abstracts may be as brief as a one-paragraph summarizing introduction, or as long as a full page. Executive summaries are three to five pages long. Both provide a manager with an overview of the report so that she or he will be better able to understand the information presented in the report.

The four stages of the life cycle of reports are conception, inception, maturity, and moribundity.

▷ EXERCISES

Review and Discussion Questions

1. What are the three advantages of written reports?

2. How do reports help solve business problems?

3. What are the six common methods of classifying reports?

4. What are the differences between informational and analytical reports?

5. What are the six guidelines for achieving accuracy and objectivity in reports?

6. When should report writers use deductive order? When should they use inductive order?

7.   What is the relationship between outlining and headings?

8.   What are the four stages of the life cycle of reports?

Problems

1.   Consult the *Annual Abstract of Statistics, Business Statistics, Statistical Abstract of the United States,* the *World Almanac,* or other references approved by your instructor. Select data that interest you and prepare
     a.   A line graph.
     b.   A bar graph.
     c.   A pie chart.

2.   Document the information prepared for Problem 1 above.

3.   Interview at least one business person to learn when and how that person uses business reports. Write a memo describing your findings.

4.   Prepare an abstract or executive summary of an article appearing in a recent issue of a professional journal. Make sure that the article is long enough to warrant an abstract or executive summary.

Additional report problems and cases appear in Chapters 13 and 14.

CHAPTER THIRTEEN

Defining and Researching Report Problems

Because the problems addressed in reports are usually more complex than those addressed in letters or memos, they require greater effort at defining and researching them. This chapter presents the common techniques for defining problems and for gathering the information required to solve them.

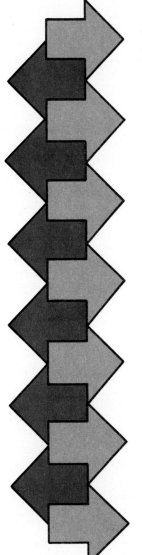

COMMUNICATION CHALLENGE

Suppose that you have been assigned the task of determining whether your company should invest the many thousands of dollars necessary to install teleconferencing equipment. How would you go about gathering the information you would need to make a decision? What kind of second-

ary research would you need to conduct? What kind of primary research would be helpful? Make a list of things you would want to do now, and add to it as you read this chapter. Compare your ideas with the ones that follow the chapter summary.

▷ OVERVIEW: BASE REPORTS ON APPROPRIATE FACTS

Because a report should help a reader make a decision, it should emphasize the factors necessary for such a decision. The first step toward knowing which information to emphasize for the reader is to define the correct problem. Suppose, for example, you have been charged with the responsibility of recommending a fleet purchase of 100 automobiles for your company and that the cars will be used by executive-level managers. What is the problem from your boss's point of view? Would she or he be primarily interested in economy, prestige, or something in between? Is dealer service an important issue? Should all the cars be identical in appearance and options, or should they all be different in the interests of individuality? These are among the questions you would need to answer before you would be able to collect the kind of data your boss would find useful.

After you had defined the problem, a variety of research might be required. You might need to check secondary (published) sources to obtain the repair records of various vehicles, or you might need to conduct primary research by interviewing different dealers to see which dealer could supply the desired vehicles at the best price.

Once you had collected the necessary information, you would need to base your recommendation on an accurate interpretation of that data. You would need to know what data is significant and what is not.

Gathering the right information to solve a particular problem is one of the most important tasks in writing an effective report. The task of gathering data has been influenced tremendously in recent years by the advent of computerized databases. A manager anywhere in the country can now have access to a nearly unlimited supply of secondary information about virtually every subject.

Computers, too, are helping with the interpretation of data. Statistical programs help calculate significant differences and trends. Other programs convert statistical information into graphs and charts so that important factors can be seen. This chapter introduces you to both traditional and electronic methods of gathering and interpreting data.

◊ DEFINING THE PROBLEM

Why is defining the problem usually management's task?

Report writers usually receive specific assignments: defining the problem is almost always management's task. Report-writing assignments are often given orally, however; so the report writer must clarify the specific problem by restating it in terms of an objective to be met or a question to be answered. For example, you may be called into your boss's office:

> **Boss:** (After the usual exchange of pleasantries) Why have we been having so many accidents on the line in your department?
>
> **You:**   Well, as you know, Booker, our presses are old and replacement parts just aren't available anymore. We do the best we can at making our own parts, but the jerrybuilt substitutes don't last. Each time a part breaks, somebody gets hurt. We've been lucky that none of the injuries has been worse.
>
> **Boss:** You'd better give me a report on the situation right away, so I can send it in to the home office. We can probably get some new equipment if we can show a definite need.

You have just been given a report-writing assignment. But exactly what are you to report? Your first task is to state the problem clearly in writing so that

1.   You can be sure you are investigating and analyzing the correct problem.

2.   You can have your boss evaluate and approve your line of investigation.

3.   You can refer to the specific statement when you need to clarify for yourself the direction and progress of your investigation.

If you choose to state the problem in terms of an objective to be met, you will use an infinitive phrase:

> To analyze the high accident rate in the Production Department.

You could also state the problem as a question:

> What is causing the high accident rate in the Production Department?

COMMUNICATION TODAY...

Ten years ago, when one was engaged in an extended research project, it was considered responsible scholarly behavior to travel to a large university or industrial library. Travel can still accomplish a great deal if it brings you in personal touch with the experts; experienced points of view and new approaches [to] problems are often best acquired in the presence of the experts. However, it is no longer necessary to travel to a large holding of recorded information in a research quest. Indeed, it may be a waste of time.

Today it is possible to access any book, report, abstract, or serial published in the last 20 years and any one of the many data resource collections by means of a computer terminal and a telephone line. . . .

The place one looks for information is called a database; it is reached by means of a telecommunications network; and one can get to use such a telecommunications network by being a subscriber to an information service or to a telecommunications network that offers an information service. . . .

A database is nothing more than an organized collection of information. Your local library is a database; so is the phone book. In today's terms, a database implies an organized body of information that is got to by means of a computer-telephone link. A network is a system of communication lines and computers that connect one with a resource such as a data base. . . . Charges for database use are cheaper than air or bus fare.

Source: Frank O'Brien, Hollins College, VA. Reprinted with permission.

Once the report-writing assignment is put into specific, workable form, the report writer needs to determine what areas or items to investigate to solve the problem. The foregoing problem is simple: You already know the cause of the high accident rate, and presumably you will be able to show that each of the recent accidents in your department was caused by a press failure.

Obviously, not all problems are as simple as the one in the preceding example. In some cases defining the problem is a major issue. For example, a company's managers and members of its union might not agree on whether low productivity or low morale is the problem requiring investigation. In general, it is sound practice to have the person who assigns the report review and agree to a statement defining the problem before beginning an investigation.

▷ GATHERING AND DOCUMENTING INFORMATION

What is the difference between secondary and primary research?

After you have determined the purpose of your report and identified the problem, you will need to gather information to complete the report. Report writers need to research all the information sources available in preparing their reports. Sources of information are either secondary or primary.

Secondary Sources

Secondary sources provide information collected by other investigators. Published materials, such as the following are examples of secondary sources a writer should check before writing the report.

almanacs	documents
annual reports	encyclopedias
articles	newspapers
books	pamphlets
brochures	periodicals
dictionaries	yearbooks

A similar problem may already have been investigated and reported. The best place to search for secondary sources is a library. In addition to checking the subject entries in the card catalog and the abstracts and indexes, consult the reference librarians. Because they are experts on their libraries' collections, librarians may save you hours of searching and usually offer invaluable assistance. Many are trained to provide help with computerized data searches as well.

Guides to Secondary Sources

What is an on-line database?

The materials cited in the following list are only a sample of the hundreds of reference sources that might prove useful in research on business topics. Many materials from such fields as psychology and sociology, for example, often contain information useful to those working in business. Reference sources selected for inclusion here are the most basic ones appropriate for beginning a research project.

Researchers should keep in mind that many of the commonly used reference sources (including most of those cited here) are now available through on-line, computerized databases. Although most libraries charge a fee for this service, many patrons feel that the speed and convenience of the computer search are well worth the cost.

ABI/Inform (equivalent to *Business Periodicals Index*), Predicasts Bases (which includes the *Funk and Scott International Index* among others), PAIS International, and New York Times Information Bank are just a few examples of the many databases currently available. The number of sources available through computer databases will inevitably increase in the future, and costs will probably decrease, so be sure to check with a reference librarian if you are interested in using a computer with your search.

Printed Indexes

American Institute of Certified Public Accountants. *Accountants Index.* New York: The Institute, 1921 to date. A detailed author-subject bibliography of English language books, pamphlets, and periodical literature in accounting.

Books in Print (BIP). New York: R. R. Bowker, 1948 to date. The most comprehensive listing of currently available American books, *BIP* is issued annually with semi-annual supplements. Because books are listed not only in separate author and title volumes, but also in a separate subject volume, *BIP* is probably the best source for quickly determining what books are currently available on a given topic.

Business Periodicals Index (BPI). New York: H. W. Wilson, 1958 to date. *BPI* is a subject index to periodicals in accounting, advertising, banking and finance, insurance, labor and management, marketing and purchasing, office management, public administration, taxation, and specific businesses, industries, and trades.

Encyclopedia of Business Information Sources. Paul Wasserman, editor. Detroit: Gale, 1970. 2v. This highly useful tool lists primary and secondary sources of factual information of interest to business executives, researchers, scholars, and students of business. When you need information on a business topic and do not know of a good place to begin your research, this book will list sources to get you started.

Funk and Scott Index of Corporations and Industries. Detroit: Funk and Scott Publishing, 1960 to date. Indexes periodical articles and other references (including financial and corporation report findings) on U.S. corporations and industries as a whole.

Information Please Almanac, Atlas, and Yearbook. New York: Information Please Publishing, 1947 to date. This annual almanac is an invaluable reference tool for finding quick information on a wide variety of subjects, from an overview of events of the past year and winners of annual awards to business, economic, and sports statistics and lists of colleges and universities.

Monthly Catalog of United States Government Publications. Washington: Government Printing Office, 1895 to date. A comprehensive listing of government publications offered for sale by the U.S. Superintendent of Documents. Each catalog's contents are arranged alphabetically by the issuing agency, with an index of subjects.

New York Times Index. New York: 1913 to date. A detailed index to the contents of the *Times*.

Paperbound Books in Print. New York: R. R. Bowker, 1955 to date. Although *BIP* does include some paperbacks, this companion volume is the most complete source for paperbound books. The subject approach in this tool is not as thorough as that of *BIP*.

Public Affairs Information Service Bulletin (PAIS). New York: H. W. Wilson, 1915 to date. Indexes materials in the areas of economic, social, and political affairs selected from periodicals, papers, books, government documents, and reports published in English throughout the world.

Readers' Guide to Periodical Literature. New York: H. W. Wilson, 1900 to date. *Readers' Guide* is probably the most frequently used reference tool in any library's collection. It indexes most U.S. popular periodicals, including news magazines and subject magazines intended for a generalist or lay audience.

Statistical Abstract of the United States. Washington: Census Bureau, 1878 to date. Probably the most useful American statistical source found in any library. Anyone looking for statistics that apply to the U.S. should automatically start here.

Wall Street Journal Index. New York: Dow Jones, 1958 to date. Indexes the contents of the *Journal*.

The World Almanac and Book of Facts. New York: Newspaper Enterprise Association, 1868 to date. See annotation under *Information Please Almanac, Atlas, and Yearbook*.

Electronic (On-line) Databases

ABI/INFORM contains more than 230,000 citations with abstracts of periodicals in the business and management area. Database topics range from economics to information science. The information can be searched by key word or topic and is designed for the novice user. It is accessed through BRS, DATA-STAR, Dialog, IIT Dialsom, ESA-IRA, or SDC Information Service.

The Accountant's Index is the electronic version of the printed Accountants' Index directory. The service provides an index of literature about business and financial topics with an emphasis on accounting. The index does not abstract the cited material. It is accessed through SDC Information Services.

Bibliographic Retrieval Service (BRS) contains more than 80 data bases covering physical and social sciences, business, education, and medicine. It is accessed through BRS.

BRS After Dark contains over 30 databases of its parent BRS. It is run during non-prime hours, allowing lower cost. It is accessed through BRS.

Dow Jones News and Dow Jones Free-Text Search are on-line databases containing full-text and edited news stories from *The Wall Street Journal*, Dow Jones News Service, and *Barron's*. The News service allows searching by company stock symbol, industry, and government codes. The Free-Text service allows searching by key words on the full text. Both databases are accessed through Dow Jones and Company Inc.

HBR/Online (Harvard Business Review) contains the full-text version of the *Harvard Business Review.* It includes articles appearing in the magazine since 1976. Citations and abstracts of articles appearing between 1971 and 1976 and 700 classic articles published between 1925 and 1971 are also included. It is accessed through BRS and DIALOG.

Management Contents contains citations and abstracts from over 725 business and management publications. More than 100 of these publications deal with business law and taxation. The service is designed as an industry analysis and prediction tool. It is accessed through DIALOG, BRS, and The Source.

Figure 13.1 illustrates the range of databases available through just one of the popular information services.

FIGURE 13.1   Sample Listing of a Computer Information Service

DIALOG Databases

This unparalleled range of databases is supplied to DIALOG from a variety of widely-recognized publishers, government agencies, corporations, and associations who are responsible for database content and editorial control. Complete database supplier information is provided in the DIALOG user's manual. Brief descriptions and typical applications summarize each database.

Business, Industry, Corporate

ABI/INFORM. Extensive summaries of articles from top business and management journals—business practices, corporate strategies and trends.

ADTRACK. Descriptions of advertisements from 150 U.S. consumer magazines—competitive tracking and product announcements.

ARTHUR D. LITTLE/ONLINE. Management summaries from A.D. Little's market research reports—planning and industry research.

BI/DATA FORECASTS. Briefings on the economies, social, and political outlook for 35 major countries—economic and industry forecasting.

BI/DATA TIME SERIES. Over 300 economic indicator time series for over 130 countries—international business and banking.

BLS CONSUMER PRICE INDEX. Time series of consumer price indexes calculated by the U.S. Bureau of Labor Statistics—economic analysis.

BLS EMPLOYMENT, HOURS, AND EARNINGS. Time series on employment, hours of work, and earnings for the U.S. by industry—economic trends and analysis.

BLS PRODUCER PRICE INDEX. Time series of producer price indexes, formerly Wholesale Price Indexes, for over 2800

commodities—economic analysis.

CENDATA. News Releases from the U.S. Bureau of the Census with textual and tabular information covering Census surveys in business, agriculture, population and more—tracking current economic and demographic trends.

CHEMICAL INDUSTRY NOTES. Extracts from articles in worldwide business-oriented periodicals for chemical-processing industries—chemical industry news and tracking.

COFFEELINE. Summaries of articles and data from over 5000 publications covering all aspects of the coffee and production trade — industry research.

COMMERCE BUSINESS DAILY. Definitive source of notices from U.S. Dept. of Commerce for gov't. procurement invitations, contract awards, surplus sales, R&D requests — competitive tracking, purchasing and sales leads.

D & B — DUN'S MARKET IDENTIFIERS®. Directory of over 1,000,000 public and private companies with 10 or more employees, listing address, products, sales executives — corporate organization, subsidiaries, industry information, sales prospects.

D & B — MILLION DOLLAR DIRECTORY®. Privately-held and public companies with net worths over $500,000, includes data on sales, type of organizaton, address, employees, key executives — corporate analysis and information.

D & B — PRINCIPAL INTERNATIONAL BUSINESSES®. Directory listings, sales volume, corporate data and references to companies for non-U.S. private and public companies from 133 countries — international trade and industry prospects.

DISCLOSURE™ II. Detailed financials for over 9000 publicly-held companies, based on reports filed with the U.S. S.E.C. — sales,

profit, corporate organization, key personnel.

DISCLOSURE™/SPECTRUM OWNERSHIP. Detailed ownership information for thousands of U.S. public companies — investment analysis.

DONNELLEY DEMOGRAPHICS. U.S. demographic information including 1980 Census, current year estimates, and five-year projections, from zip code level to the U.S. summary — demographic and market analysis.

ECONOMIC LITERATURE INDEX. Index to articles from economic journals and books — economic research and teaching.

ECONOMICS ABSTRACTS INTERNATIONAL. Summaries of literature in all areas of international economic sciences — determining industries, distribution channels.

ELECTRONIC YELLOW PAGES. Unparalleled number of listings of U.S. businesses; retail, services, manufacturers, wholesalers, etc. Over 9 million listings with name, location, line of business — sales prospecting and location tool.

FIND/SVP REPORTS AND STUDIES INDEX. Summaries of industry and market research reports, surveys from U.S. and international sources — market, industry and company analyses.

FOODS ADLIBRA. Concise summaries of articles and reports on current developments in the food industry and technologies — market and food sciences research.

FOREIGN TRADERS INDEX. Directory of manufacturers, services, representatives, wholesalers, etc. in 130 non-U.S. countries — direct marketing and sales outside the U.S. (available in U.S. only).

HARFAX INDUSTRY DATA SOURCES. Descriptions of sources for financial and marketing data in major industries worldwide, including market research, investment banking studies, forecasts, etc. — industry tracking and analysis.

HARVARD BUSINESS REVIEW. Text of Harvard Business Review, covering the range of strategic management subjects — management practices and strategies.

ICC BRITISH COMPANY DIRECTORY ICC BRITISH COMPANY FINANCIAL DATABASE Listing of detailed financial information and ratios for nearly one million British companies as filed with the Companies Registry of Companies House — identification of U.K. companies and financial analysis.

INSURANCE ABSTRACTS. Brief summaries of articles

continued

FIGURE 13.1 *continued*

from life, property, and liability insurance journals — tracking insurance industry trends and practices.

INTERNATIONAL LISTING SERVICE. Directory of worldwide public and private business opportunities — buying, selling, and obtaining financing for businesses.

INVESTEXT™. The complete text of prestigious Wall Street and selected European analysts' financial and research reports on over 3000 companies and industries — corporate and industry analysis plus financial and market research.

MANAGEMENT CONTENTS®. Informative briefs on a variety of business and management related topics from business journals, proceedings, transactions, etc. — management, finance, operations decision making.

MEDIA GENERAL DATABANK. Trading information with detailed financial information on 400 publicly-held companies over a seven-year period — charting market and financial performance.

MOODY'S CORPORATE PROFILES. Equity database with financial data and business descriptions of publicly-held U.S. companies, with five-year histories, ratios and analyses on companies

with high investor interest — assess investment opportunities.

PHARMACEUTICAL NEWS INDEX. References to major report publications, covering drugs, cosmetics, health regulations, research, financial news — drug and cosmetic industry developments and regulation.

PTS ANNUAL REPORTS ABSTRACTS. Detailed statistical, financial, product, and corporate summaries from annual and 10 K reports for publicly-held U.S. corporations and selected international companies — product, industry, company identification and strategic planning.

PTS DEFENSE MARKETS AND TECHNOLOGY. Summaries of major articles and reports from defense sources, includes contracts, the industry, and more — defense industry contracting and tracking.

PTS F & S INDEXES (Funk & Scott). Brief descriptive annotations of articles and publications covering U.S. and international company, product, and industry information — company and industry tracking.

PTS INTERNATIONAL FORECASTS. Summaries of published forecasts with historical data for the world, excluding the U.S., covering

general economics, all industries, products, end use data — strategic planning for international development.

PTS INTERNATIONAL TIME SERIES. Forecast time series containing 50 key series for each of 50 major countries, excluding U.S., and projected to 1990, as well as annual data from 1957 to date — international economic analysis.

PTS PROMT. Primary source of information on product introductions, market share, corporate directions and ventures, and companies in every industry, containing detailed summaries of articles from trade and industry sources — market and strategic planning, tracking new technologies and products.

PTS U.S. FORECASTS. Summaries of published forecasts for U.S. from trade journals, businesses and financial publications, key newspapers, government reports, and special studies — short and long term forecasting.

PTS U.S. TIME SERIES. 500 time series for U.S. from 1957 and projected to 1990 and annual data from 1957 to date on production, consumption, prices, foreign trade, manufacturing, etc. — tracking economic and industry trends.

STANDARD & POOR'S CORPORATE DESCRIPTIONS. In-depth corporate descriptions of over 7800 publicly-held U.S. companies with background, income account and balance sheet figures, and stock and bond data — competitive and financial analysis of companies and products.

STANDARD & POOR'S NEWS. Late-breaking financial news on U.S. public companies, including earnings, mergers and acquisitions, joint ventures, management and corporate changes and structure — current awareness of corporate activities.

TRADE & INDUSTRY ASAP™. Indexing and complete text of articles from 85 industry trade journals

and general business publications — current awareness and industry tracking.

TRADE AND INDUSTRY INDEX™. Index with selected summaries of major trade and industry journals and the complete text of press releases from PR Newswire — industry and company information and news.

TRADE OPPORTUNITIES. Purchase requests by the international market for U.S. goods and services, describing specific products or services in demand by over 120 countries — leads to export opportunities, sales, and representation opportunities.

TRINET COMPANY DATABASE. Directory

information on U.S. and non-U.S. company headquarters with aggregate data from establishments, including sales by SIC code — headquarter analysis and industry sales.

TRINET ESTABLISHMENT DATABASE. Directory of U.S. corporate establishments with address, sales, market share, employees, and headquarters information — corporate and market analysis.

U.S. EXPORTS. Time series of U.S. Bureau of the Census statistics on exports of merchandise from the U.S. to other countries — tracking U.S. and international economies and industry-specific trends.

Computerized information services can be expensive, and you need special training to use them efficiently. Most require a series of special commands to perform a search, and these commands differ from service to service. Also, you need to enter the right *descriptors* — key search terms — to obtain useful information. If you entered the one word *teleconferencing*, for example, you might find hundreds of documents, only a few of which would be useful.

What is Boolean logic?

Most computer databases use *Boolean logic* to limit the key terms you wish to search. Boolean logic relies on *and, or, not,* and *adjacent.* The following would all be possible:

Teleconferencing *and* productivity — Would result in a listing of all articles in which both teleconferencing and productivity were discussed.

Teleconferencing *or* productivity — Would result in a listing of all articles in which either teleconferencing or productivity were mentioned.

Teleconferencing *not* productivity — Would result in a listing of all articles in which teleconferencing was mentioned but in which productivity was not — articles mentioning productivity would be excluded.

Teleconferencing *adjacent* productivity — Would result in a listing of all articles in which teleconferencing productivity was discussed, with the terms adjacent to one another.

To obtain useful information, you need to use the right descriptors in the right combination. Many corporate, university, and public librarians have had special training in electronic data retrieval; and until you are familiar with the search procedures for the information services you wish to use, you would do well to obtain the assistance of a professional.

Primary Sources

When secondary sources do not provide the answers, the report writer needs to uncover the facts and figures firsthand. Three methods for collecting primary, or original, data are experimentation, observation, and surveys. Although *experimentation* was originally the tool of the scientist, business is now using it more frequently. Of course, many business problems do not lend themselves to experimental, laboratory research, but business can use experimentation to determine the effect of chance under a given set of conditions. In experimentation, the researcher tests one variable of a problem while holding all other variables constant. Then he or she measures the results and reports them, drawing conclusions and making recommendations based on careful analysis of the data collected in the experiment. For example, to test the effectiveness of a new packaging concept for a firm's product, the experimenter would manipulate the packaging (technically known as the *independent variable*) to see what influence the change would have on sales (the *dependent variable*).

What is the difference between the independent and the dependent variables?

In research, *observation* means recognizing and noting facts. Unlike the experimenter, the observer does not manipulate the environment. In a bookstore you can determine book preferences by observing people as they make their selections. In court you can observe the procedures used by a lawyer for presenting his or her case to the judge and jury.

Observers obtain firsthand information; they use their senses to note the physical changes that occur and they report only what they have observed. One disadvantage of observation is that because we have a tendency to interpret what we see or hear based on our previous experiences, information obtained by this method may not be totally accurate.

Observation may also include a thorough search of company records for relevant information. Accountants search the financial records of a business when they prepare their audit reports.

Why is observation usually used in conjunction with experimentation or a survey?

Observation is the only means of recognizing and noting facts about the current and previous environment. Although it is often used alone to record facts—raw data—observation is more often used in conjunction with experimentation and surveys, which help explain what the facts mean.

Because observation provides the answers to the *what* questions—such as what people are doing under certain conditions—but not to the *why*

What are the advantages and disadvantages of questionnaires, personal interviews, and telephone interviews?

questions — such as why people are doing what they are doing under certain conditions — report writers need another research technique to uncover the motives of individuals to solve certain problems. *Surveys* can be conducted by means of mailed questionnaires, personal interviews, or telephone interviews. Each method has advantages and disadvantages. The report writer must determine which method of research will best provide the answers for the particular problem at hand.

Each report-writing problem presents its own set of circumstances and calls for particular investigative techniques. Also, the nature of experimentation and observation varies greatly from industry to industry, and you would need special education to conduct particular experiments and to perform specific technical observations in each industry. But however the facts are gathered, good reports present the facts in similar ways. Our discussion will focus on surveys of the kind generally used throughout business.

Sampling for a Survey

Because it would be too expensive and almost impossible to conduct a survey to find out what everyone thinks about a certain topic, you need to *sample* the appropriate population. The theory of sampling is that a sufficiently large number of items taken at random from a larger group will have the same characteristics as the larger group.

Naturally, the larger the number included in the sample, the greater the chances that the results will accurately predict the results that would be obtained from the entire population. Various statistical methods may be used to predict differences between a sample and a complete population based on the size of the sample. For a discussion of these techniques, see an introduction to business statistics or our own *Business Report Writing* (The Dryden Press, 1984), pp. 197–221. In general, samples larger than 30 will produce sufficiently accurate results for most business purposes.

What are the differences among random sampling, stratified random sampling, and systematic sampling?

In addition to preparing a *valid* survey instrument — one that measures what it is intended to measure — you need to prepare a *reliable* survey instrument — one that would give you the same results if you were to repeat the survey. If your survey instrument is not reliable, the results will not be valid. Three common sampling techniques are random sampling, stratified random sampling, and systematic sampling.

Random Sampling.   Random sampling is the method by which each item in the population has an equal chance of being selected. To conduct a random sample, you need the identity of each item. For example, if you wanted to conduct a survey of students in a school, you would need the names of all the students enrolled. You might record the names of the students on slips of paper that you would mix thoroughly in a container. You would then select a predetermined number of names from the container. Or

FIGURE 13.2
Stratified Random
Sampling

	Total	Percent of Total	Number Selected
Freshmen	496	32	48
Sophomores	434	28	42
Juniors	341	22	33
Seniors	279	18	27
	1550	100	150

you could assign each student a number and then use a list of computer-generated random numbers to select the students you would use in your sample. Either way, because each student would have an equal chance of being selected, the sampling would be random.

Stratified Random Sampling.   Stratified random sampling is achieved by taking a random sampling of the subgroups within the entire population. The number selected from each subgroup must be proportional to that subgroup's part of the whole. Students, for example, could be divided according to their classifications — freshman, sophomore, junior, or senior. If 32 percent of the students were freshmen, then 32 percent of the sample would also be freshman. Consider the illustration in Figure 13.2.

Systematic Sampling.   Systematic sampling is the method of taking selections at constant intervals from a list of the entire population. For example, if you have a list of all the members in a particular association, you would obtain a systematic sample by taking every tenth — 10, 20, 30, 40 — name on the list, or every *n*th name depending on the size of the list and the number required for the sample.

When you select the first number strictly by chance and then go through the list using all numbers containing that number, you achieve a high degree of randomness. For example, if by chance you choose five as your first number and use 10 as the *n*, you would select the 15th, 25th, 35th, 45th, 55th . . . 995th names on the list.

Constructing a Questionnaire for a Survey

What kinds of questions might result in unusable data?

When you have decided that a questionnaire would be the best method to obtain primary data, you will need to determine which questions to ask to obtain the desired facts, opinions, attitudes, and preferences. The questions you ask, and the way you word them, will determine the quality and usability of the results, so they should be developed and selected with care. Anticipate the results you might receive from a question: What would those results tell you? How would you use the results? In designing a questionnaire, follow the example of architects and engineers, who consider the possibilities and make calculations before submitting preliminary and final plans for construction. The computer programmer's maxim, "Garbage in, garbage out," is equally true of questionnaires. You may need to test the questionnaire on a small number of people before you distribute it to your sample population.

Forms of Questions.   Six types of questions most frequently used on questionnaires are as follows:

1. **Either-or.**   An either-or question gives the respondent a choice between two answers: yes or no, true or false, like or dislike, and so forth.

    Do you own a car? Yes _____ No _____

    Would you favor a four-day work week?
    Yes _____ No _____ Not Sure _____

    Reading improves one's vocabulary.
    True _____ False _____ Don't know _____

    Traveling: Like _____ Dislike _____

2. **Checklists.**   A checklist provides the respondent with a list of possible answers to be checked. Checklists are frequently used because they are easy to complete and fast to tabulate. The respondent may check more than one item.

    Check the duties you believe a secretary should be responsible for

    _____ Compose letters

    _____ File

    _____ Take dictation at 80 words a minute

    _____ Type at least 50 words a minute

    _____ Get boss's coffee

    _____ Run errands

    _____ Keep boss's calendar

3. **Multiple-choice.**   Closely related to the checklist is the multiple-choice question, which gives the respondent several possible choices but forces him or her to choose one.

    Which method of travel do you prefer? Check one.

    _____ Airplane

    _____ Bus

    _____ Car

    _____ Train

    _____ Other (please specify) _____

What is your classification? Circle one.

Freshman   Sophomore   Junior   Senior

Other (please specify) _____

Which one of the following restaurants is your favorite?

_____ Anderson Tea Room

_____ Dockside

_____ Pier 10

_____ Stacy's Steak House

_____ Velvet Hammer

_____ Pineapple Palace

_____ Other (please specify) _____

4. **Ranking.**   A ranking question permits the respondent to rank several choices in order of preference.

Indicate your order of preference by placing 1 (first choice), 2, 3, and so forth before the qualifications you believe a writer should possess.

_____ Ability to write clearly

_____ Ability to write concisely

_____ Ability to write under pressure

_____ Command of the English language

_____ Technical expertise in a particular area

If you were asked to transfer to another department, what would be your order of preference? (1 = first choice)

_____ Accounting

_____ Purchasing

_____ Sales

_____ Traffic

To measure the intensity of the respondent's feelings about a particular question, use some form of scaling. A rating scale sets up the complete range of possible feelings on a topic and assigns each a number value so that the respondent can rate his or her feelings quickly and easily. Rating scales are also useful for determining a respondent's perceptions of events difficult to measure objectively.

What is your opinion of the proposed promotion plan?

Strongly Oppose	Moderately Oppose	Mildly Oppose	Neutral	Mildly Favor	Moderately Favor	Strongly Favor
/	/	/	/	/	/	/
-3	-2	-1	0	1	2	3

When you complete a project, does your immediate supervisor comment on it?

Never				Seldom			Often				Always
1	2	3	4	5	6	7	8	9	10	11	12

5. **Fill-in-the-blanks.** Fill-in-the-blank questions permit the respondent to supply short-answer questions.

How many years have you lived in El Paso? _____

How many times have you visited the Kennedy Center? _____

How many books have you written? _____ If none, write "none."

6. **Open-ended.** Open-ended questions give the respondent freedom in expressing his or her views. Open-ended questions are difficult to tabulate, but they provide unstructured and individual responses that may provide valuable information and new perspectives on a given problem.

When you arrive late for work, your supervisor. . . .

The part of my job I like best is. . . .

I would like to see improvements in. . . .

My suggestions for improving the parking situation are. . . .

Guidelines. The following guidelines will help you prepare a questionnaire:

1. Make your questions easy to understand. Ambiguous words, vague expressions, technical words, words with several meanings, and the like can only confuse the respondent. Most people would find the following questions confusing:

   a. Why did you buy your house? (Too many possible reasons.)
   b. How do you write? (Too many possible interpretations.)
   c. Do you have a codicil on your will? (Not everyone would know what a codicil is.)
   d. Do you regularly attend meetings? (What does *regular* mean?)
   e. What type of car do you drive? (Too many possible interpretations for *type*.)

2. Make your questions easy to answer. When questions are easy to answer, respondents do not mind taking the time to complete the questionnaire.

What is wrong with asking a two-part question?

3. Limit each question to one topic only. When respondents are asked a question that has two parts, they will not know how to respond and may ignore it. Consider the following:

    Would you like an assistant in the afternoon?

    If the respondent answers no, does it mean that he or she does not want an assistant, or does not want an assistant in the afternoon? Perhaps the respondent wants an assistant in the morning.

How are categories for answers made mutually exclusive? Why is that necessary?

4. Avoid personal questions. Respondents do not like to answer personal questions. When you need to know the respondent's age, salary, or personal habits, provide mutually exclusive ranges for your answers (for the ranges to be mutually exclusive, the same numbers must not appear in more than one category). Consider these questions:

    Indicate your age bracket by checking one of the following:

    _____ under 21   _____ 21–29

    _____ 30–39   _____ 40–49

    _____ 50–59   _____ 60–65

    _____ 66 and over

    Your current income is

    _____ under $10,000   _____ $10,000–$15,999

    _____ $16,000–$20,999   _____ $21,000–$25,999

    _____ $26,000–$30,999   _____ $31,000–$35,000

    _____ over $35,000

5. Avoid leading questions. Leading questions are those that suggest an answer. They often produce an inaccurate response. For example, if secretaries were asked, "Is your favorite typewriter an IBM Correcting Selectric?" most would respond with a yes. On the other hand, if you were to ask secretaries to name the manufacturer of their favorite typewriters, they may name another brand. Rather than ask, "Is your favorite toothpaste Crest?" ask "What brand of toothpaste do you use?"

6. Ask questions that the respondent can easily recall. If you were to ask the question, "How much do you spend each year on groceries?" the respondent would probably not take the time to add the cash register slips even if she or he had saved them.

7. Arrange your questions in a logical sequence; progress from the simple to the complex. Ask the easy questions first so that your respondent will not be discouraged before she or he has the opportunity to review the topic covered by your questionnaire.

8. Keep the questionnaire short — one to two pages. Most people will not take the time to answer a long (three or more pages) questionnaire.

9. Ask only those questions that will provide useful information. Anticipate the answers you might receive, and determine in advance how you will use the information. Delete or rephrase questions that will result in useless data.

10. Provide a stamped, addressed envelope when you use a mail questionnaire.

What function does a cover letter perform for a mailed questionnaire?

Mailed questionnaires must have an accompanying cover letter. The organizational pattern for the cover letter should usually be that of a direct request (see Chapter 6) because the recipient will usually be interested in the topic of the questionnaire. The cover letter is also a *letter of transmittal* (see Chapter 6) with the purpose of introducing the questionnaire, explaining its importance, and providing necessary instructions for completing and returning the questionnaire. Write a persuasive request (see Chapter 10) only when you believe the respondents would be reluctant to complete the questionnaire because of its length or contents.

In addition to all the foregoing precautions, remember that you may need to ensure anonymity to obtain accurate information. This is especially true when you are seeking answers to personal questions or when a person's private beliefs and publicly expressed opinions are likely to differ.

Personal Interviews for a Survey

Why should you use a prepared questionnaire in conducting a personal interview?

Personal interviews are another method of obtaining primary information. The same care should be taken in the development of questions for personal interviews as for the questionnaire. Preparing questions in advance helps ensure that you will cover all the important topics and still permits you to ask additional questions that may occur along the way. The personal interview, however, permits greater flexibility in pursuing answers to specific questions. Although it has the advantage of allowing you to ask in-depth questions and receive lengthy, informative answers, the personal interviews are time-consuming and costly. They are best used when the population to be sampled is small and is in one geographic area. The main disadvantage of personal interviewing is the possibility of reporting inaccurate information. People may express a popular view of a subject rather than reveal their own true feelings when talking with an interviewer. Also, unless the interviewer is skilled in interviewing techniques, his or her biases may influence the respondent's answers.

Telephone Interviews for a Survey

Over the years, telephone interviews have been popular for several reasons.

1. They are fast. You can reach people quickly.

For what group(s)
of people would
telephone inter-
views be inappro-
priate?

2.   They are inexpensive when calls are local.

3.   They can provide a random sample when all members of the entire group being studied have telephones.

Telephone interviews do have limitations, however. Because of the frequent use of telephones for selling, people are inclined to hang up rather than answer questions. A limited number of questions can be asked because people are reluctant to answer more than just a few. To overcome these problems, avoid personal questions and those that are long and complex.

Documentation

What is the func-
tion of documenta-
tion?

Many reports require that sources of information be documented in a formal way so that readers may verify the accuracy of the data presented. When ideas, opinions, and statement of facts are obtained from a previously published source, that source should be cited in one of four ways: (1) within the text, (2) as a footnote, (3) as an endnote, or (4) as a reference to a bibliographic entry. The organization for which you work may have a preferred form. If not, use the form that you prefer, but be sure to use the same form throughout a report.

What are the differ-
ences among cita-
tions within the
text, footnotes, end-
notes, and refer-
ences to biblio-
graphic entries?

Regardless of the form of the documentation, references to secondary sources should include the following information (if known):

What information
should be included
in a citation of a
secondary source?

1.   Name(s) of author(s).

2.   Title of book or titles of the article and of the publication in which the article appeared.

3.   Place and date of publication.

4.   Appropriate volume and issue numbers.

5.   Appropriate page references.

Citation within Text.   Citation within the text is a convenient, informal way to document secondary source material. Source references included within the text should be as brief and as inconspicuous as possible.

In "Techniques of Convention Planning" (The Trainer, Sep 1983, p. 27), Virgil Wade points out that hotel selection should be complete at least a year in advance of the convention.

According to Alex Hargrave ("Changing Marketing Strategies, 1975–1985," Marketing Management, 17:4, Dec 84, 14–23) the me generation that marked the 70s is being replaced by a we generation in which people are much less self-absorbed.

Citation as Footnote.   A footnote is a reference to a secondary source appearing at the bottom — or *foot* — of a page. Some formal reports may require footnotes, but because other forms of documentation are generally

Why have footnotes essentially been replaced by endnotes or references to bibliographic entries?

more convenient for both reader and writer, footnotes have largely been replaced by endnotes or references to bibliographic entries.

Footnotes are separated from the text by a line 1½ inches long (typed with the underline key), one line space below the last line of the text. The footnote itself begins a doublespace below the line and is indented five spaces.

Footnotes are usually numbered consecutively throughout a report, article, or chapter, with reference numbers being placed one-half line above the line of text and above the footnote entry (for this, use the *superscript* function on most word processors). The footnote itself should be single-spaced. The last line of the last footnote on the page should occur at the bottom margin.

Footnotes should be complete on the page on which the reference occurs. For this reason, close attention to vertical spacing is necessary. Footnotes on pages on which the text does not extend to the bottom should be placed so that the last line of the last footnote occurs on the bottom margin.

Imagine that we have two footnotes[2] to which we must refer.[3]

_____

[2]Wilma During, Corporate Planning and The Economy, (Hinsdale, IL: The Dryden Press, 1984), p. 147.

[3]Robert Fuller and Andrew Devine, "The Grapevine," Organizational Communication Quarterly, 9:2 (Summer 1983), 58–59.

Citation as Endnote.   Endnotes are both more modern and more convenient than footnotes. Endnotes follow the same basic format as footnotes, but instead of appearing at the bottom of each page, endnotes appear at the end of a report, article, or chapter. They are placed on a page (or pages) by themselves under a first-degree heading, *ENDNOTES*, or more simply, *NOTES* (use the same form as for other first-degree headings). The notes should be single-spaced, with double-spacing between notes. Figure 13.3 illustrates the proper entry form for a variety of note situations.

What should be included in a citation referring to a bibliographic entry?

Citation as Bibliographic Entry.   Secondary sources listed in a bibliography may be cited by a reference placed within the text. Because the bibliography contains the complete source information, the reference within the text may be brief and unobtrusive. Two forms are common: reference by number and reference by author's last name.

For reference by number, each item in the bibliography must be numbered consecutively. The reference within the text includes only the entry number and the page number(s). Bibliographies employing this method frequently list entries in the order they appear within the document rather than in alphabetical order according to the author's last name. Otherwise, it is necessary to wait until all sources are known before preparing any section of the document.

For reference by author's name, the citation within the text includes the author's last name or other significant identifying term (first author in series, issuing association or institute, name of public body, name of editor, or key

**FIGURE 13.3
Sample Entries
for Notes**

Book with one author
[1]Herman Melville, Moby-Dick, (Boston: Houghton Mifflin Company,
1956), pp. 97–99.

Article with two authors
[2]Karen Kinzer and James Waxler, "Computer Applications for Small
Businesses," The Better Small Business Quarterly, 45:1 (Jan 83), 34–35.

Article with three authors
[3]Rosemary Entrup, Lester Diez, and Mildred Neel, "Organizational
Communication Strategies," The Journal of Organizational Communication,
20:4 (Fall 1982), 17.

Book with more than three authors
[4]Larry Smart et al., Tax Shelters Anyone Can Afford (New York:
Brinkman and Knox, 1985), pp. 203–205.

Book with editors but no author
[5]William James and Henry James, eds., The Socio-psychology of the
American Male (Boston: Creative Thought Press, 1981), pp. 590–591.

Report issued by a committee, association, or public body
[6]Task Force on Venture Capital Formation, Venture Capital
Formation for Entrepreneurs (New York: American Institute of Venture
Capitalists, 1985), p. 3.

Article by unknown author
[7]"Desalinization and the Southwest," Phoenix Gazette, p. A-16,
cols. 4–5, July 4, 1985.

Common abbreviations for missing information
n.p.   —no place of publication provided
n.p.   —no publisher information provided
n.d.   —no date of publication provided
n.pag—no pagination provided

portion of title) and the relevant page number(s). The bibliography is prepared in the traditional way, alphabetized by author's last name or other
initial entry word.

> In 1984 more than 700,000 people purchased personal computers (4, 22). [Reference
> by number.]

> In 1984 more than 700,000 people purchased personal computers (Brown,
> p. 22). [Reference by author.]

Figure 13.4 illustrates sample bibliographic entries.

What is a style
sheet?

Common Style Sheets.   While the guides for documenting secondary
sources we have presented here would be sufficient for most business reports, some organizations and nearly all professional journals require reports

FIGURE 13.4
Sample
Bibliographic
Entries

Book with one author
Melville, Herman. Moby-Dick. Boston: Houghton Mifflin Company,
    1956.

Article with two authors
Kinzer, Karen and James Waxler. "Computer Applications for Small
    Businesses," The Better Small Business Quarterly, 45:1 (Jan 83),
    34–45.

Article with three authors
Entrup, Rosemary, Lester Diez, and Mildred Neel. "Organizational
    Communication Strategies," The Journal of Organizational Communication, 20:4
    (Fall 1982), 16–22.

Book with more than three authors
Smart, Larry et al. Tax Shelters Anyone Can Afford. New York:
    Brinkman and Knox, 1985.

Book with editors but no author
James, William and Henry James, eds. The Socio-psychology of the
    American Male. Boston: Creative Thought Press, 1981.

Report issued by a committee, association, or public body
Task Force on Venture Capital Formation. Venture Capital Formation for
    Entrepreneurs. New York: American Institute of Venture Capitalists, 1985.

Article by unknown author
"Desalinization and the Southwest," Phoenix Gazette. A-16, cols. 4–5,
    July 4, 1985.

and articles to be prepared according to a specific style sheet. The following
are the most common:

Campbell, William Giles and Stephen Vaughan Ballou. *Form and Style: Theses,
Reports, Term Papers.* 6th ed. Boston: Houghton Mifflin, 1981.

The Chicago Manual of Style. 13th ed. rev. Chicago: The University of Chicago
Press, 1982.

Keithley, Erwin M. and Philip J. Schreiner. *A Manual of Style for the Preparation
of Papers & Reports.* 3d ed. Cincinnati: South-Western, 1980.

MLA Handbook for Writers of Research Papers. 2d ed. New York: Modern Language
Association, 1984.

Publication Manual of the American Psychological Association. 3d ed. Washington,
DC: 1984.

Turabian, Kate L. *A Manual for Writers of Term Papers, Theses, and Dissertations.*
4th ed. Chicago: University of Chicago Press, 1973.

Although differences among these style sheets are few and often subtle,
you need to check documentation and paper preparation recommendations

carefully before preparing the final version of your report or article for one of these organizations or journals. Deviation from the required form could result in rejection of your document.

▷ INTERPRETING DATA, DRAWING CONCLUSIONS, AND MAKING RECOMMENDATIONS

What kinds of mistakes is a writer likely to make when interpreting data?

After you have completed your research and gathered all your information, you need to organize and interpret the data for your reader by using an appropriate report form. The kinds of errors that occur in interpreting data fall into three general categories.

1. **Perceptual errors.**   Have you taken the precautions necessary to ensure the accuracy and objectivity of your perceptions?

2. **Mechanical errors.**   Have you added, subtracted, multiplied, and divided correctly? Have you transposed numbers in typing?

3. **Semantic errors.**   Have you reached the wrong conclusions because you are using language inappropriately?

Of these common problems, perceptual and semantic errors are the most difficult to control.

Problems with Perception

Perceptual errors can stem from any aspect of the sender or receiver that interferes with their accurate perception of the world. Deficiencies causing perceptual problems may be physical or mental. Physical deficiencies occur during *primary mediation,* which is the act of perceiving the environment with our physical senses: seeing, hearing, touching, tasting, and smelling. If you are myopic and you remove your corrective lenses, you will be unable to report distant visual perceptions accurately because you cannot observe them accurately. If you have a hearing impairment, you will have difficulty perceiving oral messages accurately.

What are the differences between primary mediation and secondary mediation? Which type is more likely to cause problems for report writers?

Physical deficiencies are usually obvious and correctable. Other perceptual barriers, however, are more subtle. Our perceptions are influenced not only by the powers and limitations of our senses but also by our previous experiences, attitudes, beliefs, and expectations. Our minds select from and alter the information (stimuli) our senses perceive. This influence is called *secondary mediation.*

We never perceive anything in its entirety. We select or abstract from the whole those things that seem important to us; our minds work like a filter, refusing to recognize that which seems unimportant. An example of this point is the story of the six blind men who each tried to describe an elephant after examining only one part:

> After examining the elephant's tusk, one said that the elephant was like a spear.
>
> After examining the elephant's knee, one said that the elephant was like a tree.
>
> After examining the elephant's side, one said that the elephant was like a wall.
>
> After examining the elephant's trunk, one said that the elephant was like a snake.
>
> After examining the elephant's tail, one said that the elephant was like a rope.
>
> After examining the elephant's ear, one said that the elephant was like a fan.

What is projection?

Because our perceptions seem so obviously correct to us, we are inclined to believe that others perceive the world in the same way that we do. We attribute similar perceptions to others. This psychological principal is known as *projection.*

What is a mental filter, and how does it influence perception?

But because no two people are alike, each person's mental filter—based on experiences, attitudes, and expectations—selects different aspects of the environment. It is frequently difficult to remember that our own perceptions may not be complete. **The other person's perceptions are also part of the truth.** Everyone's perceptions are partially correct—sometimes we may think that the other person's portion of truth is minuscule, but we must still acknowledge that portion, regardless of its size.

We should also remember that we have a natural tendency to resist perceptions we find unpleasant. We find it difficult to accept ideas that do not agree with what we already think, believe, or feel. In days of old, bearers of bad tidings were frequently put to death. Even today, our inclination is to reject the sender of an unpleasant message along with the message. For example, if we hear from a stranger that a friend of ours cannot be trusted, we will probably not believe the message—and we will dislike the person delivering it.

Problems with Semantics

What is semantics?

Semantics—the way we use the spoken language—can also cause communication difficulties. Because language, like mathematics, is a symbol system, **language has meaning only in the minds of its users.** Semanticists are fond of saying that the map is not the territory. Just as the map is not the territory but merely represents it, the words we use represent or symbolize our view of reality. We run into difficulty when we forget that our words and the words of others are symbolic rather than "real." Problems with semantics are as much a matter of faulty thinking as they are of faulty communicating. We forget that the mere act of thinking something is true does not make it so. The following guidelines can help us focus on the symbolic nature of language.

1. **No statement tells the whole story.**   We cannot perceive totally or with complete accuracy; therefore we cannot make statements that are totally or completely accurate. By the time we have made a statement, we are twice removed from the actual event. When we think we are telling the whole story, we are committing the *allness fallacy*. Consider, for example, any simple object around you — your desk, a chair, or the floor. How many readily observable facts can you think of that apply to that object? Consider its uses, its measurements, its physical and chemical properties, its history, its evolution, its manufacturing process, its marketing, and even its future. Effective communicators need to remember that nothing is as simple as it seems.

What is the allness fallacy?

2. **No two things are identical.**   The human mind works by a process of generalization and differentiation. When things are similar, we tend to class them together. We divide the world into groups of things by pigeonholing and stereotyping. These groupings are useful. But we run into difficulties when we forget that each thing in any group is different from every other thing in the group. The human mind tends to overlook small differences. We need to remember that because nothing is simple, the smallest differences between things may well be significant. A very small pinhole makes a ping-pong ball unusable — and unsalable. For this reason, analogies should be used to illustrate only; they do not prove.

What is an analogy, and why should one be used to illustrate rather than prove?

3. **Observations, assumptions, and opinions are not the same.**   You have heard the phrase "jumping to conclusions," and you know that it is something to avoid. A *fact* or *observation* is something that has been verified by some form of measurement or sense data. (Keep in mind that perception is selective, and our sense data may not be entirely accurate.) *Assumptions* or *inferences* are conclusions based on certain observations. The more relevant observations we make, the greater the chances are that our assumptions will prove correct. For example, our assumption that the sun will come up tomorrow has an excellent chance of being correct. If, on the other hand, we assume that it will not rain tomorrow because it did not rain today, we have jumped to a conclusion. *Opinions* are based on observations and assumptions, but they are *value judgments* unrelated to fact. Opinions or value judgments are feelings or beliefs not substantiated by knowledge or proof. You may have observed in the past that you did not like Kool Kola. That is a fact. You may assume that you still do not like Kool Kola. This is an inference.

"The sun will come up tomorrow" — fact or assumption?

But when you say, "Kool Kola tastes awful," that's an opinion. Your opinion has to do with you, not with Kool Kola.

How many mutually exclusive categories can you think of?

4. **Few things are either-or.**   Most things are matters of degree rather than absolutes. One example often used to illustrate this point is the term "slightly pregnant." Pregnancy is one of life's few absolutes. Every day, science reduces the number of things that can be considered *mutually exclusive*. Life and death were once considered absolutes; now scientists are not so sure. Recent medical discoveries have made it difficult to draw a definite line between the two. We must remember that most things are relative. A person is tall only in comparison with someone or something else; a person is intelligent only in comparison with someone else; a decision is good only in comparison with another decision.

Why should report writers be careful to date and index data, saying both when and where data were collected?

5. **Time changes all things—especially people.**   You are not the same person today that you were yesterday. The changes in you from yesterday to today may not be dramatic or even significant, but you *have* changed. And the further back in time you go from your point of comparison, the more you have changed. Each day's perceptions give you new experiences against which to evaluate each new perception. But people are not the only things that change: laws, interest rates, institutions, and even solid rock are subject to the influence of time.

What is the post hoc fallacy?

6. **Time sequence alone does not establish a cause-and-effect relationship.**   Commonly known as the *post hoc fallacy*, cause-and-effect confusion can result when two events occur in sequence. Before you assume that the first event caused the second, you should eliminate the possibilities of the events being unrelated, coincidental, or caused by a third event that you have not identified.

Conclusions and Recommendations

Why is one fact meaningless until you have at least one other fact to compare it with?

Facts are valuable only in relation to other facts. The fact that one computer system might cost $5000, for example, does not mean much unless we know that a similar computer system able to perform the same functions costs $4000. To draw conclusions, you need to recognize relationships among different sets of facts. The final interpretation of data is the drawing of conclusions based on these observed relationships.

What is the relationship between the facts and the conclusions?

Conclusions are assumptions based on the facts gathered; they are not themselves facts. Conclusions should be based only on the facts gathered and not on your preconceptions or on other evidence you are not presenting in the report. What, for example, would you conclude from the following set of facts:

Employee turnover on the swing shift is twice as high as that for the day shift.

The employees on the swing shift receive no additional compensation for their less convenient hours.

Most workers with seniority request the day shift.

A questionnaire revealed that 58 percent of those on the swing shift would prefer days.

The same questionnaire revealed that the two least popular supervisors are responsible for the swing shift.

Would you conclude that the two unpopular supervisors were the cause of the high rate of turnover on the swing shift? Or would you conclude that the unpopularity of the swing shift influenced the employees' attitudes toward the supervisors? Either of those assumptions could be correct, but further study would be necessary before you could make either with confidence. At this point you do not have any evidence that indicates whether the supervisors' unpopularity is the cause of the problem or merely a coincidental effect.

What is the relationship between conclusions and recommendations?

Just as your conclusions must be based on the facts actually presented, your recommendations should also be logical extensions of those facts. Remember that the recommendations are value judgments, or opinions, that you are making as a result of your conclusions. They cannot be arbitrary; they must have a sound foundation in fact. Is Brand A better for your company than Brand B? Why? Your opinion should be based on objective evidence. It is, of course, perfectly acceptable to include intangibles as facts. For example, a certain computer may "feel" better to you than another, and it is legitimate for you to use that fact in making your recommendation. You should, however, be careful to explicitly acknowledge the intangible nature of that fact and the influence it has on your conclusions and recommendations.

The final interpretation of data is the drawing of conclusions based on observed relationships among different sets of facts. The conclusions are assumptions based on the facts already gathered; they are not themselves facts. Just as your conclusions must be based on the facts actually presented, your recommendations should also be logical extensions of those facts. The recommendations are value judgments, which you are making as a result of your conclusions.

Once you have defined the problem, gathered the appropriate information, and organized and interpreted the data, you are ready to begin writing the report.

▷ SUMMARY

Defining the problem to be addressed by a report is almost always management's task. The report writer may need to clarify the specific problem by restating it in terms of an objective to be met or a question to be answered.

Once the report-writing assignment is put into specific, workable form, the report writer needs to determine what areas or items to investigate to solve the problem.

Information may be gathered from either secondary or primary sources. Secondary sources provide information collected by other investigators. When they do not provide the answers, the report writer needs to uncover the facts and figures firsthand, from primary sources. Some methods for collecting primary, or original, data are experimentation, observation, and surveys.

In experimentation the researcher tests one variable of a problem while holding all other variables constant. Observation means recognizing and noting facts. Unlike the experimenter, the observer does not manipulate the environment. Surveys provide answers to the *why* questions—why do people react in a certain way, why do people perform better under certain conditions.

Because it would be too expensive to find out what everyone thinks about a certain topic, surveys require a *sample* of a particular group. Three common sampling techniques are random sampling, stratified random sampling, and systematic sampling.

Random sampling is the method by which each item in the population has an equal chance of being selected. Stratified random sampling uses a random sampling of the subgroups within the entire population. Systematic sampling is the method of taking selections at constant intervals from a list of the entire population.

Six types of questions most frequently used on questionnaires are (1) either-or, (2) checklists, (3) multiple-choice, (4) ranking, (5) fill-in-the-blanks, and (6) open-ended.

Telephone interviews are popular because they are fast; they are inexpensive when calls are local; and can provide a random sample when all members of the entire group being studied have telephones.

Many reports require formal documentation of secondary source data. Information for documentation may be cited (1) as a reference within the text, (2) as a footnote, (3) as an endnote, or (4) as a bibliographic reference. Regardless of the form, documentation should include the name(s) of the author(s), the title of the book or titles of the article and publication, the place and date of publication, appropriate volume and issue numbers, and the appropriate page references.

The kinds of errors that occur in interpreting data fall into three general categories: (1) perceptual errors, (2) mechanical errors, and (3) semantic errors.

Perceptual problems may be due to a physical deficiency or a mental one. Physical deficiencies occur during primary mediation, which is the act of perceiving the environment with our physical senses. Our perceptions are influenced not only by the powers and limitations of our senses but also by our previous experiences, attitudes, beliefs, and expectations. Our minds select from and alter the information our senses perceive. This influence is called secondary mediation.

COMMUNICATION SOLUTION

To determine whether your company would benefit from investing in teleconferencing equipment, you would need to conduct both secondary and primary research. You might begin with an informal search through literature readily available to you—your own business and computer magazines. From these sources you could begin collecting the names of organizations using teleconferencing equipment and the names of vendors. You could also begin forming general impressions of the advantages and disadvantages of the equipment and developing a set of criteria to help you make your determination.

As a second step, you might conduct a search of the computerized databases, using such descriptors as *teleconferencing and productivity* and *teleconferencing and business*. By using an in-formation source like BRS or Dialog, you would be able to search ABI/Inform, Harvard Business Review, Management Contents, and other business references. From the titles the computer search revealed, you could select those that looked promising and request abstracts, and then request complete articles based on the abstracts.

You might also want to conduct primary research by obtaining information directly from companies using the equipment and vendors supplying it. You could conduct personal interviews, telephone interviews, or a mail survey depending on how many companies have the kind of equipment that would meet the needs of your company.

Semantics—the way we use the spoken language—can also cause communication difficulties. The following guidelines can help remind us of the symbolic nature of language and its pitfalls: (1) no statement tells the whole story, (2) no two things are identical, (3) observations, assumptions, and opinions are not the same, (4) few things are either-or, (5) time changes all things—especially people, and (6) time sequence alone does not establish a cause-and-effect relationship.

▷ Exercises

Review and Discussion Questions

1. What is the difference between primary sources and secondary sources of information?

2. Identify and explain the three methods for collecting primary data.

3. Identify and explain the three common sampling techniques.

4. Name six types of questions most frequently used on questionnaires, and write two examples for each kind of question.

5. What are the four guidelines for preparing questionnaires?

6. The kinds of errors that occur in interpreting data fall into three general categories. Name them.

7. What are the six guidelines that help remind us of the symbolic nature of language? Discuss each.

Problems

1. Construct a questionnaire using the six types of questions most commonly used in questionnaires. Select a topic of your choice or one of the following:
   a. Reasons for absenteeism
   b. Initial job requirements
   c. Ways to delegate responsibility
   d. Professional organizations
   e. Home repairs
   f. Outdoor sports
   g. Productivity
   h. Computer usage
   i. Salaries for various occupations
   j. Recommendations for
      (1) Improving morale
      (2) Writing reports
      (3) Hiring personnel
      (4) Selecting an office site
   k. Should ABC Company purchase . . .
   l. Why should XZY Corporation . . .
   m. Women in business
   n. Networking
   o. Young entrepreneurs
   p. Young urban professionals

2. Find five articles in business periodicals dealing with the United States/Japan trade deficit.

3. Select four problems in your class, school, community, or area of study and write problem definitions to facilitate their study.

4. For each of the problems you selected in Problem 3, prepare a list of five periodicals that would be sources of information for solving the problems.

5. What are the common features of text editors for microcomputers?

6. Find the author, title, and publisher of three books on management by objectives.

7. Find five recent articles on zero-based budgeting.

8. How many books by Peter Drucker are currently in print?

9. Locate five current articles on direct mail advertising.

10. What did *The Wall Street Journal* and the *New York Times* predict for the U.S. economy at the beginning of 1980 and 1985?

11. What have the popular news magazines reported in the last five years about motivation among new managers in U.S. companies? (Note: Canadian, Japanese, and other readers from countries other than the U.S. should use equivalent sources for this and similar problems.)

12. Find statistics specifying the leading exporter of crude oil to the United States since 1960.

13. Find statistics on how U.S. consumers spend their dollars.

14. Find a list of U.S. commercial banks with deposits over $1 billion.

15. Find a list of the highest paid executives of U.S. corporations.

16. Locate five recent publications of the U.S. Department of Energy.

17. Find five current articles on The Upjohn Company.

18. Use *Moody's Manuals* or Standard and Poor's *Corporation Records* to find out the names of the chief executive officers of five corporations in the United States.

19. Select an annual report of a corporation of your choosing and prepare a list of its major topics.

20. Make a list of the ten most desirable places to live based on five criteria of your choosing.

CASES

1. What information sources are available "on line" through libraries in your area? What are the charges for using them? Present your findings in a memo using headings and at least one graphic aid.

2. What research is available on the relationship between morale and productivity? Are "happy" employees more productive? Compile a bibliography on this subject. Select the earliest and most recent articles in your bibliography and write 100-word summarizing abstracts of them.

3. What were the five most profitable U.S. corporations last year? How much money did each earn, and how did each company distribute its profits? Prepare a memo for your instructor detailing your research methodology and your findings. Use headings and at least one graphic aid.

4. How would you determine in which sports business executives participate? Prepare a memo describing the research methodology you would use, providing the rationale for your selections, and some preliminary findings. Use headings and at least one graphic aid.

5. How does the business climate in your state compare with the business climate in other states? Prepare a memo describing the methodology you employed to discover your data and your findings. Use headings and at least one graphic aid.

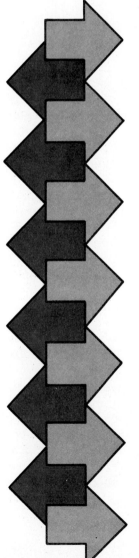

CHAPTER FOURTEEN
Common Business Reports

Each organization has its own specific requirements for particular kinds of reports. Because reports are functional pieces of writing designed to help a reader or readers make a decision, the presentation of the reported information will vary to meet the needs of different readers. The types of reports discussed in this chapter are nearly universal, though their formats may vary from organization to organization.

Topics

COMMUNICATION CHALLENGE

Examine four or five recent annual reports from different organizations. Most libraries have collections of annual reports, or you may obtain these directly from the organization. What do these reports communicate to whom? What are their purposes, and what techniques do they employ to achieve them? You may wish to review Chapters 12 and 13 as well as this chapter as you examine the annual reports. Compare your observations with those that follow the chapter summary.

▷ OVERVIEW: REPORTS SHOULD MEET SPECIFIC NEEDS

As the preceding chapters have suggested, the form and content of reports in modern organizations can be infinitely varied. Some of the reports common in business are identified primarily by their physical form: memo reports, letter reports, and formal reports. Others are identified primarily by purpose or content: justification reports, proposals, progress reports, expense reports, and personnel evaluations. Some reports do not fall neatly into any of the standard classifications. And a report that is called one thing at one organization may be called something else at another.

Fortunately, most of the same writing techniques apply regardless of the specific function or format a report requires. This chapter introduces you to the most common types of reports by their most frequently used names, beginning with two forms with which you are already familiar — the memo and the letter — and then progressing from simple to complex.

The short reports covered in this chapter do not usually require extensive efforts at problem definition or research. With the exception of formal reports, these reports are written as the need arises and are based on readily available information.

In general, the simple reports are periodic, or maintenance, reports and are required on a regular basis in most organizations. They are often available as printed forms, which the report writer simply completes. The reports of greater complexity are usually special, task reports, assigned to solve a specific problem. These reports usually require at least some research, and the report writer frequently must draw conclusions and make recommendations. Because they are longer and more complex than routine reports, they employ more of the special techniques discussed in Chapter 12. Those who assign and receive these reports frequently use them to evaluate the personnel responsible for writing them.

COMMUNICATION TODAY. . .

"One Minute Goal Setting is the first [of the secrets of One Minute Management] and is the foundation for One Minute Management. You see, in most organizations when you ask people what they do and then ask their boss, all too often you get two different lists. In fact, in some organizations I've worked in, any relationship between what I thought my job responsibilities were and what my boss through they were, was purely coincidental. And then I would get in trouble for not doing something I didn't even think was my job."

"Does that ever happen here?" asked the young man.

"No!" Trenell said. "It never happens here. The One Minute Manager always makes it clear what our responsibilities are and what we are being held accountable for."

"Just how does he do that?" the young man wanted to know.

"Efficiently," Trenell said with a smile.

Trenell began to explain. "Once he has told me what needs to be done or we have agreed on what needs to be done, then each goal is recorded on no more than a single page. The One Minute Manager feels that a goal, and its performance standard, should take no more than 250 words to express. He insists that anyone should be able to read it within a minute. He keeps a copy and I keep a copy so everything is clear and so we can both periodically check the progress."

Source: Adapted from pp. 27–28 in *The One Minute Manager* by Kenneth Blanchard and Spencer Johnson. Copyright © 1982 by Blanchard Family Partnership and Candle Communications Corporation. By permission of William Morrow & Co.

▷ MEMO REPORTS

Why are memos frequently called internal letters?

Memo reports may well be the most common means of exchanging written business information. Memos are short, informal messages that provide a rapid, convenient means of communication between employees within the same organization. Most memos are purely informational; many are handwritten. In some ways they serve the same function within the company as letters serve for communication outside the company (see Chapters 6 through 10).

Memos serve to communicate vertically (from managers to employees and from employees to managers) and horizontally (between personnel of equal rank). They also serve to communicate messages that range from extremely informal to extremely formal. Some companies use letter format to convey important, formal information that otherwise might be communicated in memo format.

When memos are used to convey complex information, they include the special techniques we discussed in Chapter 12. Figure 14.1 shows a formal memo including headings, itemizations, and a table.

FIGURE 14.1
A Memo Report

Armatron, Inc.   Interoffice Correspondence

16 Jan xx

To: All Department Heads

From: Pamela Ladendorf, Branch Manager *pl*

Subject: Recruiting a New Director of Communication

Do you know someone who would make a good Director of Communication?

Corporate has just authorized the Chicago Branch to hire its own Director of Communication. The new Director will have Department Head rank and status.

Budget Allocation

The annual budget for the new Director will be as follows:

Salaries

Director	$57,000	
Administrative Assistant	25,000	
Secretary	17,500	
Clerk-typist	10,500	$109,000
Office Equipment		5,500
Office Supplies		8,000
		$122,500

In addition, Corporate will contribute $50,000 toward the purchase or rental of word processing equipment for the new Director and staff.

Office Space

The Director of Communication and his or her staff will occupy Rooms 314-316, which are currently used for equipment storage.

All Department Heads   16 Jan xx   2

Duties and Responsibilities

The Director of Communication will be responsible for the following:

1. All Chicago Branch publications

2. Planning, organizing, and coordinating leadership training programs

3. Coordination of MBO programs

4. Supervision of intra- and extracompany correspondence.

Qualifications

The person we hire must be self-motivated and innovative, with training and/or experience in all phases of publishing:

    planning
    article research
    writing
    copy editing
    layout and design
    printing
    distribution

Also, the person must have demonstrated leadership abilities in previous jobs and have formal training in organizational communication systems. An understanding of the electronics industry is also essential.

Recruiting

The right person for this job would make all our jobs easier. Please help with the search. Send your recommendations to me, or have candidates apply directly to me. Corporate wants the job filled by 30 June, so if we haven't found the right candidates by 15 March, we'll have to go public.

▷ LETTER REPORTS

When does a letter become a letter report?

A letter report is a report written in the form of a regular business letter. Unlike the internal memo report, the letter report is an external means of communication between organizations. They may be used for personnel references, credit evaluations, or auditor recommendations. Many letters requesting or transmitting information are essentially letter reports, but we do not usually call them reports unless they are fairly long and make use of some of the basic report-writing techniques.

Letter reports differ from typical business letters in that they are formal and primarily factual. Their objective is to provide the information requested as clearly as possible. Graphs, charts, tables, or drawings may be used to illustrate specific points, as Figure 14.2 illustrates.

▷ AGENDA, MINUTES, AND ITINERARIES

Why are agenda, minutes, and itineraries considered informational reports?

Agenda, minutes, and itineraries are common informational reports. Because they provide information without analysis or conclusions and recommendations, they are frequently written in semi-outline form. These reports are perhaps the easiest to write. **NOTE:** Agenda, a plural word, is usually considered a collective noun, taking a singular article and either a singular or plural verb.

Agenda

An agenda, sometimes called the *order of business,* is a list of topics arranged in the order that they are to be discussed at a meeting. (See Figure 14.3.) The following order of business is typical for most meetings:

1. Call to order by presiding officer.
2. Roll call.
3. Minutes of the previous meeting.
4. Reading of correspondence.
5. Officers' reports.
6. Committee reports.
7. Special committee reports.
8. Unfinished business.
9. New business.
10. Announcements.
11. Adjournment.

Minutes

Under what circumstances might minutes be considered a legal document? How would that influence their preparation?

Minutes are the official records of a meeting. Depending on the organization, minutes may need to be a complete record of all that took place at the meeting, for legal purposes, or they can be a summary, as Figure 14.4 illustrates. In more complicated cases—a committee meeting discussing a serious accident in an organization, for example—the minutes may need to include a full record of who said what to whom when.

Minutes vary in form from one organization to another. Generally, the content and order are standard.

1. Name of the organization.

2. Date, time, and place.

3. Attendance.

4. Name of presiding officer.

5. A record of
    a. All announcements.
    b. Reports.
    c. Motions.
    d. Resolutions.

6. Date of next meeting.

7. Time of adjournment.

Itineraries

How can an itinerary help an executive? How can it help the organization in the executive's absence?

An itinerary is a combination of travel and appointment schedules. The usual travel itinerary shows when, where, and how a person will travel. It may also include daily appointments and contain helpful reminders of where the individual is to be at certain times, of names of people he or she may encounter in the course of conducting business, and—in the case of foreign travel—of local customs. The itinerary gives the day, time of departure, name of airport or station, flight number, time of arrival, and hotel names and addresses. (See Figure 14.5.)

▷ EXPENSE REPORT

Why are expense reports almost always printed forms?

Expense reports are almost always printed forms because they are used on a regular basis and the same information is required each time for the organization's financial records. A sample expense report is shown in Figure 14.6. Should you work for a company that does not provide forms for expense reports, be sure to specify how much you spent, the date you spent it, and the service you received. Also, be sure to keep and submit copies of your receipts.

FIGURE 14.2
A Letter Report

TIME AND MOTION STUDIES INC.
430 Water Street, Flagstaff, AZ 86001

October 1, 19xx

Mr. Francis W. Walczak
Arizona Manufacturing Company
4305 Avenue Palmetto
Flagstaff, AZ 86001

Dear Mr. Walczak:

As you suspected, you could increase both the efficiency and the
capacity of your production line by 30 percent if you installed
modern equipment.

We recommend the following substitutions:

IN USE:

Number	Stock Number	Item
15	L-1245-65-11	Power Lathe
14	DP-9321-59-01	Drill Press

SUGGESTED REPLACEMENT:

Number	Manufacturer	Item	Cost
1	Smythson	Master Lathe	$15,000
15	Smythson	Slave Units	1,200 ea
1	Olgivie	Master Press	11,000
19	Olgivie	Duplicators	900 ea

By reassigning and retraining personnel, you could effect the
increase in efficiency and capacity without reducing your work
force. We recommend that the personnel who become unnecessary in
production be transferred to Quality Control and Packaging.
Dorsaneo Management Consultants, 197 Main Street, Flagstaff, is
well equipped to help you reassign and retrain your personnel.

Mr. Francis W. Walczak   October 1, 19xx   2

Our services and charges are itemized on the enclosed invoice.
When we can help futher, please call us at 555-1983.

Sincerely,

Linda R. Armbruster

Linda R. Armbruster
President

enc

FIGURE 14.3
An Agenda

```
                        Women's Services
              Agenda for the Advisory Board Meeting
                    Thursday, March 13, 19xx
                   3:30 p.m. Knaus Hall, Room 5




    1.   Call to order--Lorraine Jenco, President

    2.   Roll Call

    3.   Minutes of the February 8 meeting

    4.   Reading of correspondence

    5.   Treasurer's report--Elaine Vavrek

    6.   Report of Ad Hoc Committee on new programs

    7.   New business

         a.   Proposal for assertiveness program

         b.   Suggestions for program for women returning to
              work

    8.   Announcements

         a.   Next meeting--April 15

         b.   Seminar on stress--April 14

    9.   Adjournment
```

**FIGURE 14.4
Minutes of a
Meeting**

Bell Corporation

MINUTES OF THE ADVISORY COMMITTEE FOR WOMEN'S SERVICES

August 17, 19xx

	The monthly meeting of the Advisory Committee for Women's Services, Bell Corporation, was held at three o'clock on Friday, August 15, 19xx, in Building B, Room 202.
CALL TO ORDER	The meeting was called to order by Ms. Karen Powers, President.
PRESENT	Members present were Susan Branch, Kathleen Goodwin, Karen Moltzen, Margaret Murphy, David Salisbury, and Joel Wells.
ABSENT	Members absent were Luella Kraft, Mark Pitkin, and Judy Valdez.
MINUTES APPROVED	The minutes of the November 2 meeting were read and approved.
PRESIDENT'S REPORT	President Powers read the annual report. After questions, the report was approved and placed on file.
TREASURER'S REPORT	Ms. Branch, treasurer, read the treasurer's report. The balance for November was $145. The report was accepted and placed on file.
NEW BUSINESS	After a lengthy discussion on conducting workshops and seminars for women in management, Murphy moved and Powers seconded that the Center sponsor a monthly seminar beginning next fall. Motion carried.
ANNOUNCEMENTS	The program for the new year will be distributed at the January meeting. Several new programs have been added, including one on interpersonal relations.
ADJOURNMENT	There being no further business, the meeting was adjourned at 5:00 p.m.

Kathleen Goodwin

Kathleen Goodwin, Secretary

FIGURE 14.5
An Itinerary

```
              ITINERARY FOR FRANK KAROCIK
                 September 1-3, 19xx



    MONDAY, SEPTEMBER 1

    7:30 a.m.    Leave San Francisco airport on Delta
                 Flight #468 to Dallas.
    10:45 a.m.   Arrive in Dallas.  Lyle Dole will meet
                 you at the airport.  Lunch with Steve
                 Ackley and Lyle.
    3:00 p.m.    Meeting with President Banner.
                 Reservations:  Hilton Inn, 1914 Commerce
                 Street, Dallas, TX 75201, (214) 555-2011.

    TUESDAY, SEPTEMBER 2

    8:15 a.m.    Leave Dallas airport on TWA Flight #303
                 to Chicago O'Hare airport.
    11:15 a.m.   Arrive in Chicago.  Sam Marsh and Don
                 Roberts will meet you at the airport.
    2:30 p.m.    Board meeting at the Marriott Hotel.
    6:30 p.m.    Dinner meeting with trustees.
                 Reservations:  Marriott Hotel, 411 Adams
                 Street, Chicago, IL 60632 (312) 555-3411.

    WEDNESDAY, SEPTEMBER 3

    8:00 a.m.    Breakfast with Craig Docell and Margaret
                 Shultz.
    10:00 a.m.   Meeting with Bob Archer on program
                 development.
    Noon         Lunch with committee members.
    3:15 p.m.    Leave O'Hare airport on TWA Flight #606
                 for San Francisco.
    4:30 p.m.    Arrive in San Francisco.
```

FIGURE 14.6
An Expense Report

EXPENSE REPORT

ATTACH BILL OR ITEMIZED RECEIPT FOR ITEMS OF $10 OR MORE. ITEMS CHARGED THROUGH AMERICAN EXPRESS SHOULD BE ENTERED WITH "A" PRECEDING THE AMOUNT.

1638 REV. 11/82

NAME	IDENTIFYING NO.	DIVISION	DEPARTMENT	LOCATION	ACCOUNT TO BE CHARGED	PERIOD ENDED MONTH DAY YEAR
Greg Martin	031764	Midwest	Auditing	Cincinnati	23 495608 4359	03 31 XX

IN-TOWN EXPENSES

DATE	MEAL ALLOW-ANCE	AUTO	TELE-PHONE	TAXIS	OTHER	EXPLANATIONS
3/10	12 50	895				2-day meeting: tax law changes and
3/11	8 35	895				new auditing procedures

| TOTALS | 20 85 | 17 90 | | | | TOTAL IN-TOWN EXPENSES (Enter in Summary 2) | 38 75 |

FOR ACCOUNTING USE ONLY

☐ PROPER RECEIPTS ☐ EXTENSIONS ☐ SUMMARY
☐ AUTO DISCOUNT ☐ PREV. BAL. & ADV. ☐ BUDGET COMP.
☐ AUTO INSURANCE ☐ USE OF AMEX ☐ PROPER APPROVAL
☐ UNUSED TICKETS ☐ TOTAL AMEX ☐ POLICY EXCEPTION

DATE RECEIVED   AUDITED BY/DATE

BUDGET COMPARISON

BUDGETED YEAR-TO-DATE EXPENSES

ACTUAL YEAR-TO-DATE EXPENSES

ADVANCES AND AMOUNTS PAID BY COMPANY

DATE	DESCRIPTION	AMOUNT
	PREVIOUS BAL. DUE COMPANY (EMPLOYEE)	
3/1	cash advance	500 00

AMERICAN EXPRESS CHARGES (Enter as one amount the total of all receipts attached)

DEDUCT UNUSED TRANSPORTATION

NET ADVANCES   500 00

EXPENSE REPORT SUMMARY

TOTAL IN-TOWN EXPENSES	38 75
TOTAL OUT-OF-TOWN EXPENSES	663 78
TOTAL BUSINESS MEETING EXPENSES	
TOTAL EXPENSES	702 53

BALANCE DUE   ☐ COMPANY (1 Minus 5)   ☒ EMPLOYEE (5 Minus 1)   202 53

EMPLOYEE SIGNATURE   *Greg Martin*   DATE 3/31/XX

APPROVALS/DATES   *George Marshall* 3/4/XX   *Jody Blankson* 4/4/XX

OUT-OF-TOWN EXPENSES
(ATTACH TO EXPENSE REPORT)

ATTACH BILL OR ITEMIZED RECEIPT FOR ITEMS OF $10 OR MORE. ITEMS CHARGED THROUGH AMERICAN EXPRESS SHOULD BE ENTERED WITH "A" PRECEDING THE AMOUNT.

NAME	IDENTIFYING NO.	DIVISION	DEPARTMENT	LOCATION	ACCOUNT TO BE CHARGED	PERIOD ENDED MONTH DAY YEAR
Greg Martin	031764	Midwest	Auditing	Cincinnati	23 495608 4359	03 31 XX

DATE	CITY	AIR/TRAIN	AUTO	HOTEL	BREAK-FAST	LUNCH	DINNER	TELE-PHONE	TIPS	TAXIS	OTHER	EXPLANATIONS
TRIP 1 PURPOSE: Audit Midway Molds, Inc.												
3/1	Cincinnati-				5 15	8 12	22 10					
3/2	Ann Arbor,				4 89	5 13	18 95					
3/3	MI				5 85	6 20	19 50					
3/4					6 12	4 50	14 20					
3/5					4 25	12 86	26 35					
3/6					5 45	8 50	10 50					
3/7			128 70	301 00	6 17	9 75	29 54					
TOTALS			128 70	301 00	37 88	55 06	141 14					TOTAL TRIP 1 663 78

TRIP 2 PURPOSE:												
TOTALS												TOTAL TRIP 2

TRIP 3 PURPOSE:												
TOTALS												TOTAL TRIP 3

| TOTAL ALL TRIPS | | | 128 70 | 301 00 | 37 88 | 55 06 | 141 14 | | | | | TOTAL OUT-OF-TOWN EXPENSES (Enter in Summary 3) 663 78 |

1638A REV. 11/82

▷ PERSONNEL EVALUATIONS

Under what circumstances might personnel evaluations be considered legal documents? How would that influence their preparation?

Managers routinely evaluate employees to inform them of their job performance and to inform higher management of each person's abilities and promotability. Most companies use forms to help ensure objectivity and thoroughness in the evaluation procedure. Objectivity and thoroughness may be especially important when an individual's performance is not up to standards or expectations. Personnel evaluations may be required to demonstrate justification for dismissal.

Figures 14.7 and 14.8 show typical evaluation forms used for business employees and for school teachers. Note that the concerns expressed in the evaluation forms vary according to professions.

▷ PROGRESS REPORTS

Why does management require progress reports?

A progress report is a strictly informational report that tells how a project is coming along. Management may have several projects under way at one time, so information about the progress of each of the projects is necessary at various intervals. Progress reports provide management with the following:

1.   A brief background of the project.

2.   A detailed account of the time period covered.

3.   A projection of the work to be done.

Management needs these reports not only to keep track of what is going on but also to determine whether the project is progressing as planned, whether it is worth continuing, and whether it is encountering any difficulties. When research is involved, progress reports frequently contain preliminary findings and tentative conclusions. Formats for progress reports vary a great deal from organization to organization. Some are printed forms (many sales reports, for example), most are memos between one and five pages long, and some are short, formal reports.

The format—and to a certain extent the content—depends on who is going to receive the report and to what use she or he will put it. Progress reports may need to explain and justify delays or failures of technical experiments. Most are arranged chronologically according to (1) what has been done, (2) what is being done, and (3) what will be done. Others may be organized according to topics or areas of concern, although time sequence may still be emphasized within each of the topics. Figure 14.9 illustrates a progress report.

FIGURE 14.7 An Employee Evaluation Form

WESTERN MICHIGAN UNIVERSITY

PERFORMANCE APPRAISAL

(Covering All Non-Bargaining Employees)

GENERAL INFORMATION

Name: _____ Social Security Number: _____

Department: _____ Service Date in Current Position: _____

Current Position Title: _____ Job Number:_____

Current Salary Grade:_____ Supervisor's Name: _____

Review Period: _____ _____ Supervisor's Job Number: _____
             (From)   (To)

All supervisors of non-bargaining University employees review the performance of their staff members at least once each year. The process provides an opportunity for the supervisor and employee to review and evaluate the previous year's accomplishments and to establish future performance objectives.

Performance appraisal is not only a salary determination tool but also a process that enables the University to maximize the potential of each employee. It provides a method of determining the training and assistance needed to make each job a rewarding and satisfying experience.

OVERALL EVALUATION SCALE DEFINITIONS

4.50-5.00 = **Outstanding.** Outstanding overall performance level. Obvious exceptional performance has been accomplished. This level is clearly exceptional to all normal standards.

3.50-4.49 = **Superior.** Performance clearly exceeds the average (competent) level of performance. Normal expectations for the position have been clearly exceeded.

2.50-3.49 = **Competent.** Fully satisfactory level of performance. All important performance standards are being met at a competent or better level. This is the standard/normal/average performance level. Most employees should expect to be rated at this level.

1.50-2.49 = ***Provisional.** Weak/substandard performance level. Important improvements are required to bring rating up to the competent level. Performance weaknesses must be corrected. Uncorrected performance problems will eventually result in a rating at the unsatisfactory level.

1.00-1.49 = ***Unsatisfactory.** Performance warning level. Overall performance is well below the acceptable level. Termination may occur after two (2) consecutive ratings at this level.

*Next review date: _____
All Unsatisfactory or Provisional evaluations require follow-up appraisal(s) in addition to the normal University review period. The next review should be not less than one month or longer than six months from the date of this appraisal.

DATE OF OVERALL SCORE: _____ OVERALL SCORE (this evaluation period): _____

NOTE: COPIES MUST BE DISTRIBUTED AT THE **BEGINNING AND END** OF THE REVIEW PERIOD.

cc: Supervisor
     Employee
     Personnel Department

Equal Opportunity/Affirmative Action Employer

Source: Courtesy of Western Michigan University.

FIGURE 14.7
(Continued)

SECTION I POSITION ACCOUNTABILITIES			SECTION II EVALUATION		
Accountability (from job description)	Performance Measure(s)	Weight (10-25%)	Eval. Rtg.*	Score = Weight x Eval. Rtg.	Comments

Total Score ÷ 100

OVERALL SCORE
(transfer to front page)

Overall Evaluation Score:

** 4.50-5.00 = Outstanding
    3.50-4.49 = Superior
    2.50-3.49 = Competent
    1.50-2.49 = Provisional
** 1.00-1.49 = Unsatisfactory

Reviewer **must provide written comments in Section IV for any overall score of 1.00-1.49 or 4.50-5.00; other comments are optional.

Must Total 100%

SIGNATURES FOR ACCOUNTABILITY AND MEASURE(S) SECTIONS

Immediate Supervisor's Signature   date

Reviewer's Supervisor's Signature   date

Employee's Signature   date

*ACCOUNTABILITIES RATING EVALUATION DEFINITIONS

(5.0 Rating)— **Outstanding.** Exceptional performance. Greatly exceeded performance of normal accomplishments. This level is awarded only for clearly exceptional performance. (Written comments are required for this rating.)

(4.0 Rating)— **Superior.** Clearly exceeded satisfactory level of performance standards. Superior performance which exceeds the normal expectations.

(3.0 Rating)— **Competent.** Fully satisfactory level of performance. Normal accomplishment standards met. (This rating is expected to be the dominant rating level for all normal performance accomplishments.)

(2.0 Rating)— **Provisional.** Substandard performance level. Important aspects of the accountability were not accomplished, or the overall level of accomplishment was substandard.

(1.0 Rating)— **Unsatisfactory.** Unsatisfactory performance evaluation. Staff members did not achieve important requirements of performance standards. (Written comments are required for this rating.)

SECTION III: ADDITIONAL FACTORS INFLUENCING PERFORMANCE

Supervisors should review and comment on factors such as attendance, punctuality, courtesy, and affirmative action as they relate to job performance. Factors which are critical to the position should be specifically incorporated into the accountabilities and measures sections of the review form—Section I.

_____

_____

_____

_____

_____

- -

SECTION IV: SUPERVISOR'S COMMENTS
(Use additional sheets if necessary)

_____

_____

_____

_____

_____

- -

SECTION V: EMPLOYEE'S COMMENTS
(Use additional sheets if necessary)

_____

_____

_____

_____

_____

- -

SECTION VI: SIGNATURE AREA

AT END OF REVIEW PERIOD
(evaluation of employee's performance according to measures)

_____   _____
Immediate Supervisor's Signature   date

_____   _____
Reviewer's Supervisor's Signature   date

_____   _____
Employee's Signature   date

P-012
Rev. 2/84   The Employee's signature is required to attest to the fact that the performance has been reviewed with the Employee. The signature does not imply agreement or disagreement with the evaluation.

FIGURE 14.8 A Teacher Evaluation Form

TEACHER PERFORMANCE EVALUATION

Teacher_____ Class_____
      LAST NAME   FIRST   INITIAL

School_____ Date and Time of Visit_____

A. TEACHING TECHNIQUES
1. Utilizes Teacher's Manual or guide effectively. . .
2. Demonstrates sufficient mastery of content. . . .
3. Makes effective use of a variety of materials. . . .
4. Makes clear, practical demonstrations and/or explanations.
5. Provides for pupil participation. . . . .
6. Uses logical, purposeful and thought-provoking questions. . . . .
7. Provides interesting and adequate reinforcement.
8. Varies procedures in working with pupils of varying abilities. . . . .
9. Provides for creative expression. . . . .
10. Makes pupils feel tasks are purposeful . . . . . .
11. Provides motivation. . . . .

B. EFFECTIVE PLANNING
1. Displays evidence of teacher prepared material. . .
2. Directions to students are clearly thought out and well stated. . . . .
3. Materials for class are organized and available . . .
4. Originality is shown in presentation. . . . . . .
5. Individual lessons are part of a logic sequence of learning unit. . . . .
6. Provides enrichment. . . . .
7. Is aware of adequate pacing. . . . .
8. Carefully plans purposeful pupil assignment. . . . .
9. Key questions prepared in advance. . . . .

C. PUPIL TEACHER RELATIONSHIPS
1. Maintains pupil interest and attention . . . . . .
2. Works constructively with individual or group. . .
3. Uses democratic techniques and processes when appropriate. . . . .

4. Manages routine so as to avoid confusion . . . . .
5. Exhibits poise, voice control, tact and integrity. . .
6. Graciously accepts less than the "right" response from a slow student. . . . .
7. Avoids the use of sarcasm or ridicule. . . . . . .
8. Discourages students use of sarcasm or ridicule. . .
9. Uses positive statements to pupils. . . . .
10. Makes supportive statements to pupils. . . . . . .
11. Maintains a friendly and respectful teacher pupil relationship. . . . .

D. CLASSROOM ENVIRONMENT
1. Environment is generally neat and attractive. . . .
2. Furniture arrangement is conductive to learning. . .
3. Bulletin boards and displays have teaching value. . .
4. Teacher is continually aware of proper heat, light and ventilation. . . . .

E. PERSONAL ATTRIBUTES
1. Dresses appropriately. . . . .
2. Is neat and well groomed. . . . .
3. Uses good oral and written language. . . . . . .
4. Is poised and refined in actions-sits, stands and moves about with good posture. . . . . .
5. Is industrious and shows initiative. . . . .
6. Evidence loyalty toward established programs, policies and procedures. . . . .
7. Is prompt with reports. . . . .
8. Evidence warm, sincere interest in all students. . . .
9. Willingness to perform on committees and other extra curricular functions. . . . .
10. Cooperates with fellow staff members. . . . . . .
11. Discreet and professional in communication. . . . .

SUGGESTED CODE FOR THOSE DESIRING A SPECIFIC RATING: 1 – Outstanding;   2 – Above Average;   3 – Average;   4 – Below Average;   5 – Unsatisfactory;

COMMENTS BY THE EVALUATOR

_____

_____

_____

_____

_____

_____

_____

_____

_____

_____

    SIGNATURE OF TEACHER RECEIVING COPY OF REPORT   SIGNATURE OF PERSON MAKING EVALUATION

ORDER BY FORM NO. 5-125 NCR – TEACHER PERFORMANCE EVALUATION USING NCR PAPER.
COPYRIGHT 1966 BY DOUBLEDAY BROS. & CO., KALAMAZOO, MICHIGAN   SCHOOL FORM PRINTERS

Source: Used by permission of Doubleday Bros. & Co., Kalamazoo, MI.

**FIGURE 14.9
Sample Progress
Report**

WOLF Construction
25 East 40 Street, Beaumont, TX   77710

30 Sep 19xx

To: Tom Wolf, President

From: Jack Evans, Project Manager   *je*

Subject: Progress on Hillcrest Apartments During September

Current Status

1. Construction on the Hillcrest Apartments remains three
    weeks behind schedule because of the heavy rains during
    August. During September we lost an additional four days
    because of rain, but close supervision and some overtime
    have prevented us from falling further behind.

2. The foundation for the entire complex is complete.
    Framing on the 14 townhouses is complete, and the framers
    will begin work on the two-bedroom units on Monday, 4
    October. The electrical and plumbing subcontractors
    will also begin work on Monday.

Expected Progress

1. During November, framing, roofing, and siding will be
    completed. We still expect to be inside all units by
    the middle of November, when the early winter rains will
    probably begin.

2. By November 15 we should be able to reduce our work force
    by 50 percent.

3. By the first week in December, the electrical and plumbing
    work should be finished.

▷ RECOMMENDATION AND JUSTIFICATION REPORTS

Recommendation and justification reports present a problem and then submit data to justify a recommended solution to that problem. Unlike most reports, which are written at the request of management, recommendation and justification reports are often initiated by the writer, who has observed a problem and wishes to suggest a solution. They are always direct messages and should begin with a clear statement of purpose or of a problem to be solved.

Recommendation reports, more often than justification reports, may be assigned tasks. Whether reader-initiated or writer-initiated, however, a recommendation report employs the following structure:

Problem:	What is it, and how will the reader benefit if it is solved?
Facts:	What is known about the situation? Where and how was that information obtained?
Assumptions:	What can be assumed on the basis of the facts?
Recommendations:	What should the reader do, and why will that action (or those actions) solve the problem?

Figure 14.10 illustrates a typical recommendation report. Note that the headings for the report are not simply "Problem," "Facts," and so forth, but that they specify *what* problem, facts, and assumptions. As a rule, specific headings, which apply only to *one* section of *one* report, are more useful than generic headings, which could be used in almost any report about any subject. Use generic headings only when your reader expects them.

Justification reports serve essentially the same function as recommendation reports. The problems they attempt to solve, however, are usually financial — solving the problem will result in saving money. Justification reports typically use the following generic headings (rather than specific ones):

1. Purpose.

2. Cost and Savings (or Advantages).

3. Method (or Procedure).

4. Conclusions.

5. Discussion.

The conclusions of a justification report should show convincingly that the recommendation is justified by the advantages that will be realized. (See Figure 14.11.)

**FIGURE 14.10
Sample
Recommendation
Report**

GOLDHABER INDUSTRIES   *Internal Correspondence*

October 10, 19xx

TO: President William Goldhaber

FROM: Michael MacBeth   *mm*

SUBJECT: Recommendation for Increased Computer Security

Now that Goldhaber Industries has networked its microcomputers to
the mainframe and the entire system is accessible through public
telephone lines, we need to add at least one level of security to
prevent the loss of critical data.

Computer Hackers

Any computer system accessible through public telephone lines is
subject to attack by hackers whose chief pleasure in life is
cracking security codes on corporate computers. Some of them also
deliberately delete or alter data so that it becomes unusable
or--worse--misleading. Because virtually every Company record is
kept on the computer, we cannot afford to run the risk that some
hacker will find a combination of access code and password that
would permit him or her access to our files.

Recent Examples

You've no doubt read the newspaper and newsweekly stories about
hackers breaking into computers owned by banks, other companies,
and even the Pentagon. Most of the hackers are young men (some
still in their early teens) who break into corporate computers
essentially as a hobby. A few are professionals who are doing it
for personal gain. Regardless of the hacker's intentions, however,
companies can suffer tremendous losses.

Right here in River City, for example, Preston's Precision Parts
lost the master control for 60 assembly robots when a hacker
cracked their security code and entered a so-called "worm" program,
which "eats" all the other programming and data on a system. By
the time Preston discovered that the worm was at work, it was too
late. To add insult to injury, when it was finished, the worm
program printed "Gotcha" on every terminal in the plant.

President William Goldhaber   Oct 10, 19xx   2

Goldhaber's Vulnerability

Because our sales personnel and executives use external computers to download reports and to upload product data, we cannot simply eliminate remote capabilities. Further, because only a project number and a password are required to gain access to our computer, it is only a mater of time before someone hits on a workable combination. Now that our computer is connected to the public phone system, anyone with a computer and modem anywhere in the country, is free to attempt gaining access.

Some hackers, in fact, have special programs that try every possible number until one is accepted as a legitimate project number and then try series of common passwords until they find a combination that works. Even though very little of the data on our computer would be of interest or use to anyone except our direct competitors, leaving our files so exposed is simply asking for trouble.

Possible Solutions

I recommend that we do two things to increase the security of our computer: institute a dial-back procedure and require individual names as well as project numbers and passwords.

1. The dial-back procedure would prevent a direct log-on. An individual would call our computer, which would ask for the phone number he or she was calling from. The computer would then disconnect, and the individual would have two minutes to set his or her modem and software to receive a call. Our computer would then return the call, recording both the number called and the time of the call.

2. Requiring individual user names would give us an additional cross-check against project numbers and passwords. After our computer has called back and established the connection with the remote terminal, we would require the user to enter his or her name. We would check the name against a list of authorized users, and then check for the corresponding project number and password. We would be able to break the connection at any time the user's responses were suspicious.

If you approve, I'll begin developing the necessary programming immediately. We can have the new procedures tested and in place in about three months.

FIGURE 14.11
A Justification
Report

HOW SAFETY GOGGLES WOULD SAVE
JACKSON ELECTRONICS $500 A YEAR

Purpose

To save Jackson Electronics $500 a year, I recommend that we
purchase 25 pairs of clear glass safety goggles and require the
line technicians to wear them during soldering operations.

Cost and Savings

Twenty-five pairs of safety goggles would cost about $750. This
investment would save Jackson an estimated $2,000 over the next
three years in medical costs and worker's compensation expenses.

Procedure

Each of the 20 line technicians would sign for and receive a pair
of safety goggles. The five extra pairs would be available for
replacements. Zimmer Glass makes safety glasses appropriate for
our needs, and by purchasing 25 we would receive a 10 percent
discount. Zimmer's price for 25 would be $748.75. We could have
immediate delivery.

Conclusions

Although eye injuries caused by soldering operations do not happen
frequently, they are expensive when they do happen. In the last
three years two injuries have cost Jackson more than $2,700. The
safety goggles would eliminate the eye injuries and associated
expenses.

Discussion

In June 1984 a soldering accident cost Robert Johnson the sight in
his left eye. Jackson Electronics paid $1,200 for emergency
medical treatment, and our insurance costs for the following year
increased 15 percent. Though not so serious, our most recent
accident, in September, has already cost Jackson $940.

Even though the line technicians are always more careful to follow
safety precautions after an accident occurs, it's only a matter of
time until someone becomes careless while soldering. Safety goggles
should eliminate future eye injuries, and by purchasing goggles
now we may be able to avoid a costly increase in insurance premiums.

▷ PROPOSALS

How are proposals different from rec- ommendation and justification reports?

Unlike recommendation and justification reports for particular actions, pro- posals attempt to persuade. They may be either requested or volunteered, but they always propose to solve a problem for the reader, and they are written because the writer will benefit if the reader accepts the proposal. In this respect proposals are different from all other reports. In spite of their persuasive component, however, proposals should still be accurate, reliable, and objective so that the reader can make an informed decision. Whether based on a request (usually called a *request for proposal,* or RFP) or submitted without specific solicitation, proposals should be clear about the problem to be solved and the procedures for solving it. Proposals usually contain the following parts:

1. **A summarizing introduction.** Give the reader a broad but quick overview. This may be the only part of the proposal your audience reads, so do it well. Articulate your objective and approach, present your reasoning with as little technical material as possible, state your own viewpoint and opinions about the problem, summarize your pro- posed solution, and give the main reasons that you are the best person to solve the problem.

2. **A detailed problem statement.** Because every proposal is written to provide a solution to a problem, your writing should indicate a thorough understanding of the problem. Whether the proposal is a response to a request or an initial statement, the problem statement should include both the problem as the reader sees it and *your* problem as you wish the reader to see it.

3. **A work statement.** Tell your reader what you will do to solve the problem. Be specific. Include the results and conclusions of your pre- liminary research in the text, and place documentation (computer print- outs, questionnaires, engineering calculations, and other supporting evidence) in an appendix. Give reasons and reader benefits behind the facts and figures.

4. **A project management statement.** Tell your reader how and when you propose to accomplish what you have said you will do. Who will report to whom? Who will do what jobs? Who will provide materials and other resources? How long will the project take? How will you measure your progress? At what intervals will you inform your reader of your progress?

5. **A statement of your qualifications.** When you are not well known to your reader, your qualifications and those of your organization are

necessary to provide credibility. What training do you and other personnel involved have? What resources do you have? Do you have the facilities required? Consider including the resumes of key personnel.

Any one of these parts may be omitted or modified depending on how much the reader (or readers) already knows or wants to know. Formal requests for proposals may specify additional details or alter the order of presentation. If you have a request for a proposal, be sure to follow its directions exactly and completely.

Whether requested or volunteered, a proposal must usually compete with others for acceptance. Your company, for example, may submit a proposal to construct a building according to a set of architectural specifications. Other companies would also submit proposals — or *bids* — for the work. In addition to cost, the architects and engineers who would review the proposals would be influenced by their confidence in your ability to do the job, to do it correctly, to do it on time, and to do it for the amount specified. Your proposal needs to show that you can deliver what you promise.

If accepted, your proposal and the acceptance may constitute a contract, so be sure that you can meet all the specifications you include. Figure 14.12 is an example of a proposal.

DESCRIPTIONS AND SPECIFICATIONS

Under what circumstances might job descriptions be considered legal documents? How would that influence their preparation?

Responsibilities and functions of personnel, offices, and departments frequently require describing or specifying. Also, materials and services often require exact specifications if they are to meet the needs of the company. By helping to define and clarify company goals and needs, descriptions and specifications not only help people understand their positions within the company but also help provide a mechanism for measuring achievement and defining standards. Descriptions and specifications will obviously vary from industry to industry and company to company.

Job Descriptions

Job descriptions (see Figure 14.13) are probably the most common descriptions in business, and should contain the following information.

1.   Job title (See the *Dictionary of Occupational Titles*).

2.   Description of duties.

3.   List of equipment and materials necessary.

4.   Special requirements of work.

FIGURE 14.12
Sample Proposal
with Memo of
Transmittal

The Sinclair Company   Memorandum

30 March 19xx

TO: Mr. Henry J. Hessler, Vice President

FROM: David L. Thornley *dt*

PROPOSAL FOR INTERPERSONAL COMMUNICATION SEMINAR

Here is the proposal I agreed to develop for you when we met on Monday,
27 February 19xx.

The two-day seminar covers all the concepts I discussed with you and
Alice Halseth. I agree that the first seminar should be conducted with
department managers, with subsequent seminars contingent on how well the
first sessions are received. Should the seminar prove successful, we
may wish to consider hiring an outside consultant to conduct it on a
regular basis.

Before the seminar, participants should receive copies of The New Guide
to Rational Living by Albert Ellis and Robert Harper (Wilshire Book
Company--paperback). As soon as I receive your final approval, I will
order the books.

The dates and the schedule you mentioned during our meeting are fine
with me. I will plan to begin each day at 8:15 a.m. and end at 4:15
p.m., with an hour's break at noon for lunch and a 15-minute coffee
break in the morning and afternoon.

Should you decide that additional or different topics should be included
in the seminar, please let me know.

enc

FIGURE 14.12
(Continued)

The Sinclair Company
St. Louis, Missouri

PROPOSAL

For a two-day seminar on interpersonal communication

Prepared for Mr. Henry J. Hessler, Vice President
Employee Development and Planning

30 March 19xx

Objectives

The proposed two-day seminar in interpersonal communication will help
participants achieve the following objectives:

* Understand the role self-image plays in interpersonal communication.
* Evaluate personal strengths and weaknesses.
* Understand and appreciate the differences among people.
* Develop specific skills to overcome communication barriers.
* Learn techniques for resolving conflicts in the work environment.
* Identify and apply specific techniques for motivating themselves
  and others.
* Set goals for personal growth and organizational success.

Two-day Seminar

To achieve these objectives, I would conduct a two-day seminar covering the
following topics:

May 26:   I.   Understanding Self
                A.   Roles and Goals
                B.   Self-image
                C.   Internalized Belief Systems

          II.   Understanding Others
                A.   Perceptions
                B.   Gut-level Programming
                C.   The Nature of Relationships

         III.   Communicating
                A.   Process
                B.   Barriers
                C.   Techniques
                D.   Mind-Reading

**FIGURE 14.12
(Continued)**

```
Proposal                          30 March 19xx                     2


              E.  Agreements
                  1.  Spoken
                  2.  Unspoken
              F.  Active Listening

June 1:   IV.  Resolving Conflicts
              A.  Whose Problem
              B.  I-You Statements
              C.  Negotiations
                  (Lose-lose, win-lose, win-win)
              D.  Team Efforts

           V.  Motivating Self and Others
              A.  Self-management by Objectives
              B.  Constructive Criticism
              C.  Constructive Praise

          VI.  Relating for Success and Personal Growth
              A.  Who Are You?
              B.  Who Do You Wish to Be?
              C.  How Can You Help Yourself?
              D.  How Can Others Help You?
```

Procedures

```
Each training module will include four specific steps:  (1) opening exercise,
(2) discussion, (3) explanation, and (4) application.  The purpose of the
opening exercise and following discussion will be to stimulate interest in
the topic.  The explanation phase of the module will present the learning
concepts and rationale.  The application phase will allow participants to
apply what they have learned through self-analysis, role playing, group
exercises, or individual applications.
```

Materials

```
I will prepare camera-ready copy for all materials and worksheets.  Each
participant should receive a copy of A New Guide to Rational Living by
Albert Ellis and Robert Harper (Wilshire Book Company).
```

Program Administration and Costs

```
I will assume responsibility for the two days of the seminar.  With a seminar
size of 20 or fewer, the cost for each individual will be less than $100 a
person, 80 percent of which can be charged back to departmental budgets.  The
remaining 20 percent will be charged against our service budget.
```

FIGURE 14.13
Job Description

ARMATRON, INC.

JOB DESCRIPTION

Department: Communication and Public Relations

Job Title: Director of Communication

Date: July 1, 19xx

Primary Function: Assume responsibility for all Branch
communication activities, both internal and external,
and to report directly to the Branch manager.

Duties include: Being responsible for

1. Publishing Chicago Branch newsletter

2. Planning, organizing, and coordinating
    leadership training programs

3. Coordinating MBO programs

4. Supervising intra- and extracompany
    correspondence

Equipment Skills: Photographic, printing, and word
processing.

Supervisor: Branch manager

Supervising Responsibilities: Initially the Department
of Communication and Public Relations will contain the
following staff support:

1. Administrative Assistant

2. Secretary

3. Clerk-typist

Additional specialists may be added when it is cost
effective to do so.

Responsibilities also entail supervising Branch staff
in areas of authority.

Work Flow: To be determined.

**FIGURE 14.13
(Continued)**

2

Salary: $50,000-$60,000

Expense Account: American Express--$10,000 a year.

Promotional Route: Corporation Vice President when
warranted.

Qualifications: College degree in advertising,
communication, journalism, or related field; experience
or training in all areas of publishing; demonstrated
leadership and supervising skills; and the ability to
develop new organizational development programs.

5.   Organizational role.
      a. Supervisor.
      b. Supervisory responsibilities.
      c. Work flow—sent to and received from.
      d. Promotional route.

6.   Qualifications.
      a. Education.
      b. Experience.
      c. Special exams or licenses.
      d. When appropriate
          (1) Height.
          (2) Weight.
          (3) Sex.
          (4) Vision (color and/or acuity).
          (5) Hearing.
          (6) Strength.

Specifications

Why might specifi-
cations be impor-
tant to an organiza-
tion? What kinds of
organizations might
be especially con-
cerned with specifi-
cations?

Specifications are detailed descriptions of procedures, mechanisms, or services. How specific specifications need to be depends on the nature of the procedure, mechanism, or service. General specifications are usually called *standards*, which may apply broadly to an industry or company. Specifications should cover the following subjects.:

1.   A general description of what you want, including physical properties and the use or service you expect to obtain.

2.   The date you expect the procedure, mechanism, or service to be complete and operational.

3.   The deadline for proposals or other preliminary reports and the date for announcing contracts or other approvals.

4.   Any monetary considerations.

5.   Special requirements for personnel involved.

6.   Technical clauses covering all aspects of the procedure, mechanism, or service.

7.   Provisions for changes after the contract is awarded.

To write specifications for your company, you will need to be completely knowledgeable in the technical area involved. A miscalculation could prove costly. To prevent miscalculations and misinterpretations, observe the following guidelines:

1.   Have all technical clauses checked by specialists.

2. Use a simple, direct writing style. Use technical language only when the technical terms are more specific than the common words.

3. Specify well-known standards and procedures.

4. Use graphic aids to help illustrate technical descriptions.

5. Proofread carefully. A comma or period out of place could cost thousands of dollars or result in a dangerous mechanical failure.

▷ DOCUMENTATION WRITING

What is documentation writing, and when is it necessary?

The term *documentation writing* is most often used to describe materials explaining computer programs to their users. Business and other organizations, however, must document—establish a permanent record of—a wide variety of things every day. Agenda, minutes of meetings, job descriptions, and product specifications are all forms of documentation writing. Whenever you assemble information that others must have access to and be able to use, or whenever you otherwise create a record for future reference, you are engaged in documentation writing. In addition to the manuals accompanying computer equipment and computer software, another obvious example of documentation writing is this textbook; it documents the procedures for solving business communication problems.

Why should computer programs be documented?

As with any type of report writing, effective documentation writing requires a specific objective: what purpose will the document serve? It also requires a good understanding of the audience: who will use the document? Will your document be used, for example, as record of how and why the program came to be written in the first place, or will it serve as a guide for users of a computerized database storing information about inventory or personnel? If so, will the users be familiar with computer operations and terminology? Will the users be trained in the use of computerized databases? How much will you have to teach them about computers and databases before they will understand how the program controls information?

The format for a document should also be designed to facilitate achieving a specific purpose with a specific audience. In many cases documentation is presented as a manual and follows a step-by-step outline. The document may include some or all of the following components:

1. **Statement of purpose.**   The purpose of the document should be stated explicitly.

2. **Statement of audience.**   For whom is the document being prepared? This statement may also include an explicit reference to those who should not have access to the document.

3. **Statement of usage.**   What requirements must be met before the document can be used? Equipment lists; training requirements; directions for using the document; and the objectives of the procedure, event, or equipment documented should all be stated explicitly.

4. **Instructions or documentation.**   What is the user to do or know? Definitions, descriptions, and required actions should be specified.

5. **Graphic aids.**   Time charts, flow charts, decision trees, photographs, sample computer screens, and other graphic aids may be required to document steps in a procedure or to clarify definitions or descriptions.

6. **Statement of feedback procedures.**   What should the user do when something goes wrong? What kinds of records should the user keep to document her or his use of the original document?

7. **Appendixes.**   What additional information will help the user? If the document contains many technical terms, a *glossary* may help. Sample forms, sample computer screens, technical explanations not necessary to actual use, sample computer printouts, and other supplemental information may help the user understand the document and its use.

8. **Index.**   Because most documents of this variety are used as reference tools, users should be able to find key terms, procedures, and descriptions quickly and easily.

▷ FORMAL REPORTS

Why are formal reports often more difficult to write than informal reports?

In addition to the informal reports just discussed, many organizations require formal reports on a fairly regular basis. These reports are almost always special assignments, and they are almost always analytical. Because they deal with topics of importance to the organization and because they become an important part of the company's operations and records, the physical presentation of these reports is more formal than those we discussed in the preceding sections. For these reasons, formal reports include some additional parts to help the reader keep track of the mass of information. These parts are

Prefatory parts: Cover

Title fly

Title page

Letter of authorization

Letter of acceptance

Letter of transmittal

Contents

Abstract (or synopsis)

Body of the report:	Introduction
	Text
	Summary, conclusions, and recommendations
Supplemental parts:	Appendix
	Bibliography

In general, the longer the report, the more of these parts it would include. A short formal report (fewer than ten pages) would probably include only a title page, letter of transmittal, abstract, and bibliography in addition to the body. Key parts of the report are illustrated in Figures 14.14 through 14.19.

Prefatory Parts

What are the functions of the prefatory parts?

1. **Cover.**   The cover protects the report and announces its title. Covers may have designs to attract attention, but they should be simple. Keep the cover title short — no more than eight words.

2. **Title fly.**   The title fly, the first sheet of the report, carries only the report title. Your title should be worded to include the *how* of the report and as many of the five Ws *(who, what, where, when, why)* as possible.

3. **Title page.**   The title page includes the title of the report, the name and professional title of the person (or group, department, or organization) for whom the report was prepared, the name and professional title of the person (or group, department, or organization) who prepared the report, and the completion date (Figure 14.14).

4. **Letter of authorization.**   The letter of authorization authorizes investigation of the problem. It states the problem and the objectives of the investigation clearly and, in addition, specifies the scope and limitations of the problem (Figure 14.15).

5. **Letter of acceptance.**   Although the letter of acceptance is not usually included in the report, it is the answer to the letter of authorization. It may change or revise the original letter of authorization. The two letters — authorization and acceptance — serve as a contractual agreement between the person (or group, department, or organization) requesting the report and the person (or group, department, or organization) conducting the investigation.

6. **Letter of transmittal.**   The letter of transmittal sends, or transmits, the report from the person conducting the research to the person who authorized it. In addition to saying, in effect, "here is the report," the letter of transmittal may state other relevant issues: (1) the authorization for the study; (2) the statement of the problem, its scope, and its limitations; (3) methods of procedure; (4) a summary of the findings, conclusions, and recommendations; (5) acknowledgments to individuals

FIGURE 14.14
Title Page

HOW MACDOUGAL'S RESTAURANTS COULD INCREASE PROFITS

20 PERCENT BY SERVING BREAKFASTS

Prepared for
William J. MacDougal
President, MacDougal's Restaurants

Prepared by
Sally K. DeRyke, Associate Director
Field Studies Division

Omaha Management Consultants Inc.
691 Westlake Road
Omaha, NE 68100

16 February 19xx

FIGURE 14.15
Letter of
Authorization

MacDougal's *Restaurants*
1120 Short Road, Omaha, NE 68100
William J. MacDougal, President
(402) 555-3318

December 4, 19xx

Dr. Kathleen M. Saxby, Director
Omaha Management Consultants Inc.
691 Westlake Road
Omaha, NE 68100

Dear Dr. Saxby:

This letter confirms our phone conversation of
December 3. For a fee of $8,500 Omaha Management
Consultants will investigate the operations of
the 14 MacDougal restaurants in Nebraska and
recommend ways for MacDougal's to increase
efficiency and achieve higher profits.

The subjects for in-depth study should include

       1. Opening for breakfast;
       2. Restaurant operation; and
       3. Training program.

I understand that you will complete the first
report on the feasibility of opening for breakfast
no later than February 20 and that the other
reports will follow at 30-day intervals. I agree
to pay Omaha Management Consultants $2,833.34
upon receipt of each report.

Sincerely,

William J. MacDougal

who helped with the project; and finally, (6) an offer to discuss the project further or to conduct future studies (Figure 14.16).

7.   **Contents.**   A contents page should be included if the report is lengthy and has several subdivisions. The purpose of the contents page is to show the reader at a glance on what page a particular division or subdivision begins. The contents page must be prepared last because it gives the page numbers for the various divisions (Figure 14.17). If the report contains several charts, tables, and illustrations, a separate list may be made for each of them. These pages would be called *Figures, Tables,* and so forth.

8.   **Abstract.**   The abstract (or synopsis) is a brief overview of the entire report. Because it is a summary, it must be prepared after the report has been completed; it should be no longer than one page. The abstract gives the busy reader a quick, comprehensive survey of the report (Figure 14.18).

A descriptive abstract *describes* the contents of the report; it *tells* the reader what is there. A summarizing abstract *restates* the information contained in the report in reduced form; it *shows* the reader what the report contains. Because summarizing abstracts are generally more useful, they are more common than descriptive abstracts. See Chapter 12.

For all but the most formal internal reports, many companies use memo format to authorize, accept, and transmit reports. This information may also be exchanged by phone (though a written follow-up is usually necessary, and more than one letter of authorization and/or acceptance may be necessary).

Body of the Report

The body of a report generally consists of the summary, conclusions, and recommendations. Figure 14.19 illustrates sample pages from a formal report.

1.   **Introduction.**   In addition to giving the reader the background of the report and detailing its authorization and subject, the introduction orients the reader to the problem, purpose, scope, limitations, and procedure. It also defines key terms.

2.   **Text.**   The text of the report presents the data gathered and the analysis. This is the central and largest part of the report.

3.   **Summary, conclusions, and recommendations.**   The summary of the report restates its main points; the conclusions are objective statements based on the findings of the report; and the recommendations are somewhat subjective statements suggesting a particular course of action based on the conclusions.

FIGURE 14.16
Letter of
Transmittal

OMAHA MANAGEMENT CONSULTANTS, INC.
691 Westlake Road   Omaha, NE 68100

8 February 19xx

Mr. William J. MacDougal, President
MacDougal's Restaurants
1120 Short Road
Omaha, NE 68100

Dear Mr. MacDougal:

Here is the report you requested on 4 December studying the
feasibility of opening MacDougal's Restaurants for breakfast.
Other members of Omaha Management Consultants are now preparing
the reports about your operation and training program.

This report shows that with only a small investment in new
equipment and a slight increase in personnel, MacDougal's could
increase its profits by about 20 percent. As a fast-food chain,
MacDougal's is in a good position to compete for breakfast
business.

At present, the large motel chains capture most of the breakfast
market. This is true primarily because those restaurants must
open to accommodate their guests, whereas most other restaurants
in Nebraska do not open until 11 a.m. Many commuters who now
eat at home or in motel restaurants would prefer the prompt,
courteous service offered by MacDougal's.

I have enjoyed preparing this report for you, Mr. MacDougal, and
I have learned some interesting things about the restaurant
business and MacDougal's while preparing it. Please call me
directly at 555-7761 when I can be of further help.

Sincerely,

Sally K. DeRyke

Sally K. DeRyke

s

enc

FIGURE 14.17
Contents Page

CONTENTS

FIGURE 14.18
Abstract

Abstract

With a total investment of only $158,000, MacDougal's restaurants could begin providing breakfast at its 14 locations in Nebraska and increase its annual profits by approximately 20 percent.

According to surveys of potential customers in Omaha, Lincoln, Kearney, and David City, the demand for a fast-food breakfast restaurant is high and currently unsatisfied. As an established fast-food chain, MacDougal's could easily meet this need.

At present the large motel chains capture most of the breakfast market. This is true primarily because those restaurants must open to accommodate their guests, whereas most other restaurants in Nebraska do not open until 11:00 a.m. Many commuters who now eat at home or in motel restaurants would prefer the prompt, courteous service offered by MacDougal's. This is especially true because the restaurants currently open for breakfast are nearly all located close to freeway entrances, which forces many local commuters to go out of their way for breakfast.

MacDougal's should convert its five restaurants in Omaha first. Because the Omaha restaurants already open at 9:00 a.m., two hours earlier than the restaurants in other cities, and because they now offer some breakfast foods, the conversion to an earlier, full-time breakfast operation will be easiest in Omaha. Also, many Omaha residents already view MacDougal's as the best place to have a quick, late breakfast, so repositioning MacDougal's in the market will be easiest to achieve in Omaha as well. Once profitability is achieved in Omaha, the details of converting the remaining MacDougal's throughout Nebraska could be established.

The initial investment in Omaha would amount to only $55,000. Advertising and personnel costs (primarily for new hires and training) would account for the largest percentage of that investment. Some new equipment would be required (additional toasters and increased refrigerator space), and a new food contract would need to be obtained.

Eight weeks would be the minimum amount of lead time required between the date of your decision and opening for breakfast, but as long as 90 days may be necessary, depending on the time required to develop appropriate advertising and to hire and train the additional employees required to cover the early morning hours. MacDougal's could expect its breakfast trade to be producing a profit within six months.

**FIGURE 14.19
Extracts from the
Text of a Formal
Report**

The Breakfast Business

Providing breakfast service would increase MacDougal's annual profits
by approximately 20 percent. This report shows why and how the
increase is possible.

Purpose

The purpose of this report is to discuss the feasibility of opening
MacDougal's Restaurants for breakfast. During my investigation,
I discovered that in the four cities in which MacDougal's are
located, the demand for a fast-food breakfast establishment is
high.

Methodology and Limitations

To determine whether MacDougal's should compete for the breakfast
business, I studied the competition, the clientele, the required
investments and changes, and the potential for increased profits.
For three weeks I surveyed customers eating breakfast at
restaurants in each of the four cities, and in each city Omaha
Management Consultants conducted a random-sample telephone survey
to determine the breakfast market.

* * * * * * * *

The Competition

At present, no fast-food restaurant in Nebraska offers breakfast.
Restaurants that offer breakfast fall into three general
categories: hotel/motel coffee shops, hotel/motel restaurants,
and family-owned downtown coffee shops. Each of these
establishments caters to a particular clientele....

In Omaha

Omaha presents a unique opportunity for MacDougal's because only
three coffee shops offer....

Supplemental Parts

What are the func-
tions of the supple-
mental parts?

1. **Appendix.**   Appendixes contain copies of the letters, questionnaires,
    forms, or blueprints used in obtaining information for the report. They
    also contain other supplementary material that is not actually used in
    the report itself. The report may direct the reader to an appendix for
    further reference or clarification. Because readers do not usually read
    appendixes, nothing important should be put in an appendix.

2. **Bibliography.**   The bibliography lists all the references—books, pe-
    riodicals, journals, speeches, interviews, and newspapers—used in the
    report.

▷ SUMMARY

Each organization has its own requirements for particular kinds of reports.
Reports are functional pieces of writing designed to help a reader make a
decision.

The memo report may well be the most common means of exchanging
written business information. These are short, informal messages that provide a rapid, convenient means of communication between employees within
the same organization.

A letter report is a report written in the form of a regular business letter.
They may be used for personnel references, credit evaluations, or auditor
recommendations. Letter reports differ from typical business letters in that
they are formal and primarily factual.

Recommendation and justification reports present a problem and then
submit data to justify a recommended solution to that problem. They are
often initiated by the writer, who has observed a problem and wishes to
suggest a solution.

The purpose of a proposal is to persuade somebody to let you do something. Proposals can be either requested or volunteered, but they always
propose to solve a problem for the reader.

An agenda is a list of topics arranged in the order that they are to be
discussed at a meeting. Minutes are the official records of a meeting. Agenda
and minutes vary in form from one organization to another. An itinerary is
a combination of travel and appointment schedules, showing when, where,
and how a person will travel.

Descriptions and specifications not only help define and clarify company goals and needs, but also help provide a mechanism for measuring
achievement. Specifications are detailed descriptions of procedures, mechanisms, or services.

COMMUNICATION SOLUTION

The principal function of annual reports is to communicate financial and investment data about companies to stockholders and other interested parties. Some annual reports are essentially public relations publications — using many color photographs, stories about key employees, and stories about company successes to create a favorable impression for the company.

Other annual reports provide little more than a brief overview of the financial health of the organization and, together with the standard auditor's short-form report listing assets and liabilities, a confirmation that the auditor has checked the organization's books and found them to be in accordance with standard accounting procedures and without "material" (significant) errors. The principal function of an annual report is to provide investors with the information required to make a decision about whether to invest (or continue to invest) in an organization.

Most annual reports use several of the common report-writing techniques:

1. Headings for major divisions and subdivisions.

2. Graphic aids (perhaps numbered and labeled) to help illustrate the text.

3. Numbered or unnumbered lists.

4. Tabulation of monetary and other figures to aid readability.

5. Summarizing statements to clarify major organizational accomplishments.

In your study of various companies' annual reports, as suggested in the Communication Challenge, you perhaps noticed the use of some or all of the preceding techniques.

In addition, some annual reports provide a table of contents and other prefatory and supplemental parts. One typical prefatory part is the letter of transmittal, usually written by the president of the organization. If the annual reports you examined contained this feature, examine the letters to see where any negative information appears. Almost always it will be placed in the middle of the letter and presented using positive language so that positive factors might receive greater emphasis.

Can you tell from any one of the reports what kind of audience the writer thought she or he was addressing? Some writers assume that the only people who will read them are serious investors who understand the technical language common to accountants and financial analysts. Others prepare their annual reports for a broader audience, assuming that many people who do not understand financial language may wish to invest in a company they can feel proud of.

Annual reports can be expensive to produce and distribute. In some companies, a staff of several people will work on an annual report for months. Color photographs, special typesetting, and high quality paper can greatly increase the cost of an annual report. Even postage, when annual reports are mailed to stockholders, can be a significant expense. In general, the expensive annual reports try to reach a broader, less sophisticated audience than the brief reports, which concentrate on financial data. The emphasis in the fancy reports is on public relations. They "sell" the organization as an organization of people rather than as a collection of assets and liabilities.

So that each employee has a good knowledge of his or her performance and so that higher management can be aware of each person's abilities and promotability, managers evaluate employees. Most companies use forms to help ensure objectivity and thoroughness in the evaluation procedure.

Formal reports usually deal with more complex problems and involve more data than informal reports. For this reason, formal reports include some additional parts to help the reader keep track of the mass of information. A cover sheet protects the report and announces its title. The title fly carries only the report title. The title page includes the title of the report, the name and professional title of the person for whom the report was prepared, the name and professional title of the person who prepared the report, and the completion date. The letter of authorization authorizes investigation of the problem. It states the problem and the objectives of the investigation. The letter of acceptance is the answer to the letter of authorization. The letter of transmittal transmits the report from the person conducting the research to the person who authorized it.

The body of a report consists of the introduction; the text; and the summary, conclusions, and recommendations. Appendixes contain copies of the letters, questionnaires, forms, blueprints, or other items used in obtaining information for the report. The bibliography lists all the references used in the report.

▷ EXERCISES

Review and Discussion Questions

1. Why are memos called internal letters?

2. When are letter reports useful?

3. What functions do agenda, minutes, and itineraries perform?

4. Why are expense reports and personnel evaluations usually handled by forms?

5. How do progress reports help management make decisions?

6. What are the differences among recommendation reports, justification reports, and proposals?

7. Why are descriptions and specifications classified as reports?

8. What is documentation writing?

9. What makes a formal report formal?

10. Identify the prefatory parts of a long, formal report.

11. Which of the parts of a formal report are essential? Nonessential? Why?

12. The body of a report consists of what three parts, and what are their functions?

13. What are the differences between conclusions and recommendations?

14. Identify the supplemental parts of a long report and explain the functions of each.

Problems for Informal Reports

1. You are the personnel manager of Mendel's Department Store and have received several complaints about the dress, appearance, and manners of your sales personnel. Write a memo to all employees stating your concerns and giving advice.

2. As the football coach at Eastern Midwest University, prepare a memo to go to all instructors who have football players in class. Tell them that football players will miss class on Friday, September 17; Friday, October 9; Friday, October 23; and Friday, November 5. The football players are expected to complete their work early the weeks the team will be traveling.

3. Prepare a memo for your instructor indicating your class, study, and work schedule for the current term.

4. Using the information in Problem 3 and other pertinent material, write a letter to the director of financial aid applying for financial assistance.

5. Write an informational memo to your instructor explaining the advantages and disadvantages of your major field of study.

6. Select a popular magazine and categorize the articles and/or stories in at least six issues according to subject matter. Present your findings
   a. In an informational report to your instructor.
   b. In an informational report to the magazine publisher.
   c. In an analytical report to your instructor.
   d. In an analytical report to the publisher.

7. Obtain four job descriptions from companies in your area, and analyze them for completeness and clarity. Report your findings to your instructor.

8. As the Los Angeles Branch Manager for Quality Insurance Company, submit a report to the home office in Chicago (address it to Wade Carlson, Vice-President — West) justifying the purchase of business communication textbooks for all branch personnel who have communication responsibilities (about 200 currently).

9. What trip would you most like to take? Prepare your itinerary.

10. Attend a business meeting of your field's professional or honorary fraternity or association and prepare minutes of the meeting.

11. Write a possible agenda for the next meeting of the group studied in Problem 10.

12. Write a memo to the members of your fraternity, sorority, or association encouraging them to give blood. The county Bloodmobile will be on your campus for one week. Give specific times and locations.

13. Because your employer refunds expenses for tuition, books, and study materials, submit an expense report for one of your current classes. List appropriate enclosures.

14. You believe that the company you work for should reimburse employees for expenses incurred in furthering their education. Write a report to Paul Madelinski, the President of Escanaba Manufacturing, recommending the adoption of such a program.

15. Your professional association holds its annual convention every December. Last December the convention chairperson asked you to submit a proposal for a presentation. Write a proposal on an appropriate subject.

16. Write a job description for the job you expect to have when you complete your education.

17. Write the description of the job you expect to have ten years from now.

18. Write specifications for one of the following:
    a. A sound system for an auditorium.
    b. A music system for a department store.
    c. An addition to a house (bedroom and bath, family room, recreation room, or garage).
    d. Clothes for a period movie.
    e. A model railroad set.
    f. A doll house.
    g. A comfortable work area (for the kind of work with which you are most familiar).
    h. A modern word processing station.
    i. Packaging requirements for a new product (select a specific product).
    j. A distribution system for perishable goods. Include appropriate illustrations and other visual aids.

19. As the Director of Management Communications Inc., send a proposal to Dr. William Massey, President of Calhoun County School Employees,

outlining the communication program you plan for the 200 school administrators in the county. You will need to cover written communication, oral communication, human relations, and dictation skills. In conversation with Dr. Massey, you have learned that two-hour sessions on Wednesday afternoons (3:00 to 5:00) would be best. Also, Dr. Massey wants the program to last six to eight weeks. Your usual fee for seminars is $125 an hour plus expenses. Dr. Massey has asked for your best "package price," and cost may be a factor in whether you get the contract.

20.   Write a progress report on your education thus far. Include plans for completion.

21.   Assume that it is ten years from now. Write a progress report on your career development. Include goals and plans.

22.   Select a term project for one of your classes and prepare weekly reports on your progress.

23.   Recommend a change in procedures at your college or university. (Be sure to select the appropriate audience, but submit your report to your instructor for his or her approval before sending it.)

24.   Propose to write a report for your instructor on a topic of your choosing.

25.   After your instructor approves your proposal (see Problem 23), write a short formal report on a topic of your choice. Consult Chapter 12 for appropriate methods of research. You may consider the following possibilities.
   a.   Comparing two products or services for the purpose of purchasing.
   b.   Comparing two businesses for prices, convenience, and customer satisfaction.
   c.   Recommending a professional journal for company personnel.
   d.   Comparing two possible sites for the location of the new Toy and Hobby Shop you would like to own. (You may build, remodel, or lease.)
   e.   Comparing actual business letters (or reports) with the ideal.
   f.   Comparing the average starting salaries for graduates in several areas (business and nonbusiness).
   g.   Recommending a change in course content or major field curriculum.
   h.   Comparing the cost-effectiveness of modes of transportation — either local or long distance.

CASES FOR FORMAL REPORTS

Write a formal report on a topic of your choice using appropriate secondary sources and at least one primary source and using the special techniques of report writing. The following are possible topics:

1. Career possibilities in your major/minor field of study.

2. Impact of technology on your major/minor field of study.

3. A plan for an organizational development program in an organization of your choice.

4. The effectiveness of the present layout of a local supermarket.

5. The communication system in a local business.

6. The purchase of equipment and/or furniture for a new office.

7. The advisability of initiating a flexible work schedule for a large university or business. Some individuals would start work at 7:00 a.m. and leave at 3:00 p.m.; others would start work at 8:00 a.m. and leave at 4:00 p.m.; and others would start work at 9:00 a.m. and leave at 5:00 p.m.

8. Absenteeism at a local factory.

9. Motivation problem at a local business.

10. Improved procedures for distributing a product of your choice:

Records	Sewing machines
Food	Electric typewriters
Petroleum	Textbooks
Automobiles	Television sets

11. Lack of involvement in student groups (either professional or social).

12. The rights of smokers and nonsmokers in a local organization.

13. The need for curriculum change in an area of study with which you are familiar.

14. Word processing software for microcomputers.

15. The value of in-house education and training programs.

16. The advantages and disadvantages of using an electronic mail system for internal correspondence.

17. Available building sites in your area (recommend the one most suitable for a specific kind of business).

18. Road conditions and priorities for major resurfacing in your area.

19. Classroom use at your college or university (which classrooms are occupied at what times, and which classrooms are available for what kind of use at what times).

20. Employee (or student) integrity (who will cheat under what circumstances and what kinds of controls might be necessary to prevent dishonesty).

Before you begin work, submit a proposal to your instructor for approval. Remember to write a report, not a term paper. Help someone make a decision about the topic of your choice. Your report may be informational, interpretive, or analytical, whichever your instructor requests, but the information presented, the interpretation, and any conclusions and recommendations should all be designed to contribute to a managerial or administrative decision.

CHAPTER FIFTEEN
Oral Presentations

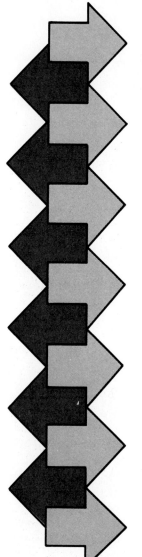

Oral presentations are common in business, and they often play an extremely important role in the success of an organization. Few individuals in business escape the need to make an oral presentation at least once in a while, so it is a skill every business person should have. Indeed, a willingness to make oral presentations and expertise at them can make a big difference in an individual's career. This chapter focuses on the aspects of communication involved in this endeavor.

Topics

COMMUNICATION CHALLENGE

Select a two- or three-column article from a weekly news magazine. Read it to yourself two or three times, and then read it aloud on a tape recording. Listen to the tape recording and see what you noticed about your delivery. List your strengths, weaknesses, and questions now. As you read the chapter, add to or change your lists as necessary.

If time and equipment permit, record your reading on a video recorder. Also, try having a friend evaluate the tape with you — does he or she agree with you on the pronunciation of all words?

Oral presentations are much like written reports. They can be short or long, informal or formal. They are prepared and delivered under a wide variety of circumstances. Except for very informal oral reports, most oral presentations are based on written information to which the presenter may refer. Even so, oral communication skills play an important role in the success of an oral presentation.

▷ OVERVIEW: MAKE A GOOD IMPRESSION

Our ability or inability to use language well is something we cannot hide. This is especially true in oral communication. In written communication we can go over our message word by word, and perhaps have others go over it as well, to weed out mistakes before delivering it, and our audience may never know how many mistakes our original version contained. In an oral presentation, however, our command of the language is immediately apparent. This may be one reason that speaking before a group is a common fear.

Yet oral communication — including the dreaded public speech or presentation—is an important means of communicating in business. It allows for immediate feedback and for the kind of give-and-take that often brings better understanding among individuals.

The term *oral communication* covers a broad range of activity, from essentially private conversations between two friends to platform speeches delivered to an audience of thousands. It includes interviews, group discussions, debates, and sales presentations. In each case the oral communication is influenced by the setting and circumstances, the purpose, and the audience.

The setting and the circumstances convey nonverbal messages to both the sender and the audience that will either help or hinder the communication. The purpose and the audience determine the degree of formality required and the appropriateness of certain techniques. This chapter will show you how to evaluate these factors to deliver a wide variety of effective oral messages.

COMMUNICATION TODAY...

The 14 Worst Human Fears

1. Speaking before a group
2. Heights
3. Insects and bugs
3. Financial problems
3. Deep water
6. Sickness
6. Death

8. Flying
9. Loneliness
10. Dogs
11. Driving/riding in a car
12. Darkness
12. Elevators
14. Escalators

Source: David Wallechinsky et al., *The Book of Lists* (New York: Bantam Books, 1977), pp. 469–470.

▷ IMPORTANCE OF ORAL COMMUNICATION

What is the relationship between written and oral communication?

Oral communication is both much older and much more common than written communication. Long before writing was developed, primitive civilizations had highly refined oral communication skills. In fact, the widespread use of writing is a fairly recent occurrence in the history of civilization. Before use of the printing press became common in the sixteenth century, written communication required laborious transcribing with quill pens on parchment. For the few who could read and write, letters took a lot of time. Although churches, courts, and a few businesses had scribes whose duty was to record important transactions, almost all business was conducted orally.

What are the differences between oral communication and listening to radio or watching television?

As long as oral communication was the primary means of sending and receiving information, people were very careful to develop their speaking and listening skills. At the turn of the twentieth century, for example, the oral communication skills of the educated were excellent. Because people still relied primarily on oral communication to convey complex messages, conversation was a well-developed art. Reading aloud, dinner time discussions, and conversations about current events, politics, and religion occupied people's attention in the same way television and radio do today. Activities involving oral communication, of course, differ greatly from passive enjoyment of radio and television, since oral communication is an active, two-way process.

Today we are not likely to be so careful about our oral communication as our turn-of-the-century relatives were, even though most communication is still oral. We spend much more time speaking and listening than we do writing and reading. It is true that in modern businesses writing and reading are generally preferred to speaking and listening for more important, more complex messages. But this, too, is a recent phenomenon.

How did the typewriter influence the use of oral communication in business?

The invention of the typewriter is primarily responsible for the reliance of modern business on written communication. At the turn of the century, oral agreements constituted the only contracts in a wide variety of business situations because written contracts were too much trouble to produce unless warranted by a complex situation and large sums of money. But relying on oral communication presented problems.

People tend to hear what they want to hear, regardless of their intentions. And with the passage of time, people tend to change and interpret oral messages in light of their own desires. The necessity for easier-to-produce written records was the mother of the invention of the typewriter.

In what way might the human aspect of a business relationship prove more important than the legal aspect?

Before the typewriter, people probably paid closer attention to what others said and took more care with what they said themselves. Literal veracity was expected, assumed, and relied on. We still value that kind of oral honesty—we all admire someone "whose word is his or her bond." But the need for records in modern business, the increasing ease with which records can be made and stored, and the fact that no two people ever remember the same conversation the same way have combined to decrease the importance of oral communication. Also, in a reaction against the way business had been conducted in the past, twentieth-century business became overprotective. Until the past few years, business has tended to emphasize the legal aspect of any relationship, especially as embodied in written agreements. Only very recently has the human aspect of relationships begun to receive its due attention again. The business world is beginning to realize that the human aspect may sometimes prove even more important than the legal aspect. Does it matter what two people *said* about something once the contract has been written and signed? You bet it does.

Is it important to be able to articulate ideas about complex subjects orally, even though we know that most people will better grasp our message when we put it in writing? You bet it is.

The written contract may be the legal instrument that finally determines who performs what action for what compensation, but the *quality* — and meaning—of the relationship between the people will be determined by what they say to each other and how they say it.

Skillfully handled, oral communication can provide a clearer insight into the meaning of a message because message transmission and feedback are immediate. In most oral situations, we need not quit until we understand and have been understood. The give-and-take of a discussion, for example, can achieve consensus much more readily — and quickly — than a written exchange of the same information.

▷ FACTORS INFLUENCING ORAL COMMUNICATION

Oral communication covers a broad spectrum of activity. The greeting given in passing and the formal platform speech are both oral communication activities, but they have as many differences as similarities. These differences are caused by the following factors:

1.   The setting and circumstances.

2.   The purpose of the communication.

3.   The size and attitudes of the audience.

4.   The techniques used in delivering the message.

5.   The observation and analysis of feedback.

Setting and Circumstances

How do the setting and the circumstances influence the physical and psychological environment of oral communication?

The setting and circumstances that make up the physical and psychological environment — excluding the audience's attitudes toward the speaker and the subject, which we shall discuss separately — are nonverbal aspects of the communication situation to which the oral communicator should pay particular attention. Setting and circumstances cannot usually be changed; they are "givens" to which the communicator must adjust.

Setting.   The nonverbal message of the setting influences both the sender and the audience, even though they may be doing their best to concentrate on the oral message. When you can select a warm, soft, environment conducive to effective oral communication — whether it is an informal interview or a formal presentation — you should consider yourself lucky. Most of the time the environment will be selected for you, and the setting frequently will work against you rather than for you.

What might make one room "warm" and another "cold" from a psychological standpoint?

If the room is not conducive to effective communication because it is cold, hard, noisy, or excessively large for the number of people present, a skilled communicator attempts to compensate for the setting's shortcomings by

1.   Keeping the message as short as possible.

2.   Deliberately drawing attention to the sources of difficulty and asking the audience to help overcome the barriers.

3.   Emphasizing the most important points of the message by using repetition, nonverbal cues, and strict organization.

4.   Watching carefully for nonverbal feedback.

5.   Soliciting and listening carefully to verbal feedback.

Circumstances.   Some people and events are "a hard act to follow," and sometimes even the best of communicators must yield to circumstances.

> You are supposed to address the convention at the same time that the social hour is scheduled to begin.

> Just as you are about to ask your boss for a raise, her husband calls and tells her that he has driven their new Lincoln Continental through the garage and greenhouse and into the swimming pool.

For effective communication, you need to be aware of the circumstances that establish the psychological atmosphere of your setting. It is important to recognize that circumstances influence, though do not solely determine, your audience's attitude toward you or your subject. The circumstances of a funeral are not the best for a humorous anecdote. You may have a well-planned speech to give on the importance of life insurance, but who would listen during a tornado?

What would make one circumstance "informal" and another "formal"?

Circumstances can vary so greatly that it is impossible to catalog them completely. In general, however, circumstances are either formal or informal; and your message as you have planned it will be appropriate, appropriate with modifications, or inappropriate for the circumstances. Only after you have considered the circumstances should you decide to forge ahead as planned, modify your message to suit the current mood, or postpone your message until the circumstances are more favorable.

The Message: Purpose and Structure

Why should an oral communicator be concerned with the purpose of the message?

In situations calling for written communication, it is easy to overlook the fact that if we fail to answer a letter we are sending a very definite message. In face-to-face communication, however, failure to respond to an oral greeting is an even stronger message; it is an immediate, direct insult. Because most oral messages contain many more emotional components than written messages, oral communicators should be just as careful to identify the main purpose of any oral communication as they would be with a written message. But obviously, many oral situations leave you little time to think about the purpose and presentation of your message: you will be asked a question and you will have to answer, or you will be asked to "say a few words" when you did not expect to be called on.

Fortunately, the less formal the situation is, the less critical your audience will be of your message presentation. In informal situations you will receive more and better feedback, and you will have greater opportunity to clarify your message. On the other hand, as a rule, the more formal a situation is, the more opportunity you will have to prepare. You make appointments for important interviews, for example; and you know in advance if you are to deliver a platform speech.

Regardless of the formality of the situation, the logical organization of thoughts is just as important to effective oral communication as it is to written communication. And effective organization of oral messages depends on the purpose of the message: to inquire, to inform, to persuade, or to entertain.

When Your Purpose Is to Inquire.   Inquiries range from extremely informal ("How's the wife, Joe?") to extremely formal (employment interviews). We have learned how to handle most informal inquiries during the process of growing up. In general, however, we would obtain better results from our formal inquiries if we would remember that the quality of the answers received depends directly on what is asked and how well it is asked. Following are some guidelines to better inquiries.

Ask Questions Rather Than Make Statements.   It seems obvious that the way to obtain information is to ask for it. But because all of us are self-centered, we tend to find our own observations and opinions more interesting than those of others; and unless we are careful, we end up giving more information than we receive.

Ask Only Those Questions Necessary to Obtain the Information.   Most people do not like to answer a long string of questions. Although one of the main advantages of oral communication is that you can ask for clarification when you do not understand something, even your best friends will not appreciate "the third degree." When you must ask several questions, break them up by explaining why you need the information and what you will do with it and by giving positive feedback for useful answers and cooperation.

Avoid Questions That Trap Your Audience.   Remember that you want to obtain information rather than make your audience defensive. Stick to questions the audience can answer without self-incrimination. Do not force your audience to justify a particular behavior. For example, rather than asking, "Why didn't you tell me you received a D in your business communication course?" you should ask, "How do you feel about your communication skills?" or, "What have you done to improve your communication skills since you took business communication?"

Ask Easy Questions First.   When you have several questions to ask, ask the easy ones first. You would also be wise to keep related questions together and to save personal questions until you have established rapport with your audience. Simple questions — those that are clear without any explanation and that elicit short answers — should precede difficult questions (frequently involving *how* or *why*) which require extended answers. Give your audience a chance to warm up.

When an inquiry is lengthy, it is usually impossible to plan or suggest a specific structure in advance. Answers may suggest questions not included in the original structure. Therefore, in addition to the foregoing suggestions, the two main keys to successful inquiries are as follows:

Remain flexible.

Practice the techniques of effective listening.

Margin notes:

What factors influence the quality of information received when the communicator's purpose is to inquire?

What is wrong with asking "why didn't you" questions?

When Your Purpose Is to Inform.   Most of us know how to convey simple information in most informal situations. We run into trouble only when the information is fairly complex or when the situation is quite formal. It's easy to see why this is so.

What is narration, and under what circumstances is it an effective oral communication strategy?

Most informal messages use the technique of *narration*—storytelling—along with chronological and descriptive patterns of organization that represent the way most people tend to observe and remember things. Each of these patterns presents particular problems, however, when the message becomes complex or formal.

Guidelines for improving our use of the chronological pattern are

1.   **Include the Audience.**   The story is based on our own observations and interests rather than on the audience's, so make a special effort to include the audience's interests and to emphasize those points of greatest interest to the audience.

2.   **Make Transitions Explicit.**   Unless we make transitions and time references absolutely clear, the chronology will not be clear to our audience. Use transitional words and phrases (*next, while, two weeks later*) so your audience will be able to follow your story.

3.   **Make a Point.**   The story needs an identifiable point or message if it is to have meaning for the audience.

Guidelines for improving our use of the descriptive pattern are

1.   **Be specific.**   Whether you are conveying technical information, attitudes, feelings, or sensory experiences, select words that will convey your meaning precisely. You can describe a daffodil, for example, either technically—"a narcissus that has long, narrow leaves and yellow flowers with a trumpetlike corona"—or, as Wordsworth did, experientially:

A host, of golden daffodils;
Beside the lake, beneath the trees,
Fluttering and dancing in the breeze.

Both descriptions are good; both are useful, but they have different uses. What makes each one good and useful in its context is its specificity for a particular audience. A poor description is one that lacks specificity. "Turn left at the third stop light" is better for *any* audience than "Go down here a ways and turn left."

How can an analogy help explain something?

2.   **Use analogies.**   When you are describing something that's unfamiliar to your audience, begin by relating it to something familiar. An analogy is especially useful when you need to explain a technical subject to a nontechnical person. Remember, though, that analogies merely illustrate; they do not prove.

As the formality of the communication situation increases, the organizational structure of the message must also become more formal; and as it does so, its organizational pattern increasingly resembles that used for written messages.

When your audience is likely to accept your information, you should use some form of direct presentation, stating your main point (which may be a conclusion or recommendation) first and the supporting details second. When your audience is likely to object to your information, use some form of indirect presentation, saving your conclusions and recommendations until after you have presented supporting material.

When Your Purpose Is to Persuade.   When the main purpose of your oral message is to persuade, use the same basic pattern you would use in writing a persuasive message. The main difference between delivering a persuasive speech and writing a persuasive letter is that when you deliver your message orally, your degree of personal involvement and conviction are more obvious to your audience. It is easier to fake conviction when you write than when you speak.

How does persuading in person differ from persuading by mail?

You must keep in mind that persuading a group is in many ways very different from persuading one person, because in any group the members are under internal and external pressures to conform. Zealots sometimes "plant" people in their audiences who will act when the appropriate time comes to help others in the audience overcome their reluctance to act. Keeping in mind that the setting and circumstances are also important variables, consider the size of the group in planning an oral presentation. The larger the group (1) the more formal you will have to be, (2) the more important it is that you assume a leadership role before attempting to persuade, and (3) the greater your chances of encountering resistance to your message.

In any situation, you should end your persuasive message by asking for the most decisive action you can expect. If you cannot achieve full commitment in one message, strive for partial commitment, which frequently leads to full commitment with additional messages.

Why would a business communicator ever be concerned with speaking to entertain?

When Your Purpose Is to Entertain.   Speaking for the sole purpose of entertaining is not usually appropriate in business. But whether your purpose is to inquire, inform, or persuade, a little "comic relief" almost always makes oral communication more enjoyable and therefore more effective. Stories and jokes can help make the listener's job easier. Humor is tricky, however. Not everyone can tell the same joke with the same success. And some people feel foolish telling stories. You will have to discover for yourself what works best for you, but we can give you a few hints to get you started.

1.   **Stories and jokes can be effective icebreakers.** When you begin your presentation with a story or joke, both you and your audience have a

chance to relax and become comfortable with each other before the more difficult message begins. But unless you are comfortable with jokes and stories, do not attempt them. Break the ice in some other way.

2. **Make sure that your material is current.** An old joke is worse than no joke at all. It does not help to ask your audience to stop you if they have heard it before. Even if they have heard it, they will not stop you—they will let you make a fool of yourself.

3. **Make sure that your entertainment material is kept separate from your main message.** Emphasize the points of your message; use the entertainment material only as filler. The point of your joke or story, however, should relate to the topic of your presentation so that you can make clear transitions.

4. **Keep the material in good taste.** Avoid ethnic and sexist jokes and stories. What your audience will appreciate will vary greatly from group to group. If there is any doubt in your mind about whether the audience is "ready" for a particular joke or story, do not use it.

SIDEBAR

Choosing Your Image

Our image depends to a certain extent on the labels others attach to us because of our occupation, income level, marital status, age, color, nationality, religious beliefs, and so on. We cannot control the preconceived image other people have of us based on those labels, but when we meet another person, we immediately project an additional impression — our visual image. We exercise a great deal of control over this image because it is determined by much more than the physical features we were born with. It is determined by the way we dress, move, groom ourselves and style our hair, by our weight, our physical condition, our posture and our facial expressions.

We think of the image-conscious person as the meticulous groomer, the person in designer clothes or wearing the latest fad. But whether or not we think of ourselves as image-conscious, with all the advertising hype that implies, we all make conscious choices about the way we present ourselves to the world. "Not caring" what we wear, or choosing clothes for comfort rather than style, are also image-conscious choices. We are simply choosing a different image.

The choices we make about our visual image determine to a great extent how other people perceive us — until we open our mouths and speak. At that moment, many of us destroy our carefully constructed facades, because few of us are as completely in control of our spoken image as we are of our visual image. The minute we begin to speak, our spoken image becomes dominant and overrides our visual image and all our other images based on job, age, sex, color, class and nationality.

Source: Sandy Livner as told to Loral Dean, *Speak Easy*, pp. 17–18. Copyright © 1978 by Speakeasy, Inc. Reprinted by permission of Summit Books, a division of Simon & Schuster, Inc.

The Audience

Why is analyzing an audience for an oral presentation easier than analyzing an audience for a written communication?

The audience is an important variable in any communication situation; but as a rule, analyzing an audience for an oral presentation is easier than analyzing an audience for a written communication. You and your audience are in the same place at the same time, frequently for a specific purpose. You have at least that one interest in common. You also usually have some information about your audience's other interests as well as their ages, sex, educational level, and perhaps occupations. Based on analysis of this information, you should be able to make some predictions about how the audience will receive you and your message.

The attributes of your audience that will have the greatest influence on the presentation of your oral message are size, attitude toward you and your subject, and previous knowledge about the subject.

How does the size of an audience influence an oral communication situation?

Audience Size.   The size of the audience is an important influence on any oral communication. People behave differently in group situations than in one-to-one relationships. In general, the larger the group, the more difficult it will be for you to get your message across. In fact, just gaining the attention of a large group can prove difficult. Three qualities of large audiences that cause problems for the oral communicator are

1.   The members of a large group are less cohesive — willing to stick together — than members of a smaller group.

2.   The members of a large group are likely to have less in common with one another than members of a smaller group.

3.   The members of a large group have a greater variation in attitudes, knowledge about the subject, and educational level than members of a smaller group.

For the communicator, the preceding qualities mean that every increase in the size of the audience, presents an increased possibility of failure to communicate with some of the audience. You cannot please all the people all the time. You should, however, try to maximize your effectiveness by

1.   Making sure that your entire audience can hear you.

2.   Adapting your message so it will have meaning for everyone in your audience. Explain technical terms for nontechnical audience members.

3.   Avoiding jokes and references that only a few in your audience will appreciate.

How does the attitude of an audience influence an oral communication situation?

Audience Attitude.   The attitude of the audience toward you and your subject can vary in several ways. The audience may

Like you and like your subject.

Like you but dislike your subject.

Dislike you but like your subject.

Dislike both you and your subject.

Like or dislike you and be neutral about your subject.

Be neutral about you and like or dislike your subject.

Be neutral about you and your subject.

A previous experience of one sort or another is the usual explanation for audience attitudes other than neutrality. If the audience has a positive attitude toward either you or your subject, you are off to a good start. If your audience dislikes you or your subject, try to discover the source of the negative attitude. Have you made an unpopular decision? Is your audience known to oppose the subject you are advocating?

When you know beforehand that your audience has a negative attitude, you must make a special effort to be positive at the beginning of the message. If you have discovered the reason for the negative attitude, can you deal with it directly and eliminate it as an influence? Or can you overcome the negative attitude by focusing on the future rather than the past?

When you cannot discover the reason for the negative attitude, or when you do not discover it until you have already begun delivering your message . . . keep smiling anyway. Someone in your audience may like your smile, and that's a start.

Audience Knowledge.   What does your audience know about your subject? What is the educational level of your audience? The answers to these questions determine how a message, oral or written, should be adapted to fit an audience. Adapting an oral message to your audience requires all the techniques for adapting written messages and more. When a written message is complex and introduces new ideas, the audience has the opportunity to read slowly, reread, underline, and use the dictionary. A speaker's audience, on the other hand, must struggle to grasp the message as it is delivered. Make it easy for your audience by following these guidelines:

What are the similarities and differences between adaptation for oral messages and adaptation for written messages?

1.   Use a vocabulary that all will understand.

2.   Explain technical terms.

3.   Use an organizational pattern appropriate for your purpose.

4.   Make your organizational plan obvious.

5.   Repeat and emphasize key points.

Oral Communication Techniques

In the foregoing sections of this chapter, we have presented the chief variables you will encounter in oral communication situations and discussed some of the ways you can respond to those variables. But whatever situation you find yourself in, the techniques you need to be an effective oral communicator remain the same. Regardless of the situation, you must (1) plan, (2) establish credibility, (3) deliver the message, and (4) obtain feedback.

Plan.　　　In planning an oral communication, observe the following principles:

In oral communication, what is planning?

1. **Think before speaking.**　　At its simplest level, planning means thinking before you speak. And at one time or another, we have all suffered the consequences of speaking first and thinking later. In face-to-face communication, that is a good way to lose a friend or make an enemy. In business groups, it is a good way to get fired. Not being careful enough about what we say may earn us the nickname "blabbermouth." On the other hand, being too careful robs us of spontaneity and earns us a reputation for "never saying what we think." The question is, how do we keep the mouth hinged to the brain? Unfortunately, there is no easy answer. Many mistakes can be avoided, however, by pausing to think before speaking.

2. **Be positive.**　　In general, avoid saying anything negative about a person, place, idea, or thing. Ask yourself what purpose you will serve by making a negative statement — weigh the advantages against the disadvantages — and if the negative statement is necessary, word it as positively as possible and include a positive statement with it if possible.

Under what circumstances should you audibly rehearse what you wish to say?

3. **Rehearse.**　　How much planning you must do before you speak depends on the complexity of the subject and the formality of the situation. Complex subjects require more planning than simple ones, and formal situations give you less margin for error than informal situations. In an interpersonal situation, for example, you may need to practice what you wish to say when the situation is important by engaging in *role playing* (see Chapter 18). Some complex situations may require months of research, preparation, and rehearsing. Rehearsing is tricky business, since you should rehearse enough to be familiar and comfortable with your message, but not so much that your delivery is stiff and tired.

　　Planning also includes preparing whatever notes you will need. Effective oral communication precludes the reading of a manuscript or the memorization of a speech. Well-prepared notes let you bring the results of your preparation with you but do not interfere with your natural relationship with the audience. See the section on "Notes" later in this chapter.

4. **Be clear, truthful, and interesting.**　　As you plan, do not expect to make your message perfect. You cannot prepare for every contingency; you cannot know everything about your subject, the circumstances, or the audience. But you owe it to your audience to present what you do know about your subject in a clear, truthful, and interesting way.

What is credibility, and how is it established?

Establish Credibility.   Your credibility as a message source has an important influence on the reception an audience gives your message. You can establish *long-term credibility* only by becoming a recognized expert in a given area. Once you have established yourself as an authority, you carry this credibility with you into new situations calling for your expertise. Long-term credibility in one area has a *halo effect*, increasing credibility in other areas as well. An audience assumes that if you have always been truthful and knowledgeable in one area, you will probably be truthful and knowledgeable in other areas as well. For example, movie stars who have established credibility with audiences sometimes find it easy to become politicians because of this halo effect.

Even if you possess long-term credibility, you will need to establish *short-term credibility* with your audience each time you speak. You do this by making clear distinctions among facts, inferences, and value judgments and by telling your audience how you know what the facts are. For more information about credibility, see Chapters 1 and 9.

How might the way a message is delivered influence the way it is received?

Deliver the Message Effectively.   In addition to the structure and content of your message, the way you deliver it will also have an influence on its reception. Whatever the size of your audience, the skills you need to make an effective delivery are essentially the same as the conversational skills you have been using all your life. Anything that makes your communication effective on a one-to-one basis will also make it effective with larger groups. Unfortunately, the larger the audience is, the easier it is to forget those basic conversational skills. For some reason, most of us find large audiences at least a little intimidating. To counteract this intimidating effect, follow these guidelines:

1.   **Relax.**   Remind yourself that even if your audience has a negative attitude toward you or your subject, your message is worth your time to deliver it and worth your audience's time to hear it. Use natural gestures and movements, but avoid pacing, fiddling with your hair, snapping your fingers, and other nervous mannerisms that might detract from the content of your message.

2.   **Involve everyone.**   Whatever the size of the group, look around the room, and take the time to establish eye contact with as many people as possible. Smile. Talk to individuals, not to the group as a whole. Make people move—have them applaud someone, ask them questions, ask them to raise their hands, have them stand, or have them shake hands with each other. Ask for a volunteer to take part in a demonstration. After the demonstration, have the audience applaud that person.

3.   **Be positive.**   If you are interested in your message, your audience will perceive this interest and will find you interesting. Your voice should

Under what circumstances should you use a sound system?

indicate your interest. Project. No one likes to listen to a mumbler. You should be heard clearly and distinctly by everyone in your audience, but do not shout. If your natural voice, well projected, cannot be heard by the entire audience, use a sound system. Your appearance should also show your interest in your message and the audience. Dress that is inappropriate for the occasion will detract from the content of your message. Let your audience know that you like and respect them and appreciate the opportunity to speak to them. Always begin with something positive. Save any limitations or negative material until after you are off to a good start.

4. **Stick to your subject.** Jokes, stories, and other material inserted for entertainment purposes must be related to your message closely enough that the audience can see the connection. After all, your message is the reason you are speaking. The entertainment material is useful only if it helps you convey your message. Do not let it compete with your message.

Observation and Analysis of Feedback

What is feedback? How do you obtain it, and to what use should you put it once you have it?

You need to obtain feedback for two distinct reasons. First, you need feedback to make sure that your audience is hearing and understanding your message. Second, you need feedback to help you do a better job on the next oral message.

To obtain feedback for the first objective of making sure that your audience is hearing and understanding your message:

1. **Use eye contact.** If the entire back row has fallen asleep, you are probably not speaking loud enough. If people can hear you, their attention should be focused on you. Only by maintaining eye contact with your audience can you know how they are reacting to your message.

2. **Invite questions.** Let your audience know in advance when you want to receive questions: at the end of the entire message, at the end of each logical division in the message, or as you go along. Some speakers think that in formal situations questions should wait until the end of the message or at least until the end of logical units. We think, however, that an audience should be able to ask questions whenever they arise, because the clarity of the message is more important than the formality of the situation.

To obtain feedback for the second objective of doing a better job next time:

1. **Analyze questions.** Your audience's questions in response to an informal message will let you know where you need to improve.

2.   **Invite evaluation.**   In formal situations, you should arrange in advance for your boss to keep track of how you are doing, or prepare an evaluation sheet for your audience to complete.

Remember that feedback does you no good unless you act on what you have learned. Paying attention to feedback — listening — is part of your responsibility as a communicator.

▷ The Nature of Formal Presentations

How do formal presentations differ from other kinds of oral communication?

Formal presentations differ from other kinds of oral communication primarily because one person — the source — speaks for an extended time without receiving much oral feedback. In most other oral communication situations the participants exchange a series of short messages until they reach an agreement of one sort or another. In a formal presentation the source is expected to deliver a fully planned, well-organized, extended message on a topic usually announced in advance to the audience. Restricted oral feedback is a criterion of a formal presentation. Sometimes the medium used for the presentation — such as television — may make feedback virtually impossible. Other formal presentations may permit questions and answers during the presentation itself; even in these cases, however, feedback is restricted to help ensure the orderly presentation of ideas.

Degree of Formality

Planned presentation and restricted feedback are among the characteristics that make formal presentations formal. Contributing to the formality are the serious intent of both sender and receivers (remember that our concern is with communication for practical purposes rather than for entertainment), the distance maintained between the sender and the audience, and the fact that a specific time and place have been selected for the presentation.

What are the most common business functions of formal presentations?

The degree of formality can vary greatly, however. The most formal kind of presentation, the reading of a paper, is rarely used in business. Academic scholars attending professional meetings read papers because the material is far too complex for the reader to risk deviating from the prepared text. In addition, to help ensure the accurate transfer of a complex message, the audience is often given copies of the entire text before the presentation. In business, however, the following kinds of presentations, listed in order of decreasing formality, are most common.

1.   **Public speech or lecture.**   Public presentations are prepared completely in advance and delivered with the aid of notes. Verbal feedback is restricted to the end of the presentation, if any is permitted at all.

2. **Sales presentation.**   Sales presentations may be invited or uninvited, depending on whether the speaker has been specially asked to describe the product or service. In either case the speaker must prepare a wide variety of material in advance and select appropriate material for the situation as the presentation progresses. After the essential message is delivered, questions are encouraged.

3. **Education and training presentation.**   Education and training presentations combine characteristics of the lecture and the discussion. The speaker must be fully prepared both to deliver a specific message and to deal with a wide range of questions about related subject matter. Verbal feedback is encouraged during and after the presentation and sometimes even before it.

4. **Discussion sessions.**   Because they permit the most interaction between the speaker (or speakers) and the audience, discussion sessions are the least formal of formal presentations. Even for these presentations, time, place, and topic are determined in advance, however; and the speakers must prepare an organized message.

5. **Informal oral reports.**   A common occurrence in business is for managers to ask members of their staffs about their progress with a particular problem. These questions can be either a "See me in my office" or a "How are you doing with . . . ?" Reports of this nature allow little time for preparation and are usually informal. The sender and the audience typically explore the problem together, and the audience may contribute as much to the discussion as the person who was asked to make the report. Staff meetings usually require informal progress reports on projects.

From your own experience with presentations of each of these types, you can probably verify that as the degree of formality decreases, the responsibility of the speaker decreases and the responsibility of the audience increases.

Presentation Objective

In formal presentations the sender of the message is either trying to *inform* the audience or to *persuade* the audience to change an attitude, belief, or behavior. The organization of the message reflects its objective in ways already discussed for written messages; but because the message is delivered orally, the sender must take unusual care to help the audience receive and understand the message. Preparation is the key to success in attaining the objective of an oral presentation.

◁ PREPARATION

No one can give an effective oral presentation, whatever the degree of formality, without extensive preparation. The speaker must know the subject, analyze the audience, and have notes and nerves ready for the delivery.

The Subject

What kinds of preparation help ensure the success of an oral presentation?

You cannot give an effective presentation if you do not know what you are talking about. Yet for some reason, many speakers attempt to lecture an audience without doing the research necessary to guarantee current, accurate information. An informational presentation is the oral equivalent of a written report. Your information should be — *must* be — accurate, reliable, and objective. And you must have enough of it to continue presenting specific information throughout the time you have been allotted. Just like informational presentations, sales and other persuasive presentations also require complete, accurate knowledge about the product, service, or concept involved.

The Audience

The audience for a formal presentation is invariably a select group. Formal presentations are always announced in advance, so the audience arrives with certain expectations. These expectations depend primarily on whether attendance is required and on the nature of the subject. The degree of interest the audience has in the subject may vary from intense, enthusiastic interest to complete apathy. The audience may know a great deal — or nothing at all — about the topic. The audience may have strong current beliefs about the topic, or it may have a neutral attitude.

Because these factors determine what a speaker must do to communicate effectively with an audience, the speaker should do everything possible to discover the audience's expectations, degree of interest, knowledge, and current beliefs about the topic. Although the presentation must usually go on even if the audience is openly hostile, with opinions diametrically opposed to those of the speaker, a speaker should know what reception to expect from the audience and be prepared to take advantage of it — or deal with it.

The Speaker's Nerves

What is stage fright, and what can you do about it?

One of the greatest difficulties about making a formal presentation is dealing with your own nerves. Getting up in front of an audience the first few times is unpleasant for some, difficult for most, and nearly impossible for a few others. Stage fright can be very real. If you had a dollar for every word that has been written about the causes and cures of stage fright, you could retire right now. Yet with everything that has been written, the only two guaranteed cures for stage fright are preparation and practice.

Preparation: Know your material and what you intend to do with it forwards and backwards, inside and out. But, except for short sales presentations, do not attempt to memorize an entire speech. Even if your memory works perfectly, your presentation will be stilted and awkward. And you also risk having your memory fail. When that happens, you are left with nothing to say and nowhere to go. Prepare good notes; they are safer than memorizing a complete speech.

Practice: The first presentation is the hardest; each subsequent time will get a bit easier. But regardless of how many presentations you give, you will always have to practice. For your first presentation, practice is especially important. Try practicing your speech in front of a mirror. Pronouncing the words clearly will help you develop a smooth delivery. When you are out walking, read your notes aloud. Throughout the day and before going to bed at night, picture yourself in front of your audience.

Use your imagination to picture yourself as a successful speaker, and you will be the successful speaker you want to be. Some speakers actually set up rows of chairs and practice delivering their speeches to an imaginary audience. Such a practice helps them develop a feeling for standing in front of a real audience and helps them develop the kind of natural body movements that can greatly contribute to an effective presentation.

In addition to these guaranteed cures, here are a few points that may help you deal with stage fright while you are preparing and practicing:

1. You were asked to make your presentation because you know something about the subject that the audience does not. Focus on that aspect of the subject; give the audience something that will benefit them.

2. Your subject and your audience are more important than you are. Think about your audience and your subject rather than about yourself.

3. No presentation is perfect. You are bound to make a mistake or two—everyone does. Keep going forward rather than looking back.

4. You cannot please all the people all the time. No matter how well (or poorly) you actually perform, somebody in the audience will think you are wonderful, and somebody will think you are awful. Do not let the one who thinks you are wonderful blind you to your mistakes or let the one who thinks you are awful undermine your confidence.

What factors should be checked the day of the presentation?

When the day of your presentation arrives, check the place for your presentation early so that you can make any required changes. In particular, check the following items:

1. **The sound system.**   Does it work? Is the microphone a lavaliere or handheld one so that you can walk around with it? Or is the microphone stationary so that you will need to stand in one place?

2. **The lighting.**   Will you have enough light to follow your outline or read your notes?

3. **The room arrangement.**   Are the chairs for the audience arranged appropriately for your presentation? Will people in the back of the room be able to see and hear you?

4. **Audiovisual equipment.**   Will you need an overhead, slide, or movie projector, a tape recorder, a video recorder and monitor, or other equipment for visual aids? Is the equipment there, and does it work properly? If you are using an overhead projector, check to see whether a spare is available.

Why should you avoid apologizing for being nervous?

If you are still nervous once you start, do not apologize for it or make any comment that suggests that you are inexperienced or poorly prepared. Concentrate on your message and your audience. If your throat gets dry, drink water rather than coffee or carbonated drinks, which may make the throat feel even drier. A pause now and then is perfectly acceptable, and you may wish to practice pausing after your key points.

How can movement help a speaker be more effective?

Remember to move naturally. Even if you are stuck behind a lecturn with a stationary microphone, you can use gestures for emphasis and step back from the microphone for a pause. Movement helps hold the attention of the audience and may help you relax as well.

The Speaker's Voice

A good speaking voice can be cultivated. Use a tape recorder and listen to yourself. Tape your presentation as you plan to give it. Check for the following:

1. **Enunciation.**   Are you pronouncing all words clearly and distinctly? Check words you are unsure of in the dictionary. Be especially careful with words ending in -ing — doing sounds more professional than doin'.

2. **Modulation.**   Your voice should rise and fall naturally — increasing in volume to emphasize important points and decreasing from time to time to provide variety.

3. **Paralanguage.**   Paralanguage consists of all vocalized sounds that are not words, such as laughter, throat-clearing, umm, and other fillers. Avoid all paralanguage that does not contribute to your purpose. The

random use of *okay* and *you know* would also be considered unessential paralanguage.

4.　　**Projection.**　　Does you voice carry well enough for you to be heard at the back of the room? If not, use a microphone. It is better to use a mike than to strain your voice.

The Speaker's Notes

Why should a presenter use notes? What kind of notes are most effective? Least effective?

Of the kinds of formal presentations mentioned, only the sales presentation does not require the use of notes. To be effective, a sales representative must know her or his material cold. The speaker may, of course, refer to notes for specific details, but the audience will expect the speaker to know about the product or service and about its competition. Formal presentations of the other types require some kind of notes so that the speaker can bring the results of planning to the presentation.

Previously we said that at its simplest level, planning means thinking before you speak. Formal presentations, however, require a *written* record of the research and the thinking you do in advance because without notes or memorization, you will not be able to remember everything.

People who do a lot of public speaking develop their own personal techniques for taking and using notes; as you gain experience, you will undoubtedly develop your own technique. We suggest that you begin developing a comfortable style based on one of the two most widely used formats: 3″ × 5″ cards or 8½″ × 11″ sheets of paper.

Many speakers prefer to keep their notes on 3″ × 5″ cards, which can be held easily and unobtrusively in the palm of the hand, and which leaves them free to move about in a natural manner while talking. The disadvantage of cards is that each one holds only a small amount of information, so a complex subject may require a large stack of cards.

Other speakers prefer to type their notes on regular 8½″ × 11″ sheets of paper. Because audiences expect some use of notes, the visibility of the sheets need not be distracting. One disadvantage of such typed notes is that inexperienced speakers tend to rely too heavily on them, *reading* rather than *presenting* the material. Because of this heavy reliance on notes, these speakers remain fixed behind a lectern, creating unnecessary distance between speaker and audience. Also, once a speaker begins reading, he or she tends to focus exclusively on the notes, and eye contact is lost, which creates even more distance.

If you choose to keep your notes on 8½″ × 11″ sheets of paper, emphasize the outline (with a red felt-tip marker, perhaps) rather than the specifics of the presentation. If you prepare well enough that you are not tempted to read, you can move about naturally, using notes to stay organized and to provide the specific details that will make your presentation interesting and convincing. Your notes should give structure to your talk but leave you flexible enough to change the details of your presentation to suit your particular audience.

▷ MESSAGE ORGANIZATION

Why does a speaker need to make listening "easy" for the audience?

Because we have already discussed general patterns of message organization, we will concentrate here on the few things you must do in a formal oral presentation that are not so vital in other forms of communication. When giving a formal presentation, remember that listening is difficult. Even when the members of your audience have good intentions, they will find it easier to think about last night's dinner or about Paris in the spring than to concentrate on your message. As a speaker, you must make listening as easy and as pleasant for your audience as possible. Message organization and clarity will help you most in holding the audience's attention, and to be effective, your pattern of organization must be clear from the beginning.

Opening

What are the most effective openings for a public speech or formal presentation?

We have said already that the beginning and the end of your message are the places of natural emphasis. The opening is especially critical in a formal presentation because the way you handle your opening will usually determine the audience's attitude toward you and your material. How might you begin?

1. **With a joke.**   If you are good with jokes *and* you have a joke that makes an appropriate point *and* you are certain that no one in your audience has heard it before, a joke can be an effective icebreaker. If you cannot satisfy all three of those criteria, avoid jokes. Jokes about introductions and about the subject or setting usually work the best. Because your audience wants to obtain ideas and useful information rather than be entertained, limit the number and length of the jokes.

2. **With a story.**   Human interest stories usually work better than jokes if they make an appropriate point and if that point is absolutely clear to the audience. Avoid telling your own life story, however.

3. **With background information.**   Merely introductory material is a waste of time. Explanations are generally not interesting, and background information is essentially explanation. If background information must be presented, interweave it with something of more interest to your audience.

4. **With a preview.**   Give the audience a quick look at the main points of your presentation.

5.   **With a benefit.**   Tell the members of your audience how they will benefit from your presentation. Explain what information they will get from it and how they can use the information.

6.   **With a goodwill statement.**   Express appreciation for being invited to speak and make reference to the importance of the occasion.

The first three items in this list work sometimes; the last three work all the time.

Body

What techniques can you employ to help an audience keep track of the main points in a presentation?

The body of a presentation consists of the facts, figures, and principles you wish to convey. Because your organizational pattern must be clear to your audience, use explicit transitions from one point to the next. Tell the audience how each part contributes to the whole, and how the whole is equal to the sum of the parts. From time to time refer to your purpose, showing how what you have already said and what you are about to say contribute to your overall purpose. Transitions that appear artificial in written messages are beneficial and desirable in oral presentations. You do not need to be subtle; be straightforward and say, "Now that we've seen how X influences Y, let's briefly consider how X influences Z."

Whenever you have resistance to overcome, or when you wish to persuade an audience to change opinions or actions, build your case slowly and carefully. If there are two sides to a subject, present both of them. Your audience will become aware of the other opinion sooner or later, and the fact that you neglected to mention the other side of the story will work against you.

Do not be afraid to repeat important points. An oral message is not the same as a written message in this regard. Because your audience cannot "look back" to see what you said before, you will need to repeat the important points to help them remember. Work your repetitions in naturally, however, so that the audience will not feel that you are talking down to them.

Closing

Why should your closing remarks be forceful?

Because it is a natural point of emphasis and because it is the last impression your audience will have of you, the closing of your presentation deserves special attention. End with a bang rather than a whimper, a flourish rather than a fade-out.

1.   **Do not quit before you are finished.**   Continue to speak clearly, distinctly, and forcefully throughout your entire message. Do not let your voice fade. Do not act tired; look alert.

2.   **Summarize.**   Review the main points for your audience. Emphasize the benefits of doing what you have suggested, or explain why knowing about your subject will be useful.

3.   **Invite questions.**   If the audience has questions, answer them. When you are finished with the questions, or if there are none, add a brief reminder of the main point as a definite conclusion.

4.   **Specify any action desired.**   If you want your audience to act, ask for that action. Explain exactly what you want your audience to do and how you want them to do it. Make the action sound easy. Attempt to get some kind of immediate commitment from them—signing a petition, leaving names and phone numbers, or making a public statement, for example.

5.   **Be positive and forward-looking.**   If you end your message on a negative note, your audience will associate you with that negative element rather than with positive elements that may have preceded it. No matter how gloomy your topic happens to be, find some hope for the future and focus on it as you conclude your presentation.

6.   **Conclude when you say you will.**   Your ending should be on time, definite, and emphatic: restate your main point, specify an action, and quit!

▷ SPECIAL TECHNIQUES

What are visual aids, and how can they help a speaker?

When an oral presentation must include complex information, physical communication aids are frequently needed to help the audience follow and digest the information presented. The best and most common visual aids are boards and charts, projectors, handouts, models, and audience participation. You should remember, however, that these special techniques are only aids; they cannot substitute for a thorough oral presentation of the material.

Prepare your complete presentation first, and then review it to see whether a special technique might clarify your material. Do you need to present a lot of statistics? Your audience will not remember a column of figures if you just read it. Do you need to clarify construction problems at an awkward building site? A visual supplement would be a great help in letting your audience "see" exactly what the problems are.

Boards and Charts

What are the advantages and disadvantages of a chalkboard?

Two common and convenient categories of visual aids are boards and charts.

Chalkboard.   The chalkboard is an old, familiar teaching device. It is such a standard communication aid that almost any place you might give an oral presentation will have a permanent or portable chalkboard available. The main advantage of the chalkboard is that it is inexpensive to use. It is a time-consuming device, however, because messages must continually be written and erased. If you have just one set of figures or concepts that will remain important throughout your presentation, you can prepare a chalkboard supplement in advance and refer to it at appropriate points in your presentation. When using the chalkboard, remember to do the following:

1. **Write legibly.**   Make sure that everyone in the room can read the board. Start at the left side of the board, and work toward the right.

2. **Keep the message simple.**   Too much information clutters the board and confuses the audience.

3. **Do not stand in the way.**   Make sure that the audience can see what you have written. Use a pointer to indicate appropriate parts of the message.

4. **Keep the board clean.**   Do not clutter the board with several separate messages; it should present a single, unified message.

5. **Erase the board when you are finished.**

The chalkboard is most useful for spontaneous illustration of particular points your audience has questions about. When you can prepare your aids in advance, other aids are usually superior to the chalkboard.

What are the advantages and disadvantages of a flip-chart?

Flip Chart.   Flip charts consist of a pad of paper (usually 28" × 34") mounted on an easel. Like the chalkboard, the flip chart is inexpensive and can be used spontaneously. The main advantage of a flip chart is that it requires no erasing. You simply flip the used page over; if you need it again, you can flip it right back. You can also use colors much more effectively on the flip chart than on the chalkboard, and they may be prepared in advance. In fact, for important presentations, they definitely should be prepared in advance by someone with a high degree of artistic skill. The main disadvantage of flip charts is that their small size makes them inappropriate for all but the smallest conference rooms.

What are the advantages and disadvantages of display boards?

Display Boards.   Felt or magnetic display boards are useful for displaying short messages that will remain constant throughout a presentation. They are most widely used for sales presentations to small audiences. Their main disadvantage is that they are not flexible. Display materials for these boards should be prepared in advance by someone with graphic skills so that full advantage can be taken of color, graphs, photographs, and other nonverbal aspects of communication.

Charts.   Charts can display almost anything that can be put on paper. Charts are still used for some presentations when graphs, sales figures, or other supplements must be included in a presentation. They may be almost any size and shape, and they are usually prepared in advance. In most companies, however, overhead projectors are replacing charts, display boards, and flip charts.

Projectors

Why is the overhead projector one of the most popular devices for graphic aids?

Overhead Projectors.   The overhead projector is an exceptionally useful device for presenting a wide variety of supplemental information. You can prepare transparencies in advance, or you can write on clear acetate during your presentation. You can emphasize important points by marking them with felt pens in a variety of colors. Such emphasis can be either permanent and prepared in advance, or it can be washable and added as you proceed. Because the overhead works well with only a small reduction in normal lighting, your audience will be able to see well enough to take notes. Transparencies for the overhead are relatively inexpensive, and almost anything that can be put on paper can be placed on transparencies in many different colors.

The disadvantages of the overhead projector are that it calls for an initial investment — so that its use must justify the expense — and that it is a mechanical device subject to breakdowns. Also, the overhead should be used in conjunction with a separate screen, which is an additional expense and one more item to worry about when setting up for your presentation. A light-colored wall will reflect an acceptable image when a screen is not available.

When you use an overhead projector, remember to do the following:

1.   **Organize your transparencies in advance.**   Keep them arranged so you will not have trouble finding the right one when its time comes.

2.   **Keep each transparency simple and easy to read.**   Make graphs and charts large, and use large type. For complex information, use more than one chart. Prepare transparencies for those sitting at the back of the room, not for those in the front. As a rule, do not read the transparency for the audience. Let them read it. Read only portions when you wish to focus on something specific.

3.   **Coordinate the transparencies with your presentation.**   You may use a plain piece of paper to block out information on a transparency until you need it, or you may *overlay* one transparency on another to add further information to a basic message. Graphs and charts, for example, can be presented section by section as your presentation progresses. Each section can even be in a different color.

4.   **Turn off the projector when you are not using it.**   Do not, however, develop the habit of turning the projector on and off for each transparency. Rapid switching on and off distracts the audience.

5.   **Use a pencil as a pointer** by placing it on the transparency.   Stay clear of the screen.

6.   **Keep a spare lamp available.**

What are the advantages and disadvantages of opaque projectors and slide projectors?

Opaque Projectors.   Opaque projectors do everything an overhead projector does, using plain white paper rather than transparencies. They do not do it as well, however. Also, they are expensive, cumbersome, noisy, and require a dark room. For most purposes, the overhead is a better choice.

Slide Projectors.   Slide projectors are useful primarily for showing photographs of people, events, and objects. When presenting information that includes photographs, you might consider photographing the material that would normally be presented on the overhead projector and using the slide projector for all of your supplemental material. The disadvantage of slide projectors is that the room must be darkened. The darkened room makes note-taking difficult and tends to separate the sender from the audience, making feedback difficult to send and receive.

Why should presenters avoid using movies and prerecorded videotapes?

Movies and Tapes.   Movie projectors and video tape recorders are substitutes for oral presentations rather than supplements to them. Use movies and videotapes only when you must present special material in an exceptionally authentic or authoritative way.

Handouts

How can handouts help a presenter? Under what circumstances can they hurt?

Handouts are written supplements that a speaker hands out to the audience —anything from a single page of material to copies of whole books or magazines. Handouts have a wide variety of uses, including the following:

1.   To provide details you don't have time to cover.

2.   To illustrate specific points of your presentation.

3.   To serve as worksheets for your audience.

4.   To outline the key points of your presentation and thus help your audience follow your argument more easily.

5.   To provide a summary of your presentation.

6.   To provide statistical data that support your generalizations.

7.   To present information that is too complex to present with other special techniques.

8.   To obtain the feedback you need to do a better job next time.

When you use handouts, remember that too much information frequently has the same effect as too little. If you distribute too many handouts, your audience will not separate the useful from the less important — it all will be thrown out together. When you are passing out several items of handout material, color-code them to help your audience keep track. Avoid the temptation to read handout material; the members of your audience can read it for themselves. Use handouts only as a supplement, an illustration, or a reminder of your presentation. Distribute handouts in advance only when the audience will need to use the materials as you make your presentation.

Models

A model is a symbolic representation. Some presentations require models to illustrate the real thing. In fact, some presentations may require the real thing (a new-car sales presentation, for example). The use of models in presentations is largely limited to special applications familiar to those who need them — primarily certain areas of advertising, sales, architecture, and engineering.

Audience Participation

Why should a presenter encourage audience participation?

Although it is not a mechanical device as the foregoing communication aids are, audience participation serves the same functions as the other special techniques: it keeps the attention of the audience focused on your presentation and helps ensure the successful transfer of meaning. Even when your situation is formal and feedback is severely restricted, you can keep your audience involved by continually giving them something "new" to think about.

1.   Use an overhead projector and handout material to break up the "sameness" of an oral presentation. A straight lecture may be hard on both speaker and audience.

2.   As the speaker, you should control the audience's attention. Change the pace of your presentation from time to time to permit your audience to relax for a minute. Make the members of your audience focus their attention when you most want it focused — but give them an opportunity to relax their attention from time to time, or they will be relaxing when you want and need their full attention.

3.   Ask real and rhetorical questions to force the audience to summarize the material you have just presented or anticipate the material you are about to present.

4.   Get the audience to *do* something: Stand up, raise their hands, applaud, move to a different seat, complete a quiz (about your topic), or almost anything that encourages physical activity. Physical movement actually reinforces memory and increases attention.

▷ FEEDBACK FOR THE NEXT TIME

Naturally you will want to do a better job each time you make a formal presentation, so you should take steps to ensure that you obtain the feedback you will need to improve. Most formal presentations require some kind of formal feedback system. Many public speeches and lectures, for example, are reviewed by newspapers. Sales presentations are evaluated by their success—did the audience buy?

Whenever formal feedback is not built into the context of your presentation, you should consider preparing an evaluation sheet, distributed as a handout, for your audience to complete. Such sheets are most frequently used to help those giving education and training presentations. Figure 15.1 illustrates an evaluation sheet used for a typical formal presentation, and Figure 15.2 illustrates an evaluation sheet used for a communication seminar.

▷ SUMMARY

Oral reports are much like written reports. Except for very informal oral reports, most are based on written information to which the reporter may refer. Even so, oral communication skills play an important role in the success of an oral report.

Oral communication is influenced by the setting and circumstances, the purpose of the communication, the size and attitudes of the audience, the techniques used in delivering the message, and the gathering and analysis of feedback.

The logical organization of thoughts is just as important to effective oral communication as it is to written communication. Effective organization of oral messages depends on the purpose of the message: to inquire, to inform, to persuade, or to entertain.

The audience is an important variable in any oral communication situation. You should know something about the interests, ages, sex, education, and perhaps occupations of your audience; and based on that analysis, you should be able to make some prediction about how they will receive you and your message. Regardless of the situation, the techniques for oral communication are (1) planning, (2) establishing credibility, (3) delivering the message effectively, and (4) obtaining feedback.

Formal presentations differ from other kinds of oral communication primarily because one person speaks for an extended time without receiving much oral feedback. The planned presentation and the restricted feedback are among the characteristics that make formal presentations formal.

**FIGURE 15.1
Evaluation Sheet for
Formal
Presentations**

FORMAL PRESENTATION EVALUATION FORM

	Poor	Fair	Good	Very Good	Excellent
1. CONTENT					
Clear Transitions	___	___	___	___	___
Definite Conclusions	___	___	___	___	___
Explicit Facts and Opinions	___	___	___	___	___
Interesting Opening	___	___	___	___	___
Good Organization	___	___	___	___	___
2. NONVERBAL SKILLS					
Appearance	___	___	___	___	___
Eye Contact	___	___	___	___	___
Gestures	___	___	___	___	___
Posture	___	___	___	___	___
3. GRAPHIC AIDS					
Appearance	___	___	___	___	___
Coordination	___	___	___	___	___
Readability	___	___	___	___	___
Relevance	___	___	___	___	___
4. VOICE					
Enunciation	___	___	___	___	___
Modulation	___	___	___	___	___
Paralanguage	___	___	___	___	___
Projection	___	___	___	___	___

**FIGURE 15.2
Evaluation Sheet for
Training Seminars**

SEMINAR EVALUATION

1. Do you think that we should repeat this seminar for others?

   _____ Yes   _____ No

2. If yes, please indicate your topic preference in the appropriate column:

Topic	More	Less
Nature of Communication	_____	_____
Writing Skills	_____	_____
Letters	_____	_____
Reports	_____	_____
Reading and Listening	_____	_____
Nonverbal Communication	_____	_____
Oral Communication	_____	_____
Interpersonal Communication	_____	_____
Small Groups	_____	_____
Formal Presentations	_____	_____
Organizational Communication	_____	_____
Job Applications	_____	_____

3. What other topics would you like to see included?

   _____

4. How would you rate the instructors?

	Poor	Fair	Good	Very Good	Excellent
Knowledge of Subject	_____	_____	_____	_____	_____
Success in Stimulating Interest	_____	_____	_____	_____	_____
Clarity of Presentation	_____	_____	_____	_____	_____
Encouragement of Audience Participation	_____	_____	_____	_____	_____
Overall Effectiveness	_____	_____	_____	_____	_____

5. What did you like most about this seminar?

6. What improvements would you suggest?

7. Additional Comments:

   _____

   _____

   _____

COMMUNICATION SOLUTION

The main things you would be able to observe from your taped reading of a news story would be qualities of voice and your pronunciation. Do you say *umh* or *ah* too often? Do you clear your throat too often? Does your voice sound the way you thought it would?

Would you be interested in listening to a speaker who sounds the way you do? If you are at all disappointed with your delivery, reread this chapter and practice, practice, practice.

No one can give an effective formal presentation without extensive preparation. To give a successful presentation, you must know your subject, analyze your audience, and have notes and nerves ready for your delivery.

As a speaker, you must make listening as easy and as pleasant for your audience as possible. Message organization and clarity will help you most in holding the audience's attention; but to be effective, your pattern of organization must be clear from the beginning.

When an oral presentation must include complex information, physical communication aids are frequently needed to help the audience. The best and most common communication aids are boards and charts, projectors, handouts, models, and audience participation.

▷ EXERCISES

Review and Discussion Questions

1. What factors influence oral communication?

2. Identify and explain the four techniques that help ensure effective oral communication.

3. What are the differences between formal presentations and other kinds of oral communication?

4. Name and explain five kinds of formal presentations.

5. What physical or mechanical aids would you prefer to use for a presentation? Why?

Problems

If possible, use a video camera and recorder to tape the presentations given to solve these problems and cases so that presenters can view themselves and improve their deliveries.

1. Plan and deliver a short oral message (less than five minutes). Immediately after your presentation, have your audience evaluate it both orally and in writing.

2. Use a tape recorder to record a lecture or a class discussion. Analyze the speaker's presentation or the oral communication skills of the class members. Listen for evidence of planning. What parts of the lecture or discussion went especially well? Why?

3. Select any of the cases from Chapters 6 through 11 and explain to your class how you would go about solving the problem. Answer any questions the audience has about your solution.

4. Imagine that you are responsible for introducing a speaker of national importance. (Select one of your choosing.) Prepare the introduction, and deliver it to your business communication class.

5. Select a product with which you are familiar. Sell it to the members of your class.

CASES

1. Plan and deliver a formal presentation on a subject of your choice. (See Problems and Cases in Chapter 14 for suggestions.) Your presentation should be about ten minutes long and should use at least two special techniques. Prepare an evaluation sheet, and have your audience use it in rating your presentation.

2. Using the information you are preparing for a written report (see Problems and Cases in Chapter 14), complete Case 1.

3. Form a team of five people and present a brief introduction to business communication. Each person should present for about ten minutes, with one person being responsible for the introductions, opening, and closing remarks.

4. Find a topic of current interest on which you and a classmate disagree. Present both sides of the issue in presentation form. Have a third student serve as moderator.

5. Attend a local lecture and present a summary and evaluation to your class.

PART FOUR

The Job Application Process

Most people go through the job search process not once but several times in the course of their careers. The material presented in Part Four is designed to help you prepare yourself for the process and sell yourself to the right person at the right time.

Whether you are finishing an associate's degree, a bachelor's degree, an advanced degree; changing jobs or careers; or returning to work after a period of being unemployed, the basic steps for finding and landing a satisfying job are the same.

Chapter 16 discusses the steps you need to take before a job interview, and Chapter 17 covers the interview and follow-up correspondence.

PART FOUR

The Job Application
Process

CHAPTER SIXTEEN
Preparing Yourself

Preparing to find a job may well be your most important task. While some people — either because they know someone or because they happen to be in the right place at the right time — end up in an ideal job by chance, most people have to work hard at finding the job that best suits their skills and aspirations. This chapter presents the steps for achieving that goal.

COMMUNICATION CHALLENGE

What is wrong with the following portions of resumes and letters of application? What would you do to improve them? Make your initial evaluation now, and then change your answers if necessary as you read through this chapter. Compare your answers with those that follow the chapter summary.

1. Job Objective: Desire position in management for major corporation.

2. Job Objective: Desire to begin work in sales, management training program, or computer programming.

3. Education: Advanced courses include English 311, English 312, Psychology 307, Sociology 347, German 216, and Philosophy 257.

4. Waitress: Responsible for taking food orders, serving food, waiting on customers, presenting checks, clearing tables, and set-ups.

5. References:
   Dr. Jeanne Roberts, Department of Accountancy, Midwest University, Columbus, OH.

Dr. James Hurst, Department of General Business, Midwest University, Columbus, OH.

Sally McRand, Director of Personnel, First National Bank, 1414 Main Street, Columbus, OH.

6. Are you looking for a new employee who is eager to watch and learn?

7. Do you have a vacancy I could fill?

8. Although I don't have the experience you require, I am a fast learner and would try hard to do a good job.

9. I could quickly spot flaws in your automatic manufacturing procedures and reprogram your robot assemblers for greater speed and efficiency.

10. I would certainly appreciate it if you could give me a job and hope that you will call me at your earliest convenience.

▷ OVERVIEW: DO YOUR HOMEWORK

Unless you know someone who has an ideal job waiting for you, you will need to submit written job applications to several organizations that might be able to offer you employment. A good job application requires preparation — preparation that ideally begins early in your college career. You will be competing against others with every job application, so you should plan early to distinguish yourself in some way.

Employers are looking for people who have demonstrated their willingness to work, initiative, perseverance, some kind of entry-level job skill, and good communication skills. You will need to demonstrate these qualities on a resume, which should be no longer than two pages, and in a letter, which should not exceed one page.

Remember that for you to be of value to an organization, your productivity must exceed the cost of your salary and fringe benefits. You will need to make a contribution to the organization's profits (however those "profits" may be measured). Your resume and letter of application must prove that you have the education, previous experience, and personal qualities necessary to make such a contribution.

Before you begin writing your resume and letter, assess your qualifications and the job opportunities available to you. Then match your skills with the requirements of the available jobs, and design your resume and letter to emphasize your best qualifications for the kind of work you wish to do. If space permits, you may wish to mention any special interests that contribute to your qualifications or that demonstrate important personal qualities. This chapter will guide you through the process of assessing your qualifications and the job market and preparing an effective resume and letter of application.

▷ WRITTEN JOB APPLICATIONS

What should a job application package contain?

A job application package is a persuasive message consisting of a resume and a cover letter that is usually called a letter of transmittal or letter of application. Written applications for jobs have been around for a long time, and they are still widely used because they work. Your job application package may be the most important piece of business correspondence you undertake. The finished product should show that you took its preparation seriously. The best application package in the world cannot guarantee you a job, but a poorly prepared application can certainly prevent you from being selected for an interview. We have saved this discussion of job applications until now because you will use many of the skills presented in the previous chapters to prepare your application package and to handle the job interview.

What Do Employers Want?

How can your job package convince the readers that you are willing to work and that you get along well with others?

All employers want to hire persons with a history of willingness to work, the ability to perform the required task, the ability to get along well with others, and sufficient potential to merit promotion. Your application package should support your claim that you satisfy each of these requirements.

The readers of your applications will be in one of two categories: either they will have asked for your application (and perhaps hundreds of others at the same time) or they will not have asked for it. Your application, then, will be either *invited* or *uninvited*. In either case you should apply for one particular job. In an invited application you have a want ad, job description, or specific request to go by; in an uninvited application, you should apply

COMMUNICATION TODAY...

The increasingly sophisticated development in computer hardware and software that made possible such advances as electronic banking, computer games, and electronic shopping has created a new application: the computerized resume. "It's not a substitute for traditional job-hunting techniques. But it is a good way to supplement your job search," says Bill Dickson, associate dean for career planning and placement at Vanderbilt University's Owen Graduate School of Management.

The big advantage of going on-line with your resume is that you have the option of putting it before many more companies with the kind of job openings you're looking for than you can by using the traditional resume-mailing method. Another advantage is that you'll hear from employers who are as interested in you as you are in them, which is a psychological advantage in an interview situation.

Computerized recruiting is the term often used to describe the process of matching job candidates and employers through resume databases. Here's how it works. If you're interested in having your credentials listed on a resume database, you fill out a form, which asks for information such as job objective, area of study, degree(s), geographic preferences, special skills, and date available. A printout of your electronic resume (as it will be seen by employers on their terminals) is sent to you for your approval.

Getting your resume listed is inexpensive ($8), and sometimes free, depending on the service you sign up with. That's because the employers who subscribe to the resume database services foot most of the bill by paying for on-line computer access time and/or annual fees. When they're looking for a particular type of candidate, they type their requirements into their computer or terminal.

Source: Peggy Schmidt, "New! Electronic Resumes," pp. 45–47. Reprinted from December 1984/ January 1985 issue of *Business Week's Guide to Careers* by special permission © 1985 by McGraw-Hill, Inc. All rights reserved.

What are the differences between invited and uninvited applications?

Under what circumstances should you apply for a specific job? Should you ever offer to fill "any opening" the organization has available?

for the job you can do best. With invited applications, job descriptions sometimes ask for more qualifications than any one applicant could reasonably be expected to have. *Five years' experience desired* does not mean, however, that an employer will not settle for less if you show that you can do the job.

With uninvited applications, you may fear that if you apply for a particular job, the person hiring or the personnel department will not consider you for other jobs that happen to be open. This is usually not true. Most people responsible for hiring attempt to match applicants and their qualifications to the jobs that are open, and the strong applications will be given first consideration, whether they match the available job exactly or not.

Nothing sounds weaker in an application than *If you have a vacancy, I'll take it.* Job applicants—especially college graduates—should be mature enough to have some idea of what they want to do with their lives, and the application package should reflect this sense of purpose. On the other hand, your package should also reflect the you-attitude by showing a willingness to do work useful to your prospective employer. In addition, your package should show self-confidence and competence (do not misspell any words). All the tricks (such as singeing the edges of your resume to show that you are a hot prospect) have been tried; most employers want a conventional presentation. But a conventional job application package can—and should—reflect your individuality.

The Basics of a Written Job Application

A job application package has two basic parts, as follows:

What are the differences among a resume, data sheet, and vita?

1. **The resume, data sheet, or vita.**   Authorities do not agree on which term to use for the first part of the job application package, but the various terms generally attempt to differentiate among degrees of sophistication. The *data sheet* is the least sophisticated, usually presenting only the most fundamental facts with no accompanying interpretation. The *resume* (from the French *résumé*, meaning a *summary*) offers more interpretation of the bare facts. The *vita* (Latin for *life*) is much longer than either a data sheet or a resume, usually including a lengthy summary of professional accomplishments, publications, and the like. Vitas are appropriate only for important positions requiring that applicants have many professional accomplishments.

2. **The letter.**   Usually called a letter of application, the second part of the job application package may also be referred to as a letter of transmittal or as a cover letter when used with a resume or vita. A letter of application is longer and more persuasive than a cover letter. New college graduates usually require letters of application to present themselves effectively.

Why should the letter of application be written only after the resume has been prepared?

Even though the letter is the persuasive part of the package, you should not try to write it until you have completed your data sheet or resume. You can consider the resume as an informative enclosure to accompany the letter, if you wish. It is a critical informative enclosure, however, because it indicates your ability to select important information, organize it in a useful way, and present it in an attractive, readable manner.

The data sheet or resume should usually be printed from typeset copy or a typewritten original. Printed resumes may be used for more than one application. However, to be effective, they must be specific enough to show your sense of purpose without limiting you any more than necessary. Resumes designed specifically for one organization and printed by a word processor using a letter-quality printer have been a popular, and for many people a successful choice in recent years.

Every now and then a person is qualified for work in two completely unrelated fields, such as banking and food processing. Such an individual should, of course, prepare separate resumes for the different applications. Usually, however, the kinds of jobs for which an applicant would be qualified are sufficiently related that one resume can suffice for all applications.

▷ ANALYZING BEFORE YOU WRITE

What categories of qualifications are most important to employers?

Before you can begin preparing your resume and letter of application you must determine your goals, analyze your qualifications for achieving those goals, and develop a strategy for selling yourself to prospective employers.

Assessing Your Qualifications

Answer the following questions as honestly as you can:

1. **Professional objectives.**   What occupational goals have you set for yourself? Why do you wish to pursue these goals? Are your goals realistic? Are they flexible? Do you have an entry-level job skill? What are your long-term career plans?

2. **Education.**   What has your education prepared you to do? How do your major and minor fields of study relate to one another? How do they relate to your professional objectives? Can you do what your education suggests that you can without a great deal of in-service training?

3. **Experience.**   Do you have work experience related to the kind of work for which you are applying? Have any of your jobs taught you specific skills required for the kind of work you want to do? Do you have a well-developed work history? Does your previous experience show a willingness to work hard?

4. **Personal qualities.**   Do you have any special personal attributes that make you especially well suited for the kind of work you are seeking? Do you enjoy working with people? With numbers? With books? Have any of your hobbies taught you something about the kind of work you are applying for? Did you work to finance your college education? Can you cooperate, follow instructions, and work as a member of a team? Have you demonstrated initiative in the past?

Assessing Job Opportunities

Once you have clarified what you want to do and what you are able to do, you must locate companies that not only need your skills but also will give you the opportunity to achieve your professional goals.

1. **What kind of company would you like to work for?**   You should consider size, location, opportunities for travel (or for staying put), the product or service, and the company's history, operations, and policies. If you want further education, will the company support your efforts to obtain it?

2. **How do you find job openings?**   Use the *College Placement Annual,*

published by the Regional Placement Associations (available from College Placement Council, Box 2263, Bethlehem, PA 18001); use your own college placement office; use classified ads (*Help Wanted* and *Situations Wanted*) in newspapers and professional journals; check the yellow pages in the telephone book; make direct application to the companies of your choice; ask your friends and relatives; and file with public (state) and private employment agencies.

How can you determine what kinds of companies would provide you with the best opportunity for achieving your professional goals?

3. **How do you select the best possibilities?**   Once you have found job openings in companies that appeal to you, consider what each of those companies offers you. What is the company's position in the industry? Has the company's growth rate been stable? Does the company have good prospects for the future? Does the company promote from within?

Marketing Your Qualifications

What must you prove for an organization to be interested in hiring you?

After you know which company or companies you would like to work for, you must market yourself to your selected audience. A company will hire you because someone there decides that you can do useful work for the company and that the company will be better off for adding you to the payroll. Thus, you must *convince* that person that your education and experience qualify you to do certain useful work and that your attitude toward work will ensure that you perform it well. The following guidelines can help you market yourself.

1. What aspects of your education contribute most directly to your ability to do the work required? Make a list of the job duties you would have in the job you are applying for, and make a separate list of the course work that applies to each. Subject matter learned is more important than course titles. Concentrate on the advanced work in your area of study — beginning and intermediate courses and work are generally assumed.

2. What aspects of your work experience contribute most directly to your ability to do the work you would be required to do? Even if your experience is limited, you can find important qualities to stress: sense of responsibility, ability to work well with people, and ability to make decisions.

3. In spite of pertinent education and experience, companies will not hire you unless you demonstrate the kind of personal qualities that will make you useful to the firm. Have you demonstrated a willingness to work hard? Do you have a well-developed work history?

Remember that the person who hires you is thinking primarily about what you can do for the company. Consequently, what counts is that person's view of your skills. Fortunately, you can control that view to a certain extent. You-attitude and positive tone will help you create the kind of favorable impression that will get you hired.

What sales tools can you use to sell yourself for a job?

You have three basic tools to work with in making your presentation: your job application package, the interview, and follow-up correspondence. Each of these tools has a specific use. The job application package is designed to obtain an interview; the purpose of the interview is to persuade the interviewer that you are the right person for the job; and the follow-up letter should remind the interviewer, after seeing your competition, that you are the best person for the job.

▷ THE RESUME

Your resume must cover four broad categories: personal details, education, experience, and references. Whether typewritten or printed, your resume should be either one or two pages long. College graduates probably cannot give a full picture of themselves in one page, and employers dislike reading more than two pages of resume, so make intelligent use of space in covering the four categories. A one-and-a-half page resume will be less successful than either a one-page or a two-page resume. Using all the space available to you, whether the resume is one page or two, shows good organizational skills.

Personal Details

Under what circumstances should you include personal details on a resume?

Your name, address, and phone number (including the area code), should be listed first because most personnel directors expect to see them first. Some personnel directors still expect to see height, weight, date of birth, and marital status (married or single; never classify yourself as divorced). However, because Title VII of the Civil Rights Act of 1964 prohibits employers from discriminating against job applicants because of age, sex, race, or place of national origin, employers usually cannot ask for this information or for a photograph. Some employers are even disqualifying applicants whose resumes contain this information.

Your height, weight, and other personal details do not say much about your qualifications for most jobs and should not be included unless they are important for job selection — as vision would be for a pilot. Your spouse's name and occupation and the number and ages of your children should not be included either.

Education

Unless you have four or more years of full-time experience in the kind of work for which you are applying, education will probably be your most important division. It deserves a major heading and several subheads. Some

Why is it important to include some specific details about your educational background?

categories you might use are schools attended (listed in reverse chronological order), honors earned, grade-point average (if noteworthy), major and minor fields, and activities. If you earned at least part of your college expenses, be sure to say so. Working your way through school demonstrates your willingness to work.

Give special emphasis to those courses that make you exceptionally well qualified. All accounting majors take introductory accounting, wherever they go to school and whatever the specific title of the course may be. So instead of listing introductory courses for an accounting job, you would be wiser to concentrate on upper-division work that indicated the range and depth of your educational background.

Experience

What sorts of information about your previous jobs would be significant to employers?

Stress job-related experience, but even if none of your working experience is job-related, showing that you have worked is important. Be sure to tell where and when you worked and what you did. List your job duties in a way that will have meaning for your reader, but do not state the obvious: if you worked as a waiter, you do not need to specify that you carried food to tables, took orders, and so forth. Mention any special responsibilities, such as closing up at night. If your work was part-time, say so. Full-time summer work should be listed as such. Prospective employers frequently expect to see your reasons for having left previous jobs. Use reverse chronological order in listing your work experience, with the most recent work being listed first.

References

Why should a new college graduate avoid saying, "References furnished upon request"?

A few years back, when the job market was not so tight, it was sufficient to say *References will be furnished upon request.* Today new college graduates are generally better off if they list their references on their resumes. Most employers give serious consideration to applications without references, but some consider it presumptuous to be told that they must ask for them if they want them. Listing references gives you a slight edge when competing with other applicants; that edge may prove important in obtaining the interview. Be sure to get each person's permission before listing him or her as a reference — no one likes to be taken by surprise. You may also find that your reference's opinion of you is not what you thought it was.

In listing your references, give the person's courtesy title (Mr., Mrs., Miss, Ms., Dr.); full name; professional title (personnel director, office manager, department chairperson); business mailing address; business telephone number; *and* connection to you. In some cases the person's title will make the connection clear: *Dr. Harvey Hallister, Professor, Department of Accountancy, University of Florida* should be sufficient to show that Harvey Hallister was your teacher. If Dr. Hallister also was the director of your senior independent study, you should add that detail.

Under what circumstances should you list a rabbi, minister, or priest as a job reference?

The best references are academic and employment references. Personal references, such as friends, relatives, church leaders, and family physicians usually cannot give employers the information they seek and should not be listed on a resume. Personal references of that variety, however, may be required on job application forms, when companies may want the names and addresses of people who have known you for several years.

College students should anticipate the need for references before the date of graduation approaches. Instructors need to be able to say more about you than, "So and So was in my class and earned an A." To provide useful information, the instructor will need to know something about you as a person. Try to take two or three classes from instructors you would like to have serve as your references, and in at least one of those classes complete a long-term, complex project requiring good time-management skills, initiative, and perseverance. When asking instructors for a reference, provide them with a brief job description and a summary of your experiences in their classes. Be sure to give the details of any special projects you completed for them.

Those of you who are already working may — for good reason — not want a current employer to know about your job search. Employers understandably prefer that their personnel not look for work elsewhere, and they may retaliate against those who plan to leave. If you are currently employed and do not want your employer to know you are leaving, omit references from your resume. It will be better for you to be rejected by a few firms for not listing references than to have your current employer surprised by a telephone call requesting information about you.

Special Interests and Other Optional Entries

Under what circumstances should you include your hobbies and special interests on a resume?

Should you mention special interests that are not job-related? Yes, but only if you have room on your one- or two-page resume after covering the more important details. The personnel director reviewing your resume may share a hobby with you, which may help you establish empathy. If you include any of the optional entries, be specific. Instead of listing *music;* specify whether you sing, play, collect, or listen. Specify also the kind of music. If you have had military experience, hold special licenses (private pilot's, FCC, real estate), have received special honors or awards, mention them at least briefly. Some of the more common optional entries are as follows:

1. **Professional objective (or *qualified by* statement).**   Many employers expect to see either a specific statement of what your plans are or a brief overview of your principal qualifications. If you use the professional objective entry, include an entry-level objective and a longer-range objective as well. Indicate your career plan.

2. **Honors and awards.**   Emphasize scholastic achievement, but awards that indicate leadership, perseverance, and other outstanding personal

qualities should also be included. Indicate when you received the honor or award, and use its correct title.

3. **Military service.**   If you have military experience, you should list it. Explain your duties and responsibilities but avoid military jargon (few civilians would understand *MOS 71H20*). Stress supervisory experience and the civilian equivalent of military skills.

4. **Publications.**   Few undergraduate students have had an article or book published. If you have, say so. Most organizations value writing skills and also appreciate the initiative it takes to write for publication.

5. **Offices held.**   Most organizations prefer to hire applicants with leadership skills. Both elected and appointed leadership positions can indicate your potential for promotion. Include a description of your responsibilities and accomplishments.

6. **Memberships.**   Membership in professional and preprofessional organizations can demonstrate initiative. Alpha Kappa Psi (the national business fraternity), Beta Alpha Psi (the national accounting honorary society), Beta Gamma Sigma (the national honorary business administration fraternity), Sigma Iota Epsilon (the national honorary management fraternity) and a wide variety of other organizations are available on many college campuses. Specify your participation in the organization so that readers will see that you benefited professionally from your affiliation with the organization.

7. **Special recognition.**   Have you received any special recognition that cannot be called an honor or an award? Perhaps one of your professors cited your project as an example of excellence. Perhaps a volunteer organization cited your efforts on its behalf. Be specific about your accomplishments and the nature of the recognition.

8. **Special qualifications and licenses held.**   Do you have any special qualifications that might cause an organization to take a special interest in you? Perhaps in addition to your degree in accountancy, you have good computer programming skills and are familiar with accounting applications for microcomputers. Or perhaps you have your private pilot's license. Extras of this variety are especially helpful because they demonstrate both initiative and perseverance.

9. **Activities, hobbies, travel, and special interests.**   Membership in social fraternities or sororities, participation in sports, hobbies that demonstrate special skills, domestic and foreign travel, and interests in reading or music can demonstrate a well-rounded personality. Do not, however, list dangerous hobbies (sky diving, motorcycle ice racing, and the like) unless the job for which you are applying is equally dangerous.

10. **Date resume was prepared.**   The last entry on the resume should be the month and year the resume was prepared. Dating the resume assures the reader that the material is current.

Appearance

What are the advantages of using a conservative format for your resume?

Most successful resumes are fairly conservative in appearance because the business persons who read job applications usually prefer resumes that establish individuality through content rather than appearance. Some fields (most nobably advertising) require more innovation in appearance than others. Do not attempt to copy someone else's resume. Your resume should reflect your own personality and style. Use the suggestions we have prescribed as guidelines rather than absolute rules.

People skim resumes rather than read them. Arrange your material so that a reader will be able to spot your most important skills in two or three minutes. Neatness counts. So does readability. Major headings should stand out. Dates and other numbers should be placed where they are visible but so that they do not interfere with more important information. Emphasize skills that show your flexibility, such as communication (both written and oral skills) and electronic data processing.

Also, watch your use of space. As mentioned previously, arrange your material so that you cover all of one page or all of two pages. Blank space on a resume has a negative implication. Your resume should not exceed two pages unless your career advancement requires a fully developed vita. Never send a photograph unless the job requires one, as modeling would.

Under what circumstances should you use an unusual layout or a nonstandard paper size or shape for your resume?

Even in those fields permitting creativity and innovation, fairly conservative resumes usually prove more successful than the bizarre. Unusual layouts and nonstandard paper shapes or sizes, for example, force a reader to spend more time locating information on your resume than he or she would normally spend. In some circumstances, this might work for you. More often, however, it does not because the reader is in a hurry to reduce a stack of 100 applications to the 10 or so worthy of serious consideration.

Before you innovate, analyze your audience. What will appeal to readers of the type who will receive your materials? How many others will be competing for the job you desire? How much time will your reader have to decide whether your resume is discarded or kept for a closer look? Only you can decide which approach is best for you, but try to avoid giving a reader excuses for not reading your resume carefully. Be sure to adhere to the basic rules of having your material well-organized and making the important points easy to find and read.

Printed resumes should not use fancy type fonts. A simple, *serif* typeface (with smaller lines added to main strokes to make the letters seem ''warmer'') is best. Resumes prepared on a word processor should make judicious use of boldface print and underscoring. Do not overuse either of them, however, and be consistent in the way you use them.

Writing Style

Why are action verbs important for a resume?

To make your resume easier and faster to read, use action verbs like those listed in Figure 16.1 rather than using complete sentences.

Avoid negative words. Should you need to explain lack of experience or some other obvious lack of qualification, do so in the letter of application. The resume should be entirely positive, emphasizing your best qualifications.

Organization

What are the differences between functional resumes and chronological resumes?

Two basic organizational patterns for resumes are the functional and the chronological. Functional resumes emphasize job skills; chronological resumes tend to emphasize when jobs were performed or skills were attained. Because employers are generally interested in a well-devleoped work history, the chronological resume is more common. The functional resume is useful for subordinating periods of unemployment, and people who have been out of the labor force for a while or who have changed jobs many times may prefer to use a functional resume. The organization for each type of resume is as follows:

Functional Resume	Chronological Resume
1. Name, address, and telephone number	1. Name, address, and telephone number
2. Job objective or "qualified by" statement (optional)	2. Job objective or "qualified by" statement (optional)
3. Important Job Skill 1 (for example, editing)	3. Education (or experience) by dates in reverse chronological order
4. Important Job Skill 2 (for example, supervising)	4. Experience (or education) by dates in reverse chronological order
5. Important Job Skill 3 (for example, planning)	5. Optional entries
6. Appropriate personal details (optional)	6. Appropriate personal details (optional)
7. References	7. References

Examples of Successful Resumes

The resumes shown in Figures 16.2 through 16.4 (pages 520–525) are all based on real, successful resumes. We have changed names, locations, and other minor details. Each entry, however, is authentic and helped ensure the success of the original resume.

Why do most employers prefer chronological resumes?

As mentioned, most employers prefer chronological resumes because they are concerned about an applicant's job history. Some personnel directors, in fact, refer to functional resumes as "the unemployed person's resume." For this reason, you should use a chronological organizational pattern if at all possible. If you have periods of unemployment, try to be creative in the way you present that information. If you changed jobs several times

**FIGURE 16.1
Action Verbs**

Accomplished	Drew up	Oversaw
Achieved	Edited	Performed
Administered	Eliminated	Photographed
Advised	Enlarged	Planned
Analyzed	Equipped	Prepared
Arbitrated	Established	Presented
Arranged	Evaluated	Processed
Assembled	Examined	Produced
Assisted	Expanded	Promoted
Audited	Financed	Provided
Built	Formulated	Purchased
Calculated	Founded	Raised
Charted	Generated	Realized
Coached	Guided	Received
Collected	Hired	Recommended
Completed	Identified	Recorded
Composed	Implemented	Reduced
Conducted	Improved	Referred
Consolidated	Increased	Reported
Constructed	Initiated	Represented
Consulted	Installed	Researched
Controlled	Instituted	Resolved
Coordinated	Instructed	Restored
Corresponded	Interpreted	Reviewed
Counseled	Interviewed	Routed
Created	Invented	Selected
Delivered	Learned	Served
Demonstrated	Lectured	Sold
Designed	Logged	Solved
Detected	Maintained	Studied
Determined	Managed	Supervised
Developed	Navigated	Supplied
Devised	Negotiated	Taught
Diagnosed	Obtained	Tested
Directed	Operated	Trained
Discovered	Ordered	Translated
Dispensed	Organized	Volunteered
Disproved	Outlined	Wrote
Distributed		

during one period, for example, you might combine those jobs into one entry, stating that you *worked a variety of jobs to earn money to finance your college education.*

If you feel that you must use a functional resume, be sure to make your major skills highly visible (see Figure 16.2) and be prepared to account for the chronology during the interview. Remember also that you may be required to complete a job application form, which will demand a chronological listing of your previous jobs and dates of employment.

◇ THE LETTER OF APPLICATION AND FOLLOW-UP CORRESPONDENCE

Why is the letter of application usually an extremely important part of the job application process?

For your job correspondence to be effective, you need to recognize that letters about jobs—like all business correspondence—have specific objectives. They fall into two general categories: (1) those written to secure an interview, and (2) those written after the interview has taken place. Letters written to arrange an interview are usually called letters of application (also called transmittal and cover letters). Follow-up correspondence includes thank-you letters, requests for information, requests for more time, and job-acceptance and job-refusal letters.

Once you have prepared your resume, your next step is to write the accompanying letter of application. Each application letter should be individually typed and prepared for a particular audience. It should follow the same principles as other letters, so we suggest that before reading this chapter, you review Chapter 1, "Understanding the Communication Process," and Chapter 5, "Letters and Memos: Format and Appearance."

What is the main purpose of a letter of application?

Because employers usually receive a great number — sometimes hundreds — of applications for each available job, how your job letter looks will make a big difference in the attention it receives. The initial perception of you by the people who receive your job letter will be created by the image you present on paper. Before they invite you to an interview, prospective employers will have concluded from your job correspondence whether you are neat, courteous, well-organized, confident, and competent.

Because letters about jobs are personal letters, you should never use your school's letterhead or the letterhead of your current employer. A printed personal letterhead is acceptable but not necessary. Prepare employment correspondence on high quality paper (16- to 20-pound stock in white or off-white). Place your return address, including your phone number, approximately 1½ inches (nine line spaces) from the top of the page on the left margin. The phone number is helpful in case the letter and the resume become separated. Your name, which appears in the signature block, is *not* part of your return address. Use block format throughout the letter (see Chapter 5).

**FIGURE 16.2
A Functional
Resume**

                              Nancy E. Hurt
                            1345 Royale Drive
                            Gautier, MS 39553
                            (606) 734-9811

Career Objective

To work as an administrative assistant specializing in word processing
management.

Education

Gautier Community College, 3 Hyde Park Drive, Gautier, MS 39553. Associate's
Degree expected in June 19xx. Grade point average: 3.7 (4.0 = A).

Business courses: Accountancy, Advanced Keyboarding, Business Law,
                     Marketing, Management, Secretarial Procedures,
                     Business Communication, Report Writing, Records
                     Management, and Finance.

Related courses: Interpersonal Communication, Organizational Communi-
                     cation, Computer Programming, and Fundamentals of
                     Economics.

Experience

Managerial   Coordinated fund-raising efforts of more than 200
Skills   Red Cross volunteers covering all West Gautier
                     neighborhoods. Responsible for recruiting, scheduling,
                     recording donations, and coordinating with Red Cross
                     state headquarters.

Administrative   More than four years' experience as a volunteer
Skills   in the Administrative Office of the Gautier Memorial
                     Hospital. Responsible for assisting patients complete
                     and submit insurance forms and medical records, drafting
                     correspondence, maintaining personnel time charts, and
                     managing hospital records.

Supervisory   Supervised staff of eight part-time volunteer
Skills   secretaries while working at Gautier Memorial Hospital.
                     Responsible for scheduling, advising, and checking work
                     to ensure accuracy and timeliness.

Secretarial   Typing--80 words a minute with 95 percent accuracy.
Skills   Shorthand--140 words a minute with 95 percent accuracy.
                     Word processing--Familiar with Wang, IBM, and Xerox.
                     Reprographics--Familiar with all standard procedures.

**FIGURE 16.2
(Continued)**

Nancy E. Hurt   2

Group Memberships

           Member, Parent Teacher Association. Offices held:
              President and Vice President.
           Member, Volunteer Community Action League
           Member, League of Women Voters. Offices held:
              Treasurer
           Member, Gautier Garden Club. Offices held:
              President and Vice President.
           Member, Zonta Club of Gautier. Ways and Means
              Chairperson
           Member, Parents Without Partners

Special Projects

           Chaired the 1984 Annual District Convention of League
           of Women Voters. Responsible for planning, organizing,
           and scheduling all activities and speakers.

           Inititated the Scholarship Program for the Zonta Club
           of Gautier. Designed application form; distributed
           forms to local schools; prepared press releases for
           newspapers, radio, and televsion; invited local
           educators and businesspeople to serve on selection
           committee; responsible for all correspondence.

Special Interests

           Reading, gourmet cooking, playing tournament bridge,
           aerobic dancing, and gardening.

References

Dr. Randolf Lang, Chairman, Department of Business, Gautier Community
College, Gautier, MS 39553, (601) 733-1703.

Alicia Williams, M.D., Gautier Memorial Hospital, Gautier, MS 39553,
(601) 734-7761.

Mr. Reginald Jackson, American Fidelity Trust and Savings, 396 Louisana Blvd,
Gautier, MS 39553, (601) 734-1593 (State Coordinator for Red Cross fund
raising).

Ms. Martha Griffins, President, League of Women Voters, 458 North Clark
Street, Gautier, MS 39355, (601) 734--2740.

Prepared May 19xx

FIGURE 16.3   A Chronological Resume

JUDY A. NAZARIAN

Present Address	**Mailing Address**
1323 Greenwood, #304	After 23 June 19XX
Kalamazoo, MI 49007	740 Locust Road
(616) 555-7792	Wilmette, IL 60091
	(312) 555-5856

QUALIFIED BY   A thorough education in all aspects of **marketing** and **business communication** combined with an excellent background in general business and more than four years of part-time work, including a **retail internship** with Marshall Field and Company and a **research internship** for business communication.

EDUCATION

Sep 19XX
to
Jun 19XX

College of Business, Western Michigan University, Kalamazoo, MI 49008. BBA Degree June 19XX.

Double
Major

Marketing. Advanced courses include Marketing, Advertising, Sales Administration, Retailing, Marketing Research, Marketing Strategies, Retail Promotion.

Business Communication. Advanced courses include Business Communication, Interpersonal Communication, Consumer Principles and Practices, Organizational Communication, Advanced Business Writing, Organizational Communication Strategies, Communication Systems.

Minor

General Business. Advanced courses include Statistics, Finance, Accounting, Business Law, Management.

EXPERIENCE

Jun 19XX
to
Aug 19XX

Sales Internship. Marshall Field and Company, Old Orchard, Skokie, IL. Worked 40 hours a week selling men's clothing, linens, and housewares.

Jan 19XX
to
Mar 19XX

Administrative Assistant. Administration Building, Western Michigan University, Kalamazoo, MI 49008. Worked 10 hours a week checking transcripts for accuracy.

FIGURE 16.3   (Continued)

Judy A. Nazarian   2

Apr 19XX to Aug 19XX	**Printing and Duplicating.** Northwestern University, Evanston, IL 60201. Worked 40 hours a week in the bindery department. Resigned position to continue education.
Jun 19XX to Aug 19XX	**Sales Representative.** Carson Pirie Scott and Company, Edens Plaza, Wilmette, IL 60091. Worked 32 hours a week selling in the juniors department. Resigned position to continue education.

EXTRACURRICULAR

Sep 19XX
to
Jan 19XX
Chi Omega social sorority. Offices held: Executive Board Secretary, Corresponding Secretary. Marketing Club. Dean's list. College teaching experience with business communication department. Sent to Armenia to study for one month.

PROFESSIONAL MEMBERSHIP

Association for Business Communication. Committee work: Ad Hoc Committee on Careers.

REFERENCES

Mr. David Rozelle, Department of Accountancy, Western Michigan University, Kalamazoo, MI 49008 (616) 555-8041.

Dr. Glenda Smith, Department of Business Information Systems, Western Michigan University, Kalamazoo, MI 49008 (616) 555-1983.

Dr. Charles A. Shull, Department of Business Information Systems, Western Michigan University, Kalamazoo, MI 49008 (616) 555-1983.

Mr. Richard Embertson, Department of Marketing, Western Michigan University, Kalamazoo, MI 49008 (616) 555-1929.

Mrs. Jane Gaessler, Carson Pirie Scott and Company, Edens Plaza, Wilmette, IL 60091 (312) 555-4800.

Prepared April 19XX

**FIGURE 16.4
A Chronological
Resume Stressing
Special Education
Projects**

DONALD D. KEYES

Present Address
1842 So. 11th Street, Apt. 2A
Carbondale, IL 62901
(618) 555-5917

Mailing Address
605 East Indiana Street
Wheaton, IL 60187
(312) 555-8924

QUALIFIED BY

A thorough education in all aspects of **management** including **field projects** and **case method analyses** combined with an excellent background in **business communication, general business,** and more than five years of full- and part-time work.

EDUCATION

Sep 19XX
to
Dec 19XX

College of Business, Department of Management, Southern Illinois University, Carbondale, IL 62901. BBA Degree cum laude (3.55/4.0 GPA) December 19XX.

Major   Management

Minors   Business Communication
         General Business

College education financed through academic scholarship and full- and part-time work.

FIELD PROJECTS

Sep 19XX
to
Jun 19XX

The Solar Solution, Department of Management. Investigated the need for and potential of solar energy and formulated my findings into an analysis of available passive and active solar energy systems for energy-conscious consumers.

Feasibility Studies, Department of Management. Assuming the roles of Manager, Supervisor, and Subordinate, task groups conducted feasibility studies integrating relevant variables, analyses, and data into an operating subsidiary company.

Case Method Analyses, Department of Management. Assuming the role of assistant to the central decision-making manager in an actual business situation, task groups identified problem areas, analyzed facts, developed strategic alternatives and recommended the best solution in light of organizational objectives and environmental constraints.

Systems Analysis, Department of Business Education and Administrative Services. Investigated communication difficulties within an actual business and developed possible remedies.

**FIGURE
16.4   (Continued)**

Donald D. Keyes   2

EXPERIENCE

Sep – Apr
19XX to
19XX
Assistant Manager, Mall Security Systems, 305 E. Illinois Street, Carbondale, IL 62901. Worked approximately 20 hours a week while attending school. Began work in Sep 19XX as Security Guard. Promoted to Shift Supervisor after nine months. Promoted to Assistant Manager (Jan 19XX) with full responsibilities for evening and weekend security at Oak Wood Mall, Carbondale, IL. Supervised and scheduled ten part-time security personnel.

May 19XX
to
Aug 19XX
Detail/Design Draftsman and Technical Illustrator, Industrial Graphics Service, 480 W. Lovell, Glen Ellyn, IL 60137. Produced technical illustrations for service manuals, US Patent Office drawings, tooling fixtures, recreational vehicles, heavy equipment, and pharmaceutical machinery. Job required patience and close attention to detail. Full-time summer work.

May 19XX
to
Aug 19XX
Technical Illustrator, Industrial Graphics Service, 480 W. Lovell, Glen Ellyn, IL 60137. Produced technical illustrations for service manuals. Full-time summer work.

May 19XX
to
Aug 19XX
Grounds Keeper and General Office Helper, Industrial Graphics Service, 480 W. Lovell, Glen Ellyn, IL 60137. Responsible for maintenance of lawns and shrubs, deliveries, and general office work, including some beginning work as a technical illustrator.

HONORS, AWARDS, AND MEMBERSHIPS
Southern Illinois University Scholarship (eight semesters)
Dean's List (four semesters)
President's List (two semesters)
Member, Alpha Kappa Psi (business fraternity)
Member, The Management Club. Offices held: Treasurer and Vice President

INTERESTS
Skiing, camping, racket ball, running, and personal computing.

REFERENCES
Dr. James W. Hill, Department of Management, Southern Illinois University, Carbondale, IL 62901 (618) 555-6058.

Dr. Stephen J. Zelinger, Department of Management, Southern Illinois University, Carbondale, IL 62901 (618) 555-6086.

Mr. Michael A. Cotteleer, Industrial Graphics Service, 480 W. Lovell, Glen Ellyn, IL 60137 (312) 555-0966.

Mr. R. L. Huszagh, Mall Security Systems, 305 E. Illinois Street, Carbondale, IL 62901 (618) 555-6800.

Prepared April 19XX

What are employers looking for in job applicants?

All employers want employees who have demonstrated a willingness to work, the skills required to perform a required task, the ability to get along well with others, and sufficient potential to merit promotion. A letter of application cannot succeed unless it demonstrates that the writer possesses these qualities. To demonstrate these qualities in your letter, you need to assess your qualifications as discussed earlier in this chapter. Obviously you should stress the information to which your reader will respond favorably and subordinate the information to which she or he will respond unfavorably.

Just as a sales letter is either solicited or unsolicited (see Chapter 10), a letter of application is either invited or uninvited depending on whether the reader expects — and desires — to receive it. Whether your letter of application is invited or uninvited, you need to give careful consideration to what your reader already knows and expects and to what your reader (and your reader's company) needs. Because the main objective of the letter of application, whether invited or uninvited, is to persuade the reader to act in a certain way, it follows the basic organizational pattern for persuasive messages: *Attention, Interest, Conviction, Action.*

How should a letter of application begin?

1.   **Attention.**   Place the message in its communication context right away by telling the reader that you are applying for a job. Subordinate that information to something of greater reader interest (a benefit perhaps) when possible. Invited letters of application should mention the source of the invitation: newspaper or journal ad, mutual friend, or special invitation. Uninvited applications should mention a way in which you can help the reader achieve certain job objectives.

Why is it important to indicate a knowledge of the special language used by those working in the kind of job you are seeking?

2.   **Interest.**   Show what you know about the reader's company. Show your reader how you would fit into the company structure. Also, show your reader that you understand the special language of the job you are seeking. Finally, provide a transition to the next step (conviction) by introducing your education and experience.

How can you prove that you can do the job for which you are applying?

3.   **Conviction.**   Use your education, experience, and personal qualities to show your reader that you can fill specific job requirements. Avoid lecturing your reader *(You need a person who . . .)* and concentrate on showing your reader that you are qualified *(Because I am a person who . . . I could make a valuable contribution to . . .).* Because you will be using a resume as an informative enclosure, select and amplify those aspects of your background most appropriate for the company addressed. In invited applications be sure to say something about each job requirement listed in the ad or other information source. In uninvited letters say something about each job requirement you assume will apply to the work you are seeking. Omit negative factors your reader would have no way of knowing about, and subordinate any negative information that must be included.

How should a letter of application end?

4. **Action.** The business objective of the letter of application is to secure an interview. Do not ask for a job; ask for an interview instead. Keep in mind that your reader is not obligated to see you. If a specific time or day would be convenient for you, suggest it for the interview. Do not, however, imply that the reader must accept your suggestion. Invite the reader to suggest alternatives.

Under what circumstances should you use gimmicks to attract special attention to your letter and resume?

As with all sales letters, you must attract your reader's attention to succeed. With uninvited applications, or when the job market is especially tight, consider using an oversized envelope so that your application will be more visible than most of the others coming in. Even when the secretary opens the mail and passes the material to someone else, your presentation will stand out because it will be unfolded. The extra neatness may give you a small but important edge. Do not, however, use other tricks or gimmicks to attract attention — your letter should be neat, nicely typed, and conservative in appearance.

In general, you should use the words *job* and *work*. The words *vacancy* and *opportunity* suggest either you do not care what you do or that you are concerned only with what the company can do for you. The word *position* also has special connotations — it implies high status in the business world. The person to whom you are writing may well want you to start with a *job* and work your way up to a *position*.

The letters shown in Figures 16.5 through 16.7 illustrate most of the previous points. Note that each of the letter writers has adapted the basic components of application letters to meet the needs and expectations of a particular reader. The salesperson's letter (Figure 16.6), for example, is more aggressive and "I" oriented than the management trainee's letter (Figure 16.7).

How can word processing equipment simplify the task of preparing job-application packages?

Each job letter you write, regardless of how many you send, should be individually prepared and typed. You may use the same basic letter to apply for several jobs, but each letter should be personalized so that the person who receives it can see that you prepared the letter with one particular reader in mind. Note, for example, the way two of the sample letters use the reader's name or the name of the reader's company in the body of the letter. As a rule, your letter should be no more than one page long.

▷ SUMMARY

A job application package is a persuasive message consisting of a resume and a letter of application. Because the letter cannot say everything about you without becoming so long that prospective employers would find it unreadable, you should put much of the general information about yourself in

**FIGURE 16.5
Sample Letter of
Application**

```
1345 Royal Drive
Gautier, MS 39553
(606) 555-9811

7 May  19xx


Mr. Anthony LeBarron
Personnel Director
Barrington Manufacturing Company
83 Lincoln Avenue
Lawrence, KS 66045

Dear Mr. LeBarron:

Please consider me for the job of Administrative Assistant you advertised in
the Lawrence Gazette.

My administrative and secretarial skills, combined with my education in business
and communication, make me especially well suited to work as an administrative
assistant for the Barrington Manufacturing Company.

I have experience in program development and implementation and the knowledge
required to manage personnel and resources in spite of limited budgets.  At
Gautier Memorial Hospital I received practical experience in meeting the public,
preparing budgets and schedules, managing records, and writing letters and
reports.  My having been selected for a wide variety of responsible positions,
including that of coordinator of fund-raising for more than 200 Red Cross
volunteers, demonstrates my well-developed oral and interpersonal communication
skills.

My recent successful return to school demonstrates my abilities to set goals and
to adapt quickly to new environments.  I also offer maturity, a well-developed
sense of responsibility, and the willingness to work hard.  I believe that I
would make an excellent administrative assistant for the Barrington Manufacturing
Company.

I would be available for an interview in Lawrence on short notice and would
welcome the opportunity to discuss my qualifications with you.  After you've
had a chance to review the skills listed on the enclosed resume, please call
me to let me know your decision.

Sincerely,

Nancy E. Hurt

Nancy E. Hurt

enc
```

**FIGURE 16.6
Sample Letter of
Application — Jobs
in Sales**

```
                    1323 Greenwood, #304
                    Kalamazoo, MI 49007
                    (616) 555-7792

                    March 15, 19xx



                    Ms. Jean Major
                    Shull's Incorporated
                    45 Shady Lane
                    Atlanta, GA 30302

                    Dear Ms. Major:

                    I am interested in discussing career opportunities with Shull's.

                    Your company's recent growth indicates an expanding need for young,
                    aggressive college graduates--graduates with a strong background in
                    marketing and business communication who possess imagination and
                    leadership skills.  I have these qualifications.

                    And when you combine the enthusiasm and hard work I would put
                    forth in your executive training program with

                         *  My educational background,
                         *  My recent experience in retailing with Marshall Field and
                            Company,
                         *  And my tremendous desire to excel,

                    I feel that I would be able to make a significant contribution to
                    your marketing management team.

                    Ms. Major, I would greatly appreciate your serious consideration
                    of my application and would welcome the opportunity to talk with
                    you.  I'll be looking forward to hearing from you after you have
                    evaluated the enclosed resume.

                    Sincerely,

                    Judy A. Nazarian

                    Judy A. Nazarian

                    enc
```

**FIGURE 16.7
Sample Letter of
Application**

Apartment 2A
1842 South 11th Street
Carbondale, IL 62901
(618) 555-5917

March 1, 19xx

Ms. Geraldine Erickson
Director of Personnel
Roddenberg Broadcasting Company
7 South Dearborn Street
Chicago, IL 60603

Dear Ms. Erickson:

Please consider me for the management trainee job you advertised in the March
Placement Bulletin at Southern Illinois University.

Because of my thorough education in management, business communication, and
general business subjects, I believe that I could make a significant contribution to Roddenberg's excellent management program. My course work
management and business communication have taught me how to work with and to
motivate others. I have the well-developed written and oral communication
skills that will enable me to meet the special requirements for success in
the broadcasting industry.

As the enclosed resume shows, I am the kind of person who accepts challenges
and responsibilities with the enthusiasm of a professional. In both my
summer jobs and my part-time employment during the school years, I earned
several promotions and was able to work for the same companies throughout
my college years. I have demonstrated both professionalism and loyalty on
my previous jobs, and I would do the same for Roddenberg Broadcasting
Company.

Please call one or more of the people listed on my resume. After you have
confirmed my willingness to work hard and to adapt to the specific needs of
your management training program, I would enjoy discussing my qualifications
with you and would be available for an interview on short notice.

Sincerely,

Donald D. Keyes

Donald D. Keyes

enc

COMMUNICATION SOLUTION

1. This job objective is too broad. *What kind* of management position? New college graduates should specify both an entry-level job and a long-term career objective.

2. This job objective is too scattered. Can the person really be equally qualified in all three areas? Perhaps this person should use a *qualified by* line to show breadth of experience without seeming to be applying for jobs in three unrelated areas.

3. Do not list college courses by their numbers. Use the actual course name (not *English 311*, but *Advanced Business Writing*), and explain the content of the course if it is not clear from the title.

4. Avoid listing the obvious. Everyone knows the basic job duties of a waitress. List only those responsibilities that would not be obvious — responsibilities for supervising or training others, for opening and closing, for helping keep the books, and so on.

5. Give complete business addresses and phone numbers for all references, including zip and area codes. Also, use the appropriate courtesy titles for all references. Note that this entry uses the appropriate academic titles but omits the title for the bank employee. It should read: Ms. (or Mrs. or Miss depending on her preference) Sally McRand.

6. Organizations prefer to hire employees who

can do useful work rather than those who desire to *watch* others work. Be specific about the kind of work you would like to do.

7. A block of wood can fill a vacancy. What can you *do* for the reader and his or her company? Avoid the words *vacancy* and *opening* — apply for a *job* and talk about the *work* you will do.

8. Do not emphasize your shortcomings. Stress your qualifications instead.

    My two years of experience in a related industry, combined with my education, would enable me to contribute to the success of your hydrology project.

9. You do not know your prospective employer's business better than she or he does. It is arrogant to presume that you could enter an organization and solve all its problems in two weeks. Remember that people with more training and experience than you have are already working to solve the problems you may see and that if a solution were easy, they would have already found it.

10. Do not ask for a job; ask for an *interview*, and ask for it with confidence.

    As I will be in St. Louis from May 10 to May 15, I would appreciate meeting with you that week to discuss the possibilities of my working for Warrington Energizers. Please call me at (616) 555-7879 and suggest a convenient time.

the resume, which you send with the letter as an informative enclosure. The resume must cover four broad categories of information: (1) personal details, (2) education, (3) experience, and (4) references. In addition to the major categories, you may include other information under optional divisions.

All employers want employees who have demonstrated a willingness to work, the skills required to perform a required task, the ability to get along well with others, and sufficient potential to merit promotion. A job application cannot succeed unless it demonstrates that the writer possesses these qualities. To demonstrate these qualities, you need to assess the following: (1) your professional objectives, (2) your education, (3) your experience, and (4) your personal qualities.

After you have analyzed your own qualifications and desires, analyze companies, jobs, and opportunities. Prepare your resume first, focusing on a specific job category. Write your letter after you have prepared the resume. Each letter should be as specific as you can make it. Your resume may be printed, and copies will go to several companies. You should write each letter for a specific company, however, and preferably for a specific person in a specific company.

While one purpose of the letter of application is to transmit the resume to the reader, its main purpose is to persuade the reader to invite the applicant for an interview. Regardless of whether your application is invited or uninvited, you should use the same basic organizational pattern: (1) attention, (2) interest, (3) conviction, and (4) action.

The letter should demonstrate the you-attitude by showing the reader that you are willing and able to perform useful work. Use your education and experience to provide the necessary proof of job skills. Close by asking for an interview.

▷ EXERCISES

Review and Discussion Questions

1. What are the two general categories of job-search letters?

2. What is the purpose of a letter of application? What is its organizational pattern?

3. In the letter of application you need to assess four general areas to demonstrate your qualifications for the job. What are they?

4. Why is a resume included with the letter of application?

5. What four categories should be included in the resume?

Problem

Collect samples of five resumes and their respective cover letters and analyze them for their effectiveness. What do you like, what do you dislike, and why? Which resume and letter do you think would be the most effective — would appeal to the most readers — and why?

CASE

Using your current qualifications or the qualifications you expect to have when you finish school, prepare a letter of application and resume for the company and job of your choice. Use your college catalog to ensure accuracy in listing the courses you plan to take.

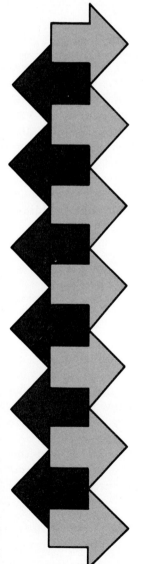

CHAPTER SEVENTEEN
Selling Yourself

Obtaining an interview is only half the battle of securing the job you want. Your written application may have opened the door for you, but to sell yourself to a particular employer, you also need to make a favorable and memorable impression in the job interview — or interviews. This chapter shows you how to be successful during an interview and how to follow through after an interview.

Topics

COMMUNICATION CHALLENGE

What do you want to do with the rest of your life? In one way or another, this question will come up in your interview. How are you going to answer it? Commit an answer to writing now, and then add to or change it as you read this chapter. Compare your answer with the guidelines that follow the chapter summary.

▷ OVERVIEW: SELLING YOURSELF

Organizations are usually able to select from a number of qualified applicants. Why should they choose you? You need to know some reasons that you should be the one hired, and then you need to present those reasons to the persons who interview you. In short, you need to sell yourself to the organization.

The impression you make during the interview, your ability to demonstrate your understanding of the organization and its needs, and your interpersonal and social skills are the important factors contributing to hiring decisions. This chapter will show you how to prepare for success in each of these areas.

▷ THE FIRST INTERVIEW

What does an employer hope to learn from job interviews?

By the time of your interview, the company has usually narrowed the candidates to the few who seem most attractive. Some of your competition for the job has been eliminated; however, those who remain will all have similar qualifications. The interview helps the employer explore qualifications that may not show up in written applications, such as attitude toward work, sense of humor, interest in a particular job or company, willingness to cooperate with others, and other personality traits.

A successful interview depends as much on what is done *before* the interview as what happens *during* it. An interviewee who is well prepared has much more control over the interview than the poorly prepared person.

Preparation

If your letter of application and resume are successful in obtaining you an invitation to an interview, you will probably receive that invitation in a letter

What can you do to prepare for job interviews?

asking you to call and arrange for an appointment. If you are asked to call, you should make the following preparations:

1.   Safeguard against possible memory loss by having a pen and note pad handy before you call for the appointment. Jot down the name, address, and phone number of the company you are about to call. On the same sheet of paper, write *who, when,* and *where,* so you can fill in this information as you talk on the phone.

2.   After you dial the number, ask for the person in charge of hiring. When the operator gives you the name, jot it on your sheet of paper. Be sure to get the correct spelling and pronunciation. Ask the operator for the person's title as well.

3.   When you are connected to the appropriate person, introduce yourself and request a specific time, date, and place for the interview. Be flexible. Repeat and record the information. Express appreciation.

In case you receive a call instead of a letter from the company, you should also make these preparations:

1.   Keep a copy of your resume and a list of the companies to which you have sent applications near your phone. The list should include the name and title of the person, the name and address of the company, and the specific job for which you have applied.

2.   Take notes during the conversation. Make sure that you record the information correctly. More than one qualified job applicant has shown up at the wrong company at the wrong time.

Research

What should you know about the organization before you arrive at the interview?

After making the appointment, do some research. Obtain information about the organization from the library, school placement office, current employees or the organization's annual report. Knowing something about the company will help give you the confidence you need to relax during the interview. Find out the location of the organization's main plants and offices and its branch offices. Find answers to the following questions:

1.   Does the organization have subsidiaries?

2.   What type of products does it manufacture? What kind of services does it offer?

3.   What are the organization's growth patterns and its prospects for the future?

4.   Have any articles been written about the organization in the past two or three years? (Check especially *The Wall Street Journal Index* and the *Business Periodicals Index.*)

COMMUNICATION TODAY...

When you walk into that job interview, you're not the only tense person in the room. Chances are the interviewer is tense too. The reason? The job of the interviewer is to screen and recommend individuals who will do well on the job — if they are hired. If the interviewer recommends too many applicants who are hired and fail on the job, that interviewer's position may be in jeopardy.

That's why interviewers ask those intimidating questions. What they really want to know is: (1) Will you do the job competently if hired? (2) Will you get along well with other members of the staff? (3) Do you have the temperament — stability, flexibility, and dependability — required for the job? If you can convince the interviewer that the answer to each of these questions is "yes," you will take the pressure off that person.

Source: Shirley Sloan Fader, "Those Intimidating Interview Questions," p. 46. Reprinted from October 1984 issue of *Business Week's Guide to Careers* by special permission © 1984 by McGraw-Hill, Inc. All rights reserved.

5.   What is the organization's style of management? Does it encourage continued education? Does it provide the training necessary for promotion from within? Are most mid- and higher-level managers long-term employees?

6.   What salaries are typical of people with your educational background and work experience starting work with this and similar organizations? Know the range (low to high).

7.   What exactly will you do for the organization? If the job you are interviewing for has an unusual title, check the *Dictionary of Occupational Titles* to see what the job involves. Be prepared to discuss typical job duties and your ability to perform them.

What kinds of questions should you ask the interviewer?

As you do this research, prepare a list of questions you would like to ask the interviewer. Be sure to avoid asking anything you should already know about the organization. Ask instead about things of interest that you learned from reading about the organization. Ask also about things that would naturally interest you: organization training programs; the way the job you would be doing fits in with the organization as a whole, and the normal career path for someone hired in the type of job you are applying for.

You may also ask specific job-related questions concerning the computer hardware or software used, the flow of work activity, what laboratory equipment or other equipment is available, and so forth.

Do not mention salary unless the interviewer asks you what salary you require. Then specify a range (a little on the high side of what your research indicated was common for people in your occupational area). A new employee should be more interested in the job and working conditions than in his or her first vacation, so do not ask about vacations.

First Impressions

Why is appearance such an important consideration for employment?

Prepare yourself for the day of the interview. Get a good night's sleep. Allow yourself plenty of time in the morning to get ready. Appearance always counts—be neat and clean. Professional employment officers report that they often make their decisions on whether to hire a particular person on the basis of appearance alone, and poor personal appearance is the most often cited reason for rejecting an applicant. The *image* you present says a great deal about you and about the way in which you will fit into a particular organization.

When possible, find out before the interview how current employees of the organization dress. Most organizations still prefer their employees to present a conservative image, and most interviewers expect the interview to be more formal than normal working conditions. For this reason, when you do not know how employees of a particular organization dress, it is better to guess on the conservative side than to present too informal an appearance.

Your *psychological appearance* is also important. Many other reasons for rejecting applicants are based on the psychological impression applicants make. Here are some common mistakes:

How does your psychological appearance influence a job interview?

1. A superior, know-it-all attitude.

2. Absence of purpose, no plans or career goals.

3. Too lazy (How do you spend your spare time? Vacations?).

4. Greed—too concerned with obtaining the highest salary.

5. Poor manners—lack of courtesy, concern for others.

6. Poor human relations skills—evidence of inability to get along with others; history of conflict with teachers and former employers.

7. Lack of outside interests—no interest in national and international affairs or current events.

8. Desire for special treatment—expects to be hired on the basis of who one is or knows or makes excuses for lack of normal achievement.

9. Poor academic skills (one's attitude toward school work is a good indicator of one's attitude toward employment).

10. Negative attitudes (cynicism, racial or sexual bias, or other signs of hostility).

The Meeting

Why should you avoid smoking or chewing gum while waiting for the interviewer?

Be punctual. To be on the safe side, arrive 10 to 15 minutes early. When you arrive at the office, introduce yourself to the receptionist. Observe the physical surroundings and the office environment while you wait. Is it a place where you would enjoy working?

When the interviewer (or panel of interviewers) is ready for you, the receptionist may direct you to the appropriate office, or the interviewer may come directly to you. In either case, when you first meet with the interviewer, greet him or her by name and extend your hand for a handshake. Your grasp should not be too strong, nor should it be limp. Do not sit down until you are asked. Sit erectly in your chair, looking alert and interested. Do not smoke or chew gum. Look your interviewer in the eye. Smile.

The first interview for most jobs takes less than 30 minutes. Be alert to terminating signs from the interviewer; take the hint and prepare to leave. Make sure that the interviewer has a good copy of your resume. Thank the interviewer and leave graciously.

Interview Hints

Why should you go to job interviews alone?

In addition to the general interviewing procedures described in Chapter 18, you should follow these guidelines in job interviews:

1. Go to the interview alone.
2. Be patient while waiting in the reception area.
3. Be pleasant and poised. Smile. Watch your posture and control nervous mannerisms.
4. Watch your grammar, pronunciation, and nonverbal behavior.
5. Neither brag nor boast. Do not try to bribe.
6. Express appreciation for the interview.
7. Thank the receptionist as you leave the main office.
8. Follow up with a letter of appreciation.

Frequently Asked Interview Questions

Why are the questions listed here asked so often? What do they have in common?

The following questions are asked often enough that you should determine in advance how you will answer them:

1. Tell me a bit about yourself.
2. What are your goals? Or, have you established any new goals recently?
3. Why do you want to work for our company?

4. Would you rather work with others or by yourself?

5. Have you ever had any problems with your parents, fellow students, or faculty members?

6. Would you rather make money or serve humanity?

7. When did you become self-supporting?

8. How important is salary to you?

9. What have you learned on your previous jobs?

10. Are you in good physical condition?

11. What are your plans to further your education?

12. What books do you read for pleasure?

13. How was your education financed?

14. What do you think will determine your progress in our company?

15. What do you think of our company? Or, how long do you plan to work for us?

16. Do you prefer any specific geographic location?

17. What are your weaknesses? Your strengths? Or, how do others describe you?

18. Do you enjoy traveling?

19. What have you accomplished that shows initiative and willingness to work? Or, how have you demonstrated leadership skills?

20. If you could have any job in this company, which would it be? Why?

21. What is your idea of success?

22. How did you rank in your graduating class in high school? College?

23. What do you want to do with the rest of your life?

24. Why did you major in . . . ? Or, what was your senior project?

25. What do you want to be doing five years from now?

Is honesty really the best policy? Why not lie a little if it will help get you the job?

Students frequently want to know the "right" answers to some of the foregoing questions. In general, the right answer is the *honest* answer thoughtfully given. Businesses want people who

1. Are willing to work.

2. Have demonstrated initiative and flexibility.

3.   Work well both with others and independently.

4.   Expect to be well rewarded (but not necessarily with money only) for their efforts.

5.   Are interested in learning new things and in mastering new skills.

You can *learn* to be this sort of person, but it is nearly impossible to *pretend* to be this sort of person during an interview.

One mistake students often make is assuming that they could solve all of a company's problems because they wrote a term paper about similar problems for one of their classes. While you should mention what you have learned in college, avoid the temptation to offer instant solutions to problems that have been plaguing a company or industry for years.

How can *positive tone* help you answer some of the more difficult questions?

As you prepare your responses to the preceding questions, note that some suggest the interviewer's expectations. "What books do you read for pleasure," for example, implies that you do read books. Why would an interviewer care? She or he is probably looking for signs of an active mind, so if you do not read books, perhaps you can convince the interviewer that you are mentally alive by focusing on what you do read.

The most common question, "Tell me about yourself," can be answered in two ways: with a brief life history or with a current personality profile. Develop answers for both possibilities, and find out which answer the interviewer would prefer: "Would you prefer to hear a little of my life history or about my current activities, interests, and plans?

What three qualities are universally sought by organizations of all types?

When given the opportunity to sell yourself (Questions 1, 13, 14, 17, 19, 20, 23, 25) emphasize your strengths. Mention activities that demonstrate initiative, perseverance, and leadership.

How can you answer a forced-choice question correctly without knowing in advance which choice the interviewer desires?

If asked a forced-choice question (Questions 4 and 6), try to avoid being trapped into defending either side. You may prefer to work by yourself, but working with others is also required on most jobs. You may prefer making money, but serving humanity is necessary for most organizations to stay in business. Show that you understand the true nature of forced-choice questions by addressing both sides of the issue.

The Stress Interview

What would you say if the interviewer simply said, "Go ahead and start." Or if the interviewer simply sat and waited, saying nothing? Some interviewers will deliberately employ techniques that will prevent you from using the answers you have rehearsed for the questions asked most often. The theory behind stress interviews is that they force the applicant to think quickly and permit the interviewer to see the applicant as she or he really is. Certainly stress interviews will reveal how well you deal with the unexpected, and almost certainly they will be unpleasant. Here are some of the more common stress-interview questions and techniques:

1. What makes you better than the 200 others I've interviewed for this job?

2. Why should I be interested in you?

3. That's the ugliest tie (or blouse) I've ever seen. Do you always dress like that?

4. How do I compare with the other interviewers you've met?

5. I've never interviewed a (your major) major who knows what he (or she) was doing. What makes you different?

6. Can't you talk a little faster? Our time is limited.

7. I think (a course you just said you thought was valuable) is a complete waste of time.

8. Everyone lies on job application forms. What are your lies?

9. Where did you get a crazy idea like that?

10. See that (any common object in the room)? Sell it to me.

One of the main things to remember about stress interviews is that staying calm and rational is more important than anything you say or do. Be prepared to emphasize your strengths. Be well prepared with stories that illustrate these strengths by *showing* how you have applied these strengths in the past. Consider a "Go ahead and start" statement to be the same as the "Tell me a bit about yourself" question, and begin to sell yourself.

If you are greeted by silence, simply ask the interviewer if she or he is ready to begin. If you receive no response, say that you assume that she or he is using silence as a stress technique and that you understand the purpose of the technique. Then begin by providing the information you have prepared for the "Tell me about yourself" question. Remember that there are no "right" answers in stress interviews, except the one used on television to sell deodorant: "Never let them see you sweat."

If you are asked an offensive question, refuse to answer it, while letting the interviewer know that you recognize questions of that sort as a common stress technique. Remember, too, that the interview is your opportunity to evaluate the organization and the people who work for it. If the interviewer, who has been especially selected to represent his or her organization, is obnoxious and disrespectful, what will the rest of the organization be like?

Conducted properly, a stress interview still demonstrates respect for the applicant. If the person is too offensive, leave. No law says you must remain. You may tell the interviewer that you find his or her technique offensive. Avoid the temptation, however, of uttering a few choice offensive words of your own. Keep your cool, and maintain your self-respect.

Illegal Interview Questions

Affirmative Action guidelines have put certain limits on the kinds of questions interviewers are permitted to ask. Title VII of the Civil Rights Act of 1964, "Equal Employment Opportunity," and Title IX of The Education Amendments of 1972, "Prohibition of Sex Discrimination," both limit the information companies may request before hiring an applicant.

Under what circumstances should you answer an illegal pre-employment interview question?

The following questions, for example, are all illegal before employment. They may result in discrimination against an applicant because of race, age, sex, religion, or place of national origin.

1. What is your maiden name?

2. Have you ever used another name when employed?

3. What is your marital status?

4. Where were you born? When were you born? How old are you?

5. Can you work Saturdays? Sundays? (Legal if the job requires it.)

6. What organizations, associations, clubs, societies, and fraternities do you belong to?

7. Other than your immediate family, what are the names of three of your relatives?

8. What is the name of your nearest relative whom we can notify in case of an emergency?

9. Where did you learn to read, write, or speak a foreign language?

10. Have you ever been arrested for a crime? If yes, where?

11. What are the names of your dependent children under 18 years of age?

12. Who will take care of your minor children while you work?

13. What is the minimum salary you would accept?

14. How tall are you? What is your weight?

15. Were your wages ever garnished?

16. Are you a homeowner?

17. Do you own a car? (Legal if the job requires it.)

18. Do you have charge accounts?

19. Where is your spouse employed?

20. Please submit a recent photograph of yourself.

Not all interviewers, however, are sufficiently informed of the law to avoid all illegal questions. Some illegal questions may occur naturally in the course of your conversation with the interviewer:

1.   What does your husband/wife do?

2.   What school do your children attend?

3.   Oh, really? Where did you learn to speak French?

If you are asked an illegal question, you should try to determine the *intent* behind the question. Does the interviewer intend to use your answer to discriminate against you (perhaps pay you less than a person of another race or sex for doing the same work), or is the interviewer merely doing her or his best to conduct a friendly interview?

How can you refuse to answer an illegal question without offending the interviewer?

After employment, a company may require some of the above information to be able to demonstrate that it is meeting Affirmative Action guidelines. Before employment, however, you have the right to refuse to answer questions you believe will result in the company's discriminating against you. But refuse gently. You may insult an interviewer who had no intention of discriminating against you and thereby miss a job opportunity. Ask why the interviewer wants the information before telling him or her that the question is illegal. Stay friendly. Be willing to express your fears that the employer may unintentionally use that information to discriminate against you. Most interviewers will be sympathetic.

Poor Interview Questions

How should you answer "closed" questions?

You may encounter an interviewer who phrases questions poorly so that you are encouraged to answer yes or no rather than provide the kind of complete answers that would help you sell yourself. If this happens, answer the question the interviewer should have asked rather than the one actually asked.

If asked this:	Answer this:
Are you qualified for this job?	What have you accomplished that illustrates your qualifications for this job?
Can you accept criticism?	How do you respond to criticism? Give me some examples.
Do you have leadership skills?	What have you done that illustrates your leadership skills? Do the groups to which you belong look to you for leadership? Why do you think this is so?
Do you get along with others?	What is your interpersonal style? How do you handle interpersonal conflict?
Did you enjoy your job at XYZ?	What did you like about your job at XYZ?
Are you ambitious?	What are your goals? What does success mean to you?

In general, try to provide more than a minimal answer, but be alert to the possibility that the interviewer really prefers a brief answer. Watch for nonverbal signs indicating whether the interviewer desires a longer answer than the question as phrased calls for.

▷ THE SECOND INTERVIEW

Why might a second interview be more difficult than the first?

Some hiring decisions for entry-level jobs are based on one interview. Most companies, however, prefer to use the initial interview—especially when it was conducted by a recruiter on a college campus—as a screening technique. They use it to eliminate candidates so that the final decision can be based on more intensive interviews with the most qualified applicants.

Second interviews usually last several hours and many include either a meal or a tour of the facilities or both. This gives both you and your prospective employer an excellent opportunity to see what the other is like. The time limitation of first interviews does not permit an extensive exploration of many of the factors that will contribute to your success in a company. By the time of the second interview, the company is fairly well convinced that you have the technical qualifications to perform (or to learn to perform) the job you are applying for. The second interview will tell them whether your social skills, attitude toward work, attitude toward the company, and adaptability will make you an asset to the company.

Social Skills

Why should an employer be concerned about your social skills?

Second interviews test your skills at meeting people—learning and remembering names, being cordial with and accepting of others, and answering questions from a variety of people. Social manners—and mannerisms—are important.

While you will not be expected to remember everyone's name and job title after brief introductions, be prepared to learn the names and titles of several people during the course of the interview. Those interviewing you will watch to see how well you interact with others. Do you wait until others are through speaking, or do you interrupt? Do you use eye contact to make all members of the group feel included? Do you hold the door for others or let it slam behind you?

Your table manners will also be important, should your interview include a meal. Are you able to eat and carry on a conversation at the same time? Do you talk with your mouth full? Do you hold your utensils correctly? Do you have three drinks before others have finished their first? Your social skills at the table will tell your interviewer a great deal about you. Should you feel insecure about your table manners, consult a book on etiquette and practice good manners until they become automatic.

If you have not had much restaurant experience, it would be helpful to have lunch (or dinner) in two or three of your area's nicer restaurants. Go with a group of friends who will also be interviewing, wear the clothes you plan to wear to the interview, and discuss current events, the economy, and other factors concerning the business climate. Avoid topics more typical of student conversations.

Attitude Toward Work

What factors will indicate your attitude toward work?

The second interview will also give the interviewer a good opportunity to explore your attitude toward work. Organizations would rather hire people who work primarily because they *want* to and only secondarily because they *have* to. Your degree of interest in your previous jobs and in the kind of work for which you are applying will be important indicators of your attitude toward work.

Ask yourself which of your previous jobs you enjoyed the most and why, what job you would enjoy doing the most if you could do anything you wanted to, and how much you enjoyed taking classes in your major area of study. People who have enjoyed previous jobs, have specific ideas about the kind of work they enjoy the most, and have enjoyed academic preparation for a particular career are more likely than others to continue to enjoy working and learning new skills.

Attitude Toward the Company

How can you indicate a positive attitude toward the organization with which you are interviewing?

A company will also be interested in your attitude toward it. How familiar are you with its products or services? Do you have faith in the quality of the company's products or services? (Did you drive a General Motors car to your interview with the Ford Motor Company?)

Do your homework before your interview to learn about the company and its products or services. This preparation is especially critical for a second interview, because the second interview will permit you more opportunity to ask questions and exchange ideas and opinions than the initial interview did. You will be expected to hold up your end of the conversation. Your interviewers will infer your attitude toward the company from what you say about it and the kind of questions you ask about its operations and policies.

Adaptability

How can you indicate that you have what it takes to earn promotions within the organization?

By the time of the second interview your technical skills in a particular job area will probably be assumed, and the company will want to explore your promotability. As you move up the ladder in any company, the skills required for success on the job will change. Generally speaking, the path of promotion will take you from (1) doing the work, to (2) supervising others who do the work, to (3) planning how the work should be done, to (4) deciding what work should be done.

As you are promoted from one job level to another, your duties will become less specific and less concerned with technique and more general and more concerned with people. During the second interview, your interviewer will try to determine whether you have the human relations potential for success at higher job levels. Following are some negative behaviors that the interviewer may look for to see if you should be eliminated from consideration for the job.

1.   **Personal complaints.**   People who have numerous personal complaints (and they can be about anything — from school, to family, to working conditions, to the weather) rarely succeed as managers. Managers must actively seek the solutions to problems, and people who spend a great deal of time complaining rarely have the time to work on solving problems.

2.   **Excuses.**   A legitimate reason for a failure or problem is different from an alibi for failure to make an effort. Such excuses mark a person as unsuitable for management positions. The worst kinds of excuses are those blaming others.

3.   **Unwillingness to share information.**   Management is a cooperative task. People who attempt to make themselves look good by concealing negative information — either from their bosses or from their associates — may succeed for a while, but bad news eventually surfaces. It is much better to share potentially important information early so that appropriate action is possible.

4.   **History of insubordination.**   To maintain their own authority, managers need to respect the authority of those who supervise them. Going over a manager's head (except as a last resort when the problem is serious), offering contradictory opinions, and other signs of disrespect for a manager will disqualify a person for managerial consideration.

The following attitudes indicate your adaptability and thus your promotability:

1.   **Positiveness.**   While honesty prevents you from ignoring negative elements around you, you should focus more on the positive aspects of any situation than the negative ones. A previous job, for example, may have been unpleasant in many respects, but you should have been able to learn something of value, make friends, or earn money to further your education. Emphasize those positive aspects when you speak to the interviewer.

2.   **Fairness.**   In discussing problems and possible solutions, focus on facts rather than on personalities. Be fair with others even when you disagree with them.

3. **Helpfulness.** Show that you are willing to do what you can to make your supervisor's job easier. Express a willingness to assume appropriate responsibilities; show that you understand that the manager has his or her own job to be concerned with and that your needs are only a part of your manager's responsibilities—perhaps only a *small* part.

▷ THE JOB APPLICATION FORM

What is the function of the job application form? What are the most common mistakes applicants make in filling out application forms?

Somewhere along the way to being hired, you will need to complete an application form. You may do this before or after either the first or second interview. While the forms you will encounter may vary from company to company and from industry to industry, they all serve the same purpose. In addition to providing needed information, they show the company whether you are able to follow directions in a neat, orderly way.

Figure 17.1 is a commonly used form. It seems simple enough, yet countless people make mistakes in completing similar forms and consequently are refused further consideration for particular jobs. In filling out forms of this variety, be sure to

1. Read the instructions carefully and follow all directions. For example, note whether the form asks for *reverse* chronological order for your job history, and if so, be sure to list your most recent job first. If the form asks you to print, be sure to print rather than using cursive writing.

2. Answer every question, even when the answer may be *none* or *not applicable.*

3. Be specific. Especially for broad categories, such as type of work and subjects of special study, have definite answers in mind. For questions about salary, make sure you know your market value.

▷ POSTINTERVIEW ACTIVITIES

What actions should you take after you have had a job interview?

The objective of the job application package, consisting of the cover letter and resume, is to secure an interview. The objectives of being interviewed are to (1) determine whether you want the job and (2) secure the job if you decide that you want it. Naturally, if your first application package to a particular company does not secure the interview and you are very interested in working for that company, you should send a second letter of application and resume to demonstrate your seriousness.

FIGURE 17.1
Application for
Employment

ORDER BY FORM NO. CL C100
REVISED 1984
(50 FORMS PER PAD)
DOUBLEDAY BROS. & CO., KALAMAZOO, MICH.

APPLICATION FOR EMPLOYMENT
(PRE-EMPLOYMENT QUESTIONNAIRE)   (AN EQUAL OPPORTUNITY EMPLOYER)

PERSONAL INFORMATION

DATE _____

NAME _____

PRESENT ADDRESS _____
                          Street   City
_____ TELEPHONE _____
        State   Zip
HOW LONG HAVE YOU LIVED AT THIS ADDRESS? _____

PERMANENT MAILING ADDRESS _____
                                   Street   City
_____ TELEPHONE _____
        State   Zip
SOCIAL SECURITY NUMBER _____ ARE YOU 18 YEARS OLD OR OLDER? _____

ARE YOU A CITIZEN OF U.S.? _____

HAVE YOU EVER BEEN CONVICTED OF A CRIME? IF SO, WHEN, WHERE, AND NATURE OF OFFENSE? _____
_____
_____

ARE THERE ANY FELONY CHARGES PENDING AGAINST YOU? _____

EMPLOYMENT DESIRED

POSITION _____   DATE YOU CAN START _____   SALARY DESIRED _____

ARE YOU EMPLOYED NOW? _____   IF SO MAY WE INQUIRE OF YOUR PRESENT EMPLOYER? _____

EVER APPLIED TO THIS COMPANY BEFORE? _____   WHERE? _____   WHEN? _____

EDUCATION	NAME AND LOCATION OF SCHOOL	YEARS ATTENDED	DID YOU GRADUATE	SUBJECTS STUDIED
GRAMMAR SCHOOL				
HIGH SCHOOL				
COLLEGE				
TRADE, BUSINESS OR CORRESPONDENCE SCHOOL				

GENERAL
SUBJECTS OF SPECIAL STUDY OR RESEARCH WORK
_____

WHAT SPECIAL WORK EXPERIENCES HAVE YOU HAD?
_____
_____

WHAT FOREIGN LANGUAGES DO YOU SPEAK OR WRITE FLUENTLY?
_____
U.S. MILITARY OR NAVAL SERVICE _____   RANK _____   PRESENT MEMBERSHIP IN NATIONAL GUARD OR RESERVES _____

(CONTINUED ON OTHER SIDE)

LAST   FIRST   MIDDLE

SAMPLE

FORMER EMPLOYERS   (LIST BELOW LAST FOUR EMPLOYERS, STARTING WITH LAST ONE FIRST)

DATE MONTH AND YEAR	NAME AND ADDRESS OF EMPLOYER	SALARY	POSITION	REASON FOR LEAVING
FROM				
TO				
FROM				
TO				
FROM				
TO				
FROM				
TO				

REFERENCES: GIVE BELOW THE NAMES OF THREE PERSONS NOT RELATED TO YOU, WHOM YOU HAVE KNOWN AT LEAST ONE YEAR.

	NAME	ADDRESS	BUSINESS	YEARS ACQUAINTED
1				
2				
3				

HEALTH RECORD: DO YOU HAVE ANY IMPAIRMENTS PHYSICAL, MENTAL, OR MEDICAL WHICH WOULD INTERFERE WITH YOUR ABILITY TO DO THE JOB FOR WHICH YOU HAVE APPLIED? *

* Completion of this part of the application is optional and will not result in adverse treatment.

IN CASE OF
EMERGENCY NOTIFY

Name   Address   Phone No.

I AUTHORIZE INVESTIGATION OF ALL STATEMENTS CONTAINED IN THIS APPLICATION. I UNDERSTAND THAT MISREPRESENTATION OR OMISSION OF FACTS CALLED FOR IS CAUSE FOR DISMISSAL. FURTHER, I UNDERSTAND AND AGREE THAT MY EMPLOYMENT IS FOR NO DEFINITE PERIOD AND MAY, REGARDLESS OF THE DATE OF PAYMENT OF MY WAGES AND SALARY, BE TERMINATED AT ANY TIME WITHOUT ANY PREVIOUS NOTICE.

DATE   SIGNATURE

DO NOT WRITE BELOW THIS LINE

INTERVIEWED BY   DATE

REMARKS:

NEATNESS		CHARACTER	
PERSONALITY		ABILITY	

HIRED   FOR DEPT.   POSITION   WILL REPORT   SALARY/ WAGES

APPROVED: 1.   2.   3.
EMPLOYMENT MANAGER   DEPT. HEAD   GENERAL MANAGER

This form has been designed to strictly comply with State and Federal fair employment practice laws prohibiting discrimination on the basis of an applicant's race, color, national origin, sex, age, marital status, height, weight or the handicapped. DOUBLEDAY BROS. & CO. does not assume responsibility and hereby disclaims any liability for inclusion in this form, of any questions upon which a violation of State and Federal fair employment practice laws may be based.

Source: Courtesy of Doubleday Bros. & Co.

While your second letter requesting an interview should be essentially the same as the first (especially if several months have elapsed), you should mention that you are writing a second time because of your serious interest in the company and your belief that you can make a significant contribution to the organization's ability to achieve its objectives.

Even though one objective of the interview is to secure the job for you, your task is not over with the interview. You should pursue your objective until you have been hired, rejected, or have decided that you would be better off working for another company. Correspondence after the interview has one or more of the following objectives:

1.   To bring your name to the attention of the interviewer one more time.

2.   To improve your interviewer's opinion of you by
     a.   Expressing appreciation for the interview.
     b.   Overcoming deficiencies discovered during the interview.
     c.   Offering new information to strengthen your application.

3.   To express continued interest in a particular job.

4.   To find out more about a particular job or company.

5.   To negotiate for
     a.   More money.
     b.   More time to decide about a job.
     c.   A change in some aspect of the job.
     d.   A more rapid decision about your status.

6.   To accept a job offer.

7.   To refuse a job offer.

Thank-You Letters

How can you use a postinterview thank-you letter to overcome an objection the interviewer had to hiring you?

Thank-you letters are the most frequently used follow-up letters. Every interview you have — regardless of whether you still want the job or of how you were treated in the interview — deserves to be followed with a letter of thanks. Thank-you letters can be either simple or complex, depending on how much work they need to do. When you are no longer interested in the job, you could simply write the following:

> Thank you for discussing the junior accountant's job with me last Tuesday. I was glad to meet you and greatly appreciated your frank discussion of the duties involved.
>
> As we agreed in the interview, I would be happier working for a company that would expose me to a variety of accounting functions. I did enjoy talking with you, and I'm sure you'll find the ideal candidate for the job.

When you still want the job, and the interview went well (that is, you are fairly convinced that the company will offer you the job), a short thank-you letter expressing your continued interest will suffice. It is more often the case, however, that you will need to improve your interviewer's opinion of you either by overcoming deficiencies that were discovered during the interview or by offering some new information that you believe will strengthen your application. In such cases you will need to write a complex follow-up letter, which is essentially a mixed message (see Chapter 11), according to the following organizational pattern:

1. **Positive opening.**   Thank the reader for having taken the time to interview you. Your thanks is a positive opening that places your letter in its specific communication context.

2. **Explanation.**   Deal in a direct manner with the deficiencies that came up during the interview. The damage was done during the interview, and your objective is to overcome the negative element by stating what you have done or are doing to correct the deficiency or by offering a fuller explanation for the problem than you did during the interview. Present any new information you have to offer (Have you completed or enrolled in additional courses or other training programs? Have you learned something new that would help you on the job?). Focus on the contribution you can make to the company based on what you learned in the interview.

3. **Action.**   Do not push. It is all right to assert yourself and to desire to know more, but do not be aggressive. Express your continued interest and ask whether you might answer additional questions.

Figure 17.2 illustrates the foregoing points:

Inquiries and Negotiations

What are the hazards of negotiating for a higher starting salary?

While your initial thank-you letter following the interview may easily and naturally contain questions about aspects of the job that you were not able to learn during the interview, it is more difficult to write a letter (after the initial thank-you letter) with no other purpose than to ask further questions about the job. Also, the current tight job market makes it difficult to negotiate with a prospective employer for more money, more time to decide about taking a job, a change in some aspect of the job, or a more rapid decision about your application.

Some people may feel that requesting more information about a company or a particular job may be viewed as criticism. Actually, the reverse is true. As long as your inquiry is legitimate — about something you should know before accepting a job with the company or about something for which

**FIGURE 17.2
Sample Follow-up
Letter**

Thank the reader
for the interview.

Overcome any ob-
jections to hiring
you by correcting
any false impres-
sions and by show-
ing that you learned
something in the
interview.

Express continued
interest in the job.

1522 Evelyn Byrd Road
Richmond, VA 23225

June 9, 19xx

Mr. Ron Dunne
Director of Personnel
Communication Unlimited
Box 18902
Knoxville, TN 37919

Dear Mr. Dunne:

Thank you for the time you spent with me when you visited
Purdue University last week. I enjoyed talking with you
about the possibility of working as the Assistant Personnel
Director for Communication Unlimited.

Since we talked, I've given further thought to the questions you asked about my lack of formal training in
communication. As you stated in the interview, your
main concern is to hire someone who can handle the
correspondence and face-to-face communication the job of
Assistant Personnel Director entails; and though my
formal training is limited to the three basic courses
offered at Purdue University, those courses were thorough
and demanding.

In addition to my formal training, my extracurricular
activities have called for well-developed communication
skills. In my role of Secretary of Pi Omega Pi, I wrote
many letters--including the most successful fund-raising
letter in the history of the fraternity--and chaired many
meetings. I would be able to bring this on-the-job
experience with me to Communication Unlimited. I am also
following your suggestion and reading several of the
communication books you mentioned.

I believe that I can make a valuable contribution to
Communication Unlimited, and I would appreciate it if you
would let me know if there is anything else I can do or
tell you about myself to help you decide about my
application.

Sincerely,

Mary Ellen Gurchiek

Mary Ellen Gurchiek

the information is not readily available elsewhere (the company's annual report, for example)—it will demonstrate your real interest in the company and place your name before the interviewer one more time. Treat inquiries about job matters the same as you would other inquiries, and use the organizational pattern presented in Chapter 6.

Negotiations also present problems. Every negotiation is a risk, and when you negotiate, you should be prepared to lose. By asking for more money or a change in some job duties, for example, you run the risk of not getting what you want and of creating resentment in your reader that will reduce your chances of getting the job at all. For this reason, most letters of negotiation are mixed messages with two or more business objectives. Because each letter of negotiation will contain information that the reader will resent and/or resist, it should also contain enough positive information to prevent the writer from losing what he or she has already gained. Suppose you received the following letter:

Thank you for the prompt return of the completed application form. This expression of your continued interest is sincerely appreciated.

We are still interested in your background and would like to consider you for our September 10 Sales Management Development training class. However, because your graduation isn't until August, I would like to delay further consideration until July. If this presents a problem, please drop me a note.

You really want to work for this particular company, but other good companies have made you more definite and attractive offers already, and they require your answer by mid-June. How do you answer the letter? Here is how one of our students handled the situation:

Thank you for your letter.

Because I am particularly interested in the job you described at Steele, I would be grateful if you would make a final decision on my eligibility for your Sales Management Development class by early June.

As you probably know, I am at present interviewing with several other companies, and I have been asked to give these companies my decision by the middle of June. While Steele is the company for which I would prefer to work, I would like to know what my opportunities with Steele will be before I refuse other offers.

Please let me know if another interview would help you decide. The University of Illinois has spring vacation from April 14 to April 23, and I could see you any time during the week. Or, with only short notice, I could visit La Crosse at some other time convenient to you.

What is the basic premise of negotiating?

Note that the student does not explicitly state that the situation requires an either/or decision. The letter implies that if the Steele Company does not make a definite job offer by early June, the student will have to accept one of the other job offers. This illustrates a basic premise of negotiations: you cannot negotiate unless you have something with which to negotiate. In this case the student had other job offers. When you negotiate for more money, you must be able to offer tangible evidence that you are worth more money. When you negotiate for more time to decide about a job or for a change in some aspect of the job duties, you must be able to provide evidence to support the worthiness of your request. And in all cases, do not negotiate unless you are prepared to lose.

Job-Acceptance and Job-Refusal Letters

Why should you bother writing courteous job-refusal letters?

Job-acceptance letters rarely present problems. They use a direct structure, beginning with the acceptance itself. Because the letter offering the job and the letter accepting it will constitute a contract, you need to make sure that you understand exactly what is being offered before you accept. Also, your letter of acceptance should include those aspects of the job, its responsibilities, and its rewards that you consider essential parts of the offer. See Figure 17.3 for an example of a job-acceptance letter.

Job-refusal letters are negative messages and therefore use the indirect structure shown in Chapter 8. The reader undoubtedly has other qualified applicants to choose from, but his or her feelings can still be hurt by your refusal. Try to keep the reader on your side. Base your refusal on reasons that leave the door open for possible future employment with the company, and express continued interest in the firm. Do not, however, imply that you may at some later date leave the company whose offer you are accepting. See Figure 17.4 for an example of a job-refusal letter.

Letters of Resignation

What functions should a letter of resignation perform?

Like job-refusal letters, job-resignation letters are negative messages and therefore use the indirect structure shown in Chapter 8. In most cases you will announce your resignation orally, and the letter will be useful primarily as a matter of record. Even when your employer knows in advance that you are resigning, you should use the letter to help retain good feelings between you and your employer in spite of the fact that you are resigning. You can do this by

1.   Showing that you learned something while working for the company.

2.   Providing ample notice (depends on the job level—the higher the job level, the more notice is required).

3.   Expressing willingness to train a replacement.

4.   Explaining your reasons for leaving.

5.   Offering constructive suggestions when possible.

FIGURE 17.3
Job-Acceptance
Letter

```
               119 Woodland Avenue, #3b
               East Orange, NJ 07017

               December 11, 19xx



               Mr. T. J. Haggblade, Personnel
               Antracene Coal Company
               Box 3340
               Indiana, PA 15705

               Dear Mr. Haggblade:

               Yes, I do want to work as Executive Secretary for the Anthracene
               Coal Company, and I'm glad to accept your offer.

               The conditions specified in your letter of November 15, 19xx,
               including the $23,000 salary, the six-month probation, and
               your overtime policy are all agreeable to me.  I've completed
               and enclosed the insurance and medical forms you sent.  Should
               I do anything else before reporting for work?

               I will be glad to see you at 8:00 a.m. Monday, January 3,
               when I report for work.

               Sincerely,

               Sydney D. Henshall
```

FIGURE 17.4
Job-Refusal Letter

468 Pennsfield, 12C
Thousand Oaks, CA 91360

May 22, 19xx

Mr. Frank Tailor, President
Resartus Industries
396 Bestar Boulevard
Pacific Palisades, CA 90272

Dear Mr. Tailor:

Discussing the job of District Sales Manager of Resartus
Industries with you was one of my more interesting interviews. You make the job at Resartus sound challenging,
and I'm sure that the opportunity is a good one. Thank
you for giving me such serious consideration.

As you know from our interview, in addition to my interest
in sales, I also have a strong interest in management
motivation. Because I believe that I can be most useful
in a job that will permit me to spend most of my time
working on problems of employee morale and motivation,
I have decided to accept a job with the Carlyle Conglomerate
which will allow me to work on such problems.

Thank you for the time you spent with me.

Cordially,

Alex Korinek

Alex Korinek

▷ Summary

Your written application may open the door for you, but to sell yourself to a particular employer, you also need to make a favorable and memorable impression in the job interview.

The interview helps the employer explore qualifications that may not show up in written applications, such as attitude toward work, sense of humor, interest in a particular job or company, willingness to cooperate with others, and other personality traits.

A successful interview depends as much on what is done *before* the interview as what happens *during* it. After making the appointment for the interview, do some research. Obtain information about the company from the library, school placement office, company employees, or the company's annual report. Prepare yourself for the day of the interview. Get a good night's sleep. Allow yourself plenty of time in the morning to get ready. Arrive 10 to 15 minutes early. Be prepared to answer frequently asked questions.

Many companies prefer to use the initial interview as a screening technique. A second interview tells the employer whether you have the social skills, attitude toward work, attitude toward the company, and adaptability that will make you an asset to the company.

Before or after either the first or second interview, you will probably be asked to complete an application form. In filling out forms of this type, answer every question, follow all directions, and be specific.

If your first application package to a particular company does not secure the interview and you are really interested in working for that company, you should send a second letter of application and resume to demonstrate your seriousness.

Your task is not over with the interview. You should pursue your objective with follow-up correspondence until you have been hired, rejected, or have decided that you would be better off working for another company. Thank-you letters are the most frequently used follow-up correspondence. Every interview you have deserves to be followed with a letter of thanks. Requesting more information about a company or a particular job, as long as your inquiry is legitimate, demonstrates your real interest in the company and places your name before the interviewer one more time.

Job-acceptance letters use a direct structure, beginning with the acceptance itself. Because the letter offering the job and the letter accepting it will constitute a contract, you need to make sure that you understand exactly what is being offered before you accept. Your letter of acceptance should include those aspects of the job, its responsibilities, and its rewards that you consider essential parts of the offer.

Job-refusal letters are negative messages and therefore use an indirect structure. Base your refusal on reasons that leave the door open for possible future employment with the company, and express continued interest in the firm.

COMMUNICATION SOLUTION

Organizations are looking for people who wish to make a positive contribution to life. Questions like "What are your goals," "What do you want to be doing five years from now," "What are your ideas of success," and "What do you want to do with the rest of your life" are all designed to see whether you have set specific goals and whether your goals are essentially selfish.

It is acceptable to want to earn money, but money should not be your only objective. What kind of contribution would you like to make to the world? Does your plan for making that contribution indicate the steps necessary to achieve your long-term objective? A good goal statement includes the following:

1. A specific, measurable, long-term objective.

2. A time for achieving the objective.

3. A plan for achieving the objective that specifies what you are willing to do to achieve the objective.

For example, a good goal statement might be "My professional goal is to be a certified public accountant for Ernst & Whinney by the year 19XX. I am willing to take additional college classes and to devote one night a week to preparing for the national examinations."

How does the organization with which you are interviewing fit into your long-range plans? Are your objectives compatible with organizational objectives? When you can show relationships between your goals and those of the organizations, do so.

Like job-refusal letters, job-resignation letters are negative messages. Use the letter to help retain good feelings between you and your employer in spite of the fact that you are resigning.

▷ EXERCISES

Review and Discussion Questions

1.   What are the purposes of job interviews?

2.   Why should you do some research on a company before the interview?

3.   Why do interviewers conduct a second interview?

4.   Give seven reasons for writing follow-up letters.

5.   Why are letters of negotiation a risk?

Problems

1.   Assume that you have interviewed for the job you applied for in Chapter 16.

      a. Write a thank-you letter based on a smooth, successful interview and your continued interest in the job.

      b. Write a thank-you letter based on your continued interest in the job and on an interview in which the interviewer expressed concern about your lack of formal education in report writing.

      c. Write a thank-you letter based on an interview in which you discovered that you are not really interested in the job.

2. Assume that two months have gone by since your interview and you have heard nothing. Write to your interviewer and persuade him or her to make a faster decision.

3. Assume that you have been offered the job you applied for in Chapter 16 and that your prospective employer wants your answer in one week. You are already committed to interviewing with a competing firm, and that interview will not take place until the day of your deadline. Write to the firm that offered you the job and request an additional week to make your decision.

4. The company has just offered you the job, but for $2,000 a year less than the usual rate for people at your level in your line of work. You have no other job offers at the moment, but you do have several promising interviews coming up in the next two weeks. Negotiate for a higher salary.

5. You have been offered two jobs at a suitable salary. Providing the specific details appropriate for your line of work, write to one company and accept its offer. Write to the other and refuse.

6. Assume you have worked for the company for five years and wish to accept a much better paying job that offers more challenges with a new company. Resign your job, giving 60 days' notice.

CASES

1. Prepare for job interviews with three organizations of your choosing. Begin by selecting three appropriate job titles for the kind of work you would like to do and researching the duties and responsibilities involved. Prepare files of information on each of the three organizations, and use appropriate forms of documentation to indicate the sources of your information. Present your findings in report format.

2. Prepare written answers to the 25 most commonly asked job interview questions, and submit them to your instructor for review.

PART FIVE

Communication Strategies at Work

Business communication involves more than writing letters and reports. In your day-to-day activities as well as in your planning for the future, you need to be adept at a wide variety of other communication skills to succeed in business.

Whether you are communicating on a one-to-one basis, in a group, or planning your organization's communication systems, you need a full understanding of the coordinating role of communication in business.

Chapters 18 and 19 will show you the rules governing communication exchanges, beginnning with interpersonal communication and progressing through group communication and leadership to organizational communication systems.

Chapter 20 will show you how modern office technology is changing the ways in which business people communicate.

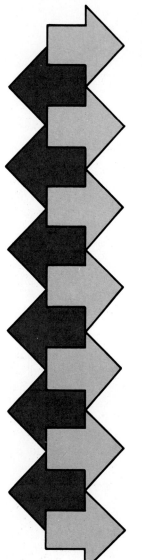

CHAPTER EIGHTEEN
Human Relations

Dale Carnegie's *How to Win Friends and Influence People* has been a best seller since it was originally published in 1936. For years people have recognized that effective human relations are essential for success in business—and in life. This chapter covers a variety of topics associated with human relations in the work place, from interpersonal communication to conflict resolution.

Topics

COMMUNICATION CHALLENGE

Conduct a *dyadic* (two-person, two-way) interview with someone in your class whom you do not know well and who seems quite different from you (different sex, age, race, religion, or cultural background). Discuss the similarities and differences in your belief systems—find points of difference and try to make your beliefs clear and to understand the other's beliefs.

Keep a summary of your conversations and your feelings about them. What happens to your communication when you are excited or upset? Draw some conclusions, and formulate some recommendations. Add to or change your ideas as you read through this chapter, and then check the Communication Solution that follows the chapter summary for additional ideas.

▷ OVERVIEW: MANAGEMENT *Is* COMMUNICATION

Management is working with and through people. Communication makes that possible. Letters and reports are only two of the broad range of management communication activities. Managers need to be effective at one-to-one conversation, in group discussions, at reading, at listening, at resolving conflicts and negotiating, and at understanding and communicating with members of other cultures.

Regardless of the communication situation, two rules always apply: be clear so that others will understand you, and be courteous so that others have the opportunity to make themselves understood. In communication your *attitude* is often the most important factor in determining your success. In general, people who really want to achieve an understanding can do so, as long as they are willing to accept some differences as natural and work to resolve those differences before they create problems.

This chapter discusses many of the communication situations and problems encountered in modern organizations. Some of the communication activities discussed—negotiations, for example—require extensive practice before you can expect to do well consistently, and others require additional training. If you are going to conduct much business with the Japanese, for example, you will need to learn to speak, read, and write Japanese. You need to be fluent in the language of the people with whom you expect to do business—clarity and courtesy both require it.

▷ INTERPERSONAL COMMUNICATION IN BUSINESS

To be successful in business, you need to master more communication skills than letter and report writing. Interpersonal communication skills and group leadership skills are essential to effective management. You also need to understand and manage the communication systems your company uses to communicate with its own employees and with the outside world.

What is interpersonal communication?

All communication is interpersonal in the sense that it takes place between people, but the term *interpersonal communication* has a generally accepted, more limited meaning. It is communication in which the communicators go beyond understanding each other's message to understand their common humanity.

Most interpersonal communication is face-to-face and takes place in dyadic — two-person — situations. Interpersonal communication, however, also includes other situations in which the communication behavior is similar to that in dyads. Three or four good friends talking together are probably communicating interpersonally rather than as a small group. Telephone conversations are interpersonal communication, though they are not face-to-face.

For communication to be interpersonal, it must involve an exploration of human psychology. Using what is already known about another person's psychology is not interpersonal communication. When we use psychological insights to motivate a person or to reduce the impact of a negative message, we are applying information learned in an interpersonal context to another, more structured communication situation. Interpersonal communication requires exploration and discovery — the learning of something new.

How does interpersonal communication determine relationships?

Interpersonal communication is the foundation of all human relationships. Because it usually takes place on a face-to-face basis, its success depends on our skill at listening, speaking, and sending and interpreting nonverbal messages.

How do the assumptions we make about others influence our interpersonal communication?

In addition to the way we listen, speak, and handle nonverbal messages, our interpersonal communication is influenced by the assumptions we make about ourselves and other people.

Fortunately, we do not have to fully understand our own behavior or that of others to achieve successful interpersonal communication. In fact, were we to understand others — or ourselves — fully, we would have no need to communicate. Our differences and our lack of knowledge about one another make communication necessary.

This lack of knowledge also makes the behavior of others often appear irrational and mysterious. We may fail to understand not only the reason someone has acted in a particular way, but also the person's explanation of that action. To compensate for this lack of knowledge, we should make five assumptions when engaging in interpersonal communication.

In what sense is behavior always meaningful?

1. The actions and communications of others have meaning to them, even if we do not know what that meaning is. In some cases the psychoanalysts are right — the "meaning" of a behavior or statement is an unconscious, inarticulate feeling that is *displaced* from one time and place to another. A frequently cited example of this is the man who has had a hard time at the office and who vents his anger and frustration on his

COMMUNICATION TODAY...

In a recent psychological study, when a random sample of male adults were asked to rank themselves on "the ability to get along with others," *all* subjects, 100 percent, put themselves in the top half of the population. Sixty percent rated themselves in the top 10 percent of the population, and a full 25 percent ever so humbly thought that they were in the top 1 percent of the population. In a parallel finding, 70 percent rated themselves in the top quartile in leadership; only 2 percent felt they were below average leaders. Finally, in an area in which self-deception should be hard for most males, at least 60 percent said they were in the top quartile of athletic ability; only 6 percent said they were below average.

We all think we're tops. We're exuberantly, wildly irrational about ourselves. And that has sweeping implications for organizing. Yet most organizations, we find, take a negative view of their people. They verbally berate participants for poor performance.... They call for risk taking but punish even tiny failures....

The message that comes through so poignantly in the studies we reviewed is that we like to think of ourselves as winners. The lesson that the excellent companies have to teach is that there is no reason why we can't design systems that continually reinforce this notion; most of their people are made to feel that they are winners. Their populations are distributed around a normal curve, just like every other large population, but the difference is that their systems reinforce degrees of winning rather than degrees of losing.

wife and children after going home. The man's anger is meaningful although misdirected.

A person's behavior is always meaningful in the sense that the person expects to receive some kind of pleasure (or relief from pain) as a result of that behavior. The gratification may not be fully conscious. In the foregoing example the man knows that he is angry, and he probably knows that his hard day at the office made him angry. What he almost certainly does not realize is that he is attempting to bolster his own self-image by hurting the self-images of his wife and children.

How does communication contribute to our control over our environment?

2. We communicate to increase the control we have over our own behavior and the behavior of others. We communicate to find out why someone — either ourselves or someone else — does something, so that in the future we can control, influence, predict, cause, or avoid that behavior. We are all more comfortable in an environment we can understand and make predictions about. We feel better when we know what is likely to happen next.

3. Regardless of the content of a message, all acts of communication are significant in that they have either a positive or a negative influence on

How does communication influence an individual's self-image?

the self-images of the sender and the receiver. Whenever we communicate, we make our receivers feel either better or worse about themselves. No communication is neutral. A simple "Good morning" may make your receiver feel better or worse, depending on whether you say it as though the person is important or unimportant to you. The sender's self-image also changes for better or worse with each act of communication—in the same direction, and to about the same degree, as the self-image of the receiver.

What is the relationship between perception and communication?

4.   All people have the same basic biological and psychological needs, but their perceptions of what constitutes satisfaction of those needs varies for cultural and personal reasons.

5.   For any of us to satisfy many of our needs for any length of time, we must cooperate—and communicate—with others. Because most people are not mind readers, we must begin by

a.   Asking questions to discover what the needs of others are and doing what we can to help them fulfill their needs and improve their self-images.

b.   Letting others know what our needs are and specifying ways they can help us achieve our goals.

▷ THE NATURE OF DYADS

What is a dyad?

Two people in face-to-face communication form a *dyad*. The major variables in dyadic communication are how well the people know each other and whether they perceive one another as equals.

Dyadic Life Cycle

Any dyad, inside or outside an organization, has a life cycle that begins when two people first meet and ends when the two no longer engage in interpersonal communication. The life cycle is composed of four general stages: initial, formative, mature, and severance.

Why are first impressions so important?

1.   **The initial stage** is very short, lasting at most about ten minutes. But the character of the dyad is usually fully established by the end of this stage. First impressions do count. The initial stage of interpersonal communication generally includes exchanges of demographic information, such as where and when the people were born, grew up, and went to school. At this phase each participant has the power to terminate the dyad; the exchange of demographic information helps the participants make inferences about differences of opinion, other matters of potential conflict, and common interests and beliefs. Some self-disclosure at this

stage helps to ensure the continuation of the relationship, but excessive self-disclosure discourages a lasting relationship.

What is dyadic equilibrium?

2. **The formative stage** may last for an indefinite period, beginning after the initial stage is over and continuing until the equilibrium of the mature stage is achieved. In the formative period, the participants discuss attitudes and opinions and establish the emotional tone of the relationship. Several types of conflict may arise at this stage. For example, one person may wish to be more intimate than the other; one may wish to control the other more than the other wishes to be controlled; or one may respond to situations in ways that the other finds inappropriate.

What are the characteristics of a mature dyadic relationship?

3. **The mature stage** also lasts an indefinite period. At this point the participants have "defined" each other and their relationship. They have reached a perceived equilibrium: they think they agree about how intimate they will be, about who will control whom, about how decisions affecting both of them will be reached, and about what jokes are funny.

    Some relationships never reach true equilibrium. The participants behave as though they agree about matters of importance to the relationship, but in actuality they disagree. This happens when one participant does not engage in honest self-disclosure. **A dyad based on inaccurate information cannot last.** The amount of self-disclosure can vary greatly in ongoing relationships, but the information must be accurate if the dyad is to continue. This is true of any dyad, from a purely professional relationship in which a bare minimum of personal information is disclosed to the fully intimate relationship of lovers.

    In mature dyadic relationships, each participant can judge with fair accuracy how the other will respond in any exchange between them. It is possible, however, for one participant to upset the equilibrium by altering an established conception of the relationship. Suppose, for example, that after 15 years of marriage and raising three children, a wife tells her husband that she wants to go back to school and become a microbiologist. The husband liked things the way they were. When this sort of conflict arises, the dyad returns to the formative stage and the participants must work to reestablish equilibrium if the relationship is to continue.

    If the dyad is important or valued, it is generally worthwhile to change the equilibrium slowly rather than dramatically. (It is easier to climb stairs than to leap tall buildings in a single bound.) In the foregoing example, the wife could achieve her objective by letting her husband adjust first to her taking a few courses, then to her working toward a degree, and then to her completion of a graduate program.

4. **The severence stage** is the final stage. Ours is a mobile society: people not only change their residences fairly often, but also sometimes change their values, beliefs, and expectations quite rapidly. These changes greatly

How are relation-
ships affected by
the mobility of peo-
ple in our society?

increase the complexity of interpersonal communication. Some people
respond to the uncertainty of future changes in relationships by avoiding intimacy; others respond by trying to effect intimacy in all relationships. Any interpersonal relationship involves some risk, of course, and
the more intimate the relationship, the greater the risk that severance
will be painful.

The Mature Organizational Dyad

How does interper-
sonal communica-
tion influence the
morale of an or-
ganization?

Dyads in the organizational setting follow the same life cycle as other dyads.
Mature dyads (good interpersonal relationships) greatly boost the efficiency
and the morale of a company. A company's success is often determined by
who communicates with whom and how well those people get along with
each other. Three factors control dyadic communication in organizations:

1.   The communication climate.

2.   The formality of the dyad.

3.   The dyad's ratio of surface to hidden meanings.

What are the differ-
ences between open
and closed commu-
nication climates?

Communication Climate.   Dyads tend to establish either an open or
closed communication climate. Some variation occurs from day to day, but
most dyads are fairly consistent with respect to the amount and kind of
communication that take place. The people in a dyad usually reach an agreement about the way they will treat one another, though the agreement may
not necessarily please both people.

Closed communication climates — those that discourage communication — give people the feeling that they are being judged and criticized. In
this type of communication climate even the most innocuous piece of constructive criticism will probably be perceived as a threat. In an open communication climate, people perceive communication more accurately and are
more willing to communicate honestly.

Although it takes two people to form a dyad, the person in the superior
position usually has a greater influence on the communication climate. Management and first-line supervisors have the organizational authority to establish the communication climate because their occupational superiority can
readily be perceived. High social status functions the same way. Compare
these approaches:

> **Boss 1:**   You've only been back from vacation three
> days, and you've already fallen behind in
> your work. I want the report on the John-
> son account on my desk by 9:00 a.m. to-
> morrow, and I won't take any excuses. Is
> that clear?

> **Boss 2:**   I know you've only been back from vaca-
> tion three days, but I have an important
> meeting with Johnson tomorrow morning
> at 10:00. I'll need the report you're work-
> ing on by 9:00 to make an effective presen-
> tation. Can you do it?

Boss 1, at the time of this statement at least, has established a closed communication climate. The tone is accusatory, judgmental, and absolute, emphasizing the superior-subordinate relationship and manipulating the receiver. The closing question does not solicit honest feedback but simply emphasizes the superior position of the boss.

Boss 2, at the time of this statement at least, has established an open communication climate. The information here is essentially the same as in the first statement, but Boss 2 gives a reason to support the request. This puts the emphasis on problem solving rather than on the superior-subordinate relationship. The judgmental tone is absent, and the statement solicits honest feedback.

Neither of these statements would occur in isolation, of course. Each would have a communication history. Boss 1 may have learned the hard way that the person addressed will not do the work unless challenged by ultimatums. In general, however, open communication climates produce higher morale and higher quality work than closed climates.

Open communication climates lead participants to feel that they are part of a problem-solving team, making valuable contributions. Closed communication climates lead participants to feel that they are on trial, defending themselves against attack. See Chapter 1 for a full discussion of communication climates.

What are the differences between formal and informal dyads?

Formality.   A mature dyad has a fairly consistent degree of formality, established almost entirely by the participant who is higher in the organizational hierarchy or who has the higher social status. The main difference between formal and informal dyads is that the former discourages self-disclosure, whereas the latter encourages it. Other aspects of communication are not necessarily influenced by the degree of formality. Generally speaking, however, long-lasting, valued relationships are less formal than relationships the participants feel will be temporary and unimportant.

Dress and outward appearance do not indicate degrees of formality. Two businessmen in blue suits, white shirts, and conservative ties may be much less formal with each other than two college students wearing cutoffs and T-shirts. The conventions of the business dyad differ from those of the college-student dyad, but formality is measured not by the conventions of behavior themselves but rather by which — or how many — conventions the participants ignore in their dealings with one another.

SIDEBAR

MBWA

Manager A and Manager B decide that the oil should be checked in their respective company's cars every week because the use of the cars has increased. Manager A uses the chain of command to implement the idea. After going through three levels of management, the idea becomes a message that one of the big bosses got a car that was low on oil and had to put oil in himself. Oil has to be checked every week just to be sure that doesn't happen again.

Manager B uses Management By Walking About (MBWA) to implement the idea. He goes

to the motor pool to visit with the employees. Manager B finds out that the employees have been checking the oil every month but are concerned about all the extra miles being put on the cars lately. The employees and Manager B agree that the oil should be checked weekly. Manager B also compliments the employees for being so observant. Manager B not only implements his oil-checking idea, but also implants a "caring for the cars" idea.

Increased communication and decreased distortion facilitate the implanting of ideas.

Source: Theresa E. Field, Wilson Hill Associates, Inc. Reprinted with permission.

How does excessive formality influence a relationship?

Although inappropriate informality in the initial or formative stages of a dyad might lead to an imbalanced relationship, informality in a mature relationship is a sign of trust. The participants in such a relationship have agreed that the absence of certain conventional forms of behavior does not endanger the relationship. Excessive formality, on the other hand, is an element of distance that may indicate a closed communication climate. For example, if one participant in the dyad tends to use a written channel rather than an oral channel for routine communication, the message "keep your distance" is clear.

The appropriate degree of formality can be established only by the two people in the dyad, but for the dyad to be successful, the participants must agree about how much formality is required.

How do hidden meanings influence interpersonal communication?

Surface and Hidden Meanings.   We are more comfortable in interpersonal communication with surface meanings rather than hidden meanings. Surface meanings include all those communication components—both verbal and nonverbal messages—that one participant in the dyad offers to the other with the intent of conveying clear information. Surface meanings may be either explicit or implicit, but they are clear to the intended receiver. A private joke, for example, has surface meaning even though it is implicit rather than explicit.

Hidden meanings are those that are unclear to the receiver, leading him or her to speculate on more than one possibility. Suppose, for example, that a co-worker says to you, "I've heard that if the new company president has his way, your department won't need its typewriters any more." When pressed for details, the co-worker says, "I don't know any more; besides, I've said too much already." Because the surface meaning does not make complete sense to you, you are left to speculate about possible hidden meanings, such as

Did your co-workers make up the story?

Is there any truth to the story?

Where did your co-worker hear the story?

Does the new president want to eliminate your department?

Will your department receive new word processing equipment?

Will your secretaries be moved to a word processing center?

And so on.

When a meaning is unclear, you might also speculate about the sender's veracity and motives. Prevarication and hypocrisy are both possible in a communication containing hidden meanings. Both make interpersonal relationships unpleasant.

How can you iden-
tify a manipulative
personality?

More typical in organizational situations than outright prevarication or malicious hypocrisy are dyads in which one or both participants use statements with hidden meanings to conceal, reveal, or test for the truth. This behavior is typical of the formative stage of the dyad's life cycle, but in the mature stage it indicates a manipulative personality and creates an atmosphere of mistrust. The communicators are acknowledging that they do not fully trust one another, at least with some category of information.

Your co-worker with the story about your department's typewriters may want to let you know that your job is insecure without telling you directly. On the other hand, he may want to convince you that your job is insecure to cause trouble between you and higher management. All you can be sure of is that, for one purpose or another, you are being manipulated.

People who habitually manipulate others in this way tend to assume that all messages contain hidden meanings. They become like the two psychiatrists who were walking down the street when a third psychiatrist passed them saying, "Good morning." When the third psychiatrist was out of earshot, the first said to the second, "I wonder what she meant by that?"

Accurate communication, good interpersonal relationships, and organizational efficiency cannot be based on speculation and mistrust. No one likes to be manipulated, and manipulation fosters countermanipulation. When this goes on, everyone in the organization suffers.

▷ Formal Interpersonal Communication: The Interview

How do interviews differ from other dyads?

Most of what we have said about dyads applies to the interviewing process, but interviews differ from other dyads in that they usually have a more definite, formal structure. Although interviews vary in their degree of formality and are conducted for various purposes, their similarities are more notable than their differences.

Interview Purposes

What are the usual purposes of interviews?

In arranging for an interview, one of the participants always has a specific purpose in mind. The specific purposes usually fall into one of the following six categories:

What three objectives should job interviews accomplish?

1. **Employment.**   The employment interview is probably the best-known of all interview types. It is unusual to get a job without some kind of interview, so most of us have had at least limited experience with an employment interview. Employment interviews have three specific purposes. First, the interviewer should determine whether the applicant is the right person for the job. Second, the interviewer should give the applicant enough information about the job and the company so the applicant can make a decision about the job on the basis of personal goals and the prospects for advancement with that company. And third, the employment interview should create goodwill for the company.

2. **Orientation.**   The orientation interview functions to supply or obtain facts, policy information, or other job-related data. Orientation interviews are routinely used to introduce new employees to the work situation. They also serve to acquaint employees with pertinent, new information.

How do performance-appraisal interviews help both employer and employee?

3. **Performance-appraisal.**   The performance-appraisal interview is used to help evaluate job performance. It is also used to discuss job, personal, and performance goals and to define job-related problems and expectations. Most companies conduct formal performance-appraisal interviews on a regular basis. At the end of the interview, both employer and employee should have a clear understanding of the other's expectations.

4. **Problem-solving.**   In problem-solving interviews, the interviewer and the interviewee discuss a job-related problem and explore possible solutions. This type of interview is also used when either the employer or the employee needs to familiarize the other with a particular problem.

5. **Counseling/grievance.**   When the employer or the employee has a particular problem that the other can solve, a counseling/grievance in-

terview is helpful. Counseling includes not only advice about personal problems, but also advice about correcting identifiable job performance deficiencies. Grievance interviews reflect the employee's "right to petition" the employer to change a particular behavior.

6. **Exit.**   The main purpose of an exit interview is to help the employer understand the reasons for employee turnover. Exit interviews also serve to express appreciation for the employee's work and to ensure that the employee leaves with a positive attitude toward the company.

Interview Structure

Why is planning necessary to conduct a successful interview?

A successful interview follows a particular pattern planned by the interviewer, although the structure must be flexible enough to allow for some unscheduled discussion. Planning, then, is essential to the interview. A specific purpose must be clarified for the interview, pertinent information collected, the main questions prepared, and a time allotment determined.

What should be accomplished in the opening phase of an interview? In the body? In the closing?

An interview consists of four parts: the opening, the body, the close, and the follow-up. The opening of the interview should make the purpose of the interview clear and establish an open climate for communication (comfortable rather than threatening).

The body of the interview is that portion in which the participants exchange pertinent information by means of questions and answers. The main requirements for success are clearly worded statements and careful listening. Participants must resist the temptation to argue or lecture. Both interviewer and interviewee should remember that each can gain from the other, whatever the circumstances or the nature of the interview. Each must remember that the other may not be capable of expressing observations or inferences adequately, and each should seek clarification on matters of disagreement or misunderstanding before making an evaluation.

The close of the interview provides the interviewer the opportunity to review and summarize the key points of the discussion, emphasizing points of agreement and follow-up actions that the participants are to undertake. Both participants should express appreciation for the interview.

What should be done as follow-up for interviews?

The follow-up consists of recording important decisions and agreements and initiating any follow-up action necessary. In performance-appraisal and counseling/grievance interviews, both participants should receive copies of the written summary and evaluation.

Types of Questions

Why is creating an open communication climate especially important in an interview?

Because all interviews consist of a series of questions and answers, the success of an interview depends primarily on the kinds of questions asked. The serious nature of an interview makes it a potentially threatening situation for many people, so the interviewer must be especially careful to create and maintain an open communication climate if he or she wishes to elicit clear, accurate information. Certain kinds of questions help to establish an open climate; other kinds of questions cut communication off.

Open-climate questions include leading questions, direct questions, open questions, probes, mirror questions, and hypothetical questions.

What are the differences between open-climate questions and closed-climate questions?

1. **Leading questions** guide the interviewee to a specific response. The interviewer should avoid leading questions unless certain that the socially approved response will result. When used to confirm known information, leading questions help the interviewer and interviewee relax with one another. "You went to Iowa State University, didn't you?" "You majored in marketing, didn't you?" "Isn't it true that you received a football scholarship?"

2. **Direct questions** call for a limited response, often yes or no. "Where were you born?" "Did that influence your decision to apply for a job with us?" Some direct questions, such as "Did you go to college?" are open-climate questions only in certain contexts. If a direct question poses a possible threat, it should be asked only after an open climate has been established.

3. **Open questions** require the interviewee to develop an extended answer. They are therefore the interviewer's main tool for discovering what the interviewee is like. "Tell me a bit about yourself." "What do you expect to be doing ten years from now?" "What do you do for relaxation?" "What would you consider your major accomplishments during the past year?"

4. **Probes** are direct or open questions that pursue some aspect of a previous response. "Why would you like to be a district manager?" "Which do you prefer, fishing or hunting?"

5. **Mirror questions,** like probes, serve to elicit more information about a certain aspect of a previous response. The question "mirrors" some part of the response.

Interviewee:	. . . and then I went to Iowa State University for about a year . . .
Interviewer:	Iowa State University?
Interviewee:	Yes, in Ames. That's where . . .

6. **Hypothetical questions** are used most frequently in employment and performance-appraisal interviews. They permit the interviewee to develop an extended response exploring a particular possibility. "What changes would you make if you were district manager?" "Let's assume that we could find the money for new equipment. What would you like to see installed?"

Closed-climate questions include loaded questions, double-bind questions, forced-choice questions, and why-didn't-you questions.

1. **Loaded questions** show evidence of an assumption or a value judgment that predetermines what is an acceptable response. "How do you feel about Melvin Crane's stupid behavior?" "What makes you think that you could run the company better?" An interviewer who has not done required homework may asked loaded questions inadvertently—as when a person with only a high school education is asked where she or he went to college.

2. **Double-bind questions** tend to force the interviewee to choose between two unacceptable answers. One classic double-bind question is, "Do you still beat your wife?" A modern version is, "Do you prefer to get drunk or get high?" Other questions that seem innocuous at first may be in effect double-bind questions: "Do you drink alcoholic beverages?" If you say no, you may be considered antisocial. If you say yes, you may be considered a lush.

3. **Forced-choice questions** are like double-bind questions in that they tend to force the interviewee to choose and defend a response. "Which is more important to you, serving humanity or making money?" "Which secretary, Susan or William, do you think should be fired?" "Would you rather read *Playboy* or *Religious Opinion* magazine?" The difference between double-bind and forced-choice questions is one of complexity. The double-bind question has no right answers; whereas either answer to the forced-choice question may be correct if it is adequately explained.

4. **Why-didn't-you questions** accuse the interviewee of some shortcoming —usually failure to provide important information. "Why didn't you tell me about your arrest record?" "Why didn't you tell me that you failed mathematics in college?" "Why didn't you turn off the stamping press before going on coffee break?" "Why didn't you complete the report on time?"

Control of Interview

How does the control of an interview influence the kind of information received?

The interviewer controls the direction and duration of the interview by asking questions, providing support, and responding to the interviewee's questions and answers. Interviews may be tightly or moderately controlled or open.

Tightly Controlled.   Tightly controlled interviews, consisting primarily of direct questions, are best when only specific, factual information is required. The interviewer usually asks all the questions; the interviewee is confined to giving the answers requested.

Moderately Controlled.   Moderately controlled interviews, consisting of some direct and some open questions, are fairly flexible. The great majority of interviews are moderately controlled, 15- to 30-minute interviews. The time span is long enough to allow the interviewer to clarify important points and to allow the interviewee to ask and receive answers to some questions as well. Moderately controlled interviews are best when time is limited but the interviewer must explore the ideas, attitudes, and beliefs of the interviewee.

Open.   Open interviews, which include many open questions, are used primarily for high-level employment interviews and for problem-solving interviews. The open interview, however, is not uncontrolled. The interviewer has an objective and a plan, but the interviewee is allowed to do most of the talking in a way that forces him or her to develop extended answers in a clear, logical, coherent fashion. This style of interviewing is best for discovering what someone is like, but it is time-consuming. The importance of the interview purpose must make the investment of time worthwhile.

Being Interviewed

What are the interviewee's responsibilities during the interview?

Most of the information presented in the foregoing discussion was from the interviewer's perspective. But in addition to understanding the interviewer's responsibilities, business communicators should also have a clear understanding of the role of the interviewee. An interview with a skilled interviewer is quite painless, but being interviewed by an unskilled person can be an awkward, uncomfortable experience. Because you will never know in advance what your interviewer may be like, be prepared by doing the following:

1. **Understand the purpose.**   When you can, find out *before* the interview what its purpose is. Sometimes, of course, you may be called in unexpectedly with no opportunity to discover the purpose before you are interviewed. In that case, find out early in the interview whether it has a specific purpose and, if so, what that purpose is.

2. **Present the right image.**   In addition to dressing appropriately for the interview, make sure that you have done your homework. If it is an employment interview, find out all you can about the company, including its policies, products, and personnel. If it is a performance-appraisal interview, analyze your strengths and weaknesses before the interview takes place.

3. **Convey the information.**   As the interviewee, your main role is to provide the answers. In most interviewing situations, you will also be expected to ask some questions. You can either work your questions in when they fit naturally or save them for the end. But make sure that you answer the questions you are asked in a clear, specific way and at

a reasonable length. Make sure that you understand each question before you launch yourself on the sea of language.

Interviewer:	Tell me a bit about yourself.
Interviewee:	Do you mean my life history or what I'm like now?

4. **Handle the difficult questions.**   If you are asked a closed-climate question, deal with it as best you can. Do not get angry or attack, and do not defend yourself. Delay. If possible, ask for a clarification; you may then be able to answer a more favorable question. If the question is so clear that asking for clarification would be ridiculous, qualify your answer. See Chapter 17 for typical stress-interview questions.

Interviewer:	Would you rather make money or serve humanity?
Interviewee:	I believe that those are compatible goals and that I can do both by . . .

▷ INFORMATION SOURCES: READING AND LISTENING

Why are reading and listening skills essential for successful communication?

So far in this book we have been concerned primarily with showing you how to improve your communication by concentrating on your responsibilities as a sender of messages. As we indicated in Chapter 1, however, your responsibilities as a receiver of messages are also important. Two of the primary means you have for receiving messages are reading and listening. You speak and write to inform, to inquire, and to persuade; but you read and listen to *learn*.

You cannot possibly communicate effectively unless you can read and listen effectively. The quality of your communication output depends completely on the quality of your communication input. What you read and hear — and the conclusions you draw because of what you have read and heard — controls what you write and say.

Even more than with speaking and writing, most of us tend to think of our reading and listening skills as well-developed; indeed, reading and listening are so fundamental that we frequently take these skills for granted. Most of us read and listen inefficiently, however, missing much that we should learn from the messages we receive.

The act of receiving messages can be broken into three phases, all necessary for full understanding. First, we must observe the message in its entirety; second, we must analyze the message; and third, we must draw certain specific conclusions on the basis of our observations and analysis.

Observation

What is observation?

What is the process of *abstracting,* and how does it influence the act of observing?

Most of us are in the habit of ignoring much of our environment. How often, for example, have you caught yourself "reading" a book — looking at and turning each page — without understanding a word you have read? How often have you been "listening" to a lecture, only to catch yourself lost in thought about some completely unrelated topic?

Observation begins with attention, and as we discussed in Chapter 1, attention is a selective process. We can pay attention only to a limited part of our environment. By a process of *abstracting,* we select and focus on certain stimuli and ignore others. For us either to read or to listen effectively, we must make a conscious effort to focus our attention on the subject matter and ignore distracting stimuli, such as background noise, the uncomfortable chair we are sitting in, or our increasing hunger pangs. We must also be aware of the following human tendencies that can serve as barriers to full observation. We pay closer attention to

1. Aspects of the environment that we consider directly relevant to our goals and objectives than to those for which we can see no immediate use.

2. Stimuli that confirm our world-view than to those that contradict it.

3. Unexpected or unfamiliar stimuli (such as a loud bang) than to expected stimuli (such as the ticking of a clock).

4. Stimuli from sources we consider especially credible than to stimuli from unknown or routine sources.

The selective process of observation has its advantages. We do not need to read or listen to everything with full attention. But we do need the ability to give full attention to a book, lecture, or conversation when the situation requires it.

Analysis

What are the differences among facts, inferences, and value judgments?

By itself, observation is not sufficient for us to grasp the meaning of written and spoken messages. We must also analyze the message, examine each of its parts, and find and separate facts, inferences, and value judgments. In the process of analysis, we ask ourselves questions about the message:

What are the facts?

How do we know what is fact and what is opinion?

Do we agree with the message?

What is our attitude toward the source? Toward the content? Is our attitude toward the source or content influencing our reception of the message?

Conclusions

At what point is the act of receiving a message complete?

The final phase in receiving messages is the formulation of conclusions. The answers we reach in our analysis will largely determine our conclusions. We may, for example, conclude that the message has no meaning for us and promptly forget it. Or we may conclude that some parts have no meaning, some are meaningful and true, and still others would be meaningful if true, but we do not judge them to be true.

In reaching conclusions and summarizing the content of the message, we organize the material in the way that will best enable us to remember it. The act of receiving the message is not complete until we have come to some conclusion about it.

Reading

In what ways is the act of receiving a written message different from that of receiving an oral message? How does the channel influence the communication process?

Both reading and listening may entail problems with the reception and understanding of messages, but the problems differ because of the different characteristics of the communication channels involved in reading as opposed to listening. With written messages, for example, receivers do not have the same opportunity to request clarification as they usually do when listening; but readers can reexamine the message as many times as necessary to reach a full understanding, as opposed to the listener's single opportunity.

In some ways reading is a less complicated activity than listening. In listening we must observe two channels of communication, oral and nonverbal, and weigh them both in our analysis. In reading we can usually focus directly on the message itself; also, as most of us have had much more formal training in reading than in listening, we are more attuned to careful reading than to careful listening.

Because reading is our primary means of learning complex material, we can benefit greatly from improving the efficiency with which we read. We spend more time listening than reading, but the time spent reading is usually more concentrated, because the written message was sufficiently important or complex to be put in writing in the first place, and because all extraneous matter has supposedly been eliminated from the central aspect of the message.

What are the differences among reading speed, accuracy, and comprehension? How does each influence what is remembered?

Techniques of Effective Reading.   Effective reading calls for mastery of three related but essentially separate skills: speed, accuracy, and comprehension. Speed is determined by the number of words we can read a minute. This aspect of reading is the easiest to measure. Reading accuracy is determined by how correctly we perceive the contents of the message, and comprehension is measured by how well we understand the message. Accuracy and comprehension are easily confused, but they are actually separate skills.

Accurate reading consists of seeing each word for what it is. Reading with comprehension consists of grasping the meaning of the message as a whole, whether or not each word is seen specifically. Suppose that you read this sentence: *Communication is essential for all human relations; it makes civilized, cooperative life possible, and it gives us our ability to build and shape our environment.* You can read somewhat inaccurately, omitting a few words entirely (*human*, either *civilized* or *cooperative*, either *build* or *shape*) and still comprehend the idea the sentence conveys.

The better you read, the faster you will be able to read with complete accuracy and full comprehension. But all readers have a point beyond which every increase in speed results in a loss of accuracy, if not comprehension. To be a good reader, you need the ability to read everything at the fastest speed that will permit the degree of accuracy and comprehension required. If you must understand something fully, and if each word is crucial for that understanding, you will have to sacrifice speed for greater accuracy and comprehension. But when all you need is the gist of something, you can increase speed by sacrificing some degree of accuracy or settling for less than complete comprehension.

Improving Speed.   Improving speed requires practice and determination. You cannot read faster without forcing yourself to do so, and you cannot read faster without suffering at least a temporary reduction in accuracy and comprehension. If you are already reading 400 words a minute, you cannot read any faster with absolute accuracy, since this is the highest rate at which the brain can process words.

Effective reading requires a direct relationship between eye and brain. Using other muscles (except for using your hands to turn the pages) can only slow you down. If, for example, you tend to use your finger to follow the text, you are limiting yourself to the speed with which you can point to individual words.

What are vocalization and subvocalization, and how do they influence reading?

If you vocalize by moving your lips or by reading almost aloud, you are limiting yourself to reading at a speaking rate, about 125 words a minute. You can test yourself for vocalizing by placing the fingers of one hand lightly over your lips as you read. If you detect any tendency toward lip movement, make a conscious effort to read without vocalizing, keeping your fingers over your lips as a constant reminder.

Even if you are not vocalizing, you may still be slowing your reading speed by subvocalization, the forming of words with the vocal cords without moving the lips. You can test for any tendency toward subvocalization by placing your fingers lightly on your larynx (Adam's apple) and checking for movement.

What is skimming?

What is scanning and how does it differ from skimming?

When you have practiced until reading is a direct act involving only the eye and the brain, you should be able to achieve a maximum reading rate of about 400 words a minute. At speeds faster than 400 words a minute, you are either *scanning* or *skimming* the material rather than reading it. Scanning is looking quickly through material to find specific points or answer specific questions. Skimming is looking quickly through material to note the central ideas.

What kinds of materials should be skimmed rather than read carefully?

Readers accustomed to placing a premium on accuracy and comprehension are often uncomfortable when they try to read more quickly than the rate that lets them read each word and consider its meaning carefully. Overcoming this discomfort is usually their biggest obstacle to reading faster. You do not need to read everything with the same kind of care, however. You may, on one hand, need to read a subordinate's market analysis report for your company's new product with extreme care, but on the other hand, you may learn all you need to know about current events by skimming a daily newspaper and one or two news weeklies.

What techniques can you use to increase both speed and accuracy in reading?

If you are currently reading at a rate of less than 400 words a minute, you can improve your speed by selecting material that you do not need to know thoroughly and forcing yourself to read it faster than you find comfortable. Cultivate the habit of skimming when the material does not warrant more careful reading. Remember, however, that it is a waste of time to skim something so rapidly that you understand and remember nothing about it. So you should test yourself for accuracy and comprehension. A news weekly that you are going to read anyway is probably the most convenient material to use for self-help in improving speed. Pick an article. Read it as quickly as you can, timing yourself (use a stopwatch if you have one, but absolute exactness is not essential). Use the following techniques:

1. Pay close attention to headings, the first paragraph, and the last paragraph.

2. Look for main ideas. The topic sentence of a paragraph is often the first sentence in the paragraph.

3. Look for names of people, places, events, and things.

4. Ask yourself the five W questions—*who, what, when, why,* and *where*—and also *how.*

5. If you miss something, do not worry about it. Forge ahead.

When you have finished skimming, note the time it took to skim the article, then write down everything you can remember about the article. Next, estimate the number of words in the article by counting the words in five lines, dividing that total by 5, and multiplying that answer by the number of lines in the whole article. When you have calculated the number of words in the article, divide that figure by the number of minutes it took you to read the article.

Now reread the article carefully. List the specific facts in the article. Comparing your original list with the list you have prepared from the article will reveal your accuracy. To determine your comprehension, add the number of correct facts in your original list (the central ideas must be substantially correct, and it is okay to count two "half-right" facts as one correct one). Then divide by the total number of facts in the article. Your answer will be a percentage that indicates your level of comprehension.

If, for example, you skim an article containing 4,275 words in 3.75 minutes, you would compute your speed and comprehension as follows:

Speed:　　4,275 words divided by 3.75 minutes equals 1,140 words a minute.

Comprehension:　　12 remembered facts essentially correct divided by 18 facts actually in the article equals 67 percent.

You should strive for a skimming rate of about 2,000 words a minute, with a comprehension level of about 80 percent. It is impossible to achieve or maintain such a level without regular practice, but the time spent mastering this technique will save you many hours that you would otherwise spend reading some material much more closely than is useful to you.

Why does vocabulary play such an important role in reading speed? In reading accuracy?

Another way to (indirectly) improve reading speed is to improve your vocabulary. A good vocabulary will enable you to read even the most complex material at close to the maximum rate of 400 words a minute because you will recognize all the words instantly and understand how they are being used in the sentence.

Unfortunately, there is no short cut to building vocabulary. If you already have a fairly well-developed vocabulary, you can probably expand it by writing down words you are not absolutely sure of when you encounter them, looking them up, and memorizing them—including spelling, pronunciation, definition, and use. If your vocabulary needs a lot of work, several good paperback books are available that can help you start to build your working vocabulary in just a few weeks. As with the other exercises for improving speed, you must invest some time, but the return you will receive in improved reading ability will make it a worthwhile investment.

What kinds of materials should be read carefully, with emphasis on accuracy rather than speed?

Improving Accuracy.　　Although you should always strive to read everything as quickly as the material and its importance will permit, accuracy and comprehension must sometimes take precedence. Some messages are so important that you cannot afford to skim them; you must observe and comprehend the entire message correctly. You may, in fact, need to take notes so that you can commit the most important facts to memory, or you may need to read the material more than once.

The key to accurate reading is, once again, a well-developed vocabulary. It is difficult, and sometimes impossible, to correctly perceive facts that are presented with words unfamiliar to you (unless you look up every unfamiliar word in the dictionary).

How can prereading help improve reading comprehension?

Improving Comprehension.

Comprehension and accuracy are closely related. You must perceive the message accurately before you can achieve total comprehension, so vocabulary, by affecting accuracy, also affects comprehension. Sometimes you may be able to comprehend the main thrust of the message despite inaccurate perceptions of some details. You run the risk, however, obviously, of misunderstanding something important. You can improve your comprehension if you pay special attention to the following:

1. **Getting ready.**   *Preread* the material by surveying the title, table of contents, chapter headings, main headings, and introductory comments. Write down questions you anticipate finding answers for in the message.

2. **Searching for main ideas and details.**   Make sure that you understand the vocabulary being used. Look for topic sentences and key paragraphs, and try to discover the organizational pattern of the material.

3. **Analyzing and interpreting.**   Pay special attention to the author's principal statements. Are they facts, inferences, or value judgments? Do you agree or disagree with the author? Is the author a recognized, unbiased authority? Is the research sound, including sufficient facts to support generalizations?

4. **Organizing and remembering.**   After you have read the entire message, can you recall the major points in their proper order? If the message is important enough, you should probably take notes, either in brief outline form or as a quick summary.

Listening

Why is effective listening often more difficult than effective reading?

Reading and listening have a lot in common, but effective listening is probably more difficult to achieve. In reading you can proceed at a pace that permits you to understand the message, and you can always go back and reread sections that you do not fully comprehend.

In listening you must adapt to the speaker's pace; although you can sometimes ask the speaker to repeat something, the repetition will probably be a paraphrase rather than an exact statement of what was said earlier, and it may not convey exactly the same idea. In addition, most of us have been taught a greater respect for written messages than for speech. We tend to pay closer attention to material that has been put into writing, and we certainly give it greater credibility.

Importance of Listening.

The importance of listening is frequently underemphasized. Throughout school you learn more about reading every year; but you are generally expected to know how to listen when you begin school. Yet studies of listening activity have shown that of the 70 percent of the waking day that most of us spend in communication activity, we spend more time listening—about 45 percent—than reading, writing, or speaking. Studies have also shown that **most of us listen with about 25 percent efficiency;** that is, we remember about 25 percent of what we hear, forgetting 75 percent almost immediately after hearing it.

What are the differences between listening and hearing?

Listening and Hearing.   Listening is much more than hearing. Hearing is a physical, passive communication process; listening is a mental, active communication process. We hear words, but we listen for meaning. Hearing is easy; listening is work.

We hear with our ears; we listen not only with our ears, but with our eyes and mind as well. As we listen we also search for nonverbal signs of communication. We study the speaker's facial expressions, body movements, gestures, tone of voice, and voice inflections. We are born with hearing abilities, but we must develop our listening skills through practice. Hearing is a gift; listening is an art.

One of the reasons listening is a more complex activity than reading is that it occurs in a wide variety of situations. Reading is essentially a private affair. If distractions interfere with your reading, you can always reread the material at a more opportune time. Listeners, however, must deal with distractions as they occur.

Although listening situations range from extremely informal to very formal, listening tasks fall into two broad categories, public and interpersonal. Public listening situations are those in which listeners are attempting to learn everything they can from a formal presentation, lecture, or media (television or radio) speech. Interpersonal listening situations are those that encourage exchange—questions, answers, or conversation—between speakers and listeners. In public listening situations, the listener has little chance for *personal* interchange with the speaker.

Listening in public situations requires many of the same skills as reading. In public situations, the listener's main tasks are to observe, analyze, draw conclusions, and remember what has been said. In interpersonal situations, listening involves an additional set of tasks: nonverbal messages must be observed, analyzed, and weighed against the spoken message. The techniques we suggest here for improving your listening effectiveness apply whether the situation is public or interpersonal.

What are the common barriers to listening effectiveness?

Listening Barriers.   Barriers to effective listening may be caused by either external or internal distractions of one sort or another. The following list is not by any means complete.

External	**Internal**
Hearing problems	Emotions
Physical condition	Attitudes
Fatigue	Biases
Hunger	Opinions
Distractions	Prejudices
Noise	Semantics
Voice inflections	Assumptions
Accents	Cultural differences
Volume changes	Social differences
Interruptions	Inferences

Techniques of Effective Listening

Effective listening in a formal situation is an eight-step process. In some situations you will not need all eight steps, but if you master them all, you will be able to handle any listening situation.

Which of the eight steps of effective listening are often neglected and why?

1. **Prepare.**   Before you enter a listening situation, make sure that you know enough about the subject to understand what will be said. You cannot always do this, of course, but when you know that you will be listening to a message about a difficult subject, *prelisten* by reading enough about the subject that the vocabulary and concepts will be somewhat familiar to you. Relate the subject matter to your goals and objectives and explore your attitude toward the subject. Prepare to deal with your internal barriers to perceiving the message accurately.

2. **Pay attention.**   Stop talking and concentrate. Listen to the speaker's full message without interrupting; save your own ideas for later. Whether you are listening to a formal speech or an informal discussion, identify the central subject matter and the organizational pattern. Formal speeches are usually arranged either inductively (specifics followed by conclusions) or deductively (generalizations supported by specifics). The pattern in informal discussions is associational and often chronological.

     Be alert for main points, topic sentences, and transitions. Focus on the message rather than the speaker, the delivery, or your own feelings. As an aid to focusing your attention and remembering the message, identify each point as evidence (specific facts) or conclusions (generalizations or inferences), and assign one or two key words to each point to serve as memory aids.

3. **Summarize.**   Keep track of what the speaker has been saying. Use your key words to help you summarize what the speaker has already

covered. As each new point is added, review the points that have led up to it. Each time you review your lengthening list, you are reinforcing the key points.

4. **Anticipate.**   Guessing the speaker's next remarks will help you pay attention to the message whether or not you anticipate correctly. If you guess correctly, the confirmation of your expectation will help you to focus on the message; if you guess incorrectly, the contrast between your expectation and the actual message will help you to observe and remember the message delivered.

5. **Listen between the lines.**   Listen not only to what is said, but also to how it is said. Watch for emotionally charged words that form a "smoke screen." Is the speaker attempting to convince you by using language that arouses strong emotional responses and thus interferes with your objectivity? While you are listening between the lines, question yourself about the message. Do you agree or disagree with what is being said? Can you think of additional supporting evidence? (Your *feelings* about the subject and speaker do not count.) A speaker who uses emotional language that your feelings object to may still have a valid point. See if you can discover the real message underneath the bombast.

6. **Ask questions.**   When you have the opportunity to ask for clarification and amplification, do so. Make sure that you understand the speaker's use of language to eliminate as many semantic barriers to communication as possible. You should also provide other kinds of feedback to help the speaker. In both formal and informal situations, smile at the speaker. When appropriate, you can also indicate your interest in the speaker by providing other verbal and nonverbal cues. Eye contact, nodding your head, and saying "Uh huh," "Yes," "I see," and other short "I'm listening" comments will encourage the speaker to make a complete statement.

7. **Take notes.**   When you need to remember the message for any length of time, you should take notes. The key to good note-taking is to listen more and write less. You cannot possibly take down every word a speaker utters, and attempting to will only cause you to fall behind, become confused, and miss most of what is said. Restrict yourself to recording the most important principles. Use the key words you have selected (see Point 2 in this list) to stand for the principles. Usually, listing one or two supporting facts for each principle will be enough to help you recall the other supporting evidence. As soon after the speech as possible, review your notes and type a more complete summary of the message for your records.

8.   **Evaluate.**   You are ready to make an accurate judgment or a fair, sensible reply after you have heard the entire speech or discussion; after you have had a chance to question the speaker, examine the evidence, and consider the usefulness of the material; and after you have made sure that barriers have not distorted your perception of the message.

Active Listening

What is active listening, and when should it be used?

Effective listening in an informal situation requires a different set of skills. Dr. Carl Rogers and other nondirective psychologists have developed the technique of *active listening* to help others solve their problems. Active listening can also help improve interpersonal communication by clarifying misunderstandings and by helping two people reach a mutually satisfying solution to a problem.

As the term implies, active listening requires the listener to participate actively in the communication process, primarily by encouraging the other person to talk. The following behaviors are essential to active listening.

1.   **Maintain eye contact.**   Eye contact lets the other person know that you are paying attention.

2.   **Provide regular feedback.**   Nod your head; smile; say "uh, huh," "I see," and other brief comments to show that you are listening.

3.   **Clarify important points.**   Summarize what the other person has said so that she or he can confirm that you heard correctly. Ask questions about parts of the problem that are not clear to you.

4.   **Explore feelings.**   Every problem has two components: the external (the situation or event) and the internal (the emotional response—how the people involved *feel* about the external component). An active listener explores both components and recognizes that the feeling component is the one with greater impact on human relations.

5.   **Do not evaluate or give advice.**   Judgments or advice both end the conversation, and both put the listener in a superior position to that of the speaker. Let the speaker reach his or her own conclusions—which you can facilitate only by listening and asking questions.

How can active listening help in the process of conflict resolution?

While one objective of active listening may be to reach an agreement about how to solve a problem, active listening is designed primarily to produce understanding. Agreement may follow understanding, but more typically, active listening results in a clear definition of a problem that must then be solved using the techniques of conflict resolution, which are discussed later in this chapter.

◇ CONFLICT RESOLUTION AND NEGOTIATIONS

What causes con-
flict?

Interpersonal communication skills are put to the test only in situations involving some kind of conflict. When people are getting along well, they are
building each other's self-images and making themselves feel good at the
same time. When everybody agrees, communication comes easily. When
conflict arises, however, people tend to engage in simultaneous monologues
rather than in dialogue.

Conflict is the result of our inability to alter a behavior we *perceive* as a
threat to our well-being or to our self-image. Because we are all defensive to
some extent, we frequently perceive a threat where none actually exists; and
because we are all self-centered, we tend to try to control the behavior of
others without first trying to understand them. If, for example, a supervisor
asks a subordinate, "Have you finished the report yet?" the subordinate may
view the question as a threat — a comment on his or her efficiency — and
conflict might result. In this case both the supervisor and the subordinate
might be trying to control the behavior of the other — the supervisor to get
the report written more quickly and the subordinate to convince the supervisor to reduce the work load. The unexpressed messages cause conflict.

Rational differences of opinion do not result in conflict. For conflict to
result from differences of opinion, the emotional self-images of the persons
must be involved. We are not defensive about our ideas in themselves. We
are defensive about our self-image. When someone criticizes an idea or attribute of ours, we may respond in one of the following three ways if our
self-image is involved.

1.   Defend or deny the idea or attribute.

2.   Attack the criticism.

3.   Delay the conflict by trying to discover whether a threat actually exists.

How does self-im-
age influence the
response to a differ-
ence of opinion?

In general, our response to a perceived threat depends on the way our
self-image compares with our image of the other person. When we perceive
the other person as our superior, we tend to defend. When we perceive the
other person as our inferior, we tend to attack. When we perceive the other
person as an equal, we tend to delay. In some instances, of course, people
may respond to a perceived threat by attacking a superior or defending against
an inferior. Context is an important influencing factor. Either attacking or
defending, however, cuts off the exploration required for effective interpersonal communication.

Because the constructive resolution of conflict requires that all parties
achieve an enhanced self-image, the third response — delay — always produces better results than either of the others. Effective interpersonal com-

munication requires more intelligent questions and attentive listening than self-expression. If we delay our response by exploring what the other person means, we may discover that what we heard was not what the other person meant. Of course, we might discover that some defense or attack is necessary because the threat is real; but because we delayed our response, we should be in a position to respond more intelligently.

Conflict resolution is a three-step process of (1) determining who has the problem, (2) communicating about the problem, and (3) taking the action necessary to eliminate the problem.

Determining Who Has the Problem

How can you determine who "has the problem" in a conflict situation?

Conflicts may cause two—or several—people to feel uncomfortable, or they may be a problem primarily for one person. The person who is most uncomfortable or most unhappy is usually the one who must assume the responsibility for initiating the process of conflict resolution.

If you are Joe's supervisor, for example, and Joe is consistently late for work, your inclination may be to assume that Joe has a problem with punctuality. If you attempt to convince Joe that his lateness is *his* problem and that he should change his behavior for that reason, you are likely to communicate an evaluation ("Joe is *bad* because he is late") and create resentment. In this and similar situations, you should first recognize that Joe does not have a problem with his lateness (though he may have other problems); *you* have a problem with Joe's lateness, and your task is to enable Joe to see why you have a problem with it.

Communicating About the Problem

How can confrontation and active listening be used to help resolve conflicts?

Once you have determined who has the problem, use communication skills to clarify the problem for all the people involved. The communication techniques useful at this stage are *confrontation* and *active listening*. When you recognize that *you* have the problem, confront the other person in a way that demonstrates that recognition. Avoid accusing the person of personal shortcomings; focus on the behavior rather than on the person. Let the other person know both why her or his behavior is causing you a problem and how you feel about it.

Poor: "Everyone else can get here on time, Joe. Why can't you?"

Poor: "I can't stand it when you're late, Joe."

Better: "When you're late and I have to reassign your work to people who arrived on time, I feel resentful, and I'm sure that the others do, too. We need to discuss the problems caused by your lateness.

What might happen
if a boss frequently
ordered an em-
ployee to perform
various tasks?

The objective of confronting the other person is to open the problem for discussion so that a mutually satisfactory agreement can be reached. An agreement forced on either party or reached by manipulation will not last. The person who comes out on the losing end of such an agreement will find a way to break it or subvert it.

When the other person has the problem, you have the responsibility to listen, using the techniques of active listening already discussed. In the case of Joe's lateness, for example, you may discover that Joe is responsible for taking two young children to a day care center in the morning. To solve *your* problem of dealing with Joe's lateness, you'll need to help him find a way to solve *his* problem of caring for the children while still being able to make it to work on time.

Because most of us like to give advice, active listening is difficult under the best of circumstances. It is even more difficult to listen actively when the other person perceives that *we* are the cause of her or his problem. The natural tendency when attacked is to counterattack or defend by explaining:

Henry: I can't possibly finish this report by 5:00. You're being unreasonable.

Julie: I'm sorry, but I have to give it to the VP at 8:00 tomorrow, so you'll just have to finish it tonight. (Defends by apologizing and counterattacks by ordering.)

How can active lis-
tening improve
human relations?

Active listening, however, will result in improved human relations and often produce a more satisfactory solution at the same time.

Henry: I can't possibly finish this report by 5:00. You're being unreasonable.

Julie: Are you worried about having to stay late tonight? (Responds to feelings by asking a question.)

Henry: Yes, I am. I have a dinner date at 7:00 tonight, and I'll never make it if I have to do the report tonight.

Julie: I have to give the complete report to the VP tomorrow at 8:00, and that's a deadline that can't be changed.

Henry: Suppose I do as much as I can tonight and come in early tomorrow and finish it?

Julie: Could you finish by 7:30 so that we would have time to check for errors before I have to sign off on it?

| Henry: | I think so. If necessary, I can change my dinner reservations for 7:30. That should give me plenty of time. |

Do not assume that all your efforts at active listening—especially your first efforts—will go as smoothly as the conversation between Henry and Julie. Neither confrontation nor active listening is a guarantee that the other person will see your point of view or that he or she will do things your way. After active listening, you may agree to do things the other person's way, or you may decide to compromise or to try a new way of solving the problem. The main advantages of these skills is that they help improve human relations, which may result in an open communication climate favorable to problem solving.

Taking Appropriate Action

In what way do "actions speak louder than words"?

Once an agreement has been reached, take whatever action is necessary to follow through on the agreement. If, as a result of active listening, you agree to change a particular procedure, be sure to change it. As mentioned in Chapter 1, when nonverbal behavior and verbal communication are in conflict, the nonverbal behavior is believed. Failure to follow through on an agreement will undermine your efforts to establish effective human relations. Do not make promises you cannot keep, and make sure that you keep the promises you make. A person who is not believed is not trusted, and a person who is not trusted has no real authority and cannot command either respect or loyalty.

Negotiating Agreements

Why are negotiators wrong to think that winning is everything?

Many organizational situations require negotiations similar to those required to resolve conflicts between individuals, and the same basic techniques apply. Neither side can "win" a negotiation unless both sides are satisfied with the outcome. Too many organizational negotiators fail to recognize that the well-being of the relationship between the parties may be more important to the health of the organization than any other aspect of the negotiations.

Roger Fisher and William Ury have identified four components of what they term *principled negotiation:*

1. **People.** Separate the people from the problem.

2. **Interests.** Focus on interests, not positions.

3. **Options.** Generate a variety of possibilities before deciding what to do.

4. **Criteria.** Insist that the result be based on some objective standard.

What is mutual gain bargaining?

Negotiating following these guidelines is often called *mutual gain bargaining.* Figure 18.1 illustrates the differences between traditional hard and soft styles of bargaining and negotiating based on merits.

FIGURE 18.1
Styles of
Negotiating

PROBLEM Positional Bargaining: Which Game Should You Play?		**SOLUTION** Change the Game— Negotiate on the Merits
SOFT	**HARD**	**PRINCIPLED**
Participants are friends.	Participants are adversaries.	Participants are problem solvers.
The goal is agreement.	The goal is victory.	The goal is a wise outcome reached efficiently and amicably.
Make concessions to cultivate the relationship.	Demand concessions as a condition of the relationship.	**Separate the people from the problem.**
Be soft on the people and the problem.	Be hard on the problem and the people.	Be soft on the people, hard on the problem.
Trust others.	Distrust others.	Proceed independent of trust.
Change your position easily.	Dig in to your position.	**Focus on interests, not positions.**
Make offers.	Make threats.	Explore interests.
Disclose your bottom line.	Mislead as to your bottom line.	Avoid having a bottom line.
Accept one-sided losses to reach agreement.	Demand one-sided gains as the price of agreement.	**Invent options for mutual gain.**
Search for the single answer: the one *they* will accept.	Search for the single answer: the one *you* will accept.	Develop multiple options to choose from; decide later.
Insist on agreement.	Insist on your position.	**Insist on using objective criteria.**
Try to avoid a contest of will.	Try to win a contest of will.	Try to reach a result based on standards independent of will.
Yield to pressure.	Apply pressure.	Reason and be open to reasons; yield to principle, not pressure.

Source: From *Getting To Yes* by Roger Fisher and William Ury, p. 13. Copyright © 1981 by Roger Fisher and William Ury. Reprinted by permission of Houghton Mifflin Company.

▷ INTERNATIONAL COMMUNICATION

Why do many people in foreign countries dislike North Americans?

When Edward T. Hall wrote *The Silent Language* (Fawcett, 1959), few North Americans engaged in international communication. North Americans abroad, in fact, were usually considered self-centered and boorish for their lack of understanding of other cultures. As a result of increased world trade, most business people can now expect to be involved in intercultural communication at some point in their careers. Both large and small businesses export and import goods. Nonprofit organizations, too, have international branches, and only rare individuals will not need to communicate with their counterparts from other cultures.

Why is it important to know the language of a country with which you want to do business?

Communicating with someone from a different culture is more difficult than communicating with someone from your own for two reasons. First, even if you speak the other language or — which is more likely — the other person speaks English, no one "thinks" in a foreign language in quite the same way as does a native. Obviously, the better you know the language of the country you are visiting, the better off you will be — even if all your conversations are in English. The French, Germans, Spanish, Italians, Japanese, Chinese, and every other cultural group with whom you may do business in the future have distinct perspectives of the environment, unique ways of looking at things. Their use of language will reflect that unique perspective, even when they speak in English.

In addition to the increased difficulty of communicating with someone whose native language is different from your own, intercultural communication presents problems because cultural expectations may be significantly different. Attitudes toward time, space, food, appearance, religion, and manners will all be different from what Americans have come to accept as normal.

Time

North Americans may be considered rude because of the way they treat time. Why?

North Americans value punctuality and like to reach business decisions quickly. In general, people from Latin America or the Middle East are casual about time; they frequently arrive at social and business meetings late by North American standards and are slow to make business decisions, preferring to get acquainted with somebody socially before discussing business matters. The Japanese, although extremely punctual, also prefer to spend time socializing before discussing business matters. North Americans who expect to have one lunch, one dinner, and then conclude a multimillion dollar deal when abroad are bound to be disappointed.

Space

North Americans may be considered rude because of the way they treat personal space. Why?

How much space do you require to feel comfortable? Most Americans prefer to keep at least 18 inches between themselves and another person with whom they are conversing. We are uncomfortable when we cannot avoid closer contact, such as in a crowded elevator. In many countries, however, much closer contact is the norm. Conversational distance in much of the Middle East allows for very little distance between people. In Japan, India, and much of the Far East, the people are accustomed to and comfortable with being in what Americans would consider crowded, confined conditions.

Food

In what parts of the world would drink-

Although McDonald's has demonstrated the international popularity of the hamburger, the rest of the world eats many types of food that North Amering alcoholic beverage be considered unacceptable behavior? In what parts would *not* drinking alcoholic beverages be considered unacceptable?

icans find unpalatable, or lacks food that many North Americans expect to have regularly. In the Far East you might have to drink tea rather than coffee. In much of the Middle East you would have to go without your morning bacon or sausage because pork is forbidden. Also, in Moslem countries the possession and use of alcoholic beverages would be a serious crime. Be sure to study the food preferences and prohibitions of countries you will visit, and be prepared to accept the standards of the host country.

Appearance

How can your reactions to the traditional clothing of a country influence communication?

The Western business suit (whether for males or females) is usually considered acceptable dress for business, regardless of where you may be. Blue jeans, too, have become an acceptable international uniform for young people. Business people may be invited to social functions, however, where natives will wear traditional clothing, such as the Japanese kimono or a Scottish kilt. When you are scheduled to travel abroad, study the clothing style of the countries you will be visiting so that you will know what to expect. Your business negotiations will not go well if you communicate the attitude that Western dress is somehow superior to the traditional clothing of your host country.

Religion

History is replete with wars fought over religious beliefs, and in spite of the fact that the United States was founded on the principle of religious freedom, too many Americans forget that most of the peoples of the world are neither Christians nor Jews. Buddhism, Hinduism, and the Moslem religion have all profoundly influenced the cultures in large parts of the world. Beware of communicating the attitude that the religion and values of your host country are inferior to your own, regardless of how different they may be.

Manners

What should you learn about the manners and customs of a country before you attempt to conduct business there?

Americans tend to be casual and open in their relationships, often calling each other by first names only a few minutes after first meeting. Many other cultures are more formal. In Japan, for example, only a Japanese man's mother has the right to use his first name; others would be considered impolite for using it.

In many cultures, including the Japanese, the bow rather than (or in addition to) a handshake is the traditional greeting. In some cultures, eye contact is considered impolite; in others, the *lack* of eye contact is considered impolite. In some cultures, you are expected to bring a gift to your host or hostess. In other cultures, such gifts would be considered attempted bribes. Some cultures expect the young to defer to their elders, while others allow for a free exchange of ideas regardless of age. Not all cultures regard women the equal of men, nor do all cultures regard men the equal of women.

Obviously, the more you know about the culture of the country you will be visiting, or of the people with whom you will be dealing, the better

COMMUNICATION SOLUTION

Communication is put to the test only when conflict is present, at which time one's ability to communicate is often diminished. In your dyadic interview, did you find it difficult to understand and make yourself understood? What communication strategies did you employ? Was active listening one of them? Obviously, there is no definitive answer to the Communication Challenge in this chapter, but you should know whether your attempts at communication succeeded or failed in the exercise. Only when you are aware of the point at which you lose your objectivity, can you begin to develop the skills necessary to communicate effectively in conflict situations.

off you will be. When people do not understand each other because of cultural differences, feelings are bound to be hurt. Even when people have great differences, however, they can communicate successfully if they are willing to accept each other's world-view and work at the process of mutual understanding.

▷ SUMMARY

Interpersonal communication is the foundation of all our human relationships. Our communication depends on our assumptions about motivation and behavior. To achieve effective interpersonal communication, we must begin with the assumption that the actions and communication of others are meaningful to them, even if we do not perceive that meaning. The reason we communicate is to increase the control we have over our own behavior and the behavior of others; all acts of communication have either a positive or a negative influence on the self-images of the sender and the receiver.

Two people in a face-to-face communication situation form a dyad. The life cycle of a dyad consists of four general stages: initial, formative, mature, and severance. Dyads have a tendency to be either open or closed to communication.

Interviews differ from other dyads in that they have a more definite, formal structure. The six specific purposes of interviews are: employment, orientation, performance appraisal, problem solving, counseling or grievance, and exit. An interview consists of a series of questions. Some kinds of questions—leading questions, direct questions, open questions, probes, mirror questions, and hypothetical questions—contribute to an open climate. Closed-climate questions include loaded questions, double-bind questions, forced-choice questions, and why-didn't-you questions.

Reading and listening are the two primary means of receiving information. We will learn more from reading and listening if we learn to overcome barriers to accurate observation, analyze the information we receive, and organize material into meaningful patterns. Effective readers know when to skim material and when to read carefully for accuracy and understanding. Effective listeners work to overcome both internal and external barriers to the listening process. Active listening is a special technique for understanding other people and helping them solve their problems.

Conflict resolution is the most critical application of interpersonal communication techniques. Conflict results from the inability to alter a behavior perceived as threatening. Conflict resolution is a three-step process consisting of (1) determining who has the problem, (2) communicating about the problem, and (3) taking the action necessary to eliminate the problem. Confrontation and active listening are the principal techniques for communicating about the problem.

Negotiating organizational differences is essentially the same process as resolving interpersonal conflicts. Organizational differences should be resolved so that all parties gain. Principled negotiations, or mutual gain bargaining, is a four-step process: (1) Separate the people from the problem; (2) focus on interests, not positions; (3) generate a variety of possibilities before deciding what to do; and (4) insist that the result be based on some objective standard.

The amount of international communication increases every year. As a result of increased world trade, nearly everyone in business must eventually communicate with people from different cultures. Most of these cultures have different communication conventions, which greatly complicates the communication process. People who will be responsible for intercultural communication should study the language and the culture of the people before they communicate, even if all the actual communicating will be in English. People who are able to accept cultural differences and accept others as they are can become effective intercultural communicators.

▷ **EXERCISES**

Review and Discussion Questions

1. Explain the importance of interpersonal communication.

2. How does communication help us control our environment?

3. Describe the four stages of a dyadic life style.

4. Name and explain the three factors that control dyadic communication in organizations.

5. Describe the six interview types.

6. Describe the four parts of an interview's structure.

7. What are the differences among tightly controlled, moderately controlled, and open interviews?

8. What four factors influence the act of observation?

9. Name and explain the three skills essential for effective reading.

10. In what way is listening different from hearing?

11. Describe the eight techniques of effective listening.

12. What is conflict?

13. How is confrontation helpful in resolving conflicts?

14. How is active listening helpful in resolving conflicts?

Problems

1. What is the *Johari Window,* and what does it suggest for interpersonal relationships? (Library research may be required for you to answer this question.)

2. What is Management By Walking About (MBWA), where did the term originate, and in what way is good communication necessary to make it work? (Library research may be required for you to answer this question.)

3. Calculate your reading speed and document the technique you used to do it.

4. Take turns with your classmates describing problems and practicing active listening.

5. Take turns with one of your classmates negotiating a higher salary for the jobs of your choice. (Your instructor may wish to set a limit on the dollar amount or the time.)

CASES

1. Write a short report (no more than ten pages) analyzing the role interpersonal communication plays in modern organizations. Use at least five secondary sources.

2. Plan and conduct two moderately controlled performance-appraisal interviews, one using all open questions and the other using all closed questions. Write a short report analyzing the differences you observe between the types of interviews. Include the questions for each interview type in an appendix.

3. Analyze a conflict you are currently having and develop a strategy for resolving the conflict. Role-play confrontation and active listening until you are satisfied with your ability to communicate about the problem, and then apply the techniques. Write a brief report about your experiences.

CHAPTER NINETEEN

Small Group and Organizational Communication

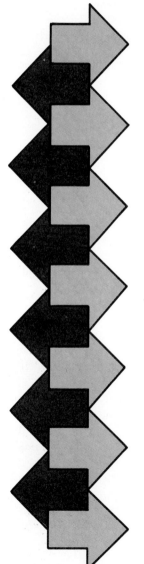

Meetings, conferences, discussions . . . in any organization the members must get together periodically to decide how to solve important problems and to exchange the information necessary to coordinate their activities. This chapter will help you understand how communication functions in small groups and in larger organizational structures.

COMMUNICATION CHALLENGE

Suppose that the president of your organization has called you into his office and asked you to form a committee to help control rumors on the organizational grapevine. Lately the rumors, which involve both personal relationships between some high-ranking organizational officers and a variety of matters concerning organizational operations, have been commanding a lot of attention from employees despite their utter falsity.

Whom do you ask to serve on your committee, and what should your committee do? How should you decide on a course of action? Take a few minutes now to jot down your ideas. If you wish, change or add to your ideas as you read this chapter, and then compare your final answer with the ideas that follow the chapter summary.

▷ OVERVIEW: MAKE A POSITIVE CONTRIBUTION

Small group and organizational communication are more complex and difficult to control than any of the forms of communication we have discussed so far. The same rules for effective communication, however, still apply, and by following them you can make a positive contribution to the small groups of which you are a member and to the organization as a whole.

Small groups play an increasingly important role in modern organizations as decisions become more complex and require a wider variety of expertise. In the course of your career you will be part of innumerable small groups, either as a member or as a group leader. The more you understand about how the group situation influences communication, the more effective you will be, either as member or leader.

As you rise in the organizational hierarchy, you will have increasing responsibility for ensuring that the organization's communication systems are functioning as well as they should. Is the grapevine in your organization running wild? Is your rumor-control center doing its job properly, or has it lost its credibility?

This chapter will introduce you to the communication concepts you need to know to understand group dynamics and to run a small group meeting effectively. It will also provide an overview of typical organizational communication systems so that you will be able to identify and improve those aspects of organizational communication for which you are responsible.

▷ THE IMPORTANCE OF SMALL GROUPS

Why are so many organizational decisions made by small groups rather than by one individual?

In modern organizations almost all important decisions are made in small groups. This trend undoubtedly results, in part, from the increasing complexity of society and technology; but it is reinforced by the fact that small groups produce reliably better decisions than any one person can produce. Although in some cases a highly skilled person can analyze a problem and reach a solution more efficiently than a group, the complex nature of many business problems makes it difficult to determine in advance who might have the required skills to solve a particular problem. And when small groups function as they should, more information is brought to bear on the problem in question than any one individual could bring.

Why is most small group communication task-oriented?

Unlike most interpersonal communication, communication in a small group is primarily task-oriented in that the group has been assembled to solve a particular problem. The participants are usually selected because they are directly concerned with the particular topic under consideration. The essential interpersonal communication skills are still required, however, for effective small group communication. These skills include the ability to

1. Read and control nonverbal messages.

2. Listen.

3. Communicate orally.

4. Establish an open communication climate.

In addition to these skills, effective small group communication requires an understanding of group characteristics, group influences on the communication process, group dynamics, and group communication and leadership.

▷ GROUP CHARACTERISTICS

What is a small group?

The variety possible in the size, type, and purpose of small groups is virtually inexhaustible. A board of directors is a small group. A jury is a small group. A committee to protect the tsetse fly would be a small group. A small group consists of any number of people from two to about twenty who have some need or purpose in common and who can communicate face to face with each other without the need for parliamentary procedure to control behavior. A small group may, of course, choose to use parliamentary procedure without ceasing to be a small group. But when the group becomes so large that parliamentary procedure is required to maintain order, the group is no longer

COMMUNICATION TODAY...

Treat people as adults. Treat them as partners; treat them with respect. Treat *them* — not capital spending and automation — as the primary source of productivity gains. These are fundamental lessons from the excellent companies research. In other words, if you want productivity and the financial reward that goes with it, you must treat your workers as your most important asset. In *A Business and Its Beliefs,* Thomas J. Watson, Jr., puts it well: "IBM's philosophy is largely contained in three simple beliefs. I want to begin with what I think is the most important: *our respect for the individual.* This is a simple concept, but in IBM it occupies a major portion of management time. We devote more effort to it than anything else. This belief was bone-deep in my father."

There was hardly a more pervasive theme in the excellent companies than *respect for the individual.* That basic belief and assumption were omnipresent. But like so much else we have talked about, it's not any one thing — one assumption, belief, statement, goal, value, system, or program — that makes the theme come to life. What makes it live at these companies is a plethora of structural devices, systems, styles, and values, all reinforcing one another so that the companies are truly unusual in their ability to achieve extraordinary results through ordinary people. The message goes right back to our early chapter on man and motivation. These companies give people control over their destinies; they make meaning for people. They turn the average Joe and the average Jane into winners. They let, even

insist that, people stick out. They accentuate the positive.

Let us make clear one final prefatory point. We are not talking about mollycoddling. We are talking about tough-minded respect for the individual and the willingness to train him, to set reasonable and clear expectations for him, and to grant him practical autonomy to step out and contribute directly to his job.

Genuine people orientation is in marked contrast to the two major alternatives all too often seen in companies: the lip service disaster and the gimmicks disaster.

The lip service disaster is arguably the worse of the two. Almost every management we've been around says that people are important — vital, in fact. But having said that, they then don't pay much attention to their people. In fact, they probably don't even realize their omissions. "People issues take up all my time," is the typical rejoinder. What they often really mean is, "This business would be so easy if it weren't for people."

Only when we look at the excellent companies do we see the contrast. The orientation toward people in these companies often started decades ago — full employment policies in times of recession, extraordinary amounts of training when no training was the norm, everybody on a first-name basis in times much more formal than ours, and so on. Caring runs in the veins of the managers of these institutions. People are why those managers are there, and they know it and live it.

Source: From *In Search of Excellence: Lessons from America's Best-Run Companies,* pp. 238–239, by Thomas J. Peters and Robert H. Waterman, Jr. Copyright © 1982 by Thomas J. Peters and Robert H. Waterman, Jr. Reprinted by permission of Harper & Row, Publishers, Inc.

small. The U.S. Senate is obviously not a small group. We are concerned here with groups small enough to establish flexible procedural rules, even if the group is so formal that its behavior is in other ways just as rigid as that of the Senate or House of Representatives.

Dyads are sometimes considered small groups. Even when dyads have a specific purpose, however, the interaction involved differs from that in groups of three or more because the presence of other people influences the communication process. The group situation puts certain pressures on participants that do not occur in dyads; perhaps because of this, groups tend to be more formal than dyads.

Purpose

What are the differences among primary, informal, and formal groups?

Groups always have a reason for being. The almost endless variety of reasons people form small groups can be divided into three general categories:

1. Primary.

2. Informal.

3. Formal.

Primary groups consist of family and close friends. The reason for continued existence of a primary group is essentially the self-satisfaction of the group members. Although it is possible for some individuals to form primary groups on the job, primary groups are not typical of organizations. We will not discuss them here.

Informal groups are formed to foster improved interpersonal relationships rather than to accomplish any particular task or objective. Coffee-break gatherings, group lunches, and company bowling and softball teams are among the most common informal groups in organizations. The communication skills necessary in informal groups are essentially interpersonal skills. It is only when an informal group assumes a task—becoming for the moment a formal group—that other skills are required.

What purposes do formal groups serve?

Formal groups are those that have a specific task or objective. People may belong to formal groups either because they share a common concern or because they are assigned to the group by their organizations. The most common formal groups in organizations are the following:

1. **Informational.** Staff meetings, conferences, and briefings are examples of informational groups. These groups are useful when the group members need the same information at the same time and when management wants to ensure exposure to the information and provide opportunity for questions and discussion.

2. **Education-and-training.** Most large organizations have entire departments whose sole purpose is to discover what employees need to

know and to arrange for education and training. These departments orient employees to new programs, correct educational deficiencies, and introduce new and pertinent information. Almost any class in any school is an example of an education-and-training group. Organizational in-service seminars are another example.

3.   **Problem-solving.**   Any group with a particular task or a specific objective is a problem-solving group. It may be formal or informal. The problem to be solved may range from preliminary discussions, to planning, to the carrying out of decisions.

Group Roles

What are the key group roles? How do these roles influence group communication?

Group behavior differs from interpersonal behavior primarily in its degree of formality. Participants in interpersonal situations have greater freedom in satisfying personal needs than group participants do. Groups can, however, help their members satisfy personal needs. For example, groups give people a sense of belonging and importance. In groups people can contribute to the accomplishment of a goal without assuming the risk of an independent decision.

Participants in groups tend to assume certain stylized roles that help them to satisfy psychological needs. These behavior patterns can either contribute to solving the group's problem or block the solution. The key roles are as follows:

What is leadership? What are the differences between ascribed and earned leadership?

1.   **Leadership.**   Leadership may be either *ascribed* or *earned*. Ascribed leadership results from a person's position or status in the organization, whereas earned leadership occurs when an individual assumes the responsibility for facilitating communication and goal achievement.

2.   **Task specialist.**   Persons performing the task specialist role are goal-oriented; their chief concern is with the facts and nature of the problem.

3.   **Human relations specialists.**   Human relations specialists attempt to resolve conflicts by including participants who might otherwise be left out, offering compromises, supporting the ideas of others, and testing for consensus.

4.   **Self-serving.**   Any dysfunctional behavior—behavior that works to prevent the group from accomplishing its goal—is essentially self-serving. Refusing to cooperate by rejecting the ideas of other participants, withdrawing from the discussion, and attempting to monopolize the discussion are typical examples.

Although these role behaviors are easy to identify and observe, most people do not fit neatly into any one pattern. Under certain circumstances, the person who normally functions as a task specialist may well engage in self-serving behavior. For a group to function well, the individuals within it must agree on roles and task achievement. Leaders, task specialists, and human relations specialists all perform necessary functions. Of course, the key roles as we have described them are obviously neater (and more academic) than behavior would ever be in a real situation, but group members should recognize that the psychological roles do exist and that to a certain extent they can be controlled.

Group Influence

What are norms, and how do they influence group behavior?

All group settings include certain assumptions about the behavior of participants. These assumptions—*norms*—may be either explicit (verbalized rules and regulations) or implicit (unspoken but agreed upon). In a group situation, each participant feels conflicting needs to conform to and to resist the group's norms. Because participants seek prestige, acceptance, and status within the group, the situation also produces competition and conflict.

These factors—conformity, resistance, competition, and conflict—interrelate in complex ways. We all tend to conform most closely to the norms of the groups that are most important to us; we risk deviation in groups that are less important. Competition and conflict between groups usually promote greater conformity within each group, but intragroup conflict tends to reduce conformity and productivity.

What is a cohesive group?

A group in which the participants adhere strictly to the norms is said to be *cohesive*. Cohesive groups, which are generally more productive than noncohesive groups, are marked by a greater willingness to communicate, to accept the ideas of all participants, and to work toward specific goals. A certain degree of resistance, competition, and conflict can also be productive, however. A person who is willing to deviate from the group's norms may make suggestions and raise objections that would not occur to, or be expressed by, group conformists.

How does status within the group influence group communication?

Another important influence is the perceived power of certain group members. Group members with high status usually send and receive more messages than members with low status, but high-status members sometimes use their power to criticize and manipulate others rather than to achieve the group's objective. High-status members also have more freedom to establish and to deviate from group norms should they choose to do so.

▷ Group Dynamics

Groups have two definite patterns of movement, one approximating a life cycle and the other involving a process of decision making. Despite variations from group to group, successful groups demonstrate similar progressions through phases of interaction and through the decision-making process.

Group Life Cycle

How does the group life cycle compare with the dyadic life cycle?

Just as interpersonal relationships have a particular life cycle, groups—especially problem-solving groups—also undergo cyclic changes. The stages in the group life cycle are initiation, exploration and clarification, conflict, resolution, and dissolution.

Initiation.   Initiation, the first stage in the life cycle of any group, consists of introductions, statement of purpose, and efforts on the part of participants to become acquainted with one another. The group members become familiar with the expectations of the others; some basic norms are established. The length of time required for this stage depends upon the complexity of the problem; the size of the group; and the personal, social, and organizational differences among members. If the members have had previous experiences with each other, this stage may be quite short.

Exploration and Clarification.   Exploration and clarification is a testing stage in which members define the problem (if there is one), discover who the leaders are, and find out how the members will relate to one another. Norms and expectations are further defined. The group decides, for example, who will introduce what ideas in what way and how decisions will be made.

Why might conflict occur in groups?

Conflict.   Conflict may occur because of differences between ascribed leaders and those with earned leadership. Conflict can also arise over norms, the definition of the problem or task, or proposed solutions or actions.

Resolution.   Resolution is the "performing" stage. Norms and leadership have been established, most conflicts have been resolved, and the group is ready to pursue the decision-making process.

Dissolution.   Dissolution brings the group to a close. The group may lose its reason for being in a number of ways. With a problem-solving group, the successful completion of the task eliminates the need for the group. An informal group may dissolve when it no longer satisfies the psychological needs of its individual members.

How might a group attempt to control deviant behavior?

Deviant Behavior and Group Life Cycle.   From the communication standpoint, one of the most interesting features of the way the life cycle influences group behavior is in the treatment of deviant behavior. In the early stages, participants who consistently deviate from group norms—perhaps by bringing up personal matters at inappropriate times—receive a great deal of communication, most of it persuasive. But the member who continues to refuse to cooperate into the later stages will be cut off from further communication. If a group member cooperates and conforms in the early stages, however, he or she will have much greater freedom to deviate in the later stages.

Decision-Making Patterns

Under what circumstances would each of the five ways of reaching a decision be most appropriate? When is consensus better than a vote? When is decision by authority or default better than the other methods?

One of the most important steps for any task-oriented group is decision making, which occurs during the resolution stage of the group's life cycle. Group norms, communication structure, and leadership determine which of the following ways of reaching a decision will be used:

1. **Consensus.** Members reach agreement by discussion of alternatives.

2. **Majority vote.** Members vote, and the plan with more than half the votes is chosen.

3. **Plurality.** Members vote, but no plan receives a majority. The plan with the most votes is selected.

4. **Authority.** The leadership insists on a particular decision.

5. **Default.** The group avoids discussion and decision making.

The decision-making process itself follows these five steps:

1. **Defining and analyzing the problem.** This process actually begins in the initiation stage, but not until the resolution stage do the group members reach agreement on a definition of the problem and isolate its probable causes.

2. **Establishing criteria for a solution.** These criteria may be formulated explicitly or implicitly, or they may be self-evident. How the group decides on the criteria will depend on the complexity of the task, the time available for reaching a decision, and the familiarity of the group members with each other and with the problem.

What is brainstorming?

3. **Proposing possible solutions.** Group norms usually determine who submits what solutions in what way. Ways in which solutions arise may range from a discussion of only those solutions proposed by the official leadership to a *brainstorming* session, in which all members propose as many solutions as possible regardless of their immediate practicality and criticism is withheld until all ideas have been listed for later evaluation.

4. **Evaluating possible solutions.** Solutions are evaluated by measuring them against the criteria established in Step 2 and weighing them against each other. New criteria may be established, and parts of two or more solutions may be combined to provide the best alternative. Although the final selection of a solution should be based on objective criteria, subjective criteria (such as who made the suggestion) frequently influence the decision.

5.   **Plotting a course of action.**   The group decides how to put the proposed solution into action. The membership must usually assume responsibility for taking some kind of action. Responsibility may be assumed voluntarily or directed by the leader.

6.   **Evaluating results.**   Some groups will also have the responsibility for determining the success of the action and making any required changes. In other cases the evaluation of results would be the responsibility of another group.

▷ GROUP COMMUNICATION AND LEADERSHIP

How do communication structures influence group behavior and morale?

Group characteristics and group dynamics influence the communication process indirectly, depending on the reasons for the group's existence and the personalities of its members. Three factors that directly influence the communication process can be selected and controlled to achieve a good flow of communication:

1.   Communication structures.

2.   Communication climate.

3.   Group leadership.

Communication Structures

What are the differences between centralized and decentralized communication structures?

Group communication structures may be centralized or decentralized; each structure or network is particularly well suited to solving certain kinds of problems. In centralized systems the individual members have only limited access to the ideas and opinions of others. Communication flow is controlled by a leader. In some cases the group members are actually isolated from each other, and the leader controls a flow of written messages. More frequently, the leader succeeds in establishing group norms that encourage a centralized communication network. In decentralized structures group members have full access to the ideas and opinions of other members.

Centralized communication structures are generally referred to as the *wheel*, the *chain*, or the *Y*. Decentralized structures are all based on variations of the circle. Figure 19.1 shows diagrams of these patterns.

The differences between centralized and decentralized structures are important. In centralized networks the person in the central position tends to become the leader regardless of other qualifications. Leadership in decentralized groups is usually assumed by those with the proper qualifications. Centralized structures waste less time in preliminary organization, and decisions are usually reached more quickly. Decentralized structures take longer

**FIGURE 19.1
Communication
Structures**

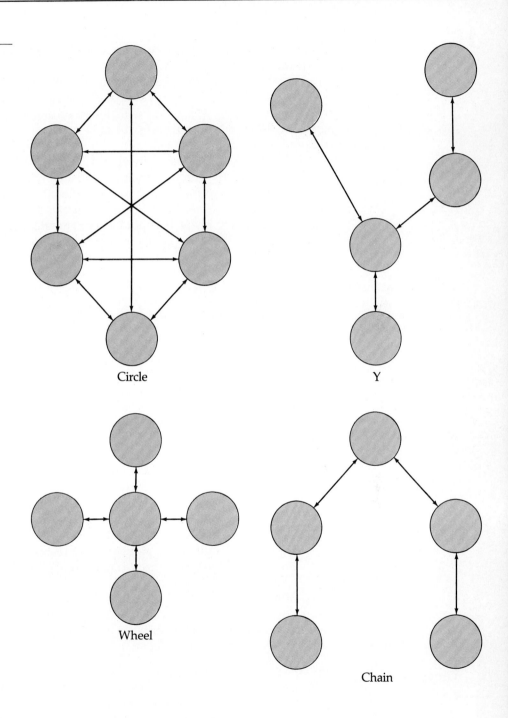

Circle

Y

Wheel

Chain

to organize, but once organized, a decentralized group can work as efficiently as a group with a centralized network.

Less flexible than decentralized groups, centralized groups are best suited to solving simple problems. For simple problems centralized structures generally produce faster responses with fewer errors. For complex problems, however, decentralized structures usually produce higher quality answers and produce them more quickly.

The communication structure also influences group morale. In centralized groups, only the central person or persons have consistently high morale. Because a group member's morale is directly related to how valuable that person feels, the farther from the central position a person is in the structure, the lower his or her morale. The morale of all members of a decentralized group tends to be about the same; it depends primarily on the nature and importance of the task.

Communication Climate

What factors influence the communication climate in a group?

The communication climate in a group situation is established in essentially the same way as it is in interpersonal communication situations (dyads). See Chapter 1 for a review of the differences between open and closed communication climates before beginning the following discussion of motivation and participation in small groups.

Group size and diversity of membership are the two most important influences on motivation and participation. The nature and importance of the task also influence motivation, but those factors are usually beyond the control of the people responsible for establishing a group. Size and diversity, however, can usually be controlled.

As the size of a group increases, the group becomes less cohesive. Group members become less willing to participate in discussion and in the decision-making process. As group size increases, the possibilities for conflict increase and the possibilities for any individual to contribute meaningfully to the solution of the problem decrease; as a result, participants are less motivated to participate. Motivation and participation are highest in groups of about five members; both decline in groups of more than eight members.

The diversity of the group is another important influence. Groups composed of members who consider themselves equals exhibit increased participation and produce higher motivation than groups whose members perceive their status as unequal. Differences in age, intelligence, and expertise inhibit participation and group interaction.

Group Leadership

Leadership consists of facilitating group interaction, member participation, and completion of the task. As we stated earlier, leadership may be ascribed or earned. Ascribed leadership is inherent in a person's status or position,

FIGURE 19.2   Leadership Styles

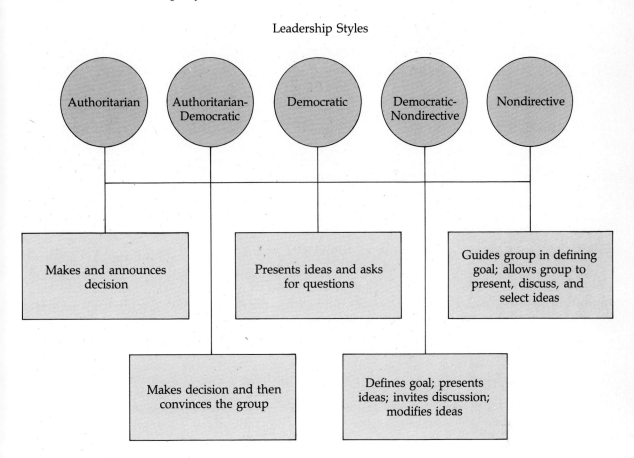

Leadership Styles

What is the relationship between leadership styles and communication structures?

whereas earned leadership is functional. The question of leadership is usually the first problem a group considers, and until the members agree on a leader or style of leadership, the group cannot devote full attention to the task. However the selection process proceeds, leadership styles may vary from complete authoritarianism to complete permissiveness. Authoritarian or directive leadership exerts a high degree of control over other group members, whereas permissive or nondirective leadership encourages the full participation of the group membership (see Figure 19.2).

Authoritarian leaders produce faster decisions, partly because they encourage centralized communication networks, and nondirective leaders prefer decentralized networks. On the other hand, nondirective leaders produce decisions of higher quality. Under authoritarian leadership, morale is lower than under nondirective leadership. Only the circumstances surrounding a particular task can determine which leadership style is more suitable for it, but the long-range interests of any organization are served by encouraging nondirective leadership and decentralized communication structures whenever possible. High quality decisions and high morale help organizations achieve their long-range objectives.

People accustomed to nondirective leadership respond well to authoritarian leadership when they know that a speedy decision is more important than a high quality decision. People accustomed to authoritarian leadership have a difficult time adjusting to nondirective leadership, and while authoritarian leaders can deal efficiently with simple problems, nondirective leaders do a far better job with complex problems.

▷ IMPROVING SMALL GROUP COMMUNICATION

What is the first question a group leader should ask?

The leader's task is to ensure effective communication in the small group, and the first question a leader must ask is, "Is this group necessary?" Group decisions have certain advantages, but they also have certain disadvantages. When a group decision is called for, the leader must establish an environment favorable for group interaction and participation, clarify the group's purpose, and provide the necessary planning and organization.

Advantages and Disadvantages of Groups

What are the advantages and disadvantages of groups?

Groups are best for complex problems requiring high quality decisions. When the problem is simple or when a rapid decision is essential, a manager would do well to make the decision alone or in consultation with an expert. Group decisions take time and cost money. In addition to the quality of the decision needed, a manager should consider the importance of morale. Group decisions result in greater acceptance of the solution than the manager would obtain without group participation.

Environment

Physical and psychological environments are both important to successful small group communication. Participants must feel comfortable in the setting of the discussion, and they must feel comfortable with one another. Decentralized communication structures, pleasant surroundings, and nondirective leadership maximize the advantages of small group decision making. If the leadership is authoritarian and communication flow is centralized, the group's time is wasted. Authoritarian leaders should make independent decisions without pretense of group participation and thus maximize the advantages of authoritarian decisions.

It is the leader's responsibility to ensure interaction, participation, and discussion. Participants should be selected for the knowledge, skill, or area of expertise they can bring to the group. The leader should include all members in the discussion, encouraging participation from those who hesitate. To achieve high quality decisions, the group requires ideas and corrective feedback from all participants.

Importance of Ideas

Because the main advantage of a group is its ability to develop a higher quality decision than one person can usually provide, leaders need to be especially aware that groups usually contain more critics than creators. If the group is to encourage creative solutions to problems, the leader has to ensure that ideas are not dismissed prematurely. If a person comes up with an idea, and everyone else in the group immediately says that it was a bad idea, no one else in the group is likely to volunteer another idea.

For this reason, many groups set aside a period soon after their formation for brainstorming, which, as explained earlier in this chapter, is a process in which everyone in the group comes up with as many ideas as possible, and criticism is withheld until after all the ideas have been listed. Ideas are then evaluated, with some being dismissed, others being combined, and some being rephrased as they are measured against the criteria established for evaluating the solution.

No group leader can afford to be an "idea killer." New and good ideas are hard to come by, and it is the leader's responsibility to ensure that good ideas have the opportunity to be developed.

Purpose, Planning, and Organization

What can a leader do to maximize the effectiveness of a group?

Even though nondirective leadership produces higher quality decisions than authoritarian leadership, the group's leader must exercise certain responsibilities if the effectiveness of the group is to be maintained. The discussion should have direction and purpose, and group members should feel a sense of accomplishment. Specifically, it is the leader's responsibility to

1. Notify everyone of the time, place, and purpose of each meeting.

2. Stick to the problem.

3. Encourage contributions.

4. Reinforce points of agreement.

5. Adjourn on time.

SIDEBAR

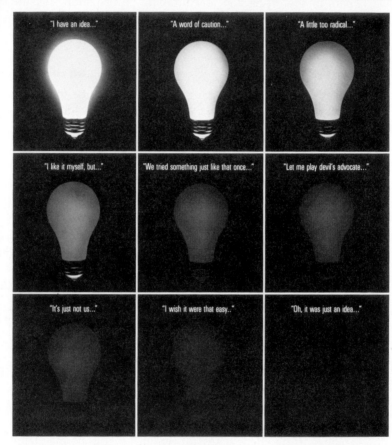

Source: Courtesy of TRW INC.

6. Ensure adequate follow-up by
   a. Providing for a written record.
   b. Encouraging appropriate further action.

The Meeting

What are a group leader's specific responsibilities?

It is the leader's responsibility to run the meeting. Most task groups require an agenda, and many require that some kind of minutes be kept to ensure an accurate record of group activities. Agenda, minutes, and the order of business are covered in Chapter 14.

Under what circumstances should a group follow parliamentary procedure?

Although most small groups do not follow parliamentary procedure, many do incorporate the basic principles of those procedures, which are designed to ensure

Equal rights for all.

Rule of the majority.

Rights of the minority.

Discussion of one item at a time.

For meetings to be productive, they should focus on one specific problem or a small group of related problems and concentrate on that. The most common complaints of group members about meetings are that the meetings waste too much time and that no problems are ever solved.

Under what circumstances should a group have an agenda for a meeting and keep minutes?

It is the leader's responsibility to keep wasted time to a minimum and to ensure that the group's contributions to solving the problem receive appropriate recognition. The leader should have a printed agenda and stick to it unless a group member has discovered an important problem that should logically take precedence over the agenda items. The leader should also beware of using the group to legitimize decisions that have already been made. If the group is not going to play an important role in solving the problem, the meeting should not be called.

When the group is making a decision about a course of action, the leader may wish to follow parliamentary procedure in calling for a formal vote. Votes are taken on specific motions, which set forth a proposal.

Main motions define the basic proposal on which the group will vote. Motions must be seconded before they can be discussed.

Subsidiary motions modify main motions. They may alter the language of the main motion, refer the main motion to a committee for further study, postpone it, or *table* it (postpone discussing it).

Privileged motions, which are urgent, may be introduced at any time. The two most common privileged motions are adjournment and recess.

Incidental motions permit temporary interruptions. A group member may raise a *point of order* if parliamentary procedure is not being followed, or a member may raise a *point of information* to request or supply additional information about the main motion being discussed.

In general, groups will discuss a topic until they reach some sense of how the problem should be solved. At that point the leader may call for a motion, or a group member may offer the motion. After the motion has been seconded, additional discussion may take place, and the motion may be altered, postponed, or tabled.

Groups striving for decision by consensus may still use this procedure, but the motions finally voted on will have been established by consensus, and the vote will be unanimous.

Groups can help satisfy social needs, but the leader should try to ensure that the meeting sticks to the task at hand and is over as quickly as possible. Those who wish to have a social period may do so after the meeting has adjourned.

▷ ORGANIZATIONAL COMMUNICATION SYSTEMS

What are the differences between formal and informal communication networks?

Organizations establish communication systems to achieve objectives. The establishment of the communication systems is, however, rarely a deliberate process. Those people who *need* to communicate to get a job done find a way. Those people who *want* to communicate manage to find the time.

Just as individual communications tend to be formal or informal, the entire organizational structure has networks of formal and informal communication.

Formal Communication Networks

What is the function of an organization chart?

No small group can begin to achieve its task objectives until the internal matter of leadership is resolved. This is also true of larger groups. All organizations have some kind of official hierarchy to provide the necessary leadership. The official hierarchy, represented by the company's organization chart, establishes a formal communication network: superiors tell subordinates what to do, subordinates report to superiors about what they have done, and departments ask one another for specialized help. Formal communication flows vertically—downward and upward—and horizontally.

The chart in Figure 19.3 illustrates a typical organizational structure. The number 1 indicates the person in charge, and numbers 2 through 6 indicate relative levels of organizational status. The solid lines indicate officially sanctioned lines of communication; the dotted lines represent unofficial communication networks. Note that some organizational relationships require both official and unofficial lines of communication.

Downward Communication.   Downward communication includes all official messages that go from superiors to subordinates in the organization.

FIGURE 19.3
A Typical
Organization Chart
Titles associated
with chart numbers
would vary from
organization to
organization.

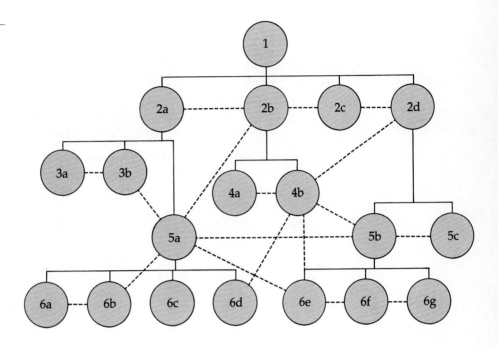

Downward communication establishes the communication climate in the organization and determines the quality and quantity of upward communication. Because downward communication is so important in the overall success of the organization, management must be especially careful to recognize and overcome the barriers caused by differences in attitude and perception inherent in communicating down the chain of command. Some examples of downward communication are the following:

1. **Job descriptions:** Lists and definitions of duties and responsibilities.

2. **Job instructions:** How to do it, what not to do, whom to call.

3. **Job indoctrination:** Explanations of the relationship between the job goals and organizational goals and motivation for specific tasks.

4. **Job performance:** Feedback about how well a person is doing in general or has done with a particular task.

To be successful, downward communication must accomplish the following:

What is required for
downward commu-
nication to be effec-
tive?

1. **Demonstrate empathy.**   Like all other communication, downward communication must take account of the receivers' values, beliefs, and problems. The fact that management wants something done may not be reason enough for an employee to do it. Management should also consider the timing of messages from the receivers' point of view because poor timing often suggests the presence of a hidden meaning.

2. **Be accurate.**   Any communication that is less than truthful undermines management's credibility as an information source. Like the boy of the folk tale, a company can "cry wolf" only so often and still expect a response.

3. **Be definite.**   The receivers must understand the message in its context. They must understand not only their action but also the way that action fits into the company's operation as a whole.

4. **Take selective perception into account.**   The farther a message has to travel, the greater the chance that it will be altered. Written messages supplemented by face-to-face discussions provide the greatest accuracy of transmission.

5. **Provide for feedback.**   Management frequently relies too heavily on written directives and other formal forms for downward communication. Manuals, newsletters, and public address systems are best when supplemented by face-to-face discussions of problems and procedures. Suggestion boxes and a reward system for employee problem solving are frequently used organizational feedback systems.

What is message overload, and how can it be avoided?

6. **Avoid message overload.**   Duplicating machines, especially photocopiers, have made it possible for companies to send countless messages at a cost that seems relatively low. But just as you cannot emphasize everything in a letter, you cannot emphasize all messages equally. Employees who receive too many messages tend to pay little attention to any of them. Save written communication for important messages.

What can management do to ensure that it receives accurate information?

Upward Communication.   Upward communication includes all messages that flow from employees to supervisors. Good communication systems start at the top and proceed down; inadequate upward communication results from management's failure to provide good downward communication. Supervisors who neglect downward communication invite employees to conceal or distort information pertinent to the well-being of the organization. The functions of upward communication are to accomplish the following:

1. Keep management informed in general, and in particular provide management with the information required to make decisions about such items as products, policies, and employees.

2. Provide employees with the opportunity to submit ideas and to participate in the decision-making process. This increases their willingness to accept decisions and downward communication.

3. Provide management with feedback about the effectiveness of downward communication.

Counseling, grievance systems, suggestion boxes, open-door policies, social gatherings, and staff meetings are all communication situations that encourage upward communication. All are primarily the responsibility of management. For management to obtain the accurate, reliable, and objective information it needs, a communication climate that encourages upward flow is essential. Successful upward communication requires the following:

1. Frequent face-to-face contact between supervisors and employees. Supervisors who isolate themselves from their employees risk cutting off the flow of communication.

2. Recognition of and rewards for accomplishment. An employee who recognizes a problem and finds a solution deserves rapid recognition and full credit. The employee should not have to battle company red tape because someone higher in the corporate structure wants to appear more knowledgeable than the employee who originated the idea.

3. The ability to listen. Managers should take the time to listen, even to criticism. They must assume that even the least fair criticism contains a small truth and should encourage employees to share ideas, problems, and criticisms. Supervisors should recognize that employees may partially withhold bad news and exaggerate good news, especially when a supervisor is known to be judgmental.

4. The ability to treat upward communication without condescension. Employees appreciate having management recognize special, individual areas of expertise. For example, the president of an electronics company should pay close attention if a technician says that a certain capacitor in the power supply of a new solid state device will not work, even if the electronic engineers who designed the device say it will.

5. Action. Superiors should follow through on promises made to subordinates. When a complaint cannot be resolved or an idea cannot be accepted, the employee involved deserves a reasonably full and honest explanation. Problems that can be solved should be acted on immediately.

How can increased horizontal communication improve the effectiveness of an organization? Why do some organizations discourage horizontal communication?

Horizontal Communication.   Horizontal communication is the flow of messages among people of equal status in the organizational hierarchy. Such messages can be exchanged for purposes of cooperation or conflict. Horizontal communication has three formal functions:

1. **Coordination.**   Because organizational units must coordinate activities and share information about joint projects, regular meetings of organizational equals are necessary.

FIGURE 19.4
The Chain
Communication
Pattern

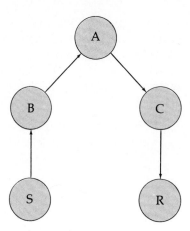

2.   **Problem solving.**   When the same problem faces a group of organizational equals, horizontal communication helps in discovering a solution.

3.   **Conflict resolution.**   When departments or organizational equals have a conflict, horizontal communication increases mutual trust and discourages rivalry between departments or groups.

Horizontal communication tends to be faster, more accurate, and less threatening than vertical communication. Organizations often discourage much horizontal communication, however, because excessive horizontal communication disrupts the organizational hierarchy and results in message overload. Many organizations prefer that messages pass up the chain of command from the sender until a common superior is informed, and then back down the chain until the receiver is finally informed (see Figure 19.4).

This kind of communication structure, known as a *chain*, helps person A in the figure retain authority. It is a pattern good for A's morale, but not very good for the morale of either S or R. If S and R need to communicate frequently, however, they will bypass the formal system and establish their own informal communication network.

Informal Communication Networks

What is the grapevine, and what contribution does it make to organizational communication?

Even in some organizations that discourage horizontal communication, more communication flows horizontally than vertically. Where formal horizontal networks do not exist, employees establish an informal network, usually called the *grapevine*, to provide rapid and flexible communication. Formal and informal networks are difficult to distinguish on the basis of message content.

Vertical communication is formal because it is frequently written, almost always "official," and carefully controlled. Horizontal communication—official or unofficial—is almost always oral, and it is not always carefully controlled.

What can an organization do to prevent the grapevine from being used to spread rumors?

The grapevine develops out of need and the accident of special relationships. People who must talk to each other do so. When people share offices or have adjacent offices, they talk to each other. Some informal communication complements and substitutes for communication that might otherwise use slower, formal channels, but the informal communication system also carries a great deal of extraorganizational information.

The advantages of the grapevine are its speed and—even considering rumors—its relative accuracy. The informal communication network transmits messages by clusters: one person passes the message to many receivers in a short time. Not everyone receiving the information passes it on, but enough people do to make transmission quite rapid. Of course, each time the message is transmitted from a sender to a receiver, part of it may be lost or distorted. Nevertheless, the grapevine is a surprisingly accurate medium for noncontroversial organizational information.

The grapevine has earned a bad reputation because rumors—information consisting mainly of inferences based on few facts—will spread just as rapidly through the information network as will any other message. Also, because the accuracy of the grapevine is well known to those who use it, rumors are readily accepted as valid. Controversial organizational information—or any information that is important, but about which there has been little official communication—becomes the subject of speculation and rumor.

Because the grapevine is a permanent fact of organizational life, management should make use of its advantages and establish procedures to control its disadvantages. If the persons who serve as liaisons by transmitting information from cluster to cluster can be identified, management can use the grapevine to accomplish the following:

1. Disseminate information that should not be sent over official channels.

2. Collect critical feedback that is not available through official channels.

3. Provide rapid clarification for official messages that have not been well received or understood.

What can a rumor-control center do to ensure high credibility?

Most large organizations would do well to establish an official *rumor-control center* to deal with the grapevine's only real disadvantage. Unless some official way of controlling rumors is established, rumors will spread unchecked to damage morale and undermine the effectiveness of the official communication network. To ensure the success of a rumor-control center, management must provide for anonymous reporting of rumors (usually by telephone) and for prompt, accurate replies. The rumor-control center must establish and maintain high credibility.

System Goals

Why are communication systems important to the success of an organization?

In addition to the specific objectives of individual messages and of message systems, organizations must achieve three general objectives if communication is to flow smoothly and efficiently. The entire effort of organizational communication should be directed toward establishing the following:

1. Open communication climate.

2. Accurate information.

3. Competition rather than conflict.

Open Climate.   As mentioned previously, open communication climates encourage communication, whereas closed climates discourage communication. Because an organization requires the cooperation of its members for long-term survival, it is management's responsibility to encourage employee communication. All employees in the organization should feel that they can express their observations and criticisms both vertically and horizontally.

In an open communication climate, employees believe that

1. They will receive credit for their ideas and contributions.

2. Their complaints will be taken seriously, investigated, and either resolved or explained in a satisfactory manner.

3. Supervisors are not manipulating communication flow to control employees.

4. Supervisors value employees as human beings whose needs and aspirations go beyond their organizational function.

How does an organization benefit from an open communication climate?

An organization benefits from an open communication climate in a variety of ways. The open climate improves morale and increases employee participation in the achievement of organizational goals. It also enables supervisors to discover the personal goals of employees; thus job assignments can be coordinated to ensure maximum contribution to both personal and organizational goals.

An open climate builds employee loyalty to the company; this not only increases organizational efficiency but also leads to employee efforts to establish goodwill for the organization. Employees who dislike the company can counteract quite a few advertising dollars. Finally, a company with an open climate can rely on employees to treat confidential information as confidential. In a closed communication climate, where management considers much information confidential, employees cannot distinguish what is legitimately confidential from what is not. Under such circumstances, what is known (as well as all sorts of speculation) is widely transmitted, both inside and outside the company.

How can manage-
ment avoid being
lied to by employ-
ees?

Accurate Information.   One result of an open communication climate is that both vertical and horizontal information tend to be more accurate. In a nonthreatening atmosphere of trust, people tell the truth. If employees believe that management is manipulating them, they engage in counterman-ipulation. This can result in managers making decisions on the basis of faulty information. The only way management can ensure accurate upward com-munication is by providing accurate downward information and rewarding accurate upward communication, even when it involves criticism.

Rewarding honest criticism is not always easy, because honest criticism is the kind that hurts the most and thus makes any of us more defensive. Even so, if management does not encourage and reward honest criticism, its best source of corrective feedback is effectively cut off. When management welcomes only good news, employees quickly learn to keep bad news to themselves. Management may not learn that a project is in trouble until it is too late to correct the difficulty quickly and inexpensively.

How can communi-
cation be used to
reduce conflict with-
in an organization?

Cooperation Rather Than Conflict.   The third goal for organizational communication systems is to encourage cooperative competition and reduce conflict within the organization. Each part of the organization depends on every other part, and the well-being of the entire organization depends on the well-being of its parts.

Because resources and status are limited in any organization, their dis-tribution is a matter of great importance to employees. It is natural for people to want their fair share, and each person's opinion (based on perceptions) of what constitutes fair distribution will be different. When people know what resources and status are available, know what objectives must be met to earn desired resources or status, and know that they will receive full credit for their achievements, they will compete openly for resources by striving to meet their objectives and by cooperating with others who are striving to meet organizational goals.

On the other hand, people who are uncertain about what resources and status are available, about what must be done to earn an increase in resources or status, and about whether they will receive full credit for achievements, will manipulate others in their efforts to achieve personal goals. Conflict arises when the ways of earning increased status and resources are not clear. Conflict also arises out of differences in perception of resources, status, and their distribution.

Manipulation fosters countermanipulation, and countermanipulation is the first sign of latent conflict. Latent conflict is in some ways the most difficult kind of conflict with which an organization must deal. It reduces organizational efficiency without being recognized, acknowledged, discussed, or resolved. Again, an open communication climate is an organization's best method of reducing conflict.

Coordinated Communication Systems

What can an organization do to improve its communication as a whole?

Organizations have known for a long time that promotion potential and the ability to communicate are closely related. In general, the best communicators gravitate toward higher levels of management. Even so, the ability to communicate effectively has been considered primarily an individual trait—something belonging to particular individuals and not to the company as a whole. In the past few years, however, companies have begun to realize that they can control the quality of their communication systems much as they control the quality of their products.

Because communication is so important in organizational life, management should assume the responsibility for establishing a formal communication policy, complete with written objectives. No company would think of manufacturing television sets without specific objectives and measurements for cost, production, and performance. Likewise, no company should engage in communication without setting similar specific objectives and measurements for both internal and external communication systems.

What is necessary for intracompany communication systems to be effective?

Intracompany Systems.   To develop successful internal communication systems that govern communication flow within the company, management must make its commitment to good communication obvious by requiring each individual manager to practice good communication and by obtaining or training individuals who can supervise internal communication. Unless management indicates commitment to quality communication by expressing concern for it and by establishing an open communication climate, employees cannot be expected to communicate openly.

Establishing effective intracompany communication systems is essentially a three-step process.

1.   Write and distribute objectives for upward, downward, and horizontal communication flow. Open communication works to everyone's advantage, so the specific objectives should be stated in terms of employees' benefits. The general goals—an open communication climate, accurate information, and competition rather than conflict—should be stressed.

2.   Establish education-and-training programs to ensure adequate communication skills. Good communication is not always easy. If, for example, an employee said, "You sure made a rotten decision when you bought the Willard heat press," even a trained manager would tend to become defensive. But for good communication, the manager must resist the temptation to become defensive. Managers must really believe that it is in their long-range interest to listen (not just *hear*, but *listen*) to

whatever criticism is offered, or their training program cannot be considered to have been successful.

3. Practice independent communication auditing. Because the perceptions of supervisors and subordinates differ, management has difficulty measuring the success of its own communication. The absence of observable negative feedback may not be an indication of a successful communication program. Independent communication auditing would permit employees to complete questionnaires anonymously and to communicate face to face with someone who would protect the confidentiality of their statements.

What is necessary for extracompany communication systems to be effective?

Extracompany Systems.   In many ways a company can achieve high quality communication with the outside world more easily than it can with and among its own employees. Most external communication has specific, identifiable goals. Companies want to sell products or services, to be well thought of, and to make a profit. Companies have long recognized that each contact with the public should contribute to the company's advertising and public relations programs.

If organization policies concerning external communication have a failing, it is that they make little or no provision for measuring the communication efforts of specific individuals. The company's efforts as a whole — advertising and formal public relations efforts — tend to be well planned, coordinated, and evaluated. For example, companies hire experts to write letters for mass mailings. But it is a rare company that monitors the letter-writing efforts of employees who routinely correspond in the company's name.

As with intracompany communication, education and training and a formal means of measuring communication performance are the keys to effective extracompany communication. Any communication education and training program should teach both the specific objectives of messages and channels and the general goals of effective communication. Whatever the communication situation, the key factors for success of the program are (1) credibility, (2) clarity, and (3) empathy. To communicate effectively you must be believed, be clear, and see things from the receiver's point of view.

▷ SUCCESSFUL COMMUNICATION IN BUSINESS

How much communication actually takes place in an organization?

Even when management fully recognizes the importance of communication, the many variables in the communication process make it difficult to study and improve communication systems. Consider a common and fairly simple example of an organizational activity: the introduction of a new product. What kinds of communication flow are required at each step?

1. **The idea.**   Whose idea is it? Is the product completely new or only new to the company? Does a need for the product exist, or will the company have to advertise to create a need?

2. **Research and development.**   How expensive is the product? Can it meet the company's quality requirements? How long will it take to develop the product? Must the idea be changed to meet certain production requirements?

3. **Production.**   Does everyone involved in production of the new product understand any new job duties? Who is responsible for quality control? Does the finished product do what it is supposed to do?

4. **Marketing.**   Who wants the product? Why should the public buy it? How will it be packaged? How will it be distributed?

5. **Evaluation.**   Will you be able to make a profit? Should you continue producing the product? Can you make any improvements in it? Can it be made for less? What should you tell the stockholders?

A tremendous amount of intracompany communication is obviously required at each of the five steps, including proposals, interpersonal and small group discussions, formal presentations, and reports.

Extracompany communication is also required to gather information about the manufacture and sales of related products, to determine the need for and interest in the product, to secure raw materials, to hire any new employees manufacturing may require, to patent key elements, to advertise the product, and to handle customers' questions and complaints.

When you consider how much of your time you will spend communicating — both on and off the job — it is easy to see that every increase you can make in the efficiency with which you communicate will be of tremendous benefit. To be a successful communicator, you need to remember that effective communication meets two objectives: first, it accomplishes a business purpose; and second, it accomplishes a human purpose. Successful communication means human cooperation. We will not pretend that successful communication is easy. People do not share the same perceptions and the same values. Differences of opinion can — and often do — cause hard feelings, but these differences of perception and opinion make communication necessary and interesting.

▷ Summary

A small group consists of any number of people from two to about twenty who have some need or purpose in common and who can communicate face to face with each other without the need for parliamentary procedure to control behavior.

Primary groups consist of family and very close friends; informal groups are formed to foster interpersonal relationships rather than to accomplish any particular task or objective; and formal groups are those that have a specific task or objective. The most common formal groups in organizations are informational, education-and-training, and problem-solving groups.

Groups give people a sense of belonging and importance. Group members adopt behavior patterns they think will lead to the satisfaction of needs. The key psychological roles are leadership, task specialist, human relations specialist, and self-serving.

Groups have two definite patterns of movement: one is a life cycle and the other is a decision-making pattern. The five stages in the group life cycle are initiation, exploration and clarification, conflict, resolution, and dissolution.

When a group decision is called for, the leader has the responsibility of establishing an environment favorable for group interaction and participation, clarifying the group's purpose, and providing the necessary planning and organization.

The organizational communication systems in business are important for business efficiency. The entire effort of organizational communication should be directed toward establishing an open communication climate, accurate information, and competition rather than conflict.

Because communication is so important in organizational life, management should assume the responsibility for establishing a formal communication policy, complete with written objectives. No company should engage in communication without setting similar specific objectives and measurements for both intracompany and extracompany communication systems.

▷ EXERCISES

Review and Discussion Questions

1. What role do small groups play in organizations?

2. What are some important differences between interpersonal communication and small group communication?

3. Identify and explain three objectives of primary, informal, and formal groups.

4. Identify and explain four group roles.

5. Identify and explain the five stages in a group life cycle.

6. Explain the decision-making process and describe each of the five steps a group must go through to reach a decision.

COMMUNICATION SOLUTION

Rumors become a problem in the absence of sufficient and accurate organizational information. People guess at what they do not know about operational matters, and then they pass their guesses along the grapevine. Establishing legitimate channels of organizational communication helps to stop the rumors about organizational operations.

Gossip — which centers on people — is another matter. Rumors about people are difficult to stop, and denials often seem to confirm rather than refute the rumor.

As the one responsible for solving this problem, you would want your committee to represent the broad areas of your organization. You would need representatives from all levels of the hierarchy and from each operational area. If possible, you would select the opinion leaders from each area.

Because rumor control is a problem that requires the cooperation of most members of the organization, if it is to be solved, you would need to ensure that everyone's ideas were considered. Your committee might want to have a brainstorming session to generate possible solutions. Then you might want to present the best of those solutions to every member of the organization and obtain reactions to those ideas and additional ideas.

An organizational newsletter, departmental meetings for disseminating information and answering questions, and a rumor-control center are some communication techniques that might be appropriate. Ideally, your group should reach consensus on the best course(s) of action.

Each of these communication techniques would help dispel rumors about organizational operations. Gossip is probably best ignored unless it becomes slanderous, and then those responsible for spreading the rumors should be made aware of the possible legal consequences.

7.   What are the advantages of a centralized communication structure? Of a decentralized structure?

8.   How are communication structures, climate, and leadership interrelated?

9.   What are the differences between formal and informal communication networks?

10. Name and explain the factors involved in successful downward communication.

11. Name and explain the factors involved in successful upward communication.

12. What are the advantages and disadvantages of horizontal communication?

13. How can a company improve its internal communication flow?

14. How do the objectives of specific messages relate to the general objectives of organizational communication systems?

Problems

1. Attend three to five business meetings of local organizations (either campus or community). What procedures are used to run the meeting? How much time is wasted? Does the leader stick to the agenda? How are decisions made? What procedure is established for followup? Present your findings, analysis, and conclusions in report form.

2. As a department manager in a large manufacturing company, you are responsible for printing most of the company's promotional literature, product labels, and assorted internal and external pieces of communication (brochures, contracts, informational pieces, etc.). Because your department does so much printing, you must maintain a large inventory of papers, inks, and printing paraphernalia. Because your presses are almost always running and almost every printed item requires experimentation, which results in some spoilage, it is difficult to maintain absolute control over your inventory.

   Over the past six months, you have noticed that your shortages seem higher than they should be, and a comparison with previous years indicates that your shortages are greater than would be expected as a result of the increases in volume of work. Furthermore, for the last four months your department has been over budget, and you know that you are going to have to get the inventory problem under control before the vice president of production (your boss) begins asking questions about it.

   Twenty employees work in your department (including a secretary and records clerk). The employees have varied backgrounds. Some are college educated, and some are attending a local college on a part-time basis. Most have been with the company for several years, and all of them have been generally reliable, doing their jobs well and meeting deadlines. Pilferage could be part of your problem, and certainly some employees must be wasting materials. One employee was transferred into your department about six months ago (when your shortages first became a serious problem), but he had an excellent record as a driver for the company for more than ten years. He transferred into your department after a leg injury made it difficult for him to drive. What would you do and why?

CASES

1. Visit with a member of top management at an organization of your choice to discuss the objectives of the company's communication systems. Write a report of whatever length your instructor requests analyzing your findings.

2. Visit with lower-ranking members of the organization used in Case 1. Are their perceptions of the communication flow in the organization the same as those of top management? If not, why not? Write a report of whatever length your instructor requests, analyzing your findings. Do you have any recommendations for the company?

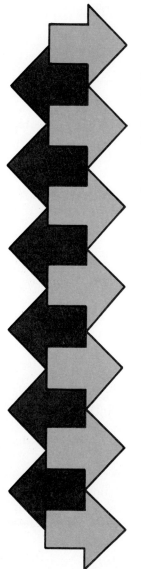

CHAPTER TWENTY
Communication Technology

Not too long ago, communication technology consisted of the telephone and the typewriter. Both of these communication tools are still with us, of course, and they will be with us for some time to come. Neither, however, has been untouched by the technological revolution that has brought us color television, solid state stereo systems, and the home computer. Most of the communication skills that made the original devices effective communication tools still apply, but the modern business communicator needs to supplement his or her basic business communication skills with an understanding of the newer modes of communication and their advantages and disadvantages.

COMMUNICATION CHALLENGE

Can you find a local electronic bulletin board system, and either post a bulletin or use the service to send electronic mail? Take a few minutes now to write down the procedure you would use to meet this challenge, and add to or change it if necessary as you read this chapter. As usual, our suggestions follow the chapter summary.

▷ OVERVIEW: THE BASIC RULES STILL APPLY

Technology is changing the face of communication. New telephone equipment, word processing programs for microcomputers, telecommunications, voice mail, videoconferencing, and national computerized databases all require new sets of skills to be used effectively. For those who are not familiar and comfortable with the trappings of technology, the equipment and terminology can be intimidating.

Regardless of the kind of organization you intend to work for, there is a computer in your future. If you are planning to work for a larger organization (one of the Fortune 1000), you will doubtless use most of the new communication technology before advancing very far in your career. Fortunately, the basic rules that you have learned for letters, memos, reports, oral presentations, and group communication still apply. Being clear and courteous, stressing the positive aspects of a situation or relationship, and encouraging feedback are just as appropriate for the new forms of communication as they were for the old.

This chapter will introduce you to the terminology and special techniques you will need to understand communication technology. Using this technology, however, is a skill that you can master only through practice. Understanding the principles involved is a good first step, but to become efficient at sending and receiving electronic mail, for example, you have to work with a specific system long enough to be familiar with its peculiar features—and every system has its peculiar features.

If you own a microcomputer, or have a friend who has one, or your school has equipment available for student use, take the time to learn the common business applications programs: word processing, spreadsheet, database, graphics, and communications. The time you invest in learning these programs will be well worth it.

▷ TELEPHONE AND DICTATION EQUIPMENT

What are the advantages and disadvantages of communicating by telephone?

The telephone is an extremely versatile, effective tool for business communication. Telephone communication is often the fastest, most effective way to reach an agreement with someone. Virtually every office in both the public and private sectors has at least one telephone, and the chances are excellent that it will be used several times every day. In fact, it is difficult to conceive of what life would be like today without telephones.

The telephone is also an economical means of communicating. Even long-distance phone calls can be inexpensive when they save the cost of writing a letter, prevent a misunderstanding, or help establish (or reestablish) goodwill.

Furthermore, modern telephone equipment offers expanded services such as teleconferencing, videoconferencing, and voice store-and-forward capabilities in addition to traditional one-to-one conversation.

Telephone Services

What are common telephone services, and how are they used?

The following services increase the usefulness of the telephone to businesses and many individuals.

- **WATS:** Wide-area telephone service reduces the cost of long-distance telephone service to companies that make many calls.

- **INWATS (800 service):** Incoming long-distance calls can be made without charge to the caller, which helps businesses establish and maintain customer goodwill.

- **Mobile phone service:** Both local and long-distance can be made to and/or from automobiles, trucks, boats, and—more recently—aircraft.

- **FAX (facsimile transmission):** Special equipment is available to transmit drawings, graphs, pictures, and written messages over the telephone lines.

- **Pagers:** A wide variety of equipment is available to let users know when they have a call waiting. Pagers use a radio signal to "beep" the user, and, as a result they have earned the nickname, "beepers."

- **Intercom service:** Most businesses telephone systems provide an intercom service so that members of the organization can have direct telephone connections with each other simply by dialing a short code number.

- **Speaker phones:** Speaker phones enable more than one person to participate in a telephone conversation.

COMMUNICATION TODAY...

Terms such as system emulation, database interchange, electronic posting, source origination, and file access sound like jargonistic descriptions of a modern Orwell's *1984,* but they are not. These are terms associated with basic communication systems and fundamental communication skills functioning in many businesses and communication systems **NOW!** . . .

Business managers do create their own reports and letters on terminals at their desks!

Dictation skills are essential in established word processing communication systems!

Letters, memos, reports and instructions are created at the desk and stored and transmitted electronically anywhere within a network system at night!

Editing, formatting, proofreading and correcting messages on microcomputers, word processors, or other electronic terminals are accepted fundamental skills in today's businesses! . . .

Teleconferencing, videoconferencing and computerconferencing permit immediate access and instant feedback for business decision makers. These systems exist and are available in private businesses and are available for hire in hotels with national and international chains!

Source: Larry Hartman, "What a Future!" *Information Systems and Business Communication,* Raymond W. Beswick and Alfred B. Williams, eds., (Urbana, IL: The American Business Communication Association, 1983), p. i.

- **Automatic sending and receiving equipment:** Special equipment is available to automate the process of dialing phone numbers and delivering a recorded message. Other automated equipment is available to answer the telephone and record incoming messages.

Teleconferencing and Videoconferencing

What is an audio teleconference? What techniques will help ensure the success of an audio teleconference?

Audio teleconferencing is simply a telephone conversation involving several people, perhaps at several locations. A teleconference may be arranged either through the appropriate telephone company or through an organization's private communication network. Standard telephones may be used, or speaker phones may be more appropriate if several people at each location will be participating.

As a rule, a telecommunications specialist (an operator with the phone company, for example) will assist in placing the conference call at a prearranged time. Successful communication during a teleconference is a little more difficult to achieve than during a typical phone call because several people may speak at once, and more information is exchanged. The following procedure will help ensure the success of an audio teleconference:

1. **Make arrangements in advance.** Each participant should know when he or she needs to call the designated operator. Allow enough time for equipment difficulties to be overcome.

2. **Prepare for the conference.** Know the names of the others who will be participating. Study the issues. As much as possible, know what questions you wish to ask and what answers you wish to provide to the questions you may be asked. Organize your notes.

3. **Begin with introductions.** Have each participant introduce himself or herself so that participants can begin to recognize each other's voices. Appoint one person the moderator, who will have the responsibility of determining whose turn it will be to speak.

4. **Let each person have a turn.** Allow each participant a set amount of time (equal to the time allowed the others) for making an initial statement. Questions and answers should follow a predetermined order so that each participant has an equal opportunity.

5. **Summarize the conference and follow through.** Before the teleconference is concluded, the moderator should summarize points of agreement, required actions, and the responsibilities of each of the participants. Follow through by preparing and distributing a written summary of the points of agreement and necessary actions.

What is a videoconference?

The procedures for videoconferencing, which allows participants at two or more locations to see as well as hear each other, are essentially the same as those for audio teleconferencing. The obvious difference is that appearance is more important as a result of the visual component. Because the participants can see each other, their nonverbal communication plays an important role in how their message is perceived by the others.

Videoconferencing is not yet as common in business as audio teleconferencing because the equipment is both expensive and complex, often requiring the use of satellite transmissions. The use of videoconferencing, however, is sure to increase because it is such a powerful communication tool for a wide variety of presentations and decision-making activities.

If you have ever had one of your presentations videotaped, you have some idea of how you will appear to others on a television screen. Were you happy with the image you presented? If not, you may wish to improve your areas of weakness and try again. Figure 20.1 illustrates a typical videoconference room so that you can approximate the conditions under which your future videoconferences may well take place.

Voice Store-and-Forward Equipment

As useful as they are, telephones have three problems: (1) they ring when you do not want them to; (2) it is often difficult to think of exactly the right thing to say on the spur of the moment, which is required in telephone

FIGURE 20.1
Videoconference
Room

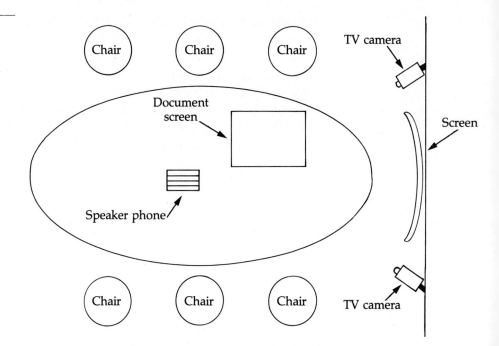

How can voice store-and-forward equipment solve common problems of communicating by mail?

conversations; and (3) the other person may not be available to answer your telephone call, and when she or he returns the call, you may not be available to answer it. The answer to these problems is voice store-and-forward equipment.

Voice store-and-forward equipment provides the equivalent of an audio mail system. It is, in fact, similar to a wide-area dictation service, allowing the sender of a message to dictate the message, listen to it and edit it before sending it to the receiver. Unlike the regular telephone system, voice store-and-forward systems are *closed*, that is, you must know a special phone number and the identification number of your receiver to be able to use the system to send or receive messages.

Each person with access to the system can check his or her "mailbox" for messages when convenient to do so. A message may be listened to several times if necessary, and a reply may be dictated at any time.

Voice store-and-forward equipment is both practical and economical. It eliminates much of the unnecessary chit-chat included in regular telephone conversations, and it eliminates the time wasted through *telephone tag*, in which the parties keep missing each other and leaving "call back" messages. By reducing the time spent on each phone conversation, voice store-and-forward equipment may also reduce the cost of telephone service.

What is telephone tag?

Dictation Equipment and Skills

Under what circumstances might dictating correspondence be more efficient than preparing it directly on a microcomputer?

Although executive use of personal and portable computers has reduced the importance of dictation in recent years, many executives still prefer to dictate letters, memos, instructions, and other short messages. Many executives, for example, use a cassette tape recorder to dictate material while commuting to and from work. Others use dictation equipment while traveling, and some dictate material for later preparation in a word processing center.

Regardless of its type, dictation equipment allows the user to stop and start the recording medium (magnetic belt or tape) quickly and easily, to edit specific portions of the recorded message, and to transmit the recorded message (either physically or electronically) to the place it will be transcribed. In some companies the telephone equipment has a special number for dictation. Other companies prefer to use standard or microcassette recorders. The following procedures apply regardless of the type of equipment you are using:

What techniques will help ensure that dictated material is transcribed correctly?

1. **Prepare before you begin.**   Write an outline for your message according to the principles presented in Part Two. Your notes should include all the major points you wish to make.

2. **Provide all necessary instructions for message preparation at the *beginning* of the message.**   Will it be a memo or a letter? Should it be a final copy or only a rough draft? Should it be double spaced or single spaced? Will you be sending copies to anyone? Will you need envelopes?

3. **Speak up and enunciate clearly.**   Listen to what you have dictated before sending it to be transcribed. Would you be able to understand the message if you were not already familiar with it? Do not smoke, chew gum, or suck on candy while dictating. Repeat or spell difficult words. Distinguish clearly between singular and plural forms of words. Repeat monetary amounts and other figures (but tell the typist to omit the repetition). If you have many figures, submit them separately and in writing.

4. **Spell names, unusual words, and homonyms.**   Let the transcriber know whether you mean *there* or *their*, *who's* or *whose*, *site*, *sight* or *cite*. While a good secretary will often be able to determine what you mean from the context, it only takes one mistake for both of you to look foolish. Do not take the chance.

5. **Dictate unusual punctuation.**   If you want a semicolon instead of a comma, or instead of a period and a new sentence, say so. Indicate quotation marks, new paragraphs, parentheses (open and close).

6. **Avoid irrelevant commments.**   Irrelevant comments have a way of turning up on the typed document. Letters have been mailed including

such comments as, "Who does this SOB think we are, anyway." Editorialize *before* you begin to dictate.

7. **Let the secretary make appropriate changes in grammar and punctuation.**   Your message may sound acceptable when you play it back, but some grammatical errors, such as lack of parallel construction and mismodification, may become noticeable in the printed document. Delegate responsibility for correcting errors in grammar and mechanics to the secretary.

8. **Read documents before signing or sending them.**   Because you *think* you know what the document says, it is easy to overlook mistakes. Something as small as a misplaced decimal point could cause you very big trouble.

▷ COMPUTER HARDWARE AND SOFTWARE

How is technology changing communication, records management, and other office activities?

Most modern office equipment is based on computer technology. Modern duplicating equipment reduces, enlarges, prints on both sides, and collates materials; modern word processing equipment greatly facilitates the production of written materials. Electronic storage media reduce both the cost and space required for storing large amounts of information.

The equipment, regardless of function, is known as *hardware*. The term *software* refers to a special set of instructions — a computer program — required to make some hardware function. Complicated duplicating machines, for example, may contain a computer chip known as a *microprocessor* to control their various operations. All the possible functions are encoded into the microprocessor. A personal computer, on the other hand, is capable of performing a wide variety of functions, depending on the software the user selects.

What is a microprocessor?

Why are technical terms frequently used in discussing computer hardware and software?

The same computer may be used for word processing, financial calculations, mail list management, or telecommunications, depending on the software selected by the user. You should be familiar with the following types of hardware, software, and related terms frequently used in business:

• **ASCII:**   The American Standard Code for Information Interchange allows information to be exchanged between different kinds of computers.

• **Baud:**   Computers transmit data at high rates of speed measured in baud, a figure equal to the number of characters being transmitted each second times 10. Common rates are 300 baud (30 cps); 1200 baud (120 cps); 2400 baud (240 cps); and 9600 baud (960 cps). Most telecommunications programs using public telephone lines operate at either 300 baud or 1200 baud.

- **Communications programs:**   Communications programs enable one computer to communicate with another (by a *modem* — explained later in this list). Computers that are otherwise incompatible may exchange information by using communications software. Communications software may allow two microcomputers to "talk" to one another or a micro to talk to a *mainframe* (explained later in this list). Communications software also allows individual users to access national information sources, such as CompuServe, The Source, or Dialog.

- **Configuration:**   Computers and their peripheral devices must be *configured* to work with each other. The user must tell the computer which device is connected in which place and what kind of signals that device expects to send and receive. Special cables may be required to connect a computer with its peripheral devices.

- **CRT or video display:**   A CRT is simply a television-like screen for viewing certain computer operations. CRTs have higher resolution than standard television screens so that they will be easier to read. CRTs are also referred to as *monitors*.

- **Database management programs:**   Information that must be compared with other information is usually stored in some kind of database. A list of a company's customers showing where they live, what they have bought, and when they made their last purchase may be accessed in a variety of ways: by the name of the customer, by zip code, by purchase date, or by the amount of the purchase. *Relational database programs,* which allow the user to check for multiple relationships, are extremely useful in business.

- **Disk drive:**   A disk drive is the device that enables the computer to record and "read" the information on a disk.

- **File server:**   A file server is a particular set of instructions that controls access to the files on a hard disk. A file server prevents two people from attempting to change the same information (file) at the same time.

- **Floppy disk:**   Information for microcomputers and minicomputers is stored on a record-shaped sheet of specially coated mylar with a cardboard cover. A disk is able to record magnetic impulses from the computer. The computer may also "read" the impulses that have been stored on (*saved to*) the disk. Floppy disks may be commercially prepared with programs (program or turnkey disks), or they may be used to store user-generated data (data disks).

- **Graphics programs:**   A graphics program can turn information from a spreadsheet into a neat bar graph or pie chart and print the result.

- **Hard disk:**   A hard disk serves the same purpose as a floppy disk, but compared with a floppy disk, it holds more information and is able to access it faster. Hard disks may hold millions of bytes of data (typically 10 to 40 *mega*bytes), and they are capable of accessing the information so quickly that they can support many users simultaneously.

- **Integrated programs:**   Several programs are available that combine two or more of the common functions. The most complex of the programs contain word processing, database management, spreadsheet, graphics, and communications. At least one program adds project management to the more common functions. Integrated programs have the advantage of allowing the user to move quickly and easily from one application to another, moving data as necessary. Sometimes, however, the integrated packages do not perform any of the applications as well as separate programs would.

- **Interface:**   The connection between a computer and its *peripheral devices* is known as an interface. One of the current problems with computer equipment is that special interfaces may be required to make one device compatible with another.

- **Keyboard:**   The keyboard is the typewriter-like input device for a computer. It allows the user to communicate with the computer.

- **LAN:**   LANS, or local-area networks, are means of connecting microcomputers so that they can share the same peripheral devices. Computers on a LAN, for example, may share the same hard disk, allowing many people to use the same programs and files and allowing them to send and receive electronic mail.

- **Macro:**   A mainframe computer or a single-key command that initiates a preset sequence of other commands or characters. Macros (single-key commands) are useful for entering complex data required on a regular basis.

- **Mainframe:**   The largest computers are known as mainframes or *macros*. They are large multi-user, multi-tasking computers designed for organizational or research applications requiring either greater storage or greater computing power than is available in minicomputers.

- **Microcomputer:**   Computers are available in three basic sizes: small, medium, and large. Microcomputers, the smallest, are designed primarily for individual use. The smallest microcomputers are severely limited in their applications, while the largest of them rival minicomputers in power and versatility. Microcomputers are also known as personal computers or home computers.

- **Minicomputer:**   Minicomputers are designed primarily for business use and can usually accommodate several users and perform more than one operation at a time.

- **Modem:**   A modem (MOdulator-DEModulator) is a device that converts computer signals into a form that can be transmitted over telephone lines and converts incoming signals back into a form readable by the computer. Most modems are designed to operate at either 300 or 1200 baud. Newer modems may operate at 2400 baud.

- **Photocopiers:**   Photocopiers have all but replaced ditto and mimeograph machines for reproducing documents. Photocopiers duplicate an original by transferring the image electrostatically to a blank piece of paper. The better machines can duplicate on both sides, copy colors, copy multiple sheets automatically, collate pages in their correct order, and staple them.

- **Phototypesetters:**   Phototypesetters automatically prepare material entered on a computer keyboard for printing.

- **Printer:**   A printer converts computer signals into images on paper. Letter-quality, or correspondence-quality, printers use a daisy wheel or print thimble to transfer ink from a ribbon in the same way that typewriters put characters on paper. Dot matrix printers form their characters with a configuration of pins, which transfer the ink to the paper in corresponding dots. Laser printers use beams of light to transfer the ink to the paper.

- **Programming language:**   A special language designed to give computers instructions. The most common programming languages used in business include BASIC, COBOL, FORTRAN, Pascal, and APL. Each language has certain advantages and disadvantages.

- **RAM:**   RAM, or Random Access Memory, is the storage area of the computer. When people speak of a "128 K" computer, they are referring to the amount of RAM it contains. A 128 K machine contains roughly 128 *thousand* bytes of RAM. A computer stores both the application software and any documents produced with the software in its RAM. In general, the larger the RAM, the more powerful the computer is. RAM is *volatile memory*: everything in it disappears when the computer is turned off.

- **ROM:**   ROM, or Read Only Memory, refers to the instructions built into a computer. ROM is *fixed* memory. It is "there" when the computer is turned on, and changing computer operations does not affect it.

- **Spreadsheets:**   Financial spreadsheets are also extremely useful in business because they allow the user to perform a wide variety of financial (and other mathematical) functions quickly and easily. Rows and columns of figures can be calculated, recalculated, and printed in numerous ways to demonstrate the possible consequences of specific business decisions.

- **Video recorders:**   A video recorder is a large-size tape recorder designed to record a video (television) signal. They are widely used in business in training programs.

- **Word processing programs:**   Word processing or *text editing* software is especially designed to allow the user to create, alter, store, and print written documents. We discuss various word processing applications more fully later in this chapter.

▷ WORD PROCESSING EQUIPMENT AND ELECTRONIC MAIL

What is word processing? How is it different from composing on a typewriter?

Using word processing (WP) equipment and electronic mail (EMAIL) greatly simplifies the process of preparing and sending written communications. It is not, however, magically different than writing with pen and paper or composing on a typewriter. Words, sentences, and paragraphs still have to be put together, and that will remain your responsibility. What a word processor will do is amplify your ability to produce written material (whether good writing or bad) by automating many of the tasks that had to be performed manually before its advent.

Regardless of type or brand, WP equipment usually consists of a keyboard (for entering data — typing); a computer program, which allows the equipment to perform the word processing operations; a memory system for saving (storing) created materials (usually a magnetic disk); and a printer for producing a "typed" (or *hard*) copy of created materials. WP equipment may be *dedicated,* or designed specifically for word processing, or it may be a text editing program used with a microcomputer or minicomputer designed for general use.

What hardware and software are necessary for word processing?

In spite of their similarities, each word processor (or text editing program for microcomputers) is different, and you will have to read the manuals accompanying your equipment and program and experiment with using it if you are to realize its full potential. The techniques we suggest here will work with most of the equipment and programs currently on the market, but you may need to alter the procedure to achieve the same result. Expect to take some time to learn a WP program. Even those computers advertised as "user friendly" will require some study and trial-and-error experimentation. The investment of time, however, will pay off.

Because they represent such an increase in efficiency over hand-drafted or dictated (even machine-dictated) letters, many organizations are beginning to require management personnel to produce their own documents using WP equipment. For people planning to enter management ranks this means two things: (1) You will need to know how to type, and (2) you—and you alone—will have full responsibility for the appearance, correctness, and content of your written work. In the very near future, only a few managers will have the luxury of secretaries or administrative assistants to help with written materials.

The Composition Process

How does using a word processor simplify the task of composing?

One of the main advantages of using a word processor is the ease with which material can be written, deleted, and moved. The writer is freed from worries about conserving time and energy while writing, allowing him or her to concentrate on developing an effective message. Material can be created and changed very quickly and easily.

Most WP keyboards are very fast, and typing on them is a pleasure. If you do not like what you have written, it is just as easy to delete material as it is to add it. You do not have to pull the sheet out, wad it up, and throw it away. You simply delete the material you do not want and save the rest.

Most WP equipment will also allow you to move blocks of information from one location to another with the press of a key or two. Would your third paragraph be better as the opening paragraph? Simply mark the paragraph and move it from one position to the other. The complete document, as corrected, can be reviewed for errors before it is printed. It is easier to review "clean copy" for errors than a marked-up manuscript. And should additional revision be required, only those few changes will need to be made before reprinting affected pages.

Form and Guide Letters

What are the differences between form and guide letters? When should each be used?

As mentioned previously, business frequently uses form and guide letters to reduce the cost of preparing correspondence. WP equipment is especially useful for producing form and guide letters, memos, and reports. The user is able to prepare the basic document, save it (by following the instructions in the manual that accompanies the program), and change only those parts of the document necessary for a particular reader. Some WP programs will automatically insert new names, addresses, and specific information in a document before printing. With other programs, the operator must make the appropriate changes manually.

Special Features

Most word processing and text editing programs contain a number of special features to facilitate the writing and revising process. The following features are the most common and the most useful.

What features are
common to most
word processing
programs? What
does each feature
do?

1. **Block move.**   With a WP program, rearranging text is usually a matter of marking the beginning and end of the section to be moved and indicating the place to which it should be moved. The document will be reformatted automatically with the section in its new location.

2. **Editing.**   Virtually all WP programs allow the user to insert and delete material by moving the *cursor* (position marker on screen) to the appropriate location and making the changes. The entire document will be automatically adjusted to accommodate the changes.

3. **Formatting.**   WP programs and equipment vary in formatting options. Some programs do not, for example, display boldfaced and underlined text as it will appear, but instead mark the beginning and end of printing features with special characters. Some programs do not indicate where page breaks (divisions between pages) are going to occur, which makes avoiding *widows* (single lines appearing by themselves at the top or bottom of a page) difficult. Most WP programs allow the user to indicate where pages should end if the naturally occurring page breaks are awkward. Some programs will insert footnotes automatically at the bottom of the page on which the note occurs.

4. **Global search and replace.**   Most WP programs allow the user to search a complete document for a specific term and, if necessary, replace it with another. This feature can help locate overused words. It also can be used to save time in the composition process and in preparing form documents. Suppose, for example, you need to prepare a form report for a number of companies in which you will mention the name of the addressed company several times. Simply prepare the original document with [company name] (or any convenient designation) in the places the name should occur, and before printing each copy of the report, initiate a global-search-and-replace command to replace all occurrences of [company name] with the appropriate company name.

   If you have a scientific document to prepare that includes several occurrences of a long, difficult-to-type formula, you could simply enter X at each point the formula should appear, and replace each occurrence of X with the formula after the document is complete, typing the formula once instead of many times. Or perhaps you have used a word incorrectly throughout the document or misspelled a word consistently. Simply replace all occurrences of the erroneous word with the correct one with one command.

5. **Mailing list programs.**   Many WP programs come with (or have available) special supplements for maintaining mailing lists. The mailing list program can usually be used in combination with the WP program to produce individualized form letters.

6. **Programmable keys.**   Many WP programs have a *glossary, macro,* or programmable-keys function that allows the user to define certain keys to represent text for insertion or formatting functions. By using this feature, an operator may call up a complete paragraph, complex scientific formula, or specific format with a simple keystroke or two.

7. **Spelling checkers.**   Some WP programs come with (or have available) spelling checkers. The spelling checker will "read" through a document looking for misspelled words, stopping at those words it "recognizes" as misspelled and allowing the operator to make the required correction.

If you use a spelling checker, remember that it is an *aid* to proofreading and not a substitute for it. The computer cannot read and understand content. It merely matches the words it finds against words in a dictionary and flags any word not found in the dictionary. This is a tremendous help in finding typographical errors and genuinely misspelled words. The computer cannot tell, however, when a key word has been omitted from a sentence, when the incorrect homonym has been used, when an apostrophe has been omitted, or when a correctly spelled word has been used incorrectly.

Some spelling checkers permit correction of the misspelled word when it is found. Others simply mark the word and require the user to correct it after the completion of the marking.

8. **Split screen.**   Some WP programs will allow the user to view two or more parts of the document at once, which facilitates checking correlated parts for consistency.

9. **Top and bottom lines (headers and footers).**   Most WP programs allow the user to insert special material automatically at the top and/or bottom line of each page. Top-line entries, for example, are useful for second (and following) page headings on letters and for running heads on reports. Most WP programs will automatically count pages and insert the appropriate number into either a top or bottom line.

10. **Wordwrap.**   Most WP programs require a carriage return only when the writer wishes to begin a new paragraph. Within paragraphs, the text automatically continues to (*wraps* around to) the next line. Some WP programs give the writer the opportunity to hyphenate words at the ends of lines, but that option may defeat the automatic wordwrap.

Selecting a WP Program

If you already have a WP package, you will have to learn how to achieve the results you desire by working around any of the program's shortcomings. If you will have the opportunity to select or recommend a word processor or WP program for a microcomputer, read the manuals for different programs closely before you make your decision. Select on the basis of which program will make it easiest for you to accomplish the kinds of things you desire to do.

Electronic Mail

What is electronic mail? What are its advantages and disadvantages?

The term *electronic mail* refers to the sending and receiving of written documents using electronic media. The most common electronic medium for electronic mail is a computer network consisting of two or more computers or word processors connected by wire (either special wires or telephone lines) or radio transmission. Local-area networks (LANs) are now common in large organizations, and they are increasingly common in small and medium sized organizations as well. Computer networks allow one person to compose a message at one computer, and through a series of commands, send it to another person at another computer—in another office in the same building, across the country, or around the world.

Electronic mail is not only much faster than traditional postal systems but also more economical. It also puts greater pressure on business communicators to be concise. Business people using electronic mail have a tendency to neglect the human objectives present in many communication situations because of the emphasis on speed and succinctness. If you are working with electronic mail, review your complete message in the same way you would a typed or hard copy before you send it. The psychological impact of a negative message, for example, can be as devastating electronically as it is when written on paper. The electronic message deserves every bit as much care as a paper message.

What are uploading and downloading?

Electronic mail frequently uses memo format. Also, most systems automatically record the name of the sender and the time that the message was sent. Messages may be prepared in advance using word processing software and *uploaded* (transmitted or sent) into the electronic mail system; or they may be prepared on-line, using the text editing program built into the electronic mail system. Messages waiting in an individual's mailbox can also be *downloaded* onto a disk (captured or saved) for later review and printing.

What are problems that may need to be overcome for electronic mail to be effective?

Electronic mail systems do not offer all the text editing or printing functions that word processing programs typically offer. Most, for example, do not provide wordwrap, so they require a carriage return at the end of each line. Most also will not accept printing commands, such as underline and boldface, because those commands do not employ standard ASCII characters. Users may indicate added emphasis by using solid capital letters, an asterisk before and after a word, or an underline mark before and after a word:

We must do it SOON.
We must do it *soon*.
We must do it _soon_.

Formatting may also pose problems in electronic mail. Some programs, for example, will not accept a blank line, so creating the appearance of a standard paragraph may be difficult. Some programs will accept blank spaces (which are indicated by a standard ASCII character) as a "line," and others may accept a period as a line. In other systems, however, you may have to use solid single-spacing and simply indent to indicate a new paragraph.

Only by using a specific system can you learn its commands, advantages, and disadvantages. Each system is at least a little different from all others, but all are fast and economical, and they are increasing in number at a phenomenal rate.

▷ COMPUTER INFORMATION SOURCES

What are national computer information services? How can they be useful to business?

National computer information sources are really complex databases available for private and business use. CompuServe, The Source, Delphi, Dow Jones, and Dialog are among the better known national services. See Chapter 13 for descriptions and examples of some typical electronic databases. For a fee, which may be based either on membership or on usage (known as *connect time*), the user may access information contained in the "host" computer.

The information may be general (of interest to many) or specialized (of interest to only a few) and may include current news, weather, sports, airline schedules, financial data, or medical information. Special databases are available to those who must remain current in specialized fields, such as business, law, medicine, agriculture, or energy conservation. As a rule, both general and specialized information sources provide the users with an EMAIL service so that they can communicate with each other quickly and easily.

Public and college libraries frequently provide access to databases useful for business research. Many companies also subscribe to electronic data bases. The process of locating useful information may be greatly simplified by using an electronic database. Inform, for example, a commonly used business database contains citations and abstracts from nearly 600 business journals, including *Business Week, Harvard Business Review, Forbes, Fortune, Euromoney,* and many others. The abstracts are clear and concise, enabling the researcher to select the most useful articles for further study.

Information in the database, however, may lag behind the most current information. The computer may work quickly, but it takes time for the human users to abstract the information and to enter it in the electronic database. Another difficulty in using databases is that the researcher must know how to select both the correct database and the correct keywords if the search is to result in useful information.

COMMUNICATION SOLUTION

To contact a local bulletin board — or a bulletin board anywhere — you need a computer with a modem connected to the public telephone system and an appropriate communications program. The only other thing you need is a telephone number. Your friends who have computers with modems can probably give you a list of numbers, or you can check with employees in local computer stores (hardware and software), your school computer club, the local chapter of DPMA (Data Processing Management Associa-

tion) or the data processing instructors on your campus.

Before you will be allowed to post a bulletin or leave electronic mail, you will probably have to apply for a password. Public bulletin boards need to ensure that those who leave messages are legitimate so that they can prevent illegal material from being posted. Once you have applied for a password and have had it validated, you will be able to post bulletins and to send and receive electronic mail.

▷ SUMMARY

The telephone is an extremely versatile, effective tool for business communication. It is also the most common and fairly economical. Modern telephone services include incoming and outgoing wide-area services, mobile services, data and facsimile transmissions, automatic dialing and receiving services, and teleconferencing. Teleconferencing allows several people from different locations to discuss matters of importance together. Videoconferencing allows participants to see as well as hear each other. The use of videoconferencing will increase because it is such a powerful communication tool.

Voice store-and-forward equipment solves many of the problems often associated with telephone equipment. Users may send and receive messages when they wish, and they may edit a message before sending it.

Dictation skills are still important. Whether a cassette tape recorder or special dictation equipment is used, the dictator should (1) prepare before beginning; (2) provide formatting and other instructions at the beginning of the message; (3) speak clearly; (4) spell names, unusual words, and homonyms; (5) dictate unusual punctuation; (6) let the secretary make appropriate changes; and (7) read documents before signing or sending them.

The computer is now playing a central role in office activities. Document production, duplication, distribution, and storage have all been automated. The equipment is called *hardware*. The programs that tell the hardware what actions to perform are known as *software*. Virtually every communication operation in an office may be facilitated by computer technology, which brings a new vocabulary into the office.

Word processing (WP) equipment and electronic mail (EMAIL) greatly simplify the process of preparing and sending written documents. Word processors amplify the writer's ability to produce written materials. Each word processor text editing program is different and requires some experimentation to master. WP equipment allows the user to create and change material quickly and easily. It is especially useful for preparing and sending form and guide letters. Most word processing programs provide numerous editing and formatting features.

The term *electronic mail* refers to the sending and receiving of written documents using electronic media. The sender and receiver may be in adjacent offices, across the country from one another, or on different continents. EMAIL is faster and more economical than traditional postal systems and has the added advantage of encouraging conciseness.

National computer information sources are complex databases providing users with access to a wide variety of general and specialized information. Current news, weather, sports, airline schedules, and financial information are just a few of the databases available to private and business members. Computer information sources are ideal for academic and business research, though the information in the database may lag behind what is available in print media.

▷ EXERCISES

Review and Discussion Questions

1. Under what circumstances are long-distance phone calls inexpensive?

2. Name and describe eight modern telephone services.

3. Define teleconferencing.

4. List and explain the five steps required for a successful teleconference.

5. Define videoconferencing, and explain its advantages and disadvantages.

6. What are three common disadvantages of telephone communication, and how can they be overcome with voice store-and-forward equipment?

7. List and explain the eight procedures necessary for high quality dictation.

8. In what ways are microcomputers, minicomputers, and mainframes different?

9. List and explain ten common word processing features.

10. What are the advantages and disadvantages of computer information sources?

Problems

1. Arrange to visit your local telephone company (or a local business with the required equipment) for a demonstration of a teleconference (or videoconference, if available). Write a brief report of your experience, reporting both your observations and your analysis of events.

2. Use a portable cassette tape recorder or professional dictation equipment to dictate a letter or memo. Use word processing equipment to transcribe the message. Submit both the tape and the finished document for evaluation by your instructor.

3. Use word processing equipment to produce a form letter ready for individualization.

4. Collect literature (advertisements, reviews, or manuals) on at least five word processing programs, analyze their features, and write a short report recommending a specific program based on its intended application.

5. Conduct an on-line data search on any topic approved by your instructor through a computer information source. You may do this either through a library or with your own (or a friend's) computer.

CASES

1. Use a mail merge program or a suitable database program to produce a series of five individualized form letters based on the letter created for Problem 3.

2. Dictate a letter and a memo (based, perhaps, on problems or cases in Part Two) using a cassette tape recorder. Include everything necessary for someone else to transcribe the message. Exchange tapes with another student in your class and transcribe the tape *exactly* as she or he prepared it.

3. What is the Christensen protocol? As the Director of the Department of Communication Technology for the Raymond Vee Corporation, you have been asked by president Raymond Vee to decide whether your company should be using the Christensen protocol. Present your findings and recommendations in memo format. (NOTE: Both primary and secondary research may be necessary for you to solve this case satisfactorily.)

4. Once again as Director of the Department of Communication Technology for the Raymond Vee Corporation, you have been asked for a recommendation. This time Raymond Vee wants to know whether your company should be using *synchronous* or *asynchronous* transmission of data. You need to let him know what they are and the advantages and disadvantages of each in addition to making your recommendation.

5. If your school has the equipment available, use two television cameras, microphones, and monitors to simulate a videoconference. Place the cameras and monitors in separate rooms so that the video equipment alone provides the link between the two individuals or groups (up to about five participants in a group). The topic of the conference is "Electronic Mediated Exchanges." Do the appropriate research before the conference takes place.

INDEX

Correction Symbols

Ab	Abbreviation	Exp	Expletive	Red	Redundant
Adapt	Adaptation	Fig	Figure	Ref	Reference
Agr	Agreement	F	Format	RO	Run-on sentence
Amb	Ambiguity	Frag	Fragment	SB	Should be
Ap	Appearance	Gob	Gobbledygook	SS	Single space
Apos	Apostrophe	Jar	Jargon	Sp	Spelling error
BC	Be consistent	K	Awkward	Spec	Specificity
Cap	Capitalize	lc	lowercase	Sub	Subordinate
Case	Grammatical case	Log	Logic	Syl	Syllabication
Chop	Choppy	MM	Misplaced modifier	T	Tense; tone
Cl	Clarity	N	Number	TR	Transpose
Coh	Coherence	Neg	Negative	TS	Triple space
Con	Conciseness	Obv	Obvious	V	Variety
CS	Comma splice	Org	Organization	W	Wordy
D	Diction	P	Punctuation	WC	Word choice
Emp	Emphasis	Pas	Passive voice	X	Obvious error
Enc	Enclosure	RB	Reader benefit	YA	You attitude